P9-DMO-426

OS/2 Presentation Manager Programming

OS/2 Presentation Manager Programming

Charles Petzold

Ziff-Davis Press
Emeryville, California

Editor	Deborah Craig
Technical Reviewer	Robert Hummel
Project Coordinators	Kim Haglund and Cort Day
Proofreaders	Kayla Sussell and Carol Burbo
Cover Illustration	Carrie English
Cover Design	Carrie English
Book Design	Gary Suen
Screen Graphics Editor	Cat Haglund
Technical Illustration	Cherie Plumlee
Word Processing	Howard Blechman
Page Layout	Tony Jonick
Indexer	David Heiret

Ziff-Davis Press books are produced on a Macintosh computer system with the following applications: FrameMaker®, Microsoft® Word, QuarkXPress®, Adobe Illustrator®, Adobe Photoshop®, Adobe Streamline™, MacLink®*Plus*, Aldus® FreeHand™, Collage Plus™.

If you have comments or questions or would like to receive a free catalog, call or write:
Ziff-Davis Press
5903 Christie Avenue
Emeryville, CA 94608
1-800-688-0448

ISBN 1-56276-123-4

Manufactured in the United States of America
10 9 8 7 6 5 4 3 2

Contents at a Glance

Table of Contents

Chapter 14 Dialog Boxes 704

Part 5 Miscellaneous Topics

ACKNOWLEDGMENTS

Over the years, so many fine people have helped make this book a reality that I can't begin to list them all.

For the first edition, a number of people at Microsoft helped in various ways. These folks are listed in the first Microsoft Press edition of this book, so I won't repeat their names here.

I'd like to thank everyone at Ziff-Davis Press for their proddings, help, and error-detection skills, and particularly for their patience as I discovered that the revision of this book for the 32-bit environment of OS/2 2.1 would take a bit longer than I had anticipated.

You wouldn't be reading these words without the help of my literary agent, Claudette Moore, whose knowledge of the computer-book industry was instrumental in easing the transition of this book between publishers.

Finally, I want to thank my friends—those within the computer and computer-book industries, those who benefit from these strange machines, and those who remain totally and happily dissociated from computers. My friends are such an important part of my life that to them I dedicate this book.

INTRODUCTION

This book covers the basics of programming in C for the OS/2 2.1 Presentation Manager—the graphical windowing environment included in IBM's OS/2.

Presentation Manager builds upon 0S/2, a powerful 32-bit protected-mode multitasking operating system, to provide windowing, a consistent user interface, and a sophisticated graphics programming system. OS/2 2.1 runs on IBM (and compatible) PCs and PS/2s that are based on Intel 386 and 486 microprocessors.

The success of the OS/2 Presentation Manager is dependent upon programmers writing applications for the environment. The purpose of this book is to help aspiring Presentation Manager programmers get started in that job.

MY ASSUMPTIONS ABOUT YOU

I assume that you know how to program in C. If you don't, programming for the OS/2 Presentation Manager is probably not a good place to begin, and I suggest that you first learn C programming for a more conventional environment, such as the OS/2 kernel or DOS. You should be familiar and comfortable with C pointers and structures—these are crucial to Presentation Manager programming.

I'm also assuming that you have some experience *using* the Presentation Manager. If not, take some time to familiarize yourself with it.

I do *not* assume that you have experience with programming for other graphical windowing environments such as the Apple Macintosh or Microsoft Windows. Experience with these environments might help with some of the initial conceptual hurdles, but it's not necessary. Don't worry—I'll help you through the weird stuff.

WHAT YOU'LL NEED

To compile and run the programs in this book, you must have the following software installed on your hard disk:

- IBM OS/2 2.1
- The IBM C Developer's WorkSet/2 *or* Borland C++ for OS/2.

Both the IBM and Borland packages have the header files you'll need for Presentation Manager programming, as well as import libraries, a resource compiler, development utilities for creating icons, dialog boxes and such, and technical documentation. Although this book shows you how to use many of the Presentation Manager function calls, it is not a replacement for the complete technical documentation.

The hardware you'll need to run the development environments is the same hardware you need to run OS/2 2.1. However, beefing up your memory to 8MB or more will certainly help performance.

The companion disk

I believe that programming is best learned by analyzing existing programs and experimenting with them by changing and expanding the code. For that reason, this book includes 99 complete executable programs and 3 dynamic link libraries. Rather than typing in the source code yourself, you can copy all the source code (and executables) from the companion diskette to your hard disk. See the Appendix for detailed instructions on how to do this. You are welcome to use any or all of the enclosed files in your own Presentation Manager programming.

How this book came to be

This book has an unusual genesis that may or may not be of interest to persons other than historians of computer literature. It began life as the very first Presentation Manager programming book.

In July 1987—3 months after OS/2 was first announced by IBM and Microsoft, 5 months before OS/2 1.0 was released, and 16 months before OS/2 1.1 (the first version to include the Presentation Manager) was released—the Microsoft Systems Software group approached Microsoft Press with the idea of developing a Presentation Manager programming book to include with beta versions of the OS/2 Software Development Kit. Having just completed the first edition of *Programming Windows*, I was the logical choice for the job.

In August 1987, I became one of a very few people outside of IBM and Microsoft to receive copies of the OS/2 Presentation Manager, still in the early stages of development.

These early versions of the Presentation Manager were definitely not yet ready for prime time—they didn't even have a Presentation Manager shell. When you booted the system, you'd get an normal OS/2 command line interface, and that is where you would edit and compile a Presentation Manager program. When you ran such a program, dynamic link libraries were invoked that would shift into a graphics mode and let the program run by itself in the PM environment. Unfortunately, when you terminated your program, the graphical environment did not go away. Thus, the normal edit-compile-run cycle of programming became an edit-compile-run-reboot cycle. This tended to hinder productivity.

Things improved over the months, of course, and by the end of October, 1987, I had completed something that vaguely resembled a book. It had 11 chapters, 371 pages, and no index. The pages were assembled in a binder under the title *Programming the OS/2 Presentation Manager: Preview Edition.* I understand that these binders are now collector items, because the distribution was limited to a few thousand software developers working with beta versions of OS/2 1.1 in 1988.

As the Presentation Manager evolved over 1988, the book grew. The first real edition of *Programming the OS/2 Presentation Manager* was published in early 1989, just a few months after OS/2 1.1 became a retail product.

Operating-system politics being what they are, it eventually became necessary for me to take the book to another publisher, namely Ziff-Davis Press. I've been working with various divisions of Ziff-Davis Publishing for 10 years now, having sold my first article to *PC Magazine* (a Ziff-Davis magazine) in early 1984. Doing a book for ZD Press seemed inevitable and natural.

For this edition, I've revised the book for the 32-bit architecture of OS/2 2.1 and added some additional information. Chapter 7 originally discussed AVIO, which stands for "advanced video input/output," a method of using character-mode video functions in a Presentation Manager program. For the most part, AVIO has become obsolete, so I've replaced Chapter 7 with an extensive discussion of advanced graphics programming techniques. Chapter 18 (on printing) is also new.

After much agonizing, I decided not to get into the subject of SOM, the System Object Model. SOM is not strictly a part of the Presentation Manager, and its eventual impact on Presentation Manager programming is not yet clear. This book restricts itself to "classical" Presentatin Manager programming.

If any questions arise, or you find any errors in these pages, or if you simply want to exchange hot movie tips, the best way to get in touch with me is through MCI Mail. I'm CPETZOLD or 143-6815. The gateway address through Internet is 1436815@mcimail.com.

Part 1

Basic Concepts

OS/2 and the Presentation Manager

THE BIG PICTURE

PRESENTATION MANAGER PROGRAMMING

Chapter 1

OS/2 2.0 is IBM's 32-bit operating system intended to replace DOS on IBM-compatible personal computers built around the Intel 386 and 486 microprocessors. The primary application environment under OS/2 is called the Presentation Manager (PM). Application programs written for the OS/2 Presentation Manager share the video display with other programs in a graphical windowing environment. Presentation Manager programs are characterized by a consistent user interface involving menus, dialog boxes, scroll bars, and other visual devices that are accessible through either the keyboard or a pointing device such as a mouse. Users generally find such an interface to be easily learned and mastered. Figure 1.1 shows several programs from this book running under the Presentation Manager.

The Presentation Manager user environment is reminiscent of systems developed at the Xerox Palo Alto Research Center (PARC) in the 1970s and early 1980s. In recent years, windowing environments have been popularized by the Apple Macintosh and, under DOS, by Microsoft Windows. The user interface of programs written for the OS/2 Presentation Manager is often similar to Windows.

For the program developer, the Presentation Manager has an extensive application program interface (API) that includes many high-level functions for creating windows and implementing the user interface. This API was originally derived from Microsoft Windows, and although the Windows and PM APIs diverged quite a bit during the original development of PM, the two systems retain many structural and conceptual similarities.

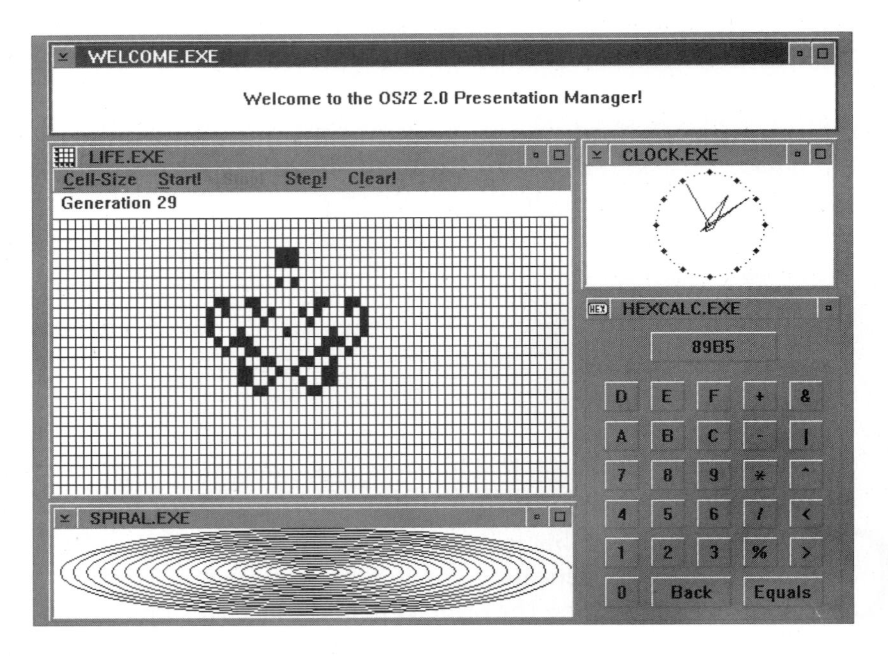

Figure 1.1: An OS/2 Presentation Manager screen

The OS/2 Presentation Manager also includes the Graphics Programming Interface (GPI), a sophisticated graphics system adapted from IBM's Graphics Data Display Manager (GDDM) and the 3270 Graphics Control Program (GCP), with some elements inherited from the Windows Graphics Device Interface (GDI).

Because the Presentation Manager runs under OS/2 2.0, programs designed for the environment can take advantage of preemptive and priority-based multitasking, 32-bit protected-mode addressing, virtual memory management, and interprocess communication.

This book shows you how to write programs for the OS/2 Presentation Manager. If you have some experience programming for Microsoft Windows or the Apple Macintosh, you're in good shape. But if your programming experience is limited to more conventional operating systems such as DOS, the OS/2 kernel, or UNIX, you need to put aside your preconceptions of how computer programs work and brace yourself for some strange ideas. We're off on a voyage to a new world.

THE BIG PICTURE

OS/2 has a history going back several years. It is a history filled with cooperation and conflict, successes and failures, continuity and change. The full story of OS/2 is probably best left to the historians of the personal computer industry rather than its programmers, yet some overall perspective will help you understand where OS/2 has been and where it is going.

Just about the only thing that most people agree on is that DOS must someday be replaced with something better. DOS has proven unable to satisfy the growing needs of users and program developers, and it is inhibiting future progress in software. To be tolerable, DOS requires various add-on kludges such as bank-switched memory or control programs based on the virtual-8086 mode of the 80386 microprocessor.

Protected multitasking operating systems such as OS/2 represent a critical turning point for the entire industry that has grown up around the IBM PC and compatibles. OS/2 and the Presentation Manager give the PC industry an opportunity to pull free of the DOS quagmire and take a major step forward.

THE OS/2 KERNEL

The initial version of OS/2 (OS/2 1.0) was developed by Microsoft and IBM for the 16-bit Intel 286 microprocessor, and the operating system was announced on April 2, 1987. Microsoft released version 1.0 to original equipment manufacturers in December 1987, and IBM released it for retail sale the same month. Unlike DOS, OS/2 1.0 used the protected-mode operation of the 286 microprocessor to unleash a 16Mb address space and implement efficient and safe multitasking.

OS/2 1.0 contained only what we now call the OS/2 *kernel*, and not the graphical Presentation Manager. OS/2 1.0 was a traditional environment for both users and programmers. The command-line interface and most internal and external commands were inherited from DOS.

From the programmer's perspective, the functionality of the OS/2 kernel resembles DOS, UNIX, and traditional minicomputer operating systems. The kernel handles file I/O, memory management, and multitasking. The API includes facilities for keyboard and mouse input and a fast full-screen character-mode video I/O (VIO) system.

The OS/2 kernel supports multiple full-screen sessions (sometimes also called *screen groups*). Each session runs one or more processes that use the video display in either a teletype or full-screen fashion. A user can switch between sessions by pressing the Alt-Esc key combination. (In OS/2 2.0, these sessions can also support DOS programs and Windows programs.)

Very few people actually used or programmed for OS/2 1.0. The DOS compatibility support was poor and the operating system was widely (and correctly) perceived as unfinished and incomplete. It needed a graphical environment.

THE OS/2 PRESENTATION MANAGER

At first, the graphical environment of OS/2 was supposed to be a protected-mode version of Microsoft Windows, which was first released for DOS in November, 1985. However, over the course of 1987, it metamorphosed into the Presentation Manager. Development of the Presentation Manager throughout 1987 and 1988 took place in three sites: Microsoft headquarters in Redmond, Washington, and IBM labs in Boca Raton, Florida and Hursley, England.

The Presentation Manager was slated for release by the end of October, 1988. Working at breakneck speed, the IBM and Microsoft developers made the date and OS/2 1.1 was officially released on October 31.

Beginning with OS/2 1.1, one OS/2 session runs in a graphics mode and is devoted to the Presentation Manager. All Presentation Manager applications run in this session. The addition of the Presentation Manager to OS/2 required little in the way of changes to the OS/2 kernel. Instead, the Presentation Manager is basically a collection of dynamic link libraries (.DLL files) that extend the functionality of OS/2 to include window management and graphics.

Although the Presentation Manager session is primarily for Presentation Manager programs, many programs written for the OS/2 kernel or DOS can also run in *text windows* in this session. However, these programs can't use graphics or take advantage of menus, dialog boxes, and other aspects of the user interface.

While program developers began taking an interest in OS/2 1.1, users in general did not. OS/2 1.1 was hampered by the same poor DOS support as OS/2 1.0, a paucity of printer drivers, and a plethora of bugs.

FROM 16 TO 32

Following the release of OS/2 1.1 in October of 1988, two more versions of OS/2 were released by Microsoft and IBM over the next two years. However, these versions were mostly devoted to fixing bugs, fine-tuning, and providing better hardware support. Everyone agreed that the real future of OS/2 was to go beyond the 16-bit Intel 286 and support true 32-bit processing under the 386 and 486.

The release of the 32-bit version of OS/2 was originally slated for year-end, 1990. However, by 1989 many industry observers considered the operating system to be "dead" and without a future. Microsoft found a different route to success with the release of Windows 3.0 in May, 1990, and this proved very popular with users.

By September, 1990, conflicts between IBM and Microsoft caused the joint development agreement to break down, and the two companies went their separate ways. Future development of OS/2 went to IBM, while Microsoft decided to focus on Windows and extend it into a different 32-bit operating system eventually known as Windows NT.

The release of OS/2 2.0—the first 32-bit version of OS/2—was delayed until spring 1992, but it shipped with a whole new look and feel (called the Workplace Shell) and a new object-oriented programming interface (called the System Object Model) in addition to the Presentation Manager. Moreover, OS/2 was marketed by what seemed to be a new company, dubbed the "new IBM." IBM surprised almost everyone by shipping over a million copies of OS/2 2.0 within several months of its release.

With the release of OS/2 2.0, the operating system has captured new attention, both from users and program developers. IBM has raised OS/2 from the dead and given it a bright new future.

FREEDOM OF CHOICE

Programmers have a choice of developing applications for either the OS/2 kernel or the OS/2 Presentation Manager. Each environment has distinct advantages and disadvantages.

For some applications, the OS/2 kernel is obviously preferable. For example, an existing DOS character-mode text editor or word processor that is known for its speed should probably be ported to the OS/2 kernel rather than to the Presentation Manager. Because the Presentation Manager runs in a graphics mode, a Presentation Manager version of the program will run more slowly with existing video display adapters. The kernel is also a better choice for developers who have designed a unique and well-known user interface for their DOS programs and feel reluctant to abandon it.

Developers who want to port their DOS programs to OS/2 as quickly as possible will find the kernel to be an easier path. Presentation Manager programs are more difficult to develop and debug than traditionally structured programs. Porting an existing DOS program to the Presentation Manager often requires turning the program inside out to accommodate the Presentation Manager architecture.

But for many sophisticated applications—particularly those that use graphics—the Presentation Manager is clearly the better environment. Let's see why.

The graphical environment The proof is in the programs. The graphical environment of the Presentation Manager is rich in functionality—programs can use graphics and formatted text to convey a high density of information to the user.

A traditional program gets user input from the keyboard and displays output on the screen. But with the addition of a mouse, the screen itself becomes a potential source of user input. Logic within the Presentation Manager assists the application in obtaining user input from various controls on the screen, such as menus, scroll bars, buttons, and dialog boxes. The interaction between the mouse and the screen narrows the gap between user and program.

The consistent user interface Because the menu and dialog box interface is built into the Presentation Manager rather than into each individual application, the interface is consistent across applications. This means that if you have experience with one Presentation Manager program (or with Microsoft Windows) you can easily learn a new PM program. In some cases, you don't need to even read a manual. If you know how menus and dialog boxes work with other PM programs, you can learn most functions of a new program solely from experimentation.

Some people dread that a system such as the Presentation Manager will lead to an undesirable uniformity of programs. Every program will look like every other program, they say, and designer creativity will be inhibited. But this has just not happened. Although the menus and dialog boxes are certainly the most obvious aspects of the user interface, much more important interaction between the user and program occurs within the window itself. The programmer is liberated from worrying about the mundane aspects of the user interface and is free to spend more time where it really counts.

Device-independent graphics The IBM PC was designed according to the principle of open architecture. Third-party manufacturers have responded to this by developing many different—and often incompatible—graphics output devices. Under DOS, program developers have faced the problem of writing their own device drivers for the CGA, the Hercules Graphics Card, the EGA, and the VGA, as well as for a number of high-resolution video adapters. The problem of printers is even worse: Some DOS word-processing packages include one or two disks containing nothing but printer drivers.

With the Presentation Manager, this all goes away. The Graphics Programming Interface of the Presentation Manager is device independent. An application need not identify the output device in order to use it. If a Presentation

Manager driver exists for the output device, all Presentation Manager programs can use the device. This also helps to protect programs from obsolescence. Video technology is advancing very quickly, but Presentation Manager programs written today will run without change on the video adapters of the future.

The SAA future Aside from their important role in OS/2, the Presentation Manager user interface and API are also part of IBM's ambitious Systems Application Architecture (SAA). SAA attempts to correct a historical weakness in IBM's line of computers and operating systems by setting user interface and API standards. The Presentation Manager is one of the first products to be a part of SAA. If the goals of SAA come to pass, the Presentation Manager user interface will become a common sight on IBM minicomputer and mainframe terminals. Just as important for the program developer, it may one day be possible to write a Presentation Manager program in a high-level language and compile it to run on a variety of computers from the IBM PS/2 series to the IBM 370.

Of course, this isn't going to happen next month or even the month after that. Porting Presentation Manager programs to other operating systems involves problems that PC programmers usually don't need to worry about. Nonetheless, SAA indicates the potential importance of the Presentation Manager in the future of the personal computer and not-quite-personal computers as well.

Presentation Manager programming

At first glance, a typical Presentation Manager program seems to be written in an unfamiliar programming language. The programs are full of uppercase identifiers and variable types, strange-looking variable names, nested *switch* statements, and many calls to Presentation Manager functions. Those odd-looking Presentation Manager programs are usually written in C. Although it is possible to use other languages, C will probably remain the preferred language for Presentation Manager programming, largely because of its flexibility in pointer and structure manipulation.

If you don't know C, programming for the Presentation Manager is probably not a good place to start learning the language. I recommend that you learn C by programming for a more traditional environment, such as the OS/2 kernel. If your C is a little rusty, brushing up on structures and pointers is a must.

THE HEADER FILES

C programs for the Presentation Manager require the use of header files supplied with OS/2 compilers. The main header file is called OS2.H. It uses *#include* statements to include other header files, which also may include other header files. The nesting of the most significant OS/2 header files is shown here:

Header File	Description
OS2.H	Includes other header files
OS2DEF.H	Common type and macro definitions
BSE.H	Includes other header files
BSEDOS.H	*Dos* functions and structures
BSETIB.H	Thread information structures
BSEMEMF.H	Memory allocation flags
BSEXCPT.H	Exception functions and structures
BSEDEV.H	I/O control structures
BSESUB.H	*Vio*, *Kbd*, and *Mou* functions
PM.H	Includes other header files
PMWIN.H	Most *Win* functions and structures
PMMLE.H	Multiline edit control support
PMSHL.H	Presentation Manager shell
PMHELP.H	The help manager
OS2NLS.H	National language support
PMGPI.H	Most *Gpi* functions and structures
PMBITMAP.H	Bitmap structures and definitions
PMDEV.H	Device context information
PMWP.H	Workplace shell support
PMAVIO.H	*Vio* functions for Advanced VIO
PMSPL.H	Print spooler
PMSTDDLG.H	Standard dialog boxes

I'll explain the meaning of those italicized three-letter abbreviations shortly.

In a very real sense, these header files define the limits of what you can do in the OS/2 Presentation Manager, and thus, they are an important part of PM documentation. You may want to print copies for reference or have a text browser within easy reach.

Many Presentation Manager functions require numeric constants as parameters. You rarely need to remember the actual values of these constants because the header files contain hundreds of *#define* statements that define identifiers for the constants. These identifiers are in uppercase letters. Most begin with a two-letter, three-letter, or four-letter prefix that indicates a general group of identifiers. The header files also define identifiers for most of the data types you use in your Presentation Manager programs, as well as numerous data structures used in passing information between the application and the Presentation Manager. I'll discuss these as we encounter them in the chapters ahead.

Programmers working with the Presentation Manager often find helpful a convention for naming variables that is known as *Hungarian notation*, in honor of its inventor, the legendary Microsoft programmer Charles Simonyi. This convention adds a lowercase abbreviation of the data type to the beginning of the variable name. Again, I'll discuss this system in context as we begin writing Presentation Manager programs.

All OS/2 and Presentation Manager functions available to an application are declared in the header files. These function declarations provide type checking during compilation. Most OS/2 functions begin with a three-letter prefix that identifies a large group of functions. The header files are generally organized around these groups of functions:

Prefix	Function Group
Dos	File I/O, memory management, and tasking
Vio	Video I/O in kernel (and some PM) programs
Kbd	Keyboard input in kernel programs
Mou	Mouse input in kernel programs
Nls	National language support
Win	PM windowing and user interface
Gpi	PM Graphics Programming Interface
Dev	PM device context interface

Prefix	Function Group
Spl	PM print spooler
Prf	PM program profile functions
Ddf	PM dynamic data formatting functions
Drg	PM drag-and-drop functions

The *Kbd* and *Mou* functions aren't used at all in Presentation Manager programs. *Vio* functions are used only in a Presentation Manager text output system called *Advanced VIO*, which has proven to be one of the least popular parts of the PM interface.

MESSAGE-BASED ARCHITECTURE

Most traditional operating systems provide a set of functions that a program calls for various system services. That is still the case in the Presentation Manager, but a Presentation Manager program also gets information from the operating system in a very different way: through *messages*. For example, in an OS/2 kernel program you use *Kbd* and *Mou* functions to obtain keyboard and mouse input. In the Presentation Manager, a program obtains keyboard and mouse input through messages that the Presentation Manager sends to the program.

But it's not only simple keyboard and mouse input that are delivered to a program in the form of messages. Messages also inform a program when a user has selected an item from a menu, when the program's window has been resized, and even when the program should repaint part of its window. In fact, Presentation Manager programs are largely message-driven. A program remains dormant most of the time until it receives a message; it thus does little but process messages. Coming to terms with this message architecture is a major hurdle of learning to program for the Presentation Manager. But don't worry about understanding this architecture right off the bat. We'll spend most of this book learning how to process messages.

EASY OR HARD?

Graphical user interfaces such as the OS/2 Presentation Manager have the reputation of being difficult systems for programmers to learn. I've already spoken of the hurdle of moving from a traditional operating system to a message-based architecture. That's only part of the problem. The steep learning curve also results from the sheer bulk of Presentation Manager function calls—about 800 of them, excluding the kernel calls.

But what's the alternative? Would you rather learn how to use the menu logic built into the Presentation Manager, or would you prefer to write your own menu routines? Would you rather learn how to draw circles using GPI functions, or would you prefer to write your own circle-drawing routines and adapt them for every video adapter and printer your program may encounter?

Out of necessity, application programs have become more complex in the past few years. Programs have been made easier to operate for naive users and, at the same time, more powerful for sophisticated users. As the user base expands to encompass less sophisticated users, applications, application program interfaces, and programmers must become more sophisticated. Program developers can no longer require users to spend many hours reading manuals before they begin to use an application. The application's interface must be obvious and intuitively clear. By programming for the Presentation Manager, you begin with an interface that is already familiar to the user. In short, learning to program for the Presentation Manager may be hard, but it's easier than the alternative.

So enough of this propaganda. Let's start pounding out some code.

Welcome to Presentation Manager Programming

W—The do-nothing program

WE—Obtaining an anchor block handle

WEL—Creating a message queue

WELC—Creating a standard window

WELCO—Looping through the messages

WELCOM—Creating a client window

WELCOME—Painting the client window

Chapter 2

Books that teach you how to program in C often begin with a "do-nothing" program and proceed quickly to the traditional "Hello world" program. The Presentation Manager analog of the "Hello world" program isn't quite as straightforward, so we'll spend this entire chapter creating it. We'll begin with a "do-nothing" program called W and progressively develop it into a program called WELCOME that creates a window, displays some text in it, and (as a bonus) plays a little music.

W—The do-nothing program

A Presentation Manager program is usually constructed from several files. Listing 2.1 shows the three files that make up the W program:

- W.MAK (a make file)
- W.C (the program source code file)
- W.DEF (a module definition file)

As you will see, these three types of files are normal for all Presentation Manager programs.

Because the W program itself does nothing interesting, we'll instead take a moment to examine the mechanics of compiling and linking an OS/2 program.

THE MAKE FILE

The first file is a make file named W.MAK. A *make file* is a text file that contains a series of commands to create an .EXE (executable) file from one or

Listing 2.1: The W program

The W.MAK File

```
#-----------------
# W.MAK make file
#-----------------

w.exe : w.obj w.def
     $(PRGLINK) w, w, NUL, $(PRGLIB), w

w.obj : w.c
     $(PRGCC) w.c
```

The W.C File

```
/*----------------------------------
   W.C -- A Do-Nothing Program
          (c) Charles Petzold, 1993
  ----------------------------------*/

int main (void)
     {
     return 0 ;
     }
```

The W.DEF File

```
;-------------------------------
; W.DEF module definition file
;-------------------------------

NAME           W         WINDOWCOMPAT

DESCRIPTION    'Welcome to PM -- Program No. 1 (c) Charles Petzold, 1993'
PROTMODE
```

more source code files. By convention, a make file has the same name as the program it creates but with the .MAK extension.

The make files in this book have been generalized somewhat so they can be used with both the IBM C Developer's WorkSet/2 and Borland C++ for OS/2. The identifiers in W.MAK that are enclosed within parentheses and prefaced by dollar signs are macros. These macros are defined in environment variables that you can set by running one of the two command files shown in Listing 2.2.

If you're using the IBM compiler, run IBM.CMD on the OS/2 command line before attempting to make the program. If you're using the Borland compiler, run BOR.CMD. The command file assumes that the Borland compiler is set up on the current drive in the directory BCOS2 (the installation default).

Listing 2.2: Command files to set environment variables

The IBM.CMD File

```
REM -------------------------------------------------------------
REM  IBM.CMD -- Set up environment for IBM C Developer's WorkSet/2
REM -------------------------------------------------------------
SET PRGCC=icc -C -Kbcpr -Ss
SET PRGLINK=link386 /BASE:0x10000
SET PRGLIB=
SET PRGRC=rc -r
```

The BOR.CMD File

```
REM ------------------------------------------------------
REM  BOR.CMD -- Set up environment for Borland C++ for OS/2
REM ------------------------------------------------------
SET PRGCC=bcc -c -I\bcos2\include
SET PRGLINK=tlink -c -L\bcos2\lib \bcos2\lib\c02.obj
SET PRGLIB=c2 + os2
SET PRGRC=rc -r -i \bcos2\include
```

A make file is usually divided into several sections. Each section begins with the name of a *target* file, followed by a colon, followed by one or more *dependent* files. The dependent files contribute to the target file. If any of the dependent files have been changed more recently than the target file, the target file needs to be recreated. The target file is recreated by running the indented commands that follow. In addition, if any dependent file is a target file in a later section of the make file, that dependent file may have to be updated first.

Assuming you have one of the C compilers and associated files properly installed, you can create W.EXE from W.MAK, W.C, and W.DEF by running the IBM NMAKE program or the Borland MAKE program on an OS/2 command line, either in a full-screen or windowed character-mode session. Run NMAKE like this if you're using the IBM compiler:

```
NMAKE W.MAK
```

Use this line if you're running the Borland compiler:

```
MAKE -f W.MAK
```

When you first run NMAKE or MAKE on W.MAK, it will discover that it needs to recreate W.EXE because one of its dependent files (W.OBJ) doesn't exist. However, W.OBJ is also a target file dependent on W.C. So, the first step is to run the C compiler to create the W.OBJ object module from W.C.

Compiling If you're using the IBM C compiler, the compile step looks like this:

```
icc -C -Kbcpr -Ss w.c
```

The -C switch causes the C compiler to compile the program (creating W.OBJ) but not to link it. The link comes later. The various -K switches determine what warning and diagnostic messages will be reported by the compiler. The -Ss switch allows the use of double slashes (//) for single-line comments.

If you're using the Borland compiler, the compile step looks like this:

```
bcc -c -I\bcos2\include w.c
```

The -c switch instructs the compiler to compile the program but not to link it. The -I switch indicates a directory in which the compiler can find header (.H) files. The header files include the normal C header files plus the OS/2 header files.

Linking If the compilation is successful, the W.OBJ object module is linked with library files to create the executable W.EXE file. If you're using the IBM compiler, the link step looks like this:

```
link386 /BASE:0x10000 w, w, NUL,, w
```

The /BASE flag tells the linker that when OS/2 runs the program, the program will be loaded in memory with a base address of 0x10000. This is true of all OS/2 2.0 programs, and using this flag will produce a smaller executable file than otherwise. The /BASE flag is followed by the name of the W.OBJ object code file. The .OBJ extension is assumed. The next field is the name of the .EXE file. Again, the extension is assumed. The third parameter is the name of a map file. Specifying NUL prevents the map file from being created.

The fourth parameter normally lists the names of the libraries to be linked with the .OBJ file. However, the IBM C compiler embeds the names of these libraries in the W.OBJ file and the linker uses those libraries automatically. The libraries are DDE4SBS.LIB, which is the single-threaded C runtime library, and OS2386.LIB, an import library for OS/2 functions. An *import library* doesn't contain code, but simply allows the linker to construct the .EXE file so that it contains dynamic link information. When you run an OS/2 program, OS/2 uses this information in the .EXE files to link calls to OS/2 functions within the program with the functions themselves. Although the W program doesn't seem to make any OS/2 function calls, the start-up code makes a few.

The fifth parameter to the linker is the name of the program's module definition file, W.DEF. The .DEF extension is assumed. (More on the module definition file shortly.)

If you're using the Borland compiler, the link step looks like this:

```
tlink -c -L\bcos2\lib \bcos2\lib\c02.obj w, w, NUL, c2 + os2, w
```

The parameter ordering of the Borland linker is the same as the IBM linker: flags, object files, executable file, map file, libraries, and module definition file. The -c switch preserves case sensitivity, and the -L switch tells the linker where to find the libraries. The first object file (C02.OBJ) is provided with the Borland compiler and contains the program start-up code. The library field indicates two libraries: C2.LIB is the single-threaded C runtime library, and OS2.LIB is the import library.

THE MODULE DEFINITION FILE

Although it isn't strictly required for this simple do-nothing program, Presentation Manager applications should usually include a *module definition file.* This is a simple text file that the linker uses when constructing the program's .EXE file. The module definition file commonly has the same name as the program, but with a .DEF extension. For OS/2 2.0, the importance (and size) of the module definition file has decreased a lot from the time it was first invented for Microsoft Windows 1.0, but the file still serves some purposes.

The W.DEF file shown in Listing 2.1 begins with a NAME statement. This identifies the module as a program rather than a dynamic link library and gives it a module name of W. The module should have the same name as the program's .EXE file. The keyword WINDOWCOMPAT causes the linker to set a flag in the W.EXE file. This flag tells OS/2 that, although the program is not a Presentation Manager program, it *can* be run in a text window within the Presentation Manager session.

The text in the DESCRIPTION line is embedded by the linker at the end of the .EXE file. This is an excellent place for a copyright notice or other information about the program. The PROTMODE keyword indicates that the program will be run only in OS/2 protected mode. This often allows the linker to shorten the .EXE file.

We'll change the module definition file slightly before this chapter is completed, but the general information shown in the W.DEF file will remain about the same for most programs in this book.

RUNNING W.EXE

After creating W.EXE, you can run the program in a variety of ways, most easily by executing it from the OS/2 command-line prompt, either in a full-screen character-mode session or in a Presentation Manager window. You can also run the program from a disk drive window or by creating a program window for it. Regardless, W.EXE doesn't do much of anything besides start up and quickly terminate.

WE—OBTAINING AN ANCHOR BLOCK HANDLE

A Presentation Manager program makes many calls to Presentation Manager functions. But the very first Presentation Manager function that the program must call is *WinInitialize*. This function registers the program with the system and returns the anchor block handle. (The term *anchor block* has origins in the mainframe world but has no significant meaning in the context of OS/2 or the Presentation Manager.) Before the program terminates, it should call *WinTerminate* to free the anchor block handle. The WE program in Listing 2.3 shows how this is done. WE is still basically a do-nothing program, but it's now a do-nothing program that could use some Presentation Manager functions.

You can create WE.EXE from the three files by executing

```
NMAKE WE.MAK
```

using the IBM compiler or

```
MAKE -f WE.MAK
```

using the Borland compiler. You can run WE.EXE in the same way you run W.EXE. The program still doesn't do much of anything.

In going from W to WE, the changes made to the three standard files at first look innocuous. But you'll find when creating WE.EXE that the compilation takes a little longer than it did previously. It's almost as if the compiler has to digest several other files in addition to WE.C. As you'll see in the following discussion, that's exactly the case.

THE HEADER FILES

Near the top of WE.C is the preprocessor statement:

```
#include <os2.h>
```

OS2.H is a master header file that contains other *#include* statements for other OS/2 and Presentation Manager header files. When you use the IBM compiler, all of these header files should be located in a subdirectory listed in your INCLUDE environment string. (With the Borland compiler, the appropriate directory is part of the command line when you run the compiler.) These header files are extremely important. As I mentioned in Chapter 1, you should treat them as primary documentation for the Presentation Manager. Even for a program as simple as WE, these header files supply function declarations

Listing 2.3: The WE program

The WE.MAK File

```
#-----------------
# WE.MAK make file
#-----------------

we.exe : we.obj we.def
     $(PRGLINK) we, we, NUL, $(PRGLIB), we

we.obj : we.c
     $(PRGCC) we.c
```

The WE.C File

```
/*-------------------------------------------------------
   WE.C -- A Program that Obtains an Anchor Block Handle
           (c) Charles Petzold, 1993
  -------------------------------------------------------*/

#include <os2.h>

int main (void)
     {
     HAB  hab ;

     hab = WinInitialize (0) ;

     WinTerminate (hab) ;
     return 0 ;
     }
```

The WE.DEF File

```
;------------------------------
; WE.DEF module definition file
;------------------------------

NAME           WE        WINDOWCOMPAT

DESCRIPTION    'Welcome to PM -- Program No. 2 (c) Charles Petzold, 1993'
PROTMODE
```

and definitions of identifiers used in the program. Let's examine how the header files affect the compilation of WE.C.

The WE.C program defines one variable (*hab*) and calls two Presentation Manager functions, *WinInitialize* and *WinTerminate*. These two functions are located in the PMWIN.DLL dynamic link library that OS/2 links your program with when you run the program. The *hab* variable is defined within the *main* function of WE.C:

```
HAB hab ;
```

The data type of *hab* is HAB, which stands for "handle to an anchor block." (I'll discuss what a handle is shortly.) This HAB type is defined by a *typedef* statement in OS2DEF.H:

```
typedef LHANDLE HAB ;
```

The LHANDLE data type is defined like this:

```
typedef unsigned long LHANDLE ;
```

Thus the C compiler will treat the variable *hab* as a 32-bit unsigned long integer.
The *WinInitialize* and *WinTerminate* functions are declared in PMWIN.H:

```
HAB APIENTRY WinInitialize (ULONG flOptions) ;
BOOL APIENTRY WinTerminate (HAB hab) ;
```

(By the way, although the parameter for *WinInitialize* is defined as allowing options to be specified, the only allowable parameter is 0.) BOOL and ULONG are data types defined in OS2DEF.H:

```
typedef unsigned long BOOL ;
typedef unsigned long ULONG ;
```

Thus the *WinInitialize* function takes an unsigned long parameter and returns an unsigned long value of type HAB, a handle to an anchor block. The *WinTerminate* function accepts an anchor block handle as a parameter and returns an unsigned long. The program treats this return value as a BOOL (Boolean), which is interpreted as being either 0 (FALSE) or 1 (TRUE).
For the IBM compiler, the APIENTRY identifier is defined in OS2DEF.H like this:

```
#define APIENTRY _System
```

For the Borland compiler, it's defined like so:

```
#define APIENTRY _syscall
```

These keywords are recognized by the IBM and Borland compilers (respectively) and indicate what conventions the compiler should use in generating the function call. This is important because the *WinInitialize* and *WinTerminate* calls will go to entry points in a dynamic link library, and the calling convention must be consistent.

If you wrote WE.C without using the header files or any *#define* or *typedef* statements, it would look like this:

```
unsigned long _Syscall WinInitialize (unsigned long) ;
unsigned long _Syscall WinTerminate (unsigned long) ;

int main (void)
     {
     unsigned long hab ;

     hab = WinInitialize (0) ;
     WinTerminate (hab) ;
     return 0 ;
     }
```

In one sense, this is easier to read, because it uses only standard C data types (and one IBM extension). However, in many ways this version is much more obscure than the version that uses the Presentation Manager header files.

For example, the *WinTerminate* function is declared in PMWIN.H as returning a BOOL, indicating that the function returns a 0 if it fails and a 1 if it succeeds. This fact could be important, and yet it's not at all intuitive if the *WinTerminate* function is declared as returning an unsigned long. Likewise, the return value of *WinInitialize* isn't just any old unsigned long; it's a handle to an anchor block. It's not even important for you to know that an anchor block handle is really an unsigned long. All you need to know is that it's an anchor block handle. You should use this value only in other functions that accept an anchor block handle as a parameter, such as *WinTerminate.*

THE PROPER HANDLING OF HANDLES

When you program for the Presentation Manager, you're really engaged in a primitive form of object-oriented programming. Many Presentation Manager functions obtain information about an object, act on an object, or cause an object to act on itself. A *handle* is a number that refers to an object. Almost every Presentation Manager function call—one exception is *WinInitialize*—requires a handle as the first parameter.

Although this requirement implies that every Presentation Manager function acts on an object, this is really not the case. Presentation Manager function calls require a handle as the first parameter because of the requirements of IBM's Systems Application Architecture, of which the Presentation Manager is a part. As you'll see, some functions really don't need a handle to anything. These functions sometimes require the anchor block handle as the first parameter.

The concept of a handle shouldn't be new to you. If you've done assembly-language programming under DOS or the OS/2 kernel, or if you've ever used the C file I/O functions *open*, *read*, *write*, and *close*, you're familiar with file handles. Under the OS/2 kernel, a program can obtain a file handle from the *DosOpen* function call. The open file is an object to which the file handle refers. You use the handle when calling *DosRead*, *DosWrite*, or other functions that act on the open file. You eventually close the file using *DosClose*. After the *DosClose* call, the file handle is invalid. Although the file handle is a number, the actual value of the handle returned from *DosOpen* isn't important to your program. It is meaningful only to the OS/2 kernel. Obviously, the OS/2 kernel maintains a table of open files, and the file handle somehow references that table. But your program doesn't need to know this. OS/2 hides this data from your program.

The handles you use in the Presentation Manager are similar to file handles. But in the Presentation Manager almost everything has a handle. Before we're finished with this chapter, we'll have encountered several:

- Anchor block handles
- Message queue handles
- Window handles
- Presentation space handles

Every handle is first obtained from a Presentation Manager function. You save the handle in a variable, and then use this handle in other Presentation Manager functions. At some point, you usually call a function that destroys the resources connected with the handle. At that time the handle becomes invalid.

Most handles are 32 bits long, but some are 16 bits long. Often handles indirectly reference information in structures maintained internally by the Presentation Manager. But your program doesn't access these structures directly. You don't even have to know which handles are 32 bits long and which are 16 bits long, because you use the data types defined in the header files (such as HAB) to define variables to store the handles.

A handle with a value of 0 is called a NULL handle. In C programming, a NULL pointer is often an invalid pointer. Similarly, in Presentation Manager programming, a NULL handle returned from a function is usually an indication of an error. In some cases, however, you can use a NULL handle as a default parameter to a function that requires a handle. We'll examine these cases as they arise. To specify a NULL handle, you can use the identifier NULLHANDLE.

The anchor block handle is a peculiar sort of handle. I've already mentioned that handles refer to objects. The anchor block handle is a little different. The object to which the anchor block handle refers is the program itself; the program that calls *WinInitialize*. Let's be more precise. What we call a program is usually the .EXE file. But the program can be run multiple times. While a particular instance of a program is running, it is called a process. The anchor block handle refers to the particular process that calls *WinInitialize*. Let's be even more precise. A process can have multiple threads of execution. Each of these threads could have its own anchor block handle. (However, don't confuse the anchor block handle with a process ID or a thread ID.)

Usually, a Presentation Manager program calls *WinInitialize* when it begins execution. The program can then call other Presentation Manager functions. Right before the program is ready to terminate, it pulls up its anchor with *WinTerminate* and departs.

RUNNING WE.EXE

I have some bad news for you. Although we are gathered here to write Presentation Manager programs, we're not there yet. You might think that calling the magic function *WinInitialize* turns an ordinary OS/2 program into a Presentation Manager program, but it's not so. Like W.EXE, WE.EXE is an OS/2 kernel program. Although a call to *WinInitialize* is necessary in a Presentation Manager program, it isn't sufficient. You can call *WinInitialize* from an old-fashioned character-mode OS/2 program also. Getting that anchor block handle only lets you access some Presentation Manager functions that are not directly connected with the windowing or graphics facilities of the Presentation Manager. But don't fret: Although we're not quite there yet, the next step will get us there.

WEL—Creating a Message Queue

Calling *WinInitialize* to get an anchor block handle is like getting a pass to the pool. The next step—creating a message queue—is like jumping in. (We'll soon be swimming laps.) As you know, OS/2 supports multiple sessions, one being the Presentation Manager session. A program that creates a message queue is always run in the Presentation Manager session along with other Presentation Manager programs. The WEL program in Listing 2.4 shows how to create this message queue.

Listing 2.4: The WEL program

The WEL.MAK File

```
#-------------------
# WEL.MAK make file
#-------------------

wel.exe : wel.obj wel.def
     $(PRGLINK) wel, wel, NUL, $(PRGLIB), wel

wel.obj : wel.c
     $(PRGCC) wel.c
```

The WEL.C File

```
/*-------------------------------------------------
   WEL.C -- A Program that Creates a Message Queue
            (c) Charles Petzold, 1993
  -------------------------------------------------*/

#include <os2.h>

int main (void)
     {
     HAB  hab ;
     HMQ  hmq ;

     hab = WinInitialize (0) ;
     hmq = WinCreateMsgQueue (hab, 0) ;

     WinDestroyMsgQueue (hmq) ;
     WinTerminate (hab) ;
     return 0 ;
     }
```

The WEL.DEF File

```
;-------------------------------
; WEL.DEF module definition file
;-------------------------------

NAME           WEL       WINDOWAPI

DESCRIPTION    'Welcome to PM -- Program No. 3 (c) Charles Petzold, 1993'
PROTMODE
```

THE MESSAGE QUEUE DIFFERENCE

As you'll see, Presentation Manager programs are based on a message-driven input model. Programs receive all input in the form of messages. We're not quite ready to look at this message system in detail, but after working with it, you'll probably realize that this input model is a necessary part of a windowing environment like the Presentation Manager.

Many messages that a program receives from the Presentation Manager are stored in a message queue. The program must create this message queue explicitly with a call to the Presentation Manager. This call establishes the program as a Presentation Manager application.

Following the *WinInitialize* call, WEL.C makes this call:

```
hmq = WinCreateMsgQueue (hab, 0) ;
```

As its name implies, this call creates a message queue. Like most Presentation Manager functions, *WinCreateMsgQueue* requires a handle as the first parameter. This is the anchor block handle, which is the only handle we have so far. The second parameter indicates the size of the queue, where 0 means a default size that is sufficient for most programs. The value returned from the function is the handle to the message queue. This is stored in a variable named *hmq* of type HMQ. The program destroys the queue like this:

```
WinDestroyMsgQueue (hmq) ;
```

Following this call, the *hmq* handle is invalid.

Message queues get a little more complex for programs with multiple threads of execution. A message queue is always associated with a particular thread—the thread that creates it. A thread can have only one message queue. In a multithread program, some threads can create message queues, but others don't have to (and usually don't).

When OS/2 is booted, the first program that calls *WinCreateMsgQueue* (normally, the Presentation Manager desktop shell) establishes a session as the Presentation Manager session. It is during the *WinCreateMsgQueue* call that the screen display is switched from character mode to graphics mode. Later programs that call *WinCreateMsgQueue*—even if executed from an OS/2 command-line prompt in a character-mode session—are run in this same session.

Notice also that the WINDOWCOMPAT keyword in W.DEF and WE.DEF has been changed to WINDOWAPI in WEL.DEF. This causes the linker to set a flag in the WEL.EXE file to inform OS/2 that this is truly a Presentation Manager program.

However, although WEL is now a true Presentation Manager program, it still doesn't do anything visually interesting. Let's fix that.

WELC—CREATING A STANDARD WINDOW

A program running in the Presentation Manager session occupies one or more windows. In simple terms, a *window* is a rectangular area of the screen that the program uses to receive input and display its output. A window is like a virtual terminal. A user can move and resize the windows on the screen and select one window (and hence one program) as the active, or foreground, window. A Presentation Manager program must create the window that the program uses. The WELC program in Listing 2.5 shows how this is done.

WELC.EXE is the first version of the program we are creating that has a substantial, visible result. When you run WELC, a window appears that looks much like the windows of other programs running under the Presentation Manager. The window contains a thick resizing border, a system menu button in the upper-left corner, a minimize and maximize button in the upper-right corner, and a title bar across the top containing the name of the program, WELC.EXE. Not bad, but not perfect. The problem is that this window disappears almost immediately after it's created. We'll fix that problem in the next version of our program, but first, let's examine what we've done to get this far.

THE *WINCREATESTDWINDOW* FUNCTION

WELC.C calls two Presentation Manager functions in addition to those introduced earlier: *WinCreateStdWindow* creates a standard window, and *WinDestroyWindow* destroys it. *WinCreateStdWindow* is the function normally used to create a main window for a Presentation Manager application. This isn't the only way to create an application window, but it's certainly the easiest. The *WinCreateStdWindow* function requires nine parameters, which are identified with comments in WELC.C. (The double slashes are recognized by the IBM and Borland C compilers as setting off single-line comments.) Six of the parameters are set to 0 or NULL in this example. Certainly, we're not yet taking advantage of *WinCreateStdWindow*'s full potential.

WinCreateStdWindow creates a type of window known as a "frame window." We'll examine what this means a little later. The function returns a handle to the frame window. In WELC.C this handle is stored in a variable named *hwndFrame* and defined as type HWND ("handle to a window"). This handle must be used in other Presentation Manager functions to refer to the window. For example, in WELC.C this window handle is passed to *WinDestroyWindow* to destroy the window, which means that the Presentation Manager frees all the resources associated with the window and removes it from the screen. The window handle then becomes invalid.

Listing 2.5: The WELC program

The WELC.MAK File

```
#-------------------
# WELC.MAK make file
#-------------------

welc.exe : welc.obj welc.def
     $(PRGLINK) welc, welc, NUL, $(PRGLIB), welc

welc.obj : welc.c
     $(PRGCC) welc.c
```

The WELC.C File

```
/*-----------------------------------------------------------
   WELC.C -- A Program that Creates a Standard Frame Window
             (c) Charles Petzold, 1993
  -----------------------------------------------------------*/

#include <os2.h>

int main (void)
     {
     static ULONG flFrameFlags = FCF_TITLEBAR      | FCF_SYSMENU |
                                 FCF_SIZEBORDER    | FCF_MINMAX  |
                                 FCF_SHELLPOSITION | FCF_TASKLIST ;
     HAB          hab ;
     HMQ          hmq ;
     HWND         hwndFrame ;

     hab = WinInitialize (0) ;
     hmq = WinCreateMsgQueue (hab, 0) ;

     hwndFrame = WinCreateStdWindow (
                    HWND_DESKTOP,        // Parent window handle
                    WS_VISIBLE,          // Style of frame window
                    &flFrameFlags,       // Pointer to control data
                    NULL,                // Client window class name
                    NULL,                // Title bar text
                    0L,                  // Style of client window
                    0,                   // Module handle for resources
                    0,                   // ID of resources
                    NULL) ;              // Pointer to client window handle

     WinDestroyWindow (hwndFrame) ;
     WinDestroyMsgQueue (hmq) ;
     WinTerminate (hab) ;
     return 0 ;
     }
```

Listing 2.5: The WELC program (Continued)

The WELC.DEF File

```
;---------------------------------
; WELC.DEF module definition file
;---------------------------------

NAME           WELC      WINDOWAPI

DESCRIPTION    'Welcome to PM -- Program No. 4 (c) Charles Petzold, 1993'
PROTMODE
```

The first parameter to *WinCreateStdWindow* is the identifier known as HWND_DESKTOP (defined in PMWIN.H as 1), which specifies the "parent" of the frame window. The concept of a parent window will be explored in more detail in the next chapter.

The second parameter specifies the style of the window. The parameter is the identifier WS_VISIBLE (which is defined in PMWIN.H as the value 0x80000000L). The WS prefix stands for "window style." This value instructs the *WinCreateStdWindow* function to make the window visible when it is created.

The third parameter is a pointer to the variable *flFrameFlags*. The "fl" prefix is an example of Hungarian notation, which I alluded to in Chapter 1. The "f" indicates that the variable is a series of flags, and the "l" indicates that the flags are encoded in a 32-bit long integer. The *flFrameFlags* variable is defined as a ULONG (unsigned long). This parameter tells *WinCreateStdWindow* what the standard window should include. I've initialized *flFrameFlags* like this:

```
static ULONG flFrameFlags = FCF_TITLEBAR      | FCF_SYSMENU |
                            FCF_SIZEBORDER    | FCF_MINMAX  |
                            FCF_SHELLPOSITION | FCF_TASKLIST ;
```

The FCF ("frame creation flags") identifiers are defined in PMWIN.H. Some of these identifiers are almost self-explanatory: FCF_TITLEBAR means that we want a title bar across the top of the window; FCF_SYSMENU, a system menu box to the left of the title bar; FCF_SIZEBORDER, a thick sizing border around the window; and FCF_MINMAX, a minimize and maximize button to the right of the title bar. FCF_SHELLPOSITION instructs the Presentation Manager shell to give the window a default size and position on the screen. FCF_TASKLIST installs the program on the Window List.

Here's how these six identifiers are defined in PMWIN.H:

```
#define FCF_TITLEBAR      0x00000001L
#define FCF_SYSMENU       0x00000002L
#define FCF_SIZEBORDER    0x00000008L
#define FCF_MINMAX        0x00000030L
#define FCF_SHELLPOSITION 0x00000400L
#define FCF_TASKLIST      0x00000800L
```

Each identifier is a 32-bit constant with one or two bits set to 1 and the other bits set to 0. These identifiers are combined into one 32-bit number using the C bitwise OR operator (|). Many identifiers defined in the OS/2 header files work this way.

Of course, most windows created by Presentation Manager programs remain on the screen longer than the window in WELC. Our first priority is to fix that problem.

WELCO—LOOPING THROUGH THE MESSAGES

The problem with WELC is that we don't have a chance to enjoy the wonderful window we've created. The program calls *WinCreateStdWindow* to create the frame window but then calls *WinDestroyWindow* to blow it away. Obviously, we have to insert some code between those two function calls to keep the window up on the screen a little longer. If this were a conventional OS/2 program, you might set up a little loop to call *KbdCharIn* and then wait for a keystroke before destroying the window. But the *KbdCharIn* function isn't allowed in Presentation Manager programs. Nor are any of the other keyboard functions provided by the OS/2 kernel. What we can do instead is add a message loop. This *message loop* is something like a loop that reads the keyboard, but it is much, much more. A program with a message loop—WELCO—is shown in Listing 2.6.

When you run WELCO.EXE under the Presentation Manager, you'll be treated to a real Presentation Manager window, as shown in Figure 2.1. With this window you can

- Press the mouse button when the pointer is positioned over the title bar and drag the window around the screen.
- Drag the sizing border to change the size of the window.
- Click on the maximize button and expand the window to full screen.
- Click on the minimize button and compress the window into a little icon displayed in the Minimized Window Viewer.

Listing 2.6: The WELCO program

The WELCO.MAK File

```
#---------------------
# WELCO.MAK make file
#---------------------

welco.exe : welco.obj welco.def
     $(PRGLINK) welco, welco, NUL, $(PRGLIB), welco

welco.obj : welco.c
     $(PRGCC) welco.c
```

The WELCO.C File

```
/*------------------------------------------
   WELCO.C -- A Program with a Message Loop
              (c) Charles Petzold, 1993
  ------------------------------------------*/

#include <os2.h>

int main (void)
     {
     static ULONG flFrameFlags = FCF_TITLEBAR      | FCF_SYSMENU |
                                 FCF_SIZEBORDER    | FCF_MINMAX  |
                                 FCF_SHELLPOSITION | FCF_TASKLIST ;
     HAB          hab ;
     HMQ          hmq ;
     HWND         hwndFrame ;
     QMSG         qmsg ;

     hab = WinInitialize (0) ;
     hmq = WinCreateMsgQueue (hab, 0) ;

     hwndFrame = WinCreateStdWindow (
                    HWND_DESKTOP,        // Parent window handle
                    WS_VISIBLE,          // Style of frame window
                    &flFrameFlags,       // Pointer to control data
                    NULL,                // Client window class name
                    NULL,                // Title bar text
                    0L,                  // Style of client window
                    0,                   // Module handle for resources
                    0,                   // ID of resources
                    NULL) ;              // Pointer to client window handle

     while (WinGetMsg (hab, &qmsg, NULLHANDLE, 0, 0))
          WinDispatchMsg (hab, &qmsg) ;

     WinDestroyWindow (hwndFrame) ;
     WinDestroyMsgQueue (hmq) ;
```

Listing 2.6: The WELCO program (Continued)

```
     WinTerminate (hab) ;
     return 0 ;
     }
```

The WELCO.DEF File

```
;---------------------------------
; WELCO.DEF module definition file
;---------------------------------

NAME           WELCO     WINDOWAPI

DESCRIPTION    'Welcome to PM -- Program No. 5 (c) Charles Petzold, 1993'
PROTMODE
```

- Use the mouse or keyboard to invoke the system menu.
- Size or move the window with the keyboard.
- Use Alt with a function key to invoke system menu options.
- Close the window, removing it from the screen.

Figure 2.1: The WELCO display

That's a considerable improvement, considering that we added only three lines to the program.

ANATOMY OF A WINDOW

As we develop a Presentation Manager program in this chapter, we will encounter three major concepts that are central to Presentation Manager programming:

- Windows
- Messages
- Presentation spaces

These three concepts are closely related: A window receives input in the form of messages and displays output to a presentation space. This entire book is about receiving messages and writing to presentation spaces. The window is at the center of it all.

Earlier I said that a window is a rectangular area on the screen. That's too easy. Sure, a window occupies an area on the screen, but that's what the window *looks like*, not what it *is*. As you start programming for the Presentation Manager, windows will seem to take on life. You will use anthropomorphic language when thinking and talking about windows. You will say that a window does something, a window responds in a certain way, and a window has a style. A window has a parent and can also have children. A window can talk to another window. And yes, a window occupies a rectangular area on the screen.

You'll find it helpful to think of windows in terms common in object-oriented programming. For example, you might now believe that some code someplace in the Presentation Manager draws the sizing border, system menu box, title bar, and minimize/maximize button so that they look the way they do. Yes, but no; you're closer to reality if you think of the window as drawing itself. The window itself determines how it will look.

This may become clearer if I discuss the *WinCreateStdWindow* function in more depth. I've been speaking about the window that *WinCreateStdWindow* creates as if it were a single window. Actually, *WinCreateStdWindow* is a high-level function that does the work of several other functions. As used in WELCO, *WinCreateStdWindow* creates four windows:

- A frame window
- A title bar window
- A system menu window
- A minimize/maximize window

(*WinCreateStdWindow* also creates a fifth window—the drop-down menu displayed from the system menu. But let's ignore that menu for now.)

These are separate windows. They are certainly bound together into one tidy unit, and they certainly have some relationship with each other, but in other ways these windows are distinct and independent.

The *WinCreateStdWindow* function creates the frame window, and the frame window creates the other three windows. These three windows correspond to the FCF_TITLEBAR, FCF_SYSMENU, and FCF_MINMAX flags set in the *flFrameFlags* parameter that is passed to *WinCreateStdWindow*. Each of these four windows has its own window handle. *WinCreateStdWindow* returns only the window handle of the frame window, but the other handles are available if you need them.

The frame window is like a base on which the other three windows are arranged. Each of these four windows draws itself. The frame window draws itself as a solid background surrounded by a sizing border. The title bar window, system menu window, and minimize/maximize window are relatively small windows that sit on top of the frame window.

Each of these four windows is distinct in appearance because each window draws itself in a unique way. Each window responds to input in a distinct way because each window processes its own input. This input takes the form of messages.

MESSAGES

In a conventional operating system, you must always ask for information. In the Presentation Manager, information is delivered to your program in the form of messages. For example, in a conventional OS/2 kernel program, you can determine the size of the screen display in units of characters or pixels by calling the *VioGetMode* function. In a Presentation Manager program, the size of the screen is less important than the size of one of your program's windows. The size of these windows can change. The window is notified of such a change through messages. Messages are notifications of user input and everything else that affects the program's windows.

A Presentation Manager program works by processing messages. In fact, it does little else except process messages. We say that a Presentation Manager program is *message-driven.*

A message is a data structure of type QMSG (queue message), which is defined in PMWIN.H as shown here:

```
typedef struct _QMSG
     {
     HWND   hwnd ;
     ULONG  msg ;
     MPARAM mp1 ;
     MPARAM mp2 ;
     ULONG  time ;
     POINTL ptl ;
     ULONG  reserved ;
     }
     QMSG ;
```

A message is usually directed to a particular window. The handle of the intended recipient of a message is given in the *hwnd* field of the structure.

The *msg* field (defined as type ULONG, or unsigned long) identifies the message. All messages have identifiers defined in PMWIN.H. Many of them begin with the letters WM ("window message"). Examples of these identifiers are WM_CREATE, WM_SIZE, WM_CHAR, WM_MOUSEMOVE, WM_PAINT, WM_DESTROY, and WM_QUIT. The *mp1* and *mp2* fields (defined as type MPARAM, which is a 32-bit pointer) are *message parameters.* They contain information connected with the particular message. The *time* field is the time the message was sent, and *ptl* (a POINTL structure) indicates the position of the mouse pointer at the time the message was sent. The following table summarizes this information:

The Message Structure

The message is addressed to	*hwnd*
The message is	*msg*
More detailed information is found in	*mp1* & *mp2*
The time of the message is	*time*
The mouse pointer was positioned at	*ptl*

When a message is addressed to a particular window (the usual case), the window processes the message. Everything a window does is the result of processing messages.

The message queue is a place where messages are stored. After a thread creates a message queue by calling *WinCreateMsgQueue*, the Presentation Manager uses this queue to store messages to all windows created in that thread. Not all messages are stored in the message queue (a distinction I'll discuss a little later in this chapter), but most messages relating directly to user input are stored there. The message queue created by WELCO stores messages for the frame window, the title bar window, the system menu window, and the minimize/maximize window.

THE MESSAGE LOOP

After a thread creates a message queue, it can create windows. Messages for the windows created in the thread are stored in the thread's message queue. Messages are retrieved from the message queue in a two-line piece of code called the *message loop*. The program first must define a variable of type QMSG, the message structure:

```
QMSG qmsg ;
```

After creating its windows, the program enters the message loop:

```
while (WinGetMsg (hab, &qmsg, NULLHANDLE, 0, 0))
     WinDispatchMsg (hab, &qmsg) ;
```

Notice that the last three parameters in the *WinGetMsg* call are set to 0 or NULLHANDLE (which is defined as equal to 0). This is normal: It indicates that *WinGetMsg* should retrieve all messages to all windows created in that thread.

WinGetMsg passes to the Presentation Manager a pointer to a QMSG message structure. The Presentation Manager fills the fields of the structure with the next message from the queue and returns control to the program. When *WinGetMsg* returns, the QMSG structure holds a valid message from the message queue. The program then "dispatches" the message to the appropriate window by calling *WinDispatchMsg*. When *WinDispatchMsg* returns, the program again calls *WinGetMsg*. If there are no messages in the queue, *WinGetMsg* waits until one is available. For all messages except WM_QUIT, *WinGetMsg* returns a nonzero value. WM_QUIT is a very special message. It causes *WinGetMsg* to return a 0 value and fall out of the *while* loop. (The WM_QUIT message is put into the queue when you select Close from the system menu of a program or otherwise exit it.) The program then makes calls to *WinDestroyWindow*, *WinDestroyMsgQueue*, and *WinTerminate* and exits *main*, ending the program.

Do you find this message loop code a little peculiar? The program fetches a message from the queue with *WinGetMsg*. That's OK. But the program is seemingly not doing anything with the message. It's simply throwing the message away by calling *WinDispatchMsg*. If the message is actually being dispatched somewhere, who's getting it? Where does the message go? Well, the message is addressed to a particular window, so obviously that window gets the message. *WinDispatchMsg* sends a message to a window.

Perhaps this is still bothering you. Maybe you're not quite comfortable with the concept of a window getting messages—it's much too abstract. Would it make more sense if I said that *WinDispatchMsg* causes a function to be called? And that the message being dispatched takes the form of parameters to the function? And that this function interprets these parameters and does something to process the message? Would you be more comfortable with the idea that this function, in a very real sense, *is* the window?

THE WINDOW PROCEDURE

Every window has an associated window procedure that processes messages for the window. The window procedure determines how the window responds to user input (in the form of messages) and what the window looks like.

WinGetMsg retrieves messages addressed to all windows that have been created in the thread of the process. During the *WinDispatchMsg* call, the Presentation Manager determines the address of the window procedure for the window whose handle is in the *hwnd* field of the message structure. It then calls this window procedure. The window procedure processes the message and returns control to the Presentation Manager, which then returns control to the program that called *WinDispatchMsg*.

The window procedures for the four windows created in WELCO are located in PMWIN.DLL, one of the dynamic link library modules that constitute the Presentation Manager. PMWIN.DLL contains window procedures that process messages for all frame windows, title bars, system menus, and so forth created by all programs currently running under the Presentation Manager. The title bar window displays text because that happens to be the way the window procedure draws its window. The title bar changes color to indicate that the program (or more precisely, the frame window) is active because the frame window sends the title bar window a message telling it to change the color. The title bar window responds to mouse input in its own specialized way to allow the window to be repositioned on the screen, and it then sends a message to the frame window informing it of the new position.

A typical window procedure is shown in Listing 2.7. Note that the four parameters to the window procedure are the first four fields of the message structure: the window handle, the message identifier, and the two MPARAM values that provide message-specific information. When the *WinDispatchMsg* function calls the window procedure, it extracts these four fields from the structure to pass to the window procedure.

A window procedure generally processes messages using a *switch* and *case* construction. For each type of message, the *mp1* and *mp2* parameters provide additional information about the message.

Listing 2.7: A typical window procedure

```
MRESULT EXPENTRY DoodadWndProc (HWND hwnd, ULONG msg, MPARAM mp1, MPARAM mp2)
     {
          [ definitions of local variables ]
     switch (msg)
          {
          case WM_CREATE:
                    [ do initialization ]
               return 0 ;

          case WM_PAINT:
                    [ paint the window ]
               return 0 ;

          case WM_CHAR:
                    [ process keyboard messages ]
               return 0 ;

          case WM_MOUSEMOVE:
                    [ process mouse movement messages ]
               return 0 ;

          case WM_DESTROY:
                    [ clean up ]
               return 0 ;
          }
     return WinDefWindowProc (hwnd, msg, mp1, mp2) ;
     }
```

The value the window procedure returns depends on the message. Usually it's a 0. Any message the window doesn't process must be passed on to a function called *WinDefWindowProc.* This function does default processing of all messages that a window procedure chooses to ignore.

Why are we spending time looking at the structure of window procedures that are internal to the Presentation Manager? It's not just an academic exercise. Not all window procedures are inside the Presentation Manager. Presentation Manager programs can also contain window procedures. In fact, they almost always do. And that's why we will soon add a window procedure—and a new window—to our program.

WELCOM—CREATING A CLIENT WINDOW

The four windows in WELCO seem to get along OK. But it's like a party in your house to which you weren't invited. After WELCO creates the four windows, it just retrieves messages from the message queue and dispatches them to window procedures located somewhere in PMWIN.DLL.

Let's get in on this action. In the WELCOM version of our program, shown in Listing 2.8, I've changed the *WinCreateStdWindow* call slightly so that it creates a fifth window. This window will fill that large area between the title bar and the visible parts of the sizing border, covering the still-visible part of the frame window. This fifth window is *our* window—we process the messages to it.

This new window is called a *client window.* Messages for this client window are stored in the message queue just like messages for the other four windows created by *WinCreateStdWindow.* The messages are retrieved from the queue with *WinGetMsg* and dispatched to the appropriate window procedure with *WinDispatchMsg.* But the window procedure for the client window is not in PMWIN.DLL. This window procedure is located in WELCOM itself.

REGISTERING A WINDOW CLASS

Every window has an associated window procedure. More precisely, every window is based on a particular *window class.* It's the window class that defines the window procedure used to process messages for all windows created based on that class.

The Presentation Manager has 19 predefined window classes. (One of them, for example, is the class called WC_TITLEBAR, using the PMWIN.H identifier.) Each of these window classes has a window procedure located in PMWIN.DLL or another dynamic link library. When *WinCreateStdWindow* was called in previous versions of the program, it created four windows based on four of these predefined window classes. Messages to these windows go to the window procedure for the window class.

If you want *WinCreateStdWindow* to create a client window with a window procedure in your own program, you must first register a new window class that identifies this window procedure. You do this by calling *WinRegisterClass,* as shown in the WELCOM.C program. The second and third parameters to *WinRegisterClass* are the most important: They specify the name of the window class and the address of the window procedure for that class. The window procedure processes messages to all windows that are based on that class.

Listing 2.8: The WELCOM program

The WELCOM.MAK File

```
#---------------------
# WELCOM.MAK make file
#---------------------

welcom.exe : welcom.obj welcom.def
     $(PRGLINK) welcom, welcom, NUL, $(PRGLIB), welcom

welcom.obj : welcom.c
     $(PRGCC) welcom.c
```

The WELCOM.C File

```
/*----------------------------------------------------
   WELCOM.C -- A Program that Creates a Client Window
               (c) Charles Petzold, 1993
  ----------------------------------------------------*/

#include <os2.h>

MRESULT EXPENTRY ClientWndProc (HWND, ULONG, MPARAM, MPARAM) ;

int main (void)
     {
     static CHAR  szClientClass [] = "Welcome" ;
     static ULONG flFrameFlags = FCF_TITLEBAR      | FCF_SYSMENU |
                                 FCF_SIZEBORDER    | FCF_MINMAX  |
                                 FCF_SHELLPOSITION | FCF_TASKLIST ;
     HAB          hab ;
     HMQ          hmq ;
     HWND         hwndFrame, hwndClient ;
     QMSG         qmsg ;

     hab = WinInitialize (0) ;
     hmq = WinCreateMsgQueue (hab, 0) ;

     WinRegisterClass (
                    hab,                 // Anchor block handle
                    szClientClass,       // Name of class being registered
                    ClientWndProc,       // Window procedure for class
                    0L,                  // Class style
                    0) ;                 // Extra bytes to reserve

     hwndFrame = WinCreateStdWindow (
                    HWND_DESKTOP,        // Parent window handle
                    WS_VISIBLE,          // Style of frame window
                    &flFrameFlags,       // Pointer to control data
```

Listing 2.8: The WELCOM program (Continued)

```
                    szClientClass,      // Client window class name
                    NULL,               // Title bar text
                    ØL,                 // Style of client window
                    Ø,                  // Module handle for resources
                    Ø,                  // ID of resources
                    &hwndClient) ;      // Pointer to client window handle

     while (WinGetMsg (hab, &qmsg, NULLHANDLE, Ø, Ø))
          WinDispatchMsg (hab, &qmsg) ;

     WinDestroyWindow (hwndFrame) ;
     WinDestroyMsgQueue (hmq) ;
     WinTerminate (hab) ;
     return Ø ;
     }

MRESULT EXPENTRY ClientWndProc (HWND hwnd, ULONG msg, MPARAM mp1, MPARAM mp2)
     {
     return WinDefWindowProc (hwnd, msg, mp1, mp2) ;
     }
```

The WELCOM.DEF File

```
;-----------------------------------
; WELCOM.DEF module definition file
;-----------------------------------

NAME           WELCOM    WINDOWAPI

DESCRIPTION    'Welcome to PM -- Program No. 6 (c) Charles Petzold, 1993'
PROTMODE
```

The predefined window classes in PMWIN.DLL and other dynamic link libraries are *public* window classes: They can be used by all programs running under the Presentation Manager. When your program contains a window procedure and you register a class for it, that is a *private* class that can be used only by your program.

The name of a private window class registered in a program is generally a character string that either is the name of the program or is derived from the name of the program, but it can really be anything you want. In WELCOM, the class name is the character string "Welcom" stored in the array *szClientClass*. (The "sz" prefix indicates that the variable is a string terminated by a zero byte.) The window procedure is the function named *ClientWndProc*, which in WELCOM is located after the *main* function. You can name the window procedure whatever you like. The window procedure is declared near the top of the program with the following statement:

```
MRESULT EXPENTRY ClientWndProc (HWND, ULONG, MPARAM, MPARAM) ;
```

Declaring *ClientWndProc* before *main* lets the C compiler recognize *ClientWndProc* as a function when compiling code for the *WinRegisterClass* call. The EXPENTRY identifier stands for "exported entry point" and indicates that the function is called from outside the program. EXPENTRY is defined in OS2DEF.H in the same way as APIENTRY.

THE NEW *WINCREATESTDWINDOW* CALL

The next step is to change some of the parameters to *WinCreateStdWindow* so that it creates a client window in addition to the other five windows. The fourth parameter to *WinCreateStdWindow* (previously set to NULL) is now set to the name of the client window class, which is the character array *szClientClass*. The last parameter to *WinCreateStdWindow* is a pointer to a variable that will receive the handle of the client window when *WinCreateStdWindow* creates it. This variable is named *hwndClient* and defined as type HWND.

WinCreateStdWindow now creates five windows, four of them based on predefined window classes and the fifth—the client window—based on the "Welcom" class. *WinCreateStdWindow* returns the window handle of the frame window, but it also stores the window handle of the client window in the variable pointed to by its last parameter.

PROCESSING THE MESSAGES

The *ClientWndProc* window procedure in WELCOM is called only from the Presentation Manager, from outside the program, using the same calling conventions that programs use for calling Presentation Manager functions. The window procedure returns an MRESULT (a 32-bit pointer) to the Presentation Manager. *ClientWndProc* receives messages only for the client window. Whenever *ClientWndProc* is called, the *hwnd* parameter is the window handle of the client window. This is the same window handle stored in the *hwndClient* variable in *main*.

ClientWndProc doesn't yet process any messages itself. Any message a window procedure doesn't process must be passed on to the *WinDefWindowProc* function in the Presentation Manager. The value returned from *WinDefWindowProc* is then returned from the window procedure.

That *ClientWndProc* doesn't process any messages causes a little problem: The client window isn't painted. If you experiment with WELCOM in the Presentation

Manager, you'll find that the client window displays whatever was underneath it when it is created or resized! Of course, we'll fix this problem shortly.

THE STREAM OF PROCESSING

With the client window procedure in place, you can now get a good sense of how Presentation Manager programs are structured and how they operate. The *main* function first performs initialization. At the very least, this involves calls to *WinInitialize*, *WinCreateMsgQueue*, *WinRegisterClass*, and *WinCreateStdWindow*. It then enters the message loop. When it exits the message loop, it cleans up with *WinDestroyWindow*, *WinDestroyMsgQueue*, and *WinTerminate*, and then exits *main*, terminating the program.

In the message loop, the program calls *WinGetMsg*, which retrieves the next message from the program's message queue. These messages include user input from the keyboard and mouse. The program passes the message back to the Presentation Manager by calling *WinDispatchMsg*. The Presentation Manager determines the address of the window procedure for the particular window that must receive the message, and it then calls the window procedure. This is either a predefined window procedure within the Presentation Manager or a window procedure within the program (such as *ClientWndProc*).

The window procedure either processes the message or calls *WinDefWindowProc*. The window procedure then returns control to the Presentation Manager (still in the *WinDispatchMsg* call), which returns control to the program's message loop.

This is a considerably more complex interaction between a program and an operating system than is typical in a more conventional operating system such as the OS/2 kernel. In the Presentation Manager, programs have a more intimate connection with the operating system and (potentially) other programs running under the Presentation Manager. It's the use of messages that makes the difference. Messages are the means of communication between the Presentation Manager and windows, and between windows themselves.

QUEUED AND NONQUEUED MESSAGES

I've been discussing how messages get from the message queue to a window procedure. However, not all messages originate in the message queue. Window procedures can also be called directly from the Presentation Manager.

When a message is placed in a program's message queue, retrieved with *WinGetMsg*, and dispatched to the window procedure with *WinDispatchMsg*, that message is said to be a "queued" message. Many of the messages relating to user input (such as the WM_CHAR keyboard message and the

WM_MOUSEMOVE mouse message) are queued messages. Timer messages are queued, as are menu messages (which signal a window procedure that a menu item has been chosen). But many other messages are sent to the window procedure directly without first being placed in the message queue. For example, the WM_CREATE message—which is the first message that a window procedure receives—is sent to the window while the Presentation Manager executes the *WinCreateStdWindow* function. The WM_DESTROY message is sent to a window procedure as part of the Presentation Manager's processing of the *WinDestroyWindow* call. These are "nonqueued" messages.

Whether a message is sent directly to a window procedure or dispatched to the window procedure after being retrieved from the message queue is generally not very important. The window procedure is "message central": It gets all messages to the window. It usually doesn't matter what route the messages took to get to the window procedure.

A window can also "post" or "send" messages to other windows. The *WinPostMsg* function places a message in the message queue associated with a particular window and returns immediately. The *WinSendMsg* function causes the Presentation Manager to call the window procedure directly. *WinSendMsg* returns only after the window procedure has processed the message. (The *WinDispatchMsg* call used in the message loop is similar to the *WinSendMsg* call.)

In short, *post* means to put the message in the mail box; *send* means to hand-deliver the message to the recipient. A message that is posted becomes a queued message; a message that is sent becomes a nonqueued message. As I said, from the perspective of the window procedure, the distinction is usually not very important. When speaking about messages, the term *send* is often used for convenience even when the message is actually posted. In the chapters ahead, I'll discuss whether a message is queued or nonqueued when necessary, but otherwise I'll tend to use this convenient terminology.

Messages sometimes generate other messages. This can happen when a window procedure declines to process a message and passes the message to *WinDefWindowProc. WinDefWindowProc* sometimes does default processing of a message by sending the window procedure another message. Calling Presentation Manager functions also sometimes results in the window procedure being sent a message.

This means that the window procedure must be recursive. Generally, this doesn't cause any problems, but you should keep it in the back of your mind. If you encounter a strange bug (a static local variable in your window procedure changing when you call a Presentation Manager function, for example), perhaps your window procedure is changing the variable itself while processing another message generated by the call to the Presentation Manager function.

WELCOME—Painting the Client Window

Now that we have a client window with its very own window procedure that processes messages to the window, we are ready to process a few messages and paint the client window. The final WELCOME program in this chapter is shown in Listing 2.9.

Listing 2.9: The WELCOME program

The WELCOME.MAK File

```
#----------------------
# WELCOME.MAK make file
#----------------------

welcome.exe : welcome.obj welcome.def
     $(PRGLINK) welcome, welcome, NUL, $(PRGLIB), welcome

welcome.obj : welcome.c
     $(PRGCC) welcome.c
```

The WELCOME.C File

```
/*----------------------------------------------------------
   WELCOME.C -- A Program that Writes to its Client Window
                (c) Charles Petzold, 1993
  ----------------------------------------------------------*/

#include <os2.h>

MRESULT EXPENTRY ClientWndProc (HWND, ULONG, MPARAM, MPARAM) ;

int main (void)
     {
     static CHAR  szClientClass [] = "Welcome1" ;
     static ULONG flFrameFlags = FCF_TITLEBAR      | FCF_SYSMENU |
                                 FCF_SIZEBORDER    | FCF_MINMAX  |
                                 FCF_SHELLPOSITION | FCF_TASKLIST ;
     HAB          hab ;
     HMQ          hmq ;
     HWND         hwndFrame, hwndClient ;
     QMSG         qmsg ;

     hab = WinInitialize (0) ;
     hmq = WinCreateMsgQueue (hab, 0) ;

     WinRegisterClass (
                    hab,                // Anchor block handle
                    szClientClass,      // Name of class being registered
                    ClientWndProc,      // Window procedure for class
                    CS_SIZEREDRAW,      // Class style
```

Listing 2.9: The WELCOME program (Continued)

```
                   0) ;                      // Extra bytes to reserve

     hwndFrame = WinCreateStdWindow (
                   HWND_DESKTOP,             // Parent window handle
                   WS_VISIBLE,               // Style of frame window
                   &flFrameFlags,            // Pointer to control data
                   szClientClass,            // Client window class name
                   NULL,                     // Title bar text
                   0L,                       // Style of client window
                   0,                        // Module handle for resources
                   0,                        // ID of resources
                   &hwndClient) ;            // Pointer to client window handle

     while (WinGetMsg (hab, &qmsg, NULLHANDLE, 0, 0))
          WinDispatchMsg (hab, &qmsg) ;

     WinDestroyWindow (hwndFrame) ;
     WinDestroyMsgQueue (hmq) ;
     WinTerminate (hab) ;
     return 0 ;
     }

MRESULT EXPENTRY ClientWndProc (HWND hwnd, ULONG msg, MPARAM mp1, MPARAM mp2)
     {
     static CHAR szText [] = "Welcome to the OS/2 2.0 Presentation Manager!" ;
     HPS         hps;
     RECTL       rcl ;

     switch (msg)
          {
          case WM_CREATE:
               DosBeep (261, 100) ;
               DosBeep (330, 100) ;
               DosBeep (392, 100) ;
               DosBeep (523, 500) ;
               return 0 ;

          case WM_PAINT:
               hps = WinBeginPaint (hwnd, NULLHANDLE, NULL) ;

               WinQueryWindowRect (hwnd, &rcl) ;

               WinDrawText (hps, -1, szText, &rcl, CLR_NEUTRAL, CLR_BACKGROUND,
                            DT_CENTER | DT_VCENTER | DT_ERASERECT) ;

               WinEndPaint (hps) ;
               return 0 ;

          case WM_DESTROY:
```

Listing 2.9: The WELCOME program (Continued)

```
                    DosBeep (523, 100) ;
                    DosBeep (392, 100) ;
                    DosBeep (330, 100) ;
                    DosBeep (261, 500) ;
                    return 0 ;
               }
          return WinDefWindowProc (hwnd, msg, mp1, mp2) ;
          }
```

The WELCOME.DEF File

```
;------------------------------------
; WELCOME.DEF module definition file
;------------------------------------

NAME           WELCOME   WINDOWAPI

DESCRIPTION    'Welcome to PM -- Program No. 7 (c) Charles Petzold, 1993'
PROTMODE
```

WELCOME.EXE displays the text "Welcome to the OS/2 2.0 Presentation Manager!" in the center of its client window, as shown in Figure 2.2.

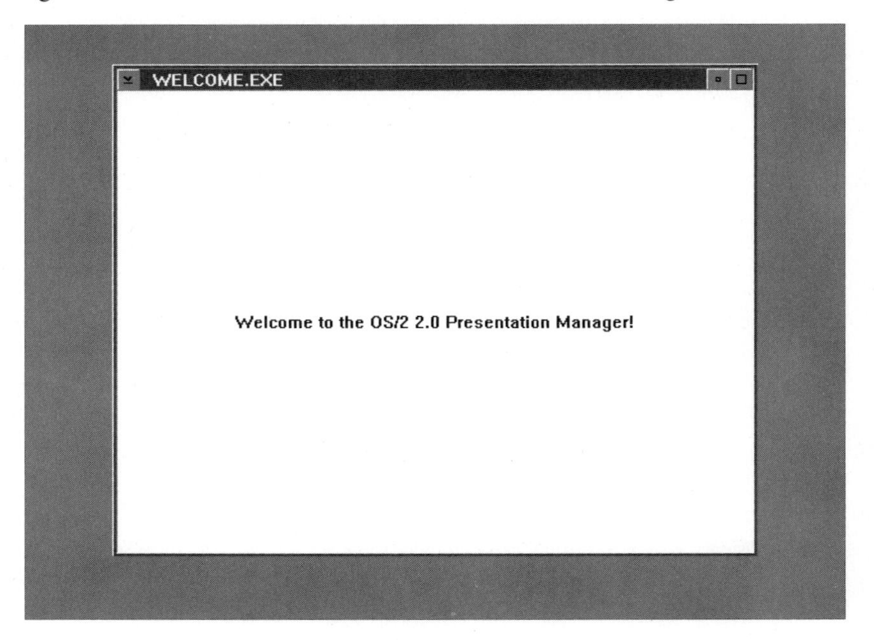

Figure 2.2: The WELCOME display

PROCESSING MESSAGES

The *ClientWndProc* window procedure in WELCOME shows the typical *switch* and *case* construction used to process messages. The *msg* parameter to the window procedure identifies the message. *ClientWndProc* processes three messages: WM_CREATE, WM_PAINT, and WM_DESTROY. In most cases, a window procedure returns 0L when it processes a message. Any message not processed must be passed on to *WinDefWindowProc*, and the value returned from *WinDefWindowProc* must be returned from the window procedure.

The WM_CREATE message is the first message that a window procedure receives. It is sent directly to the window procedure during the *WinCreateStdWindow* call. A window procedure can perform some window initialization during the WM_CREATE message. In WELCOME, *ClientWndProc* calls the OS/2 *DosBeep* function to play the notes of a C-major chord to indicate that the client window has arrived.

The WM_DESTROY message is the last message a window procedure receives. The Presentation Manager sends this message to the window procedure during the *WinDestroyWindow* call. Although window procedures can do some cleanup during the WM_DESTROY message, *ClientWndProc* again calls *DosBeep* a few times as a swan song to indicate that the client window is being destroyed.

THE WM_PAINT MESSAGE

One of the most important messages that a window procedure receives is WM_PAINT, which tells the window procedure when to display something on the window. "What?" you say. "The Presentation Manager is telling *me* when I can display something on *my* window? I have to be given permission? What kind of fascist operating system is this?" Cool down. The WM_PAINT message is simply the Presentation Manager's way of telling you that a portion of your window is invalid—that is, that part of the window's visible area contains garbage or perhaps nothing at all. The WM_PAINT message tells the window function that the window is due for a paint job.

How does the window become invalid? When a window is first created, the entire window is invalid. In fact, one of the first queued messages the client window receives is WM_PAINT. The window function can take this opportunity to display something in the window. Now suppose you minimize the window and then restore it to the original size. The Presentation Manager doesn't save the contents of the window when the window is minimized. In a graphical environment it's simply too much data. Thus when the window is restored after being minimized, it is invalid, and a WM_PAINT message is placed in the message queue. If you start rearranging several windows on the display, a window may overlap others. The Presentation Manager generally won't save the area of a window covered by another window. When the window is uncovered, the previously hidden area is invalid, and a WM_PAINT message goes into the message queue.

This is probably quite different from the way you usually think about using the video display. Under a conventional operating system, your program can display something on the screen whenever it wants and not worry about something on the screen mysteriously disappearing. Under the Presentation Manager, you can still display something on a window whenever you want. But it often makes more sense to do painting only when the window function receives the WM_PAINT message. The program must retain what it needs to re-create the appearance of the window, because it can receive a WM_PAINT message at almost any time. If the window function displays something on the window while processing a message other than WM_PAINT, it must retain that information and reexecute the same painting code when it gets a WM_PAINT message.

Normally, if you resize a window to make it smaller, the window procedure doesn't receive a WM_PAINT message. The Presentation Manager simply cuts off the edges of the window that previously extended past the new size. You'll note, however, that in WELCOME the fourth parameter to *WinRegisterClass* is set to CS_SIZEREDRAW. This is a window class style. It causes the Presentation Manager to invalidate the entire window and post a WM_PAINT message to the client window whenever the size of the window changes.

When you get a WM_PAINT message, you can obtain the coordinates of the invalid area of the window. You need update only that part of the window. We'll explore this and other aspects of the WM_PAINT message more in upcoming chapters. Right now all you have to know is that WM_PAINT informs the window procedure that it's time to update the appearance of the window.

PROCESSING WM_PAINT

The code that processes the WM_PAINT message in a window function must begin with a call to *WinBeginPaint* and end with a call to *WinEndPaint*. When *WinEndPaint* is called, the Presentation Manager validates the entire area of the window. Using a simple form of the *WinBeginPaint* call, the code looks like this:

```
case WM_PAINT:
     hps = WinBeginPaint (hwnd, NULL, NULL) ;

          [ paint the window ]

     WinEndPaint (hps) ;
     return 0 ;
```

If your program doesn't process WM_PAINT messages (as WELCOM doesn't), they are passed to *WinDefWindowProc*. *WinDefWindowProc* simply calls *WinBeginPaint* and *WinEndPaint* with nothing in between to validate the entire area of the client window. This is a good example of how *WinDefWindowProc* takes care of chores a program chooses to ignore. If *WinBeginPaint* and *WinEndPaint* aren't called during a WM_PAINT message, an area of the window remains invalid, and the WM_PAINT message isn't removed from the message queue.

The handle returned from the *WinBeginPaint* call is a handle to a presentation space. The handle is stored in a variable named *hps* of type HPS. You need this handle to the presentation space to draw on the surface of the client window. The presentation space handle is the first parameter to all the Graphics Programming Interface (GPI) drawing functions.

The presentation space is essentially a data structure that defines an abstract display surface. The presentation space is associated with a *device context*, which defines a particular physical display medium. In the form of the *WinBeginPaint* call used here, the presentation space for which we get a handle is associated with a device context for the video display—in particular, the part of the display that the client window occupies. This form of the *WinBeginPaint* call (with the second parameter set to NULL) implies that we're using a subset of GPI that is called the *cached micro-PS*.

PAINTING WELCOME'S CLIENT WINDOW

After the *WinBeginPaint* call, WELCOME obtains the dimensions of the client window by using this function:

```
WinQueryWindowRect (hwnd, &rcl) ;
```

The first parameter is *hwnd*, the handle to the client window. The *rcl* variable is a structure of type RECTL (rectangle). The RECTL structure has four fields: *xLeft*, *yBottom*, *xRight*, and *yTop*. *WinQueryWindowRect* fills the fields of the *rcl* structure with the current coordinates of the client window. These coordinates are relative to the lower-left corner of the client window, hence the *xLeft* and *yBottom* fields are set to 0. The *xRight* field is actually the width of the window in pixels, and *yTop* is the height of the window in pixels.

The *WinDrawText* function is used to display the string "Welcome to the OS/2 2.0 Presentation Manager!" in the center of the client window. It uses the *rcl* rectangle structure and the parameter DT_CENTER | DT_VCENTER | DT_ERASERECT to specify that the string is to be centered horizontally and vertically within the rectangle and that the rectangle (the entire window) is to be erased before the text is displayed. The CLR_NEUTRAL and

CLR_BACKGROUND parameters specify the text color and background color. I'll discuss these two color identifiers in Chapter 5.

TOO MUCH OVERHEAD?

This has been a long journey to write a simple program that displays some text and plays a tune. But I've covered all the facets of Presentation Manager programming. You've learned about windows. You've learned about messages. You've learned about presentation spaces.

That's it. Everything that follows is just detail.

More Fun with Windows

EXPLORING THE STANDARD WINDOW

CONTROLS AND THEIR OWNERS

REGISTERING THE WINDOW CLASS

CREATING THE STANDARD WINDOW

THE *WINCREATEWINDOW* FUNCTION

Chapter 3

In Chapter 2, our rush to create a functional window required that we ignore some details and finer points of the art of window creation. Here we'll try variations on the basic theme.

Exploring the Standard Window

The *WinCreateStdWindow* function creates one or more windows. In the final version of the WELCOME program shown in Chapter 2, *WinCreateStdWindow* creates five windows: the frame, title bar, system menu, minimize/maximize window, and the client window. The term *standard window* refers to this collection of windows organized around the frame window.

All but one of the windows that make up the standard window are created based on window classes already registered by the Presentation Manager. Messages to these windows come through the program's message queue but are dispatched to the particular window procedure in PMWIN.DLL that is defined by the window class. The client window, on the other hand, is generally based on a window class that the program itself registers, and it uses a window procedure within the program (called *ClientWndProc* in WELCOME) to process its messages.

The windows that make up the standard window receive messages from the Presentation Manager (often initiated by user input) but can also send messages to one another. They essentially carry on a family conversation.

THE FAMILY OF WINDOWS

Windows created in the Presentation Manager usually have a parent-child relationship. In the standard window, the frame window is the parent, and the other windows (including the client window) are the children of the frame window. Thus we can define a standard window as "a frame window and its children." Windows with a common parent are called *sibling* windows. A window can have many children but only one parent. A window's children, its children's children, and so forth are called the window's *descendants.*

The grand matriarch of Presentation Manager windows is the *desktop* window, which occupies the entire screen. Although it appears to be simply a background color (or perhaps a bitmapped image), the desktop window is a real window with a real window procedure somewhere in PMWIN.DLL that processes its messages. Every other window is a descendant of the desktop window. (Actually this isn't quite true. Some windows, called *object* windows, have no parent. Like other windows, object windows can send and receive messages, but they aren't visible on the screen and don't receive user input. When I discuss windows in this book I'm almost always talking about windows that are *not* object windows.)

A child of the desktop window is called a *top-level* window. Virtually every program that runs under the Presentation Manager creates at least one top-level window. When a program such as WELCOME calls *WinCreateStdWindow* to create the application's main window, the frame window is a top-level window. The other windows created by the function are children of the frame window and are not top-level windows. The family tree for the WELCOME program is shown in Figure 3.1.

A child window is affected by its parent in several ways:

- A child window is always displayed within the area of the screen occupied by its parent. We say that the child is *clipped* on the surface of its parent. This is fairly obvious in the case of the desktop window and the frame window because the desktop window encompasses the entire screen. The children of the frame window also appear within the area occupied by the frame. If the frame window tried to position part of the title bar window outside of the area that is occupied by the frame, the part of the title bar outside the frame window would not be visible.

- Child windows remain in the same position relative to the parent unless you move them explicitly. When you move the frame window around the screen, the children follow. This happens automatically: When the frame window wants to move itself (usually because it has received a message

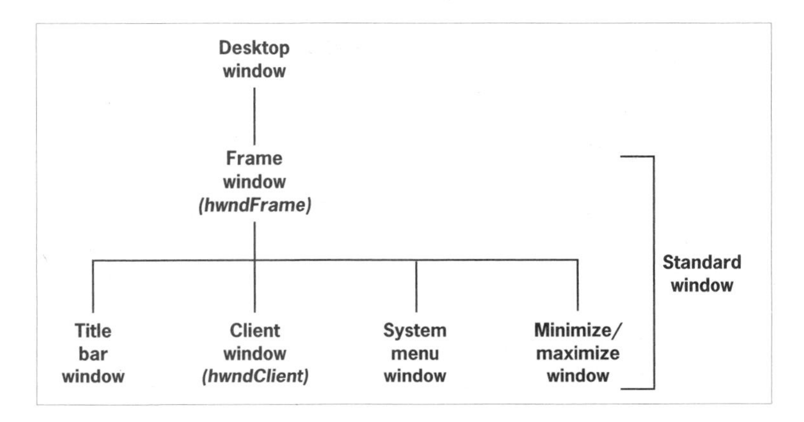

Figure 3.1: The WELCOME family tree

from the title bar window that the user has moved the window), it need only tell the Presentation Manager to move the frame. The Presentation Manager takes care of moving the children.

- When a parent window is hidden, minimized, or destroyed, all of its children (and, by extension, all its descendants) are also hidden, minimized, or destroyed. This should be partly obvious in WELCOME. If you minimize the frame window, all the children of the frame window are also removed from the screen. When the frame window is destroyed by the call to *WinDestroyWindow* after WELCOME leaves the message loop, all the children of the frame window (including the client window) are also destroyed. *ClientWndProc* receives a WM_DESTROY message at that time.
- Sibling windows can overlap on the screen. We'll see examples of overlapping siblings in the WELCOME2 and WELCOME3 programs in this chapter.

The Presentation Manager includes a function, *WinQueryWindow*, that you can use to determine a window's parent:

```
hwndParent = WinQueryWindow (hwnd, QW_PARENT) ;
```

The function call sets the variable *hwndParent* to the handle of the parent window of *hwnd*. For example, after the *WinCreateStdWindow* function returns control to your program, the following call obtains the frame window handle:

```
hwndFrame = WinQueryWindow (hwndClient, QW_PARENT) ;
```

This will be the same window handle originally returned from *WinCreateStdWindow*.

If *hwndFrame* is a top-level window, you can obtain the desktop window handle by calling:

```
hwndDesktop = WinQueryWindow (hwndFrame, QW_PARENT) ;
```

Or you can use the function specifically designed for this purpose:

```
hwndDesktop = WinQueryDesktopWindow (hab, NULLHANDLE) ;
```

In many Presentation Manager functions, the HWND_DESKTOP identifier is used to refer to the desktop window. Usually you pass HWND_DESKTOP as the first parameter to *WinCreateStdWindow*. This makes the frame a top-level window. The application often has no choice but to do this: The frame window must have a parent, but the application doesn't know about any other windows except the desktop window. The desktop is thus the only possible parent.

If the program calls *WinCreateStdWindow* a second time, it has a choice: The second frame window could be another top-level window, or it could be a child of one of the windows created in the first *WinCreateStdWindow* call (most likely a child of the first client window). Let's look at an example of the first approach.

CREATING MULTIPLE TOP-LEVEL WINDOWS

The WELCOME2 program, shown in Listing 3.1, creates two top-level standard windows. The program contains two window procedures (*Client1WndProc* and *Client2WndProc*), registers two window classes ("Welcome2.1" and "Welcome2.2"), and calls *WinCreateStdWindow* twice.

Listing 3.1: The WELCOME2 program

The WELCOME2.MAK File

```
#-----------------------
# WELCOME2.MAK make file
#-----------------------

welcome2.exe : welcome2.obj welcome2.def
     $(PRGLINK) welcome2, welcome2, NUL, $(PRGLIB), welcome2

welcome2.obj : welcome2.c
     $(PRGCC) welcome2.c
```

Listing 3.1: The WELCOME2 program (Continued)

The WELCOME2.C File

```
/*-----------------------------------------------------------
   WELCOME2.C -- A Program that Creates Two Top-Level Windows
                 (c) Charles Petzold, 1993
  -----------------------------------------------------------*/

#include <os2.h>

MRESULT EXPENTRY Client1WndProc (HWND, ULONG, MPARAM, MPARAM) ;
MRESULT EXPENTRY Client2WndProc (HWND, ULONG, MPARAM, MPARAM) ;

int main (void)
     {
     static CHAR  szClientClass1 [] = "Welcome2.1",
                  szClientClass2 [] = "Welcome2.2" ;
     static ULONG flFrameFlags = FCF_TITLEBAR      | FCF_SYSMENU |
                                 FCF_SIZEBORDER    | FCF_MINMAX  |
                                 FCF_SHELLPOSITION | FCF_TASKLIST ;
     HAB          hab ;
     HMQ          hmq ;
     HWND         hwndFrame1, hwndFrame2, hwndClient1, hwndClient2 ;
     QMSG         qmsg ;

     hab = WinInitialize (0) ;
     hmq = WinCreateMsgQueue (hab, 0) ;

     WinRegisterClass (
                    hab,                // Anchor block handle
                    szClientClass1,     // Name of class being registered
                    Client1WndProc,     // Window procedure for class
                    CS_SIZEREDRAW,      // Class style
                    0) ;                // Extra bytes to reserve

     WinRegisterClass (
                    hab,                // Anchor block handle
                    szClientClass2,     // Name of class being registered
                    Client2WndProc,     // Window procedure for class
                    CS_SIZEREDRAW,      // Class style
                    0) ;                // Extra bytes to reserve

     hwndFrame1 = WinCreateStdWindow (
                    HWND_DESKTOP,       // Parent window handle
                    WS_VISIBLE,         // Style of frame window
                    &flFrameFlags,      // Pointer to control data
                    szClientClass1,     // Client window class name
                    NULL,               // Title bar text
                    0L,                 // Style of client window
```

Listing 3.1: The WELCOME2 program (Continued)

```
                    0,                      // Module handle for resources
                    0,                      // ID of resources
                    &hwndClient1) ;         // Pointer to client window handle

     hwndFrame2 = WinCreateStdWindow (
                    HWND_DESKTOP,           // Parent window handle
                    WS_VISIBLE,             // Style of frame window
                    &flFrameFlags,          // Pointer to control data
                    szClientClass2,         // Client window class name
                    "Window No. 2",         // Title bar text
                    0L,                     // Style of client window
                    0,                      // Module handle for resources
                    0,                      // ID of resources
                    &hwndClient2) ;         // Pointer to client window handle

     while (WinGetMsg (hab, &qmsg, NULLHANDLE, 0, 0))
          WinDispatchMsg (hab, &qmsg) ;

     WinDestroyWindow (hwndFrame1) ;
     WinDestroyWindow (hwndFrame2) ;
     WinDestroyMsgQueue (hmq) ;
     WinTerminate (hab) ;
     return 0 ;
     }

MRESULT EXPENTRY Client1WndProc (HWND hwnd, ULONG msg, MPARAM mp1, MPARAM mp2)
     {
     static CHAR szText [] = "Welcome to Window No. 1" ;
     HPS         hps ;
     RECTL       rcl ;

     switch (msg)
          {
          case WM_PAINT:
               hps = WinBeginPaint (hwnd, NULLHANDLE, NULL) ;

               WinQueryWindowRect (hwnd, &rcl) ;

               WinDrawText (hps, -1, szText, &rcl, CLR_NEUTRAL, CLR_BACKGROUND,
                            DT_CENTER | DT_VCENTER | DT_ERASERECT) ;

               WinEndPaint (hps) ;
               return 0 ;
          }
     return WinDefWindowProc (hwnd, msg, mp1, mp2) ;
     }

MRESULT EXPENTRY Client2WndProc (HWND hwnd, ULONG msg, MPARAM mp1, MPARAM mp2)
     {
```

Listing 3.1: The WELCOME2 program (Continued)

```
     static CHAR szText [] = "Welcome to Window No. 2" ;
     HPS         hps ;
     RECTL       rcl ;

     switch (msg)
          {
          case WM_PAINT:
               hps = WinBeginPaint (hwnd, NULLHANDLE, NULL) ;

               WinQueryWindowRect (hwnd, &rcl) ;

               WinDrawText (hps, -1, szText, &rcl, CLR_NEUTRAL, CLR_BACKGROUND,
                            DT_CENTER | DT_VCENTER | DT_ERASERECT) ;

               WinEndPaint (hps) ;
               return 0 ;

          case WM_CLOSE:
               return 0 ;
          }
     return WinDefWindowProc (hwnd, msg, mp1, mp2) ;
     }
```

The WELCOME2.DEF File

```
;-------------------------------------
; WELCOME2.DEF module definition file
;-------------------------------------

NAME           WELCOME2  WINDOWAPI

DESCRIPTION    'Creates Two Top-Level Windows (c) Charles Petzold, 1993'
PROTMODE
```

The first parameter in the *WinCreateStdWindow* call is the parent of the frame window. In both function calls, this parameter is set to HWND_DESKTOP. The two frame windows in WELCOME2 share the same parent and are thus siblings. The WELCOME2 family tree is shown in Figure 3.2.

When you run WELCOME2 (shown in Figure 3.3), you'll find that the two top-level windows function independently, almost as if they were created in different programs. Both windows are listed on the Window List. Because all top-level windows are siblings, they can overlap. But only one top-level window is "active" at any time. You can switch between the two windows (as you can switch among all top-level windows listed on the Window List) using the Alt-Esc or Alt-Tab key combinations.

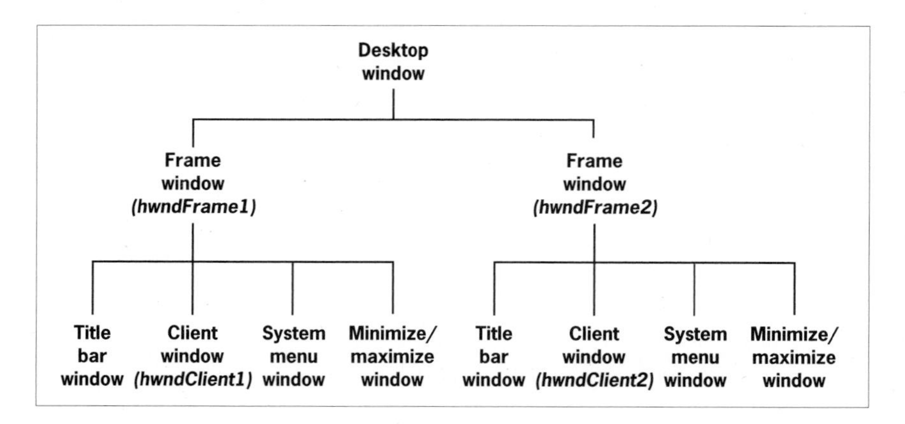

Figure 3.2: The WELCOME2 family tree

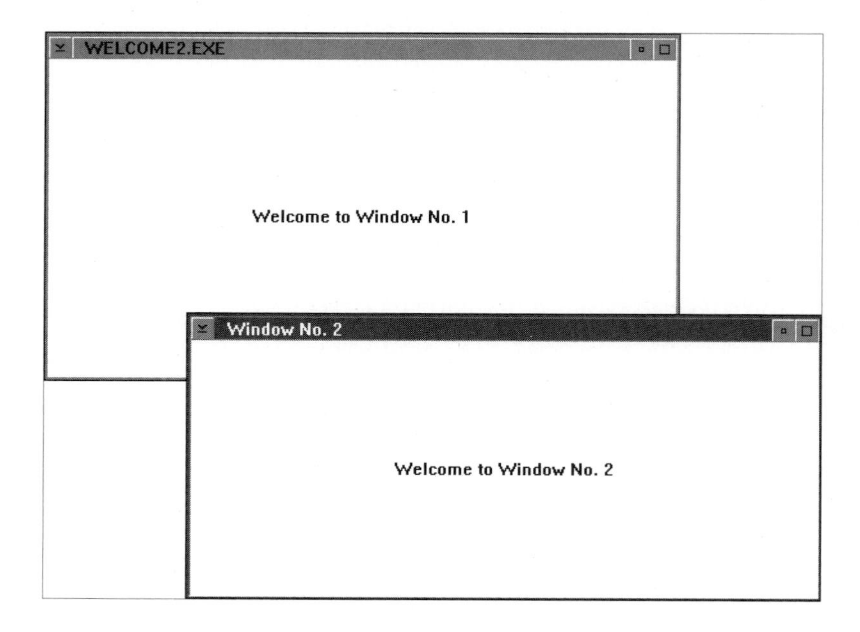

Figure 3.3: The WELCOME2 display

To simplify this demonstration program, I have both window functions in WELCOME2 perform approximately the same task, which is to display some text in the client window. However, the two window functions could perform entirely different tasks from one another. For example, it's not difficult to imagine a Presentation Manager CAD (computer-assisted design) program organized into two top-level windows. One window could be an ASCII text editor that allows you to enter and edit a series of drawing commands. The other window could display the graphical representation of these commands. If you changed one of the commands in the editor window, the change could be reflected in the graphics window; likewise, if you changed the drawing itself (perhaps using the mouse), the change could be reflected in the corresponding text command in the editor window. The two client window procedures would communicate these changes to each other with messages. You would store the two client window handles returned from the *WinCreateStdWindow* calls in global variables so that both window procedures could access them.

What messages would the two client windows send to each other? That's up to you. PMWIN.H defines the identifier WM_USER specifically for the purpose of creating your own messages. Within a program, you can define private messages that use values of WM_USER or above:

```
#define WM_MYMESSAGE0 (WM_USER + 0)
#define WM_MYMESSAGE1 (WM_USER + 1)
#define WM_MYMESSAGE2 (WM_USER + 2)
```

If *Client1WndProc* needs to send a WM_MYMESSAGE1 message to *Client2WndProc,* it can do so:

```
WinSendMsg (hwndClient2, WM_MYMESSAGE1, MPFROMLONG (lData1),
            MPFROMLONG (lData2)) ;
```

The *lData1* and *lData2* would be long integers with message-specific data. The MPFROMLONG macros convert a long integer to an MPARAM (32-bit pointer) data type. The message would be processed within *Client2WndProc* like any other message:

```
case WM_MYMESSAGE1:
          [ process message ]
     return 0 ;
```

Keep in mind that the two MPARAM values that accompany messages can be pointers to structures or big blocks of memory, so the amount of data passed in the message can be very large. The value returned from *WinSendMsg* is the value that the window procedure returns once it has processed the message. This is defined as an MRESULT, which is also a 32-bit pointer.

TITLE BAR TEXT

Notice that in Figure 3.3 the first window's title bar contains the text "WELCOME2.EXE" and the second has "Window No. 2." This is what you'll see when you run the program from the CMD.EXE prompt or the disk drive window. However, if you install WELCOME2 to be run from the Desktop Shell, you can specify a program title, and that's what you'll see in the title bar of the first window (but not the second).

This is part of what the FCF_TASKLIST flag does. The title bar text (and the Window List entry) is the name under which the program was started. For most programs in this book, I use NULL for the *WinCreateStdWindow* parameter that indicates the title bar text. This causes the title bar to display only the .EXE file name or the program title. For the second window in WELCOME2, however, I used "Window No. 2" for the title bar text in *WinCreateStdWindow*, and that overrides any other title text.

TERMINATING A PRESENTATION MANAGER PROGRAM

I've written WELCOME2 so that you cannot terminate the program by selecting Close from the second window's system menu. This requires a little explanation of how Presentation Manager programs terminate. When you select Close from the system menu, the client window procedure receives a WM_CLOSE message. If the window procedure passes WM_CLOSE to *WinDefWindowProc*, the Presentation Manager posts a WM_QUIT message to the message queue. This causes *WinGetMsg* to return 0 when the WM_QUIT message is retrieved from the queue, and the program exits the message loop.

If a window procedure simply traps WM_CLOSE messages and returns from the window procedure without calling *WinDefWindowProc*, nothing happens. This is how *Client2WndProc* essentially disables the Close option on its system menu.

WELCOME2 is somewhat unorthodox. A Presentation Manager program usually creates only one top-level main window. Any other top-level windows created in the program (such as dialog boxes) exist only for short periods of time.

CREATING CHILDREN OF THE CLIENT

A more common approach to creating multiple standard windows is demonstrated in the WELCOME3 program, which is shown in Listing 3.2.

Listing 3.2: The WELCOME3 program

The WELCOME3.MAK File

```
#-----------------------
# WELCOME3.MAK make file
#-----------------------

welcome3.exe : welcome3.obj welcome3.def
     $(PRGLINK) welcome3, welcome3, NUL, $(PRGLIB), welcome3

welcome3.obj : welcome3.c
     $(PRGCC) welcome3.c
```

The WELCOME3.C File

```
/*-----------------------------------------------------------
   WELCOME3.C -- Creates a Top-Level Window and Two Children
                 (c) Charles Petzold, 1993
  -----------------------------------------------------------*/

#define INCL_WIN
#include <os2.h>

MRESULT EXPENTRY ClientWndProc (HWND, ULONG, MPARAM, MPARAM) ;
MRESULT EXPENTRY ChildWndProc  (HWND, ULONG, MPARAM, MPARAM) ;

int main (void)
     {
     static CHAR  szClientClass [] = "Welcome3",
                  szChildClass  [] = "Welcome3.Child" ;
     static ULONG flFrameFlags = FCF_TITLEBAR      | FCF_SYSMENU  |
                                 FCF_SIZEBORDER    | FCF_MINMAX   |
                                 FCF_SHELLPOSITION | FCF_TASKLIST ;
     HAB          hab ;
     HMQ          hmq ;
     HWND         hwndFrame,  hwndClient, hwndChildClient1, hwndChildClient2 ;
     QMSG         qmsg ;

     hab = WinInitialize (0) ;
     hmq = WinCreateMsgQueue (hab, 0) ;

     WinRegisterClass (
                    hab,                 // Anchor block handle
                    szClientClass,       // Name of class being registered
                    ClientWndProc,       // Window procedure for class
                    CS_SIZEREDRAW,       // Class style
                    0) ;                 // Extra bytes to reserve

     WinRegisterClass (
```

Listing 3.2: The WELCOME3 program (Continued)

```
               hab,                 // Anchor block handle
               szChildClass,        // Name of class being registered
               ChildWndProc,        // Window procedure for class
               CS_SIZEREDRAW,       // Class style
               sizeof (PVOID)) ;    // Extra bytes to reserve

     /*-------------------------
        Create top-level window
       -------------------------*/

     hwndFrame = WinCreateStdWindow (
               HWND_DESKTOP,        // Parent window handle
               WS_VISIBLE,          // Style of frame window
               &flFrameFlags,       // Pointer to control data
               szClientClass,       // Client window class name
               NULL,                // Title bar text
               ØL,                  // Style of client window
               Ø,                   // Module handle for resources
               Ø,                   // ID of resources
               &hwndClient) ;       // Pointer to client window handle

     /*--------------------------
        Create two child windows
       --------------------------*/

     flFrameFlags &= ~FCF_TASKLIST ;

     WinCreateStdWindow (
               hwndClient,          // Parent window handle
               WS_VISIBLE,          // Style of frame window
               &flFrameFlags,       // Pointer to control data
               szChildClass,        // Client window class name
               "Child No. 1",       // Title bar text
               ØL,                  // Style of client window
               Ø,                   // Module handle for resources
               Ø,                   // ID of resources
               &hwndChildClient1) ;// Pointer to client window handle

     WinCreateStdWindow (
               hwndClient,          // Parent window handle
               WS_VISIBLE,          // Style of frame window
               &flFrameFlags,       // Pointer to control data
               szChildClass,        // Client window class name
               "Child No. 2",       // Title bar text
               ØL,                  // Style of client window
               Ø,                   // Module handle for resources
               Ø,                   // ID of resources
               &hwndChildClient2) ;// Pointer to client window handle
```

Listing 3.2: The WELCOME3 program (Continued)

```
          /*---------------------------------------------------
             Set reserved area of window to text string pointers
            ---------------------------------------------------*/

     WinSetWindowPtr (hwndChildClient1, QWL_USER, "I'm a child ...") ;
     WinSetWindowPtr (hwndChildClient2, QWL_USER, "... Me too!") ;

     while (WinGetMsg (hab, &qmsg, NULLHANDLE, 0, 0))
          WinDispatchMsg (hab, &qmsg) ;

     WinDestroyWindow (hwndFrame) ;
     WinDestroyMsgQueue (hmq) ;
     WinTerminate (hab) ;
     return 0 ;
     }

MRESULT EXPENTRY ClientWndProc (HWND hwnd, ULONG msg, MPARAM mp1, MPARAM mp2)
     {
     static CHAR szText [] = "I'm the parent of two children" ;
     HPS         hps ;
     RECTL       rcl ;

     switch (msg)
          {
          case WM_PAINT:
               hps = WinBeginPaint (hwnd, NULLHANDLE, NULL) ;

               WinQueryWindowRect (hwnd, &rcl) ;

               WinDrawText (hps, -1, szText, &rcl, CLR_NEUTRAL, CLR_BACKGROUND,
                            DT_CENTER | DT_VCENTER | DT_ERASERECT) ;

               WinEndPaint (hps) ;
               return 0 ;
          }
     return WinDefWindowProc (hwnd, msg, mp1, mp2) ;
     }

MRESULT EXPENTRY ChildWndProc (HWND hwnd, ULONG msg, MPARAM mp1, MPARAM mp2)
     {
     HPS   hps ;
     RECTL rcl ;

     switch (msg)
          {
          case WM_PAINT:
               hps = WinBeginPaint (hwnd, NULLHANDLE, NULL) ;

               WinQueryWindowRect (hwnd, &rcl) ;
```

Listing 3.2: The WELCOME3 program (Continued)

```
               WinDrawText (hps, -1, WinQueryWindowPtr (hwnd, QWL_USER), &rcl,
                            CLR_NEUTRAL, CLR_BACKGROUND,
                            DT_CENTER | DT_VCENTER | DT_ERASERECT) ;

               WinEndPaint (hps) ;
               return 0 ;

          case WM_CLOSE:
               WinDestroyWindow (WinQueryWindow (hwnd, QW_PARENT)) ;
               return 0 ;
          }
     return WinDefWindowProc (hwnd, msg, mp1, mp2) ;
     }
```

The WELCOME3.DEF File

```
;-------------------------------------
; WELCOME4.DEF module definition file
;-------------------------------------

NAME           WELCOME4  WINDOWAPI

DESCRIPTION    'Creates Top-Level and 3 Children (c) Charles Petzold, 1993'
PROTMODE
```

WELCOME3 makes three calls to *WinCreateStdWindow*. The first call creates a top-level window. The second and third calls create child standard windows of the first client window. For these children, the first parameter to *WinCreateStdWindow* is *hwndClient*—the client window handle returned from the first call. The second and third standard windows are siblings. Both client windows of these children are based on the same window class ("Welcome3.Child") and thus share the same window procedure, *ChildWndProc*, but they could easily be based on different window classes.

Figure 3.4 shows the WELCOME3 family tree, and Figure 3.5 shows the program running under the Presentation Manager. (To make the program look as it does in Figure 3.5, you'll have to select each child window using the mouse, and then use Alt-F7, Alt-F8, and the cursor keys to move and size the windows.)

This is the more common technique for creating multiple windows within a program and is the basis for the Multiple Document Interface (MDI) convention used by some programs. The top-level window is the application's main window. The client window of this top-level standard window is the application's workspace. Several other child windows can exist within this workspace.

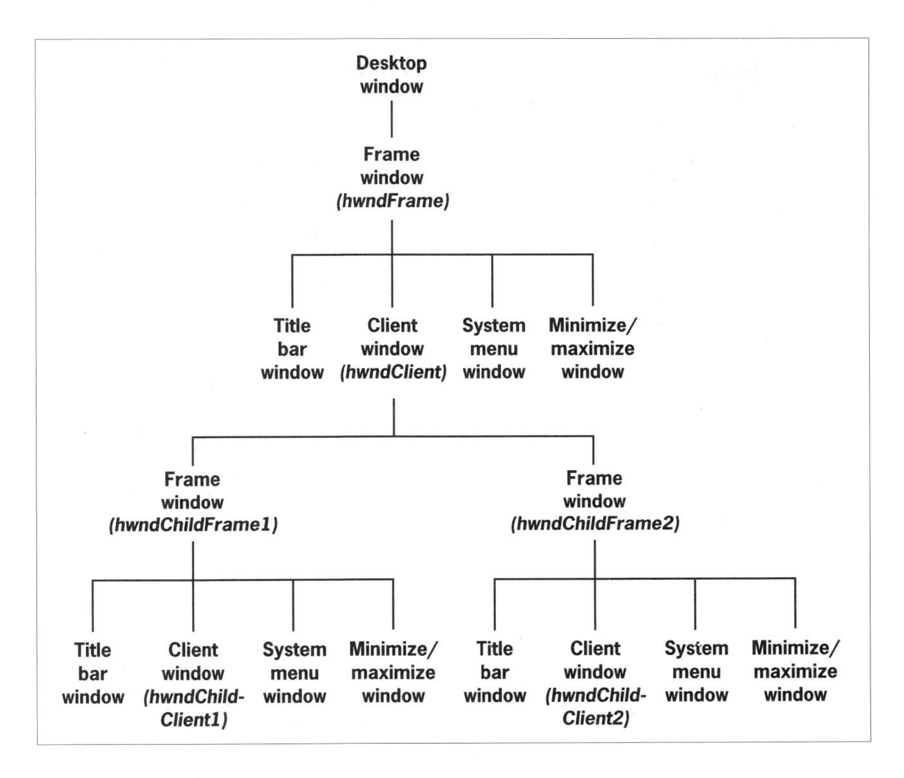

Figure 3.4: The WELCOME3 family tree

You'll notice that the two child standard windows obey the rules for child windows discussed earlier: They can be displayed only within the area occupied by their parent (the main client window); because they are siblings, they can overlap; they follow the parent when the parent is moved around the screen; and they are minimized when the parent is minimized.

You can also minimize these two children independently—a small icon-sized image of the children's client areas will appear at the bottom of the parent's client area.

Although you can use the Alt-Esc or Alt-Tab key combination to move between the top-level windows in the Presentation Manager, there is no automatic keyboard interface for moving between windows that are not top-level windows. The program would have to provide this keyboard interface. However, you can bring a particular child standard window to the top by clicking on it with the mouse.

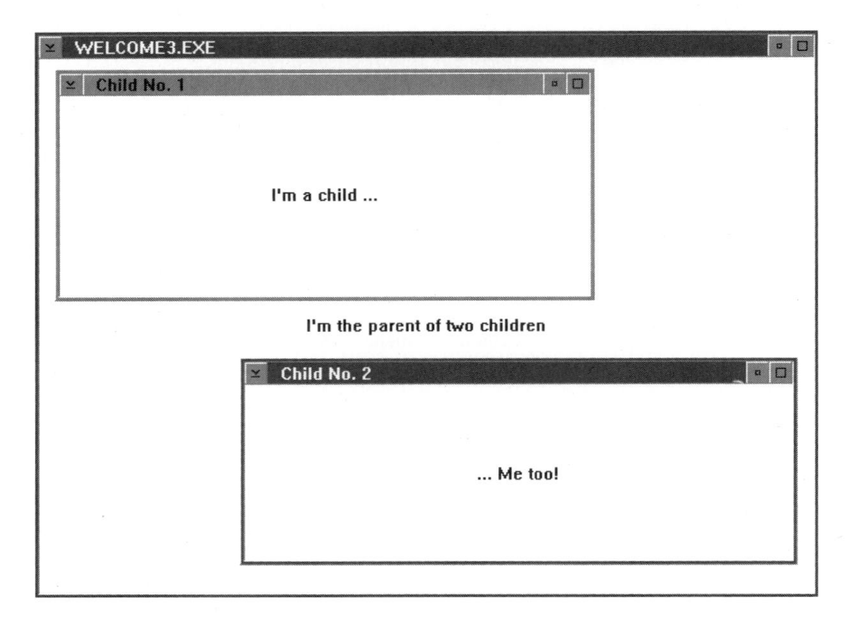

Figure 3.5: The WELCOME3 display

The two child windows are not listed on the Window List. Only top-level windows should be listed there. Before creating these child windows, WELCOME3 removes the FCF_TASKLIST flag from *flFrameFlags:*

```
flFrameFlags &= ~FCF_TASKLIST ;
```

WELCOME3 uses a little trick that allows the two child standard windows to display different text in their client windows. When the program registers the "Welcome3.Child" window class, it specifies that four bytes (the size of a PVOID or pointer) are to be reserved for use by the program for every window created based on this class. This is indicated by the fifth parameter to *WinRegisterClass:*

```
WinRegisterClass (
     hab,                  // Anchor block handle
     szChildClass,         // Name of class being registered
     ChildWndProc,         // Window procedure for class
     CS_SIZEREDRAW,        // Class style
     sizeof (PVOID)) ;     // Extra bytes to reserve
```

After the two child standard windows are created, WELCOME3 uses *WinSetWindowPtr* to store something in that area:

```
WinSetWindowPtr (hwndChildClient1, QWL_USER, "I'm a child ...") ;
WinSetWindowPtr (hwndChildClient2, QWL_USER, "... Me too!") ;
```

What is stored in this space is actually the address of the static text strings "I'm a child..." and "...Me too!". In *ChildWndProc*, these addresses are retrieved during processing of the WM_PAINT message and passed to the *WinDrawText* function:

```
WinDrawText (hps, -1, WinQueryWindowPtr (hwnd, QWL_USER), &rcl,
     CLR_NEUTRAL, CLR_BACKGROUND,
     DT_CENTER  DT_VCENTER  DT_ERASERECT) ;
```

Thus the window procedure doesn't have to figure out which child window is receiving the WM_PAINT message. Although this is a somewhat unusual application of the technique, storing window-specific data in the reserved area is often quite handy when two or more windows share the same window procedure.

The processing of the WM_CLOSE message in *ChildWndProc* destroys the window being closed but doesn't terminate the program:

```
case WM_CLOSE:
     WinDestroyWindow (WinQueryWindow (hwnd, QW_PARENT)) ;
     return 0 ;
```

WinQueryWindow obtains the parent of the client window (which is its frame window). Destroying that frame window also destroys the client window.

The program can be terminated only from the main window. After leaving the message loop, WELCOME3 destroys the program's top-level frame window as usual:

```
WinDestroyWindow (hwndFrame) ;
```

If one or both of the two child standard windows still exist, they, too, will be destroyed as a result. All windows in WELCOME3 are descendants of *hwndFrame*, so the one *WinDestroyWindow* call destroys all the windows in the program.

CONTROLS AND THEIR OWNERS

The frame window is the parent of all other windows created in the *WinCreateStdWindow* function. The frame window is also the "owner" of these other windows. A window is always displayed in the foreground of its owner (if it has one). However, it is not clipped to the surface of its owner. As with the parent/child relationship, when a window is hidden, minimized, or destroyed, the windows it owns are also hidden, minimized, or destroyed.

The owner relationship also affects how messages are sent between the windows. The title bar, system menu, and minimize/maximize windows are often called *control windows*. Control windows usually have a relatively simple appearance and function. Their primary job is to receive user input (keystrokes and mouse activity) in the form of messages and then send notification messages to the window's owner. The owner of the control window (which in all the examples so far is a frame window) then acts on the notification message.

For example, when you click on the maximize icon with the mouse, the minimize/maximize window sends a WM_SYSCOMMAND message to its owner—the frame window. The frame window then begins the process of maximizing the window. Likewise, the title bar window notifies the frame window of a new window position.

Although every window (except object windows and the desktop window itself) has a parent, windows do not need owners. The frame window created in *WinCreateStdWindow* has no owner. The frame window is the owner of the client window, but the client window doesn't really need an owner either.

You can determine the owner of a window by calling *WinQueryWindow:*

```
hwndOwner = WinQueryWindow (hwnd, QW_OWNER) ;
```

You can assign a new owner to a window by calling *WinSetOwner:*

```
WinSetOwner (hwnd, hwndNewOwner) ;
```

By setting the *hwndNewOwner* parameter to NULLHANDLE, you can cause the window whose handle is *hwnd* to have no owner.

REGISTERING THE WINDOW CLASS

Let's back up a little and examine in more detail some of the functions involved in creating a standard window. The standard window usually includes a client window. A preliminary step in creating a client window is the registering of a class for that window. The call to *WinRegisterClass* in WELCOME.C from Chapter 2 looks like this:

```
WinRegisterClass (
hab,                  // Anchor block handle
szClientClass,        // Name of class being registered
ClientWndProc,        // Window procedure for class
CS_SIZEREDRAW,        // Class style
0) ;                  // Extra bytes to reserve
```

Of these five parameters, the second and third are the most important. The second parameter is the name of the window class being registered. The name is a zero-terminated character string generally derived from the name of the program. In WELCOME the class name is "Welcome." The third parameter is the address of the window procedure for the class. This window procedure processes all messages to all windows that are later created based on this class.

The class style parameter is a 32-bit unsigned long integer that sets certain characteristics of all windows later created based on the class. You can set the class style parameter to 0L for a default class style. Or you can use one or more identifiers beginning with the letters CS ("class style") defined in PMWIN.H to specify a nondefault class style. You combine these identifiers with the C bitwise OR operator (¦). Each identifier sets one bit in the class style. For this reason, the identifiers are sometimes called *class style bits.* Ten class style bits are defined in PMWIN.H and are shown in Figure 3.6 in a diagram that indicates how each identifier contributes to the resultant 32-bit window style.

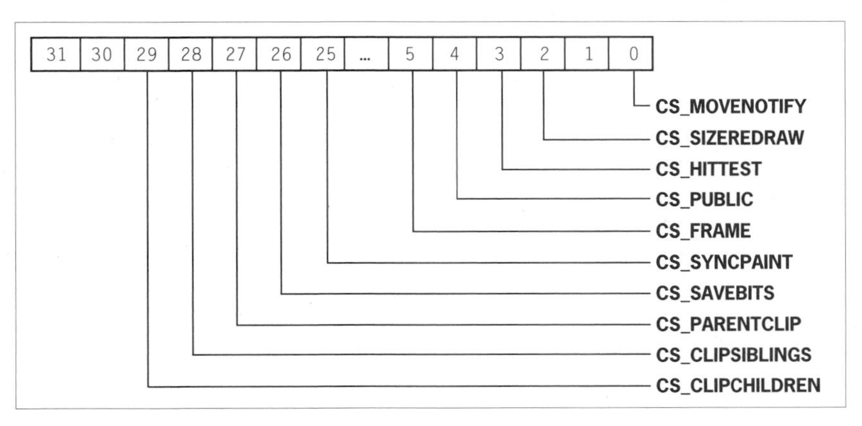

Figure 3.6: The window class style bits

Most of these class styles are not commonly used. For the programs in this book, I use only CS_SIZEREDRAW and CS_SYNCPAINT. The CS_SIZEREDRAW bit affects how the Presentation Manager should invalidate a window (and hence cause the window to receive a WM_PAINT message) when it is resized by the user. If the CS_SIZEREDRAW bit is not set and the window is reduced in size, the Presentation Manager does not need to invalidate the window. The part of the window outside the new size can simply be erased. When the CS_SIZEREDRAW bit is set, the entire window is invalidated when it is resized. You should use CS_SIZEREDRAW for all windows whose appearance depends on the size of the window. Because we have been displaying centered text in our client windows, CS_SIZEREDRAW is proper for the window class.

When CS_SYNCPAINT is set, WM_PAINT messages are sent directly to a window procedure when part of the window becomes invalid. When this bit is not set, WM_PAINT messages are posted to the message queue and retrieved later. The CS_SYNCPAINT bit is used mostly with small control windows that look best if they are repainted immediately.

The parameter to *WinRegisterClass* labeled "extra bytes to reserve" reserves a block of memory associated with each window created based on this class. You put data into this area using *WinSetWindowUShort, WinSetWindowULong,* and *WinSetWindowPtr;* you retrieve it by using *WinQueryWindowUShort, WinQueryWindowULong,* and *WinQueryWindowPtr.* You can do whatever you want with this memory. As you saw in WELCOME3, it's a handy place to store data unique to each window.

At this point, we can devise some general rules for storing data used in window procedures:

- When a variable defined in a window procedure is needed only during the processing of a message, use an automatic variable.
- To retain information from message to message, use static variables. However, if two or more windows share the same window procedure, use static variables *only* for data that can be shared among all windows.
- Use the reserved area for data unique to each window.

Creating the Standard Window

The *WinCreateStdWindow* call from the WELCOME program in Chapter 2 looks like this:

```
hwndFrame = WinCreateStdWindow (
     HWND_DESKTOP,  // Parent window handle
     WS_VISIBLE,    // Style of frame window
     &flFrameFlags, // Pointer to control data
     szClientClass, // Client window class name
     NULL,          // Title bar text
     ØL,            // Style of client window
     Ø,             // Module handle for resources
     Ø,             // ID of resources
     &hwndClient) ; // Pointer to client window handle
```

Two parameters in the *WinCreateStdWindow* function are *window styles:* The second parameter is the window style of the frame window, and the sixth parameter is the window style of the client window. A *window style* is a 32-bit unsigned long integer. Like the class style discussed previously, the window style sets certain characteristics of the window. But although the class style applies to all windows based on the class, the window style applies only to the particular window being created.

The PMWIN.H header file contains identifiers (sometimes called *window style bits*) to set bits in the window style when the identifiers are combined with the C bitwise OR operator (|).

The high 16 bits of the window style are defined in the same way for all window classes. The identifiers begin with WS ("window style"). Like the control style flags, many of these are rather rare. The WS_SYNCPAINT, WS_SAVEBITS, WS_PARENTCLIP, WS_CLIPSIBLINGS, and WS_CLIPCHILDREN bits have the same purpose as the equivalent class style bits. Thus you can create a window class without these styles but then create windows based on that class that use these styles.

The only window style that we've used so far for the frame window is the WS_VISIBLE bit. By default, a window is invisible when it's created. Specifying WS_VISIBLE overrides that default. Alternatively, you can exclude WS_VISIBLE from the frame window style when creating the window and later call *WinSetWindowPos* and *WinShowWindow*. The WS_VISIBLE bit isn't required for the client window style because the Presentation Manager specifically makes the client window visible.

The WS_MAXIMIZED bit causes a window to be maximized when it is first displayed. Similarly, the WS_MINIMIZED bit causes the window to be displayed initially as an icon. If the WS_DISABLED bit is set, the window can't receive mouse input and is generally inert. The window can be subsequently enabled by a call to *WinEnableWindow*.

The low 16 bits of the window style have different meanings depending on the window class. The window procedure for the class interprets these bits. We'll see examples of this in the WELCOME4 program coming up shortly.

THE FRAME CREATION FLAGS

The third parameter to *WinCreateStdWindow* is a pointer to a ULONG that mostly indicates what child windows should be created in the standard window. The PMWIN.H header file also defines FCF_STANDARD to be the same as:

```
FCF_TITLEBAR   | FCF_SYSMENU       | FCF_MENU   |
FCF_SIZEBORDER | FCF_MINMAX        | FCF_ICON   |
FCF_ACCELTABLE | FCF_SHELLPOSITION | FCF_TASKLIST
```

The FCF_MINMAX identifier is the same as FCF_MINBUTTON | FCF_MAXBUTTON. You can experiment with the WELCOME, WELCOME2, or WELCOME3 program (within limits) by removing some of the frame creation flags and putting in others. For example, if you exclude FCF_MINMAX, the minimize/maximize window isn't created, and the title bar fills the space. The Minimize and Maximize options are also disabled on the system menu. You can use FCF_MINBUTTON or FCF_MAXBUTTON to include one button but not the other.

If you exclude FCF_TITLEBAR, the title bar isn't created, and the Presentation Manager ignores the "title bar text" parameter of *WinCreateStdWindow*. The system menu and minimize/maximize button are created (if FCF_SYSMENU and FCF_MINMAX are specified, of course) and displayed in the normal places. But the area normally occupied by the title bar is not part of the client window. You can't even move the window, because that is a function of the title bar.

If you exclude FCF_SIZEBORDER, the sizing border window isn't created. Without the sizing border, the window not only looks a little naked, but the user can change the size of the window only by minimizing or maximizing it from the system menu or from the minimize/maximize button. You'll probably want to use FCF_BORDER to draw a thin black border around the naked window.

The FCF_DLGBORDER frame creation flag bit causes a wide border to be drawn. This is more commonly seen on dialog boxes. Like the title bar, the dialog border uses color to indicate if the window is active.

You can include FCF_VERTSCROLL or FCF_HORZSCROLL or both in the frame creation flags. The window will then include scroll bars. The vertical scroll bar appears to the right of the client window, and the horizontal scroll bar is on the bottom. We'll start using scroll bars in the next chapter.

At this time you can't use the FCF_MENU, FCF_ICON, or FCF_ACCELTABLE bits in the frame creation flags. These bits cause the Presentation Manager to attempt to load a menu, icon, or keyboard accelerator table from a module (an .EXE or .DLL file) whose module handle is indicated in the seventh parameter of the *WinCreateStdWindow* function. Menus, icons, and accelerator tables are known as *resources*. Every resource has an ID number. The ID number for all three of these resources must be the same and is specified as the eighth parameter in *WinCreateStdWindow*. We'll start using resources in Chapter 12.

Note that some frame creation flags—specifically the FCF_TITLEBAR, FCF_SYSMENU, FCF_MENU, FCF_MINBUTTON, FCF_MAXBUTTON, FCF_VERTSCROLL, and FCF_HORZSCROLL flags—cause windows to be created. Others—such as FCF_SIZEBORDER, FCF_BORDER, and FCF_DLG-BORDER—affect only the appearance and functionality of the frame window.

THE *WINCREATEWINDOW* FUNCTION

The *WinCreateStdWindow* function creates several windows organized around a frame window. Within the Presentation Manager, each window is created by a call to *WinCreateWindow*. This function is available for use by your programs also. It looks like this:

```
hwnd = WinCreateWindow (
     hwndParent,          // Parent window handle
     szClassName,         // Window class
     szText,              // Window text
     WS_...,              // Window style
     xStart, yStart,      // Initial position of window
     xSize ySize,         // Initial size of window
     hwndOwner,           // Owner window handle
     hwndOrder,           // Placement window handle
     idChild,             // Child window ID
     pControlData,        // Control data
     pPresParams) ;       // Presentation parameters
```

The parameters to this function indicate the full array of information required to create a window, and they show how *WinCreateStdWindow* makes the job of creating a standard window in your program a whole lot simpler.

You'll note here that each window has a "window text." But many control windows (such as the system menu window, sizing border window, and minimize/maximize window) don't display this text. The Presentation Manager uses the "title bar text" parameter to *WinCreateStdWindow* as the "window text" parameter to *WinCreateWindow* only when it is creating the title bar window. The title bar window procedure displays that text in its window.

Each window also has a position and size. The position is relative to the lower-left corner of the window's parent. We haven't been worrying about this so far. The Presentation Manager gives the frame window a default position and size and then organizes the other windows within that.

THE PREDEFINED WINDOW CLASSES

In the *WinCreateStdWindow* call, only one window class parameter is required: the window class of the client window. However, the Presentation Manager needs to specify a window class in each *WinCreateWindow* call it makes when creating the standard window. For the windows other than the client window, the Presentation Manager uses predefined window classes. These have identifiers in PMWIN.H. Some of the more common are shown in the following table:

Predefined Window Class	Type of Window
WC_FRAME	Standard frame window (including dialog boxes)
WC_BUTTON	Push button, check box, and so on
WC_MENU	Menu (including system menu and minimize/maximize window)
WC_STATIC	Static text or rectangle
WC_ENTRYFIELD	Single-line text editing field
WC_LISTBOX	List box
WC_SCROLLBAR	Scroll bar
WC_TITLEBAR	Standard title bar
WC_MLE	Multiline text edit control

Each of these window classes has a corresponding window procedure in PMWIN.DLL.

In the *WinCreateStdWindow* calls made in the various WELCOME programs, the Presentation Manager creates windows based on the WC_FRAME, WC_MENU, and WC_TITLEBAR styles. Perhaps it will be instructive to call *WinCreateWindow* ourselves in a program and see how this works.

CREATING CHILD CONTROL WINDOWS

The WELCOME4 program, shown in Listing 3.3, creates one standard window and three control windows as children of the client window. These three control windows are created using *WinCreateWindow* and are based on the predefined window classes of WC_BUTTON, WC_SCROLLBAR, and WC_MLE.

Listing 3.3: The WELCOME4 program

The WELCOME4.MAK File

```
#-----------------------
# WELCOME4.MAK make file
#-----------------------
```

Listing 3.3: The WELCOME4 program (Continued)

```
welcome4.exe : welcome4.obj welcome4.def
     $(PRGLINK) welcome4, welcome4, NUL, $(PRGLIB), welcome4

welcome4.obj : welcome4.c
     $(PRGCC) welcome4.c
```

The WELCOME4.C File

```
/*-------------------------------------------------------------
   WELCOME4.C -- Creates a Top-Level Window and Three Children
                 (c) Charles Petzold, 1993
  -------------------------------------------------------------*/

#define INCL_WIN
#include <os2.h>

#define ID_BUTTON 1
#define ID_SCROLL 2
#define ID_ENTRY  3

MRESULT EXPENTRY ClientWndProc (HWND, ULONG, MPARAM, MPARAM) ;

int main (void)
     {
     static CHAR  szClientClass [] = "Welcome4" ;
     static ULONG flFrameFlags = FCF_TITLEBAR      | FCF_SYSMENU   |
                                 FCF_BORDER        | FCF_MINBUTTON |
                                 FCF_SHELLPOSITION | FCF_TASKLIST ;
     HAB          hab ;
     HMQ          hmq ;
     HWND         hwndFrame,  hwndClient ;
     QMSG         qmsg ;
     RECTL        rcl ;

     hab = WinInitialize (0) ;
     hmq = WinCreateMsgQueue (hab, 0) ;

     WinRegisterClass (
                    hab,                  // Anchor block handle
                    szClientClass,        // Name of class being registered
                    ClientWndProc,        // Window procedure for class
                    CS_SIZEREDRAW,        // Class style
                    0) ;                  // Extra bytes to reserve

     hwndFrame = WinCreateStdWindow (
                    HWND_DESKTOP,         // Parent window handle
                    WS_VISIBLE,           // Style of frame window
                    &flFrameFlags,        // Pointer to control data
                    szClientClass,        // Client window class name
```

Listing 3.3: The WELCOME4 program (Continued)

```
                NULL,                 // Title bar text
                0L,                   // Style of client window
                0,                    // Module handle for resources
                0,                    // ID of resources
                &hwndClient) ;        // Pointer to client window handle

          /*--------------------------------------------------------
             Find dimensions of client window for sizes of children
            --------------------------------------------------------*/

     WinQueryWindowRect (hwndClient, &rcl) ;
     rcl.xRight /= 3 ;                                  // divide width in thirds

          /*---------------------------
             Create push button window
            ---------------------------*/

     WinCreateWindow (
                hwndClient,                             // Parent window handle
                WC_BUTTON,                              // Window class
                "Big Button",                           // Window text
                WS_VISIBLE                              // Window style
                     | BS_PUSHBUTTON,
                10,                                     // Window position
                10,
                rcl.xRight - 20,                        // Window size
                rcl.yTop - 20,
                hwndClient,                             // Owner window handle
                HWND_BOTTOM,                            // Placement window handle
                ID_BUTTON,                              // Child window ID
                NULL,                                   // Control data
                NULL) ;                                 // Presentation parameters

          /*-------------------------
             Create scroll bar window
            -------------------------*/

     WinCreateWindow (
                hwndClient,                             // Parent window handle
                WC_SCROLLBAR,                           // Window class
                NULL,                                   // Window text
                WS_VISIBLE                              // Window style
                     | SBS_VERT,
                rcl.xRight + 10,                        // Window position
                10,
                rcl.xRight - 20,                        // Window size
                rcl.yTop - 20,
                hwndClient,                             // Owner window handle
                HWND_BOTTOM,                            // Placement window handle
```

Listing 3.3: The WELCOME4 program (Continued)

```
               ID_SCROLL,                     // Child window ID
               NULL,                          // Control data
               NULL) ;                        // Presentation parameters

          /*-----------------------------------
             Create multiline entry field window
            -----------------------------------*/

     WinCreateWindow (
               hwndClient,                    // Parent window handle
               WC_MLE,                        // Window class
               NULL,                          // Window text
               WS_VISIBLE                     // Window style
                    | MLS_BORDER
                    | MLS_VSCROLL
                    | MLS_WORDWRAP,
               2 * rcl.xRight + 10,           // Window position
               10,
               rcl.xRight - 20,               // Window size
               rcl.yTop - 20,
               hwndClient,                    // Owner window handle
               HWND_BOTTOM,                   // Placement window handle
               ID_ENTRY,                      // Child window ID
               NULL,                          // Control data
               NULL) ;                        // Presentation parameters

     while (WinGetMsg (hab, &qmsg, NULLHANDLE, 0, 0))
          WinDispatchMsg (hab, &qmsg) ;

     WinDestroyWindow (hwndFrame) ;
     WinDestroyMsgQueue (hmq) ;
     WinTerminate (hab) ;
     return 0 ;
     }

MRESULT EXPENTRY ClientWndProc (HWND hwnd, ULONG msg, MPARAM mp1, MPARAM mp2)
     {
     switch (msg)
          {
          case WM_COMMAND:
               switch (COMMANDMSG(&msg)->cmd)
                    {
                    case ID_BUTTON:
                         WinAlarm (HWND_DESKTOP, WA_NOTE) ;
                         return 0 ;
                    }
               break ;

          case WM_ERASEBACKGROUND:
```

Listing 3.3: The WELCOME4 program (Continued)

```
               return MRFROMSHORT (1) ;
          }
     return WinDefWindowProc (hwnd, msg, mp1, mp2) ;
     }
```

The WELCOME4.DEF File

```
;-------------------------------------
; WELCOME4.DEF module definition file
;-------------------------------------

NAME           WELCOME4  WINDOWAPI

DESCRIPTION    'Creates Top-Level and 3 Children (c) Charles Petzold, 1993'
PROTMODE
```

To keep the size of the window constant, the main window in WELCOME4 uses FCF_BORDER rather than FCF_SIZEBORDER and has no maximize icon. The window is shown in Figure 3.7.

Figure 3.7: The WELCOME4 display

After creating the standard window, WELCOME4 makes a call to *WinQueryWindowRect* to obtain the rectangle structure that defines the size of the client window:

```
WinQueryWindowRect (hwndClient, &rcl) ;
```

The *xRight* field of this structure is the width of the client area in pixels. WELCOME4 divides it by 3 to be used in the three *WinCreateWindow* calls.

The first *WinCreateWindow* call creates a window based on the WC_BUTTON class:

```
WinCreateWindow (
     hwndClient,          // Parent window handle
     WC_BUTTON,           // Window class
     "Big Button",        // Window text
     WS_VISIBLE           // Window style
          | BS_PUSHBUTTON,
     10,                  // Window position
     10,
     rcl.xRight - 20,     // Initial size of window
     rcl.yTop - 20,
     hwndClient,          // Owner window handle
     HWND_BOTTOM,         // Placement window handle
     ID_BUTTON,           // Child window ID
     NULL,                // Control data
     NULL) ;              // Presentation parameters
```

This call creates a large push button (such as those that appear in dialog boxes) in the left third of the client window. The text inside the button is "Big Button." Both the parent and owner are set to the *hwndClient* window handle returned from the original *WinCreateStdWindow* call. The window style uses WS_VISIBLE and BS_PUSHBUTTON. Identifiers beginning with BS ("button style") are class-specific window styles for buttons. The initial position of the window is relative to the lower-left corner of the client window. These two parameters are both set to 10 pixels to provide a small margin around the push button. The size of the window is set to one-third the width of the client window and to the height of the client window, minus 20 pixels from each dimension.

The second *WinCreateWindow* call creates a vertical scroll bar in the middle third of the client window:

```
WinCreateWindow (
     hwndClient,          // Parent window handle
     WC_SCROLLBAR,        // Window class
     NULL,                // Window text
     WS_VISIBLE           // Window style
          |SBS_VERT,
     rcl.xRight + 10,     // Window position
     10,
     rcl.xRight - 20,     // Window size
     rcl.yTop - 20,
     hwndClient,          // Owner window handle
     HWND_BOTTOM,         // Placement window handle
     ID_SCROLL,           // Child window ID
```

```
     NULL,                    // Control data
     NULL) ;                  // Presentation parameters
```

The class is WC_SCROLLBAR, and the class-specific window style is SBS_VER. SBS stands for "scroll-bar style," and VERT indicates a vertical scroll bar.

The third *WinCreateWindow* call creates a multiline edit control window:

```
WinCreateWindow (
     hwndClient,                     // Parent window handle
     WC_MLE,                         // Window class
     NULL,                           // Window text
     WS_VISIBLE,                     // Window style
          | MLS_BORDER
          | MLS_VSCROLL
          | MLS_WORDWRAP,
     2 + rcl.xRight + 10,            // Window position
     10,
     rcl.xRight - 20,                // Window size
     rcl.yTop - 20,
     hwndClient,                     // Owner window handle
     HWND_BOTTOM,                    // Placement window handle
     ID_ENTRY,                       // Child window ID
     NULL,                           // Control data
     NULL) ;                         // Presentation parameters
```

The class is WC_MLE and the style bits are MLS_BORDER (to draw a border around the window), MLS_VSCROLL (to give it a vertical scroll bar), and MLS_WORDWRAP (so that text entered by the user is wrapped to the width of the window).

All three *WinCreateWindow* calls return the handle to the window they create, but WELCOME4 doesn't save these handles.

Although WELCOME4's button and scroll bar may appear to be somewhat grotesque, they are still functional. When you click on the button with the mouse, it flashes. When you click on various parts of the scroll bar, they too flash. You can even click on the text entry field and type in some text.

These three control windows created in WELCOME4 send *notification messages* to their owner (which is the client window) when they receive user input. For example, the push button sends its owner a WM_COMMAND message when the button is clicked with the mouse. *ClientWndProc* receives this message and beeps by calling *WinAlarm*. Likewise, the control windows that make up the standard window notify their owner (the frame window) of user input.

The WELCOME4 family tree is shown in Figure 3.8. This family tree shows the parent-child relationship; the owner-owned relationship is identical to this, except that the desktop window doesn't own the frame window.

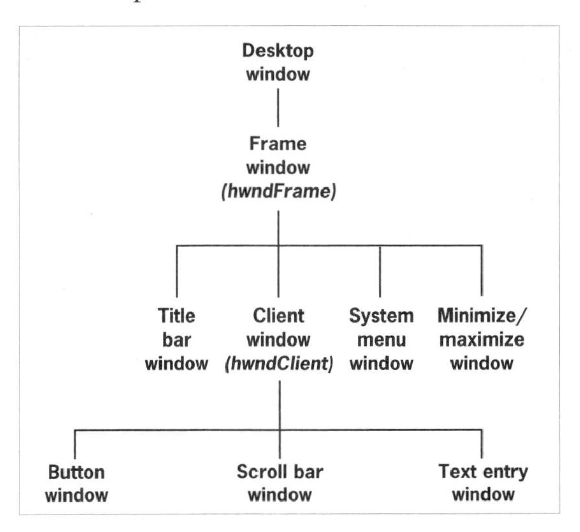

Figure 3.8: The WELCOME4 family tree

Child window ids When the Presentation Manager (or your program) creates child windows using the *WinCreateWindow* function, each child is assigned a "child window ID" that is specified as the eleventh parameter to *WinCreateWindow.* In WELCOME4, these ID numbers are set to ID_BUTTON, ID_SCROLL, and ID_ENTRY, which are defined at the top of the program as 1, 2, and 3. The control window uses this ID to identify itself to its owner when it sends a notification message. For example, in the WM_COMMAND notification message that push buttons send, the *mp1* parameter contains this ID. Thus a window can contain many push buttons or other control windows, each with a different ID. (We'll examine this in greater detail in Chapters 11, 13, and 14.)

When the frame window creates its children, each of them is assigned an ID number. As shown in the following table, these are fixed values defined in PMWIN.H, and have identifiers beginning with the letters FID (which stand for "frame ID").

FID	Type of Child Window
FID_SYSMENU	System menu
FID_TITLEBAR	Title bar
FID_MINMAX	Minimize/maximize button
FID_MENU	Program's menu
FID_VERTSCROLL	Vertical scroll bar
FID_HORZSCROLL	Horizontal scroll bar
FID_CLIENT	Client window

A program can determine the window handle of a child window based on the parent window handle and the child ID:

```
hwndChild = WinWindowFromID (hwndParent, idChild) ;
```

If you need to know the window handle of the system menu window (for example), you can easily obtain it:

```
hwndSysMenu = WinWindowFromID (hwndFrame, FID_SYSMENU) ;
```

Why would you need this information? Well, you might want to send the system menu window a message. Improbable? Not at all: we'll do it in Chapter 13.

You can also determine a window's ID from its window handle:

```
idChild = WinQueryWindowUShort (hwnd, QWS_ID) ;
```

The *WinQueryWindowUShort, WinQueryWindowULong,* and *WinQueryWindowPtr* functions also let you obtain a window's message queue handle, its style, and the address of the window procedure, as well as the reserved areas specified in the window class.

STYLES, CLASSES, AND IDS

By now you've seen similar identifiers used in various ways in connection with various parts of the standard window. For the title bar, for example, you've seen identifiers named FCF_TITLEBAR, WC_TITLEBAR, and FID_TITLEBAR. This may all be a little confusing. Here's a little table that can help you keep the identifiers straight:

Frame Creation Flag	Causes the Frame Window to Create a Child of Class	With a Child Window ID of
FCF_TITLEBAR	WC_TITLEBAR	FID_TITLEBAR
FCF_SYSMENU	WC_MENU	FID_SYSMENU
FCF_MENU	WC_MENU	FID_MENU
FCF_MINMAX	WC_MENU	FID_MINMAX
FCF_VERTSCROLL	WC_SCROLLBAR	FID_VERTSCROLL
FCF_HORZSCROLL	WC_SCROLLBAR	FID_HORZSCROLL

The FCF identifiers are used in the *WinCreateStdWindow* call to specify the window style of the frame window. Within the Presentation Manager, a call to the *WinCreateWindow* function creates each of the control windows. The window class is one of the WC identifiers, and the child window ID is an FID identifier.

Part 2

Painting the Client Window

An Exercise in Text Output

The Five GPI Primitives

Bitmaps and Bitblts

Advanced Graphics

An Exercise in Text Output

DISPLAYING TEXT ON THE CLIENT WINDOW

DEVICE-INDEPENDENT PROGRAMMING

ADDING SCROLL BARS

OPTIMIZING THE CODE

ADDING A KEYBOARD INTERFACE

Chapter 4

The Presentation Manager is a graphical environment, yet for many applications the display of text and numbers is more important than pictures. Although it would be nice to write a database program that can include bitmapped images of employees' faces, the fact remains that the employees' names, addresses, and social security numbers are still the most important data. This chapter covers the basic concepts involved with displaying plain-vanilla text in the client window. Although the chapter touches on keyboard and mouse input, these subjects are discussed in more depth in Chapters 8 and 9.

When programming for the Presentation Manager, you don't use OS/2 kernel functions such as *DosWrite* and *VioWrtTTY* or C functions such as *printf* and *puts* to write text to the screen. Instead, you use functions provided by the Graphics Programming Interface (GPI) component of the Presentation Manager. (Exceptions do exist: Several high-level drawing functions such as *WinDrawText* aren't really part of GPI, although they certainly make use of GPI.) GPI functions begin with the prefix *Gpi.* Although this chapter covers only text output, many of the concepts examined here are also applicable to graphics.

Displaying text on the client window

As a case study, let's write a Presentation Manager program that displays some information obtainable from the *WinQuerySysValue* function.

You can use *WinQuerySysValue* in a program to obtain the height and width of the screen as well as scores of other interesting pieces of information, many concerning the sizes of various windows created by the Presentation Manager. The first parameter to the function is the identifier HWND_DESKTOP, and the second parameter is one of the identifiers defined in PMWIN.H with the letters SV ("system value"). For example, the following call returns the height of the title bar in pixels:

```
WinQuerySysValue (HWND_DESKTOP, SV_CYTITLEBAR)
```

Like many of the values that *WinQuerySysValue* returns, this value depends on the resolution of the video display on which the Presentation Manager is running. In later chapters, we'll use *WinQuerySysValue* for various purposes. Here we merely want to look at some return values. We'll display this information in the client window. I've limited the list to about 50 items. They are displayed, one per line, in three columns: the SV identifier passed to *WinQuerySysValue*, a description of the item, and the value returned from the function. The first version of the program to display these values is called SYSVALS1 and is shown in Listing 4.1.

Listing 4.1: The SYSVALS1 program

The SYSVALS1.MAK File

```
#-----------------------
# SYSVALS1.MAK make file
#-----------------------

sysvals1.exe : sysvals1.obj sysvals1.def
     $(PRGLINK) sysvals1, sysvals1, NUL, $(PRGLIB), sysvals1

sysvals1.obj : sysvals1.c sysvals.h
     $(PRGCC) sysvals1.c
```

The SYSVALS.H File

```
/*-----------------------------------------------
   SYSVALS.H -- System values display structure
  -----------------------------------------------*/

#define NUMLINES ((int) (sizeof sysvals / sizeof sysvals [0]))

struct
{
SHORT   sIndex ;
CHAR  * szIdentifier ;
CHAR  * szDescription ;
}
sysvals [] =
```

Listing 4.1: The SYSVALS1 program (Continued)

```
{
SV_SWAPBUTTON,       "SV_SWAPBUTTON",       "Mouse buttons swapped flag",
SV_DBLCLKTIME,       "SV_DBLCLKTIME",       "Mouse double click time",
SV_CXDBLCLK,         "SV_CXDBLCLK",         "Mouse double click area width",
SV_CYDBLCLK,         "SV_CYDBLCLK",         "Mouse double click area height",
SV_CXSIZEBORDER,     "SV_CXSIZEBORDER",     "Sizing border width",
SV_CYSIZEBORDER,     "SV_CYSIZEBORDER",     "Sizing border height",
SV_ALARM,            "SV_ALARM",            "Alarm enabled flag",
SV_CURSORRATE,       "SV_CURSORRATE",       "Cursor blink rate",
SV_FIRSTSCROLLRATE,  "SV_FIRSTSCROLLRATE",  "Scroll bar repeat delay",
SV_SCROLLRATE,       "SV_SCROLLRATE",       "Scroll bar scroll rate",
SV_NUMBEREDLISTS,    "SV_NUMBEREDLISTS",    "Undefined",
SV_WARNINGFREQ,      "SV_WARNINGFREQ",      "Alarm frequency for warning",
SV_NOTEFREQ,         "SV_NOTEFREQ",         "Alarm frequency for note",
SV_ERRORFREQ,        "SV_ERRORFREQ",        "Alarm frequency for error",
SV_WARNINGDURATION,  "SV_WARNINGDURATION",  "Alarm duration for warning",
SV_NOTEDURATION,     "SV_NOTEDURATION",     "Alarm duration for note",
SV_ERRORDURATION,    "SV_ERRORDURATION",    "Alarm duration for error",
SV_CXSCREEN,         "SV_CXSCREEN",         "Screen width in pixels",
SV_CYSCREEN,         "SV_CYSCREEN",         "Screen height in pixels",
SV_CXVSCROLL,        "SV_CXVSCROLL",        "Vertical scroll bar width",
SV_CYHSCROLL,        "SV_CYHSCROLL",        "Horizontal scroll bar height",
SV_CYVSCROLLARROW,   "SV_CYVSCROLLARROW",   "Vertical scroll bar arrow height",
SV_CXHSCROLLARROW,   "SV_CXHSCROLLARROW",   "Horizontal scroll bar arrow width",
SV_CXBORDER,         "SV_CXBORDER",         "Border width",
SV_CYBORDER,         "SV_CYBORDER",         "Border height",
SV_CXDLGFRAME,       "SV_CXDLGFRAME",       "Dialog window frame width",
SV_CYDLGFRAME,       "SV_CYDLGFRAME",       "Dialog window frame height",
SV_CYTITLEBAR,       "SV_CYTITLEBAR",       "Title bar height",
SV_CYVSLIDER,        "SV_CYVSLIDER",        "Vertical scroll bar slider height",
SV_CXHSLIDER,        "SV_CXHSLIDER",        "Horizontal scroll bar slider width",
SV_CXMINMAXBUTTON,   "SV_CXMINMAXBUTTON",   "Minimize/maximize button width",
SV_CYMINMAXBUTTON,   "SV_CYMINMAXBUTTON",   "Minimize/maximize button height",
SV_CYMENU,           "SV_CYMENU",           "Menu bar height",
SV_CXFULLSCREEN,     "SV_CXFULLSCREEN",     "Full screen client window width",
SV_CYFULLSCREEN,     "SV_CYFULLSCREEN",     "Full screen client window height",
SV_CXICON,           "SV_CXICON",           "Icon width",
SV_CYICON,           "SV_CYICON",           "Icon height",
SV_CXPOINTER,        "SV_CXPOINTER",        "Pointer width",
SV_CYPOINTER,        "SV_CYPOINTER",        "Pointer height",
SV_DEBUG,            "SV_DEBUG",            "Debug version flag",
SV_CMOUSEBUTTONS,    "SV_CMOUSEBUTTONS",    "Number of mouse buttons",
SV_CPOINTERBUTTONS,  "SV_CPOINTERBUTTONS",  "Ditto",
SV_POINTERLEVEL,     "SV_POINTERLEVEL",     "Pointer hide level",
SV_CURSORLEVEL,      "SV_CURSORLEVEL",      "Cursor hide level",
SV_TRACKRECTLEVEL,   "SV_TRACKRECTLEVEL",   "Tracking rectangle hide level",
SV_CTIMERS,          "SV_CTIMERS",          "Number of available timers",
SV_MOUSEPRESENT,     "SV_MOUSEPRESENT",     "Mouse present flag",
SV_CXBYTEALIGN,      "SV_CXBYTEALIGN",      "Horizontal pixel alignment value",
```

Listing 4.1: The SYSVALS1 program (Continued)

```
SV_CXALIGN,          "SV_CXALIGN",          "Ditto",
SV_CYBYTEALIGN,      "SV_CYBYTEALIGN",      "Vertical pixel alignment value",
SV_CYALIGN,          "SV_CYALIGN",          "Ditto",
SV_EXTRAKEYBEEP,     "SV_EXTRAKEYBEEP",     "Extended key beep",
SV_SETLIGHTS,        "SV_SETLIGHTS",        "Lights set from keyboard state flag",
SV_INSERTMODE,       "SV_INSERTMODE",       "Insert mode flag"
} ;
```

The SYSVALS1.C File

```
/*---------------------------------------------------
   SYSVALS1.C -- System Values Display Program No. 1
                 (c) Charles Petzold, 1993
  ---------------------------------------------------*/

#define INCL_WIN
#define INCL_GPI
#include <os2.h>
#include <stdio.h>
#include <string.h>
#include "sysvals.h"

MRESULT EXPENTRY ClientWndProc (HWND, ULONG, MPARAM, MPARAM) ;

int main (void)
     {
     static CHAR  szClientClass [] = "SysVals1" ;
     static ULONG flFrameFlags = FCF_TITLEBAR      | FCF_SYSMENU |
                                 FCF_SIZEBORDER    | FCF_MINMAX  |
                                 FCF_SHELLPOSITION | FCF_TASKLIST ;
     HAB          hab ;
     HMQ          hmq ;
     HWND         hwndFrame, hwndClient ;
     QMSG         qmsg ;

     hab = WinInitialize (0) ;
     hmq = WinCreateMsgQueue (hab, 0) ;

     WinRegisterClass (hab, szClientClass, ClientWndProc, CS_SIZEREDRAW, 0) ;

     hwndFrame = WinCreateStdWindow (HWND_DESKTOP, WS_VISIBLE,
                                     &flFrameFlags, szClientClass, NULL,
                                     0L, 0, 0, &hwndClient) ;

     while (WinGetMsg (hab, &qmsg, NULLHANDLE, 0, 0))
          WinDispatchMsg (hab, &qmsg) ;

     WinDestroyWindow (hwndFrame) ;
     WinDestroyMsgQueue (hmq) ;
```

Listing 4.1: The SYSVALS1 program (Continued)

```
     WinTerminate (hab) ;
     return 0 ;
     }

MRESULT EXPENTRY ClientWndProc (HWND hwnd, ULONG msg, MPARAM mp1, MPARAM mp2)
     {
     static INT  cxChar, cxCaps, cyChar, cyDesc, cyClient ;
     CHAR        szBuffer [10] ;
     FONTMETRICS fm ;
     HPS         hps ;
     INT         iLine ;
     POINTL      ptl ;

     switch (msg)
          {
          case WM_CREATE:
               hps = WinGetPS (hwnd) ;
               GpiQueryFontMetrics (hps, sizeof fm, &fm) ;

               cxChar = fm.lAveCharWidth ;
               cxCaps = (fm.fsType & 1 ? 2 : 3) * cxChar / 2 ;
               cyChar = fm.lMaxBaselineExt ;
               cyDesc = fm.lMaxDescender ;

               WinReleasePS (hps) ;
               return 0 ;

          case WM_SIZE:
               cyClient = SHORT2FROMMP (mp2) ;
               return 0 ;

          case WM_PAINT:
               hps = WinBeginPaint (hwnd, NULLHANDLE, NULL) ;
               GpiErase (hps) ;

               for (iLine = 0 ; iLine < NUMLINES ; iLine++)
                    {
                    ptl.x = cxCaps ;
                    ptl.y = cyClient - cyChar * (iLine + 1) + cyDesc ;

                    GpiCharStringAt (hps, &ptl,
                              strlen (sysvals[iLine].szIdentifier),
                              sysvals[iLine].szIdentifier) ;

                    ptl.x += 24 * cxCaps ;
                    GpiCharStringAt (hps, &ptl,
                                   strlen (sysvals[iLine].szDescription),
                                   sysvals[iLine].szDescription) ;
```

Listing 4.1: The SYSVALS1 program (Continued)

```
                    sprintf (szBuffer, "%d",
                             WinQuerySysValue (HWND_DESKTOP,
                                               sysvals[iLine].sIndex)) ;

                    ptl.x += 38 * cxChar ;
                    GpiCharStringAt (hps, &ptl, strlen (szBuffer),
                                     szBuffer) ;
                    }
               WinEndPaint (hps) ;
               return 0 ;
          }
     return WinDefWindowProc (hwnd, msg, mp1, mp2) ;
     }
```

The SYSVALS1.DEF File

```
;-------------------------------------
; SYSVALS1.DEF module definition file
;-------------------------------------

NAME           SYSVALS1  WINDOWAPI

DESCRIPTION    'System Values Display No. 1 (c) Charles Petzold, 1993'
PROTMODE
```

The SYSVALS.H header file defines a structure named *sysvals* that contains the system value identifiers and text descriptions that SYSVALS1 needs to obtain and display the information from *WinQuerySysValue*. The same SYSVALS.H file will be used in the subsequent versions of the program in this chapter. Notice that the SYSVALS1 make file recompiles the program whenever the SYSVALS1.C or SYSVALS.H file is altered.

The definition of the INCL_WIN and INCL_GPI identifiers near the top of SYSVALS1.C is required in order to include sections of the OS/2 header files that are omitted by default.

The SYSVALS1 window is shown in Figure 4.1. You might have already noticed that SYSVALS1 is seriously flawed. Never fear: We'll hammer away at it until we get it right. Despite its flaws, SYSVALS1 illustrates many of the basic concepts involved in displaying text on your client window.

DEVICE-INDEPENDENT PROGRAMMING

One primary purpose of the Presentation Manager is to provide a "device-independent" environment for your applications. This means that your programs should run without change or special drivers on any machine—and in

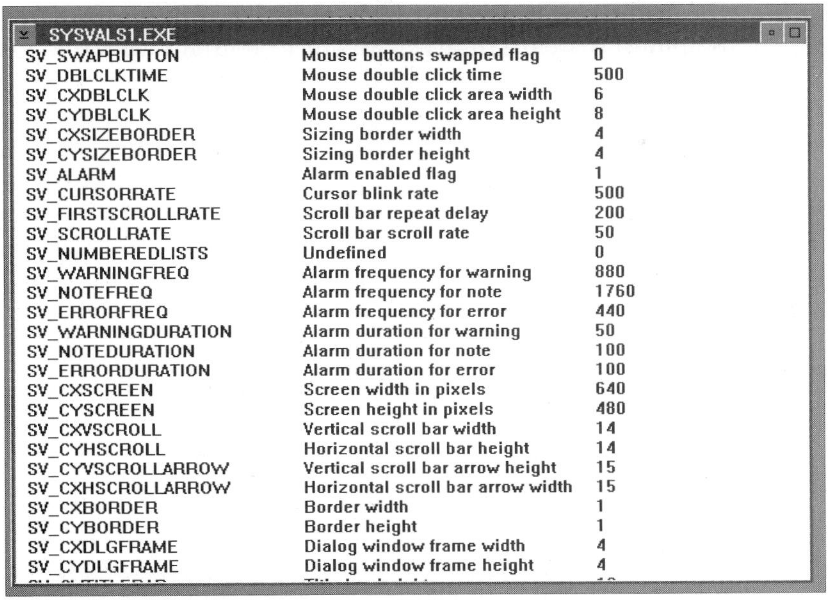

SYSVALS1.EXE

SV_SWAPBUTTON	Mouse buttons swapped flag	0
SV_DBLCLKTIME	Mouse double click time	500
SV_CXDBLCLK	Mouse double click area width	6
SV_CYDBLCLK	Mouse double click area height	8
SV_CXSIZEBORDER	Sizing border width	4
SV_CYSIZEBORDER	Sizing border height	4
SV_ALARM	Alarm enabled flag	1
SV_CURSORRATE	Cursor blink rate	500
SV_FIRSTSCROLLRATE	Scroll bar repeat delay	200
SV_SCROLLRATE	Scroll bar scroll rate	50
SV_NUMBEREDLISTS	Undefined	0
SV_WARNINGFREQ	Alarm frequency for warning	880
SV_NOTEFREQ	Alarm frequency for note	1760
SV_ERRORFREQ	Alarm frequency for error	440
SV_WARNINGDURATION	Alarm duration for warning	50
SV_NOTEDURATION	Alarm duration for note	100
SV_ERRORDURATION	Alarm duration for error	100
SV_CXSCREEN	Screen width in pixels	640
SV_CYSCREEN	Screen height in pixels	480
SV_CXVSCROLL	Vertical scroll bar width	14
SV_CYHSCROLL	Horizontal scroll bar height	14
SV_CYVSCROLLARROW	Vertical scroll bar arrow height	15
SV_CXHSCROLLARROW	Horizontal scroll bar arrow width	15
SV_CXBORDER	Border width	1
SV_CYBORDER	Border height	1
SV_CXDLGFRAME	Dialog window frame width	4
SV_CYDLGFRAME	Dialog window frame height	4

Figure 4.1: The SYSVALS1 display

particular, with any video display adapter—on which the Presentation Manager itself runs. Although the VGA (with 640 pixels horizontally by 480 scan lines vertically) is probably the most common video device your program will encounter, some high-resolution video adapters go up to 1664 by 1200.

Because a display driver is one of the dynamic link libraries in the Presentation Manager, Presentation Manager applications don't require their own video display drivers. The application makes various GPI calls, the Presentation Manager calls the display driver dynamic link library, and the display driver handles the hardware screen output. Of course, you do your part by writing Presentation Manager programs that can easily adapt themselves to different environments. This involves one basic rule: Don't assume anything.

But with the Presentation Manager, there's really no need for assumptions: All the information you need concerning the video display can be obtained through various Presentation Manager functions. For example, *WinQuerySysValue* can tell you the width and height of the video display in pixels. Just about the only guarantee you have is that the video display can accommodate at least 80 text characters across and 24 text lines down when you use the standard default *system font* (which I'll discuss shortly). Of course, this doesn't necessarily mean that you have access to the entire screen. Normally, your application must share the display with other programs. Unless this is impractical, your program should be designed to be functional in both maximized and nonmaximized windows.

Most Presentation Manager programs have a sizing border that lets the user change the size of your program's window. This has a profound consequence: Not only can you not make any assumptions about the size of your program's client window, but you can't even assume that the size will remain constant while your program is running. So the first job we'll tackle is how a program can determine the size of its client window.

THE SIZE OF THE CLIENT WINDOW

The programs presented in Chapters 2 and 3 obtained the size of the client window by calling

```
WinQueryWindowRect (hwnd, &rcl) ;
```

The *rcl* variable is a structure of type RECTL with four fields—*xLeft*, *yBottom*, *xRight*, and *yTop*. The *WinQueryWindowRect* function fills in these fields by setting the *xLeft* and *yBottom* fields to 0 and the *xRight* and *yTop* fields to the pixel width and height of the client window. This function was convenient in the earlier programs because they used *WinDrawText* to display centered text in the client window and could simply pass the RECTL pointer directly to *DrawText*.

But SYSVALS1 doesn't use the *WinDrawText* function. *WinDrawText* works well for displaying text within a rectangle, but it's less suitable for displaying multiple lines of text, as SYSVALS1 does. Instead, SYSVALS1 uses the GPI function *GpiCharStringAt* to display the text, and *GpiCharStringAt* doesn't use the RECTL structure.

Moreover, the approach used in the previous programs required that the *WinQueryWindowRect* function be called when processing every WM_PAINT message. It's more efficient to obtain the size of the client window only when the size changes. How do you know when the size of the client window changes? Simple: the Presentation Manager sends a message to the client window procedure. That message is WM_SIZE.

The window procedure receives the first WM_SIZE message during the *WinCreateStdWindow* call. Thereafter, the window procedure receives a WM_SIZE message whenever the user changes the window's size, either by using the sizing border or by maximizing or minimizing the window. The *mp1* and *mp2* parameters that accompany a WM_SIZE message indicate the previous size of the client window and the new size of the window. The width and height of the window are given in pixels. These values are encoded in *mp1* and *mp2* as shown in Figure 4.2.

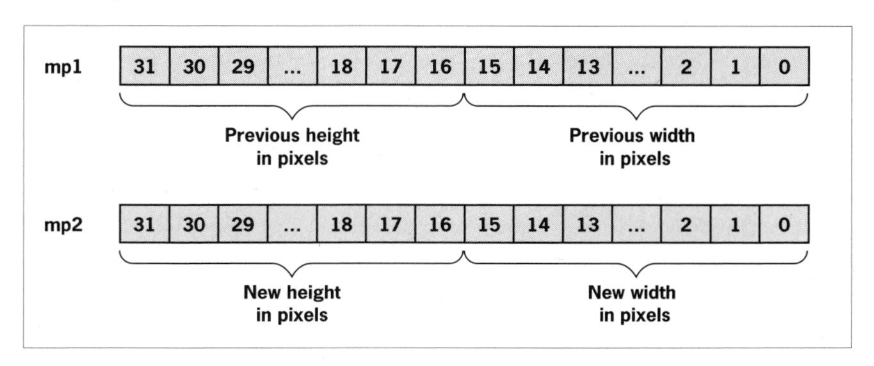

Figure 4.2: The WM_SIZE *mp1* and *mp2* parameters

WM_SIZE is a good example of a message that encodes two unsigned short integers (the USHORT type) in a 32-bit pointer (the MPARAM type). To help you extract the two USHORTs from the MPARAM, the PMWIN.H header file contains two macros: SHORT1FROMMP and SHORT2FROMMP. These are defined as follows:

```
#define SHORT1FROMMP(mp) ((USHORT) (ULONG) (mp))
#define SHORT2FROMMP(mp) ((USHORT) ((ULONG) mp >> 16))
```

For example, you can obtain the new height of the client window with

```
SHORT2FROMMP(mp2)
```

You should use these macros rather than your own code to extract the USHORT values. On some future implementations of the Presentation Manager, the two USHORT values might be encoded in the MPARAM in a different way. The macros insulate you from the implementation.

Processing the WM_SIZE message is simple. In the general case, you define two static variables in your client window procedure, named *cxClient* and *cy-Client* (for example) to store the width and height of the client window:

```
static INT cxClient, cyClient ;
```

An *x* prefix to a variable name usually indicates a horizontal position, a *y* prefix indicates a vertical position. The *c* prefix stands for "count," and when combined with *x* indicates a width, or with *y*, a height. You can process the WM_SIZE message like so:

```
case WM_SIZE:
     cxClient = SHORT1FROMMP (mp2) ;
     cyClient = SHORT2FROMMP (mp2) ;
     return Ø ;
```

The *cxClient* and *cyClient* variables must be defined as *static* because they are used later when processing other messages. After the first WM_SIZE message, the window procedure always has access to a valid client window size. In most cases you won't need to store or use the previous window size. You'll find similar WM_SIZE processing in most of the programs in this book. In SYSVALS1, however, only *cyClient* is set because the program doesn't use *cxClient.*

Note in the sample code above that the SHORT1FROMMP and SHORT2-FROMMP macros extract *unsigned* short integer values from *mp1* and *mp2*, but the values are stored in *cxClient* and *cyClient*, which are defined as *signed* integers. As you'll see, the *cxClient* and *cyClient* are often used in arithmetic manipulations for which the INT definition is safer.

THE PRESENTATION SPACE

To write to the client window, you need a handle to a presentation space. (A *presentation space* is a data structure internal to the Presentation Manager that describes an abstract display surface.) The presentation space handle is your passport to use the various GPI drawing functions, and is the first parameter to virtually all GPI function calls. The presentation space contains certain "attributes" (such as color) that influence how the GPI functions work. These attributes all have default values when the presentation space is first created. You can change these attributes with GPI functions, but often the defaults are the most convenient.

For example, in SYSVALS1 we probably want to display black text on a white background. These colors are attributes defined in the presentation space, and the defaults are black text on a white background. (Actually, the default colors are a little more complex than simply black and white, but I'll discuss that in Chapter 5.) We want the text to run from left to right rather than right to left, top to bottom, or bottom to top; this also is defined by the default presentation space. We want the letters of the text string to be positioned top side up and not tilted in some way. The default presentation space attributes define the characters to be displayed like this. The presentation space also defines the font used to display text. In the default presentation space, this is a font known as the "system font," which is the same font that the Presentation

Manager uses for text in title bars, menus, message boxes, and dialog boxes. The system font is a proportionally spaced Helvetica font. This means that characters have different widths. For example, a "W" is wider than an "I." Working with a proportionally spaced font certainly adds a layer of complexity to text output, but nothing insurmountable.

In this book, I'll most often use the type of presentation space called the *cached micro-PS*. The cached micro-PS gives a program access to only a subset of the GPI functions, but it is often easier to use in small programs.

Because a presentation space defines an abstract drawing surface, it isn't very useful by itself (unless, of course, you own an abstract display or an abstract printer). This is why a presentation space is usually "associated with" a particular device context. The *device context* refers to a device driver and the physical output device, such as the video display, a printer, or a plotter. (A device context can also describe an output device that isn't quite real, such as a "memory device context," in which a block of memory mimics a real display surface, or a "metafile device context," in which the graphics drawing functions are collected in a file.) Here's a simplified description of the relationship between a presentation space and a device context.

The presentation space describes an abstract drawing surface. The device context describes a physical output device. When the presentation space is associated with the device context, what you draw on the presentation space by calling GPI functions will appear on the device. The cached micro-PS, however, is always associated with the device context for the video display. More specifically, the cached micro-PS applies only to a particular window on the video display, typically your client window. When you obtain a handle to a cached micro-PS, you can't draw outside this window. It's not an error if you try to do so—the Presentation Manager simply ignores the attempt.

Getting a handle to a presentation space In using a cached micro-PS, you obtain the handle to the presentation space when you need to draw, and you "release" the handle when you finish drawing. After you release the handle, it's no longer valid. You have to obtain a new handle when you want to draw again. You should obtain and release the presentation space handle while processing a single message. You should not obtain the handle while processing one message and release it while processing another. Each time you obtain the handle, all attributes of the presentation space are set to default values. Changes you make to these attributes are lost when you release the handle.

In your window procedure, you define a variable (usually called *hps*) that is of type HPS, a handle to a presentation space:

```
HPS hps ;
```

There are two methods for obtaining a cached micro-PS handle for your client window. The SYSVALS1 program uses both methods.

Method one: During processing of the WM_PAINT message The first way to obtain a cached micro-PS handle is while processing the WM_PAINT message:

```
case WM_PAINT:
     hps = WinBeginPaint (hwnd, NULLHANDLE, NULL) ;
          [ call GPI functions ]
     WinEndPaint (hps) ;
     return 0 ;
```

You should always call *WinBeginPaint* and *WinEndPaint* as a pair. Don't call *WinBeginPaint* and *WinEndPaint* while processing messages other than WM_PAINT. By setting the second parameter of *WinBeginPaint* to NULLHANDLE, you request a cached micro-PS handle. Otherwise, you would set this parameter to the noncached presentation space handle you obtain from *GpiCreatePS* (a function I'll touch on in Chapters 6 and 7).

The window procedure receives a WM_PAINT message only when part of the window is invalid and must be repainted. For example, if part of your program's client window is partly off the screen and the user then moves the window so it is entirely within the screen, the area previously off the screen is marked as invalid. The Presentation Manager posts a WM_PAINT message in the window procedure's message queue.

The third parameter to *WinBeginPaint* is an optional pointer to a RECTL structure to obtain the coordinates of the rectangle encompassing the invalid area. (We'll use this in the SYSVALS3 version of the program later in this chapter.) The presentation space handle you obtain from *WinBeginPaint* allows you to draw only within this rectangle. When you call *WinEndPaint*, the Presentation Manager validates the entire area of the window.

Method two: During processing of other messages You can also obtain a cached micro-PS handle while processing messages other than WM_PAINT:

```
hps = WinGetPS (hwnd) ;
     [ call GPI functions ]
WinReleasePS (hps) ;
```

You should always call *WinGetPS* and *WinReleasePS* as a pair. With the handle from *WinGetPS*, you can draw on any part of the client window. However, unlike *WinEndPaint*, *WinReleasePS* doesn't validate any part of the window. SYSVALS1 calls *WinGetPS* and *WinReleasePS* while processing the WM_CREATE message. In a moment, I'll describe what the program does during that message.

THE COORDINATE SYSTEM

Parameters to GPI functions often specify coordinate positions and sizes. Several attributes of the presentation space define the coordinate system in effect when you draw; that is, they determine how the coordinate positions and sizes you specify in GPI functions are translated and mapped to the pixels of the output device. By default, coordinates and sizes for a cached micro-PS are specified in units of pixels, and coordinates are relative to the lower-left corner of the window, regardless of where the window is positioned on the screen. Values on the horizontal (or *x*) axis increase to the right; values on the vertical (or *y*) axis increase going up.

The notation (x,y) is often used to indicate a particular point in x and y coordinates. The point (0,0) is the lower-left corner of the client window. If you set variables *cxClient* and *cyClient* while processing the WM_SIZE message, the upper-right corner of the client window is (*cxClient-1, cyClient-1*). The coordinate system for a cached micro-PS is shown in Figure 4.3.

The size of a character Because this coordinate system has an origin at the lower-left corner of the client area, it is somewhat inconvenient for displaying text, which most of us read from the top down. But that's a relatively simple adjustment you can make when it comes time to display the text. The GPI function used in SYSVALS1 to display text is *GpiCharStringAt*. This function requires the x and y coordinates of the starting position of the text. SYSVALS1 calls *GpiCharStringAt* three times—once for each of the three columns to be displayed. Thus, to properly space successive lines and columns of text, SYSVALS1 needs to know the height and width of the characters in pixels.

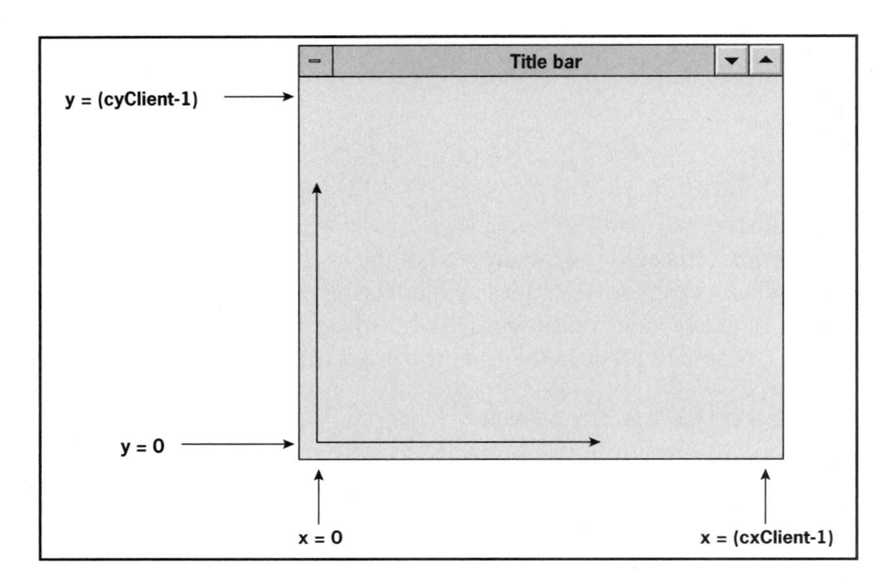

Figure 4.3: The cached micro-PS default coordinate system

When you obtain a handle to a cached micro-PS, the default presentation space includes a font. Unless you change that font, the Presentation Manager uses it for all text you write to the presentation space. The default font is called the *system font.* This is the proportionally spaced font used for normal text in the Presentation Manager. You can obtain character dimensions of the current font in the presentation space by calling *GpiQueryFontMetrics.* You first define a structure of type FONTMETRICS:

```
FONTMETRICS fm ;
```

Then you call the function:

```
GpiQueryFontMetrics (hps, (LONG) sizeof fm, &fm);
```

The second parameter is the size of the structure in bytes, and the last parameter is a pointer to the structure.

On the function's return, the fields of the *fm* structure describe many of the basic characteristics of the font. Figure 4.4 shows the fields that describe the dimensions of characters. Obviously, these fields represent much more information than you need right now, but they give you a sense of just how much information is available. All these values are LONG (32-bit) integers, as indicated by the "l" prefix.

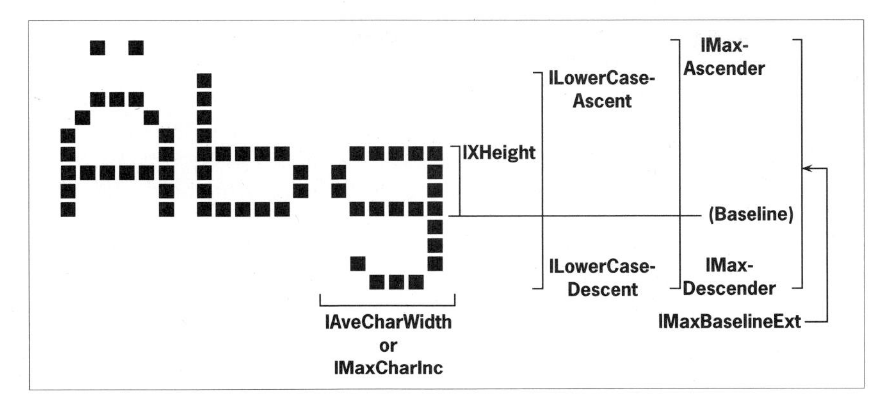

Figure 4.4: The character dimension fields from *GpiQueryFontMetrics*

Character width For a proportionally spaced font like the system font, the FONTMETRICS structure provides two fields that are valuable. The *lAveCharWidth* field is the weighted average width of lowercase letters based on the frequency of these letters in English text. The FONTMETRICS structure also includes a field called *lMaxCharInc*, which is the width of the widest character. In all cases the width includes intercharacter spacing.

Character height and line spacing When it comes to character heights, the FONTMETRICS structure provides more detailed information. The *lXHeight* value is the height above the baseline of a lowercase letter without ascenders. (The baseline is the imaginary line on which the characters sit.) The *lLowerCaseAscent* value indicates the maximum height of lowercase letters (without accent marks) above the baseline, and the *lLowerCaseDescent* value is the extent to which lowercase letters drop below the baseline.

Some characters may be taller than lowercase letters. For example, some letters have accent marks, and the line and block characters from the IBM extended character set are also taller. The maximum ascent and descent of all the characters in the character set is indicated by the *lMaxAscender* and *lMaxDescender* fields. The sum of *lMaxAscender* and *lMaxDescender* is *lMaxBaselineExt*. In most cases, you should use *lMaxBaselineExt* for spacing successive lines of text.

Some other fields of the FONTMETRICS structure are less useful. The *lEmHeight* and *lEmInc* fields indicate the point size of the font in both vertical and horizontal coordinates. (A point is 1/72 inch, but the values in the FONTMETRICS structure are given in pixels.) However, the point size of a font is a typographical concept rather than a metrical concept, and usually cannot be related to the other font metrics. If you want a tighter line spacing than *lMaxBaselineExt* indicates, and you know that the text you are displaying contains only unaccented letters, you can use *lEmHeight* to space successive lines of text.

The *lInternalLeading* field is a fudge factor; it is the difference between *lMaxBaselineExt* and *lEmHeight*. In OS/2 2.0, the *lExternalLeading* field is always 0.

Getting the information The size of the system font won't change while your program is running, so you need to obtain the character sizes only once. An excellent time to do this is while processing the WM_CREATE message, which is the approach that SYSVALS1 uses. SYSVALS1 defines four static variables to hold the average lowercase width, average uppercase width, total height, and descender height of a character:

```
static INT cxChar, cxCaps, cyChar, cyDesc, cyClient ;
```

While processing WM_CREATE, SYSVALS1 obtains a handle to the presentation space, calls *GpiQueryFontMetrics*, and saves the values of the *lAveCharWidth*, *lMaxBaselineExt*, and *lMaxDescender* fields:

```
case WM_CREATE:
     hps = WinGetPS (hwnd) ;
     GpiQueryFontMetrics (hps, (LONG) sizeof fm, &fm) ;

     cxChar = fm.lAveCharWidth ;
     cxCaps = (fm.fsType & 1 ? 2 : 3) * cxChar / 2 ;
     cyChar = fm.lMaxBaselineExt ;
     cyDesc = fm.lMaxDescender ;

     WinReleasePS (hps) ;
     return 0 ;
```

The calculation of *cxCaps* (the average width of an uppercase letter) requires a little explanation: The bottom bit of the *fsType* field is set to 1 if the font is fixed pitch—that is, all the characters have the same width. In that case, *cxCaps* is simply set to *cxChar*. Otherwise, the program sets *cxCaps* to 150 percent of *cxChar*. This is a good approximation that works for many types of fonts.

Like the processing of the WM_SIZE message, this is fairly standard code; you'll see it frequently in Presentation Manager programs that work with simple text.

During the WM_CREATE message, SYSVALS1 obtains a handle to the presentation space only to obtain information. Attempting to draw during the WM_CREATE message is unwise because the window isn't yet displayed on the screen. And be forewarned that the FONTMETRICS structure is over 200 bytes long. For purposes of clarity, I've defined *fm* as a local variable in *ClientWndProc.* In most programs, the definition of *fm* and the *GpiQueryFontMetrics* call should probably be moved to a subroutine so the structure doesn't take up stack space whenever the window procedure is called.

THE WM_PAINT MESSAGE

WM_PAINT is an extremely important message. The window procedure receives a WM_PAINT message when an area of the window becomes invalid. This can happen frequently as the user moves and resizes various windows on the screen. Your Presentation Manager programs should be structured so that they can entirely update the client window on receipt of a WM_PAINT message. In many cases, this means the program can be most efficient if it draws on the client window only during the WM_PAINT message.

This certainly isn't a hard-and-fast rule. Obviously, the program can access a presentation space by calling *WinGetPS* and paint on the client window at almost any time. But the program must be able to entirely repaint the client window when it receives the WM_PAINT message anyway, so any drawing it does during other messages has to be duplicated during WM_PAINT processing. Often, however, a window procedure will determine during a message other than WM_PAINT that part of the client window should be changed. We'll see examples of how programs can themselves generate WM_PAINT messages in the SYSVALS2 and SYSVALS3 programs presented in this chapter.

THE *GPICHARSTRINGAT* FUNCTION

SYSVALS1 uses the *GpiCharStringAt* function to write text to the client area. The *At* part of the function name indicates that the function requires specific coordinates for where the text is to begin. The general syntax of *GpiCharStringAt* is

```
GpiCharStringAt (hps, &ptl, lCount, pchString) ;
```

The first parameter is a handle to the presentation space. That's the case for virtually all GPI functions. The last parameter is a pointer to a character string (as indicated by the "pch" prefix). The third parameter is a LONG value of the number of characters in the string. Unlike *WinDrawText*, *GpiCharStringAt* doesn't recognize zero-terminated character strings.

The second parameter to *GpiCharStringAt* is a pointer to a structure of type POINTL (which stands for "a point with LONG coordinates"). The definition of the POINTL structure in OS2DEF.H looks like this:

```
typedef struct _POINTL
     {
     LONG x ;
     LONG y ;
     }
     POINTL ;
```

It's simply a structure that specifies a point in terms of x and y coordinates. You can define a variable (the name *ptl* is standard) of type POINTL in your window procedure:

```
POINTL ptl ;
```

You then set the *x* and *y* fields of this structure before you call *GpiCharStringAt*. These *x* and *y* values indicate the starting position of the string—specifically, the point corresponding to the baseline of the left side of the first character. If you use *GpiCharStringAt* with the string "go," for example, it's displayed relative to the lower-left corner of the client window, as shown in Figure 4.5.

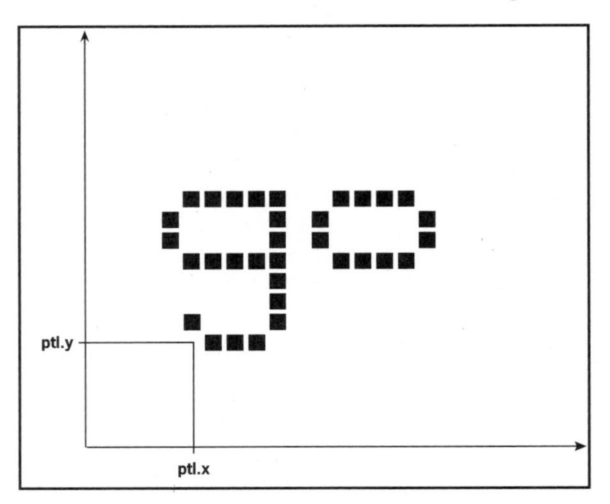

Figure 4.5: A character string with starting coordinates set by the *GpiCharStringAt* function

The use of the baseline for the y coordinate can be a little tricky. For example, to display the string "go" in the lower-left corner of the client window, you might want to use code like this:

```
ptl.x = 0 ;
ptl.y = 0 ;

GpiCharStringAt (hps, &ptl, 2, "go") ;
```

But the descender on the "g" won't be visible. Instead, you need to adjust the y coordinates for the length of the descender:

```
ptl.y = cyDesc ;
```

NUMERIC FORMATTING

If you felt disheartened when I announced at the beginning of this chapter that you can't use *printf* in a Presentation Manager program to display text to the screen, cheer up and take a look at *sprintf*. Like *printf*, *sprintf* formats numbers and text based on a formatting string. However, rather than writing the resultant formatted text to standard output, *sprintf* stores it in a character buffer that you provide. The general syntax is

```
iLength = sprintf (szBuffer, szFormat,...) ;
```

where *iLength* is the integer length of the zero-terminated output string that *sprintf* stores in *szBuffer*.

When you use *sprintf* in a Presentation Manager program, include the STDIO.H header file at the top of the C source code file:

```
#include <stdio.h>
```

You must also define a buffer large enough for the formatted text. For example, you might use

```
CHAR szBuffer [80] ;
```

You can then use *sprintf* with *GpiCharStringAt* like this:

```
iLength = sprintf (szBuffer,
                   "The sum of %d and &d is %d",
                   iNum1, iNum2, iNum1 + iNum2) ;

GpiCharStringAt (hps, &ptl, iLength, szBuffer) ;
```

Or you can dispense with the *iLength* variable and combine both statements into one:

```
GpiCharStringAt (hps, &ptl,
     sprintf (szBuffer,
              "The sum of %d and %d is %d",
              iNum1, iNum2, iNum1 + iNum2),
     szBuffer) ;
```

This may look ugly, but it's a common construction in Presentation Manager programs.

At this point, the processing of the WM_PAINT message in SYSVALS1 should be almost comprehensible:

```
case WM_PAINT:
     hps = WinBeginPaint (hwnd, NULLHANDLE, NULL) ;
     GpiErase (hps) ;

     for (iLine = 0 ; iLine < NUMLINES ; iLine++)
          {
          ptl.x = cxCaps ;
          ptl.y = cyClient - cyChar * (iLine + 1) + cyDesc ;

     GpiCharStringAt (hps, &ptl,
          strlen (sysvals[iLine].szIdentifier),
          sysvals[iLine].szIdentifier) ;

     ptl.x += 24 * cxCaps ;
     GpiCharStringAt (hps, &ptl,
          strlen (sysvals[iLine].szDescription),
          sysvals[iLine].szDescription) ;

     sprintf (szBuffer, "%d",
              WinQuerySysValue (HWND_DESKTOP,
                                sysvals[iLine].sIndex)) ;

     ptl.x += 38 * cxChar ;
     GpiCharStringAt (hps, &ptl, strlen (szBuffer),
              szBuffer) ;
     }
WinEndPaint (hps) ;
return 0 ;
```

Between the *WinBeginPaint* and *WinEndPaint* calls is a call to *GpiErase* (which erases the invalid rectangle) and a simple *for* loop. The NUMLINES identifier is defined in SYSVALS.H.

The *x* field of the POINTL structure is initially set to *cxCaps*. Thus every line is indented one character width from the left side of the client window. For the first line (*iLine* equals 0), the *y* field is set to (*cyClient-cyChar+cyDesc*), the top line of the client window. Each successive line begins *yChar* pixels below the previous line. The first *GpiCharStringAt* call displays the *szIdentifier* field of the *sysvals* structure (for example, SV_SWAPBUTTON). For the second *GpiCharStringAt* call, the *x* field of the POINTL structure is increased by 24 times the average width of an uppercase letter:

```
ptl.x += 24 * cxCaps ;
```

This value is based on the widths of the actual character strings in the structure. The *szDescription* field is then displayed. SYSVALS1 formats the value obtained from *WinQuerySysValue* by calling *sprintf*. It moves the *x* field of the POINTL structure to the right of the description column:

```
ptl.x += 38 * cxChar ;
```

It then displays the value.

THE PROBLEM WITH SYSVALS1

So that's it—SYSVALS1 obtains the width and height of a system font character while processing the WM_CREATE message, obtains the width and height of the client window from the WM_SIZE message, and paints the client window using this information during WM_PAINT. It's simple, and it's wrong: On most standard video displays, there's not enough room to display all the values obtained from *WinQuerySysValue*. SYSVALS1 always displays the values starting at the top of its client window and has no way to bring the hidden lines into view. That's a problem. But it's nothing a scroll bar can't fix.

ADDING SCROLL BARS

Scroll bars are an important part of the consistent user interface in the Presentation Manager. For users, scroll bars are easy to learn and to use, and they provide good visual feedback. Scroll bars are usually thought of as controlling the view of a document, as in a word processing program, but they can be used in any program that has more to display than can fit in the client window. A vertical scroll bar like the one shown in Figure 4.6 is normally positioned to the right of the client window.

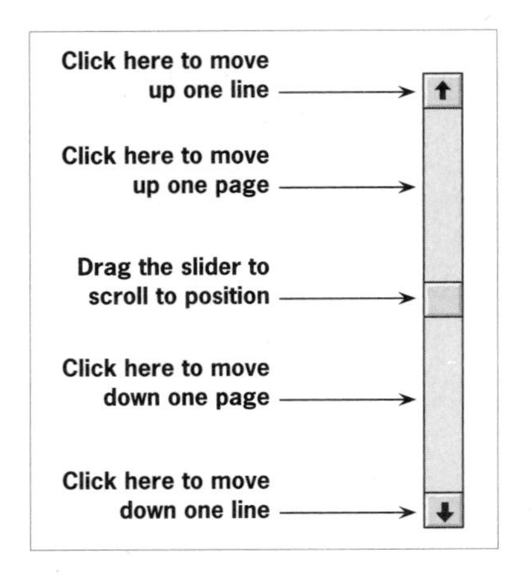

Figure 4.6: A vertical scroll bar and the actions it usually performs

A click on the arrow at the top of the scroll bar moves the view one line toward the beginning of the document. (This is called "scrolling up" in keeping with the user's perspective, even though the document actually scrolls down relative to the window.) Similarly, a click on the bottom arrow moves the view one line toward the end of the document.

Between the two arrows is a long area containing the moveable scroll-bar slider. Clicking above the slider moves the view one page toward the beginning of the document; clicking below the slider moves the view one page toward the end of the document. The slider indicates the approximate position within the entire document of the portion displayed on the screen. For example, if the slider is in the middle of the scroll bar, you're in the middle of the document. You can move to a position in the document by dragging the slider to the relative spot in the slider area. For example, you can move to the beginning of the document by dragging the slider to the top of the slider area.

Horizontal scroll bars (normally positioned at the bottom of a client window) are used in a similar fashion to scroll documents to the left and right.

CREATING THE SCROLL BAR

The first step in adding a scroll-bar interface involves changing a parameter to the *WinCreateStdWindow* call. You simply include the necessary frame creation flag identifier (FCF_HORZSCROLL, FCF_VERTSCROLL, or both) in the *flFrameFlags* variable. The Presentation Manager creates the scroll-bar windows as children of the frame window. With only this change, the scroll bars don't seem to do very much. The scroll bar colors itself with a reverse-video flash when you click on it, but that's about it.

Looks are deceiving. When you click on a scroll bar, the scroll-bar window procedure (located in the Presentation Manager) receives a mouse message. The scroll bar then posts a notification message to its owner, which is the frame window. This notification message contains information about the action of the mouse on the scroll bar. The frame window graciously sends this message to the client window procedure, which is in your program. The notification messages are WM_HSCROLL for a horizontal scroll bar and WM_-VSCROLL for a vertical scroll bar.

Your client window procedure can also send messages to the scroll-bar window. These messages set the "range" and current "position" of the scroll-bar slider. To send these messages, you need to know the window handle of the scroll bar. When the Presentation Manager creates the scroll bars as part of the standard window, they are assigned predefined child ID numbers of FID_-HORZSCROLL and FID_VERTSCROLL. Thus you can obtain the window handle of horizontal and vertical scroll bars by calling

```
hwndHscroll = WinWindowFromID (hwndFrame, FID_HORZSCROLL) ;
hwndVscroll = WinWindowFromID (hwndFrame, FID_VERTSCROLL) ;
```

The scroll bars' parent is *hwndFrame*. The frame window is also the parent of the client window, so you can obtain these handles within your client window procedure by using only the *hwnd* parameter passed to the procedure. You'll probably do this while processing the WM_CREATE message:

```
hwndHscroll = WinWindowFromID (
          WinQueryWindow (hwnd, QW_PARENT),
          FID_HORZSCROLL) ;

hWndVscroll = WinWindowFromID (
          WinQueryWindow (hwnd, QW_PARENT),
          FID_VERTSCROLL) ;
```

Within a client window procedure, these window handles should be stored in static variables of type HWND.

THE RANGE AND POSITION

After obtaining the window handle of a scroll bar, the program can initialize the scroll bar to a range and slider position. When first created, a scroll bar has a default range of 0 to 100. The position of the scroll-bar slider is always a discrete integral value within this range.

If the slider is at the top (or left) of the scroll bar, the position is 0. If the slider is at the bottom (or right) of the scroll bar, the position is 100. If that 0 to 100 range isn't appropriate for your program, you can set a different range by sending the scroll bar an SBM_SETSCROLLBAR message. SBM_SETSCROLLBAR, like other messages that begin with SBM ("scroll-bar message"), is a message understood only by scroll bars. Set the *mp1* parameter of this message to the initial position of the scroll-bar slider. Set *mp2* to contain the range of the scroll bar, with the minimum value in the low half of *mp2* and the maximum value in the high half. You can convert these values to an MPARAM data type using the MPFROM2SHORT macro. For example, suppose you want to set the vertical scroll-bar range to 10 through 40 and the initial position to 15. Here's the code:

```
iMinPos = 10 ;
iMaxPos = 40 ;
iPosition = 15 ;

WinSendMsg (hwndVscroll, SBM_SETSCROLLBAR,
            MPFROM2SHORT (iPosition, 0),
            MPFROM2SHORT (iMinPos, iMaxPos)) ;
```

If you ever need to obtain the range from the scroll bar, you can send the scroll bar an SBM_QUERYRANGE message:

```
mr = WinSendMsg (hwndVscroll, SBM_QUERYRANGE, NULL, NULL) ;
```

The minimum and maximum range positions are encoded in *mr* (a variable of type MRESULT) and can be extracted using the SHORT1FROMMR and SHORT2FROMMR macros:

```
iMinPos = SHORT1FROMMR (mr) ;
iMaxPos = SHORT2FROMMR (mr) ;
```

RECEIVING NOTIFICATION MESSAGES FROM THE SCROLL BAR

Scroll bars post notification messages to their owner (the frame window) when the various parts of the scroll bar are clicked on or dragged. The frame window sends these messages to the client window. For vertical scroll bars, the notification message is WM_VSCROLL; for horizontal scroll bars, it's WM_HSCROLL.

Messages from vertical scroll bars During a WM_VSCROLL or WM_HSCROLL message, the low half of *mp1* (which you can obtain using the SHORT1FROMMP macro) contains the child window ID. For a vertical scroll bar created as part of the standard window, this is FID_VERTSCROLL. You need to examine this value only if you create multiple vertical scroll bars as children of your client window. The high half of *mp2* indicates the action of the mouse on the scroll bar. The value corresponds to an identifier defined in PMWIN.H that begins with the letters SB. Figure 4.7 shows how these values identify the mouse actions on the vertical scroll bar. The low half of *mp2* is the current position of the slider for SB_SLIDERTRACK and SB_SLIDERPOSITION actions.

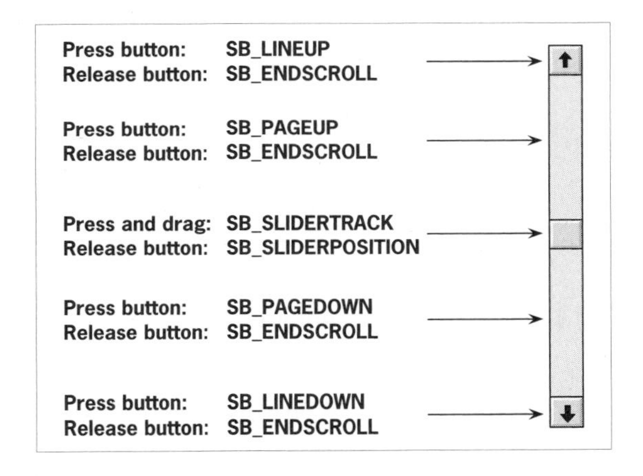

Figure 4.7: Vertical scroll-bar action identifiers

Within your client window procedure, you process the WM_VSCROLL message with code that looks like this:

```
case WM_VSCROLL:
     switch (SHORT2FROMMP (mp2))
          {
          case SB_LINEUP:
               [ process line up action ]
              break ;

          case SB_PAGEUP:
              [ process page up action ]
              break ;

          [ and so forth ]
```

Messages from horizontal scroll bars Horizontal scroll bars generate messages in the same way vertical scroll bars do: The notification message is WM_-HSCROLL, the child window ID is FID_HORZSCROLL, and the identifiers indicating the mouse actions are those shown in Figure 4.8.

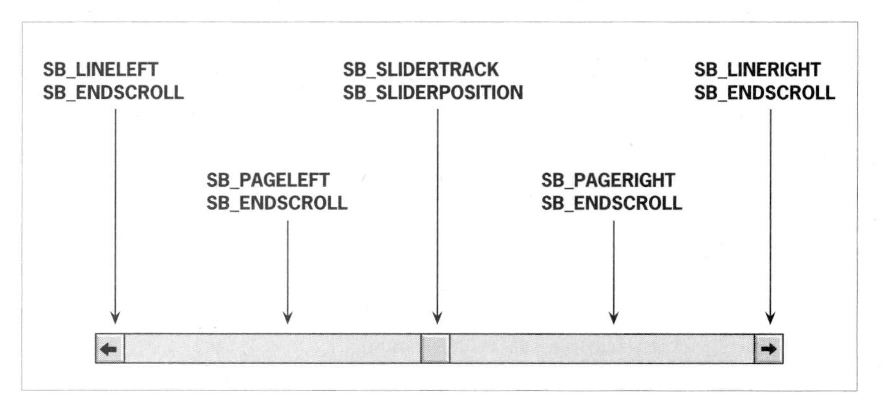

Figure 4.8: Horizontal scroll-bar action identifiers

Processing scroll-bar messages You have several options for handling scroll-bar messages. When the user clicks on the arrows or the slider area, you receive at least two WM_VSCROLL or WM_HSCROLL messages. You get the first message when the mouse button is pressed. The action identifier is SB_LINEUP, SB_PAGEUP, SB_LINEDOWN, or SB_PAGEDOWN for vertical scroll bars or one of the similar identifiers for horizontal scroll bars. When the button is released, you receive a WM_VSCROLL or WM_HSCROLL message with the SB_ENDSCROLL action identifier. As a general rule, you process the various "button down" messages and ignore SB_ENDSCROLL.

However, if your program requires a lot of time to process these actions, you might want to delay the processing until the mouse button is released. You can simply track how many messages you receive and do something that affects the client window only when you get SB_ENDSCROLL. This approach requires more complex logic and provides less feedback to the user, but it *is* an alternative.

The SB_SLIDERTRACK and SB_SLIDERPOSITION actions can be somewhat troublesome. As the user drags the slider up and down the scroll bar, your window procedure receives many SB_SLIDERTRACK actions. If your program is fast enough, you should process SB_SLIDERTRACK actions and ignore SB_SLIDERPOSITION. But if your program has a hard time keeping up, you should process SB_SLIDERPOSITION and ignore SB_SLIDERTRACK.

These two approaches are illustrated later in the chapter: SYSVALS2 is a slow, simple program that processes SB_SLIDERPOSITION; SYSVALS3 is optimized sufficiently to process SB_SLIDERTRACK actions on the vertical scroll bar.

SETTING THE NEW SLIDER POSITION

The scroll-bar window itself doesn't change the position of the scroll-bar slider unless you tell it to. To change the position of the slider, you send the scroll bar a message. Assume the variable *iPosition* contains the new position of the vertical scroll bar. You send the scroll bar an SBM_SETPOS message in which *mp1* is the new position:

```
WinSendMsg (hwndVscroll, SBM_SETPOS, MPFROMSHORT (iPosition), NULL) ;
```

You typically send the scroll bar the SBM_SETPOS message while processing the WM_VSCROLL or WM_HSCROLL notification message from the scroll bar.

If you need to obtain the current position of the scroll-bar slider, you can send the scroll bar an SBM_QUERYPOS message:

```
iPosition = SHORT1FROMMR (WinSendMsg (hwndVScroll,
                SBM_QUERYPOS, NULL, NULL)) ;
```

THE IMPLEMENTATION

Now we're ready to look at the SYSVALS2 program, shown in Listing 4.2. You'll need the SYSVALS.H header file from Listing 4.1 to compile the program.

Listing 4.2: The SYSVALS2 program

The SYSVALS2.MAK File

```
#-----------------------
# SYSVALS2.MAK make file
#-----------------------

sysvals2.exe : sysvals2.obj sysvals2.def
     $(PRGLINK) sysvals2, sysvals2, NUL, $(PRGLIB), sysvals2

sysvals2.obj : sysvals2.c sysvals.h
     $(PRGCC) sysvals2.c
```

Listing 4.2: The SYSVALS2 program (Continued)

The SYSVALS2.C File

```
/*-------------------------------------------------
   SYSVALS2.C -- System Values Display Program No. 2
                 (c) Charles Petzold, 1993
  -------------------------------------------------*/

#define INCL_WIN
#define INCL_GPI
#include <os2.h>
#include <stdio.h>
#include <stdlib.h>
#include <string.h>
#include "sysvals.h"

MRESULT EXPENTRY ClientWndProc (HWND, ULONG, MPARAM, MPARAM) ;

int main (void)
     {
     static CHAR  szClientClass [] = "SysVals2" ;
     static ULONG flFrameFlags = FCF_TITLEBAR      | FCF_SYSMENU  |
                                 FCF_SIZEBORDER    | FCF_MINMAX   |
                                 FCF_SHELLPOSITION | FCF_TASKLIST |
                                 FCF_VERTSCROLL ;
     HAB          hab ;
     HMQ          hmq ;
     HWND         hwndFrame, hwndClient ;
     QMSG         qmsg ;

     hab = WinInitialize (0) ;
     hmq = WinCreateMsgQueue (hab, 0) ;

     WinRegisterClass (hab, szClientClass, ClientWndProc, CS_SIZEREDRAW, 0) ;

     hwndFrame = WinCreateStdWindow (HWND_DESKTOP, WS_VISIBLE,
                                     &flFrameFlags, szClientClass, NULL,
                                     0L, 0, 0, &hwndClient) ;

     while (WinGetMsg (hab, &qmsg, NULLHANDLE, 0, 0))
          WinDispatchMsg (hab, &qmsg) ;

     WinDestroyWindow (hwndFrame) ;
     WinDestroyMsgQueue (hmq) ;
     WinTerminate (hab) ;
     return 0 ;
     }

MRESULT EXPENTRY ClientWndProc (HWND hwnd, ULONG msg, MPARAM mp1, MPARAM mp2)
```

Listing 4.2: The SYSVALS2 program (Continued)

```
     {
     static HWND hwndVscroll ;
     static INT  cxChar, cxCaps, cyChar, cyDesc, iVscrollPos, cyClient ;
     CHAR        szBuffer [10] ;
     FONTMETRICS fm ;
     HPS         hps ;
     INT         iLine ;
     POINTL      ptl ;

     switch (msg)
          {
          case WM_CREATE:
               hps = WinGetPS (hwnd) ;
               GpiQueryFontMetrics (hps, sizeof fm, &fm) ;

               cxChar = fm.lAveCharWidth ;
               cxCaps = (fm.fsType & 1 ? 2 : 3) * cxChar / 2 ;
               cyChar = fm.lMaxBaselineExt ;
               cyDesc = fm.lMaxDescender ;

               WinReleasePS (hps) ;

               hwndVscroll = WinWindowFromID (
                                   WinQueryWindow (hwnd, QW_PARENT),
                                   FID_VERTSCROLL) ;

               WinSendMsg (hwndVscroll, SBM_SETSCROLLBAR,
                                   MPFROM2SHORT (iVscrollPos, 0),
                                   MPFROM2SHORT (0, NUMLINES - 1)) ;
               return 0 ;

          case WM_SIZE:
               cyClient = SHORT2FROMMP (mp2) ;
               return 0 ;

          case WM_VSCROLL:
               switch (SHORT2FROMMP (mp2))
                    {
                    case SB_LINEUP:
                         iVscrollPos -= 1 ;
                         break ;

                    case SB_LINEDOWN:
                         iVscrollPos += 1 ;
                         break ;

                    case SB_PAGEUP:
                         iVscrollPos -= cyClient / cyChar ;
                         break ;
```

Listing 4.2: The SYSVALS2 program (Continued)

```
                    case SB_PAGEDOWN:
                         iVscrollPos += cyClient / cyChar ;
                         break ;

                    case SB_SLIDERPOSITION:
                         iVscrollPos = SHORT1FROMMP (mp2) ;
                         break ;

                    default:
                         return 0 ;
                    }
               iVscrollPos = max (0, min (iVscrollPos, NUMLINES - 1)) ;

               WinSendMsg (hwndVscroll, SBM_SETPOS,
                           MPFROMSHORT (iVscrollPos), NULL) ;

               WinInvalidateRect (hwnd, NULL, FALSE) ;
               return 0 ;

          case WM_PAINT:
               hps = WinBeginPaint (hwnd, NULLHANDLE, NULL) ;
               GpiErase (hps) ;

               for (iLine = 0 ; iLine < NUMLINES ; iLine++)
                    {
                    ptl.x = cxCaps ;
                    ptl.y = cyClient - cyChar * (iLine + 1 - iVscrollPos)
                                     + cyDesc ;

                    GpiCharStringAt (hps, &ptl,
                                     strlen (sysvals[iLine].szIdentifier),
                                     sysvals[iLine].szIdentifier) ;

                    ptl.x += 24 * cxCaps ;
                    GpiCharStringAt (hps, &ptl,
                                     strlen (sysvals[iLine].szDescription),
                                     sysvals[iLine].szDescription) ;

                    sprintf (szBuffer, "%d",
                             WinQuerySysValue (HWND_DESKTOP,
                                               sysvals[iLine].sIndex)) ;

                    ptl.x += 38 * cxChar ;
                    GpiCharStringAt (hps, &ptl, strlen (szBuffer),
                                     szBuffer) ;
                    }
               WinEndPaint (hps) ;
               return 0 ;
```

Listing 4.2: The SYSVALS2 program (Continued)

```
          }
     return WinDefWindowProc (hwnd, msg, mp1, mp2) ;
     }
```

The SYSVALS2.DEF File

```
;------------------------------------
; SYSVALS2.DEF module definition file
;------------------------------------

NAME           SYSVALS2  WINDOWAPI

DESCRIPTION    'System Values Display No. 2 (c) Charles Petzold, 1993'
PROTMODE
```

The SYSVALS2 window with the vertical scroll bar is shown in Figure 4.9.

SYSVALS2.EXE

SV_SWAPBUTTON	Mouse buttons swapped flag	0
SV_DBLCLKTIME	Mouse double click time	500
SV_CXDBLCLK	Mouse double click area width	6
SV_CYDBLCLK	Mouse double click area height	8
SV_CXSIZEBORDER	Sizing border width	4
SV_CYSIZEBORDER	Sizing border height	4
SV_ALARM	Alarm enabled flag	1
SV_CURSORRATE	Cursor blink rate	500
SV_FIRSTSCROLLRATE	Scroll bar repeat delay	200
SV_SCROLLRATE	Scroll bar scroll rate	50
SV_NUMBEREDLISTS	Undefined	0
SV_WARNINGFREQ	Alarm frequency for warning	880
SV_NOTEFREQ	Alarm frequency for note	1760
SV_ERRORFREQ	Alarm frequency for error	440
SV_WARNINGDURATION	Alarm duration for warning	50
SV_NOTEDURATION	Alarm duration for note	100
SV_ERRORDURATION	Alarm duration for error	100
SV_CXSCREEN	Screen width in pixels	640
SV_CYSCREEN	Screen height in pixels	480
SV_CXVSCROLL	Vertical scroll bar width	14
SV_CYHSCROLL	Horizontal scroll bar height	14
SV_CYVSCROLLARROW	Vertical scroll bar arrow height	15
SV_CXHSCROLLARROW	Horizontal scroll bar arrow width	15
SV_CXBORDER	Border width	1
SV_CYBORDER	Border height	1
SV_CXDLGFRAME	Dialog window frame width	4
SV_CYDLGFRAME	Dialog window frame height	4

Figure 4.9: The SYSVALS2 display

The only change in *main* is that the *flFrameFlags* variable now includes the identifier FCF_VERTSCROLL. This causes the Presentation Manager to create a vertical scroll bar as part of the standard window. *ClientWndProc* contains two new variables: *hwndVscroll*, which stores the handle of the scroll-bar window, and *iVscrollPos*, which stores the current position of the scroll-bar slider.

While processing the WM_CREATE message, the program obtains the window handle of the scroll bar:

```
hwndVscroll = WinWindowFromID (
          WinQueryWindow (hwnd, QW_PARENT),
          FID_VERTSCROLL) ;
```

The program then initializes the range and slider position by sending the scroll bar a message:

```
WinSendMsg (hwndVscroll, SBM_SETSCROLLBAR,
          MPFROM2SHORT (iVscrollPos, 0),
          MPFROM2SHORT (0, NUMLINES - 1)) ;
```

The range (in *mp2*) is set to a minimum position of 0 and a maximum position of NUMLINES-1. Thus the scroll bar has as many positions as there are lines of text. The initial value of *iVscrollPos* is 0 (because it is defined as a static variable but not explicitly initialized), so the slider is set to the topmost position.

SYSVALS2 uses the position of the vertical scroll-bar slider to determine how it displays the lines of text in the client window. The value of the slider position corresponds to the line that appears at the top of the client window, as shown here:

Slider Position	Line at Top of Client Window
0 (top)	First
1	Second
2	Third
⋮	
NUMLINES - 1 (bottom)	Last

The processing of the WM_VSCROLL message begins with the *iVscrollPos* variable being incremented or decremented, depending on the particular action of the mouse on the scroll bar:

```
case WM_VSCROLL:
switch (SHORT2FROMMP (mp2))
     {
     case SB_LINEUP:
          iVscrollPos -= 1 ;
          break ;
```

```
case SB_LINEDOWN:
     iVscrollPos += 1 ;
     break ;

case SB_PAGEUP:
     iVscrollPos -= cyClient / cyChar ;
     break ;

case SB_PAGEDOWN:
     iVscrollPos += cyClient / cyChar ;
     break ;

case SB_SLIDERPOSITION:
     iVscrollPos = SHORT1FROMMP (mp2) ;
     break ;
default: return 0
}
```

For SB_LINEUP and SB_LINEDOWN, *iVscrollPos* is simply decremented or incremented by 1 for a change of one line. For SB_PAGEUP and SB_PAGE-DOWN, the variable is decreased or increased by *cyClient/cyChar*, which is the number of lines that can fit in the client window. For the SB_SLIDERPOSITION action, the low USHORT encoded in *mp2* is the new slider position after the slider has been dragged and released. SYSVALS2 ignores the SB_ENDSCROLL and SB_SLIDERTRACK actions.

It's possible that the new value of *iVscrollPos* is outside the range of the scroll bar. For example, the scroll-bar slider could have been at the top of the scroll bar when the user clicked the up arrow. This statement uses the *min* and *max* macros defined in STDLIB.H to bring *iVscrollPos* within the scroll bar range:

```
iVscrollPos = max (0, min (iVscrollPos, NUMLINES - 1)) ;
```

The slider is set to the new position by sending it the SBM_SETPOS message:

```
WinSendMsg (hwndVscroll, SBM_SETPOS,
    MPFROMSHORT (iVscrollPos), NULL) ;
```

Finally, SYSVALS2 must update its client window to reflect the change. It must get a presentation space handle, erase the entire client window, rewrite all the lines of text, and then release the presentation space handle. It does all this by calling

```
WinInvalidateRect (hwnd, NULL, FALSE) ;
```

What's this? This one *WinInvalidateRect* statement does all that? It sure does, because this statement invalidates the entire client window and causes the Presentation Manager to post a WM_PAINT message in SYSVALS2's message queue. The repainting actually occurs during the WM_PAINT message.

Earlier I discussed the idea of structuring your programs so that all drawing on the client window occurs during the WM_PAINT message. The *WinInvalidateRect* function is one of the tools that help you achieve this goal. The second parameter to *WinInvalidateRect* can be a pointer to a RECTL structure to specify that only a small rectangular area of the window is to be invalidated. Specifying NULL invalidates the whole window.

WM_PAINT PROCESSING IN SYSVALS2

Now let's look at the WM_PAINT processing. If you compare it with the WM_PAINT logic in SYSVALS1, you'll find only one changed statement. The original SYSVALS1 program used the following statement to set the *y* field of the POINTL structure passed to *GpiCharStringAt*:

```
ptl.y = cyClient - cyChar * (iLine + 1) + cyDesc ;
```

SYSVALS2, on the other hand, uses this statement:

```
ptl.y = cyClient - cyChar * (iLine + 1 - iVscrollPos) + cyDesc ;
```

When the scroll-bar slider is at the top of the bar, *iVscrollPos* is 0, and *ptl.y* is set to the same value as in SYSVALS1. The first line of text is displayed at the top of the client window. When *iVscrollPos* is 1, *ptl.y* is set to (*cyClient* + *cyDesc*), which means that the first line of text is displayed right above the client window; in other words, it isn't displayed at all. The second line of text (when *iLine* equals 1) occupies the top line of the client window. Thus, SYSVALS2 calls *GpiCharStringAt* for all lines of text, but the program begins writing these lines either at the top of the client window (when *iVscrollPos* is 0) or somewhere above the client window. The Presentation Manager obligingly clips everything that falls outside the window.

This isn't very efficient WM_PAINT processing. It may not be too bad for 50 or so lines of text, but what if there were several hundred lines? Or thousands? The painting should really be restricted only to what's needed. So let's not be satisfied that we got the program working. Anybody can do that. Let's take a crack at making it better.

OPTIMIZING THE CODE

The new and improved SYSVALS3 program is shown in Listing 4.3. In addition to faster vertical scroll-bar processing and repainting, this version includes a horizontal scroll bar for left and right scrolling. The *flFrameFlags* variable in *main* includes the frame creation flag identifiers FCF_HORZSCROLL and FCF_VERTSCROLL.

Listing 4.3: The SYSVALS3 program

The SYSVALS3.MAK File

```
#------------------------
# SYSVALS3.MAK make file
#------------------------

sysvals3.exe : sysvals3.obj sysvals3.def
     $(PRGLINK) sysvals3, sysvals3, NUL, $(PRGLIB), sysvals3

sysvals3.obj : sysvals3.c sysvals.h
     $(PRGCC) sysvals3.c
```

The SYSVALS3.C File

```
/*--------------------------------------------------
   SYSVALS3.C -- System Values Display Program No. 3
                 (c) Charles Petzold, 1993
  --------------------------------------------------*/

#define INCL_WIN
#define INCL_GPI
#include <os2.h>
#include <stdio.h>
#include <stdlib.h>
#include <string.h>
#include "sysvals.h"

MRESULT EXPENTRY ClientWndProc (HWND, ULONG, MPARAM, MPARAM) ;
LONG             RtJustCharStringAt (HPS, PPOINTL, LONG, PCHAR) ;

int main (void)
     {
     static CHAR  szClientClass [] = "SysVals3" ;
     static ULONG flFrameFlags = FCF_TITLEBAR      | FCF_SYSMENU  |
                                 FCF_SIZEBORDER    | FCF_MINMAX   |
                                 FCF_SHELLPOSITION | FCF_TASKLIST |
                                 FCF_VERTSCROLL    | FCF_HORZSCROLL ;
     HAB          hab ;
     HMQ          hmq ;
```

Listing 4.3: The SYSVALS3 program (Continued)

```
     HWND        hwndFrame, hwndClient ;
     QMSG        qmsg ;

     hab = WinInitialize (0) ;
     hmq = WinCreateMsgQueue (hab, 0) ;

     WinRegisterClass (hab, szClientClass, ClientWndProc, CS_SIZEREDRAW, 0) ;

     hwndFrame = WinCreateStdWindow (HWND_DESKTOP, WS_VISIBLE,
                                     &flFrameFlags, szClientClass, NULL,
                                     0L, 0, 0, &hwndClient) ;

     while (WinGetMsg (hab, &qmsg, NULLHANDLE, 0, 0))
          WinDispatchMsg (hab, &qmsg) ;

     WinDestroyWindow (hwndFrame) ;
     WinDestroyMsgQueue (hmq) ;
     WinTerminate (hab) ;
     return 0 ;
     }

MRESULT EXPENTRY ClientWndProc (HWND hwnd, ULONG msg, MPARAM mp1, MPARAM mp2)
     {
     static HWND hwndHscroll, hwndVscroll ;
     static INT  iHscrollMax, iVscrollMax, iHscrollPos, iVscrollPos,
                 cxChar, cxCaps, cyChar, cyDesc, cxClient, cyClient,
                 cxTextTotal ;
     CHAR        szBuffer [10] ;
     FONTMETRICS fm ;
     HPS         hps ;
     INT         iLine, iPaintBeg, iPaintEnd, iHscrollInc, iVscrollInc ;
     POINTL      ptl ;
     RECTL       rclInvalid ;

     switch (msg)
          {
          case WM_CREATE:
               hps = WinGetPS (hwnd) ;
               GpiQueryFontMetrics (hps, sizeof fm, &fm) ;

               cxChar = fm.lAveCharWidth ;
               cxCaps = (fm.fsType & 1 ? 2 : 3) * cxChar / 2 ;
               cyChar = fm.lMaxBaselineExt ;
               cyDesc = fm.lMaxDescender ;

               WinReleasePS (hps) ;

               cxTextTotal = 32 * cxCaps + 38 * cxChar ;
```

Listing 4.3: The SYSVALS3 program (Continued)

```
          hwndHscroll = WinWindowFromID (
                              WinQueryWindow (hwnd, QW_PARENT),
                              FID_HORZSCROLL) ;

          hwndVscroll = WinWindowFromID (
                              WinQueryWindow (hwnd, QW_PARENT),
                              FID_VERTSCROLL) ;
          return 0 ;

     case WM_SIZE:
          cxClient = SHORT1FROMMP (mp2) ;
          cyClient = SHORT2FROMMP (mp2) ;

          iHscrollMax = max (0, cxTextTotal - cxClient) ;
          iHscrollPos = min (iHscrollPos, iHscrollMax) ;

          WinSendMsg (hwndHscroll, SBM_SETSCROLLBAR,
                                   MPFROM2SHORT (iHscrollPos, 0),
                                   MPFROM2SHORT (0, iHscrollMax)) ;

          WinSendMsg (hwndHscroll, SBM_SETTHUMBSIZE,
                                   MPFROM2SHORT (cxClient, cxTextTotal),
                                   NULL) ;

          WinEnableWindow (hwndHscroll, iHscrollMax ? TRUE : FALSE) ;

          iVscrollMax = max (0, NUMLINES - cyClient / cyChar) ;
          iVscrollPos = min (iVscrollPos, iVscrollMax) ;

          WinSendMsg (hwndVscroll, SBM_SETSCROLLBAR,
                                   MPFROM2SHORT (iVscrollPos, 0),
                                   MPFROM2SHORT (0, iVscrollMax)) ;

          WinSendMsg (hwndVscroll, SBM_SETTHUMBSIZE,
                                   MPFROM2SHORT (cyClient / cyChar,
                                                 NUMLINES),
                                   NULL) ;

          WinEnableWindow (hwndVscroll, iVscrollMax ? TRUE : FALSE) ;
          return 0 ;

     case WM_HSCROLL:
          switch (SHORT2FROMMP (mp2))
               {
               case SB_LINELEFT:
                    iHscrollInc = -cxCaps ;
                    break ;

               case SB_LINERIGHT:
```

Listing 4.3: The SYSVALS3 program (Continued)

```
                    iHscrollInc = cxCaps ;
                    break ;

               case SB_PAGELEFT:
                    iHscrollInc = -8 * cxCaps ;
                    break ;

               case SB_PAGERIGHT:
                    iHscrollInc = 8 * cxCaps ;
                    break ;

               case SB_SLIDERPOSITION:
                    iHscrollInc = SHORT1FROMMP (mp2) - iHscrollPos;
                    break ;

               default:
                    iHscrollInc = 0 ;
                    break ;
               }
          iHscrollInc = max (-iHscrollPos,
                             min (iHscrollInc, iHscrollMax - iHscrollPos)) ;

          if (iHscrollInc != 0)
               {
               iHscrollPos += iHscrollInc ;
               WinScrollWindow (hwnd, -iHscrollInc, 0,
                                NULL, NULL, NULLHANDLE, NULL,
                                SW_INVALIDATERGN) ;

               WinSendMsg (hwndHscroll, SBM_SETPOS,
                           MPFROMSHORT (iHscrollPos), NULL) ;
               }
          return 0 ;

     case WM_VSCROLL:
          switch (SHORT2FROMMP (mp2))
               {
               case SB_LINEUP:
                    iVscrollInc = -1 ;
                    break ;

               case SB_LINEDOWN:
                    iVscrollInc = 1 ;
                    break ;

               case SB_PAGEUP:
                    iVscrollInc = min (-1, -cyClient / cyChar) ;
                    break ;
```

Listing 4.3: The SYSVALS3 program (Continued)

```
          case SB_PAGEDOWN:
               iVscrollInc = max (1, cyClient / cyChar) ;
               break ;

          case SB_SLIDERTRACK:
               iVscrollInc = SHORT1FROMMP (mp2) - iVscrollPos;
               break ;

          default:
               iVscrollInc = 0 ;
               break ;
          }
     iVscrollInc = max (-iVscrollPos,
                   min (iVscrollInc, iVscrollMax - iVscrollPos)) ;

     if (iVscrollInc != 0)
          {
          iVscrollPos += iVscrollInc ;
          WinScrollWindow (hwnd, 0, cyChar * iVscrollInc,
                           NULL, NULL, NULLHANDLE, NULL,
                           SW_INVALIDATERGN) ;

          WinUpdateWindow (hwnd) ;
          }

     WinSendMsg (hwndVscroll, SBM_SETPOS,
                 MPFROMSHORT (iVscrollPos), NULL) ;
     return 0 ;

case WM_PAINT:
     hps = WinBeginPaint (hwnd, NULLHANDLE, &rclInvalid) ;
     GpiErase (hps) ;

     iPaintBeg = max (0, iVscrollPos +
                    (cyClient - rclInvalid.yTop) / cyChar) ;
     iPaintEnd = min (NUMLINES, iVscrollPos +
                    (cyClient - rclInvalid.yBottom)
                         / cyChar + 1) ;

     for (iLine = iPaintBeg ; iLine < iPaintEnd ; iLine++)
          {
          ptl.x = cxCaps - iHscrollPos ;
          ptl.y = cyClient - cyChar * (iLine + 1 - iVscrollPos)
                           + cyDesc ;

          GpiCharStringAt (hps, &ptl,
                           strlen (sysvals[iLine].szIdentifier),
                           sysvals[iLine].szIdentifier) ;
```

Listing 4.3: The SYSVALS3 program (Continued)

```
                    ptl.x += 24 * cxCaps ;
                    GpiCharStringAt (hps, &ptl,
                                     strlen (sysvals[iLine].szDescription),
                                     sysvals[iLine].szDescription) ;

                    sprintf (szBuffer, "%d",
                             WinQuerySysValue (HWND_DESKTOP,
                                               sysvals[iLine].sIndex)) ;

                    ptl.x += 38 * cxChar + 6 * cxCaps ;
                    RtJustCharStringAt (hps, &ptl, strlen (szBuffer),
                                        szBuffer) ;
                    }
               WinEndPaint (hps) ;
               return 0 ;
          }
     return WinDefWindowProc (hwnd, msg, mp1, mp2) ;
     }

LONG RtJustCharStringAt (HPS hps, PPOINTL pptl, LONG lLength, PCHAR pchText)
     {
     POINTL aptlTextBox[TXTBOX_COUNT] ;

     GpiQueryTextBox (hps, lLength, pchText, TXTBOX_COUNT, aptlTextBox) ;

     pptl->x -= aptlTextBox[TXTBOX_CONCAT].x ;

     return GpiCharStringAt (hps, pptl, lLength, pchText) ;
     }
```

The SYSVALS3.DEF File

```
;-----------------------------------
; SYSVALS3.DEF module definition file
;-----------------------------------

NAME           SYSVALS3  WINDOWAPI

DESCRIPTION    'System Values Display No. 3 (c) Charles Petzold, 1993'
PROTMODE
```

The SYSVALS3 window is shown in Figure 4.10.

RIGHT-JUSTIFIED TEXT

You'll notice I've also prettied up the display a little. In SYSVALS1 and SYSVALS2, the values returned from *WinQuerySysValue* were displayed beginning at the same horizontal pixel position. Columns of numbers are commonly displayed

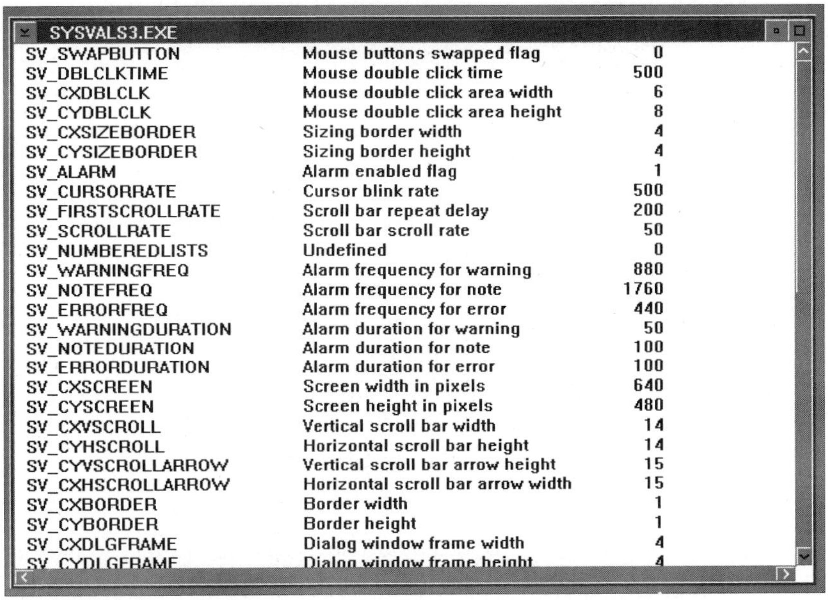

SYSVALS3.EXE

SV_SWAPBUTTON	Mouse buttons swapped flag	0
SV_DBLCLKTIME	Mouse double click time	500
SV_CXDBLCLK	Mouse double click area width	6
SV_CYDBLCLK	Mouse double click area height	8
SV_CXSIZEBORDER	Sizing border width	4
SV_CYSIZEBORDER	Sizing border height	4
SV_ALARM	Alarm enabled flag	1
SV_CURSORRATE	Cursor blink rate	500
SV_FIRSTSCROLLRATE	Scroll bar repeat delay	200
SV_SCROLLRATE	Scroll bar scroll rate	50
SV_NUMBEREDLISTS	Undefined	0
SV_WARNINGFREQ	Alarm frequency for warning	880
SV_NOTEFREQ	Alarm frequency for note	1760
SV_ERRORFREQ	Alarm frequency for error	440
SV_WARNINGDURATION	Alarm duration for warning	50
SV_NOTEDURATION	Alarm duration for note	100
SV_ERRORDURATION	Alarm duration for error	100
SV_CXSCREEN	Screen width in pixels	640
SV_CYSCREEN	Screen height in pixels	480
SV_CXVSCROLL	Vertical scroll bar width	14
SV_CYHSCROLL	Horizontal scroll bar height	14
SV_CYVSCROLLARROW	Vertical scroll bar arrow height	15
SV_CXHSCROLLARROW	Horizontal scroll bar arrow width	15
SV_CXBORDER	Border width	1
SV_CYBORDER	Border height	1
SV_CXDLGFRAME	Dialog window frame width	4
SV_CYDLGFRAME	Dialog window frame height	4

Figure 4.10: The SYSVALS3 display

right justified. In SYSVALS3, the *RtJustCharStringAt* function at the bottom of SYSVALS3.C results in right-justified text.

```
LONG RtJustCharStringAt (HPS hps, PPOINTL pptl, LONG lLength, PCHAR pchText)
     {
     POINTL aptlTextBox[TXTBOX_COUNT] ;

     GpiQueryTextBox (hps, lLength, pchText, TXTBOX_COUNT, aptlTextBox) ;

     pptl->x -= aptlTextBox[TXTBOX_CONCAT].x ;

     return GpiCharStringAt (hps, pptl, lLength, pchText) ;
     }
```

This function is defined with the same parameters as *GpiCharStringAt*, but when the function is called, the *x* field of the POINTL structure should be set to the pixel position where the text ends rather than begins. This function uses the identifiers TXTBOX_COUNT and TXTBOX_CONCAT, defined in PMGPI.H. You use these when working with the *GpiQueryTextBox* function, which obtains an array of POINTL structures that give the coordinates of the four corners of a text string, assuming that the text begins at the point (0,0). The TXTBOX_CONCAT element of the *aptl* structure contains the coordinates of the end of the string (where more text would follow). So, when the x coordinate of TXTBOX_CONCAT is subtracted from the *x* field of the POINTL structure passed to *RtJustCharStringAt*, the resulting value is the x coordinate that will result in right-justified text.

CHANGING THE RANGE BASED ON WINDOW SIZE

Another change incorporated in SYSVALS3 is that the scroll-bar range and slider position are no longer set during processing of the WM_CREATE message. Instead, a new range and position are set during each WM_SIZE message.

The goal here is to have the last line of text be visible at the bottom of the client window. So, during the WM_SIZE message, the maximum position of the vertical scroll-bar slider is calculated based on the total number of text lines and the number of lines that can fit in the client window:

```
iVscrollMax = max (0, NUMLINES - cyClient / cyChar) ;
```

The existing value of *iVscrollPos* could be outside this new range, so *iVscrollPos* is adjusted using the *min* macro:

```
iVscrollPos = min (iVscrollPos, iVscrollMax) ;
```

Then the new range and position are set by sending the scroll bar a message:

```
WinSendMsg (hwndVscroll, SBM_SETSCROLLBAR,
            MPFROM2SHORT (iVscrollPos, 0),
            MPFROM2SHORT (0, iVscrollMax)) ;
```

If all the text fits in the client window, *iVscrollMax* equals 0 and there is no need for a working scroll bar. To enable or disable the scroll bar, call *WinEnableWindow* based on the value of *iVscrollMax*:

```
WinEnableWindow (hwndVscroll, iVscrollMax ? TRUE : FALSE) ;
```

A disabled scroll bar is partly invisible and beeps if you click on it.

Yet another enhancement in SYSVALS3 is to make use of variable scroll-bar slider (or thumb) sizes. Normally, the scroll bar slider indicates the position of the displayed text within the entire document. However, there's no visual indication of how large the document actually is. A variable scroll bar slider can help. The size of the slider is made to indicate how much text is being displayed relative to the total amount of text.

A program can change the size of the slider by sending the scroll bar an SBM_SETTHUMBSIZE message:

```
WinSendMsg (hwndVscroll, SBM_SETTHUMBSIZE,
            MPFROM2SHORT (cyClient / cyChar, NUMLINES),
            NULL) ;
```

The *mp1* parameter is composed of two shorts: The size of the visible part of the document and the size of the entire document.

SCROLLING THE WINDOW

Rather than immediately altering the value of *iVscrollPos*, the new WM_-VSCROLL processing sets a variable named *iVscrollInc* to the incremental change in the slider position indicated by the mouse action:

```
case WM_VSCROLL:
     switch (SHORT2FROMMP (mp2))
          {
          case SB_LINEUP:
               iVscrollInc = - 1 ;
               break ;

          case SB_LINEDOWN:
               iVscrollInc = 1 ;
               break ;

          case SB_PAGEUP:
               iVscrollInc = min (- 1, -cyClient / cyChar) ;
               break ;

          case SB_PAGEDOWN:
               iVscrollInc = max (1, cyClient / cyChar) ;
               break ;

          case SB_SLIDERTRACK:
               iVscrollInc = SHORT1FROMMP (mp2) - iVscrollPos;
               break ;

          default:
               iVscrollInc = 0 ;
               break ;
          }
```

SYSVALS3 processes the SB_SLIDERTRACK action rather than SB_SLIDER-POSITION. This allows the program to change the client window while the user is dragging the slider with the mouse rather than after the dragging action is completed.

Next, *iVscrollInc* is adjusted based on the position of the slider and the range maximum:

```
iVscrollInc = max (-iVscrollPos,
        min (iVscrollInc, iVscrollMax - iVscrollPos));
```

If *iVscrollInc* is still nonzero, processing continues with the calculation of a new slider position:

```
iVscrollPos += iVscrollInc ;
```

In SYSVALS2, the entire window was redrawn whenever the scroll-bar position was changed. SYSVALS3 attempts to preserve part of the window by scrolling the contents of the window:

```
WinScrollWindow (hwnd, 0, cyChar * iVscrollInc,
        NULL, NULL, NULLHANDLE, NULL, SW_INVALIDATERGN) ;
```

This function can scroll a rectangular area of a window up, down, to the left, or to the right. Here we're specifying that the contents of the entire window move up by (*cyChar* * *iVscrollInc*) pixels. Thus, if the action is SB_LINEDOWN, then *iVscrollInc* is 1, and the contents of the window move up *cyChar* pixels. This means that only the last line at the bottom of the window has to be redrawn. Including SW_INVALIDATERGN as the last parameter of *WinScrollWindow* tells the Presentation Manager to invalidate the area uncovered by the scroll—the bottom line of the client window. A WM_PAINT message is placed in SYSVALS3's message queue.

Normally, SYSVALS3 would retrieve the WM_PAINT message from its message queue and repaint the window. If the scroll bar is busy receiving and processing mouse messages, however, this won't happen immediately. We can force the client window to be repainted right away with this function:

```
WinUpdateWindow (hwnd) ;
```

This causes the Presentation Manager to call *ClientWndProc* with the WM_PAINT message.

PAINTING ONLY THE INVALID RECTANGLE

When the window procedure receives a WM_PAINT message, it's likely that only a small rectangular part of the client window is invalid and needs to be repainted. When a program obtains a presentation space handle from *WinBeginPaint*, it can paint only within that rectangular invalid area. The Presentation Manager must clip all screen output that falls outside the invalid area. But for optimum efficiency, the program itself shouldn't make any GPI calls that will eventually be ignored by the Presentation Manager.

To speed up the painting, SYSVALS3 obtains the coordinates of the rectangular invalid area. It does this in the *WinBeginPaint* function:

```
hps = WinBeginPaint (hwnd, NULLHANDLE, &rclInvalid) ;
```

The Presentation Manager fills in the fields of the RECTL structure named *rclInvalid* with the coordinates of this rectangle.

SYSVALS3 then uses the *yTop* and *yBottom* fields of the RECTL structure to determine the range of lines that must be repainted:

```
iPaintBeg = max (0, iVscrollPos +
        (cyClient - rclInvalid.yTop) / cyChar) ;
iPaintEnd = min (NUMLINES, iVscrollPos +
        (cyClient - rclInvalid.yBottom) / cyChar + 1) ;
```

The *for* loop encompasses only this range:

```
for (iLine = iPaintBeg ; iLine < iPaintEnd ; iLine++)
```

The improved efficiency in processing the WM_VSCROLL and WM_PAINT messages allows SYSVALS3 to move the contents of the window during SB_-SLIDERTRACK actions from the vertical scroll bar.

ADDING A KEYBOARD INTERFACE

Of course, if your mouse is buried somewhere on your desk, you haven't been able to scroll SYSVALS2 or SYSVALS3 at all. So let's make one final change to the program to allow the mouseless among us to scroll the window using the cursor movement keys.

Scroll bars understand keyboard messages. However, the Presentation Manager posts keyboard messages to only one window—the window with the "input focus" (as you'll see in Chapter 8, when we examine the keyboard in more depth). If your program is active, then the window with the input focus is generally the client window rather than the scroll-bar window.

Earlier I mentioned that the frame window is the initial recipient of notification messages from the scroll bar, and that the frame window sends these messages to the client window. This raises an interesting question: If the frame window passes scroll-bar messages to the client window, why can't the client window pass keyboard messages to the scroll-bar window? Let's do it.

The keyboard message is called WM_CHAR. For the cursor movement keys, the high USHORT of *mp2* is a *virtual key code* (more on this in Chapter 5) that identifies the key. The PMWIN.H header file has a macro called CHARMSG that lets you extract this code. You probably want the Up Arrow, Down Arrow, Page Up, and Page Down keys to control the vertical scroll bar and the Left Arrow and Right Arrow keys to control the horizontal scroll bar. Here's the code to be added to the window procedure:

```
case WM_CHAR:
     switch (CHARMSG (&msg) ->vkey
          {
          case VK_LEFT:
          case VK_RIGHT:
               return WinSendMsg (hwndHscroll, msg, mp1, mp2) ;

          case VK_UP:
          case VK_DOWN:
          case VK_PAGEUP:
          case VK_PAGEDOWN:
               return WinSendMsg (hwndVscroll, msg, mp1, mp2) ;
          }
     break ;
```

Simple enough, wouldn't you say? With this addition, I declare the program finished. The name of the final version is simply SYSVALS without any degrading numeric suffix. The program is shown in Listing 4.4.

Listing 4.4: The final SYSVALS program

The SYSVALS.MAK File

```
#-----------------------
# SYSVALS.MAK make file
#-----------------------

sysvals.exe : sysvals.obj sysvals.def
     $(PRGLINK) sysvals, sysvals, NUL, $(PRGLIB), sysvals

sysvals.obj : sysvals.c sysvals.h
     $(PRGCC) sysvals.c
```

The SYSVALS.C File

```
/*------------------------------------------
   SYSVALS.C -- System Values Display Program
                (c) Charles Petzold, 1993
  ------------------------------------------*/

#define INCL_WIN
#define INCL_GPI
```

Listing 4.4: The final SYSVALS program (Continued)

```
#include <os2.h>
#include <stdio.h>
#include <stdlib.h>
#include <string.h>
#include "sysvals.h"

MRESULT EXPENTRY ClientWndProc (HWND, ULONG, MPARAM, MPARAM) ;
LONG             RtJustCharStringAt (HPS, PPOINTL, LONG, PCHAR) ;

int main (void)
     {
     static CHAR  szClientClass [] = "SysVals" ;
     static ULONG flFrameFlags = FCF_TITLEBAR       | FCF_SYSMENU   |
                                 FCF_SIZEBORDER     | FCF_MINMAX    |
                                 FCF_SHELLPOSITION  | FCF_TASKLIST  |
                                 FCF_VERTSCROLL     | FCF_HORZSCROLL ;
     HAB          hab ;
     HMQ          hmq ;
     HWND         hwndFrame, hwndClient ;
     QMSG         qmsg ;

     hab = WinInitialize (0) ;
     hmq = WinCreateMsgQueue (hab, 0) ;

     WinRegisterClass (hab, szClientClass, ClientWndProc, CS_SIZEREDRAW, 0) ;

     hwndFrame = WinCreateStdWindow (HWND_DESKTOP, WS_VISIBLE,
                                     &flFrameFlags, szClientClass, NULL,
                                     0L, 0, 0, &hwndClient) ;

     while (WinGetMsg (hab, &qmsg, NULLHANDLE, 0, 0))
          WinDispatchMsg (hab, &qmsg) ;

     WinDestroyWindow (hwndFrame) ;
     WinDestroyMsgQueue (hmq) ;
     WinTerminate (hab) ;
     return 0 ;
     }

MRESULT EXPENTRY ClientWndProc (HWND hwnd, ULONG msg, MPARAM mp1, MPARAM mp2)
     {
     static HWND hwndHscroll, hwndVscroll ;
     static INT  iHscrollMax, iVscrollMax, iHscrollPos, iVscrollPos,
                 cxChar, cxCaps, cyChar, cyDesc, cxClient, cyClient,
                 cxTextTotal ;
     BOOL        fUpdate ;
     CHAR        szBuffer [10] ;
     FONTMETRICS fm ;
     HPS         hps ;
```

Listing 4.4: The final SYSVALS program (Continued)

```
     INT         iLine, iPaintBeg, iPaintEnd, iHscrollInc, iVscrollInc ;
     POINTL      ptl ;
     RECTL       rclInvalid ;

     switch (msg)
          {
          case WM_CREATE:
               hps = WinGetPS (hwnd) ;

               GpiQueryFontMetrics (hps, sizeof fm, &fm) ;

               cxChar = fm.lAveCharWidth ;
               cxCaps = (fm.fsType & 1 ? 2 : 3) * cxChar / 2 ;
               cyChar = fm.lMaxBaselineExt ;
               cyDesc = fm.lMaxDescender ;

               WinReleasePS (hps) ;

               cxTextTotal = 32 * cxCaps + 38 * cxChar ;

               hwndHscroll = WinWindowFromID (
                                   WinQueryWindow (hwnd, QW_PARENT),
                                   FID_HORZSCROLL) ;

               hwndVscroll = WinWindowFromID (
                                   WinQueryWindow (hwnd, QW_PARENT),
                                   FID_VERTSCROLL) ;
               return 0 ;

          case WM_SIZE:
               cxClient = SHORT1FROMMP (mp2) ;
               cyClient = SHORT2FROMMP (mp2) ;

               iHscrollMax = max (0, cxTextTotal - cxClient) ;
               iHscrollPos = min (iHscrollPos, iHscrollMax) ;

               WinSendMsg (hwndHscroll, SBM_SETSCROLLBAR,
                                        MPFROM2SHORT (iHscrollPos, 0),
                                        MPFROM2SHORT (0, iHscrollMax)) ;

               WinSendMsg (hwndHscroll, SBM_SETTHUMBSIZE,
                                        MPFROM2SHORT (cxClient, cxTextTotal),
                                        NULL) ;

               WinEnableWindow (hwndHscroll, iHscrollMax ? TRUE : FALSE) ;

               iVscrollMax = max (0, NUMLINES - cyClient / cyChar) ;
               iVscrollPos = min (iVscrollPos, iVscrollMax) ;
```

Listing 4.4: The final SYSVALS program (Continued)

```
          WinSendMsg (hwndVscroll, SBM_SETSCROLLBAR,
                                   MPFROM2SHORT (iVscrollPos, 0),
                                   MPFROM2SHORT (0, iVscrollMax)) ;

          WinSendMsg (hwndVscroll, SBM_SETTHUMBSIZE,
                                   MPFROM2SHORT (cyClient / cyChar,
                                                 NUMLINES),
                                   NULL) ;

          WinEnableWindow (hwndVscroll, iVscrollMax ? TRUE : FALSE) ;
          return 0 ;

     case WM_HSCROLL:
          switch (SHORT2FROMMP (mp2))
               {
               case SB_LINELEFT:
                    iHscrollInc = -cxCaps ;
                    break ;

               case SB_LINERIGHT:
                    iHscrollInc = cxCaps ;
                    break ;

               case SB_PAGELEFT:
                    iHscrollInc = -8 * cxCaps ;
                    break ;

               case SB_PAGERIGHT:
                    iHscrollInc = 8 * cxCaps ;
                    break ;

               case SB_SLIDERPOSITION:
                    iHscrollInc = SHORT1FROMMP (mp2) - iHscrollPos;
                    break ;

               default:
                    iHscrollInc = 0 ;
                    break ;
               }
          iHscrollInc = max (-iHscrollPos,
                        min (iHscrollInc, iHscrollMax - iHscrollPos)) ;

          if (iHscrollInc != 0)
               {
               iHscrollPos += iHscrollInc ;
               WinScrollWindow (hwnd, -iHscrollInc, 0,
                                NULL, NULL, NULLHANDLE, NULL,
                                SW_INVALIDATERGN) ;
```

Listing 4.4: The final SYSVALS program (Continued)

```
                    WinSendMsg (hwndHscroll, SBM_SETPOS,
                                MPFROMSHORT (iHscrollPos), NULL) ;
                    }
               return 0 ;

          case WM_VSCROLL:
               fUpdate = TRUE ;

               switch (SHORT2FROMMP (mp2))
                    {
                    case SB_LINEUP:
                         iVscrollInc = -1 ;
                         break ;

                    case SB_LINEDOWN:
                         iVscrollInc = 1 ;
                         break ;

                    case SB_PAGEUP:
                         iVscrollInc = min (-1, -cyClient / cyChar) ;
                         break ;

                    case SB_PAGEDOWN:
                         iVscrollInc = max (1, cyClient / cyChar) ;
                         break ;

                    case SB_SLIDERTRACK:
                         fUpdate = FALSE ;
                         iVscrollInc = SHORT1FROMMP (mp2) - iVscrollPos;
                         break ;

                    case SB_SLIDERPOSITION:
                         iVscrollInc = SHORT1FROMMP (mp2) - iVscrollPos;
                         break ;

                    default:
                         fUpdate = FALSE ;
                         iVscrollInc = 0 ;
                         break ;
                    }

               iVscrollInc = max (-iVscrollPos,
                             min (iVscrollInc, iVscrollMax - iVscrollPos)) ;

               if (iVscrollInc != 0)
                    {
                    iVscrollPos += iVscrollInc ;
                    WinScrollWindow (hwnd, 0, cyChar * iVscrollInc,
                                     NULL, NULL, NULLHANDLE, NULL,
```

Listing 4.4: The final SYSVALS program (Continued)

```
                                  SW_INVALIDATERGN) ;

                    WinUpdateWindow (hwnd) ;
                    }

               if (fUpdate)
                    WinSendMsg (hwndVscroll, SBM_SETPOS,
                                MPFROMSHORT (iVscrollPos), NULL) ;
               return Ø ;

          case WM_CHAR:
               switch (CHARMSG(&msg)->vkey)
                    {
                    case VK_LEFT:
                    case VK_RIGHT:
                         return WinSendMsg (hwndHscroll, msg, mp1, mp2) ;
                    case VK_UP:
                    case VK_DOWN:
                    case VK_PAGEUP:
                    case VK_PAGEDOWN:
                         return WinSendMsg (hwndVscroll, msg, mp1, mp2) ;
                    }
               break ;

          case WM_PAINT:
               hps = WinBeginPaint (hwnd, NULLHANDLE, &rclInvalid) ;
               GpiErase (hps) ;

               iPaintBeg = max (Ø, iVscrollPos +
                                (cyClient - rclInvalid.yTop) / cyChar) ;
               iPaintEnd = min (NUMLINES, iVscrollPos +
                                (cyClient - rclInvalid.yBottom)
                                     / cyChar + 1) ;

               for (iLine = iPaintBeg ; iLine < iPaintEnd ; iLine++)
                    {
                    ptl.x = cxCaps - iHscrollPos ;
                    ptl.y = cyClient - cyChar * (iLine + 1 - iVscrollPos)
                                     + cyDesc ;

                    GpiCharStringAt (hps, &ptl,
                              strlen (sysvals[iLine].szIdentifier),
                              sysvals[iLine].szIdentifier) ;

                    ptl.x += 24 * cxCaps ;
                    GpiCharStringAt (hps, &ptl,
                              strlen (sysvals[iLine].szDescription),
                              sysvals[iLine].szDescription) ;
```

Listing 4.4: The final SYSVALS program (Continued)

```
                    sprintf (szBuffer, "%d",
                             WinQuerySysValue (HWND_DESKTOP,
                                               sysvals[iLine].sIndex)) ;

                    ptl.x += 38 * cxChar + 6 * cxCaps ;
                    RtJustCharStringAt (hps, &ptl, strlen (szBuffer),
                                        szBuffer) ;
                    }
               WinEndPaint (hps) ;
               return 0 ;
          }
     return WinDefWindowProc (hwnd, msg, mp1, mp2) ;
     }

LONG RtJustCharStringAt (HPS hps, PPOINTL pptl, LONG lLength, PCHAR pchText)
     {
     POINTL aptlTextBox[TXTBOX_COUNT] ;

     GpiQueryTextBox (hps, lLength, pchText, TXTBOX_COUNT, aptlTextBox) ;

     pptl->x -= aptlTextBox[TXTBOX_CONCAT].x ;

     return GpiCharStringAt (hps, pptl, lLength, pchText) ;
     }
```

The SYSVALS.DEF File

```
;-----------------------------------
; SYSVALS.DEF module definition file
;-----------------------------------

NAME           SYSVALS   WINDOWAPI

DESCRIPTION    'System Values Display (c) Charles Petzold, 1993'
PROTMODE
```

The Five GPI Primitives

GPI PRIMITIVE 1: LINES

PIXELS AND DEVICE INDEPENDENCE

GPI PRIMITIVE 2: PATTERNED AREAS

GPI PRIMITIVE 3: TEXT

GPI PRIMITIVE 4: MARKER SYMBOLS

GPI PRIMITIVE 5: IMAGES

Chapter 5

The world of computer graphics is often separated into two categories: *raster* graphics and *vector* graphics. These terms refer both to graphics output devices and to the way that an application program draws graphics objects on these devices. Raster output devices display images that are made up of dots called *pixels* or *pels* (picture elements). Video displays, dot-matrix printers, and laser printers are all raster devices. Vector output devices—such as plotters—display images made up of lines and filled areas. (Note: The distinction between raster and vector devices gets a little fuzzy with devices such as the IBM 8514/A video display adapter and PostScript laser printers: Although these devices are technically raster devices, they contain a high-level graphics interface that understands and interprets vector drawing commands.)

The OS/2 Graphics Programming Interface (one of the two major components of the Presentation Manager, the other being the windowing and user interface) is fundamentally, but not exclusively, a vector graphics system: Presentation Manager programs draw graphics in terms of lines and filled areas. This approach works for every type of graphics output device—the drawing commands need only be translated by a device driver into a format the device can understand: vector drawing commands for vector output devices and pixels for raster devices.

GPI also has several functions for working with raster graphics. These functions allow a program to draw individual pixels (or, more commonly, collections of pixels called *bitmaps*) on an output device. However, these functions are useful only with raster devices: Vector devices cannot adequately draw individual dots.

Vectors and rasters each have their place in the world of graphics. An architectural drawing is obviously a job for vector graphics, whereas the reproduction of a digitized photograph requires raster graphics. Accordingly, vector and raster graphics each have their place in this book: I cover vector graphics in this chapter and raster graphics in the next chapter.

The following sections describe the five GPI primitives that form the foundation of the GPI graphics system: lines, patterned areas, text, marker symbols, and images.

GPI PRIMITIVE 1: LINES

When drawing text in Chapter 4 we specified the starting point of a text string using a POINTL structure. You also use the POINTL structure to draw lines. POINTL is defined in OS2DEF.H like this:

```
typedef struct _POINTL
     {
     LONG x ;
     LONG y ;
     }
POINTL ;
```

The two fields *x* and *y* define a point in terms of GPI coordinates. For a cached micro-PS, these coordinates are in units of pixels relative to the lower-left corner of the presentation space, which corresponds to the lower-left corner of the window. For convenience, I'll often use the notation (x,y) to refer to a point in the presentation space. The point (0,0) is the lower-left corner of the window. The x (horizontal) coordinates increase to the right and the y (vertical) coordinates increase going up.

A structure variable of type POINTL is usually given a prefix of *ptl.* If you need only one POINTL structure variable, you can name it *ptl* and define it like this:

```
POINTL ptl ;
```

You can define an array of POINTL structures like this:

```
POINTL aptl[5] ;
```

and define a pointer to a POINTL structure like this:

```
POINTL * pptl ;
```

or this:

```
PPOINTL pptl ;
```

The *pptl* name stands for "pointer to a POINTL structure."

SIMPLE STRAIGHT LINES

To draw a straight line, you must specify the two points that indicate the beginning and end of the line. Let's assume that *cxClient* and *cyClient* have been set to the width and height of the client window. Suppose you want to draw a diagonal line from the upper-left to the lower-right corner of the client window.

After obtaining a handle to a cached micro-PS from the *WinGetPS* or *WinBeginPaint* function, you set the two fields of a POINTL structure to the beginning of the line: the point (0,cyClient). You then call *GpiMove*:

```
ptl.x = 0 ;
ptl.y = cyClient ;
GpiMove (hps, &ptl) ;
```

GpiMove does not draw anything. Instead, it sets the "current position" (defined shortly) to the specified point.

You then set the two fields of the structure to the second point and call *GpiLine*:

```
ptl.x = cxClient ;
ptl.y = 0 ;
GpiLine (hps, &ptl) ;
```

GpiLine draws the line from (0,cyClient) to (cxClient,0).

Initially, it may seem annoying that drawing a single line requires four assignment statements and two function calls. The syntax of the *GpiMove* and *GpiLine* functions is defined in this way to be consistent with the *GpiPolyLine* and *GpiQueryCurrentPosition* functions discussed later in this chapter. In actual practice, it's usually not as inconvenient as it first appears to be.

THE CURRENT POSITION

We've just seen how the *GpiMove* function does not draw anything itself. Instead, it affects the operation of a subsequent call to *GpiLine*. The *GpiMove* function is said to set an "attribute" of the presentation space. In one sense, the presentation space is simply a data structure internal to GPI. This data structure identifies the output device associated with the presentation space and also retains all the attributes of the presentation space.

The *GpiMove* function sets the current position to the point specified in the function. The current position is used by most GPI drawing functions as a starting position when drawing a graphics object such as a line.

When you first obtain a handle to a cached micro-PS by calling *WinGetPS* or *WinBeginPaint*, all the attributes are set to default values. The default current position is the point (0,0). When you release a presentation space handle by calling *WinReleasePS* or *WinEndPaint*, any changes you've made to the attributes are lost.

The *GpiLine* function uses the current position as a starting point for the line it draws and then sets the current position to the end of the line—the point specified in the *GpiLine* function. Thus, you can draw another line connected to the first by calling *GpiLine* again with a new point.

For example, suppose you want to draw a big "V" in your client window. This job requires just one call to *GpiMove* and two calls to *GpiLine*:

```
ptl.x = 0 ;
ptl.y = cyClient ;
GpiMove (hps, &ptl) ;

ptl.x = cxClient / 2 ;
ptl.y = 0 ;
GpiLine (hps, &ptl) ;

ptl.x = cxClient ;
ptl.y = cyClient ;
GpiLine (hps, &ptl) ;
```

If you enjoy typing long function names, you can use the *GpiSetCurrentPosition* function rather than *GpiMove*:

```
GpiSetCurrentPosition (hps, &ptl) ;
```

When using a cached micro-PS, there is no difference between *GpiMove* and *GpiSetCurrentPosition*. You can also obtain the current position by using this function:

```
GpiQueryCurrentPosition (hps, &ptl) ;
```

Note that all four functions covered so far have had the same parameter syntax.

Some graphics programming languages have a function that draws a line from the current position to a point relative to the current position. GPI does not include such a function, but it's easy enough to write one:

```
LONG LineRelative (HPS hps, POINTL * pptlRelative)
     {
```

```
POINTL ptl ;

GpiQueryCurrentPosition (hps, &ptl) ;
ptl.x += pptlRelative->x ;
ptl.y += pptlRelative->y ;
return GpiLine (hps, &ptl) ;
}
```

Throughout this chapter, we will work mostly with three types of GPI functions: functions that draw (like *GpiLine*), functions that set an attribute of the presentation space (like *GpiMove* and *GpiSetCurrentPosition*), and functions that query a presentation space attribute (like *GpiQueryCurrentPosition*). Most GPI functions fall into one of these three categories.

DRAWING MULTIPLE LINES

The current position stored in the presentation space allows you to draw a series of connected lines by making one call to *GpiMove* and multiple calls to *GpiLine*. However, for jobs of that type it is more efficient to use the *GpiPolyLine* function:

```
GpiPolyLine (hps, lCount, aptl) ;
```

The *aptl* parameter is an array of POINTL structures. The function draws *lCount* lines—the first from the current position to *aptl[0]*, the second from *aptl[0]* to *aptl[1]*, and so forth. The *lCount* parameter also indicates the number of points in the *aptl* array. When the function returns, the current point is set to the end of the last line it draws, the point *aptl[lCount - 1]*.

GpiPolyLine is functionally equivalent to the following:

```
for (lIndex = 0 ; lIndex < lCount ; lIndex++)
    GpiLine (hps, aptl + lIndex) ;
```

(Newcomers to C who are not yet entirely comfortable with the equivalence between array names and pointers might prefer the notation *&aptl[lIndex]* rather than *aptl+lIndex*.) However, any looping that *GpiPolyLine* performs occurs deep within a device driver. When drawing many connected lines, *GpiPolyLine* is much faster than multiple *GpiLine* calls.

The STAR5 program in Listing 5.1 shows how to draw a five-pointed star using *GpiMove* and *GpiPolyLine*.

Listing 5.1: The STAR5 program

The STAR5.MAK File

```
#--------------------
# STAR5.MAK make file
#--------------------

star5.exe : star5.obj star5.def
     $(PRGLINK) star5, star5, NUL, $(PRGLIB), star5

star5.obj : star5.c
     $(PRGCC) star5.c
```

The STAR5.C File

```
/*-------------------------------------
   STAR5.C -- Draws 5-Pointed Star
              (c) Charles Petzold, 1993
  -------------------------------------*/

#include <os2.h>

MRESULT EXPENTRY ClientWndProc (HWND, ULONG, MPARAM, MPARAM) ;

int main (void)
     {
     static CHAR  szClientClass [] = "Star5" ;
     static ULONG flFrameFlags = FCF_TITLEBAR      | FCF_SYSMENU |
                                 FCF_SIZEBORDER    | FCF_MINMAX  |
                                 FCF_SHELLPOSITION | FCF_TASKLIST ;
     HAB          hab ;
     HMQ          hmq ;
     HWND         hwndFrame, hwndClient ;
     QMSG         qmsg ;

     hab = WinInitialize (0) ;
     hmq = WinCreateMsgQueue (hab, 0) ;

     WinRegisterClass (hab, szClientClass, ClientWndProc, CS_SIZEREDRAW, 0) ;

     hwndFrame = WinCreateStdWindow (HWND_DESKTOP, WS_VISIBLE,
                                     &flFrameFlags, szClientClass, NULL,
                                     0L, 0, 0, &hwndClient) ;

     while (WinGetMsg (hab, &qmsg, NULLHANDLE, 0, 0))
          WinDispatchMsg (hab, &qmsg) ;

     WinDestroyWindow (hwndFrame) ;
     WinDestroyMsgQueue (hmq) ;
```

Listing 5.1: The STAR5 program (Continued)

```
     WinTerminate (hab) ;
     return 0 ;
     }

MRESULT EXPENTRY ClientWndProc (HWND hwnd, ULONG msg, MPARAM mp1, MPARAM mp2)
     {
     static POINTL aptlStar[5] = {-59,-81, 0,100, 59,-81, -95,31, 95,31 } ;
     static INT    cxClient, cyClient ;
     HPS           hps ;
     INT           i ;
     POINTL        aptl[5] ;

     switch (msg)
       {
          case WM_SIZE:
               cxClient = SHORT1FROMMP (mp2) ;
               cyClient = SHORT2FROMMP (mp2) ;
               return 0 ;

          case WM_PAINT:
               hps = WinBeginPaint (hwnd, NULLHANDLE, NULL) ;
               GpiErase (hps) ;

               for (i = 0 ; i < 5 ; i++)
                    {
                    aptl[i].x = cxClient / 2 + cxClient * aptlStar[i].x / 200 ;
                    aptl[i].y = cyClient / 2 + cyClient * aptlStar[i].y / 200 ;
                    }
               GpiMove (hps, aptl + 4) ;
               GpiPolyLine (hps, 5L, aptl) ;

               WinEndPaint (hps) ;
               return 0 ;
          }
     return WinDefWindowProc (hwnd, msg, mp1, mp2) ;
     }
```

The STAR5.DEF File

```
;---------------------------------
; STAR5.DEF module definition file
;---------------------------------

NAME           STAR5     WINDOWAPI

DESCRIPTION    'Draws 5-Pointed Star (c) Charles Petzold, 1993'
PROTMODE
```

The *aptlStar* array contains the five POINTL structures that define the star. These are specified in "virtual" coordinates—that is, a coordinate system that I fabricated. The point (0,0) is the center of the star, and the star extends 100 units in all four directions. STAR5 must convert these points so that the star fills the client window, as shown in Figure 5.1.

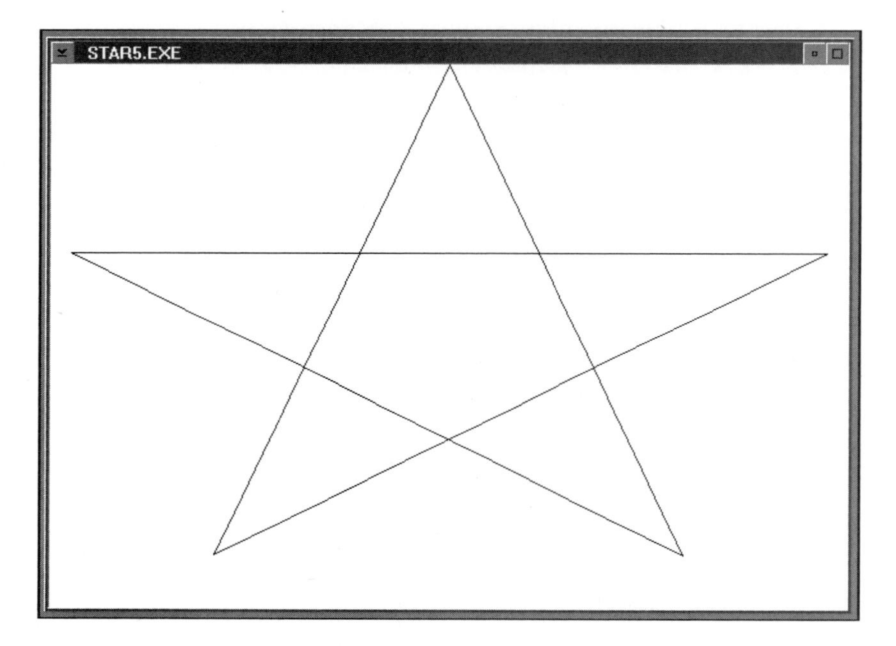

Figure 5.1: The STAR5 display

STAR5 converts the virtual coordinates to client window coordinates during the WM_PAINT message. The *x* fields of the POINTL structures are multiplied by *cxClient* and divided by 200. This adjusts for the window width. Then half of *cxClient* is added to move the center of the star to the center of the client window. The *y* fields are adjusted similarly, and the resultant points are stored in the *aptl* array.

Notice how STAR5 calls *GpiMove* and *GpiPolyLine* to draw the star. First, it sets the current position to the last point in the array:

```
GpiMove (hps, aptl + 4) ;
```

(The expression *aptl+4* is equivalent to *&aptl[4]*.) The *GpiPolyLine* function then draws five lines starting with a line to the first point in the array:

```
GpiPolyLine (hps, 5L, aptl) ;
```

GpiPolyLine draws the following five lines:

Line	Begin Point	End Point
1	aptl[4]	aptl[0]
2	aptl[0]	aptl[1]
3	aptl[1]	aptl[2]
4	aptl[2]	aptl[3]
5	aptl[3]	aptl[4]

It's necessary to initially set the current position to the last point in the array when the array defines a closed figure (like a star) and does not duplicate the first point. An alternative is to define an array of six POINTL structures, where the last point is the same as the first. In this case, you can draw the star by calling

```
GpiMove (hps, aptl) ;
GpiPolyLine (hps, 5L, aptl + 1) ;
```

DRAWING CURVES WITH GPIPOLYLINE

The *GpiPolyLine* function is deceptive. The function seems to draw a series of straight lines, and it can certainly be used for that purpose. But *GpiPolyLine* has a more important role, which is to draw curves. To do this, simply call *GpiPolyLine* with a POINTL array that defines many tiny lines.

Don't hesitate to call *GpiPolyLine* with an array of hundreds—or even thousands—of points. That's the *real* purpose of this function. Because *GpiPolyLine* is executed by the device driver, it is very fast.

Any curve that you can define mathematically you can draw as a series of straight lines using *GpiPolyLine*. For example, suppose you want to draw one cycle of a sine curve in your client window. You can define an array of 100 POINTL structures and set the points to define the sine curve:

```
#include <math>     // for sin declaration
     :
POINTL aptl[100] ;
INT iIndex ;
     :
```

```
for (iIndex = 0 ; iIndex < 100 ; iIndex++)
     {
     aptl[iIndex].x = iIndex * cxClient / 100 ;
     aptl[iIndex].y = (LONG) (cyClient / 2 * (1 + sin (iIndex * 6.28 / 100))) ;
     }
```

The *x* fields of the POINTL structures range from 0 to *cxClient*. The *y* field is the value of the *sin* function over one period, scaled to the height of the client window.

To draw the sine curve, begin by setting the current position to the first point as follows:

```
GpiMove (hps, aptl) ;
```

Then use the *GpiPolyLine* function to draw 99 lines beginning at the second point:

```
GpiPolyLine (hps, 99, aptl + 1) ;
```

CURVES AND PARAMETRIC EQUATIONS

The sine curve is relatively easy because the y coordinate is a simple function of the x coordinate. In general, however, this is not the case. There might be multiple y values for each value of x. A more generalized approach to drawing curves uses *parametric* equations.

In parametric equations, both the x and y coordinates of every point are calculated from functions based on a third variable, often called *t*. Intuitively, you can think of *t* as time or as some other abstract index necessary to define the entire curve. When you draw a curve using GPI functions, the values of *t* will range from 0 to the number of points that are in the POINTL array.

For example, suppose you want to draw an ellipse that fills your client window. You can start with parametric equations that define a unit circle:

```
x(t) = cos(t)
y(t) = sin(t)
```

For *t* ranging from 0 degrees to 2π radians, these equations define a circle around the point (0,0) with a radius of 1.

The ellipse is defined similarly:

```
x(t) = RX cos(t)
y(t) = RY sin(t)
```

The two axes of the ellipse are parallel to the horizontal and vertical axes. The horizontal ellipse axis is $2 \times$ RX in length; the vertical ellipse axis is $2 \times$ RY. The ellipse is still centered around (0,0). To center it around the point (CX,CY), the formulas are

```
x(t) = CX + RX cos(t)
y(t) = CY + RY sin(t)
```

Here's the code to draw an ellipse centered in the client window:

```
#include <math>     // for sin and cos declaration
     :

double dAngle ;
POINTL aptl[100] ;
INT iIndex ;
     :

for (iIndex = 0 ; iIndex < 100 ; iIndex ++)
     {
     dAngle = iIndex * 6.28 / 100 ;

     aptl[iIndex].x = (LONG) (cxClient / 2 * (1 + cos (dAngle))) ;
     aptl[iIndex].y = (LONG) (cyClient / 2 * (1 + sin (dAngle))) ;
     }
GpiMove (hps, aptl) ;
GpiPolyLine (hps, 99, aptl + 1) ;
```

In this case, both RX and CX are equal to *cxClient/2*, and RY and CY are equal to *cyClient/2*.

The SPIRAL program shown in Listing 5.2 uses a variation on these formulas to draw a spiral in its client window.

Listing 5.2: The SPIRAL program

The SPIRAL.MAK File

```
#---------------------
# SPIRAL.MAK make file
#---------------------

spiral.exe : spiral.obj spiral.def
     $(PRGLINK) spiral, spiral, NUL, $(PRGLIB), spiral

spiral.obj : spiral.c
     $(PRGCC) spiral.c
```

The SPIRAL.C File

Listing 5.2: The SPIRAL program (Continued)

```
/*-----------------------------------------
   SPIRAL.C -- GPI Spiral Drawing
               (c) Charles Petzold, 1993
  -----------------------------------------*/

#include <os2.h>
#include <math.h>
#include <stdlib.h>

#define NUMPOINTS 1000
#define NUMREV    20
#define PI        3.14159

MRESULT EXPENTRY ClientWndProc (HWND, ULONG, MPARAM, MPARAM) ;

int main (void)
     {
     static CHAR  szClientClass [] = "Spiral" ;
     static ULONG flFrameFlags = FCF_TITLEBAR      | FCF_SYSMENU |
                                 FCF_SIZEBORDER    | FCF_MINMAX  |
                                 FCF_SHELLPOSITION | FCF_TASKLIST ;
     HAB          hab ;
     HMQ          hmq ;
     HWND         hwndFrame, hwndClient ;
     QMSG         qmsg ;

     hab = WinInitialize (0) ;
     hmq = WinCreateMsgQueue (hab, 0) ;

     WinRegisterClass (hab, szClientClass, ClientWndProc, CS_SIZEREDRAW, 0) ;

     hwndFrame = WinCreateStdWindow (HWND_DESKTOP, WS_VISIBLE,
                                     &flFrameFlags, szClientClass, NULL,
                                     0L, 0, 0, &hwndClient) ;

     while (WinGetMsg (hab, &qmsg, NULLHANDLE, 0, 0))
          WinDispatchMsg (hab, &qmsg) ;

     WinDestroyWindow (hwndFrame) ;
     WinDestroyMsgQueue (hmq) ;
     WinTerminate (hab) ;
     return 0 ;
     }

MRESULT EXPENTRY ClientWndProc (HWND hwnd, ULONG msg, MPARAM mp1, MPARAM mp2)
     {
     static INT cxClient, cyClient ;
     double     dAngle, dScale ;
     HPS        hps ;
     INT        i ;
```

Listing 5.2: The SPIRAL program (Continued)

```
     PPOINTL    pptl ;

     switch (msg)
       {
          case WM_SIZE:
               cxClient = SHORT1FROMMP (mp2) ;
               cyClient = SHORT2FROMMP (mp2) ;
               return 0 ;

          case WM_PAINT:
               hps = WinBeginPaint (hwnd, NULLHANDLE, NULL) ;
               GpiErase (hps) ;

               if ((pptl = malloc (NUMPOINTS * sizeof (POINTL))) != NULL)
                    {
                    for (i = 0 ; i < NUMPOINTS ; i ++)
                         {
                         dAngle = i * 2 * PI / (NUMPOINTS / NUMREV) ;
                         dScale = 1 - (double) i / NUMPOINTS ;

                         pptl[i].x = (LONG) (cxClient / 2 *
                                             (1 + dScale * cos (dAngle))) ;

                         pptl[i].y = (LONG) (cyClient / 2 *
                                             (1 + dScale * sin (dAngle))) ;
                         }
                    GpiMove (hps, pptl) ;
                    GpiPolyLine (hps, NUMPOINTS - 1L, pptl + 1) ;

                    free (pptl) ;
                    }
               WinEndPaint (hps) ;
               return 0 ;
          }
     return WinDefWindowProc (hwnd, msg, mp1, mp2) ;
     }
```

The SPIRAL.DEF File

```
;----------------------------------
; SPIRAL.DEF module definition file
;----------------------------------

NAME           SPIRAL    WINDOWAPI

DESCRIPTION    'GPI Spiral Using a Polyline (c) Charles Petzold, 1993'
PROTMODE
```

In effect, SPIRAL draws 20 ellipses but uniformly decreases the length of the axes to create a spiral, as shown in Figure 5.2.

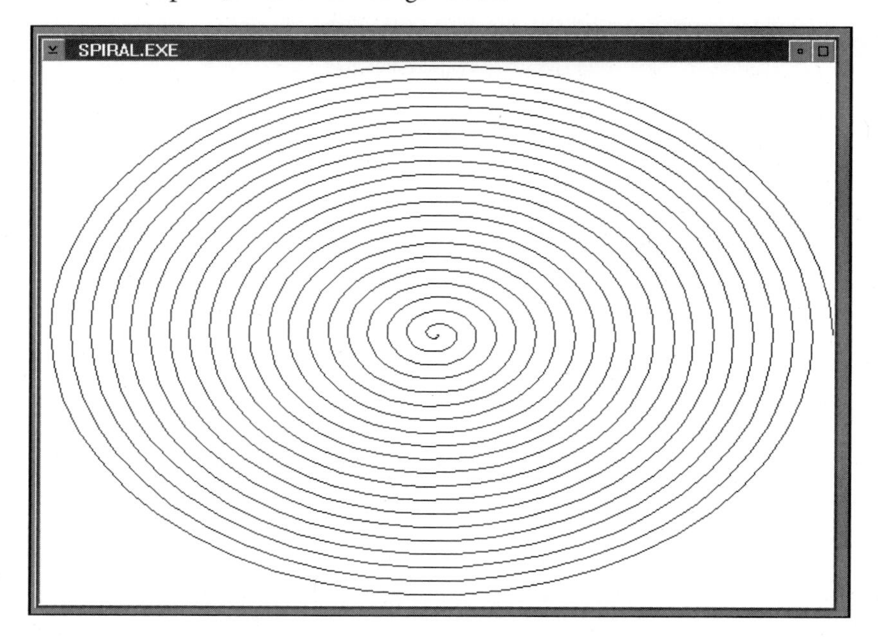

Figure 5.2: The SPIRAL display

SPIRAL uses 1,000 points to describe this figure. The program allocates a block of memory for this array by calling the normal C *malloc* function. The memory is freed after the drawing is finished.

THE LINE TYPE

Up until now we have only drawn solid lines. You can also draw lines composed of various dots and dashes. This is called the *line type attribute*, which you set with the *GpiSetLineType* function:

```
GpiSetLineType (hps, lLineType) ;
```

The *lLineType* parameter is one of the following identifiers defined in PMGPI.H:

LINETYPE_DEFAULT

LINETYPE_LONGDASH

LINETYPE_DOT

LINETYPE_DASHDOUBLEDOT

LINETYPE_SHORTDASH

LINETYPE_SOLID

LINETYPE_DASHDOT

LINETYPE_INVISIBLE

LINETYPE_DOUBLEDOT

LINETYPE_ALTERNATE

These identifiers are fairly self-explanatory. The LINETYPE_DEFAULT identifier (defined as 0L) has the same effect as LINETYPE_SOLID. The LINETYPE_ALTERNATE style draws every other pixel, giving the appearance of a gray line.

The line type is an attribute of the presentation space. When you set the line type, it affects all subsequent lines you draw until you change the line type again or release the presentation space.

You can determine the current line type by calling

```
lLineType = GpiQueryLineType (hps) ;
```

However, if you call *GpiQueryLineType* for a new presentation space without first calling *GpiSetLineType*, the function returns an identifier of LINETYPE_DEFAULT rather than LINETYPE_SOLID.

The LINETYPE program (Listing 5.3) displays lines drawn with each of these line types so that you can see what they look like.

Listing 5.3: The LINETYPE program

The LINETYPE.MAK File

```
#-----------------------
# LINETYPE.MAK make file
#-----------------------

linetype.exe : linetype.obj linetype.def
     $(PRGLINK) linetype, linetype, NUL, $(PRGLIB), linetype

linetype.obj : linetype.c
     $(PRGCC) linetype.c
```

Listing 5.3: The LINETYPE program (Continued)

The LINETYPE.C File

```
/*-----------------------------------------
   LINETYPE.C -- GPI Line Types
                 (c) Charles Petzold, 1993
  -----------------------------------------*/

#define INCL_WIN
#define INCL_GPI
#include <os2.h>
#include <string.h>

MRESULT EXPENTRY ClientWndProc (HWND, ULONG, MPARAM, MPARAM) ;

int main (void)
     {
     static CHAR  szClientClass [] = "LineType" ;
     static ULONG flFrameFlags = FCF_TITLEBAR      | FCF_SYSMENU |
                                 FCF_SIZEBORDER    | FCF_MINMAX  |
                                 FCF_SHELLPOSITION | FCF_TASKLIST ;
     HAB          hab ;
     HMQ          hmq ;
     HWND         hwndFrame, hwndClient ;
     QMSG         qmsg ;

     hab = WinInitialize (0) ;
     hmq = WinCreateMsgQueue (hab, 0) ;

     WinRegisterClass (hab, szClientClass, ClientWndProc, CS_SIZEREDRAW, 0) ;

     hwndFrame = WinCreateStdWindow (HWND_DESKTOP, WS_VISIBLE,
                                     &flFrameFlags, szClientClass, NULL,
                                     0L, 0, 0, &hwndClient) ;

     while (WinGetMsg (hab, &qmsg, NULLHANDLE, 0, 0))
          WinDispatchMsg (hab, &qmsg) ;

     WinDestroyWindow (hwndFrame) ;
     WinDestroyMsgQueue (hmq) ;
     WinTerminate (hab) ;
     return 0 ;
     }

MRESULT EXPENTRY ClientWndProc (HWND hwnd, ULONG msg, MPARAM mp1, MPARAM mp2)
     {
     static struct {
                   LONG lLineType ;
                   CHAR *szLineType ;
```

Listing 5.3: The LINETYPE program (Continued)

```
                 }
                 show [] =
                 {
                 LINETYPE_DEFAULT         , "LINETYPE_DEFAULT"         ,
                 LINETYPE_DOT             , "LINETYPE_DOT"             ,
                 LINETYPE_SHORTDASH       , "LINETYPE_SHORTDASH"       ,
                 LINETYPE_DASHDOT         , "LINETYPE_DASHDOT"         ,
                 LINETYPE_DOUBLEDOT       , "LINETYPE_DOUBLEDOT"       ,
                 LINETYPE_LONGDASH        , "LINETYPE_LONGDASH"        ,
                 LINETYPE_DASHDOUBLEDOT   , "LINETYPE_DASHDOUBLEDOT"   ,
                 LINETYPE_SOLID           , "LINETYPE_SOLID"           ,
                 LINETYPE_INVISIBLE       , "LINETYPE_INVISIBLE"       ,
                 LINETYPE_ALTERNATE       , "LINETYPE_ALTERNATE"
                 } ;
     static INT  cxClient, cyClient, cxCaps, cyChar, cyDesc,
                 iNumTypes = sizeof show / sizeof show[0] ;
     FONTMETRICS fm ;
     HPS         hps ;
     INT         i ;
     POINTL      ptl ;

     switch (msg)
          {
          case WM_CREATE:
               hps = WinGetPS (hwnd) ;
               GpiQueryFontMetrics (hps, sizeof fm, &fm) ;
               cxCaps = (fm.fsType & 1 ? 2 : 3) * fm.lAveCharWidth / 2 ;
               cyChar = fm.lMaxBaselineExt ;
               cyDesc = fm.lMaxDescender ;
               WinReleasePS (hps) ;
               return 0 ;

          case WM_SIZE:
               cxClient = SHORT1FROMMP (mp2) ;
               cyClient = SHORT2FROMMP (mp2) ;
               return 0 ;

          case WM_PAINT:
               hps = WinBeginPaint (hwnd, NULLHANDLE, NULL) ;
               GpiErase (hps) ;

               for (i = 0 ; i < iNumTypes ; i ++)
                    {
                    GpiSetLineType (hps, show [i].lLineType) ;

                    ptl.x = cxCaps ;
                    ptl.y = cyClient - 2 * (i + 1) * cyChar + cyDesc ;

                    GpiCharStringAt (hps, &ptl,
```

Listing 5.3: The LINETYPE program (Continued)

```
                              strlen (show [i].szLineType),
                              show [i].szLineType) ;

                    if (cxClient > 25 * cxCaps)
                         {
                         ptl.x = 24 * cxCaps ;
                         ptl.y += cyChar / 2 - cyDesc ;
                         GpiMove (hps, &ptl) ;

                         ptl.x = cxClient - cxCaps ;
                         GpiLine (hps, &ptl) ;
                         }
                    }
               WinEndPaint (hps) ;
               return 0 ;
          }
     return WinDefWindowProc (hwnd, msg, mp1, mp2) ;
     }
```

The LINETYPE.DEF File

```
;-----------------------------------------
; LINETYPE.DEF module definition file
;-----------------------------------------

NAME           LINETYPE  WINDOWAPI

DESCRIPTION    'GPI Line Types (c) Charles Petzold, 1993'
PROTMODE
```

The results are shown in Figure 5.3.

Each line type is a short sequence of dots or dashes that is repeated over the length of the line. You can use these line types when drawing multiple lines (even very short ones) with *GpiPolyLine*. When drawing each line, the device driver keeps track of which part of the short sequence it drew in the last line. The next line picks up the sequence where the last line ended. You can also use the line types with successive *GpiLine* calls. However, the device driver resets its position to the beginning of the sequence when you call *GpiMove*, *GpiSet-CurrentPosition*, or *GpiSetLineType*.

BOXES AND A SIMPLE ELLIPSE

Probably the most common closed figure is a rectangle. You can draw a rectangle with one *GpiMove* and four *GpiLine* calls, or you can use the function that GPI provides:

```
GpiBox (hps, lOption, &ptl, 0L, 0L) ;
```

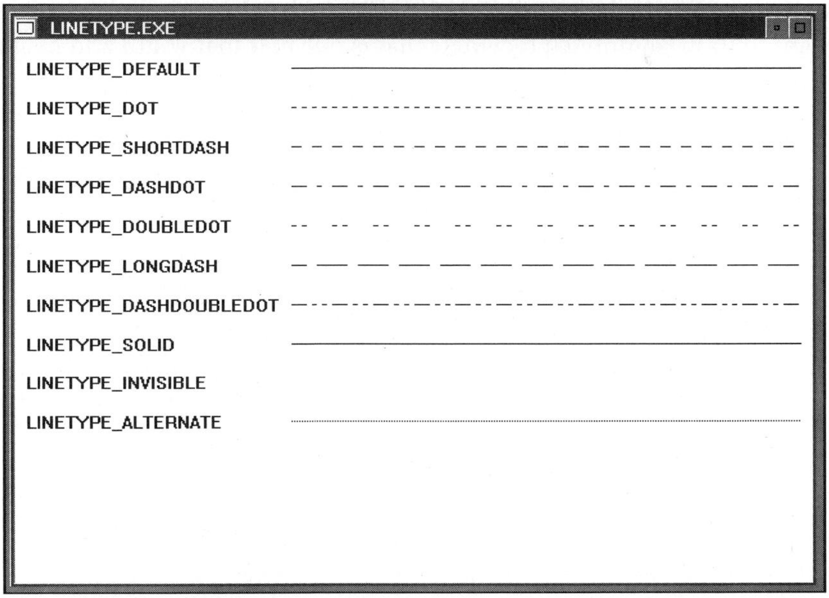

Figure 5.3: The LINETYPE display

The *GpiBox* function draws a rectangle with sides parallel to the x and y axes. The position and size of the rectangle are defined by any two opposite corners of the rectangle. *GpiBox* uses the current position for one corner and the POINTL structure passed to the function for the opposite corner. *GpiBox* does not change the current position.

The *lOption* parameter can be one of the following identifiers defined in PMGPI.H:

DRO_FILL

DRO_OUTLINE

DRO_OUTLINEFILL

DRO_FILL causes the rectangle to be filled. The DRO_OUTLINE option directs GPI to draw only the outline of the rectangle. DRO_OUTLINEFILL draws the outline and fills the rectangle. GPI uses the current line type to draw the outline. How GPI fills the interior of the rectangle is discussed in the following section on patterned areas.

Suppose *cxClient* and *cyClient* are the width and height of your client window. You want to draw an unfilled rectangle that is one half that width and height and centered in the client window. Here's the code:

```
ptl.x = xClient / 4 ;
ptl.y = yClient / 4 ;
GpiMove (hps, &ptl) ;

ptl.x *= 3 ;
ptl.y *= 3 ;
GpiBox (hps, DRO_OUTLINE, &ptl, 0L, 0L) ;
```

You can set the last two parameters of *GpiBox* to values greater than 0 to draw a rectangle with rounded corners. The general syntax of *GpiBox* is

```
GpiBox (hps, lOption, &ptl, cxEllipseAxis, cyEllipseAxis) ;
```

The last two parameters define the width and height of an ellipse. (These dimensions must be less than or equal to the width and height of the rectangle being drawn.) You can visualize GPI cutting this ellipse into four quadrants and using each quadrant of the ellipse as a corner of the box.

If *cxEllipseAxis* and *cyEllipseAxis* are set equal to the width and height of the rectangle being drawn, then *GpiBox* draws an ellipse. Here's a simple ellipse function that calculates the last two parameters of *GpiBox*:

```
#include <stdlib.;      // For labs declaration
     :
LONG Ellipse (HPS hps, LONG lOption, POINTL * pptl)
     {
     POINTL ptlCurrent ;

     GpiQueryCurrentPosition (hps, &ptlCurrent) ;

     return GpiBox (hps, lOption, pptl, labs (pptl->x - ptlCurrent.x),
                    labs (pptl->y - ptlCurrent.y)) ;
     }
```

Like *GpiBox*, this *Ellipse* function draws a figure with axes parallel to the sides of the window. GPI provides even more versatile ellipse drawing facilities with the *GpiSetArcParams*, *GpiFullArc*, *GpiPointArc*, and *GpiPartialArc* functions. Other GPI functions that draw curves are *GpiPolySpline*, *GpiPolyFillet*, and *GpiPolyFilletSharp*. I'll discuss these in Chapter 7.

PIXELS AND DEVICE INDEPENDENCE

Until now, we've been working in a coordinate system based on units of pixels. To some people familiar with other graphics programming languages, the idea of working in units of pixels may seem a contradiction to the goal of writing device-independent programs. After all, what can be more device-dependent than pixels?

Pixels certainly have problems. The first is resolution. Almost every graphics output device has a different pixel resolution. On a VGA, a 300-pixel-high image will occupy most of the screen. On a 300 dots-per-inch laser printer, it will be an inch high. Second, many video display adapters and dot-matrix printers use different horizontal and vertical resolutions.

Let's examine some ways to deal with these problems.

SIMPLE TECHNIQUES

If you draw in units of pixels, you can use pixels in a device-independent manner. One simple technique (used in the SYSVALS programs in Chapter 4 and the LINETYPE program earlier in this chapter) involves basing all coordinates and dimensions on the size of the standard system font characters.

This technique is particularly useful when a program combines text with some rudimentary graphics. For example, suppose you want to write a simple database program using an index card metaphor. Each record is displayed in a simulated 3 × 5-inch index card on the screen. How large are the index cards in pixels? Think of a typewriter. A typewriter with a pica typeface types 10 characters per inch horizontally with 6 lines to the inch vertically. Thus a 3 × 5 card can fit 18 rows of 50 characters each. If *cxChar* and *cyChar* are the average width and height of a system font character, then each card is (50 × *cxChar*) pixels wide and (18 x *cyChar*) pixels high.

Sometimes you need to display only graphics in your window and you want the size of the objects to be based on the size of the window. In this case, you can use the technique shown earlier in the STAR5 program. The five-pointed star in that program is defined in a virtual coordinate system centered around the point (0,0) with a width of 200 units and a height of 200 units. Before drawing the object, the program scales these units to the size of the client window and translates the points so that (0,0) corresponds to the center of the window.

Of course, for some applications these approaches are not satisfactory at all. For example, how do you draw a square with sides of equal length? If the output device has different horizontal and vertical resolutions, then the horizontal and vertical dimensions of the object must be scaled differently.

THE DEVICE CONTEXT AND ITS CAPABILITIES

You'll recall from Chapter 4 that a "device context" refers to a graphics output device (such as a video display or a printer) and its device driver. A presentation space is associated with a particular device context. A cached micro-PS is always associated with the device context for the video display.

A program can obtain lots of interesting information about an output device—including everything it needs to accurately scale graphics objects—by calling the *DevQueryCaps* ("query capabilities") function. To use *DevQueryCaps* for the video display, you first need a handle to the video display device context. You can obtain this easily during WM_CREATE processing by calling *WinOpenWindowDC*:

```
static HDC hdc ;
     :
hdc = WinOpenWindowDC (hwnd) ;
```

Or, you can obtain a handle to the device context associated with a presentation space by calling:

```
hdc = GpiQueryDevice (hps) ;
```

The PMDEV.H header file defines 42 identifiers, each beginning with the word CAPS, that you use with *DevQueryCaps*. Each identifer obtains a particular item that describes the device. Although you can obtain information about multiple items, it's easier to use *DevQueryCaps* for only one item at a time:

```
LONG lCapsValue ;
     :
DevQueryCaps (hdc, CAPS... , 1L, &lCapsValue) ;
```

The DEVCAPS program shown in Listing 5.4 obtains all the information available from *DevQueryCaps* and displays it in a simple two-column format.

Listing 5.4: The DEVCAPS program

The DEVCAPS.MAK File

```
#----------------------
# DEVCAPS.MAK make file
#----------------------

devcaps.exe : devcaps.obj devcaps.def
     $(PRGLINK) devcaps, devcaps, NUL, $(PRGLIB), devcaps

devcaps.obj : devcaps.c devcaps.h
     $(PRGCC) devcaps.c
```

Listing 5.4: The DEVCAPS program (Continued)

The DEVCAPS.C File

```
/*-----------------------------------------------
   DEVCAPS.C -- Device Capabilities Display Program
                (c) Charles Petzold, 1993
  -----------------------------------------------*/

#define INCL_WIN
#define INCL_GPI
#include <os2.h>
#include <stdio.h>
#include <string.h>
#include "devcaps.h"

MRESULT EXPENTRY ClientWndProc (HWND, ULONG, MPARAM, MPARAM) ;
LONG             RtJustCharStringAt (HPS, PPOINTL, LONG, PCHAR) ;

int main (void)
     {
     static CHAR  szClientClass [] = "DevCaps" ;
     static ULONG flFrameFlags = FCF_TITLEBAR       | FCF_SYSMENU |
                                 FCF_SIZEBORDER     | FCF_MINMAX  |
                                 FCF_SHELLPOSITION  | FCF_TASKLIST ;
     HAB          hab ;
     HMQ          hmq ;
     HWND         hwndFrame, hwndClient ;
     QMSG         qmsg ;

     hab = WinInitialize (0) ;
     hmq = WinCreateMsgQueue (hab, 0) ;

     WinRegisterClass (hab, szClientClass, ClientWndProc, 0L, 0) ;

     hwndFrame = WinCreateStdWindow (HWND_DESKTOP, WS_VISIBLE,
                                     &flFrameFlags, szClientClass, NULL,
                                     0L, 0, 0, &hwndClient) ;

     while (WinGetMsg (hab, &qmsg, NULLHANDLE, 0, 0))
          WinDispatchMsg (hab, &qmsg) ;

     WinDestroyWindow (hwndFrame) ;
     WinDestroyMsgQueue (hmq) ;
     WinTerminate (hab) ;
     return 0 ;
     }

MRESULT EXPENTRY ClientWndProc (HWND hwnd, ULONG msg, MPARAM mp1, MPARAM mp2)
     {
```

Listing 5.4: The DEVCAPS program (Continued)

```
     static HDC  hdc ;
     static INT  cyClient, cxCaps, cyChar, cyDesc ;
     CHAR        szBuffer [12] ;
     FONTMETRICS fm ;
     HPS         hps ;
     INT         i ;
     LONG        lValue ;
     POINTL      ptl ;

     switch (msg)
          {
          case WM_CREATE:
               hps = WinGetPS (hwnd) ;
               GpiQueryFontMetrics (hps, sizeof fm, &fm) ;
               cxCaps = fm.lEmInc ;
               cxCaps = (fm.fsType & 1 ? 2 : 3) * fm.lAveCharWidth / 2 ;
               cyChar = fm.lMaxBaselineExt ;
               cyDesc = fm.lMaxDescender ;
               WinReleasePS (hps) ;

               hdc = WinOpenWindowDC (hwnd) ;
               return 0 ;

          case WM_SIZE:
               cyClient = SHORT2FROMMP (mp2) ;
               return 0 ;

          case WM_PAINT:
               hps = WinBeginPaint (hwnd, NULLHANDLE, NULL) ;
               GpiErase (hps) ;

               for (i = 0 ; i < NUMLINES ; i++)
                    {
                    ptl.x = cxCaps ;
                    ptl.y = cyClient - cyChar * (i + 2) + cyDesc ;

                    if (i >= (NUMLINES + 1) / 2)
                         {
                         ptl.x += cxCaps * 35 ;
                         ptl.y += cyChar * ((NUMLINES + 1) / 2) ;
                         }

                    DevQueryCaps (hdc, devcaps[i].lIndex, 1L, &lValue) ;

                    GpiCharStringAt (hps, &ptl,
                                     strlen (devcaps[i].szIdentifier),
                                     devcaps[i].szIdentifier) ;

                    ptl.x += 33 * cxCaps ;
```

Listing 5.4: The DEVCAPS program (Continued)

```
                    RtJustCharStringAt (hps, &ptl,
                                sprintf (szBuffer, "%d", lValue),
                                szBuffer) ;
                    }
               WinEndPaint (hps) ;
               return 0 ;
          }
     return WinDefWindowProc (hwnd, msg, mp1, mp2) ;
     }

LONG RtJustCharStringAt (HPS hps, PPOINTL pptl, LONG lLength, PCHAR pchText)
     {
     POINTL aptlTextBox[TXTBOX_COUNT] ;

     GpiQueryTextBox (hps, lLength, pchText, TXTBOX_COUNT, aptlTextBox) ;

     pptl->x -= aptlTextBox[TXTBOX_CONCAT].x ;

     return GpiCharStringAt (hps, pptl, lLength, pchText) ;
     }
```

The DEVCAPS.H File

```
/*-----------------------
   DEVCAPS.H header file
  -----------------------*/

#define NUMLINES (sizeof devcaps / sizeof devcaps [0])

struct
     {
     LONG lIndex ;
     CHAR *szIdentifier ;
     }
     devcaps [] =
     {
     CAPS_FAMILY                   , "CAPS_FAMILY"                   ,
     CAPS_IO_CAPS                  , "CAPS_IO_CAPS"                  ,
     CAPS_TECHNOLOGY               , "CAPS_TECHNOLOGY"               ,
     CAPS_DRIVER_VERSION           , "CAPS_DRIVER_VERSION"           ,
     CAPS_HEIGHT                   , "CAPS_HEIGHT"                   ,
     CAPS_WIDTH                    , "CAPS_WIDTH"                    ,
     CAPS_HEIGHT_IN_CHARS          , "CAPS_HEIGHT_IN_CHARS"          ,
     CAPS_WIDTH_IN_CHARS           , "CAPS_WIDTH_IN_CHARS"           ,
     CAPS_VERTICAL_RESOLUTION      , "CAPS_VERTICAL_RESOLUTION"      ,
     CAPS_HORIZONTAL_RESOLUTION    , "CAPS_HORIZONTAL_RESOLUTION"    ,
     CAPS_CHAR_HEIGHT              , "CAPS_CHAR_HEIGHT"              ,
     CAPS_CHAR_WIDTH               , "CAPS_CHAR_WIDTH"               ,
     CAPS_SMALL_CHAR_HEIGHT        , "CAPS_SMALL_CHAR_HEIGHT"        ,
```

Listing 5.4: The DEVCAPS program (Continued)

```
     CAPS_SMALL_CHAR_WIDTH        , "CAPS_SMALL_CHAR_WIDTH"        ,
     CAPS_COLORS                  , "CAPS_COLORS"                  ,
     CAPS_COLOR_PLANES            , "CAPS_COLOR_PLANES"            ,
     CAPS_COLOR_BITCOUNT          , "CAPS_COLOR_BITCOUNT"          ,
     CAPS_COLOR_TABLE_SUPPORT     , "CAPS_COLOR_TABLE_SUPPORT"     ,
     CAPS_MOUSE_BUTTONS           , "CAPS_MOUSE_BUTTONS"           ,
     CAPS_FOREGROUND_MIX_SUPPORT  , "CAPS_FOREGROUND_MIX_SUPPORT"  ,
     CAPS_BACKGROUND_MIX_SUPPORT  , "CAPS_BACKGROUND_MIX_SUPPORT"  ,
     CAPS_VIO_LOADABLE_FONTS      , "CAPS_VIO_LOADABLE_FONTS"      ,
     CAPS_WINDOW_BYTE_ALIGNMENT   , "CAPS_WINDOW_BYTE_ALIGNMENT"   ,
     CAPS_BITMAP_FORMATS          , "CAPS_BITMAP_FORMATS"          ,
     CAPS_RASTER_CAPS             , "CAPS_RASTER_CAPS"             ,
     CAPS_MARKER_HEIGHT           , "CAPS_MARKER_HEIGHT"           ,
     CAPS_MARKER_WIDTH            , "CAPS_MARKER_WIDTH"            ,
     CAPS_DEVICE_FONTS            , "CAPS_DEVICE_FONTS"            ,
     CAPS_GRAPHICS_SUBSET         , "CAPS_GRAPHICS_SUBSET"         ,
     CAPS_GRAPHICS_VERSION        , "CAPS_GRAPHICS_VERSION"        ,
     CAPS_GRAPHICS_VECTOR_SUBSET  , "CAPS_GRAPHICS_VECTOR_SUBSET"  ,
     CAPS_DEVICE_WINDOWING        , "CAPS_DEVICE_WINDOWING"        ,
     CAPS_ADDITIONAL_GRAPHICS     , "CAPS_ADDITIONAL_GRAPHICS"     ,
     CAPS_PHYS_COLORS             , "CAPS_PHYS_COLORS"             ,
     CAPS_COLOR_INDEX             , "CAPS_COLOR_INDEX"             ,
     CAPS_GRAPHICS_CHAR_WIDTH     , "CAPS_GRAPHICS_CHAR_WIDTH"     ,
     CAPS_GRAPHICS_CHAR_HEIGHT    , "CAPS_GRAPHICS_CHAR_HEIGHT"    ,
     CAPS_HORIZONTAL_FONT_RES     , "CAPS_HORIZONTAL_FONT_RES"     ,
     CAPS_VERTICAL_FONT_RES       , "CAPS_VERTICAL_FONT_RES"       ,
     CAPS_DEVICE_FONT_SIM         , "CAPS_DEVICE_FONT_SIM"         ,
     CAPS_LINEWIDTH_THICK         , "CAPS_LINEWIDTH_THICK"         ,
     CAPS_DEVICE_POLYSET_POINTS   , "CAPS_DEVICE_POLYSET_POINTS"
     } ;
```

The DEVCAPS.DEF File

```
;-------------------------------------
; DEVCAPS.DEF module definition file
;-------------------------------------

NAME           DEVCAPS   WINDOWAPI

DESCRIPTION    'Device Capabilities (c) Charles Petzold, 1993'
PROTMODE
```

When the Presentation Manager is running on an IBM VGA, DEVCAPS returns the information shown in Figure 5.4.

DEVCAPS.EXE

CAPS_FAMILY	5	CAPS_VIO_LOADABLE_FONTS	0
CAPS_IO_CAPS	2	CAPS_WINDOW_BYTE_ALIGNMENT	0
CAPS_TECHNOLOGY	2	CAPS_BITMAP_FORMATS	2
CAPS_DRIVER_VERSION	512	CAPS_RASTER_CAPS	113
CAPS_HEIGHT	480	CAPS_MARKER_HEIGHT	9
CAPS_WIDTH	640	CAPS_MARKER_WIDTH	9
CAPS_HEIGHT_IN_CHARS	24	CAPS_DEVICE_FONTS	0
CAPS_WIDTH_IN_CHARS	80	CAPS_GRAPHICS_SUBSET	0
CAPS_VERTICAL_RESOLUTION	2667	CAPS_GRAPHICS_VERSION	0
CAPS_HORIZONTAL_RESOLUTION	2667	CAPS_GRAPHICS_VECTOR_SUBSET	0
CAPS_CHAR_HEIGHT	14	CAPS_DEVICE_WINDOWING	0
CAPS_CHAR_WIDTH	8	CAPS_ADDITIONAL_GRAPHICS	169
CAPS_SMALL_CHAR_HEIGHT	8	CAPS_PHYS_COLORS	16
CAPS_SMALL_CHAR_WIDTH	8	CAPS_COLOR_INDEX	63
CAPS_COLORS	16	CAPS_GRAPHICS_CHAR_WIDTH	13
CAPS_COLOR_PLANES	1	CAPS_GRAPHICS_CHAR_HEIGHT	13
CAPS_COLOR_BITCOUNT	4	CAPS_HORIZONTAL_FONT_RES	96
CAPS_COLOR_TABLE_SUPPORT	0	CAPS_VERTICAL_FONT_RES	96
CAPS_MOUSE_BUTTONS	0	CAPS_DEVICE_FONT_SIM	0
CAPS_FOREGROUND_MIX_SUPPORT	123	CAPS_LINEWIDTH_THICK	0
CAPS_BACKGROUND_MIX_SUPPORT	18	CAPS_DEVICE_POLYSET_POINTS	105

Figure 5.4: The DEVCAPS display

Some information is encoded in bits in the return values. You'll need the Presentation Manager documentation and the PMDEV.H header file in order to decode it. For now, we'll look at four items: CAPS_HEIGHT and CAPS_WIDTH give the pixel dimensions of the output device (in this case the video display). CAPS_VERTICAL_RESOLUTION and CAPS_HORIZONTAL_RESOLUTION give the resolution of the output device in the rather ungainly units of pixels per meter.

Thus, you can determine the physical dimensions of the output device (in meters) by dividing CAPS_HEIGHT by CAPS_VERTICAL_RESOLUTION and CAPS_WIDTH by CAPS_HORIZONTAL_RESOLUTION. (In most cases, these quotients will be less than 1, so you'll probably want to calculate physical dimensions in something other than meters.) You now have enough information to adjust horizontal and vertical sizes in order to draw square squares and round circles.

The CLOCK program in Chapter 10 shows how to use the CAPS_VERTICAL_RESOLUTION and CAPS_HORIZONTAL_RESOLUTION values to draw round graphics objects regardless of the different resolutions of the video display. The clock displayed by this program adjusts its size to fit the window but remains round.

USING METRIC UNITS

You may also want to draw graphic objects in specific sizes, such as units of a fraction of an inch or millimeters. These are called *metric units*.

There are a couple of ways to do this. The easy approach (described in the next section) lets GPI do most of the work. But you may prefer to retain control over metric scaling entirely within your program. For example, suppose you want to work in units of 1/100 inch. (These units are called "Low English" because they use English measurements. "High English" units are 1/1000 inch.)

You first need to obtain the horizontal and vertical resolution of the device:

```
static LONG cxPixelsPerMeter, cyPixelsPerMeter ;
     :
DevQueryCaps (hdc, CAPS_HORIZONTAL_RESOLUTION, 1L, &cxPixelsPerMeter) ;
DevQueryCaps (hdc, CAPS_VERTICAL_RESOLUTION, 1L, &cyPixelsPerMeter) ;
```

There are 2.54 centimeters to the inch and 100 centimeters to the meter. Thus you can calculate pixels per inch by using the following method:

```
static LONG cxPixelsPerInch, cyPixelsPerInch ;
     :
cxPixelsPerInch = (cxPixelsPerMeter * 254 + 5000) / 10000 ;
cyPixelsPerInch = (cyPixelsPerMeter * 254 + 5000) / 10000 ;
```

The addition of 5,000 before the division gives a rounded result.

If you want to set the current position 3 inches from the left and 1½ inches from the bottom of your client window, you start by setting *ptl.x* and *ptl.y* to these values in units of 1/100 inch:

```
ptl.x = 300 ;
ptl.y = 150 ;
```

Now convert these coordinates to pixels:

```
ptl.x = ptl.x * cxPixelsPerInch / 100 ;
ptl.y = ptl.y * cyPixelsPerInch / 100 ;
```

Then call the *GpiMove* function.

You can also translate a pixel size or position to Low English units. For example, suppose you want to save *cxClient* and *cyClient* in these units. Here's the new WM_SIZE code:

```
case WM_SIZE:
     cxClient = SHORT1FROMMP (mp2) * 100 / cxPixelsPerInch ;
     cyClient = SHORT2FROMMP (mp2) * 100 / cyPixelsPerInch ;
     return 0 ;
```

PAGE UNITS

Rather than do your own translation between metric units and pixels, you can have GPI translate points for you. You must use a function called *GpiSetPS* to set *presentation page units*, which are the units you specify in GPI functions. GPI converts these page units into *device units*, the normal coordinate system in units of pixels relative to the lower-left corner of the window.

To use *GpiSetPS*, you first define a structure of type SIZEL:

```
SIZEL sizl ;
```

The SIZEL structure has two fields named *cx* and *cy*. For our purposes, you can set both of these fields to zero:

```
sizl.cx = 0 ;
sizl.cy = 0 ;
```

You then call *GpiSetPS*:

```
GpiSetPS (hps, &sizl, lPageUnits) ;
```

The last parameter specifies the page units. It can be any of the following seven identifiers:

Page Units Identifier	Units
PU_PELS	Pixels
PU_ARBITRARY	"Square" pixels
PU_LOMETRIC	0.1 millimeter
PU_HIMETRIC	0.01 millimeter
PU_LOENGLISH	0.01 inch
PU_HIENGLISH	0.001 inch
PU_TWIPS	1/1440 inch

By default, page units are set to PU_PELS. Page units of PU_ARBITRARY result in an adjustment so that horizontal units you specify in GPI functions are the same as vertical units. This is a compromise between PU_PELS and the five metric page units. The fabricated word “twips” stands for “twentieths of a point,” and refers to a printer’s point size, 1/72 inch. Thus 1/20 point is 1/1440 inch.

Be careful with *GpiSetPS*: The function resets all attributes of the presentation space to default values. If you use *GpiSetPS*, it’s best to call it immediately after you obtain a presentation space handle using *WinBeginPaint* or *WinGetPS*.

The RULER program in Listing 5.5 shows how to use *GpiSetPS* to draw using Low English units.

Listing 5.5: The RULER program

The RULER.MAK File

```
#---------------------
# RULER.MAK make file
#---------------------

ruler.exe : ruler.obj ruler.def
     $(PRGLINK) ruler, ruler, NUL, $(PRGLIB), ruler

ruler.obj : ruler.c
     $(PRGCC) ruler.c
```

The RULER.C File

```
/*-------------------------------------
   RULER.C -- Draw a Ruler
              (c) Charles Petzold, 1993
  -------------------------------------*/

#define INCL_WIN
#define INCL_GPI
#include <os2.h>
#include <stdio.h>

MRESULT EXPENTRY ClientWndProc (HWND, ULONG, MPARAM, MPARAM) ;

int main (void)
     {
     static CHAR  szClientClass [] = "Ruler" ;
     static ULONG flFrameFlags = FCF_TITLEBAR      | FCF_SYSMENU |
                                 FCF_SIZEBORDER    | FCF_MINMAX  |
                                 FCF_SHELLPOSITION | FCF_TASKLIST ;
     HAB          hab ;
     HMQ          hmq ;
     HWND         hwndFrame, hwndClient ;
```

Listing 5.5: The RULER program (Continued)

```
     QMSG          qmsg ;

     hab = WinInitialize (0) ;
     hmq = WinCreateMsgQueue (hab, 0) ;

     WinRegisterClass (hab, szClientClass, ClientWndProc, CS_SIZEREDRAW, 0) ;

     hwndFrame = WinCreateStdWindow (HWND_DESKTOP, WS_VISIBLE,
                                     &flFrameFlags, szClientClass, NULL,
                                     0L, 0, 0, &hwndClient) ;

     while (WinGetMsg (hab, &qmsg, NULLHANDLE, 0, 0))
          WinDispatchMsg (hab, &qmsg) ;

     WinDestroyWindow (hwndFrame) ;
     WinDestroyMsgQueue (hmq) ;
     WinTerminate (hab) ;
     return 0 ;
     }

MRESULT EXPENTRY ClientWndProc (HWND hwnd, ULONG msg, MPARAM mp1, MPARAM mp2)
     {
     static INT   iTick[16] = { 100, 25, 35, 25, 50, 25, 35, 25,
                                 70, 25, 35, 25, 50, 25, 35, 25 } ;
     static INT   cxClient, cxChar, cyDesc ;
     static SIZEL sizl ;
     CHAR         szBuffer [4] ;
     FONTMETRICS  fm ;
     HPS          hps ;
     INT          i ;
     POINTL       ptl ;

     switch (msg)
          {
          case WM_CREATE:
               hps = WinGetPS (hwnd) ;
               GpiSetPS (hps, &sizl, PU_LOENGLISH) ;

               GpiQueryFontMetrics (hps, sizeof fm, &fm) ;
               cxChar = fm.lAveCharWidth ;
               cyDesc = fm.lMaxDescender ;

               WinReleasePS (hps) ;
               return 0 ;

          case WM_SIZE:
               ptl.x = SHORT1FROMMP (mp2) ;
               ptl.y = SHORT2FROMMP (mp2) ;
```

Listing 5.5: The RULER program (Continued)

```
          hps = WinGetPS (hwnd) ;
          GpiSetPS (hps, &sizl, PU_LOENGLISH) ;
          GpiConvert (hps, CVTC_DEVICE, CVTC_PAGE, 1L, &ptl) ;
          WinReleasePS (hps) ;

          cxClient = ptl.x ;
          return 0 ;

     case WM_PAINT:
          hps = WinBeginPaint (hwnd, NULLHANDLE, NULL) ;
          GpiSetPS (hps, &sizl, PU_LOENGLISH) ;
          GpiErase (hps) ;

          for (i = 0 ; i < 16 * cxClient / 100 ; i++)
               {
               ptl.x = 100 * i / 16 ;
               ptl.y = 0 ;
               GpiMove (hps, &ptl) ;

               ptl.y = iTick [i % 16] ;
               GpiLine (hps, &ptl) ;

               if (i % 16 == 0)
                    {
                    ptl.x -= cxChar / (i >= 160 ? 1 : 2) ;
                    ptl.y += cyDesc ;
                    GpiCharStringAt (hps, &ptl,
                                     sprintf (szBuffer, "%d", i / 16),
                                     szBuffer) ;
                    }
               }
          WinEndPaint (hps) ;
          return 0 ;
     }
return WinDefWindowProc (hwnd, msg, mp1, mp2) ;
}
```

The RULER.DEF File

```
;-----------------------------------
; RULER.DEF module definition file
;-----------------------------------

NAME           RULER     WINDOWAPI

DESCRIPTION    'Draw a Ruler (c) Charles Petzold, 1993'
PROTMODE
```

RULER draws a ruler with tick marks every 1/16 inch along the bottom of its client window, as shown in Figure 5.5.

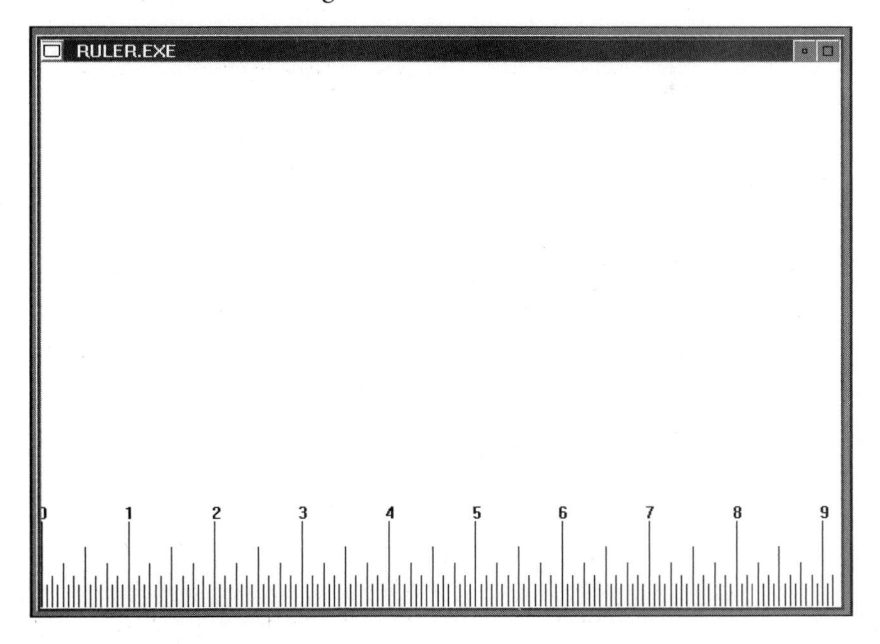

Figure 5.5: The RULER display

In RULER, the *sizl* structure is defined as a static variable and implicitly initialized to zero. *ClientWndProc* calls *GpiSetPS* with the PU_LOENGLISH parameter whenever it obtains a presentation space handle, which it does three times: during the WM_CREATE, WM_SIZE, and WM_PAINT messages.

During the WM_CREATE message, the program obtains font metrics from the *GpiQueryFontMetrics* function. Because page units have been set to Low English, these font metrics are in units of 1/100 inch.

The Low English page units don't affect nongraphics functions. For example, the WM_SIZE message will continue to report the window size in device units (pixels). For this reason, RULER must convert the window size to Low English units before saving the values in *cxClient* and *cyClient*. First, the new window size is saved in a POINTL structure:

```
ptl.x = SHORT1FROMMP (mp2) ;
ptl.y = SHORT2FROMMP (mp2) ;
```

Next, RULER gets a presention space handle and sets the page units:

```
hps = WinGetPS (hwnd) ;
GpiSetPS (hps, &sizl, PU_LOENGLISH) ;
```

The coordinates of the POINTL structure are converted to page units using *GpiConvert*, and the presentation space is released:

```
GpiConvert (hps, CVTC_DEVICE, CVTC_PAGE, 1L, &ptl) ;
WinReleasePS (hps) ;
```

The second parameter to *GpiConvert* indicates that the POINTL structure (the last parameter) is in device units. The third parameter is the units to which the POINTL structure should be converted. (You can switch these two parameters to convert from page units to device units.) The fourth parameter is the number of POINTL structures to be converted, passed as the last parameter. Finally, *cxClient* and *cyClient* are saved from the converted points as follows:

```
cxClient = ptl.x ;
cyClient = ptl.y ;
```

Thus, by the time the WM_PAINT message is processed, everything the program needs to draw the ruler (the size of the client window and the font metrics) is in units of 1/100 of an inch. The *sTick* array (which has the lengths of the ruler tick marks) has also been initialized in Low English units.

This discussion of page units only scratches the surface of GPI's various transformation functions. The points you specify in GPI functions are actually in a coordinate system called "world space" and are translated to "model space," then to page units, and then to device coordinates. The *GpiSetModelTransformMatrix* and *GpiSetDefaultViewMatrix* functions allow you to perform translation, scaling, and rotation on world coordinates for more complex drawing. I'll discuss this more in Chapter 7.

GPI PRIMITIVE 2: PATTERNED AREAS

The second GPI primitive is a pattern that fills an enclosed area. You define the area with a series of lines, and GPI fills it. The *GpiBox* function also uses a pattern to fill the box interior.

Area filling under GPI is not implemented as a "flood fill," such as that available with the PAINT statement in Microsoft's QuickBASIC. In a flood fill, you specify a point that is bounded by one or more existing lines. The graphics system fills the area with a pattern by searching for the boundary lines. Flood fills are possible only on raster output devices that allow the graphics system to read (as well as write) individual pixels. Instead, GPI accumulates the lines that you specify as boundaries to the area and then algorithmically fills the enclosed areas defined by these lines.

If you have already experimented with the DRO_FILL and DRO_OUTLINE-FILL options of *GpiBox*, you will have noticed that GPI simply fills the box with a solid color. But that's only because the default area pattern is a solid pattern. Let's look at the other available patterns and the various ways of defining and filling an area under GPI.

SELECTING THE PATTERN

To select the pattern that GPI uses to fill an area, you call

```
GpiSetPattern (hps, lPattern) ;
```

The *lPattern* parameter can be any one of the following 21 identifiers beginning with the prefix PATSYM ("pattern symbol"):

PATSYM_DEFAULT	PATSYM_DIAG1
PATSYM_DENSE1	PATSYM_DIAG2
PATSYM_DENSE2	PATSYM_DIAG3
PATSYM_DENSE3	PATSYM_DIAG4
PATSYM_DENSE4	PATSYM_NOSHADE
PATSYM_DENSE5	PATSYM_SOLID
PATSYM_DENSE6	PATSYM_HALFTONE
PATSYM_DENSE7	PATSYM_HATCH
PATSYM_DENSE8	PATSYM_DIAGHATCH
PATSYM_VERT	PATSYM_BLANK
PATSYM_HORIZ	

The PATSYM_DEFAULT and PATSYM_SOLID identifiers have the same effect; so do PATSYM_NOSHADE and PATSYM_BLANK. PATSYM_DIAG1 and PATSYM_DIAG2 are patterns composed of diagonal lines from lower left to upper right. For PATSYM_DIAG3 and PATSYM_DIAG4, the diagonal lines go from upper left to lower right.

The various PATSYM_DENSE identifiers result in shaded patterns: PATSYM_DENSE1 has the highest color density, and PATSYM_DENSE8 has the lowest color density. You can get a 50 percent shading using PATSYM_HALFTONE, which (depending on the output device) may or may not be the same as PATSYM_DENSE4 or PATSYM_DENSE5.

The PATTERNS program shown in Listing 5.6 uses the *GpiBox* function to draw all 19 patterns in its client window.

Listing 5.6: The PATTERNS program

The PATTERNS.MAK File

```
#-----------------------
# PATTERNS.MAK make file
#-----------------------

patterns.exe : patterns.obj patterns.def
     $(PRGLINK) patterns, patterns, NUL, $(PRGLIB), patterns

patterns.obj : patterns.c
     $(PRGCC) patterns.c
```

The PATTERNS.C File

```
/*-----------------------------------------
   PATTERNS.C -- GPI Area Patterns
                 (c) Charles Petzold, 1993
  -----------------------------------------*/

#define INCL_WIN
#define INCL_GPI
#include <os2.h>
#include <string.h>

MRESULT EXPENTRY ClientWndProc (HWND, ULONG, MPARAM, MPARAM) ;

int main (void)
     {
     static CHAR  szClientClass [] = "Patterns" ;
     static ULONG flFrameFlags = FCF_TITLEBAR      | FCF_SYSMENU |
                                 FCF_SIZEBORDER    | FCF_MINMAX  |
                                 FCF_SHELLPOSITION | FCF_TASKLIST ;
     HAB          hab ;
     HMQ          hmq ;
     HWND         hwndFrame, hwndClient ;
     QMSG         qmsg ;

     hab = WinInitialize (0) ;
     hmq = WinCreateMsgQueue (hab, 0) ;

     WinRegisterClass (hab, szClientClass, ClientWndProc, CS_SIZEREDRAW, 0) ;

     hwndFrame = WinCreateStdWindow (HWND_DESKTOP, WS_VISIBLE,
                                     &flFrameFlags, szClientClass, NULL,
                                     0L, 0, 0, &hwndClient) ;
```

Listing 5.6: The PATTERNS program (Continued)

```
     while (WinGetMsg (hab, &qmsg, NULLHANDLE, 0, 0))
          WinDispatchMsg (hab, &qmsg) ;

     WinDestroyWindow (hwndFrame) ;
     WinDestroyMsgQueue (hmq) ;
     WinTerminate (hab) ;
     return 0 ;
     }

MRESULT EXPENTRY ClientWndProc (HWND hwnd, ULONG msg, MPARAM mp1, MPARAM mp2)
     {
     static struct {
                   LONG lPatternSymbol ;
                   CHAR *szPatternSymbol ;
                   }
                   show [] =
                   {
                   PATSYM_DEFAULT   , "PATSYM_DEFAULT"   ,
                   PATSYM_DENSE1    , "PATSYM_DENSE1"    ,
                   PATSYM_DENSE2    , "PATSYM_DENSE2"    ,
                   PATSYM_DENSE3    , "PATSYM_DENSE3"    ,
                   PATSYM_DENSE4    , "PATSYM_DENSE4"    ,
                   PATSYM_DENSE5    , "PATSYM_DENSE5"    ,
                   PATSYM_DENSE6    , "PATSYM_DENSE6"    ,
                   PATSYM_DENSE7    , "PATSYM_DENSE7"    ,
                   PATSYM_DENSE8    , "PATSYM_DENSE8"    ,
                   PATSYM_VERT      , "PATSYM_VERT"      ,
                   PATSYM_HORIZ     , "PATSYM_HORIZ"     ,
                   PATSYM_DIAG1     , "PATSYM_DIAG1"     ,
                   PATSYM_DIAG2     , "PATSYM_DIAG2"     ,
                   PATSYM_DIAG3     , "PATSYM_DIAG3"     ,
                   PATSYM_DIAG4     , "PATSYM_DIAG4"     ,
                   PATSYM_NOSHADE   , "PATSYM_NOSHADE"   ,
                   PATSYM_SOLID     , "PATSYM_SOLID"     ,
                   PATSYM_HALFTONE  , "PATSYM_HALFTONE"  ,
                   PATSYM_HATCH     , "PATSYM_HATCH"     ,
                   PATSYM_DIAGHATCH , "PATSYM_DIAGHATCH" ,
                   PATSYM_BLANK     , "PATSYM_BLANK"
                   } ;
     static INT    cyClient, cxCaps, cyChar, cyDesc,
                   iNumTypes = sizeof show / sizeof show[0] ;
     FONTMETRICS   fm ;
     HPS           hps ;
     INT           i ;
     POINTL        ptl ;

     switch (msg)
          {
```

Listing 5.6: The PATTERNS program (Continued)

```
          case WM_CREATE:
               hps = WinGetPS (hwnd) ;
               GpiQueryFontMetrics (hps, sizeof fm, &fm) ;
               cxCaps = (fm.fsType & 1 ? 2 : 3) * fm.lAveCharWidth / 2 ;
               cyChar = fm.lMaxBaselineExt ;
               cyDesc = fm.lMaxDescender ;
               WinReleasePS (hps) ;
               return 0 ;

          case WM_SIZE:
               cyClient = SHORT2FROMMP (mp2) ;
               return 0 ;

          case WM_PAINT:
               hps = WinBeginPaint (hwnd, NULLHANDLE, NULL) ;
               GpiErase (hps) ;

               for (i = 0 ; i < iNumTypes ; i ++)
                    {
                    GpiSetPattern (hps, show [i].lPatternSymbol) ;

                    ptl.x = (i < 11 ? 1 : 33) * cxCaps ;
                    ptl.y = cyClient - (i % 11 * 5 + 4) * cyChar / 2 + cyDesc ;

                    GpiCharStringAt (hps, &ptl,
                                     strlen (show [i].szPatternSymbol),
                                     show [i].szPatternSymbol) ;

                    ptl.x  = (i < 11 ? 20 : 52) * cxCaps ;
                    ptl.y -= cyDesc + cyChar / 2 ;
                    GpiMove (hps, &ptl) ;

                    ptl.x += 10 * cxCaps ;
                    ptl.y +=  2 * cyChar ;
                    GpiBox (hps, DRO_FILL, &ptl, 0L, 0L) ;
                    }
               WinEndPaint (hps) ;
               return 0 ;
          }
     return WinDefWindowProc (hwnd, msg, mp1, mp2) ;
     }
```

The PATTERNS.DEF File

```
;-------------------------------------
; PATTERNS.DEF module definition file
;-------------------------------------
```

Listing 5.6: The PATTERNS program (Continued)

```
NAME           PATTERNS  WINDOWAPI

DESCRIPTION    'GPI Area Patterns (c) Charles Petzold, 1993'
PROTMODE
```

The various patterns drawn by this program are shown in Figure 5.6.

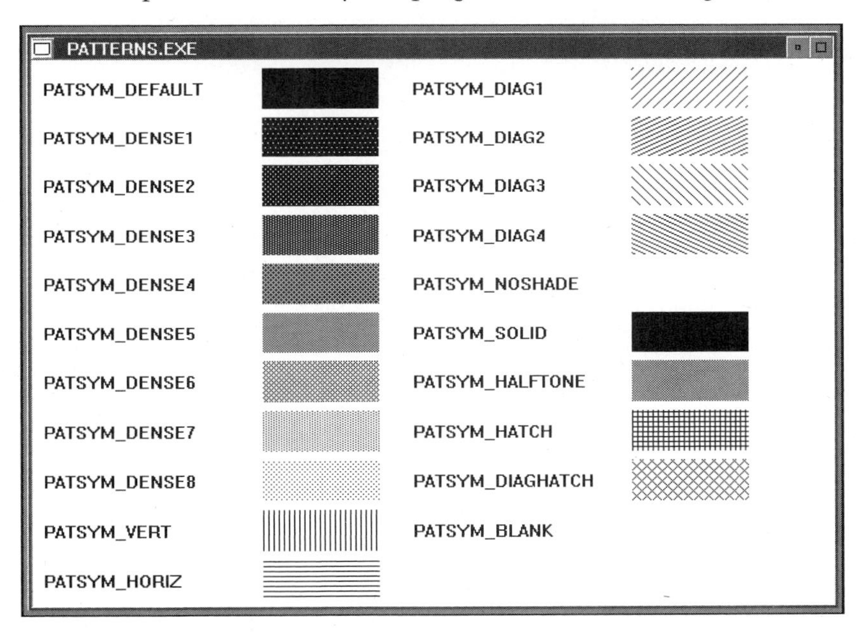

Figure 5.6: The PATTERNS display

A pattern is really only a small rectangular bitmap that is repeated horizontally and vertically to fill an area. In the next chapter I'll show you how to create your own patterns for area filling.

DEFINING AN AREA

Area filling is not limited to the *GpiBox* function. You can define any area to be filled by simply drawing a series of lines between the *GpiBeginArea* and *GpiEndArea* functions:

```
GpiBeginArea (hps, lAreaFlags) ;
     [draw lines to define the area]
GpiEndArea (hps) ;
```

This is known as an *area bracket.* GPI does not fill the area until you call the *GpiEndArea* function.

For example, suppose you want to draw a large filled triangle in your client window. If *cxClient* and *cyClient* are the dimensions of the client window, here's the code:

```
GpiBeginArea (hps, ØL) ;

ptl.x = Ø ;
ptl.y = Ø ;
GpiMove (hps, &ptl) ;

ptl.x = cxClient / 2 ;
ptl.y = cyClient ;
GpiLine (hps, &ptl) ;

ptl.x = cxClient ;
ptl.y = Ø ;
GpiLine (hps, &ptl) ;

ptl.x = Ø ;
ptl.y = Ø ;
GpiLine (hps, &ptl) ;

GpiEndArea (hps) ;
```

The last *GpiLine* call, which closes the triangle, is not required. If you do not close the figure, GPI will close it for you by drawing a straight line to the starting point.

Only a subset of GPI functions are allowed within an area bracket. All line drawing and line attribute functions are allowed, but little else. If you call *GpiBox* within an area bracket, it should be with the DRO_OUTLINE option. If you want to use a nonsolid pattern, call *GpiSetPattern* before calling *GpiBeginArea.*

You can define more than one filled area within a single area bracket. When you call *GpiMove* in an area bracket, GPI closes the previous figure (if necessary) and starts a second figure. For example, the following code draws two filled triangles side by side in the window:

```
GpiBeginArea (hps, ØL) ;

ptl.x = Ø ;
ptl.y = Ø ;
GpiMove (hps, &ptl) ;
```

```
ptl.x = cxClient / 4 ;
ptl.y = cyClient ;
GpiLine (hps, &ptl) ;

ptl.x = cxClient / 2 ;
ptl.y = 0 ;
GpiLine (hps, &ptl) ;

GpiMove (hps, &ptl) ;

ptl.x = 3 * cxClient / 4 ;
ptl.y = cyClient ;
GpiLine (hps, &ptl) ;

ptl.x = cxClient ;
ptl.y = 0 ;
GpiLine (hps, &ptl) ;

GpiEndArea (hps) ;
```

In this case I'm letting GPI close the two triangles. The *GpiMove* call in the middle of this area bracket marks the beginning of the second triangle, which is the same as the third point of the first triangle. As part of area bracket processing, GPI closes the first triangle with a line from (cxClient/2,0) to (0,0). Similarly, the *GpiEndArea* call causes GPI to construct a boundary line from (cxClient,0) to (cxClient/2,0).

In the preceding examples, the boundary lines are not actually drawn by GPI. GPI uses the lines you specify solely to define the enclosed area. Whether GPI draws the boundary lines or not is governed by the second parameter to *GpiBeginArea*. It can be one of the following identifiers:

```
BA_NOBOUNDARY
BA_BOUNDARY
```

The BA_NOBOUNDARY identifier is equal to zero, so no boundary line is drawn in the preceding examples. You can also combine these identifiers by using the C bitwise OR operator with one of the following identifiers:

```
BA_ALTERNATE
BA_WINDING
```

The BA_ALTERNATE identifier is equal to zero, so that is the default if you use neither identifier. These identifiers govern whether GPI uses "alternate" or "winding" mode to fill areas.

ALTERNATE AND WINDING MODES

When you draw a series of lines to define a filled area, the lines can cross each other, and the enclosed area can actually comprise several smaller subareas. You may not want all of these areas to be filled. The classic example is a five-pointed star that you draw with five lines. The points of the star and the interior pentagon are all subareas. You can have GPI fill that interior pentagon by specifying winding mode or leave it unfilled by specifying alternate mode. This is illustrated in the STARFILL program in Listing 5.7.

Listing 5.7: The STARFILL program

The STARFILL.MAK File

```
#-----------------------
# STARFILL.MAK make file
#-----------------------

starfill.exe : starfill.obj starfill.def
     $(PRGLINK) starfill, starfill, NUL, $(PRGLIB), starfill

starfill.obj : starfill.c
     $(PRGCC) starfill.c
```

The STARFILL.C File

```
/*-----------------------------------------
   STARFILL.C -- Alternate and Winding Modes
                 (c) Charles Petzold, 1993
  -----------------------------------------*/

#define INCL_GPI
#include <os2.h>

MRESULT EXPENTRY ClientWndProc (HWND, ULONG, MPARAM, MPARAM) ;

int main (void)
     {
     static CHAR  szClientClass [] = "StarFill" ;
     static ULONG flFrameFlags = FCF_TITLEBAR      | FCF_SYSMENU |
                                 FCF_SIZEBORDER    | FCF_MINMAX  |
                                 FCF_SHELLPOSITION | FCF_TASKLIST ;
     HAB          hab ;
     HMQ          hmq ;
     HWND         hwndFrame, hwndClient ;
     QMSG         qmsg ;

     hab = WinInitialize (0) ;
     hmq = WinCreateMsgQueue (hab, 0) ;
```

Listing 5.7: The STARFILL program (Continued)

```
     WinRegisterClass (hab, szClientClass, ClientWndProc, CS_SIZEREDRAW, 0) ;

     hwndFrame = WinCreateStdWindow (HWND_DESKTOP, WS_VISIBLE,
                                     &flFrameFlags, szClientClass, NULL,
                                     0L, 0, 0, &hwndClient) ;

     while (WinGetMsg (hab, &qmsg, NULLHANDLE, 0, 0))
          WinDispatchMsg (hab, &qmsg) ;

     WinDestroyWindow (hwndFrame) ;
     WinDestroyMsgQueue (hmq) ;
     WinTerminate (hab) ;
     return 0 ;
     }

MRESULT EXPENTRY ClientWndProc (HWND hwnd, ULONG msg, MPARAM mp1, MPARAM mp2)
     {
     static POINTL aptlStar[5] = {-59,-81, 0,100, 59,-81, -95,31, 95,31 } ;
     static INT    cxClient, cyClient ;
     HPS           hps ;
     INT           i ;
     POINTL        aptl[5] ;

     switch (msg)
     {
          case WM_SIZE:
               cxClient = SHORT1FROMMP (mp2) ;
               cyClient = SHORT2FROMMP (mp2) ;
               return 0 ;

          case WM_PAINT:
               hps = WinBeginPaint (hwnd, NULLHANDLE, NULL) ;
               GpiErase (hps) ;
               GpiSetPattern (hps, PATSYM_HALFTONE) ;

                         /*---------------------
                            Alternate Fill Mode
                           ---------------------*/

               for (i = 0 ; i < 5 ; i++)
                    {
                    aptl[i].x = cxClient / 4 + cxClient *
                                          aptlStar[i].x / 400 ;
                    aptl[i].y = cyClient / 2 + cyClient *
                                          aptlStar[i].y / 200 ;
                    }

               GpiBeginArea (hps, BA_NOBOUNDARY | BA_ALTERNATE) ;
```

Listing 5.7: The STARFILL program (Continued)

```
               GpiMove (hps, aptl) ;
               GpiPolyLine (hps, 4L, aptl + 1) ;
               GpiEndArea (hps) ;

                         /*-------------------
                            Winding Fill Mode
                           -------------------*/

               for (i = 0 ; i < 5 ; i++)
                    aptl[i].x += cxClient / 2 ;

               GpiBeginArea (hps, BA_NOBOUNDARY | BA_WINDING) ;
               GpiMove (hps, aptl) ;
               GpiPolyLine (hps, 4L, aptl + 1) ;
               GpiEndArea (hps) ;

               WinEndPaint (hps) ;
               return 0 ;
          }
     return WinDefWindowProc (hwnd, msg, mp1, mp2) ;
     }
```

The STARFILL.DEF File

```
;-------------------------------------
; STARFILL.DEF module definition file
;-------------------------------------

NAME           STARFILL  WINDOWAPI

DESCRIPTION    'Alternate and Winding Modes (c) Charles Petzold, 1993'
PROTMODE
```

As you can see in Figure 5.7, the center of the five-pointed star is filled in winding mode but not in alternate mode.

At first, the difference between alternate and winding modes seems rather simple. For alternate mode, you can imagine a line drawn from a point in an enclosed area to infinity. The enclosed area is filled only if that imaginary line crosses an odd number of boundary lines. This is why the points of the star are filled but the center is not.

The example of the five-pointed star makes winding mode seem simpler than it actually is. When you're drawing a single object in an area bracket, in most cases winding mode will cause all enclosed areas to be filled. But there are exceptions.

Figure 5.7: The STARFILL display

To determine whether an enclosed area is filled in winding mode, you again imagine a line drawn from a point in that area to infinity. If the imaginary line crosses an odd number of boundary lines, the area is filled, just as in alternate mode. If the imaginary line crosses an even number of boundary lines, the area can either be filled or not filled. The area is filled if the number of boundary lines going in one direction (relative to the imaginary line) is not equal to the number of boundary lines going in the other direction. For example, consider the object shown in Figure 5.8.

The arrows on the lines indicate the direction in which the lines are drawn. Both winding mode and alternate mode will fill the three enclosed L-shaped areas numbered 1 through 3. The two smaller interior areas, numbered 4 and 5, will not be filled in alternate mode. But in winding mode, area number 5 is filled because you must cross two lines going in the same direction to get from the inside of that area to the outside of the figure. Area number 4 is not filled. You must again cross two lines, but the two lines go in opposite directions.

Is GPI really smart enough to figure this out? Sure it is, and the ALTWIND program shown in Listing 5.8 demonstrates this.

Figure 5.9 shows the ALTWIND display.

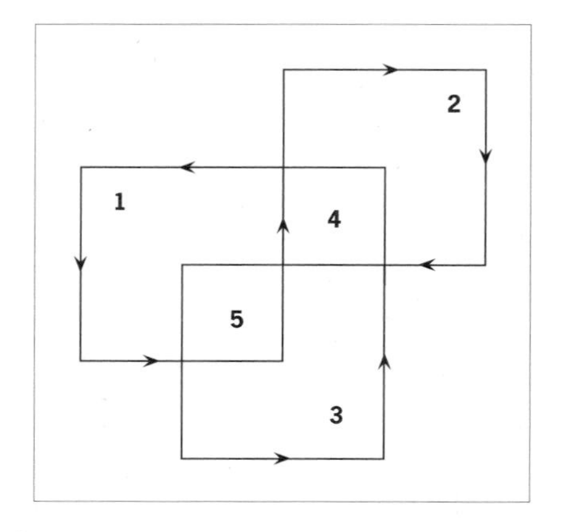

Figure 5.8: A figure in which winding mode does not fill all interior areas

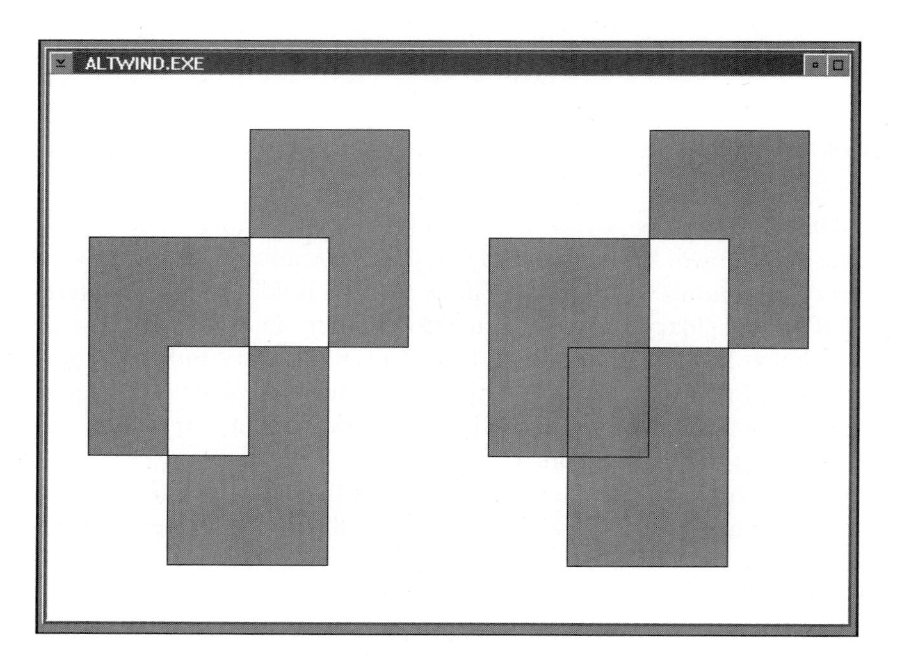

Figure 5.9: The ALTWIND display

Listing 5.8: The ALTWIND program

The ALTWIND.MAK File

```
#-----------------------
# ALTWIND.MAK make file
#-----------------------

altwind.exe : altwind.obj altwind.def
     $(PRGLINK) altwind, altwind, NUL, $(PRGLIB), altwind

altwind.obj : altwind.c
     $(PRGCC) altwind.c
```

The ALTWIND.C File

```
/*------------------------------------------
   ALTWIND.C -- Alternate and Winding Modes
                (c) Charles Petzold, 1993
  ------------------------------------------*/

#define INCL_GPI
#include <os2.h>

MRESULT EXPENTRY ClientWndProc (HWND, ULONG, MPARAM, MPARAM) ;

int main (void)
     {
     static CHAR  szClientClass [] = "AltWind" ;
     static ULONG flFrameFlags = FCF_TITLEBAR      | FCF_SYSMENU |
                                 FCF_SIZEBORDER    | FCF_MINMAX  |
                                 FCF_SHELLPOSITION | FCF_TASKLIST ;
     HAB          hab ;
     HMQ          hmq ;
     HWND         hwndFrame, hwndClient ;
     QMSG         qmsg ;

     hab = WinInitialize (0) ;
     hmq = WinCreateMsgQueue (hab, 0) ;

     WinRegisterClass (hab, szClientClass, ClientWndProc, CS_SIZEREDRAW, 0) ;

     hwndFrame = WinCreateStdWindow (HWND_DESKTOP, WS_VISIBLE,
                                    &flFrameFlags, szClientClass, NULL,
                                    0L, 0, 0, &hwndClient) ;

     while (WinGetMsg (hab, &qmsg, NULLHANDLE, 0, 0))
          WinDispatchMsg (hab, &qmsg) ;

     WinDestroyWindow (hwndFrame) ;
```

Listing 5.8: The ALTWIND program

```
     WinDestroyMsgQueue (hmq) ;
     WinTerminate (hab) ;
     return 0 ;
     }

MRESULT EXPENTRY ClientWndProc (HWND hwnd, ULONG msg, MPARAM mp1, MPARAM mp2)
     {
     static POINTL aptlFigure[10] = { 10,30, 50,30, 50,90, 90,90, 90,50,
                                      30,50, 30,10, 70,10, 70,70, 10,70 } ;
     static INT    cxClient, cyClient ;
     HPS           hps ;
     INT           i ;
     POINTL        aptl[10] ;

     switch (msg)
          {
          case WM_SIZE:
               cxClient = SHORT1FROMMP (mp2) ;
               cyClient = SHORT2FROMMP (mp2) ;
               return 0 ;

          case WM_PAINT:
               hps = WinBeginPaint (hwnd, NULLHANDLE, NULL) ;
               GpiErase (hps) ;
               GpiSetPattern (hps, PATSYM_HALFTONE) ;

                         /*---------------------
                           Alternate Fill Mode
                           ---------------------*/

               for (i = 0 ; i < 10 ; i++)
                    {
                    aptl[i].x = cxClient * aptlFigure[i].x / 200 ;
                    aptl[i].y = cyClient * aptlFigure[i].y / 100 ;
                    }

               GpiBeginArea (hps, BA_BOUNDARY | BA_ALTERNATE) ;
               GpiMove (hps, aptl) ;
               GpiPolyLine (hps, 9L, aptl + 1) ;
               GpiEndArea (hps) ;

                         /*-------------------
                           Winding Fill Mode
                           -------------------*/

               for (i = 0 ; i < 10 ; i++)
                    aptl[i].x += cxClient / 2 ;

               GpiBeginArea (hps, BA_BOUNDARY | BA_WINDING) ;
```

Listing 5.8: The ALTWIND program

```
               GpiMove (hps, aptl) ;
               GpiPolyLine (hps, 9L, aptl + 1) ;
               GpiEndArea (hps) ;

               WinEndPaint (hps) ;
               return 0 ;
          }
     return WinDefWindowProc (hwnd, msg, mp1, mp2) ;
     }
```

The ALTWIND.DEF File

```
;-----------------------------------
; ALTWIND.DEF module definition file
;-----------------------------------

NAME           ALTWIND   WINDOWAPI

DESCRIPTION    'Alternate and Winding Modes (c) Charles Petzold, 1993'
PROTMODE
```

If you use *GpiBox* with the DRO_OUTLINE option within an area bracket, you need to know how GPI draws the box in order to anticipate how the intersection of the box and other closed objects will be filled in winding mode. GPI begins drawing the box at the current position. The first line it draws is horizontal, and then the box is continued from there. Thus, if the current position is the lower-left or upper-right corner of the box, the box is drawn counterclockwise.

COLOR AND MIX

All text, lines, and areas we've drawn have appeared on the window in black on a white background. Or maybe not: If you have set different Window Background and Window Text colors using the Presentation Manager Scheme Palette window, GPI uses these colors for the background of the window and the color of text, lines, areas, and other primitives.

The color index You specify a color by calling the *GpiSetColor* function:

```
GpiSetColor (hps, lColorIndex) ;
```

The color is an attribute of the presentation space. The color you set with *GpiSetColor* affects all subsequent GPI primitives until you change the color again or release the presentation space.

Generally, the *lColorIndex* value will be one of the following identifiers:

CLR_BACKGROUND	CLR_DARKGRAY
CLR_BLUE	CLR_DARKBLUE
CLR_RED	CLR_DARKRED
CLR_PINK	CLR_DARKPINK
CLR_GREEN	CLR_DARKGREEN
CLR_CYAN	CLR_DARKCYAN
CLR_YELLOW	CLR_BROWN
CLR_NEUTRAL	CLR_PALEGRAY

Each of these color index identifiers is self-explanatory, with the exception of CLR_BACKGROUND and CLR_NEUTRAL:

CLR_BACKGROUND is the color you set in the Presentation Manager Scheme Palette window as the Window Background color. By default, this is white. The *GpiErase* function erases a window using this CLR_BACKGROUND color. CLR_NEUTRAL is the Window Text color you set in the Scheme Palette window; by default, CLR_NEUTRAL is black. For a new presentation space, all GPI primitives you draw will use the CLR_NEUTRAL color. GPI also recognizes the CLR_DEFAULT identifier, which has the same effect as CLR_NEUTRAL when used with *GpiSetColor.*

In one sense, these interpretations of the CLR_BACKGROUND and the CLR_NEUTRAL identifiers are convenient for the programmer. The user has selected these colors as his or her personal preferences for window background and foreground colors. A Presentation Manager program uses these colors by default. A user's preference, however, can sometimes defeat a feature of a program. For example, if your program uses CLR_RED text for emphasis, the text won't stand out if the user has selected red as the normal window text color.

Therefore, GPI lets you override the user's preferences and explicitly set all colors used by the program. GPI provides two additional color indexes, CLR_BLACK and CLR_WHITE, for specifying black and white.

Another pair of color indexes, CLR_FALSE and CLR_TRUE, is more appropriate for use with bitmaps. On a video display, CLR_FALSE has the same effect as CLR_BLACK, and CLR_TRUE has the same effect as CLR_WHITE; on a printer, this relationship is reversed because video displays are black background devices and printers are white background devices.

You may be familiar with the IRGB (Intensity-Red-Green-Blue) color encoding of the IBM CGA, EGA, and VGA video adapters. The following table shows how IRGB colors correspond to the GPI color indexes.

I R G B	IRGB Color Name	Equivalent Color Index
0 0 0 0	Black	CLR_BLACK
0 0 0 1	Blue	CLR_DARKBLUE
0 0 1 0	Green	CLR_DARKGREEN
0 0 1 1	Cyan	CLR_DARKCYAN
0 1 0 0	Red	CLR_DARKRED
0 1 0 1	Magenta	CLR_DARKPINK
0 1 1 0	Brown	CLR_BROWN
0 1 1 1	Light Gray	CLR_PALEGRAY
1 0 0 0	Dark Gray	CLR_DARKGRAY
1 0 0 1	Light Blue	CLR_BLUE
1 0 1 0	Light Green	CLR_GREEN
1 0 1 1	Light Cyan	CLR_CYAN
1 1 0 0	Light Red	CLR_RED
1 1 0 1	Light Magenta	CLR_PINK
1 1 1 0	Yellow	CLR_YELLOW
1 1 1 1	White	CLR_WHITE

In literature about the IBM video adapters, "magenta" is often used to describe the color known as "pink" in GPI. In technical literature on the CGA, EGA, and VGA boards, colors with the I ("intensity") bit set are traditionally referred to as "light" colors; by contrast, in GPI, most colors without the I bit set are "dark" or "pale" colors.

The COLORS program shown in Listing 5.9 displays the colors available with all 21 CLR identifiers.

This program sets the color by calling *GpiSetColor* and then calls the *GpiBox* function to draw a solid rectangle using that color.

Listing 5.9: The COLORS program

The COLORS.MAK File

```
#----------------------
# COLORS.MAK make file
#----------------------

colors.exe : colors.obj colors.def
     $(PRGLINK) colors, colors, NUL, $(PRGLIB), colors

colors.obj : colors.c
     $(PRGCC) colors.c
```

The COLORS.C File

```
/*---------------------------------------
   COLORS.C -- GPI Foreground Colors
               (c) Charles Petzold, 1993
  ---------------------------------------*/

#define INCL_WIN
#define INCL_GPI
#include <os2.h>
#include <string.h>

MRESULT EXPENTRY ClientWndProc (HWND, ULONG, MPARAM, MPARAM) ;

int main (void)
     {
     static CHAR  szClientClass [] = "Colors" ;
     static ULONG flFrameFlags = FCF_TITLEBAR      | FCF_SYSMENU |
                                 FCF_SIZEBORDER    | FCF_MINMAX  |
                                 FCF_SHELLPOSITION | FCF_TASKLIST ;
     HAB          hab ;
     HMQ          hmq ;
     HWND         hwndFrame, hwndClient ;
     QMSG         qmsg ;

     hab = WinInitialize (0) ;
     hmq = WinCreateMsgQueue (hab, 0) ;

     WinRegisterClass (hab, szClientClass, ClientWndProc, 0L, 0) ;

     hwndFrame = WinCreateStdWindow (HWND_DESKTOP, WS_VISIBLE,
                                     &flFrameFlags, szClientClass, NULL,
                                     0L, 0, 0, &hwndClient) ;

     while (WinGetMsg (hab, &qmsg, NULLHANDLE, 0, 0))
          WinDispatchMsg (hab, &qmsg) ;
```

Listing 5.9: The COLORS program (Continued)

```
     WinDestroyWindow (hwndFrame) ;
     WinDestroyMsgQueue (hmq) ;
     WinTerminate (hab) ;
     return 0 ;
     }

MRESULT EXPENTRY ClientWndProc (HWND hwnd, ULONG msg, MPARAM mp1, MPARAM mp2)
     {
     static struct {
                   LONG  lColorIndex ;
                   PCHAR szColorIndex ;
                   }
                   show [] =
                   {
                   CLR_FALSE      , "CLR_FALSE"      ,
                   CLR_TRUE       , "CLR_TRUE"       ,
                   CLR_DEFAULT    , "CLR_DEFAULT"    ,
                   CLR_WHITE      , "CLR_WHITE"      ,
                   CLR_BLACK      , "CLR_BLACK"      ,
                   CLR_BACKGROUND , "CLR_BACKGROUND" ,
                   CLR_BLUE       , "CLR_BLUE"       ,
                   CLR_RED        , "CLR_RED"        ,
                   CLR_PINK       , "CLR_PINK"       ,
                   CLR_GREEN      , "CLR_GREEN"      ,
                   CLR_CYAN       , "CLR_CYAN"       ,
                   CLR_YELLOW     , "CLR_YELLOW"     ,
                   CLR_NEUTRAL    , "CLR_NEUTRAL"    ,
                   CLR_DARKGRAY   , "CLR_DARKGRAY"   ,
                   CLR_DARKBLUE   , "CLR_DARKBLUE"   ,
                   CLR_DARKRED    , "CLR_DARKRED"    ,
                   CLR_DARKPINK   , "CLR_DARKPINK"   ,
                   CLR_DARKGREEN  , "CLR_DARKGREEN"  ,
                   CLR_DARKCYAN   , "CLR_DARKCYAN"   ,
                   CLR_BROWN      , "CLR_BROWN"      ,
                   CLR_PALEGRAY   , "CLR_PALEGRAY"
                   } ;
     static INT    cyClient, cxCaps, cyChar, cyDesc,
                   iNumColors = sizeof show / sizeof show[0] ;
     FONTMETRICS   fm ;
     HPS           hps ;
     INT           i ;
     POINTL        ptl ;

     switch (msg)
          {
          case WM_CREATE:
               hps = WinGetPS (hwnd) ;
               GpiQueryFontMetrics (hps, sizeof fm, &fm) ;
```

Listing 5.9: The COLORS program (Continued)

```
          cxCaps = (fm.fsType & 1 ? 2 : 3) * fm.lAveCharWidth / 2 ;
          cyChar = fm.lMaxBaselineExt ;
          cyDesc = fm.lMaxDescender ;
          WinReleasePS (hps) ;
          return 0 ;

     case WM_SIZE:
          cyClient = SHORT2FROMMP (mp2) ;
          return 0 ;

     case WM_PAINT:
          hps = WinBeginPaint (hwnd, NULLHANDLE, NULL) ;
          GpiErase (hps) ;

          for (i = 0 ; i < iNumColors ; i ++)
               {
               ptl.x = (i < 11 ? 1 : 33) * cxCaps ;
               ptl.y = cyClient - (i % 11 * 5 + 4) * cyChar / 2 + cyDesc ;

               GpiCharStringAt (hps, &ptl,
                                strlen (show [i].szColorIndex),
                                show [i].szColorIndex) ;

               ptl.x  = (i < 11 ? 20 : 52) * cxCaps ;
               ptl.y -= cyDesc + cyChar / 2 ;
               GpiMove (hps, &ptl) ;

               GpiSavePS (hps) ;
               GpiSetColor (hps, show [i].lColorIndex) ;

               ptl.x += 10 * cxCaps ;
               ptl.y +=  2 * cyChar ;
               GpiBox (hps, DRO_FILL, &ptl, 0L, 0L) ;

               GpiRestorePS (hps, -1L) ;
               }
          WinEndPaint (hps) ;
          return 0 ;
     }
return WinDefWindowProc (hwnd, msg, mp1, mp2) ;
}
```

The COLORS.DEF File

```
;-----------------------------------
; COLORS.DEF module definition file
;-----------------------------------
```

Listing 5.9: The COLORS program (Continued)

```
NAME            COLORS    WINDOWAPI

DESCRIPTION     'GPI Foreground Colors (c) Charles Petzold, 1993'
PROTMODE
```

The *GpiSetColor* function sets the color for all GPI primitives, including text. How does COLORS prevent the text from appearing in color? Very simple: COLORS calls the *GpiSavePS* function before calling *GpiSetColor* and calls *GpiRestorePS* after calling *GpiBox*. The *GpiSavePS* function saves all the attributes of the presentation space and *GpiRestorePS* restores them. If you remove these two functions from COLORS, you'll find that the text displayed by *GpiCharStringAt* will also appear in various colors.

I could have simplified COLORS a little by using the *WinFillRect* function:

```
WinFillRect (hps, &rcl, lColorIndex ) ;
```

The second parameter is a pointer to a RECTL structure. The function fills that rectangle with the specified color. The *WinFillRect* function is useful for coloring the background of a client window without calling *GpiErase*:

```
WinQueryWindowRect (hwnd, &rcl) ;
WinFillRect (hps, &rcl, CLR_CYAN) ;
```

WinFillRect is one of the few drawing functions that begins with a *Win* prefix rather than *Gpi*. (You encountered another of these functions—*WinDrawText*—in Chapter 2.) These are high-level drawing functions that do the work of several GPI functions. They are often convenient but can be used only on a video display. Another useful high-level drawing function is *WinDrawBorder*.

Foreground mix mode The use of color may seem fairly straightforward, but it's not. In general, GPI does not simply draw a color on the display. Instead, GPI performs a bitwise pixel operation between the foreground color of the image you're drawing (the source color) and the color already on the surface of the display (the destination color). This operation is called the *mix mode* or simply the *mix*.

Let's approach this by thinking about a monochrome video display that is capable of two colors: black and white. Each pixel on the display can be represented by either 0 (black) or 1 (white).

You want to draw a pixel on this display. This source pixel can be 0 or 1. The surface of the display where you want to draw this pixel (the destination) can also be either 0 or 1. The resultant color of the drawn pixel is defined by the mix mode.

There are 16 possible mix modes. These are represented by identifiers defined in PMGPI.H that begin with FM ("foreground mix"). The following table uses C notation to show the bitwise combinations of pixels:

Table 5.1: Mix Modes

<table>
<tr><th>Source (SRC):</th><th>0 0 1 1</th><th>Operation</th><th>Mix Mode</th></tr>
<tr><th>Destination (DEST):</th><th>0 1 0 1</th><th></th><th></th></tr>
<tr><td>Result:</td><td>0 0 0 0</td><td>0</td><td>FM_ZERO</td></tr>
<tr><td></td><td>0 0 0 1</td><td>SRC & DEST</td><td>FM_AND</td></tr>
<tr><td></td><td>0 0 1 0</td><td>SRC & ~DEST</td><td>FM_MASKSRCNOT</td></tr>
<tr><td></td><td>0 0 1 1</td><td>SRC</td><td>FM_OVERPAINT</td></tr>
<tr><td></td><td>0 1 0 0</td><td>~SRC & DEST</td><td>FM_SUBTRACT</td></tr>
<tr><td></td><td>0 1 0 1</td><td>DEST</td><td>FM_LEAVEALONE</td></tr>
<tr><td></td><td>0 1 1 0</td><td>SRC ^ DEST</td><td>FM_XOR</td></tr>
<tr><td></td><td>0 1 1 1</td><td>SRC | DEST</td><td>FM_OR</td></tr>
<tr><td></td><td>1 0 0 0</td><td>~(SRC | DEST)</td><td>FM_NOTMERGESRC</td></tr>
<tr><td></td><td>1 0 0 1</td><td>~(SRC ^ DEST)</td><td>FM_NOTXORSRC</td></tr>
<tr><td></td><td>1 0 1 0</td><td>~DEST</td><td>FM_INVERT</td></tr>
<tr><td></td><td>1 0 1 1</td><td>SRC | ~DEST</td><td>FM_MERGESRCNOT</td></tr>
<tr><td></td><td>1 1 0 0</td><td>~SRC</td><td>FM_NOTCOPYSRC</td></tr>
<tr><td></td><td>1 1 0 1</td><td>~SRC | DEST</td><td>FM_MERGENOTSRC</td></tr>
<tr><td></td><td>1 1 1 0</td><td>~(SRC & DEST)</td><td>FM_NOTMASKSRC</td></tr>
<tr><td></td><td>1 1 1 1</td><td>1</td><td>FM_ONE</td></tr>
</table>

You can change the mix mode by calling the following function:

```
GpiSetMix (hps, lMixMode)
```

where *lMixMode* is one of the FM identifiers shown in the table. The default mix mode is FM_OVERPAINT, which transfers the color specified by the *GpiSetColor* to the destination regardless of the color of the destination. This is what we intuitively expect to happen. The PMGPI.H header file also includes the identifier FM_DEFAULT, which has the same effect as FM_OVERPAINT.

If the mix mode is set to FM_XOR, the resulting pixel will be white (1) only if either the source or destination pixel (but not both) was also white. That is, the FM_XOR mix mode causes source pixels of 1 to invert the destination and source pixels of 0 to leave it unchanged.

If you set color to CLR_BLACK and the mix mode to FM_XOR, any lines you draw on a black background will be black, and any lines you draw on a white background will be white. If you set color to CLR_WHITE and the mix mode to FM_XOR, any lines you draw on a black background will be white; any lines you draw on a white background will be black.

With color, the situation gets just a little more complex. Consider the EGA and VGA display adapters in high-resolution graphics mode. These adapters use 4 bits (intensity, red, green, and blue) for each pixel. The mix mode works on each of these bits individually. For example, if a window is colored with CLR_RED, the surface of the window has its intensity and red bits set to 1 and its blue and green bits set to 0. If you set color to CLR_BLUE, the intensity and blue bits are set to 1, and the green and red bits are set to 0. You use the FM_XOR mix mode and display a line. The text is displayed in CLR_DARK-PINK. The resultant red and blue bits are set to 1, and the intensity and green bits are set to 0.

The FM_ZERO mix mode causes the GPI primitive you draw to be displayed in black regardless of the destination color and the color you set with *GpiSetColor.* Similarly, FM_ONE causes a GPI primitive to be displayed in white. The FM_LEAVEALONE mix causes the GPI primitive to be invisible.

The FM_INVERT mix mode causes a GPI primitive to invert the color of the destination regardless of the color you set. For example, text drawn on a CLR_RED destination is displayed as CLR_DARKCYAN. FM_INVERT is useful for drawing and erasing an object. When you draw the same object a second time, the destination reverts to its original color. This technique is used in the WEB program in Chapter 9.

The background color and mix GPI also has two functions for setting the background color and mix:

```
GpiSetBackColor (hps, lColorIndex) ;
```

and

```
GpiSetBackMix (hps, lMixMode) ;
```

Use of the CLR_DEFAULT as a parameter to *GpiSetBackColor* has the same effect as CLR_BACKGROUND. For the *lMixMode* parameter to *GpiSetBackMix*, you use identifiers beginning with BM ("background mix") rather than FM, but they are equivalent to the FM identifiers. However, not all mix modes are supported for background mixing. The supported background mixes are shown in the following table:

Source (SRC):	0 0 1 1	Operation	Mix Mode
Destination (DEST):	0 1 0 1		
Result:	0 0 1 1	SRC	BM_OVERPAINT
	0 1 0 1	DEST	BM_LEAVEALONE
	0 1 1 0	SRC ^ DEST	BM_XOR
	0 1 1 1	SRC | DEST	BM_OR

The default background mix is BM_LEAVEALONE. (BM_DEFAULT provides the same result.) If you want to use a background color, you'll have to change the background mix to something other than BM_LEAVEALONE. Otherwise, GPI will ignore the background color.

The background color and mix don't affect lines, but do affect patterns. You'll note that many of the patterns are composed of lines or dots. These lines and dots are drawn on the display using the foreground color and foreground mix mode. The area between the lines and dots is drawn on the display using the background color and background mix mode.

For example, suppose you make the following series of function calls:

```
GpiSetColor (hps, CLR_BLUE) ;
GpiSetMix (hps, FM_OVERPAINT) ;
GpiSetBackColor (hps, CLR_RED) ;
GpiSetBackMix (hps, BM_OVERPAINT) ;
GpiSetPattern (hps, PATSYM_VERT) ;
```

When you call *GpiBox* with an option of DRO_FILL or DRO_OUTLINEFILL, the pattern will have blue vertical lines on a red background, regardless of the original color of the display.

GPI PRIMITIVE 3: TEXT

Text is the most common GPI primitive yet potentially the most complex because of the use of various fonts. GPI allows you to enumerate all the fonts available on the system and choose different fonts for the display of text. Many of these fonts (such as the default system font) contain characters of varying widths. In addition, you can alter the default spacing of characters to achieve such effects as justified text.

THE TEXT OUTPUT FUNCTIONS

GPI has four text output functions:

- *GpiCharStringAt*
- *GpiCharString*
- *GpiCharStringPos*
- *GpiCharStringPosAt*

The GpiCharStringAt and GpiCharString functions Perhaps the most common text output function is the function introduced in Chapter 4:

```
GpiCharStringAt (hps, &ptl, lLength, &cString) ;
```

The last parameter is a character array or a pointer to a character string. The *lLength* parameter is the length of this string. The POINTL structure indicates the starting position of the text. This is usually the baseline of the left side of the first character. (We'll look at an exception to this rule shortly.)

You can also use the *GpiCharString* function to display text:

```
GpiCharString (hps, lLength, &cString) ;
```

It is the same as *GpiCharStringAt*, except that the text begins at the current position. The *GpiCharStringAt* function is equivalent to

```
GpiMove (hps, &ptl) ;
GpiCharString (hps, lLength, &cString) ;
```

Following the *GpiCharString* and *GpiCharStringAt* calls, the current position is usually set to the baseline of the right side of the last character. (Again, there are exceptions.) Therefore, you can call *GpiCharString* again to continue a line of text.

The GpiCharStringPos and GpiCharStringPosAt functions Two other text output functions have some additional parameters:

```
GpiCharStringPos (hps, &rcl, lOptions, lLength, &cString, alIncrement) ;
GpiCharStringPosAt (hps, &ptl, &rcl, lOptions, lLength, &cString, alIncrement) ;
```

The *GpiCharStringPos* function begins the text at the current position; the *GpiCharStringPosAt* function begins the string at the POINTL structure passed as the second parameter. Information in the following discussion of *GpiCharStringPos* also applies to *GpiCharStringPosAt*.

The simplest form of *GpiCharStringPos* results from setting the *&rcl* and *alIncrement* parameters to NULL and the *lOptions* parameter to 0:

```
GpiCharStringPos (hps, NULL, 0L, lLength, &cString, NULL) ;
```

In this form, the function is equivalent to *GpiCharString*. Nonzero *lOption* values cause some different results.

You can set the *lOption* parameter to CHS_LEAVEPOS:

```
GpiCharStringPos (hps, NULL, CHS_LEAVEPOS, lLength, &cString, NULL) ;
```

On return from the function, the current position will be set at the beginning of the string rather than the end. That is, the *GpiCharStringPos* function leaves the current position unchanged, but *GpiCharStringPosAt* sets the current position to the POINTL structure passed to the function.

If you include the *&rcl* parameter (a pointer to a RECTL structure), you can use the CHS_CLIP option:

```
GpiCharStringPos (hps, &rcl, CHS_CLIP, lLength, &cString, NULL) ;
```

In this case the character string will be clipped to the interior of the rectangle. Any part of the text string falling outside the rectangle will not be displayed. The *&rcl* parameter is also required for the CHS_OPAQUE option, as follows:

```
GpiCharStringPos (hps, &rcl, CHS_OPAQUE, lLength, &cString, NULL) ;
```

In this case the rectangle is colored with the current background color before the text is displayed. GPI temporarily sets the background mix to BM_OVERPAINT before coloring the rectangle.

The fourth and final option is CHS_VECTOR. This function requires that the last parameter be an array of LONG integers:

```
GpiCharStringPos (hps, NULL, CHS_VECTOR, lLength, &cString, alIncrement) ;
```

The *alIncrement* array contains *lLength* LONG values. GPI uses this array to position the successive characters in the string, thereby overriding the default spacing. The CHS_VECTOR option is the reason for the *Pos* ("position") in the function names *GpiCharStringPos* and *GpiCharStringPosAt*.

You can use any combination of the CHS_OPAQUE, CHS_VECTOR, CHS_LEAVEPOS, and CHS_CLIP identifiers by combining them with the C bitwise OR operator. The RECTL structure passed as the second parameter is required only for CHS_OPAQUE or CHS_CLIP. The array of LONG increment values passed as the last parameter is required only when you use CHS_VECTOR.

TEXT COLOR

The color and mix mode affect the display of characters in the text string. We've already seen how the CHS_OPAQUE option in *GpiCharStringPos* and *GpiCharStringPosAt* functions can cause GPI to use the background color to color a rectangle before displaying the text.

You can also use the background color and background mix with other forms of the text output functions. If you set the background mix to something other than BM_LEAVEALONE, the background color is used to color the small rectangular character cells that surround each character. You might want to do this if you are displaying text over some existing graphics and want the text to be more distinct. (However, this only works with raster fonts and not with outline fonts. I'll explain the distinction in a moment.)

FONT FILES

The subject of fonts can be quite complex, yet we must attack it. As you discovered in Chapter 4, the default system font is proportionally spaced. Although we have been successful in working with this font, it is not appropriate for all applications. For example, a programmer's text editor or a communications program should probably use a fixed-pitch font, in which every character has the same width. We at least want to be able to switch to a fixed-pitch font. The ability to use boldface and italic versions of fonts would be nice also.

GPI supports fonts in two very different formats: "Raster" or "bitmap" fonts are stored as small bitmaps with 0 bits for the background of the character and 1 bits for the character itself. "Outline" or "vector" fonts are stored as a series of straight lines and curves.

In this chapter, I'll restrict the discussion to raster fonts; I'll discuss the use of outline fonts in Chapter 7.

The OS/2 Presentation Manager includes three files that contain collections of raster fonts in various point sizes for various output devices. These files, and the raster fonts they contain, are shown in the following table:

Font File	Font Face Name	Point Sizes
COURIER.FON	Courier	8, 10, 12
HELV.FON	Helv	8, 10, 12, 14, 18, 24
TIMES.FON	Tms Rmn	8, 10, 12, 14, 18, 24

The default system font is stored in DISPLAY.DLL, the dynamic link library for the video display. It has a font face name of System Proportional and a point size of 10. A System Monospaced font (also 10 points in size) is stored in the SYSMONO.FON file.

Each font is identified by a face name and a point size. The Courier font is a fixed-pitch font similar to that produced by a typewriter. The Helv (Helvetica) and Tms Rmn (Times Roman) fonts are both proportional fonts. Helv is a sans serif font, which means that it does not have small lines finishing off the strokes of the characters. Tms Rmn has serifs and is commonly used for text in magazines and books.

The point size refers to the height of the characters. (However, point size is a typographical concept rather than a metrical concept. The maximum height of the characters may be less than or greater than the point size.) One point is 1/72 inch. However, if you set page units to Low English, High English, or Twips, the point size of the fonts will not necessarily agree with the GPI page units. For example, a 24-point font will not be 480 twips high. The size of the raster fonts is based on an ideal "font resolution" for the device. You can obtain this font resolution from *DevQueryCaps* using the CAPS_HORIZONTAL_FONT_RES and CAPS_VERTICAL_FONT_RES identifiers. As you can see from Figure 5.4, these values for the VGA are set to 96 pixels per inch. This is greater than the actual resolution of the device, to allow fonts as small as 8 points to be legible on the screen.

The EASYFONT system Working with fonts can be difficult, but I've attempted to make it a little easier for you. Listing 5.10 shows two files named EASYFONT.H and EASYFONT.C that can greatly assist you in working with raster fonts in your Presentation Manager programs.

Listing 5.10: The EASYFONT files

The EASYFONT.H File

```
/*-------------------------------------
   EASYFONT.H header file for EASYFONT.C
  -------------------------------------*/

BOOL EzfQueryFonts    (HPS hps) ;
LONG EzfCreateLogFont (HPS hps, LONG lcid, INT idFace, INT idSize,
                                           USHORT fsSelection) ;

#define FONTFACE_SYSTEM  0
#define FONTFACE_MONO    1
#define FONTFACE_COUR    2
```

Listing 5.10: The EASYFONT files

```
#define FONTFACE_HELV    3
#define FONTFACE_TIMES   4

#define FONTSIZE_8       0
#define FONTSIZE_10      1
#define FONTSIZE_12      2
#define FONTSIZE_14      3
#define FONTSIZE_18      4
#define FONTSIZE_24      5
```

The EASYFONT.C File

```
/*---------------------------------------------------
   EASYFONT.C -- Routines for Using Image Fonts
                 (c) Charles Petzold, 1993
  ---------------------------------------------------*/

#define INCL_GPI
#include <os2.h>
#include <stdlib.h>
#include <string.h>
#include "easyfont.h"

static LONG  alMatch[5][6] ;
static PCHAR szFacename[5] = { "System Proportional",
                               "System Monospaced",
                               "Courier", "Helv", "Tms Rmn" } ;
static INT   iFontSize [6] = { 80, 100, 120, 140, 180, 240 } ;

BOOL EzfQueryFonts (HPS hps)
     {
     PFONTMETRICS pfm ;
     HDC          hdc ;
     INT          iIndex, iFace, iSize ;
     LONG         lHorzRes, lVertRes, lRequestFonts, lNumberFonts ;

     hdc = GpiQueryDevice (hps) ;
     DevQueryCaps (hdc, CAPS_HORIZONTAL_FONT_RES, 1L, &lHorzRes) ;
     DevQueryCaps (hdc, CAPS_VERTICAL_FONT_RES,   1L, &lVertRes) ;

     for (iFace = 0 ; iFace < 5 ; iFace++)
          {
          lRequestFonts = 0 ;
          lNumberFonts = GpiQueryFonts (hps, QF_PUBLIC, szFacename[iFace],
                                        &lRequestFonts, 0L, NULL) ;
          if (lNumberFonts == 0)
               continue ;

          pfm = malloc (lNumberFonts * sizeof (FONTMETRICS)) ;
```

Listing 5.10: The EASYFONT files

```
          if (pfm == NULL)
               return FALSE ;

          GpiQueryFonts (hps, QF_PUBLIC, szFacename[iFace],
                         &lNumberFonts, sizeof (FONTMETRICS), pfm) ;

          for (iIndex = 0 ; iIndex < lNumberFonts ; iIndex++)
               if (pfm[iIndex].sXDeviceRes == (SHORT) lHorzRes &&
                   pfm[iIndex].sYDeviceRes == (SHORT) lVertRes &&
                  (pfm[iIndex].fsDefn & 1) == 0)
                    {
                    for (iSize = 0 ; iSize < 6 ; iSize++)
                         if (pfm[iIndex].sNominalPointSize == iFontSize[iSize])
                              break ;

                    if (iSize != 6)
                         alMatch[iFace][iSize] = pfm[iIndex].lMatch ;
                    }

          free (pfm) ;
          }
     return TRUE ;
     }

LONG EzfCreateLogFont (HPS hps, LONG lcid, INT idFace, INT idSize,
                                           USHORT fsSelection)
     {
     static FATTRS fat ;

     if (idFace > 4 || idSize > 5 || alMatch[idFace][idSize] == 0)
          return FALSE ;

     fat.usRecordLength = sizeof fat ;
     fat.fsSelection    = fsSelection ;
     fat.lMatch         = alMatch[idFace][idSize] ;

     strcpy (fat.szFacename, szFacename[idFace]) ;

     return GpiCreateLogFont (hps, NULL, lcid, &fat) ;
     }
```

EASYFONT.H contains declarations of the two functions in EASYFONT.C. These are *EzfQueryFonts* and *EzfCreateLogFont* ("create logical font"). In addition, EASYFONT.H contains a collection of identifiers you use as parameters to *EzfCreateLogFont.*

To use EASYFONT, include the EASYFONT.H header file in your .C source code file:

```
#include <easyfont.h>
```

Then compile and link EASYFONT.C with your program.

In a window procedure that uses fonts, obtain a handle to a presentation space during the WM_CREATE message and call *EzfQueryFonts*:

```
hps = WinGetPS (hwnd) ;
EzfQueryFonts (hps) ;
WinReleasePS (hps) ;
```

This performs all necessary initialization. Later on, whenever you need to use a nondefault font, obtain a handle to a presentation space and call *EzfCreateLogFont*:

```
EzfCreateLogFont (hps, lcid, idFace, idSize, fsSelection) ;
```

The *lcid* parameter is a "local ID." It can be any number between 1 and 254. The *idFace* parameter can be any of the FONTFACE identifiers defined in EASYFONT.H. The *idSize* parameter is one of the FONTSIZE identifiers also defined in EASYFONT.H.

Not all sizes are available for all font face names. In particular, the FONTFACE_SYSTEM and FONTFACE_MONO identifier can only be used with FONTSIZE_10. The FONTFACE_COUR identifier can only be used with FONTSIZE_8, FONTSIZE_10, and FONTSIZE_12. *EzfCreateLogFont* returns TRUE if the font exists and FALSE otherwise. You should check the return value before attempting to use the logical font you asked for.

The *fsSelection* parameter can be any one of the following identifiers defined in OS2DEF.H:

Identifier	Meaning
FATTR_SEL_ITALIC	Italic font
FATTR_SEL_UNDERSCORE	Underlined font
FATTR_SEL_STRIKEOUT	Line drawn through characters
FATTR_SEL_BOLD	Boldface font

Use 0 if you want a normal font without any attributes.

EzfCreateLogFont creates a logical font associated with a local ID. To use this font, you pass the local ID to *GpiSetCharSet*:

```
GpiSetCharSet (hps, lcid) ;
```

After this call, you can use *GpiQueryFontMetrics* to get the dimensions of the new font. Any text you draw will be displayed with the new font. Before releasing the presentation space, go back to the default font:

```
GpiSetCharSet (hps, LCID_DEFAULT) ;
```

Then delete the local ID you used:

```
GpiDeleteSetId (hps, lcid) ;
```

You can call *EzfCreateLogFont* multiple times to create different logical fonts, each associated with a unique local ID. You then use *GpiSetCharSet* to use any one of these fonts for text output. Be sure to set the default font and delete all local IDs before releasing the presentation space.

The *EzfQueryFonts* function in EASYFONT.C first obtains the horizontal and vertical font resolution of the output device from *DevQueryCaps*. This is necessary because the font files may contain raster fonts for various output devices. For each of the five font faces, the function calls *GpiQueryFonts* to determine how many fonts are present and then allocates memory to store that number of FONTMETRICS structures. *GpiQueryFonts* is called again to obtain the FONTMETRICS structures for all the available fonts. Each font is checked against the device resolution and the desired point sizes. The function saves a field of the FONTMETRICS structure named *lMatch* in a static array. This value is used in the *GpiCreateLogFont* call in *EzfCreateLogFont*.

Listing 5.11 shows a program called FONTS, which uses EASYFONT to display all of the bitmap fonts available for use.

Listing 5.11: The FONTS program

The FONTS.MAK File

```
#---------------------
# FONTS.MAK make file
#---------------------

fonts.exe : fonts.obj easyfont.obj fonts.def
     $(PRGLINK) fonts easyfont, fonts, NUL, $(PRGLIB), fonts

fonts.obj : fonts.c easyfont.h
     $(PRGCC) fonts.c

easyfont.obj : easyfont.c
     $(PRGCC) easyfont.c
```

Listing 5.11: The FONTS program (Continued)

The FONTS.C File

```
/*-------------------------------------
   FONTS.C -- GPI Image Fonts
              (c) Charles Petzold, 1993
  -------------------------------------*/

#define INCL_WIN
#define INCL_GPI
#include <os2.h>
#include <stdio.h>
#include <stdlib.h>
#include "easyfont.h"

#define LCID_MYFONT 1L

MRESULT EXPENTRY ClientWndProc (HWND, ULONG, MPARAM, MPARAM) ;

int main (void)
     {
     static CHAR  szClientClass [] = "Fonts" ;
     static ULONG flFrameFlags = FCF_TITLEBAR      | FCF_SYSMENU  |
                                 FCF_SIZEBORDER    | FCF_MINMAX   |
                                 FCF_SHELLPOSITION | FCF_TASKLIST |
                                 FCF_VERTSCROLL    | FCF_HORZSCROLL ;
     HAB          hab ;
     HMQ          hmq ;
     HWND         hwndFrame, hwndClient ;
     QMSG         qmsg ;

     hab = WinInitialize (0) ;
     hmq = WinCreateMsgQueue (hab, 0) ;

     WinRegisterClass (hab, szClientClass, ClientWndProc, CS_SIZEREDRAW, 0) ;

     hwndFrame = WinCreateStdWindow (HWND_DESKTOP, WS_VISIBLE,
                                     &flFrameFlags, szClientClass, NULL,
                                     0L, 0, 0, &hwndClient) ;

     while (WinGetMsg (hab, &qmsg, NULLHANDLE, 0, 0))
          WinDispatchMsg (hab, &qmsg) ;

     WinDestroyWindow (hwndFrame) ;
     WinDestroyMsgQueue (hmq) ;
     WinTerminate (hab) ;
     return 0 ;
     }
```

Listing 5.11: The FONTS program (Continued)

```
MRESULT EXPENTRY ClientWndProc (HWND hwnd, ULONG msg, MPARAM mp1, MPARAM mp2)
     {
     static CHAR *szFace[] = { "System", "Monospaced", "Courier",
                               "Helv",   "Tms Rmn" } ;
     static CHAR *szSize[] = { "8", "10", "12", "14", "18", "24" } ;
     static CHAR *szSel[]  = { "Normal",  "Italic",  "Underscore",
                               "Strike-out", "Bold" } ;
     static CHAR szBuffer[80] ;
     static HWND hwndVscroll, hwndHscroll ;
     static INT  idFace[] = { FONTFACE_SYSTEM, FONTFACE_MONO,
                              FONTFACE_COUR,   FONTFACE_HELV,
                              FONTFACE_TIMES } ;
     static INT  idSize[] = { FONTSIZE_8,  FONTSIZE_10, FONTSIZE_12,
                              FONTSIZE_14, FONTSIZE_18, FONTSIZE_24 } ;
     static INT  afiSel[] = { 0, FATTR_SEL_ITALIC,    FATTR_SEL_UNDERSCORE,
                                 FATTR_SEL_STRIKEOUT, FATTR_SEL_BOLD } ;
     static INT  iVscrollMax = sizeof idFace / sizeof idFace[0] - 1,
                 iHscrollMax = sizeof afiSel / sizeof afiSel[0] - 1,
                 cyClient, iHscrollPos, iVscrollPos ;
     FONTMETRICS fm ;
     HPS         hps;
     HWND        hwndFrame ;
     INT         iSize ;
     POINTL      ptl ;

     switch (msg)
          {
          case WM_CREATE:
               hps = WinGetPS (hwnd) ;
               EzfQueryFonts (hps) ;
               WinReleasePS (hps) ;

               hwndFrame   = WinQueryWindow (hwnd, QW_PARENT) ;
               hwndVscroll = WinWindowFromID (hwndFrame, FID_VERTSCROLL) ;
               hwndHscroll = WinWindowFromID (hwndFrame, FID_HORZSCROLL) ;

               WinSendMsg (hwndVscroll, SBM_SETSCROLLBAR,
                           MPFROM2SHORT (iVscrollPos, 0),
                           MPFROM2SHORT (0, iVscrollMax)) ;

               WinSendMsg (hwndHscroll, SBM_SETSCROLLBAR,
                           MPFROM2SHORT (iHscrollPos, 0),
                           MPFROM2SHORT (0, iHscrollMax)) ;
               return 0 ;

          case WM_SIZE:
               cyClient = SHORT2FROMMP (mp2) ;
               return 0 ;
```

Listing 5.11: The FONTS program (Continued)

```
          case WM_VSCROLL:
               switch (SHORT2FROMMP (mp2))
                    {
                    case SB_LINEUP:
                    case SB_PAGEUP:
                         iVscrollPos = max (Ø, iVscrollPos - 1) ;
                         break ;

                    case SB_LINEDOWN:
                    case SB_PAGEDOWN:
                         iVscrollPos = min (iVscrollMax, iVscrollPos + 1) ;
                         break ;

                    case SB_SLIDERPOSITION:
                         iVscrollPos = SHORT1FROMMP (mp2) ;
                         break ;

                    default:
                         return Ø ;
                    }
               WinSendMsg (hwndVscroll, SBM_SETPOS,
                           MPFROM2SHORT (iVscrollPos, Ø), NULL) ;

               WinInvalidateRect (hwnd, NULL, FALSE) ;
               return Ø ;

          case WM_HSCROLL:
               switch (SHORT2FROMMP (mp2))
                    {
                    case SB_LINELEFT:
                    case SB_PAGELEFT:
                         iHscrollPos = max (Ø, iHscrollPos - 1) ;
                         break ;

                    case SB_LINERIGHT:
                    case SB_PAGERIGHT:
                         iHscrollPos = min (iHscrollMax, iHscrollPos + 1) ;
                         break ;

                    case SB_SLIDERPOSITION:
                         iHscrollPos = SHORT1FROMMP (mp2) ;
                         break ;

                    default:
                         return Ø ;
                    }
               WinSendMsg (hwndHscroll, SBM_SETPOS,
                           MPFROM2SHORT (iHscrollPos, Ø), NULL) ;
```

Listing 5.11: The FONTS program (Continued)

```
          WinInvalidateRect (hwnd, NULL, FALSE) ;
          return 0 ;

     case WM_CHAR:
          switch (CHARMSG(&msg)->vkey)
               {
               case VK_LEFT:
               case VK_RIGHT:
                    return WinSendMsg (hwndHscroll, msg, mp1, mp2) ;
               case VK_UP:
               case VK_DOWN:
               case VK_PAGEUP:
               case VK_PAGEDOWN:
                    return WinSendMsg (hwndVscroll, msg, mp1, mp2) ;
               }
          break ;

     case WM_PAINT:
          hps = WinBeginPaint (hwnd, NULLHANDLE, NULL) ;
          GpiErase (hps) ;

          ptl.x = 0 ;
          ptl.y = cyClient ;

          for (iSize = 0 ; iSize < 6 ; iSize++)
               if (EzfCreateLogFont (hps, LCID_MYFONT,
                                     idFace [iVscrollPos],
                                     idSize [iSize],
                                     afiSel [iHscrollPos]))
                    {
                    GpiSetCharSet (hps, LCID_MYFONT) ;
                    GpiQueryFontMetrics (hps, sizeof fm, &fm) ;

                    ptl.y -= fm.lMaxBaselineExt ;

                    GpiCharStringAt (hps, &ptl,
                         sprintf (szBuffer, "%s, %s point, %s",
                                  szFace [iVscrollPos],
                                  szSize [iSize],
                                  szSel  [iHscrollPos]),
                         szBuffer) ;

                    GpiSetCharSet (hps, LCID_DEFAULT) ;
                    GpiDeleteSetId (hps, LCID_MYFONT) ;
                    }

          WinEndPaint (hps) ;
          return 0 ;
     }
```

Listing 5.11: The FONTS program (Continued)

```
     return WinDefWindowProc (hwnd, msg, mp1, mp2) ;
     }
```

The FONTS.DEF File

```
;-----------------------------------
; FONTS.DEF module definition file
;-----------------------------------

NAME           FONTS     WINDOWAPI

DESCRIPTION    'Displays GPI Image Fonts (c) Charles Petzold, 1993'
PROTMODE
```

Several programs in upcoming chapters (KEYLOOK and TYPEAWAY in Chapter 8 and HEAD in Chapter 14) use EASYFONT to obtain the system monospaced font for text output.

You'll notice that the FONTS make file also compiles EASYFONT.C and links EASYFONT.OBJ with the program. FONTS.C includes EASYFONT.H for the function declarations and definitions of the FONTFACE and FONTSIZE identifiers.

Each screen in FONTS shows all the available font sizes for a particular face name and *fsSelection* attribute (such as italics). You change the *fsSelection* attribute using the horizontal scroll bar and the face name using the vertical scroll bar. The Tms Rmn italic fonts are shown in Figure 5.10.

GPI PRIMITIVE 4: MARKER SYMBOLS

Markers are small symbols about the same size as a system font character. (To determine the size of a marker, call *DevQueryCaps* with the CAPS_MARKER_WIDTH and CAPS_MARKER_HEIGHT identifiers.) You can use markers as bullets or data points on a line graph.

DRAWING A MARKER

You can draw a marker by calling the following function:

```
GpiMarker (hps, &ptl) ;
```

GPI draws the marker with its center at the point specified in the POINTL structure. The current position is also set to that point.

You can also draw a series of markers:

```
GpiPolyMarker (hps, lNumber, aptl) ;
```

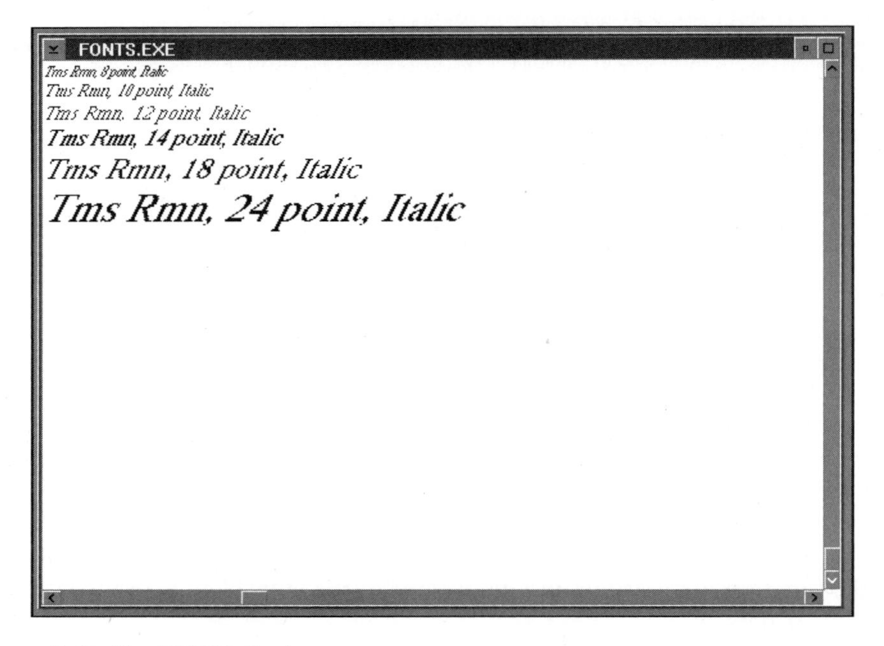

Figure 5.10: The FONTS display

The *aptl* parameter is an array of *lNumber* POINTL structures. Like *GpiPolyLine*, *GpiPolyMarker* is more efficient than multiple *GpiMarker* calls because the repetition occurs within the device driver. The current position is set to the last point.

If you use markers to indicate data points on a line graph, you can use the same array of POINTL structures for drawing the line and drawing the markers. For example, suppose *aptl* contains *iNum* data points for the graph. This code will draw the line and the markers:

```
GpiMove (hps, aptl) ;
GpiPolyLine (hps, iNum - 1L, aptl + 1) ;
GpiPolyMarker (hps, iNum, aptl) ;
```

SELECTING A DIFFERENT MARKER SYMBOL

The default marker has the appearance of a small "x" and has the name MARKSYM_CROSS. You can use the *GpiSetMarker* function to select a different marker:

```
GpiSetMarker (hps, lSymbol) ;
```

The *lSymbol* parameter can be any of the following identifiers:

MARKSYM_DEFAULT	MARKSYM_EIGHTPOINTSTAR
MARKSYM_CROSS	MARKSYM_SOLIDDIAMOND
MARKSYM_PLUS	MARKSYM_SOLIDSQUARE
MARKSYM_DIAMOND	MARKSYM_DOT
MARKSYM_SQUARE	MARKSYM_SMALLCIRCLE
MARKSYM_SIXPOINTSTAR	MARKSYM_BLANK

The MARKSYM_DEFAULT identifier has the same effect as MARKSYM_CROSS.

The marker is drawn using the current color and mix. The background of the rectangle that encompasses the marker is drawn using the current background color and background mix.

GPI PRIMITIVE 5: IMAGES

I began this chapter by noting that GPI is fundamentally a vector graphics system. But this final GPI primitive looks like it belongs more to the realm of raster graphics. An *image* is a collection of bytes whose bits define a little picture. Each bit corresponds to a display pixel.

You display an image by calling

```
GpiImage (hps, 0L, &sizl, lLength, abData) ;
```

The last parameter is an array of bytes that is *lLength* bytes long. This is the image data. The third parameter is a pointer to a SIZEL structure. The SIZEL structure is similar to the POINTL structure except that the fields are named *cx* and *cy*. This structure defines the width and height of the image in pixels.

The data in *abData* is organized with the top row of bits first. The first byte contains the 8 leftmost bits of this row. The most significant bit of the first byte is the leftmost pixel. Each row of bits must begin with a new byte; if the width of the image is not a multiple of 8, the last few bits of the last byte of each row are not used. Thus you can calculate *lLength* using the following formula:

```
lLength = (sizl.cx + 7) / 8 *  sizl.cy ;
```

The leftmost pixel of the top row is displayed at the current position. *GpiImage* does not change the current position. The 1 bits are displayed with the current foreground color and mix, and the 0 bits are displayed with the current background color and mix.

The IMAGECAT program shown in Listing 5.12 uses the *GpiImage* function to draw a little cat in the center of the client window.

Listing 5.12: The IMAGECAT program

The IMAGECAT.MAK File

```
#-------------------------
# IMAGECAT.MAK make file
#-------------------------

imagecat.exe : imagecat.obj imagecat.def
     $(PRGLINK) imagecat, imagecat, NUL, $(PRGLIB), imagecat

imagecat.obj : imagecat.c
     $(PRGCC) imagecat.c
```

The IMAGECAT.C File

```
/*----------------------------------------
   IMAGECAT.C -- Cat drawn using GpiImage
                 (c) Charles Petzold, 1993
  ----------------------------------------*/

#define INCL_WIN
#define INCL_GPI
#include <os2.h>
#include <stdlib.h>

MRESULT EXPENTRY ClientWndProc (HWND, ULONG, MPARAM, MPARAM) ;

int main (void)
     {
     static CHAR  szClientClass [] = "ImageCat" ;
     static ULONG flFrameFlags = FCF_TITLEBAR      | FCF_SYSMENU |
                                 FCF_SIZEBORDER    | FCF_MINMAX  |
                                 FCF_SHELLPOSITION | FCF_TASKLIST ;
     HAB          hab ;
     HMQ          hmq ;
     HWND         hwndFrame, hwndClient ;
     QMSG         qmsg ;

     hab = WinInitialize (0) ;
     hmq = WinCreateMsgQueue (hab, 0) ;

     WinRegisterClass (hab, szClientClass, ClientWndProc, CS_SIZEREDRAW, 0) ;

     hwndFrame = WinCreateStdWindow (HWND_DESKTOP, WS_VISIBLE,
                                     &flFrameFlags, szClientClass, NULL,
                                     0L, 0, 0, &hwndClient) ;
```

Listing 5.12: The IMAGECAT program (Continued)

```
     while (WinGetMsg (hab, &qmsg, NULLHANDLE, 0, 0))
          WinDispatchMsg (hab, &qmsg) ;

     WinDestroyWindow (hwndFrame) ;
     WinDestroyMsgQueue (hmq) ;
     WinTerminate (hab) ;
     return 0 ;
     }

MRESULT EXPENTRY ClientWndProc (HWND hwnd, ULONG msg, MPARAM mp1, MPARAM mp2)
     {
     static BYTE abCat [] = {
                              0x01, 0xF8, 0x1F, 0x80, 0x01, 0x04, 0x20, 0x80
                              0x00, 0x8F, 0xF1, 0x00, 0x00, 0x48, 0x12, 0
                              0x00, 0x28, 0x14, 0x00, 0x00, 0x1A, 0x58, 0
                              0x00, 0x08, 0x10, 0x00, 0x00, 0xFC, 0x3
                              0x00, 0x09, 0x90, 0x00, 0x00, 0xFC, 0x3
                              0x00, 0x08, 0x10, 0x00, 0x00, 0x07, 0
                              0x00, 0x08, 0x10, 0x00, 0x00, 0x08, 0
                              0x00, 0x08, 0x10, 0x20, 0x00, 0x10, 0x0
                              0x00, 0x10, 0x08, 0x08, 0x00, 0x10, 0x0
                              0x00, 0x20, 0x04, 0x04, 0x00, 0x20, 0x0
                              0x00, 0x20, 0x04, 0x04, 0x00, 0x40, 0x0
                              0x00, 0x40, 0x02, 0x04, 0x00, 0x40, 0x0
                              0x00, 0xC0, 0x03, 0x04, 0x00, 0x9C, 0x39, 0
                              0x00, 0xA2, 0x45, 0x08, 0x00, 0xA2, 0x45, 0x10
                              0x00, 0xA2, 0x45, 0xE0, 0x00, 0xA2, 0x45, 0x0
                              0x00, 0xA2, 0x45, 0x00, 0x00, 0xFF, 0xFF, 0
     static INT  cxClient, cyClient ;
     HPS         hps ;
     POINTL      ptl ;
     SIZEL       sizl ;

     switch (msg)
          {
          case WM_SIZE:
               cxClient = SHORT1FROMMP (mp2) ;
               cyClient = SHORT2FROMMP (mp2) ;
               return 0 ;

          case WM_PAINT:
               hps = WinBeginPaint (hwnd, NULLHANDLE, NULL) ;
               GpiErase (hps) ;

               ptl.x = cxClient / 2 - 16 ;
               ptl.y = cyClient / 2 + 16 ;
               GpiMove (hps, &ptl) ;
```

Listing 5.12: The IMAGECAT program (Continued)

```
               sizl.cx = 32 ;
               sizl.cy = 32 ;
               GpiImage (hps, ØL, &sizl, sizeof abCat, abCat) ;

               WinEndPaint (hps) ;
               return Ø ;
          }
     return WinDefWindowProc (hwnd, msg, mp1, mp2) ;
     }
```

The IMAGECAT.DEF File

```
;-----------------------------------
; IMAGECAT.DEF module definition file
;-----------------------------------

NAME           IMAGECAT  WINDOWAPI

DESCRIPTION    'Cat Drawn Using GpiImage (c) Charles Petzold, 1993'
PROTMODE
```

The cat is 32 pixels high and 32 pixels wide. It will look a little different on various output devices. Figure 5.11 shows what it looks like on a VGA.

Figure 5.11: The IMAGECAT display

The *GpiImage* function is easy to use but extremely limited. For example, the function cannot alter the size of the displayed image to accommodate various output devices. If *GpiImage* were the only way to display bitmapped data in GPI, it would be important despite its limitations.

Fortunately, GpiImage pales in comparison to the *WinDrawBitMap* and *GpiBitBlt* functions, which are the subject of the next chapter. Among other things, we'll use these functions to stretch that little cat to fill the entire client window.

Bitmaps and Bitblts

THE BIT-BLOCK TRANSFER

BITMAP HANDLES AND BITMAP DRAWING

WORKING WITH BITMAPS

Chapter 6

GPI is fundamentally a vector graphics drawing system and can display graphics on both vector and raster output devices. For output to a vector device, the GPI drawing commands are translated into commands that the output device understands. For output to a raster device, which displays an image composed of color dots called *pixels* or *pels*, the device driver must translate the GPI drawing commands into displayable pixels. If GPI were based on a raster model, output to a vector device would be nearly impossible.

But GPI is not limited to vector graphics. A Presentation Manager program can also draw pixels on a raster output device. Of course, drawing pixels one at a time can be very slow: The IBM Video Graphics Array (VGA) adapter running in its 640-by-480 graphics mode displays 307,200 pixels on the screen. A laser printer with 300-dots-per-inch resolution requires about 8 million pixels to define an 8½-by-11-inch page.

Instead, a Presentation Manager program that draws pixels usually works with bitmaps. A *bitmap* is an array of data organized into rows and columns in which the bits correspond to pixels on the raster output device.

A bitmap can represent either a monochrome or a color image:

- In a monochrome bitmap, each bit corresponds to one pixel. When a monochrome bitmap is displayed, a 0 bit usually corresponds to the background color and a 1 bit is the foreground color.
- In a color bitmap, each pixel requires multiple bits to represent color.

This chapter is generally restricted to monochrome bitmaps but will touch on color when necessary.

Bitmaps are most suitable for small objects that must be frequently redrawn. For example, the mouse pointer you see on the Presentation Manager screen is stored as two bitmaps. Each time you move the mouse, the Presentation Manager must redraw the two bitmaps on the display.

Bitmaps are highly device dependent. Because a bitmap represents an object as a series of pixels, it is usually designed for a particular device. A bitmap designed for the 640-by-350 resolution of the IBM Enhanced Graphics Adapter (EGA) will be distorted when displayed on a VGA. (You can compensate for this by stretching the bitmap, but that will introduce other distortions.)

Moreover, not all output devices are raster devices. Although every graphics output device attached to the Presentation Manager can handle vector graphics, only a raster output device can handle bitmaps. In short, don't expect to display a bitmap on a plotter. Even if the device driver could translate the bitmap into approximate plotter commands, the plotter would take a very long time to draw it.

THE BIT-BLOCK TRANSFER

You can think of the entire video display as one big bitmap. The pixels you see on the screen are represented by bits stored in memory on the video display adapter board. Any rectangular area of the video display is also a bitmap. Each bitmap has a size: the number of rows and columns of pixels it contains.

Let's begin our journey into the world of bitmaps by copying an image from one area of the video display to another. This is a job for the powerful *GpiBitBlt* function.

Bitblt (pronounced "bit blit") stands for "bit-block transfer." The term was first used in graphics in connection with the SmallTalk system designed at the Xerox Palo Alto Research Center (PARC). In SmallTalk, all graphics output operations are based around the bitblt. Among programmers, "blt" is often used as a verb, as in: "Blt the bitmap on the screen."

The *GpiBitBlt* function is a pixel-mover, or (more vividly) a raster-blaster. As you'll see, the term "transfer" doesn't entirely do justice to the *GpiBitBlt* function. The function actually performs a bitwise operation on pixels and can result in some interesting effects.

SIMPLE USE OF *GPIBITBLT*

The MINMAX1 program shown in Listing 6.1 uses the *GpiBitBlt* function to copy the program's minimize-maximize menu (located in the upper-right corner of the frame window) to its client window.

Listing 6.1: The MINMAX1 program

The MINMAX1.MAK File

```
#----------------------
# MINMAX1.MAK make file
#----------------------

minmax1.exe : minmax1.obj minmax1.def
     $(PRGLINK) minmax1, minmax1, NUL, $(PRGLIB), minmax1

minmax1.obj : minmax1.c
     $(PRGCC) minmax1.c
```

The MINMAX1.C File

```
/*----------------------------------------------
   MINMAX1.C -- Bitblt of Minimize-Maximize Menu
                (c) Charles Petzold, 1993
  ----------------------------------------------*/

#define INCL_WIN
#include <os2.h>

MRESULT EXPENTRY ClientWndProc (HWND, ULONG, MPARAM, MPARAM) ;

int main (void)
     {
     static CHAR  szClientClass [] = "MinMax1" ;
     static ULONG flFrameFlags = FCF_TITLEBAR      | FCF_SYSMENU |
                                 FCF_SIZEBORDER    | FCF_MINMAX  |
                                 FCF_SHELLPOSITION | FCF_TASKLIST ;
     HAB          hab ;
     HMQ          hmq ;
     HWND         hwndFrame, hwndClient ;
     QMSG         qmsg ;

     hab = WinInitialize (0) ;
     hmq = WinCreateMsgQueue (hab, 0) ;

     WinRegisterClass (hab, szClientClass, ClientWndProc, CS_SIZEREDRAW, 0) ;

     hwndFrame = WinCreateStdWindow (HWND_DESKTOP, WS_VISIBLE,
                                     &flFrameFlags, szClientClass, NULL,
```

Listing 6.1: The MINMAX1 program (Continued)

```
                                    0L, 0, 0, &hwndClient) ;

     while (WinGetMsg (hab, &qmsg, NULLHANDLE, 0, 0))
          WinDispatchMsg (hab, &qmsg) ;

     WinDestroyWindow (hwndFrame) ;
     WinDestroyMsgQueue (hmq) ;
     WinTerminate (hab) ;
     return 0 ;
     }

MRESULT EXPENTRY ClientWndProc (HWND hwnd, ULONG msg, MPARAM mp1, MPARAM mp2)
     {
     static INT  cxClient, cyClient ;
     static LONG cxMinMax, cyMinMax ;
     HPS         hps ;
     POINTL      aptl[3] ;
     INT         iRow, iCol ;

     switch (msg)
          {
          case WM_CREATE:
               cxMinMax = WinQuerySysValue (HWND_DESKTOP, SV_CXMINMAXBUTTON) ;
               cyMinMax = WinQuerySysValue (HWND_DESKTOP, SV_CYMINMAXBUTTON) ;
               return 0 ;

          case WM_SIZE:
               cxClient = SHORT1FROMMP (mp2) ;
               cyClient = SHORT2FROMMP (mp2) ;
               return 0 ;

          case WM_PAINT:
               hps = WinBeginPaint (hwnd, NULLHANDLE, NULL) ;

               GpiErase (hps) ;

               for (iRow = 0 ; iRow <= cyClient / cyMinMax ; iRow++)
                    for (iCol = 0 ; iCol <= cxClient / cxMinMax ; iCol++)
                         {
                         aptl[0].x = iCol * cxMinMax ;       // target
                         aptl[0].y = iRow * cyMinMax ;       //   lower left

                         aptl[1].x = aptl[0].x + cxMinMax ; // target
                         aptl[1].y = aptl[0].y + cyMinMax ; //   upper right

                         aptl[2].x = cxClient - cxMinMax ;  // source
                         aptl[2].y = cyClient ;              //   lower left

                         GpiBitBlt (hps, hps, 3L, aptl, ROP_SRCCOPY, BBO_AND) ;
```

Listing 6.1: The MINMAX1 program (Continued)

```
                    }
               WinEndPaint (hps) ;
               return 0 ;
          }
     return WinDefWindowProc (hwnd, msg, mp1, mp2) ;
     }
```

The MINMAX1.DEF File

```
;----------------------------------
; MINMAX1.DEF module definition file
;----------------------------------

NAME           MINMAX1   WINDOWAPI

DESCRIPTION    'Bitblt of Min-Max Menu (c) Charles Petzold, 1993'
PROTMODE
```

But why stop at one bitblt? In fact, MINMAX1 fills its client window with multiple copies of the minimize-maximize window, as shown in Figure 6.1. *GpiBitBlt* transfers pixels from a rectangular area on one presentation space (called the *source*) to a rectangular area on another presentation space (the *target*, or *destination*). In MINMAX1, the two presentation spaces are the same: the cached micro-PS associated with the program's client window. The source rectangle is the minimize-maximize menu; the destination is various rectangles on the client window.

MINMAX1's minimize-maximize menu is outside the program's client window, so you may be surprised that *GpiBitBlt* can access that area of the display. When you're using a cached micro-PS, GPI only prohibits *writing* outside the window. GPI does indeed allow *GpiBitBlt* to access an area outside the window's limits. However, if MINMAX1 tries to repaint its client window when part of the minimize-maximize menu is off the screen or partially obscured, the image within the client window will reflect that. *GpiBitBlt* is reading pixels from the screen; if the image isn't on the screen, the function can't read it.

MINMAX1 calls the *GpiBitBlt* function during the WM_PAINT message based on information obtained during WM_CREATE and WM_SIZE. During the WM_CREATE message, MINMAX1 calls *WinQuerySysValue* to get the size of the minimize-maximize menu. It saves the dimensions in *cxMinMax* and *cyMinMax*. During the WM_SIZE message, MINMAX1 saves the size of the client window in *cxClient* and *cyClient*, as usual. MINMAX1 uses these variables to determine the number of times it calls *GpiBitBlt* during the WM_PAINT message.

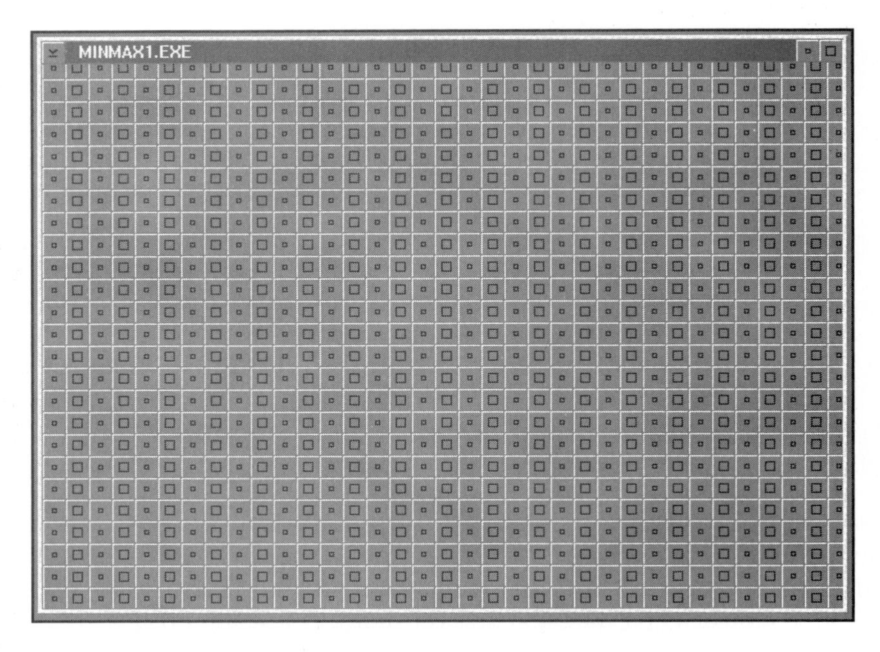

Figure 6.1: The MINMAX1 display

As used in MINMAX1, the *GpiBitBlt* function requires an array of three POINTL structures. This array is defined in *ClientWndProc* like this:

```
POINTL aptl[3] ;
```

During the WM_PAINT message, MINMAX1 sets the three POINTL structures with the coordinates (relative to the lower-left corner of the client window) of both the source and destination rectangles, as shown in the following table:

POINTL Structure	Meaning
aptl[0]	Target (or destination) of lower-left corner of bitmap
aptl[1]	Target (or destination) of upper-right corner of bitmap
aptl[2]	Lower-left corner of source bitmap

For each copy of the minimize-maximize menu that MINMAX1 draws, *aptl[2]* is set to the lower-left corner of the source rectangle (that is, the lower-left corner of the minimize-maximize menu) relative to the lower-left corner of the client window:

```
aptl[2].x = cxClient - cxMinMax ;
aptl[2].y = cyClient ;
```

For the first *GpiBitBlt* call during the WM_PAINT message, MINMAX1 sets *aptl[0]* to the point (0,0), which is the lower-left corner of the client window. The *aptl[1]* structure indicates the width and height of the destination rectangle relative to *aptl[0]*. This is shown in Figure 6.2.

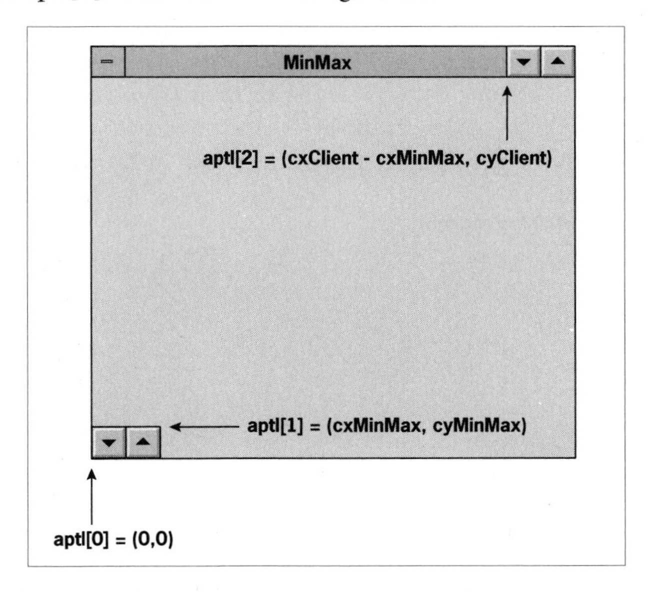

Figure 6.2: The aptl array coordinates for the first *GpiBitBlt* call in MINMAX1

For the subsequent *GpiBitBlt* calls in MINMAX1, *aptl[0]* and *aptl[1]* are the lower-left corner and upper-right corner of the target rectangle. This may be a little confusing: *aptl[1]* is documented as the upper-right corner of the destination rectangle, but in MINMAX1 it really indicates the size of the source bitmap. (We'll see why it's specified this way in this next section.)

MINMAX1 passes the *aptl* array to *GpiBitBlt*:

```
GpiBitBlt (hps, hps, 3L, aptl, ROP_SRCCOPY, BBO_AND) ;
```

The general syntax of *GpiBitBlt* is as follows:

```
GpiBitBlt (hpsDest, hpsSource, lNumPoints, aptl, lRasterOp,
          lCompressionType) ;
```

In the case of MINMAX1, the source presentation space (*hpsSource*) and the destination presentation space (*hpsDest*) are the same. The *lNumPoints* parameter indicates the number of POINTL structures passed as the fourth parameter—in this case three. I'll discuss the last two parameters later in this chapter.

STRETCHING THE BITMAP

The third parameter to *GpiBitBlt*, *lNumPoints*, indicates the number of POINTL structures in the array passed as the fourth parameter.

If you want the copy of the bitmap to be the same size and orientation as the source bitmap (as is the case in MINMAX1), set the *lNumPoints* parameter to 3L. If you want to change the size of the bitmap as it is copied, you can use a fourth POINTL structure in the array and specify *lNumPoints* as 4L. This is illustrated in the MINMAX2 program shown in Listing 6.2.

Listing 6.2: The MINMAX2 program

The MINMAX2.MAK File

```
#----------------------
# MINMAX2.MAK make file
#----------------------

minmax2.exe : minmax2.obj minmax2.def
     $(PRGLINK) minmax2, minmax2, NUL, $(PRGLIB), minmax2

minmax2.obj : minmax2.c
     $(PRGCC) minmax2.c
```

The MINMAX2.C File

```
/*---------------------------------------------
   MINMAX2.C -- Bitblt of Minimize-Maximize Menu
                (c) Charles Petzold, 1993
  ---------------------------------------------*/

#define INCL_WIN
#include <os2.h>

MRESULT EXPENTRY ClientWndProc (HWND, ULONG, MPARAM, MPARAM) ;

int main (void)
     {
     static CHAR  szClientClass [] = "MinMax2" ;
     static ULONG flFrameFlags = FCF_TITLEBAR      | FCF_SYSMENU |
                                 FCF_SIZEBORDER    | FCF_MINMAX  |
```

Listing 6.2: The MINMAX2 program (Continued)

```
                              FCF_SHELLPOSITION | FCF_TASKLIST ;
     HAB           hab ;
     HMQ           hmq ;
     HWND          hwndFrame, hwndClient ;
     QMSG          qmsg ;

     hab = WinInitialize (0) ;
     hmq = WinCreateMsgQueue (hab, 0) ;

     WinRegisterClass (hab, szClientClass, ClientWndProc, CS_SIZEREDRAW, 0) ;

     hwndFrame = WinCreateStdWindow (HWND_DESKTOP, WS_VISIBLE,
                                     &flFrameFlags, szClientClass, NULL,
                                     0L, 0, 0, &hwndClient) ;

     while (WinGetMsg (hab, &qmsg, NULLHANDLE, 0, 0))
          WinDispatchMsg (hab, &qmsg) ;

     WinDestroyWindow (hwndFrame) ;
     WinDestroyMsgQueue (hmq) ;
     WinTerminate (hab) ;
     return 0 ;
     }

MRESULT EXPENTRY ClientWndProc (HWND hwnd, ULONG msg, MPARAM mp1, MPARAM mp2)
     {
     static INT  cxClient, cyClient ;
     static LONG cxMinMax, cyMinMax ;
     HPS         hps ;
     POINTL      aptl[4] ;

     switch (msg)
          {
          case WM_CREATE:
               cxMinMax = WinQuerySysValue (HWND_DESKTOP, SV_CXMINMAXBUTTON) ;
               cyMinMax = WinQuerySysValue (HWND_DESKTOP, SV_CYMINMAXBUTTON) ;
               return 0 ;

          case WM_SIZE:
               cxClient = SHORT1FROMMP (mp2) ;
               cyClient = SHORT2FROMMP (mp2) ;
               return 0 ;

          case WM_PAINT:
               hps = WinBeginPaint (hwnd, NULLHANDLE, NULL) ;
               GpiErase (hps) ;

               aptl[0].x = 0 ;                    // target lower left
               aptl[0].y = 0 ;
```

Listing 6.2: The MINMAX2 program (Continued)

```
               aptl[1].x = cxClient ;             // target upper right
               aptl[1].y = cyClient ;

               aptl[2].x = cxClient - cxMinMax ;  // source lower left
               aptl[2].y = cyClient ;

               aptl[3].x = cxClient ;             // source upper right
               aptl[3].y = cyClient + cyMinMax ;

               GpiBitBlt (hps, hps, 4L, aptl, ROP_SRCCOPY, BBO_AND) ;

               WinEndPaint (hps) ;
               return 0 ;
          }
     return WinDefWindowProc (hwnd, msg, mp1, mp2) ;
     }
```

The MINMAX2.DEF File

```
;-----------------------------------
; MINMAX2.DEF module definition file
;-----------------------------------

NAME           MINMAX2   WINDOWAPI

DESCRIPTION    'Bitblt of Min-Max Menu (c) Charles Petzold, 1993'
PROTMODE
```

MINMAX2 calls *GpiBitBlt* only once during the WM_PAINT message, but it does so in style: The minimize-maximize menu is stretched to fill the entire client window, as shown in Figure 6.3.

When you use an array of four POINTL structures in the *GpiBitBlt* function, they are interpreted as shown in the following table:

POINTL Structure	Meaning
aptl[0]	Target (or destination) of lower-left corner of bitmap
aptl[1]	Target (or destination) of upper-right corner of bitmap
aptl[2]	Lower-left corner of source bitmap
aptl[3]	Upper-right corner of source bitmap

In MINMAX2, the destination points are the lower-left and upper-right corners of the client window. The two source points are the lower-left and the

Figure 6.3: The MINMAX2 display

upper-right corners of the minimize-maximize window. This is shown in Figure 6.4.

Now you can see that *aptl[1]* really indicates the upper-right corner of the target rectangle rather than the size of the bitmap.

FLIPPING THE BITMAP

The *aptl[0]* and *aptl[1]* elements of the POINTL array specify the points of the destination rectangle that correspond to the lower-left corner and lower-right corner of the source bitmap. The MINMAX2 program in Listing 6.2 sets *aptl[0]* and *aptl[1]* like this:

```
aptl[0].x = 0 ;
aptl[0].y = 0 ;

aptl[1].x = cxClient ;
aptl[1].y = cyClient ;
```

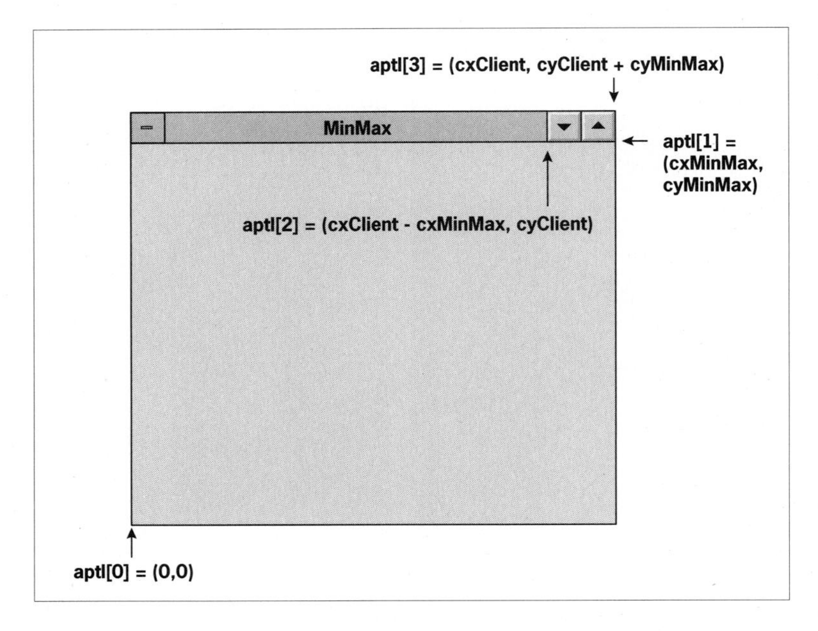

Figure 6.4: The *aptl* array coordinates for the *GpiBitBlt* call in MINMAX2

But these two points do not have to be the lower-left corner and upper-right corner of the destination rectangle. You can use any two opposite points for a variety of effects. For example, if you'd like to turn the image upside down, use

```
aptl[0].x = 0 ;
aptl[0].y = cyClient ;

aptl[1].x = cxClient ;
aptl[1].y = 0 ;
```

The lower-left corner of the source bitmap is copied to *aptl[0]*, which is now the upper-left corner of the client window. The upper-right corner of the source bitmap is copied to *aptl[1]*, the lower-right corner of the client window.

To display the minimize-maximize menu flipped around the vertical axis, use

```
aptl[0].x = cxClient ;
aptl[0].y = 0 ;

aptl[1].x = 0 ;
aptl[1].y = cyClient ;
```

To display the minimize-maximize menu flipped on both axes, use

```
aptl[0].x = cxClient ;
aptl[0].y = cyClient ;

aptl[1].x = 0 ;
aptl[1].y = 0 ;
```

When you flip a bitmap around the horizontal or vertical axis, you must specify four points in the *aptl* array, even if the bitmap is not being altered in size. The rule is simple: Use three points in the *aptl* array when you do not wish to change the size or orientation of the source bitmap. Otherwise use four points.

DIFFERENT PRESENTATION SPACES

The preceding examples use the same presentation space for both the source and the target. You can modify the MINMAX2.C source code file to use different presentation spaces. The destination presentation space is still the cached micro-PS for the client window, but the source presentation space can be the cached micro-PS for the minimize-maximize menu.

To use this approach, you need another variable of type HPS to store the source presentation space handle:

```
HPS hpsMinMax ;
```

During the WM_PAINT message, you can obtain *hpsMinMax* like this:

```
hpsMinMax = WinGetPS (
     WinWindowFromID (
          WinQueryWindow (hwnd, QW_PARENT),
               FID_MINMAX)) ;
```

The *WinQueryWindow* function obtains the handle of the frame window (which is the parent of the client window), *WinWindowFromID* returns the handle to the minimize-maximize menu window, and *WinGetPS* obtains a cached micro-PS for this window.

At first, it may seem rude to get a presentation space handle for a window that does not belong to your program. But the window really is part of your program. You created the minimize-maximize window by calling *WinCreate-StdWindow*. Although the window procedure for this window is within the Presentation Manager, the window belongs to your program. You can do what you want with it.

The *aptl[0]* and *aptl[1]* structures are set to the same values shown in MINMAX2.C. But the coordinates of the source bitmap are now relative to the lower-left corner of the source presentation space:

```
aptl[2].x = 0 ;
aptl[2].y = 0 ;

aptl[3].x = cxMinMax ;
aptl[3].y = cyMinMax ;
```

The *GpiBitBlt* call specifies *hpsMinMax* as the source presentation space:

```
GpiBitBlt (hps, hpsMinMax, 4L, aptl, ROP_SRCCOPY, BBO_AND) ;
```

Remember to release the presentation space handle of the minimize-maximize menu when you're finished with it:

```
WinReleasePS (hpsMinMax) ;
```

THE RASTER OPERATIONS

In MINMAX1 and MINMAX2, the source bitmap is simply copied from one area of the screen to another. This is the result of specifying ROP_SRCCOPY as the fifth parameter—the raster operation—to *GpiBitBlt.* ROP_SRCCOPY is only 1 of 256 raster operations you can use in *GpiBitBlt.* Let's experiment with a few others in MINMAX2 and then investigate the raster operations more methodically.

Try replacing ROP_SRCCOPY with ROP_NOTSRCCOPY. As the name suggests, this raster operation inverts the colors of the bitmap as it is copied: On the client window, the black area of the minimize-maximize menu becomes white, and the white area becomes black. Try ROP_ZERO: The entire client window is painted black. ROP_ONE causes the entire client window to be painted white.

Now try replacing the *GpiBitBlt* call in MINMAX2 with the following two statements:

```
GpiSetPattern (hps, PATSYM_HALFTONE) ;
GpiBitBlt (hps, hps, 4L, aptl, ROP_MERGECOPY, BBO_AND) ;
```

In this case, the black area of the minimize-maximize menu remains black when copied to the client window, but the white area is displayed as the PATSYM_HALFTONE pattern.

Here's another one:

```
GpiSetPattern (hps, PATSYM_HORIZ) ;
GpiBitBlt (hps, hps, 4L, aptl, ROP_PATCOPY, BBO_AND) ;
```

This simply fills the entire client window with the PATSYM_HORIZ pattern. Now try adding two more statements so that you call *GpiSetPattern* and *GpiBitBlt* twice:

```
GpiSetPattern (hps, PATSYM_HORIZ) ;
GpiBitBlt (hps, hps, 4L, aptl, ROP_PATCOPY, BBO_AND) ;
GpiSetPattern (hps, PATSYM_VERT) ;
GpiBitBlt (hps, hps, 4L, aptl, ROP_PATPAINT, BBO_AND) ;
```

This one (shown in Figure 6.5) is strange: The black area of the minimize-maximize menu is now copied as white, and the white area is a pattern of black dots which (if you think about it) appears to be an "intersection" of the horizontal and vertical line patterns.

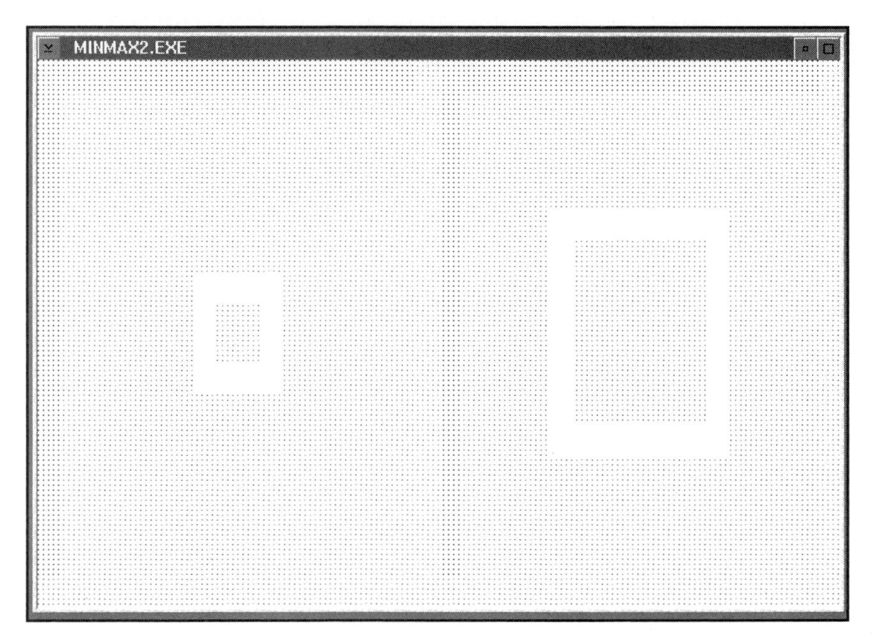

Figure 6.5: The MINMAX2 display with a different raster operation

Just what on earth is going on here?

As mentioned, the *GpiBitBlt* function is not simply a bit-transfer function. It actually performs a bitwise operation between the following three bitmaps:

- **Source** The source bitmap, expanded or compressed (if necessary) to be the same size as the destination rectangle
- **Destination** The destination rectangle before the *GpiBitBlt* call

- **Pattern** The current pattern of the destination presentation space, repeated horizontally and vertically to be the same size as the destination rectangle

The result of this bitwise operation is copied to the destination rectangle.

The raster operations are conceptually similar to the mix modes we encountered in Chapter 5. The mix modes govern the way in which a graphics object (such as a line) is combined with a destination. You'll recall that there were 16 foreground mix modes—all the unique results obtained when 0s and 1s in the object are combined with 0s and 1s in the destination.

The raster operations used in *GpiBitBlt* involve a combination of three objects, and this results in 256 raster operations. There are 256 ways to combine a source bitmap, a destination bitmap, and a pattern. Fifteen of these raster operations are common enough to be given names (some of them rather obscure) in PMGPI.H. The raster operation identifiers all begin with the prefix ROP. If you examine how they're defined in PMGPI.H, you'll see that each is defined as a number (which also seems rather obscure):

```
#define ROP_NOTSRCCOPY 0x0033L
#define ROP_SRCCOPY    0x00CCL
#define ROP_PATCOPY    0x00F0L
```

Those numbers have real meaning: They define how the source, destination, and pattern bitmaps are combined to create a result.

Table 6.1 shows the 15 raster operations that have names.

Table 6.1: The 15 Raster Operations That Have Names Defined in PMGPI.H

Pattern:	**1 1 1 1 0 0 0 0**			
Source:	**1 1 0 0 1 1 0 0**			
Destination:	**1 0 1 0 1 0 1 0**	**Operation**	**Value**	**Identifier**
Result:	0 0 0 0 0 0 0 0	0	0x00	ROP_ZERO
	0 0 0 1 0 0 0 1	~(S | D)	0x11	ROP_NOTSRCERASE
	0 0 1 1 0 0 1 1	~S	0x33	ROP_NOTSRCCOPY
	0 1 0 0 0 1 0 0	S & ~D	0x44	ROP_SRCERASE
	0 1 0 1 0 1 0 1	~D	0x55	ROP_DSTINVERT
	0 1 0 1 1 0 1 0	P ^ D	0x5A	ROP_PATINVERT
	0 1 1 0 0 1 1 0	S ^ D	0x66	ROP_SRCINVERT
	1 0 0 0 1 0 0 0	S & D	0x88	ROP_SRCAND

Table 6.1: The 15 Raster Operations That Have Names Defined in PMGPI.H (Continued)

Pattern:	**1 1 1 1 0 0 0 0**			
Source:	**1 1 0 0 1 1 0 0**			
Destination:	**1 0 1 0 1 0 1 0**	**Operation**	**Value**	**Identifier**
Result:	1 0 1 1 1 0 1 1	~S | D	0xBB	ROP_MERGEPAINT
	1 1 0 0 0 0 0 0	P & S	0xC0	ROP_MERGECOPY
	1 1 0 0 1 1 0 0	S	0xCC	ROP_SRCCOPY
	1 1 1 0 1 1 1 0	S | D	0xEE	ROP_SRCPAINT
	1 1 1 1 0 0 0 0	P	0xF0	ROP_PATCOPY
	1 1 1 1 1 0 1 1	P | ~S | D	0xFB	ROP_PATPAINT
	1 1 1 1 1 1 1 1	1	0xFF	ROP_ONE

This table is important in understanding and using raster operations, so let's spend a little time examining it.

The numeric values of the ROP identifiers are listed in the second-to-last column. These numbers are the hexadecimal representations of the "result" bits shown in the first eight columns. These bits are the result of a bitwise operation between the pattern, source, and destination bits shown at the top. The Operation column uses C syntax to show how the pattern, source, and destination are combined.

To begin understanding this table, it's easiest to assume that you're dealing with a monochrome system in which 0 is black and 1 is white. The result of the ROP_ZERO operation is all zeros regardless of the source, destination, and pattern, so the destination will be colored black. Similarly, ROP_ONE always causes the destination to be colored white.

Let's take another look at these four lines of code shown earlier:

```
GpiSetPattern (hps, PATSYM_HORIZ) ;
GpiBitBlt (hps, hps, 4L, aptl, ROP_PATCOPY, BBO_AND) ;
GpiSetPattern (hps, PATSYM_VERT) ;
GpiBitBlt (hps, hps, 4L, aptl, ROP_PATPAINT, BBO_AND) ;
```

This code was responsible for the display in Figure 6.5. As you can see from Table 6.1, ROP_PATCOPY causes the result bits to be the same as the pattern bits. The source and destination bitmaps are essentially ignored. In other words, ROP_PATCOPY simply copies the current pattern to the destination rectangle.

The ROP_PATPAINT raster operation involves a more complex operation. The result is equal to

```
P | ~S | D
```

When the source bitmap is black (a 0 bit), the result is always white (a 1 bit). Figure 6.5 verifies this. When the source is white (1), the result is also white if either the pattern or the destination is white. In other words, the result will be black only if the source is white and both the pattern and the destination are black. Again, Figure 6.5 verifies this. Black dots appeared in the white area of the source bitmap where the lines of the pattern that were already on the destination intersected the lines of the current pattern.

When a raster operation does not require a source bitmap, you can set the second parameter of *GpiBitBlt* (the handle to the source presentation space) to NULL and the third parameter (the number of POINTL structures in the array) to 2L. The preceding example can also be written as

```
GpiSetPattern (hps, PATSYM_HORIZ) ;
GpiBitBlt (hps, NULL, 2L, aptl, ROP_PATCOPY, BBO_AND) ;

GpiSetPattern (hps, PATSYM_VERT) ;
GpiBitBlt (hps, hps, 4L, aptl, ROP_PATPAINT, BBO_AND) ;
```

You don't need to use one of the predefined identifiers for the raster operation parameter to *GpiBitBlt.* You can use any number between 0 and 255. The hard part is determining what number to use for a particular effect. Here are some examples.

Suppose you want to copy the white area of a source bitmap as white, but you want to display the PATSYM_HALFTONE pattern where the bitmap is black. You set up a little table similar to the one shown at the top of Table 6.1 and work out the bits:

Pattern:	1 1 1 1 0 0 0 0	
Source:	1 1 0 0 1 1 0 0	
Destination:	1 0 1 0 1 0 1 0	Value
Result:	1 1 1 1 1 1 0 0	0xFC

When the source is 1 (white), the result is also 1. When the source is 0 (black), the result is the pattern. Thus the raster operation is 0xFC. Here's the code:

```
GpiSetPattern (hps, PATSYM_HALFTONE) ;
GpiBitBlt (hps, hps, 4L, aptl, 0xFC, BBO_AND) ;
```

Simple, right?

Let's try another. Where the source is white, you want the result to be colored with horizontal lines, and where the source is black, you want vertical lines. First, color the destination area using PATSYM_HORIZ and then set the pattern to PATSYM_VERT:

```
GpiSetPattern (hps, PATSYM_HORIZ) ;
GpiBitBlt (hps, NULL, 2L, aptl, ROP_PATCOPY, BBO_AND) ;
GpiSetPattern (hps, PATSYM_VERT) ;
```

Now all you need is a raster operation that does the following: When the source is 1 (white), the result is the destination; when the source is 0 (black), the result is the pattern. Here's the table:

Pattern:	1 1 1 1 0 0 0 0	
Source:	1 1 0 0 1 1 0 0	
Destination:	1 0 1 0 1 0 1 0	Value
Result:	1 0 1 1 1 0 0 0	0xB8

And here's the GpiBitBlt function that uses this raster operation:

```
GpiBitBlt (hps, hps, 4L, aptl, 0xB8L, BBO_AND) ;
```

RASTER OPERATIONS AND COLOR

As I discussed in Chapter 5, a color display uses multiple bits for each pixel. For example, the standard VGA uses 4 bits per pixel and can display 16 colors simultaneously. Although the VGA can map these 4 bits to any one of 262,144 possible colors, the mapping is usually defined so that the 4 bits represent an IRGB (Intensity-Red-Green-Blue) color scheme.

Like the mix mode in Chapter 5, the *GpiBitBlt* function performs the bitwise operation between each of these color bits separately. For example, if the destination is CLR_RED (intensity and red bits set to 1) and the source is CLR_PALEBLUE (blue bit set to 1), an ROP_SRCPAINT raster operation will color the destination as CLR_PINK (intensity, red, and blue bits set to 1).

If you are using a color display and you have used the Presentation Manager Scheme Palette window to set your window background and window text colors to something other than white and black, the preceding descriptions of some raster operations probably did not agree with your observations. Instead, you saw results that included the CLR_BACKGROUND and CLR_-NEUTRAL colors.

Here's why: When the *GpiBitBlt* function performs a bitwise operation on a source, destination, and pattern, all three bitmaps must have the same color format. *GpiBitBlt* performs the operation on the color bits separately.

Patterns are stored as monochrome bitmaps. They have 1 bit per pixel. During *GpiBitBlt*, the pattern must be converted to a color bitmap. That is, on the VGA, each bit of the pattern must be converted to 4 bits so that they can be combined with the source and destination. GPI does this by converting the 1 bits to the 4 IRGB bits that describe the current presentation space foreground color (the CLR_NEUTRAL color by default) and the 0 bits to the 4 IRGB bits for the current presentation space background color (CLR_BACKGROUND by default).

I guarantee that this will be confusing at first. By default, CLR_NEUTRAL is black and CLR_BACKGROUND is white. This means that 1 bits in the pattern become black and 0 bits become white, which is exactly the opposite of the interpretation of bits in a monochrome system.

For example, the PATSYM_VERT pattern is mostly 0 bits except for the vertical lines, which are 1 bits. In a monochrome system, for example, PATSYM_VERT would have white lines on a black background. But when the pattern is converted to a color bitmap (as it must be for GPI to display it on a color screen), the pattern appears as CLR_NEUTRAL lines on a CLR_BACKGROUND background, or black on white by default.

BITBLT COMPRESSION

I haven't yet discussed the last parameter to *GpiBitBlt*. This parameter governs how a source bitmap is altered when it is compressed to a smaller destination. Three options are available: BBO_OR, BBO_AND, and BBO_IGNORE.

If you considered the problem of stretching or compressing a bitmap, you probably assumed that GPI simply duplicates rows and columns of pixels to stretch a bitmap. This is correct. You may also have assumed that GPI simply eliminates rows and columns of pixels to compress a bitmap. But that's only one of the three options—the one you get when you use BBO_IGNORE, which is often not satisfactory.

For example, suppose you have a source bitmap that has a white background and a 1-pixel-wide outline of a square in black. When GPI compresses the bitmap, the rows and columns of the bitmap containing the black lines could be the rows and columns that GPI eliminates. The result will be entirely white.

When you have a bitmap with a black image on a white background, use BBO_AND. GPI will not eliminate whole rows and columns but instead will combine adjacent rows and columns of the bitmap with a bitwise AND operation. A result pixel will be white only if both adjacent pixels are also white. With a white image on a black background, use BBO_OR. Adjacent rows and columns are combined with a bitwise OR operation so that a result will be black only if adjacent pixels are black.

BBO_IGNORE is for use with color bitmaps. For color bitmaps, BBO_OR and BBO_AND can result in the creation of colors not in the original bitmap, even when you're using ROP_SRCCOPY.

BITMAP HANDLES AND BITMAP DRAWING

We've been blting bitmaps around the video display but we haven't really gotten our hands on a bitmap, and it's not quite clear what we could do with one anyway.

Let's temporarily abandon the *GpiBitBlt* function and approach bitmaps from another direction. We'll first try getting a handle to a bitmap and drawing the bitmap on the video display. After we nail down a couple of additional concepts, we can again bring *GpiBitBlt* into our collection of tools.

THE SYSTEM BITMAPS

If you've been exploring the Presentation Manager programming utilities, you may have discovered that the Icon Editor can create a bitmap file with the extension .BMP. In Chapter 12, you'll learn how to use that bitmap as a "resource" in a program, load it into memory, and display it on the screen.

But you needn't jump ahead that far yet. The Presentation Manager occasionally uses bitmaps called "system bitmaps." These bitmaps are stored as resources in DISPLAY.DLL, the device driver for the video display. As mentioned, bitmaps are very device dependent and must often be different sizes for different video display drivers. Accordingly, the bitmaps are stored in the video display device driver.

In preparation for getting your hands on a bitmap, you must define a variable to store a bitmap handle. A bitmap handle is of type HBITMAP:

```
HBITMAP hbm ;
```

An HBITMAP variable begins with *hbm* by convention. Now you can call *WinGetSysBitmap*:

```
hbm = WinGetSysBitmap (HWND_DESKTOP, idSysBitmap) ;
```

This function returns a handle to a copy of a system bitmap. The *idSysBitmap* parameter is one of the identifiers that begins with SBMP defined in PMWIN.H.

When you've finished using the bitmap, you should delete it:

```
GpiDeleteBitmap (hbm) ;
```

It's okay to delete a bitmap you obtain from *WinGetSysBitmap*. You're not deleting the system bitmap itself, only the copy that was made for you.

DRAWING A BITMAP

If you look over the identifiers beginning with SBMP, you'll find SBMP_MINBUTTON and SBMP_MAXBUTTON. Of course! The Presentation Manager has to draw the minimize-maximize menu somehow. What it uses are these system bitmaps.

This can only mean that we're not yet done with the MINMAX series of programs. It's time for MINMAX3, which is shown in Listing 6.3.

Listing 6.3: The MINMAX3 program

The MINMAX3.MAK File

```
#----------------------
# MINMAX3.MAK make file
#----------------------

minmax3.exe : minmax3.obj minmax3.def
     $(PRGLINK) minmax3, minmax3, NUL, $(PRGLIB), minmax3

minmax3.obj : minmax3.c
     $(PRGCC) minmax3.c
```

The MINMAX3.C File

```
/*---------------------------------------
   MINMAX3.C -- Minimize-Maximize Bitmap
                (c) Charles Petzold, 1993
  ---------------------------------------*/

#define INCL_WIN
#include <os2.h>

MRESULT EXPENTRY ClientWndProc (HWND, ULONG, MPARAM, MPARAM) ;

int main (void)
     {
     static CHAR  szClientClass [] = "MinMax3" ;
     static ULONG flFrameFlags = FCF_TITLEBAR      | FCF_SYSMENU |
                                 FCF_SIZEBORDER    | FCF_MINMAX  |
                                 FCF_SHELLPOSITION | FCF_TASKLIST ;
     HAB          hab ;
     HMQ          hmq ;
     HWND         hwndFrame, hwndClient ;
     QMSG         qmsg ;
```

Listing 6.3: The MINMAX3 program (Continued)

```
     hab = WinInitialize (0) ;
     hmq = WinCreateMsgQueue (hab, 0) ;

     WinRegisterClass (hab, szClientClass, ClientWndProc, CS_SIZEREDRAW, 0) ;

     hwndFrame = WinCreateStdWindow (HWND_DESKTOP, WS_VISIBLE,
                                     &flFrameFlags, szClientClass, NULL,
                                     0L, 0, 0, &hwndClient) ;

     while (WinGetMsg (hab, &qmsg, NULLHANDLE, 0, 0))
          WinDispatchMsg (hab, &qmsg) ;

     WinDestroyWindow (hwndFrame) ;
     WinDestroyMsgQueue (hmq) ;
     WinTerminate (hab) ;
     return 0 ;
     }

MRESULT EXPENTRY ClientWndProc (HWND hwnd, ULONG msg, MPARAM mp1, MPARAM mp2)
     {
     static INT cxClient, cyClient ;
     HBITMAP    hbmMin, hbmMax ;
     HPS        hps ;
     POINTL     aptl [2] ;

     switch (msg)
          {
          case WM_SIZE:
               cxClient = SHORT1FROMMP (mp2) ;
               cyClient = SHORT2FROMMP (mp2) ;
               return 0 ;

          case WM_PAINT:
               hps = WinBeginPaint (hwnd, NULLHANDLE, NULL) ;

               hbmMin = WinGetSysBitmap (HWND_DESKTOP, SBMP_MINBUTTON) ;
               hbmMax = WinGetSysBitmap (HWND_DESKTOP, SBMP_MAXBUTTON) ;

               aptl[0].x = 0 ;                // Target lower left
               aptl[0].y = 0 ;
               aptl[1].x = cxClient / 2 ;     // Target upper right
               aptl[1].y = cyClient ;

               WinDrawBitmap (hps, hbmMin, NULL, aptl,
                              CLR_NEUTRAL, CLR_BACKGROUND, DBM_STRETCH) ;

               aptl[0].x = cxClient / 2 ;     // Target left
               aptl[1].x = cxClient ;         // Target right
```

Listing 6.3: The MINMAX3 program (Continued)

```
               WinDrawBitmap (hps, hbmMax, NULL, aptl,
                              CLR_NEUTRAL, CLR_BACKGROUND, DBM_STRETCH) ;

               GpiDeleteBitmap (hbmMin) ;
               GpiDeleteBitmap (hbmMax) ;

               WinEndPaint (hps) ;
               return 0 ;
          }
     return WinDefWindowProc (hwnd, msg, mp1, mp2) ;
     }
```

The MINMAX3.DEF File

```
;-----------------------------------
; MINMAX3.DEF module definition file
;-----------------------------------

NAME           MINMAX3   WINDOWAPI

DESCRIPTION    'Min-Max Bitmap (c) Charles Petzold, 1993'
PROTMODE
```

While processing the WM_PAINT message, MINMAX3 obtains handles to the minimize and maximize bitmaps by calling *WinGetSysBitmap* twice. It stores the handles in *hbmMin* and *hbmMax*. The program then draws the two bitmaps on its client window by calling *WinDrawBitmap* and deletes the bitmaps using *GpiDeleteBitmap*. The MINMAX3 display is shown in Figure 6.6.

THE *WINDRAWBITMAP* FUNCTION

As you can tell by the *Win* prefix, *WinDrawBitmap* is a high-level drawing function. It is certainly convenient and will be welcomed by Microsoft Windows programmers. (Windows has no comparable function.) But you'll soon see that GPI offers a better approach to drawing bitmaps.

The general syntax of *WinDrawBitmap* is

```
WinDrawBitmap (hps, hbm, &rclSource, &ptlDest, clrForeground,
               clrBackground, fsOptions) ;
```

The third parameter, *&rclSource*, is a pointer to a RECTL structure defining a rectangular area of the bitmap you want to draw. If you set this parameter to NULL (as MINMAX3 does), *WinDrawBitmap* draws the entire bitmap.

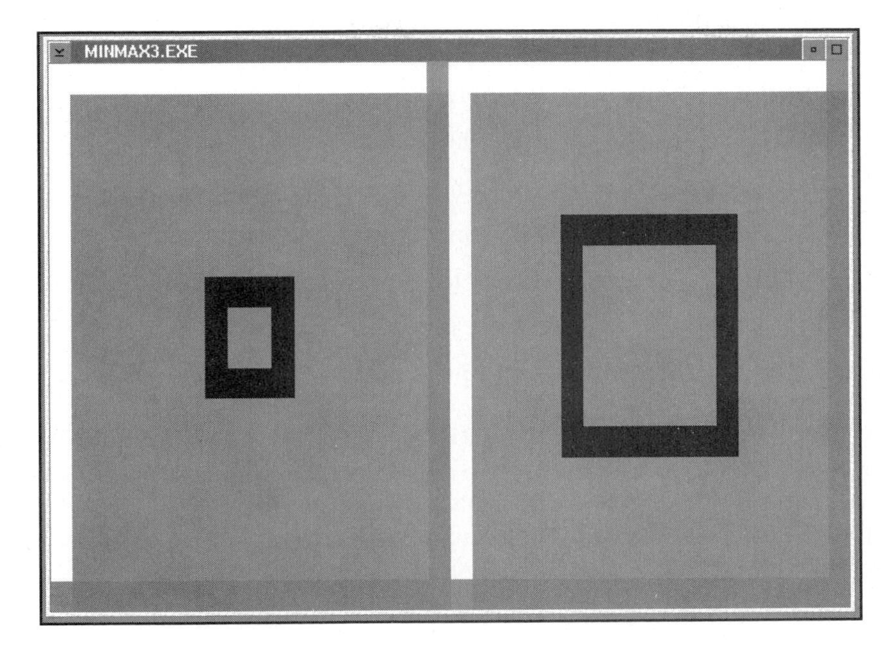

Figure 6.6: The MINMAX3 display

The fourth parameter specifies the destination coordinates. If you do not include DBM_STRETCH in the options, this parameter points to a POINTL structure specifying the lower-left corner of the destination. If you use DBM_STRETCH, the parameter is an array of two POINTL structures specifying the lower-left corner and upper-right corner. Alternatively, you can use a pointer to a RECTL structure for this parameter and cast it to a PPOINTL (a pointer to a POINTL structure).

You specify two colors for the bitmap, *clrForeground* and *clrBackground*. The *clrForeground* is used for the 1 bits of the bitmap and *clrBackground* is used for the 0 bits. (MINMAX3 uses both CLR_NEUTRAL and CLR_BACKGROUND.) If you have not changed the window background and window text colors in the Presentation Manager Scheme Palette window, the minimize and maximize bitmaps are drawn as black squares on a white background. Alternatively, you can use the DBM_IMAGEATTRS option in the final parameter to use the colors currently selected for drawing images.

The *flOptions* parameter can be a combination (using the C bitwise OR operator) of the following identifiers:

Identifier	Meaning
DBM_NORMAL	Draw the bitmap normally
DBM_INVERT	Invert the colors of the bitmap
DBM_HALFTONE	Draw only every other bit of the bitmap
DBM_STRETCH	Stretch the bitmap to fit the target area
DBM_IMAGEATTRS	Use the image attributes for color

The DBM_NORMAL identifier is defined as 0, so that is the default if you use 0 as the last parameter. Both the DBM_INVERT and DBM_HALFTONE flags allow you to use a small subset of the 256 raster operations to draw the bitmap. *WinDrawBitmap* uses the bitmap as the source and temporarily sets the current pattern to PATSYM_HALFTONE (which consists of alternating 0 and 1 bits). The last parameter to *WinDrawBitmap* is equivalent to the following raster operations:

***WinDrawBitmap* Parameter**	**Raster Operation**
DBM_NORMAL	ROP_SRCCOPY
DBM_INVERT	ROP_NOTSRCCOPY
DBM_HALFTONE	0xFC (P | S)
DBM_INVERT	DBM_HALFTONE	0x30 (P & ~S)

Remember that GPI converts both the source and pattern to a color bitmap before performing the logical operation on each set of color bits. Thus, when you use ROP_NOTSRCCOPY, the 1 bits in the bitmap are colored with the inverse of the ROP_NEUTRAL color and the 0 bits are colored with the inverse of ROP_BACKGROUND.

GETTING BITMAP INFORMATION

We managed to obtain handles to system bitmaps and draw them on the MINMAX3 client window without knowing the size of the bitmaps. If you need this information, you can obtain it. First you define a variable of type BITMAPINFOHEADER:

```
BITMAPINFOHEADER bmp ;
```

The recommended prefix for structures of this type is *bmp*, which actually stands for "bitmap parameters." The BITMAPINFOHEADER structure is defined in PMGPI.H:

```
typedef struct_BITMAPINFOHEADER
     {
     ULONG cbFix ;
     USHORT cx ;
     USHORT cy ;
     USHORT cPlanes ;
     USHORT cBitCount ;
     }
BITMAPINFOHEADER ;
```

You first set the *cbFix* field as the size of the structure, which is 12 bytes. Then you pass a pointer to this structure to *GpiQueryBitmapParameters*:

```
GpiQueryBitmapParameters (hbm, &bmp) ;
```

On return from the function, the *cx* and *cy* fields will contain the width and height of the bitmap in pixels. For a monochrome bitmap, the *cPlanes* and *cBitCount* fields are 1. For color bitmaps, these two fields describe how the bitmap is organized to represent color.

You also use the BITMAPINFOHEADER structure (or more preferably, the newer BITMAPINFOHEADER2 structure) when creating a bitmap. Let's get to it.

WORKING WITH BITMAPS

I mentioned earlier that you can create a bitmap using the Icon Editor program and store that bitmap as a resource in your program. This is certainly an easy approach to creating and using a bitmap. But we'll wait until Chapter 12 to see how that is done. Meanwhile, it's instructive to create bitmaps and work with them directly in a program.

THE BITMAP BITS

What do you need to create a bitmap that represents an image? One major requirement is obviously the bits themselves. In a program, these bits are usually stored as an array of BYTE (unsigned character) values. For a monochrome bitmap, this array is organized as follows:

- The array begins with the bottom row of bits.
- The first byte in each row is the leftmost eight pixels.

- The most significant bit in each byte is the leftmost pixel.
- The number of bits in each row must be a multiple of the size of a ULONG (32 bits). If the bitmap width is not a multiple of 32, the row must be padded at the right.
- A 1 bit generally represents the foreground color (black by default), and a 0 bit generally represents the background color (white by default).

For example, suppose you want to create a small bitmap that contains the word "HELLO." You want the letters to be colored with the foreground color (black by default). The background will be white (by default). You can picture such a bitmap like this:

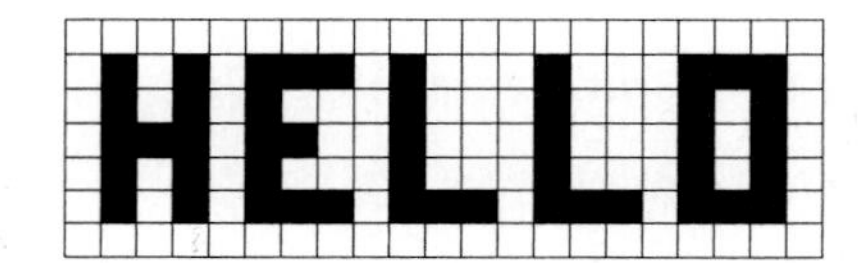

This is a 21-by-7 bitmap, with 7 rows of 21 bits each. You can represent the bitmap as a string of bits where the background bits are 0 and the foreground bits are 1:

```
0 0 0 0 0 0 0 0 0 0 0 0 0 0 0 0 0 0 0 0 0
0 1 0 1 0 1 1 1 0 1 0 0 0 1 0 0 0 1 1 1 0
0 1 0 1 0 1 0 0 0 1 0 0 0 1 0 0 0 1 0 1 0
0 1 1 1 0 1 1 0 0 1 0 0 0 1 0 0 0 1 0 1 0
0 1 0 1 0 1 0 0 0 1 0 0 0 1 0 0 0 1 0 1 0
0 1 0 1 0 1 1 1 0 1 1 1 0 1 1 1 0 1 1 1 0
0 0 0 0 0 0 0 0 0 0 0 0 0 0 0 0 0 0 0 0 0
```

Group each set of 8 bits into a byte. The leftmost bits are most significant. Each row must be padded at the right for a multiple of 4 bytes per row. It doesn't matter whether you pad the rows with 0s or 1s:

```
0x00 0x00 0x00 0x00
0x57 0x44 0x70 0x00
0x54 0x44 0x50 0x00
0x76 0x44 0x50 0x00
0x54 0x44 0x50 0x00
0x57 0x77 0x70 0x00
0x00 0x00 0x00 0x00
```

Now reverse the order of the rows so that the array begins with the bottom row. You can define the resultant array in a program like this:

```
static BYTE abHello [] = { 0x00, 0x00, 0x00, 0x00,
                           0x57, 0x77, 0x70, 0x00,
                           0x54, 0x44, 0x50, 0x00,
                           0x76, 0x44, 0x50, 0x00,
                           0x54, 0x44, 0x50, 0x00,
                           0x57, 0x44, 0x70, 0x00,
                           0x00, 0x00, 0x00, 0x00 } ;
```

BITMAP CREATION AND INITIALIZATION

To create a bitmap based on an array of bits, you use the *GpiCreateBitmap* function. This function returns a handle to the bitmap that you store in a variable of type HBITMAP.

Before calling *GpiCreateBitmap*, you need two structures that are very similar: BITMAPINFO2 and BITMAPINFOHEADER2. The first five fields of the BITMAPINFOHEADER2 structure are similar to BITMAPINFOHEADER:

```
typedef struct _BITMAPINFOHEADER2
     {
     ULONG cbFix ;
     ULONG cx ;
     ULONG cy ;
     ULONG cPlanes ;
     ULONG cBitCount ;
     :
     :
     }
BITMAPINFOHEADER2 ;
```

For all purposes, the remaining fields can be set to zero to assume their defaults. The fields of the BITMAPINFO2 structure are the same as BITMAPINFOHEADER2, but a final field—an array of one RGB2 structure—is added, as shown here:

```
typedef struct _BITMAPINFO2
     {
     ULONG cbFix ;
     ULONG cx ;
     ULONG cy ;
     ULONG cPlanes ;
     ULONG cBitCount ;
     :
     :
     RGB2  argb2Color[1] ;
```

```
     }
BITMAPINFO2 ;
```

By convention, a BITMAPINFO2 structure variable begins with *bmi*. The RGB2 structure defines a color as a combination of red, green, and blue bytes:

```
typedef struct _RGB2
     {
     BYTE bBlue ;
     BYTE bGreen ;
     BYTE bRed ;
     BYTE fcOptions ;
     }
RGB2 ;
```

The fourth field is not used with bitmaps. Each color byte can range from 0 through 0xFF (255). When all 3 bytes are set to 0, the color is black. When all 3 bytes are set to 255, the color is white. You need one RGB structure for each color in the bitmap. For example, if the bitmap has 4 color bits per pixel, you need an array of 16 RGB structures: one for each of the 16 possible colors. These structures indicate to GPI what real color corresponds to each combination of 4 bits. For a monochrome bitmap (which we'll be creating), you need an array of two RGB structures.

In both structures, the *cbFix* field is set to the size of the structure. The *cx* and *cy* fields specify the size of the bitmap in bits. The *cPlanes* and *cBitCount* fields indicate how bits in the bitmap are organized to represent color. For a monochrome bitmap, these two fields are set to 1.

So, to create a bitmap to contain the *abHello* array of bits, first define a BITMAPINFOHEADER2 structure variable and set the fields like this:

```
BITMAPINFOHEADER2 bmp ;
     ....
bmp.cbFix = sizeof (BITMAPINFOHEADER2) ;
bmp.cx = 21 ;
bmp.cy = 7 ;
bmp.cPlanes = 1 ;
bmp.cBitCount = 1 ;
```

The BITMAPINFO2 structure is set up similarly, but it needs two RGB2 values that define how the 0 and 1 bits are interpreted. For a monochrome bitmap, the three fields of the first RGB2 structure should be set to 0, and the three fields of the second structure should be set to 255.

And now we have a little problem. We need to define values of *argb2Color[0]* and *argb2Color[1]*, but the definition of the BITMAPINFO2 structure is large enough to accommodate only one RGB2 structure. We need a BITMAPINFO2 structure large enough for two RGB2 structures. Here's one way to do it. Don't define a structure of type BITMAPINFO2 like this:

```
BITMAPINFO2 bmi ;
```

Instead, define a pointer to a BITMAPINFO2 structure:

```
BITMAPINFO2 * pbmi ;
```

Then use *malloc* to allocate enough local memory for the structure:

```
pbmi = malloc (sizeof (BITMAPINFO2) + sizeof (RGB2)) ;
```

The *cbFix* field is set equal to the size of the BITMAPINFO2 structure excluding the *argb2Color* field, so you can set the fields of the structure like this:

```
pbmi->cbFix = sizeof bmp ;
pbmi->cx = 21 ;
pbmi->cy = 7
pbmi->cPlanes = 1 ;
pbmi->cBitCount = 1 ;
pbmi->argb2Color[0].bBlue  = 0 ;
pbmi->argb2Color[0].bGreen = 0 ;
pbmi->argb2Color[0].bRed   = 0 ;
pbmi->argb2Color[1].bBlue  = 255 ;
pbmi->argb2Color[1].bGreen = 255 ;
pbmi->argb2Color[1].bRed   = 255 ;
```

Now we're ready to call *GpiCreateBitmap* using the *abHello* array and these two structures:

```
hbm = GpiCreateBitmap (hps, &bmp, CBM_INIT, abHello, pbmi) ;
```

The first parameter to *GpiCreateBitmap* is a handle to a presentation space. For bitmaps to be displayed on the screen, you can use the handle returned from *WinGetPS*. If possible, GPI will use part of the video memory to store the bitmap. Even if the bitmap is stored in system memory, it is always associated with a particular device. The CBM_INIT identifier indicates that we want the bitmap to be initialized with the *abHello* data after the bitmap is created.

After you call *GpiCreateBitmap*, you want to free the memory used for the BITMAPINFO2 structure:

```
free (pbmi) ;
```

When your program is finished using a bitmap, the bitmap should be deleted:

```
GpiDeleteBitmap (hbm) ;
```

You can also create a bitmap without initializing it. In this case, the bitmap initially contains random data. If we simply wanted to create an uninitialized 21-by-7 bitmap, the *GpiCreateBitmap* function would be

```
hbm = GpiCreateBitmap (hps, &bmp, 0L, NULL, NULL) ;
```

Notice that only the BITMAPINFOHEADER2 structure is required for this variation of the *GpiCreateBitmap* call. You don't need to tell GPI how to interpret color information when creating the uninitialized bitmap.

THE BIT CAT

Now that we have some of the concepts down, let's look at a program that creates and displays a bitmap. Rather than the simple "HELLO" bitmap described previously, this program uses a more interesting bitmap. Remember the cat we displayed in Chapter 5 using *GpiImage*? We'll now display that cat as a bitmap. BITCAT1 is shown in Listing 6.4.

Listing 6.4: The BITCAT1 program

The BITCAT1.MAK File

```
#-----------------------
# BITCAT1.MAK make file
#-----------------------

bitcat1.exe : bitcat1.obj bitcat1.def
     $(PRGLINK) bitcat1, bitcat1, NUL, $(PRGLIB), bitcat1

bitcat1.obj : bitcat1.c bitcat.h
     $(PRGCC) bitcat1.c
```

The BITCAT1.C File

```
/*-----------------------------------------
   BITCAT1.C -- Bitmap Creation and Display
                (c) Charles Petzold, 1993
  -----------------------------------------*/

#define INCL_WIN
#define INCL_GPI
#include <os2.h>
#include <stdlib.h>
#include <string.h>
#include "bitcat.h"

MRESULT EXPENTRY ClientWndProc (HWND, ULONG, MPARAM, MPARAM) ;
```

Listing 6.4: The BITCAT1 program (Continued)

```
int main (void)
     {
     static CHAR  szClientClass [] = "BitCat1" ;
     static ULONG flFrameFlags = FCF_TITLEBAR       | FCF_SYSMENU |
                                 FCF_SIZEBORDER     | FCF_MINMAX  |
                                 FCF_SHELLPOSITION  | FCF_TASKLIST ;
     HAB          hab ;
     HMQ          hmq ;
     HWND         hwndFrame, hwndClient ;
     QMSG         qmsg ;

     hab = WinInitialize (0) ;
     hmq = WinCreateMsgQueue (hab, 0) ;

     WinRegisterClass (hab, szClientClass, ClientWndProc, CS_SIZEREDRAW, 0) ;

     hwndFrame = WinCreateStdWindow (HWND_DESKTOP, WS_VISIBLE,
                                     &flFrameFlags, szClientClass, NULL,
                                     0L, 0, 0, &hwndClient) ;

     while (WinGetMsg (hab, &qmsg, NULLHANDLE, 0, 0))
          WinDispatchMsg (hab, &qmsg) ;

     WinDestroyWindow (hwndFrame) ;
     WinDestroyMsgQueue (hmq) ;
     WinTerminate (hab) ;
     return 0 ;
     }

MRESULT EXPENTRY ClientWndProc (HWND hwnd, ULONG msg, MPARAM mp1, MPARAM mp2)
     {
     static HBITMAP      hbm ;
     static INT          cxClient, cyClient ;
     BITMAPINFO2       * pbmi ;
     BITMAPINFOHEADER2   bmp ;
     HPS                 hps ;
     POINTL              aptl [4] ;

     switch (msg)
          {
          case WM_CREATE:

                         // Create 32-by-32 monochrome bitmap

               memset (&bmp, 0, sizeof (BITMAPINFOHEADER2)) ;

               bmp.cbFix     = sizeof (BITMAPINFOHEADER2) ;
               bmp.cx        = 32 ;
               bmp.cy        = 32 ;
```

Listing 6.4: The BITCAT1 program (Continued)

```
          bmp.cPlanes   = 1 ;
          bmp.cBitCount = 1 ;

          pbmi = malloc (sizeof (BITMAPINFO2) + sizeof (RGB2)) ;

          memset (pbmi, 0, sizeof (BITMAPINFOHEADER2)) ;

          pbmi->cbFix     = sizeof (BITMAPINFOHEADER2) ;
          pbmi->cx        = 32 ;
          pbmi->cy        = 32 ;
          pbmi->cPlanes   = 1 ;
          pbmi->cBitCount = 1;

          pbmi->argbColor[0].bBlue   = 0x00 ;       // 0 bits (background)
          pbmi->argbColor[0].bGreen  = 0x00 ;
          pbmi->argbColor[0].bRed    = 0x00 ;
          pbmi->argbColor[0].fcOptions = 0 ;

          pbmi->argbColor[1].bBlue   = 0xFF ;       // 1 bits (foreground)
          pbmi->argbColor[1].bGreen  = 0xFF ;
          pbmi->argbColor[1].bRed    = 0xFF ;
          pbmi->argbColor[1].fcOptions = 0 ;

          hps = WinGetPS (hwnd) ;
          hbm = GpiCreateBitmap (hps, &bmp, CBM_INIT, abBitCat, pbmi) ;
          WinReleasePS (hps) ;

          free (pbmi) ;
          return 0 ;

     case WM_SIZE:
          cxClient = SHORT1FROMMP (mp2) ;
          cyClient = SHORT2FROMMP (mp2) ;
          return 0 ;

     case WM_PAINT:
          hps = WinBeginPaint (hwnd, NULLHANDLE, NULL) ;

          aptl[0].x = 0 ;                       // target lower left
          aptl[0].y = 0 ;

          aptl[1].x = cxClient ;                // target upper right
          aptl[1].y = cyClient ;

          aptl[2].x = 0 ;                       // source lower left
          aptl[2].y = 0 ;

          aptl[3].x = 32 ;                      // source upper right
          aptl[3].y = 32 ;
```

Listing 6.4: The BITCAT1 program (Continued)

```
               GpiWCBitBlt (hps, hbm, 4L, aptl, ROP_SRCCOPY, BBO_AND) ;

               aptl[1] = aptl[3] ;                // target upper right

               GpiWCBitBlt (hps, hbm, 4L, aptl, ROP_SRCCOPY, BBO_AND) ;

               WinEndPaint (hps) ;
               return 0 ;

          case WM_DESTROY:
               GpiDeleteBitmap (hbm) ;
               return 0 ;
          }
     return WinDefWindowProc (hwnd, msg, mp1, mp2) ;
     }
```

The BITCAT.H File

```
/*----------------------
   BITCAT.H header file
  ----------------------*/

static BYTE abBitCat[] = {0x00, 0xFF, 0xFF, 0x00, 0x00, 0xA2, 0x45, 0x0
                          0x00, 0xA2, 0x45, 0x00, 0x00, 0xA2, 0x45, 0xE
                          0x00, 0xA2, 0x45, 0x10, 0x00, 0xA2, 0x45, 0x0
                          0x00, 0x9C, 0x39, 0x08, 0x00, 0xC0, 0x03, 0

                          0x00, 0x40, 0x02, 0x04, 0x00, 0x40, 0x0
                          0x00, 0x40, 0x02, 0x04, 0x00, 0x20, 0x0
                          0x00, 0x20, 0x04, 0x04, 0x00, 0x20, 0x0
                          0x00, 0x10, 0x08, 0x04, 0x00, 0x10, 0x0

                          0x00, 0x10, 0x08, 0x10, 0x00, 0x08, 0x10
                          0x00, 0x08, 0x10, 0xC0, 0x00, 0x08, 0x10
                          0x00, 0x07, 0xE0, 0x00, 0x00, 0x08, 0
                          0x00, 0xFC, 0x3F, 0x00, 0x00, 0x09, 0x90,

                          0x00, 0xFC, 0x3F, 0x00, 0x00, 0x08, 0x10,
                          0x00, 0x1A, 0x58, 0x00, 0x00, 0x28, 0x14, 0x0
                          0x00, 0x48, 0x12, 0x00, 0x00, 0x8F, 0xF1, 0x0
                          0x01, 0x04, 0x20, 0x80, 0x01, 0xF8, 0x1F, 0x80
```

The BITCAT1.DEF File

```
;----------------------------------
; BITCAT1.DEF module definition file
;----------------------------------
```

Listing 6.4: The BITCAT1 program (Continued)

```
NAME            BITCAT1   WINDOWAPI

DESCRIPTION     'Bitmap Creation and Display (c) Charles Petzold, 1993'
PROTMODE
```

The *abBitCat* array in BITCAT.H contains the bytes that define the picture of the cat. Note that the rows are in reverse order from the rows used in *GpiImage*. (*GpiImage* requires the top row first.) The BITCAT1 program creates the 32-by-32 bitmap during the WM_CREATE message and deletes it during the WM_DESTROY message.

During the WM_PAINT message, BITCAT1 draws the bitmap twice using the *WinDrawBitmap* function. The first call draws the bitmap to fill the entire client window. The second call draws the bitmap in the lower-left corner of the client window in its actual pixel size. This is shown in Figure 6.7.

Figure 6.7: The BITCAT1 display

BITMAPS AND BITBLTS

I mentioned earlier that the *WinDrawBitmap* function is convenient but that GPI has a better way to draw a bitmap using our old friend, the *GpiBitBlt* function. This will be demonstrated shortly in the BITCAT2 program.

You may resist this new method at first because BITCAT2.C is longer than BITCAT1.C and somewhat more complex. However, this method unleashes all the power available in the *GpiBitBlt* function when drawing a bitmap. This is where bitmaps and bitblts come together as two related tools.

You'll recall that *GpiBitBlt* transfers a bitmap from one presentation space to another, possibly combining it with the current pattern set in the destination presentation space. There doesn't seem to be any place in the function for a handle to a bitmap. To use the *GpiBitBlt* function to draw a bitmap, we must first make the bitmap part of a presentation space. This requires a concept that is very important for working with bitmaps: the memory device context.

THE MEMORY DEVICE CONTEXT

In Chapter 5, we worked briefly with the device context for the video display. "Device context" is a term used to describe the combination of an output device and its device driver. A presentation space is associated with a device context. When you call GPI drawing functions for a particular presentation space, GPI draws the objects on the device context associated with the presentation space.

We're going to create a device context that exists only in memory. This device context is not a real output device. It is called the memory device context. To create this device context, you call *DevOpenDC* with a second parameter set to the identifier OD_MEMORY and the other parameters as shown here:

```
hdcMemory = DevOpenDC (hab, OD_MEMORY, "*", ØL, NULL, NULL) ;
```

You then create a presentation space associated with this memory device context by calling *GpiCreatePS*:

```
hpsMemory = GpiCreatePS (hab, hdcMemory, &sizl,
                         PU_PELS | GPIF_DEFAULT
                         GPIT_MICRO | GPIA_ASSOC) ;
```

This presentation space is associated with the memory device context. The third parameter is a pointer to a structure of type SIZEL with two fields named *cx* and *cy*. Before calling *GpiCreatePS*, you set these two fields to 0.

Here comes the crucial step: You call *GpiSetBitmap* to set a bitmap in this presentation space:

```
GpiSetBitmap (hpsMemory, hbm) ;
```

This function seems a little strange at first. Near the beginning of this chapter, I said that you could imagine the entire video display as one big bitmap. The video adapter board contains a large block of memory that includes (in one form or another) the digital representation of the image on the screen.

When you call *GpiSetBitmap*, the bitmap becomes the display surface of the memory device context associated with the presentation space. You can then use this presentation space as a source (or destination) with functions such as *GpiBitBlt*. Moreover, anything you draw on this presentation space is actually drawn on the bitmap.

When you are finished using the presentation space, the memory device context, and the bitmap, you destroy them in this order:

```
GpiDestroyPS (hpsMemory) ;
DevCloseDC (hdcMemory) ;
GpiDeleteBitmap (hbm) ;
```

Now let's look at BITCAT2, which uses this approach. The program is shown in Listing 6.5.

Listing 6.5: The BITCAT2 program

The BITCAT2.MAK File

```
#-----------------------
# BITCAT2.MAK make file
#-----------------------

bitcat2.exe : bitcat2.obj bitcat2.def
     $(PRGLINK) bitcat2, bitcat2, NUL, $(PRGLIB), bitcat2

bitcat2.obj : bitcat2.c bitcat.h
     $(PRGCC) bitcat2.c
```

The BITCAT2.C File

```
/*------------------------------------------
   BITCAT2.C -- Bitmap Creation and Display
                (c) Charles Petzold, 1993
  ------------------------------------------*/

#define INCL_WIN
#define INCL_GPI
#include <os2.h>
#include <stdlib.h>
#include <string.h>
#include "bitcat.h"
```

Listing 6.5: The BITCAT2 program (Continued)

```
MRESULT EXPENTRY ClientWndProc (HWND, ULONG, MPARAM, MPARAM) ;

int main (void)
     {
     static CHAR  szClientClass [] = "BitCat2" ;
     static ULONG flFrameFlags = FCF_TITLEBAR      | FCF_SYSMENU  |
                                 FCF_SIZEBORDER    | FCF_MINMAX   |
                                 FCF_SHELLPOSITION | FCF_TASKLIST ;
     HAB          hab ;
     HMQ          hmq ;
     HWND         hwndFrame, hwndClient ;
     QMSG         qmsg ;

     hab = WinInitialize (Ø) ;
     hmq = WinCreateMsgQueue (hab, Ø) ;

     WinRegisterClass (hab, szClientClass, ClientWndProc, CS_SIZEREDRAW, Ø) ;

     hwndFrame = WinCreateStdWindow (HWND_DESKTOP, WS_VISIBLE,
                                     &flFrameFlags, szClientClass, NULL,
                                     ØL, Ø, Ø, &hwndClient) ;

     while (WinGetMsg (hab, &qmsg, NULLHANDLE, Ø, Ø))
          WinDispatchMsg (hab, &qmsg) ;

     WinDestroyWindow (hwndFrame) ;
     WinDestroyMsgQueue (hmq) ;
     WinTerminate (hab) ;
     return Ø ;
     }

MRESULT EXPENTRY ClientWndProc (HWND hwnd, ULONG msg, MPARAM mp1, MPARAM mp2)
     {
     static HBITMAP      hbm ;
     static HDC          hdcMemory ;
     static HPS          hpsMemory ;
     static INT          cxClient, cyClient ;
     BITMAPINFO2       * pbmi ;
     BITMAPINFOHEADER2   bmp ;
     HAB                 hab ;
     HPS                 hps ;
     POINTL              aptl [4] ;
     SIZEL               sizl ;

     switch (msg)
          {
          case WM_CREATE:
               hab = WinQueryAnchorBlock (hwnd) ;
```

Listing 6.5: The BITCAT2 program (Continued)

```
               // Open memory DC and create PS associated with it

     hdcMemory = DevOpenDC (hab, OD_MEMORY, "*", 0L, NULL, 0) ;

     sizl.cx = 0 ;
     sizl.cy = 0 ;

     hpsMemory = GpiCreatePS (hab, hdcMemory, &sizl,
                              PU_PELS    | GPIF_DEFAULT |
                              GPIT_MICRO | GPIA_ASSOC) ;

               // Create 32-by-32 bitmap

     memset (&bmp, 0, sizeof (BITMAPINFOHEADER2)) ;

     bmp.cbFix     = sizeof (BITMAPINFOHEADER2) ;
     bmp.cx        = 32 ;
     bmp.cy        = 32 ;
     bmp.cPlanes   = 1 ;
     bmp.cBitCount = 1 ;

     hbm = GpiCreateBitmap (hpsMemory, &bmp, 0L, NULL, NULL) ;

               // Select bitmap into memory PS

     GpiSetBitmap (hpsMemory, hbm) ;

               // Set bitmap bits from abBitCat array

     pbmi = malloc (sizeof (BITMAPINFO2) + sizeof (RGB)) ;

     memset (pbmi, 0, sizeof (BITMAPINFOHEADER2)) ;

     pbmi->cbFix     = sizeof (BITMAPINFOHEADER2) ;
     pbmi->cx        = 32 ;
     pbmi->cy        = 32 ;
     pbmi->cPlanes   = 1 ;
     pbmi->cBitCount = 1 ;

     pbmi->argbColor[0].bBlue  = 0x00 ;      // 0 bits (background)
     pbmi->argbColor[0].bGreen = 0x00 ;
     pbmi->argbColor[0].bRed   = 0x00 ;
     pbmi->argbColor[0].fcOptions = 0 ;

     pbmi->argbColor[1].bBlue  = 0xFF ;      // 1 bits (foreground)
     pbmi->argbColor[1].bGreen = 0xFF ;
     pbmi->argbColor[1].bRed   = 0xFF ;
     pbmi->argbColor[0].fcOptions = 0 ;
```

Listing 6.5: The BITCAT2 program (Continued)

```
          GpiSetBitmapBits (hpsMemory, 0L, 32L, abBitCat, pbmi) ;

          free (pbmi) ;
          return 0 ;

     case WM_SIZE:
          cxClient = SHORT1FROMMP (mp2) ;
          cyClient = SHORT2FROMMP (mp2) ;
          return 0 ;

     case WM_PAINT:
          hps = WinBeginPaint (hwnd, NULLHANDLE, NULL) ;

          aptl[0].x = 0 ;                    // target lower left
          aptl[0].y = 0 ;

          aptl[1].x = cxClient ;             // target upper right
          aptl[1].y = cyClient ;

          aptl[2].x = 0 ;                    // source lower left
          aptl[2].y = 0 ;

          aptl[3].x = 32 ;                   // source upper right
          aptl[3].y = 32 ;

          GpiBitBlt (hps, hpsMemory, 4L, aptl, ROP_SRCCOPY, BBO_AND) ;

          aptl[1] = aptl[3] ;                // target upper right

          GpiBitBlt (hps, hpsMemory, 3L, aptl, ROP_SRCCOPY, BBO_AND) ;

          WinEndPaint (hps) ;
          return 0 ;

     case WM_DESTROY:
          GpiDestroyPS (hpsMemory) ;
          DevCloseDC (hdcMemory) ;
          GpiDeleteBitmap (hbm) ;
          return 0 ;
     }
return WinDefWindowProc (hwnd, msg, mp1, mp2) ;
}
```

The BITCAT2.DEF File

```
;-----------------------------------
; BITCAT2.DEF module definition file
;-----------------------------------
```

Listing 6.5: The BITCAT2 program (Continued)

```
NAME           BITCAT2   WINDOWAPI

DESCRIPTION    'Bitmap Creation and Display (c) Charles Petzold, 1993'
PROTMODE
```

The BITCAT2 program also requires the BITCAT.H header file from Listing 6.4. As you can see from Figure 6.8, the program shows the same output as BITCAT1.

Figure 6.8: The BITCAT2 display

During the WM_CREATE message, BITCAT2 opens a memory device context and creates a presentation space associated with that device context. BITCAT2 creates an initialized 32-by-32 bitmap exactly like BITCAT1. But then it calls *GpiSetBitmap* to set the bitmap in the presentation space.

During the WM_PAINT message, BITCAT2 uses the *GpiBitBlt* function to draw the bitmap on the display. The source presentation space is simply the presentation space associated with the memory device context. Although BITCAT2 uses ROP_SRCCOPY, it could also select a nondefault pattern in the destination presentation space and use *GpiBitBlt* with all 256 raster operations.

For drawing bitmaps, GPI also provides two additional functions: *GpiDrawBits* and *GpiWCBitBlt* (the *WC* stands for "world coordinates").

DRAWING ON THE MEMORY DEVICE CONTEXT

I said earlier that the bitmap is the display surface of the memory device context. Thus, when you use normal GPI functions to draw on the presentation space associated with this memory device context, you're actually drawing on the bitmap. This is one reason that you can create a bitmap without initializing it. You can create an image on the bitmap simply by drawing on the presentation space.

This is shown in the HELLOBIT program in Listing 6.6.

Listing 6.6: The HELLOBIT program

The HELLOBIT.MAK File

```
#-----------------------
# HELLOBIT.MAK make file
#-----------------------

hellobit.exe : hellobit.obj hellobit.def
     $(PRGLINK) hellobit, hellobit, NUL, $(PRGLIB), hellobit

hellobit.obj : hellobit.c
     $(PRGCC) hellobit.c
```

The HELLOBIT.C File

```
/*----------------------------------------
   HELLOBIT.C -- "Hello, world" Bitmap
                 (c) Charles Petzold, 1993
  ----------------------------------------*/

#define INCL_WIN
#define INCL_GPI
#include <os2.h>
#include <string.h>

MRESULT EXPENTRY ClientWndProc (HWND, ULONG, MPARAM, MPARAM) ;

int main (void)
     {
     static CHAR  szClientClass [] = "HelloBit" ;
     static ULONG flFrameFlags = FCF_TITLEBAR      | FCF_SYSMENU |
                                 FCF_SIZEBORDER    | FCF_MINMAX  |
                                 FCF_SHELLPOSITION | FCF_TASKLIST ;
     HAB          hab ;
```

Listing 6.6: The HELLOBIT program (Continued)

```
     HMQ          hmq ;
     HWND         hwndFrame, hwndClient ;
     QMSG         qmsg ;

     hab = WinInitialize (Ø) ;
     hmq = WinCreateMsgQueue (hab, Ø) ;

     WinRegisterClass (hab, szClientClass, ClientWndProc, CS_SIZEREDRAW, Ø) ;

     hwndFrame = WinCreateStdWindow (HWND_DESKTOP, WS_VISIBLE,
                                     &flFrameFlags, szClientClass, NULL,
                                     ØL, Ø, Ø, &hwndClient) ;

     while (WinGetMsg (hab, &qmsg, NULLHANDLE, Ø, Ø))
          WinDispatchMsg (hab, &qmsg) ;

     WinDestroyWindow (hwndFrame) ;
     WinDestroyMsgQueue (hmq) ;
     WinTerminate (hab) ;
     return Ø ;
     }

MRESULT EXPENTRY ClientWndProc (HWND hwnd, ULONG msg, MPARAM mp1, MPARAM mp2)
     {
     static CHAR       szHello [] = " Hello, world! " ;
     static HBITMAP    hbm ;
     static HDC        hdcMemory ;
     static HPS        hpsMemory ;
     static INT        cxClient, cyClient, cxString, cyString ;
     BITMAPINFOHEADER2 bmp ;
     HAB               hab ;
     HPS               hps ;
     POINTL            aptl [4], ptl ;
     INT               x, y ;
     SIZEL             sizl ;

     switch (msg)
          {
          case WM_CREATE:
               hab = WinQueryAnchorBlock (hwnd) ;

                         // Open memory DC and create PS associated with it

               hdcMemory = DevOpenDC (hab, OD_MEMORY, "*", ØL, NULL, Ø) ;

               sizl.cx = Ø ;
               sizl.cy = Ø ;
               hpsMemory = GpiCreatePS (hab, hdcMemory, &sizl,
                                        PU_PELS     | GPIF_DEFAULT |
```

Listing 6.6: The HELLOBIT program (Continued)

```
                              GPIT_MICRO | GPIA_ASSOC) ;

                    // Determine dimensions of text string

          GpiQueryTextBox (hpsMemory, sizeof szHello - 1L,
                           szHello, 4L, aptl) ;

          cxString = (SHORT) (aptl [TXTBOX_TOPRIGHT].x -
                              aptl [TXTBOX_TOPLEFT].x) ;

          cyString = (SHORT) (aptl [TXTBOX_TOPLEFT].y -
                              aptl [TXTBOX_BOTTOMLEFT].y) ;

                    // Create bitmap and set it in the memory PS

          memset (&bmp, Ø, sizeof (BITMAPINFOHEADER2)) ;

          bmp.cbFix     = sizeof (BITMAPINFOHEADER2) ;
          bmp.cx        = cxString ;
          bmp.cy        = cyString ;
          bmp.cPlanes   = 1 ;
          bmp.cBitCount = 1 ;

          hbm = GpiCreateBitmap (hpsMemory, &bmp, ØL, ØL, NULL) ;

          GpiSetBitmap (hpsMemory, hbm) ;

                    // Write the text string to the memory PS

          ptl.x = Ø ;
          ptl.y = - aptl [TXTBOX_BOTTOMLEFT].y ;

          GpiSetColor (hpsMemory, CLR_TRUE) ;
          GpiSetBackColor (hpsMemory, CLR_FALSE) ;
          GpiSetBackMix (hpsMemory, BM_OVERPAINT) ;
          GpiCharStringAt (hpsMemory, &ptl, sizeof szHello - 1L,
                           szHello) ;
          return Ø ;

     case WM_SIZE:
          cxClient = SHORT1FROMMP (mp2) ;
          cyClient = SHORT2FROMMP (mp2) ;
          return Ø ;

     case WM_PAINT:
          hps = WinBeginPaint (hwnd, NULLHANDLE, NULL) ;

          for (y = Ø ; y <= cyClient / cyString ; y++)
               for (x = Ø ; x <= cxClient / cxString ; x++)
```

Listing 6.6: The HELLOBIT program (Continued)

```
                         {
                         aptl[0].x = x * cxString ;     // target lower left
                         aptl[0].y = y * cyString ;

                         aptl[1].x = aptl[0].x + cxString ; // upper right
                         aptl[1].y = aptl[0].y + cyString ;

                         aptl[2].x = 0 ;                // source lower left
                         aptl[2].y = 0 ;

                         GpiBitBlt (hps, hpsMemory, 3L, aptl, ROP_SRCCOPY,
                                    BBO_AND) ;
                         }
               WinEndPaint (hps) ;
               return 0 ;

          case WM_DESTROY:
               GpiDestroyPS (hpsMemory) ;
               DevCloseDC (hdcMemory) ;
               GpiDeleteBitmap (hbm) ;
               return 0 ;
          }
     return WinDefWindowProc (hwnd, msg, mp1, mp2) ;
     }
```

The HELLOBIT.DEF File

```
;-----------------------------------
; HELLOBIT.DEF module definition file
;-----------------------------------

NAME           HELLOBIT  WINDOWAPI

DESCRIPTION    'Hello, world Bitmap (c) Charles Petzold, 1993'
PROTMODE
```

HELLOBIT creates a memory device context and a presentation space associated with this memory device context during the WM_CREATE message. Then it determines the dimension of the text “Hello, world!” by calling *GpiQueryTextBox*. The program creates a bitmap of these dimensions and sets the bitmap in the memory device context.

HELLOBIT then writes the text string on the presentation space by calling *GpiCharStringAt*. The bitmap is monochrome, so the foreground color is set to CLR_TRUE (1 bits), and the background color to CLR_FALSE (0 bits). These are the best color values to use with monochrome bitmaps. HELLOBIT also sets the background mix to BM_OVERPAINT so that the background is filled in with 0 bits.

During the WM_PAINT message, HELLOBIT covers the window with copies of this bitmap by calling *GpiBitBlt.* This is shown in Figure 6.9.

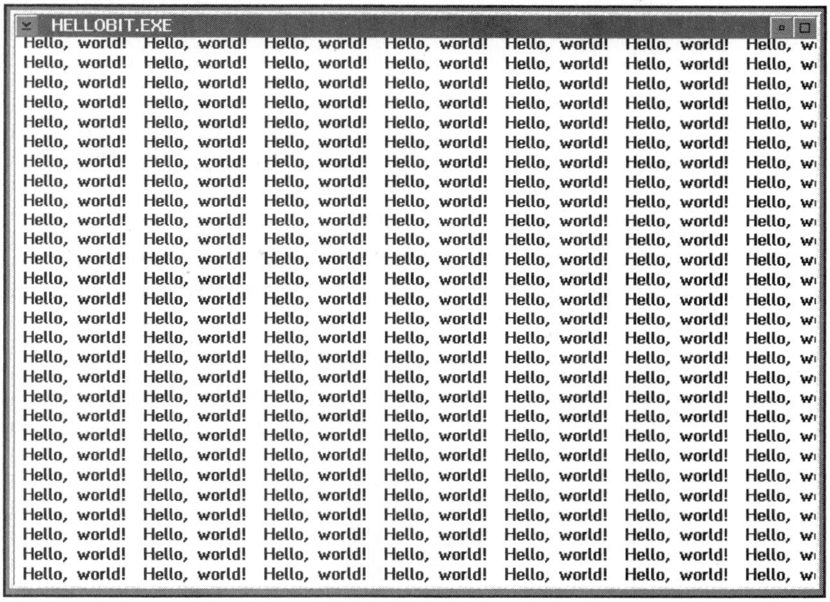

Figure 6.9: The HELLOBIT display

As in BITCAT2, the presentation space, device context, and bitmap are destroyed during the WM_DESTROY message.

You might want to try a variation of HELLOBIT that uses *WinDrawBitmap* during the WM_PAINT message. In this case, you don't need the memory device context or presentation space after you initialize the bitmap by calling *GpiCharStringAt.* You can destroy them after that call:

```
GpiDestroyPS (hpsMemory) ;
DevCloseDC (hdcMemory) ;
```

During the WM_DESTROY message you need only destroy the bitmap. Thus, the memory device context and presentation space serve simply as a mold to draw on the bitmap. You can then destroy the mold (calling *GpiDestroyPS* and *DevCloseDC*), leaving the bitmap behind.

One common use of a memory device context is for a "shadow bitmap." You create a bitmap large enough to encompass the client window and select that into a presentation space associated with a memory device context. Whenever you draw on the window, you also draw on the presentation space. During the WM_PAINT message, you can update the client window with a simple *GpiBitBlt* call. This approach is shown in the SKETCH program in Chapter 9.

When a bitmap is set in a presentation space associated with a memory device context, you can set the bitmap bits with an array of data using *GpiSetBitmapBits*. This is yet another way to initialize a bitmap. You can also obtain the bitmap bits and store them in an array by calling *GpiQueryBitmapBits*.

CUSTOMIZED PATTERNS

Another use for bitmaps is to create your own customized patterns for area filling. A pattern is based on an 8-by-8 bitmap. When a pattern is used to fill an area, the bitmap is simply repeated horizontally and vertically.

For example, suppose you want to use a pattern that looks like a brick wall. Assuming you want the brick itself to be the foreground color (1 bits) and the cement between the bricks to be the background color (0 bits), the bitmap that you begin with might look like this:

These bits (padded at the right so each row is 32 bits) are stored in the *abBrick* array in the BRICKS program in Listing 6.7.

Listing 6.7: The BRICKS program

The BRICKS.MAK File

```
#----------------------
# BRICKS.MAK make file
#----------------------

bricks.exe : bricks.obj bricks.def
     $(PRGLINK) bricks, bricks, NUL, $(PRGLIB), bricks

bricks.obj : bricks.c
     $(PRGCC) bricks.c
```

Listing 6.7: The BRICKS program (Continued)

The BRICKS.C File

```
/*-------------------------------------------
   BRICKS.C -- Customized Pattern from Bitmap
               (c) Charles Petzold, 1993
  -------------------------------------------*/

#define INCL_WIN
#define INCL_GPI
#include <os2.h>
#include <stdlib.h>
#include <string.h>

#define LCID_BRICKS_BITMAP    1L

MRESULT EXPENTRY ClientWndProc (HWND, ULONG, MPARAM, MPARAM) ;

int main (void)
     {
     static CHAR  szClientClass [] = "Bricks" ;
     static ULONG flFrameFlags = FCF_TITLEBAR      | FCF_SYSMENU |
                                 FCF_SIZEBORDER    | FCF_MINMAX  |
                                 FCF_SHELLPOSITION | FCF_TASKLIST ;
     HAB          hab ;
     HMQ          hmq ;
     HWND         hwndFrame, hwndClient ;
     QMSG         qmsg ;

     hab = WinInitialize (0) ;
     hmq = WinCreateMsgQueue (hab, 0) ;

     WinRegisterClass (hab, szClientClass, ClientWndProc, CS_SIZEREDRAW, 0) ;

     hwndFrame = WinCreateStdWindow (HWND_DESKTOP, WS_VISIBLE,
                                     &flFrameFlags, szClientClass, NULL,
                                     0L, 0, 0, &hwndClient) ;

     while (WinGetMsg (hab, &qmsg, NULLHANDLE, 0, 0))
          WinDispatchMsg (hab, &qmsg) ;

     WinDestroyWindow (hwndFrame) ;
     WinDestroyMsgQueue (hmq) ;
     WinTerminate (hab) ;
     return 0 ;
     }

MRESULT EXPENTRY ClientWndProc (HWND hwnd, ULONG msg, MPARAM mp1, MPARAM mp2)
     {
```

Listing 6.7: The BRICKS program (Continued)

```
     static BYTE          abBrick [] = {
                                          0x00, 0x00, 0x00, 0x00,
                                          0xF3, 0x00, 0x00, 0x00,
                                          0xF3, 0x00, 0x00, 0x00,
                                          0xF3, 0x00, 0x00, 0x00,
                                          0x00, 0x00, 0x00, 0x00,
                                          0x3F, 0x00, 0x00, 0x00,
                                          0x3F, 0x00, 0x00, 0x00,
                                          0x3F, 0x00, 0x00, 0x00
                                          } ;
     static HBITMAP       hbm ;
     static POINTL        aptl [2] ;
     BITMAPINFO2        * pbmi ;
     BITMAPINFOHEADER2    bmp ;
     HPS                  hps ;

     switch (msg)
          {
          case WM_CREATE:
                                        // Create 8 by 8 bitmap

               memset (&bmp, 0, sizeof (BITMAPINFOHEADER2)) ;

               bmp.cbFix     = sizeof (BITMAPINFOHEADER2) ;
               bmp.cx        = 8 ;
               bmp.cy        = 8 ;
               bmp.cPlanes   = 1 ;
               bmp.cBitCount = 1 ;

               pbmi = malloc (sizeof (BITMAPINFO2) + sizeof (RGB)) ;

               memset (pbmi, 0, sizeof (BITMAPINFOHEADER2)) ;

               pbmi->cbFix     = sizeof (BITMAPINFOHEADER2) ;
               pbmi->cx        = 8 ;
               pbmi->cy        = 8 ;
               pbmi->cPlanes   = 1 ;
               pbmi->cBitCount = 1 ;

               pbmi->argbColor[0].bBlue  = 0x00 ;
               pbmi->argbColor[0].bGreen = 0x00 ;
               pbmi->argbColor[0].bRed   = 0x00 ;
               pbmi->argbColor[0].fcOptions = 0 ;

               pbmi->argbColor[1].bBlue  = 0xFF ;
               pbmi->argbColor[1].bGreen = 0xFF ;
               pbmi->argbColor[1].bRed   = 0xFF ;
               pbmi->argbColor[1].fcOptions = 0 ;
```

Listing 6.7: The BRICKS program (Continued)

```
          hps = WinGetPS (hwnd) ;
          hbm = GpiCreateBitmap (hps, &bmp, CBM_INIT, abBrick, pbmi) ;

          WinReleasePS (hps) ;
          free (pbmi) ;
          return 0 ;

     case WM_SIZE:
          aptl[1].x = SHORT1FROMMP (mp2) ;
          aptl[1].y = SHORT2FROMMP (mp2) ;
          return 0 ;

     case WM_PAINT:
          hps = WinBeginPaint (hwnd, NULLHANDLE, NULL) ;

          GpiSetBitmapId (hps, hbm, LCID_BRICKS_BITMAP) ;
          GpiSetPatternSet (hps, LCID_BRICKS_BITMAP) ;

          GpiBitBlt (hps, NULLHANDLE, 2L, aptl, ROP_PATCOPY, BBO_AND) ;

          GpiSetPatternSet (hps, LCID_DEFAULT) ;
          GpiDeleteSetId (hps, LCID_BRICKS_BITMAP) ;

          WinEndPaint (hps) ;
          return 0 ;

     case WM_DESTROY:
          GpiDeleteBitmap (hbm) ;
          return 0 ;
     }
return WinDefWindowProc (hwnd, msg, mp1, mp2) ;
}
```

The BRICKS.DEF File

```
;-------------------------------------
; BRICKS.DEF module definition file
;-------------------------------------

NAME           BRICKS    WINDOWAPI

DESCRIPTION    'Customized Pattern from Bitmap (c) Charles Petzold, 1988'
PROTMODE
```

During the WM_CREATE message, BRICKS creates an 8-by-8 bitmap initialized with these bits. During the WM_PAINT message, the bitmap is first tagged with an ID number:

```
GpiSetBitmapId (hps, hbm, LCID_BRICKS_BITMAP) ;
```

The LCID_BRICKS_BITMAP is defined in BRICKS.C as 1. (LCID stands for "local ID.") The bitmap is now an available pattern. You can use the *GpiSetPatternSet* function to make this pattern the current pattern:

```
GpiSetPatternSet (hps, LCID_BRICKS_BITMAP) ;
```

Notice that this is the *GpiSetPatternSet* function rather than the *GpiSetPattern* function normally used for selecting a pattern.

BRICKS uses the *GpiBitBlt* function with the ROP_PATCOPY raster operation to fill the window with the bitmap, as shown in Figure 6.10.

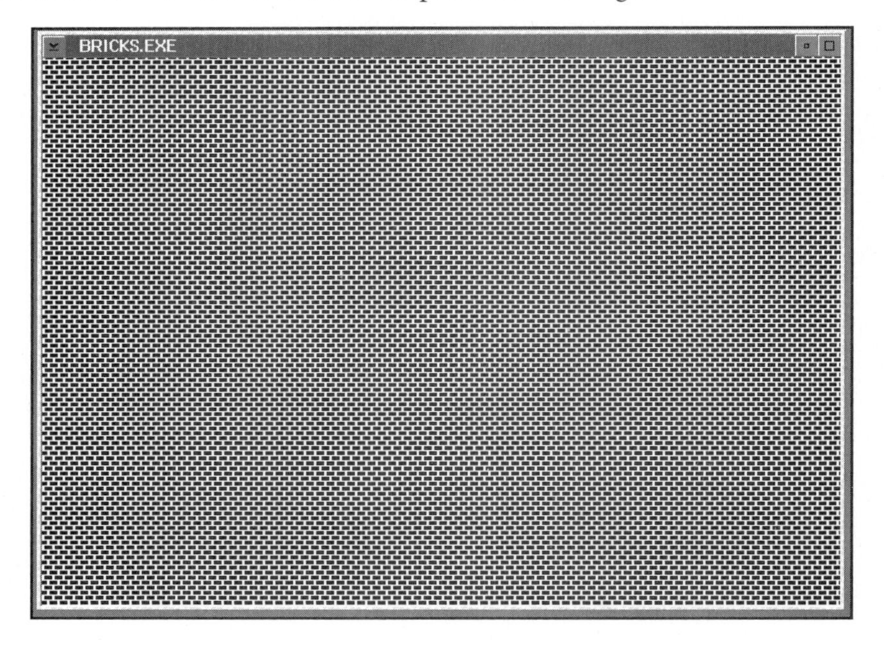

Figure 6.10: The BRICKS display

The program could also have used *GpiBox* with the DRO_FILL or DRO_OUTLINEFILL option to display the bricks pattern. After BRICKS uses the pattern, the current pattern set is established as the default pattern set (containing all predefined patterns):

```
GpiSetPatternSet (hps, LCID_DEFAULT) ;
```

The LCID_DEFAULT identifier is defined in PMGPI.H. BRICKS then deletes the local ID:

```
GpiDeleteSetId (hps, LCID_BRICKS_BITMAP) ;
```

You can define up to 254 customized patterns using local IDs ranging from 1 through 254. When you want to use a customized pattern, you call *GpiSetPatternSet* with the local ID. When you want to use a predefined pattern, you first call *GpiSetPattern* Set with LCID_DEFAULT and then use *GpiSetPattern* with a PATSYM identifier.

The local IDs for these customized patterns become part of the presentation space. Before releasing a cached micro-PS by calling *WinReleasePS* or *WinEndPaint*, you should set the pattern to the default and delete all the IDs. A bitmap cannot be deleted while it has a local ID. You can obtain the bitmap handle tagged with a local ID by calling *GpiQueryBitmapHandle*:

```
hbm = GpiQueryBitmapHandle (hps, lcid) ;
```

You'll recall from the last chapter that you use local IDs when creating fonts. You cannot use the same local ID for both a bitmap and a pattern at the same time. Also keep in mind that the *GpiSetPS* function deletes all local IDs.

DRAWING PIXELS

Finally, GPI has two functions that might seem important when you first begin programming for the OS/2 Presentation Manager. The *GpiSetPel* function sets an individual pixel to the current foreground color:

```
GpiSetPel (hps, &ptl) ;
```

The *GpiQueryPel* function obtains the color of an individual pixel:

```
lColor = GpiQueryPel (hps, &ptl) ;
```

These two functions are used so infrequently in Presentation Manager programming that you can just about ignore them.

Advanced Graphics

Bézier splines

Paths

Transforms

Outline fonts

Chapter 7

To programmers who came to OS/2 after first learning graphics under Windows or the Macintosh, the OS/2 Graphics Programming Interface was a revelation. Even the very first version of the Presentation Manager offered more advanced graphics features and, consequently, presented several new learning experiences. In this chapter, I'll cover several of these features:

- *Bézier splines*, a type of curved line very useful in interactive design
- *Paths*, a technique for drawing thick lines and creating arbitrary clipping regions
- *Transforms*, ways to scale, skew, or rotate graphics objects
- *Outline fonts*, fonts designed with vector outlines that are infinitely scalable and may be manipulated like other graphics objects

If your graphics needs are not sophisticated, you can probably get by with the material covered in Chapters 5 and 6. But the advanced graphics techniques discussed in this chapter certainly give you more flexibility in displaying visual information to the user. So let's begin.

Bézier splines

When Pierre Bézier began his pioneering work in computer modeling in the 1960s, he probably didn't realize the extent to which his work would eventually find its way into mainstream computer graphics. An engineer with the French automobile company Renault, Bézier used a computer program called UNISURF to develop methods for defining the curvature of body panels for cars.

At the time, automobile body panels were designed on paper, using simple drawing tools such as French curves. Clay models would be constructed, and, after that, stamps and dies for creating the panels. In the late 1950s, however, the advent of hardware that could create the dies directly from mathematical specifications dictated a new approach to defining shapes.

The Bézier spline was part of the mathematics developed to assist in this process. Traditionally, a *spline* was a thin, flexible, piece of wood or metal that could be anchored at noncolinear points (that is, points that do not define a straight line) to form a curve. Such mechanical devices have now gone the way of the slide rule. These days, splines are mathematical formulas processed by a computer.

In computer graphics, the Bézier spline has come to be regarded as the most important type of curved line after the ellipse. Bézier splines are a valuable tool in computer-aided design (CAD) because they are well-suited for interactive manipulation, and they are often considered pleasing to the eye. But Bézier splines also have a powerful application in a different area of computer graphics that is not at all like CAD—namely, text.

It turns out that Bézier splines are extremely useful in the definition of fonts based on vector outlines. These outline fonts (which I'll describe later in this chapter) give the programmer and user maximum flexibility in manipulating and displaying text. Bézier splines prove to be nearly ideal for defining the curves in the characters of these outline fonts.

DRAWING BEZIER SPLINES

A Bézier spline in two dimensions is a curved line uniquely described by four points: two end points and two control points. For the moment (until we start tackling the mathematics behind the definition of the Bézier spline), I'll call the end points E1 and E2 and the control points C1 and C2. The Bézier curve begins at E1 and ends at E2. The curve generally does not pass through C1 and C2; instead, the control points affect the curvature of the line by acting like magnets that pull the curve in one direction or another.

To draw a Bézier spline in a Presentation Manager program, you use the *GpiPolySpline* function. *GpiPolySpline* draws one or more connected Bézier spline curves beginning at the current position. The function has the following syntax:

```
GpiPolySpline (hps, lPoints, aptl) ;
```

The last parameter is an array of POINTL structures and the second parameter is the number of POINTL structures in this array. This is always a multiple of 3.

To draw one spline curve, you need an array of three POINTL structures. The *GpiPolySpline* function draws a curve from the current position to *aptl[2]*, using *aptl[0]* and *aptl[1]* as control points, as shown here:

```
E1 = Current Position
C1 = aptl[0]
C2 = aptl[1]
E2 = aptl[2]
```

When you specify six points in the array, the function draws two connected Bézier splines. The second curve continues from *aptl[2]*, thus:

```
E1 = aptl[2]
C1 = aptl[3]
C2 = aptl[4]
E2 = aptl[5]
```

The *GpiPolySpline* function sets the current position to the last point in the array, for example, *aptl[2]* for three points and *aptl[5]* for six points.

The use of *GpiPolySpline* to draw two or more connected Bézier splines can be a little tricky. In general, the resultant composite curve will not be smooth at the point where the curves meet. If you want a smooth composite curve (using the example of two curves shown above), *aptl[1]*, *aptl[2]*, and *aptl[3]* must be colinear (that is, lie in the same straight line), with *aptl[2]* somewhere between the other two points.

PLAYING WITH BEZIER SPLINES

So, let's see what these Bézier curves look like with an interactive program. The BEZIER program is shown in Listing 7.1.

Listing 7.1: The BEZIER Program

The BEZIER.MAK File

```
#---------------------
# BEZIER.MAK make file
#---------------------

bezier.exe : bezier.obj bezier.def
     $(PRGLINK) bezier, bezier, NUL, $(PRGLIB), bezier

bezier.obj : bezier.c
     $(PRGCC) bezier.c
```

Listing 7.1: The BEZIER Program (Continued)

The BEZIER.C File

```
/*-------------------------------------
   BEZIER.C -- Bezier Splines
               (c) Charles Petzold, 1993
  -------------------------------------*/

#define INCL_WIN
#define INCL_GPI
#include <os2.h>

MRESULT EXPENTRY ClientWndProc (HWND, ULONG, MPARAM, MPARAM) ;

int main (void)
     {
     static CHAR  szClientClass [] = "Bezier" ;
     static ULONG flFrameFlags = FCF_TITLEBAR      | FCF_SYSMENU |
                                 FCF_SIZEBORDER    | FCF_MINMAX  |
                                 FCF_SHELLPOSITION | FCF_TASKLIST ;
     HAB          hab ;
     HMQ          hmq ;
     HWND         hwndFrame, hwndClient ;
     QMSG         qmsg ;

     hab = WinInitialize (0) ;
     hmq = WinCreateMsgQueue (hab, 0) ;

     WinRegisterClass (hab, szClientClass, ClientWndProc, CS_SIZEREDRAW, 0) ;

     hwndFrame = WinCreateStdWindow (HWND_DESKTOP, WS_VISIBLE,
                                     &flFrameFlags, szClientClass, NULL,
                                     0L, 0, 0, &hwndClient) ;

     while (WinGetMsg (hab, &qmsg, NULLHANDLE, 0, 0))
          WinDispatchMsg (hab, &qmsg) ;

     WinDestroyWindow (hwndFrame) ;
     WinDestroyMsgQueue (hmq) ;
     WinTerminate (hab) ;
     return 0 ;
     }

MRESULT EXPENTRY ClientWndProc (HWND hwnd, ULONG msg, MPARAM mp1, MPARAM mp2)
     {
     static POINTL aptl[4] ;
     HPS           hps ;
     INT           cxClient, cyClient ;
```

Listing 7.1: The BEZIER Program (Continued)

```
     switch (msg)
          {
          case WM_SIZE:
               cxClient = SHORT1FROMMP (mp2) ;
               cyClient = SHORT2FROMMP (mp2) ;

               aptl[0].x = cxClient / 3 ;
               aptl[0].y = cyClient / 2 ;

               aptl[1].x = cxClient / 2 ;
               aptl[1].y = 3 * cyClient / 4 ;

               aptl[2].x = cxClient / 2 ;
               aptl[2].y = cyClient / 4 ;

               aptl[3].x = 2 * cxClient / 3 ;
               aptl[3].y = cyClient / 2 ;

               return 0 ;

          case WM_BUTTON1DOWN:
               aptl[1].x = MOUSEMSG(&msg)->x ;
               aptl[1].y = MOUSEMSG(&msg)->y ;

               WinInvalidateRect (hwnd, NULL, TRUE) ;
               break ;

          case WM_BUTTON2DOWN:
               aptl[2].x = MOUSEMSG(&msg)->x ;
               aptl[2].y = MOUSEMSG(&msg)->y ;

               WinInvalidateRect (hwnd, NULL, TRUE) ;
               break ;

          case WM_PAINT:
               hps = WinBeginPaint (hwnd, NULLHANDLE, NULL) ;
               GpiErase (hps) ;

                    // Draw dotted straight lines

               GpiSetLineType (hps, LINETYPE_DOT) ;
               GpiMove (hps, aptl + 0) ;
               GpiLine (hps, aptl + 1) ;
               GpiMove (hps, aptl + 2) ;
               GpiLine (hps, aptl + 3) ;

                    // Draw spline

               GpiSetLineType (hps, LINETYPE_SOLID) ;
```

Listing 7.1: The BEZIER Program (Continued)

```
               GpiMove (hps, aptl) ;
               GpiPolySpline (hps, 3, aptl + 1) ;

               WinEndPaint (hps) ;
               return 0 ;
          }
     return WinDefWindowProc (hwnd, msg, mp1, mp2) ;
     }
```

The BEZIER.DEF File

```
;-----------------------------------
; BEZIER.DEF module definition file
;-----------------------------------

NAME           BEZIER    WINDOWAPI

DESCRIPTION    'Bezier Splines (c) Charles Petzold, 1993'
PROTMODE
```

When the program begins, it sets the two end points halfway between the top and bottom of the client window, with E1 one-third of the distance and E2 two-thirds of the distance from the left of the window. The Bézier curve connects these two points, as shown in Figure 7.1.

The program also draws two dotted lines, the first from E1 on the left to the first control point C1, located halfway across the client window and one-quarter the distance down. The second dotted line connects E2 with the second control point C2, located towards the bottom of the client window. I'll discuss the significance of these dotted lines shortly.

The end points E1 and E2 are fixed in place by the program, depending on the size of the client window, but you can change the two control points C1 and C2 by clicking with the left and right mouse buttons, respectively. (Except for this mouse-button logic, the rest of the program is fairly straightforward. For now, you'll have to trust the mouse processing, which won't be treated in detail until Chapter 9.)

If you move the first control point to the upper-left corner of the window and the second control point to the upper-right corner, the program will draw the Bézier spline shown in Figure 7.2. Switching the positions of the two control points causes a loop to appear in the Bézier spline curve, as shown in Figure 7.3. Bézier spline curves with loops are not generally used.

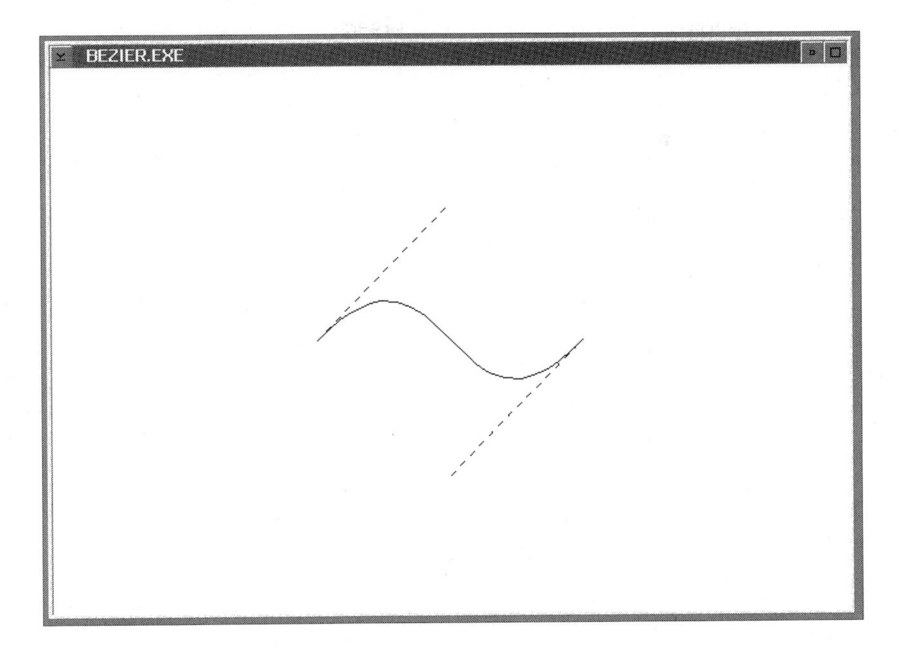

Figure 7.1: The initial BEZIER display

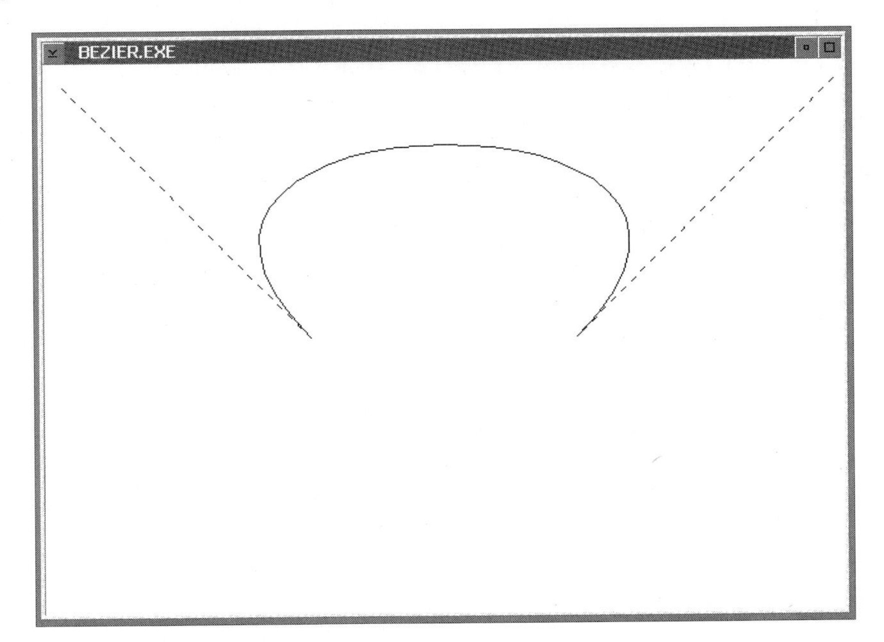

Figure 7.2: Another BEZIER display

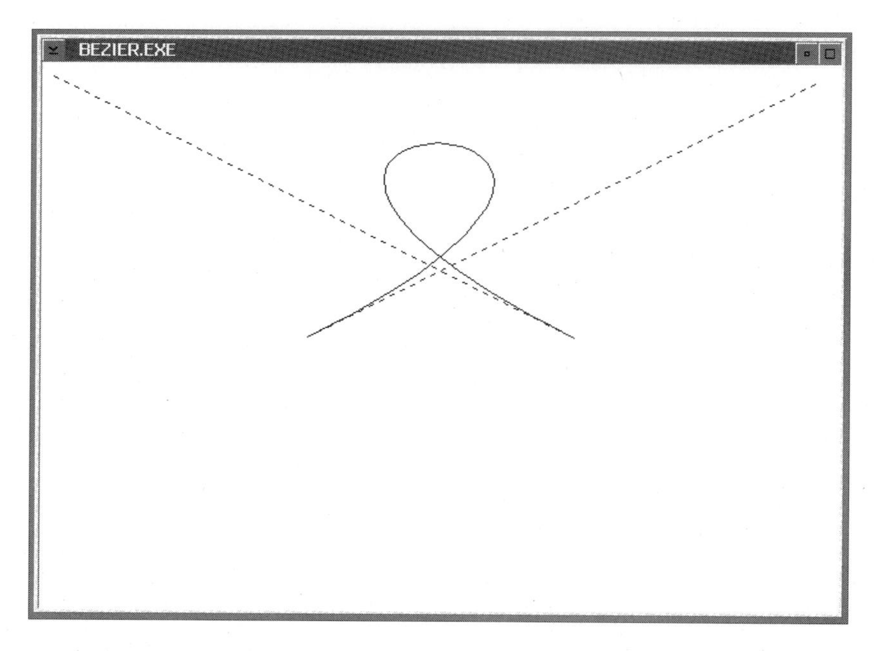

Figure 7.3: A third BEZIER display

BEZIER SPLINE CHARACTERISTICS

As you'll probably discover when experimenting with the BEZIER program, the Bézier spline lends itself well to interactive design. With a little practice, it becomes fairly easy to use the control points to pull the curve into a desired shape. The control points act like magnets on the curve in a fairly intuitive way.

Other characteristics of the Bézier spline also make it suitable for use in interactive design. Some forms of spline curves do not necessarily touch any of the points used to define them, but the Bézier curve always passes through the two end points. This anchors at least part of the curve in place.

If you think of the curve as being drawn from E1 to E2, then at E1 the curve is tangent to—and in the same direction as—a straight line that runs from E1 to C1. Similarly, at the point E2, the curve is tangent to—and in the same direction as—a straight line that runs from C2 to E2. The dotted lines drawn by the BEZIER program help indicate this.

Some complex curves have irregularities for certain combinations of points, which can cause strange behavior in the curve. For example, part of the curve could veer off into infinity. This is rarely desirable! The Bézier spline, by contrast, stays well under control. Specifically, the curve is always bound by the four-sided convex polygon (sometimes called a *convex hull*) that you can visualize by connecting the four points that define the curve.

This polygon is not always defined in the same way. For example, the Bézier spline in Figure 7.1 is bounded by the polygon formed by connecting E1 to C1 to E2 to C2 back to E1. Figure 7.2 shows a Bézier curve that is bounded by a polygon from E1 to C1 to C2 to E2 back to E1. In Figure 7.3, the bounding polygon is from E1 to C2 to C1 to E2 back to E1. These three examples account for all possibilities of how the convex hull is defined.

Most importantly, Bézier spline curves are pleasing to the eye. This is surprising, considering that so little information is required to define the curve and considering how easy it is to manipulate them.

THE MATHEMATICAL REPRESENTATION

No discussion of the Bézier spline would be complete without the mathematics involved. Although you don't have to worry about this when using Bézier splines in a Presentation Manager program, you may be surprised at the relative simplicity of the curve formulas. (On the other hand, if you're not accustomed to stuff like this, you may be surprised at the complexity of the formulas!)

The Bézier spline curve is a cubic polynomial, which means that the formulas involve variables taken to the third power. It is expressed in terms of parametric equations, in which the variables *x* and *y* are functions of a third variable, often called *t*. You can think of *t* as "time," ranging from 0 at the beginning of the line to 1 at the end of the line.

The general form of a parametric cubic polynomial in two dimensions is

$$x(t) = a_x t^3 + b_x t^2 + c_x t + d_x$$

$$y(t) = a_y t^3 + b_y t^2 + c_y t + d_y$$

where *t* ranges from 0 to 1. The *a*, *b*, *c*, and *d* values are constants. To derive these constants for the Bézier spline, we need some assumptions. To do this, I'll have to abandon my earlier notation (E1, E2, C1, and C2) at this point, and instead refer to the four points in terms of subscripted values of *x* and *y*, as shown here:

$$E1 = (x_0, y_0)$$

$$C1 = (x_1, y_1)$$

$$C2 = (x_2, y_2)$$

$$E2 = (x_3, y_3)$$

We make four assumptions. The first assumption is that the curve passes through the point (x_0, y_0) when t is 0. Thus:

$$x(0) = x_0$$

$$y(0) = y_0$$

The second assumption is that the curve passes through the point (x_3, y_3) when t is 1:

$$x(1) = x_3$$

$$y(1) = y_3$$

These two assumptions ensure that the curve begins at E1 and ends at E2. The third and fourth assumptions involve the first derivatives of the two parametric equations. This governs the slope of the line at the end points. For the beginning of the curve, the assumption is

$$x'(0) = 3(x_1 - x_0)$$

$$y'(0) = 3(y_1 - y_0)$$

Similarly, for the end of the curve, the assumption is

$$x'(1) = 3(x_3 - x_2)$$

$$y'(1) = 3(y_3 - y_2)$$

Armed with these equations, you can solve for the constants a_x, b_x, and so forth in terms of the constants x_0, x_1, and so forth. Putting these constants back into the generalized third-degree parametric formulas shown above and performing some algebraic manipulation, you can derive the common form of the Bézier spline formulas:

$$x(t) = (1-t)^3 x_0 + 3t(1-t)^2 x_1 + 3t^2(1-t)x_2 + t^3 x_3$$

$$y(t) = (1-t)^3 y_0 + 3t(1-t)^2 y_1 + 3t^2(1-t)y_2 + t^3 y_3$$

There is a certain internal symmetry in these formulas that is very appealing, don't you think?

PATHS

If you've ever done any graphics programming in PostScript, you probably already know what a path is. It's almost impossible to draw anything at all under PostScript unless you use paths. The OS/2 Graphics Programming

Interface (GPI) also supports paths. Although you don't have to use them for most drawing, they can be quite useful for advanced graphics programming.

Let's begin with a few definitions:

A *path* is a collection of straight line and curve definitions stored internally in GPI memory. Some of these lines may be connected to each other. If so, these connected lines are known collectively as a *subpath* or a *figure*. Thus, a path is composed of one or more subpaths. Each subpath is a collection of connected lines.

A subpath can be either closed or open. A subpath is *closed* if the end of the last line is connected to the beginning of the first line in the subpath. (A special function is available to close a subpath.) Otherwise, the subpath is *open*.

CREATING A PATH

To create a path in your presentation space, you first call

```
GpiBeginPath (hps, lPath) ;
```

The *lPath* parameter is documented as a *path ID*, but it must be set to 1.

The *GpiBeginPath* function marks the beginning of a *path bracket*. After calling *GpiBeginPath*, only a limited number of GPI functions are allowed in the path bracket. (The complete list is in the Presentation Manager Programming Reference.) In particular, you can call functions that draw lines and set line attributes, plus a few others. The lines are not actually drawn but instead are stored in GPI memory as the path definition. (As we'll see towards the end of this chapter, if you have an outline font selected in the presentation space, text output functions such as *GpiCharStringAt* are also allowed within the path bracket. In this case, the character outlines become part of the path definition.)

To make a closed subpath, you must call

```
GpiCloseFigure (hps) ;
```

after drawing the lines that comprise the subpath, even if you've made the end point of the last line the same as the beginning point of the first line. And if you've haven't made these two points the same, *GpiCloseFigure* will close the path with a straight line between those two points. If you don't call *GpiCloseFigure*, the subpath will be open.

GpiCloseFigure also begins a new subpath. You can also begin a new subpath by calling *GpiMove* or another function that otherwise changes the current position without drawing a line.

To end the path bracket you call

```
GpiEndPath (hps) ;
```

At this point, the entire path definition is stored in GPI memory and things are back to normal. However, you'll probably want to use the path soon after creating it by calling one of the special path functions. These functions are

- *GpiOutlinePath*
- *GpiStrokePath*
- *GpiFillPath*
- *GpiClipPath*
- *GpiPathToRegion*

Each of these functions does something with the path and then deletes it from storage. There is no explicit path deletion function. In addition, you can call *GpiModifyPath* prior to calling one of these five functions. (I'll discuss *Gpi-ModifyPath* later in this chapter.)

OUTLINING THE PATH

The simplest function that does something with a path is

```
GpiOutlinePath (hps, lPath, lOption) ;
```

As with *GpiBeginPath*, the *lPath* parameter must be set to 1. Also, the *lOption* parameter must be set to 0. This function simply renders the path on an output device (such as the video display) by drawing it as a series of lines. It then deletes the path definition from memory.

But why bother? Why not just draw the lines to begin with instead of storing them in a path definition and then calling *GpiOutlinePath?* Well, in most cases, the effects *are* exactly the same, and there is no real reason to use the path. The *GpiOutlinePath* function was actually more important in OS/2 1.1, when this function provided the only way to draw outlined (rather than filled) characters using an outline font. The addition of the FATTR_SEL_OUTLINE text attribute (discussed later in this chapter) solved that problem. But even with the addition of the FATTR_SEL_OUTLINE attribute, *GpiOutlinePath* still has a unique purpose when used in conjunction with *GpiModifyPath*, as we shall see.

As we saw in Chapter 5, lines have certain attributes. This is true whether you draw these lines using the line-drawing functions, or by calling *GpiOutlinePath*, or when you display an outline font created with the FATTR_SEL_OUTLINE function. First, there is the line type that you set using the *GpiSetLineType* function. This determines whether lines are solid (the default) or composed of various dots and dashes. Second, the lines have a width governed by use of the function

```
GpiSetLineWidth (hps, fxWidth) ;
```

The second parameter is a fixed-point value, with the high word being an integer part and the low word being a fractional part. The value 0x00010000 (the identifier LINEWIDTH_NORMAL) is the default—a line width that is "normal" for the particular output device (generally one pixel wide on video displays). You can also use LINEWIDTH_THICK (the value 0x00020000) to double the width of the lines. These are the only two values that are guaranteed to yield unique results, and indeed are the only values that work on the VGA.

The width of these lines is independent of any transforms that may be in effect. If you use a transform that, for example, doubles the sizes of all graphics objects, line widths are *not* affected. This is known as the *cosmetic* line width, to differentiate it from the *geometric* line width that I'll discuss next.

STROKING THE PATH

The second function that renders a path is

```
GpiStrokePath (hps, lPath, lOption) ;
```

As with the *GpiOutlinePath* function, the *lPath* parameter must be set to 1 and the *lOption* parameter must be set to 0.

Like the *GpiOutlinePath* function, *GpiStrokePath* renders the path on an output device by drawing it as a series of lines. However, *GpiStrokePath* draws geometric lines rather than cosmetic lines. These geometric lines are *not* affected by the *GpiSetLineType* or *GpiSetLineWidth* functions. Instead, the width of the lines is governed by the function

```
GpiSetLineWidthGeom (hps, lWidth) ;
```

The *lWidth* parameter is the desired line width in world coordinates (a concept to be discussed later in this chapter). What you need to know now is that the geometric line width is dependent on any transforms that may be in effect. The lines are actually treated as filled areas, and filled with the current area-filling pattern, which you set using *GpiSetPattern.*

COSMETIC AND GEOMETRIC LINES

The distinction between cosmetic and geometric lines is perhaps best illustrated with the following example.

Suppose you use lines to create an architectural drawing. You'll probably want to use geometric lines for the walls of the structure, because these should appear larger when you "zoom in" on the image. However, the lines that indicate measurements of the structure should be cosmetic lines—there is no reason for them to be thicker when you zoom in.

One reason why paths are very important is that you simply can't draw geometric lines otherwise! Which, of course, immediately provokes the question: "Why not?"

Once you begin drawing geometric lines that have a very thick width (say over a quarter inch or so), the *ends* and *joins* of these lines become visually important. When drawing geometic lines using the *GpiStrokePath* function, two other line-drawing attribute functions play a part. The first is

```
GpiSetLineEnd (hps, lEnd) ;
```

The *lEnd* parameter can be LINEEND_FLAT (the default), LINEEND_-SQUARE, or LINEEND_ROUND. This affects the beginning of the first line and the end of the last line in an open path. (It does not affect a closed path at all.) With LINEEND_FLAT, the end of the line is cut off flatly. With LINEEND_SQUARE, the end of the line is also flat, but it is extended half the width of the line. With LINEEND_ROUND, the end of the line is capped off with a semi-circular area.

When two lines within a subpath are joined, the appearance of the join is governed by

```
GpiSetLineJoin (hps, lJoin) ;
```

where *lJoin* can be LINEJOIN_BEVEL (the default), LINEJOIN_ROUND or LINEJOIN_MITRE. (Notice the British spelling of "miter" that reveals the origins of GPI in the IBM labs in Hursley, England.) The miter join comes to a point; the bevel join has the point chopped off; and the round join is, of course, round.

Explanations are one thing, and visuals are another. So let's look at a short program that uses geometric lines to illustrate the three types of ends and joins. This is the ENDJOIN program shown in Listing 7.2.

Listing 7.2: The ENDJOIN program

The ENDJOIN.MAK File

```
#----------------------
# ENDJOIN.MAK make file
#----------------------

endjoin.exe : endjoin.obj endjoin.def
```

Listing 7.2: The ENDJOIN program (Continued)

```
     $(PRGLINK) endjoin, endjoin, NUL, $(PRGLIB), endjoin

endjoin.obj : endjoin.c
     $(PRGCC) endjoin.c
```

The ENDJOIN.C File

```
/*---------------------------------------
   ENDJOIN.C -- Line Ends and Joins
                (c) Charles Petzold, 1993
  ---------------------------------------*/

#define INCL_WIN
#define INCL_GPI
#include <os2.h>

MRESULT EXPENTRY ClientWndProc (HWND, ULONG, MPARAM, MPARAM) ;

int main (void)
     {
     static CHAR  szClientClass [] = "EndJoin" ;
     static ULONG flFrameFlags = FCF_TITLEBAR      | FCF_SYSMENU  |
                                 FCF_SIZEBORDER    | FCF_MINMAX   |
                                 FCF_SHELLPOSITION | FCF_TASKLIST ;
     HAB          hab ;
     HMQ          hmq ;
     HWND         hwndFrame, hwndClient ;
     QMSG         qmsg ;

     hab = WinInitialize (0) ;
     hmq = WinCreateMsgQueue (hab, 0) ;

     WinRegisterClass (hab, szClientClass, ClientWndProc, CS_SIZEREDRAW, 0) ;

     hwndFrame = WinCreateStdWindow (HWND_DESKTOP, WS_VISIBLE,
                                     &flFrameFlags, szClientClass, NULL,
                                     0L, 0, 0, &hwndClient) ;

     while (WinGetMsg (hab, &qmsg, NULLHANDLE, 0, 0))
          WinDispatchMsg (hab, &qmsg) ;

     WinDestroyWindow (hwndFrame) ;
     WinDestroyMsgQueue (hmq) ;
     WinTerminate (hab) ;
     return 0 ;
     }

void DrawFigure (HPS hps, INT i, INT cxClient, INT cyClient)
     {
```

Listing 7.2: The ENDJOIN program (Continued)

```
     POINTL ptl ;

     ptl.x = (1 + 10 * i) * cxClient / 30 ;
     ptl.y = 3 * cyClient / 4 ;
     GpiMove (hps, &ptl) ;

     ptl.x = (5 + 10 * i) * cxClient / 30 ;
     ptl.y = cyClient / 4 ;
     GpiLine (hps, &ptl) ;

     ptl.x = (9 + 10 * i) * cxClient / 30 ;
     ptl.y = 3 * cyClient / 4 ;
     GpiLine (hps, &ptl) ;
     }

MRESULT EXPENTRY ClientWndProc (HWND hwnd, ULONG msg, MPARAM mp1, MPARAM mp2)
     {
     static INT  cxClient, cyClient ;
     static LONG alJoin [] = { LINEJOIN_BEVEL, LINEJOIN_ROUND, LINEJOIN_MITRE },
                 alEnd  [] = { LINEEND_FLAT, LINEEND_SQUARE, LINEEND_ROUND } ;
     HPS         hps ;
     INT         i ;

     switch (msg)
          {
          case WM_SIZE:
               cxClient = SHORT1FROMMP (mp2) ;
               cyClient = SHORT2FROMMP (mp2) ;
               return 0 ;

          case WM_PAINT:
               hps = WinBeginPaint (hwnd, NULLHANDLE, NULL) ;

               GpiErase (hps) ;

               for (i = 0 ; i < 3 ; i++)
                    {
                              // Draw the geometric line

                    GpiSetLineJoin (hps, alJoin [i]) ;
                    GpiSetLineEnd  (hps, alEnd  [i]) ;
                    GpiSetLineWidthGeom (hps, cxClient / 20) ;
                    GpiSetColor (hps, CLR_DARKGRAY) ;

                    GpiBeginPath (hps, 1) ;
                    DrawFigure (hps, i, cxClient, cyClient) ;
                    GpiEndPath (hps) ;

                    GpiStrokePath (hps, 1, 0) ;
```

Listing 7.2: The ENDJOIN program (Continued)

```
                              // Draw the cosmetic line

                    GpiSetLineWidth (hps, LINEWIDTH_THICK) ;
                    GpiSetColor (hps, CLR_BLACK) ;

                    DrawFigure (hps, i, cxClient, cyClient) ;
                    }

               WinEndPaint (hps) ;
               return 0 ;
          }
     return WinDefWindowProc (hwnd, msg, mp1, mp2) ;
     }
```

The ENDJOIN.DEF File

```
;-----------------------------------
; ENDJOIN.DEF module definition file
;-----------------------------------

NAME           ENDJOIN   WINDOWAPI

DESCRIPTION    'Line Ends and Joins (c) Charles Petzold, 1993'
PROTMODE
```

The program draws three sets of lines, to illustrate (from left to right), the flat, square, and round line ends, and the bevel, round, and miter line joins, as shown in Figure 7.4.

Actually, for each of the three images, the program draws two lines using the same coordinates—one wide dark-gray geometric line, and the other a black cosmetic line using a thick (that is, double) width. This illustrates how the ends and joins correspond to the actual geometric ends of the lines. In particular, notice how the square and round ends are extended past the actual end of the line, unlike the flat end.

This brings me back to answering the question: "Why are paths required for drawing geometric lines?" The answer is that GPI cannot properly determine if two lines are joined unless the connected lines are accumulated in a path before being drawn. For example, if GPI received a *GpiLine* call, it would have to draw the selected line-end design at the end of the line, even though another *GpiLine* call may follow it, which would indicate a line-join design.

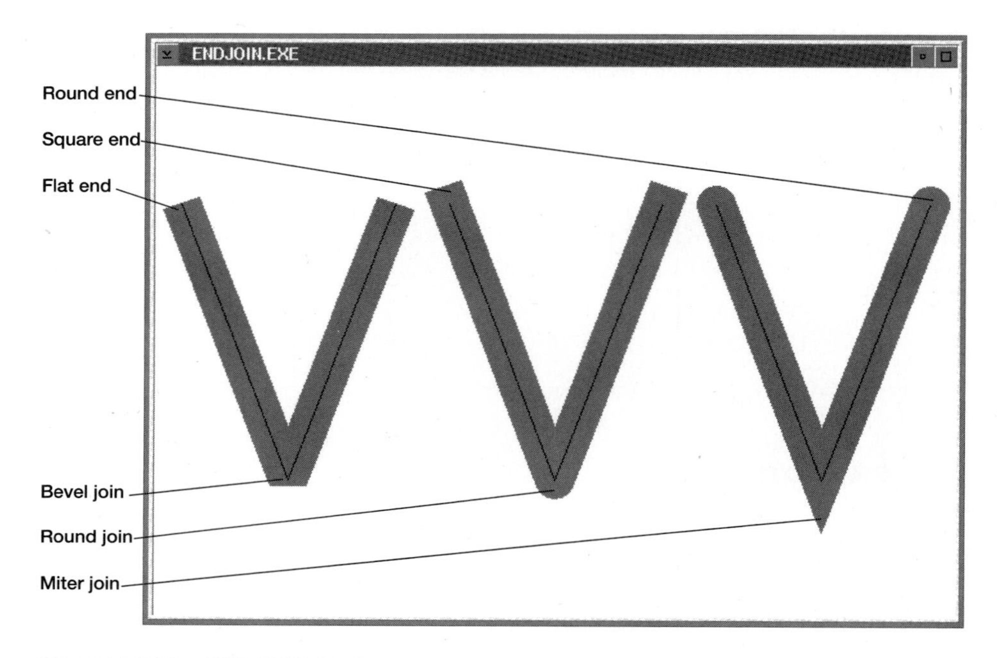

Figure 7.4: The ENDJOIN display

FILLING THE PATH

So far, we've examined outlining a path (using cosmetic lines) and stroking a path (using geometric lines). You can also fill path interiors using the function

```
GpiFillPath (hps, lPath, lOption) ;
```

As usual, the *lPath* parameter is 1. This function closes all open subpaths with straight lines. The interiors of the subpaths are filled using the current area-filling pattern.

The *lOption* parameter can be either FPATH_ALTERNATE (the default if you specify a 0 parameter) or FPATH_WINDING. This determines how subpath interiors are filled if they overlap:

- For alternate fill mode, an interior is not filled if an imaginary line drawn from the interior to infinity crosses an even number of boundaries. Otherwise the interior is filled.
- For winding fill mode, an interior is not filled if an imaginary line drawn from the interior to infinity crosses the same number of boundary lines drawn in one direction as drawn in the opposite direction. Otherwise the interior is filled.

Although GPI has functions to fill arbitrarily defined areas using an area bracket (*GpiBeginArea* and *GpiEndArea*) rather than a path, text output functions are not allowed in area brackets. With paths, you can fill characters with nonsolid patterns such as hatch-marks.

Two functions that have similar syntax to *GpiFillPath* are

```
GpiSetClipPath (hps, lPath, lOption) ;
```

where the *lOption* parameter can be either SCP_ALTERNATE or SCP_WINDING, and

```
hRgn = GpiPathToRegion (hps, lPath, lOption) ;
```

where the *lOption* parameter can be either FPATH_ALTERNATE or FPATH_WINDING.

The *GpiSetClipPath* function causes GPI to clip all drawing to the interior of the path. Thus, text characters can define a clipping area for some interesting effects (as we'll see towards the end of this chapter). *GpiPathToRegion* converts the path to a GPI region and returns a handle to the region.

MODIFYING THE PATH

So far you've seen five functions that you can call after creating a path: These functions can outline the path with a cosmetic line, stroke it with a geometric line, fill it, make it into a clipping area, or convert the path into a region. Each of these functions deletes the path from GPI memory after completing the operation.

After calling *GpiEndPath* and before calling one of the five functions discussed above, you can also call

```
GpiModifyPath (hps, lPath, lMode) ;
```

The *lPath* parameter must be 1, and *lMode* must be MPATH_STROKE.

This function creates a new path from the old path: Think of the path as being stroked by a geometric line. The new path is the outline of that thick line. Every open path is converted into a closed path, and every closed path is converted into two closed paths.

The PATHS program in Listing 7.3 illustrates combinations of modifying, outlining, stroking, and filling.

Listing 7.3: The PATHS program

The PATHS.MAK File

```
#---------------------
# PATHS.MAK make file
#---------------------

paths.exe : paths.obj paths.def
     $(PRGLINK) paths, paths, NUL, $(PRGLIB), paths

paths.obj : paths.c
     $(PRGCC) paths.c
```

The PATHS.C File

```
/*--------------------------------------
   PATHS.C -- Path Functions
              (c) Charles Petzold, 1993
  --------------------------------------*/

#define INCL_WIN
#define INCL_GPI
#include <os2.h>

MRESULT EXPENTRY ClientWndProc (HWND, ULONG, MPARAM, MPARAM) ;

int main (void)
     {
     static CHAR  szClientClass [] = "Paths" ;
     static ULONG flFrameFlags = FCF_TITLEBAR      | FCF_SYSMENU  |
                                 FCF_SIZEBORDER    | FCF_MINMAX   |
                                 FCF_SHELLPOSITION | FCF_TASKLIST ;
     HAB          hab ;
     HMQ          hmq ;
     HWND         hwndFrame, hwndClient ;
     QMSG         qmsg ;

     hab = WinInitialize (0) ;
     hmq = WinCreateMsgQueue (hab, 0) ;

     WinRegisterClass (hab, szClientClass, ClientWndProc, CS_SIZEREDRAW, 0) ;

     hwndFrame = WinCreateStdWindow (HWND_DESKTOP, WS_VISIBLE,
                                     &flFrameFlags, szClientClass, NULL,
                                     0L, 0, 0, &hwndClient) ;

     while (WinGetMsg (hab, &qmsg, NULLHANDLE, 0, 0))
          WinDispatchMsg (hab, &qmsg) ;
```

Listing 7.3: The PATHS program (Continued)

```
     WinDestroyWindow (hwndFrame) ;
     WinDestroyMsgQueue (hmq) ;
     WinTerminate (hab) ;
     return 0 ;
     }

MRESULT EXPENTRY ClientWndProc (HWND hwnd, ULONG msg, MPARAM mp1, MPARAM mp2)
     {
     static INT  cxClient, cyClient ;
     HPS         hps ;
     INT         x, y ;
     POINTL      ptl ;

     switch (msg)
          {
          case WM_SIZE:
               cxClient = SHORT1FROMMP (mp2) ;
               cyClient = SHORT2FROMMP (mp2) ;
               return 0 ;

          case WM_PAINT:
               hps = WinBeginPaint (hwnd, NULLHANDLE, NULL) ;

               GpiErase (hps) ;

               for (x = 0 ; x < 3 ; x++)
               for (y = 0 ; y < 2 ; y++)
                    {
                         // Create an open subpath

                    GpiBeginPath (hps, 1) ;

                    ptl.x = (1 + 10 * x) * cxClient / 30 ;
                    ptl.y = (4 +  5 * y) * cyClient / 10 ;
                    GpiMove (hps, &ptl) ;

                    ptl.x = (5 + 10 * x) * cxClient / 30 ;
                    ptl.y = (2 +  5 * y) * cyClient / 10 ;
                    GpiLine (hps, &ptl) ;

                    ptl.x = (9 + 10 * x) * cxClient / 30 ;
                    ptl.y = (4 +  5 * y) * cyClient / 10 ;
                    GpiLine (hps, &ptl) ;

                         // Create a closed subpath

                    ptl.x = (1 + 10 * x) * cxClient / 30 ;
                    ptl.y = (3 +  5 * y) * cyClient / 10 ;
                    GpiMove (hps, &ptl) ;
```

Listing 7.3: The PATHS program (Continued)

```
               ptl.x = (5 + 10 * x) * cxClient / 30 ;
               ptl.y = (1 +  5 * y) * cyClient / 10 ;
               GpiLine (hps, &ptl) ;

               ptl.x = (9 + 10 * x) * cxClient / 30 ;
               ptl.y = (3 +  5 * y) * cyClient / 10 ;
               GpiLine (hps, &ptl) ;

               GpiCloseFigure (hps) ;
               GpiEndPath (hps) ;

                    // Possibly modify the path

               if (y == 0)
                    {
                    GpiSetLineWidthGeom (hps, cxClient / 30) ;
                    GpiModifyPath (hps, 1, MPATH_STROKE) ;
                    }

                    // Perform the operation

               GpiSetLineWidth (hps, LINEWIDTH_THICK) ;
               GpiSetLineWidthGeom (hps, cxClient / 50) ;
               GpiSetPattern (hps, PATSYM_HALFTONE) ;

               switch (x)
                    {
                    case 0:  GpiOutlinePath (hps, 1, 0) ;
                             break ;

                    case 1:  GpiStrokePath (hps, 1, 0) ;
                             break ;

                    case 2:  GpiFillPath (hps, 1, FPATH_ALTERNATE) ;
                             break ;
                    }
               }

          WinEndPaint (hps) ;
          return 0 ;
     }
return WinDefWindowProc (hwnd, msg, mp1, mp2) ;
}
```

The PATHS.DEF File

```
;----------------------------------
; PATHS.DEF module definition file
;----------------------------------
```

Listing 7.3: The PATHS program (Continued)

```
NAME           PATHS     WINDOWAPI

DESCRIPTION    'Path Functions (c) Charles Petzold, 1993'
PROTMODE
```

The program creates a path six times; the path contains an open subpath (a V shape) and a closed subpath (a triangle). From left to right on the top of the display, the program outlines the path using a double-width cosmetic pen, strokes the path with a geometric pen that is 1/50th the width of the client area, and fills the path. Both the stroking and the filling use the halftone area-fill pattern. On the bottom, these three operations are preceded by modifying the path with a geometric pen 1/30th the width of the client area. This is shown in Figure 7.5.

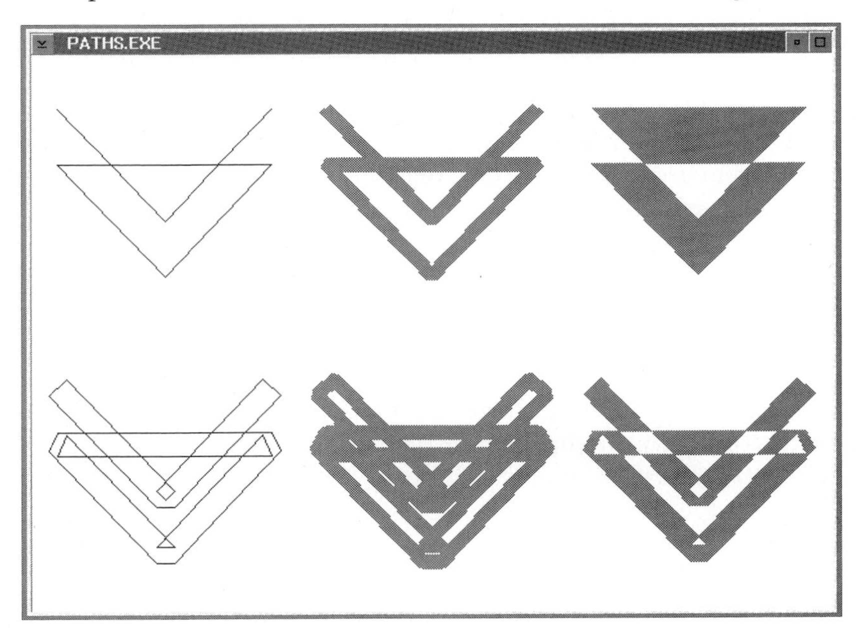

Figure 7.5: The PATHS display

The two outlined paths on the left side of the display show most clearly the effects of *GpiModifyPath*. The open V-shaped subpath is converted into a closed subpath that outlines the path as if it had been stroked with a geometric pen. The closed triangle subpath is converted into two paths, one on the outside and one on the inside of the outlines of a geometric pen stroking. Of course, the little interior loops at the apexes look rather odd, but those are the results of the algorithm that GPI uses.

TRANSFORMS

Pixels: You can't draw without them; you can't draw with them.

Pixels are the single greatest impediment to device-independent graphics programming. Draw a 100-pixel vertical line and what do you get? On the IBM Color Graphics Adapter (CGA), the line will be half the height of the video display. On a 300-dots-per-inch laser printer, it's a mere third of an inch. Moreover, some graphics output devices have unequal horizontal and vertical resolutions, and that's a problem when you want to draw round circles and square squares.

Many of the sample programs shown so far in this book have scaled their graphics output to the size of the client window or based graphics output on a character size. These techniques avoided problems of different device resolutions, but they have limited use in the real world. In real-world programming, you may want to use real-world measurements, such as inches or millimeters. Or, you may want to define an arbitrary coordinate system and treat the window as a 1000 by 1000 coordinate space. Or, you may prefer that the origin—the point (0,0)—be in the center of the window rather than the lower-left corner.

In Chapter 5, I showed how you can use the *DevQueryCaps* function to obtain all the information you need to compensate for the resolution of the output device and draw in real-world units. I also discussed the *GpiSetPS* function, which sets a GPI transform. A *transform* maps points in one coordinate space to points in another coordinate space. GPI defines a hierarchy of coordinate spaces to map the points you specify in GPI functions to the actual pixels of the output device.

FROM WORLD TO MEDIA

When you pass a POINTL structure to a GPI function, GPI must convert the point to a particular pixel on the output device. The points you specify in GPI functions are points in a *world coordinate space.* This is a common concept in graphics programming. You can think of the world coordinate space as whatever coordinate space is convenient for your application. In a micro-PS (which we've been using exclusively), GPI defines four transforms that progressively convert points from the world coordinate space to points in four other coordinate spaces, as shown in Table 7.1.

Table 7.1: The Micro-PS Coordinate Spaces and Transforms

Source Coordinate Space	Destination Coordinate Space	Transform	GPI Function
World	Model	Model	GpiSetModelTransformMatrix
Model	Presentation Page	Default Viewing	GpiSetDefaultViewMatrix
Presentation Page	Device (window pixels)	Device	GpiCreatePS, GpiSetPS, GpiSetPageViewport
Device (window pixels)	Media (screen pixels)	Windowing	(none)

To denote a point in one of these coordinate spaces, I'll use the name of the coordinate space as a subscript to *x* and *y*. For example, the point

$$(x_{world}, y_{world})$$

is a point in the world coordinate space, and

$$(x_{page}, y_{page})$$

is a point in the coordinate space known as the *presentation page.*

The transforms are mathematical formulas that convert a point in one coordinate space to a point in the next coordinate space. By default, the model transform (which converts a point in the world coordinate space to a point in model coordinate space) is a *unity transform,* which means that it leaves the point unchanged. This is expressed mathematically as:

$$x_{model} = x_{world}$$

$$y_{model} = y_{world}$$

The default viewing transform is also a unity transform by default:

$$x_{page} = x_{model}$$

$$y_{page} = y_{model}$$

For now, let's ignore the top half of Table 7.1. Points in the world coordinate space are the same as points in the model coordinate space, which are the same as points in the presentation page.

THE WINDOWING TRANSFORM

Let's begin at the bottom of the table with the windowing transform. This is the easiest one of the lot, particularly considering that you can't use a GPI function to change it. But it gives us an easy approach to the entire concept of transforms.

The windowing transform maps from the *device coordinate space* (the window) to the *media coordinate space* (the screen). Both the device space and the media space are in units of pixels. But the origin of the device space is the lower-left corner of the window, while the origin of the media space is the lower-left corner of the screen.

You can express the windowing transform mathematically as

$$x_{media} = x_{device} + WX$$

$$y_{media} = y_{device} + WY$$

where the point (*WX,WY*) is the point in media space corresponding to the lower-left corner of the window. This is a type of transform known as *translation.* Points in one coordinate space are simply shifted a constant distance to convert to points in another coordinate space.

For example, suppose the pixel at the lower-left corner of a window is at the point (50,100) relative to the lower-left corner of the screen. WX is 50 and WY is 100. The windowing transform converts the point (25,50) in device space (the window) to the point (25+WX,50+WY) or (75,150) in media space (the screen). If the window happens to be positioned so its lower-left corner is to the left of the left side of the screen or below the bottom of the screen, then WX or WY (or both) will be negative.

You cannot change the windowing transform because it is determined by the location of the window on the screen. In fact, there isn't even a *Gpi* or *Dev* function that allows you to determine where the window is located on the screen. But you can use a *Win* function called *WinMapWindowPoints* to determine this. To convert from device (window) coordinates to media (screen) coordinates, you call

```
WinMapWindowPoints (hwnd, HWND_DESKTOP, aptl,lNumPoints) ;
```

where *hwnd* is the window handle, *aptl* is an array of POINTL structures, and *lNumPoints* is the number of POINTL structures in the array. For example:

```
ptl.x = 0 ;
ptl.y = 0 ;
WinMapWindowPoints (hwnd, HWND_DESKTOP, &ptl, 1) ;
```

On return from this function, the *ptl* structure fields will be the point (WX,WY)—the screen point that corresponds the origin of the window. To convert from media (screen) coordinates to device (window) coordinates, you call

```
WinMapWindowPoints (HWND_DESKTOP, hwnd, &ptl, 1) ;
```

I've been speaking about this transform as it applies to windows. But something similar happens with the printer page also. The origin of the media coordinate space is the lower-left corner of the printer page. The origin of the device coordinate space is the lower-left corner of the *printable* area of the page. Obtaining the offset of the device space from media space requires use of the *DevQueryHardcopyCaps* function.

THE CONCEPT OF THE PRESENTATION PAGE

I mentioned earlier that the model and default viewing transforms are unity transforms by default and don't really do anything. We'll see how to set these transforms shortly, but for now, world coordinates are the same as model coordinates, which are the same as page coordinates. I've also discussed the windowing transform that maps from device coordinates to media coordinates.

This leaves us with the coordinate space called the *presentation page* (or more simply the *page*) and the *device* transform that maps from the presentation page space to device space.

GPI is a *page-oriented* graphics system. Conceptually, GPI constructs images on the presentation page and maps this page to device space. The presentation page is a rectangle that has a height and width specified in presentation page units. Presentation page units can be pixels, or units based on inches or millimeters. For example, you can create a presentation page that is 100 pixels wide and 200 pixels high, or 300 millimeters wide and 400 millimeters high, or 5 inches high and 6 inches wide—whatever is most convenient for your program.

If the model and default viewing transforms are unity transforms, the points you specify in GPI functions are in presentation page units. GPI uses the device transform to convert these points to pixels in device space. If your presentation page is 5 inches wide and 6 inches high, the device transform will be different for different devices because different devices have a different number of pixels per inch.

The point (0,0) in page space is always the lower-left corner of the presentation page. But (as we'll see) this need not map to the point (0,0) in device space.

PAGE SIZE AND PAGE UNITS

In Chapter 5, we saw how to change the device transform using the *GpiSetPS* function. Here's an example:

```
SIZEL sizlPage ;
     :
     :
sizlPage.cx = 0 ;
sizlPage.cy = 0 ;
GpiSetPS (hps, &sizlPage, PU_LOENGLISH) ;
```

Following this function call, all coordinates you specify in GPI functions are units of 0.01 inches. You can then draw a line from (0,0) to (100,200):

```
ptl.x = 0 ;
ptl.y = 0 ;
GpiMove (hps, &ptl) ;

ptl.x = 100 ;
ptl.y = 200 ;
GpiLine (hps, &ptl) ;
```

The line will begin in the lower-left corner of the window, and end one inch from the left side of the window (or printable area of the printer page) because 100 units of 0.01 inches each is one inch. The line will end two inches from the bottom of the window or printable area of the printer page.

The second parameter to *GpiSetPS* is a pointer to a SIZEL structure. This indicates the size of the presentation page. Specifying 0 for both fields of this structure means that we want the presentation page to be the size of the output media. For a window presentation space, this is the size of the screen. For a printer presentation space, this is the size of the printable area of the page.

The second parameter, a constant identifier with the prefix PU, specifies the page units:

PU_ARBITRARY	"square" pixels
PU_PELS	pixels
PU_LOMETRIC	0.1 millimeters
PU_HIMETRIC	0.01 millimeters
PU_LOENGLISH	0.01 inches
PU_HIENGLISH	0.001 inches
PU_TWIPS	1/1440 inch

I'll discuss PU_ARBITRARY a little later. The last five identifiers in the list set *metric* page units. These are page units based on millimeters and inches. The PU_LOMETRIC and PU_HIMETRIC set page units based on millimeters. (LO means *low* or coarser units; HI means *high* or finer units.) Similarly, PU_LOENGLISH and PU_HIENGLISH set page units based on inches.

PU_TWIPS requires a little more explanation: A *twip* is a fabricated word that stands for "twentieth of a point." A printer's point size is approximately 1/72 inch, but in computer graphics it is often assumed to be exactly 1/72 inch. A twentieth of a point is thus 1/1440 inch. Page units of PU_TWIPS are particularly suited for working with text.

Setting the two fields of the SIZEL structure to 0 tells GPI to set the page size to the size of the output device (the whole screen or the printable area of the printer page). But this page size is measured in page units. For example, if you call

```
GpiQueryPS (hps, &sizlPage) ;
```

after setting page units of PU_LOENGLISH, the *cx* and *cy* fields of the *sizlPage* structure will indicate the size of the output device in units of 0.01 inches, not in units of pixels.

Calling the *GpiSetPS* function has enormous repercussions. This function causes such an upheaval in the presentation space that GPI is forced to set all attributes to their default values. When you call *GpiSetPS*, GPI automatically does processing equivalent to a call to

```
GpiResetPS (hps, GRES_ALL) ;
```

All the attributes you have set are returned to their default values, just as if you had created a new presentation space.

COORDINATE CONVERSION

If you want to draw in units of inches or millimeters, you can set page units in the *GpiSetPS* functions to what you want, and simply draw in those units.

However, the page units you set in GPI do not affect functions and messages that are part of the windowing environment of the Presentation Manager. For example, the WM_SIZE message will continue to report the size of the window in pixels, not the GPI page units you select.

To help with this problem, GPI provides a function called *GpiConvert* that lets you convert POINTL structures from one coordinate space to another:

```
GpiConvert (hps, lSource, lTarget, lPoints, aptl) ;
```

With a micro-PS, the second and third parameters can be any of the following identifiers defined in PMGPI.H:

CVTC_WORLD

CVTC_MODEL

CVTC_PAGE

CVTC_DEVICE

These correspond to the first four coordinate spaces in Table 7.1.

For example, when processing a WM_SIZE message, you might want to save the dimensions of the window in page units rather than device units. Your new WM_SIZE message would begin like this:

```
case WM_SIZE:
     sizlClient.cx = SHORT1FROMMP (mp2) ;
     sizlClient.cy = SHORT2FROMMP (mp2) ;

     GpiConvert (hps, CVTC_DEVICE, CVTC_PAGE, 1L,(PPOINTL) &sizlClient) ;
```

The WM_SIZE message reports the window size in device units. Thus, the source presentation space in *GpiConvert* is CVTC_DEVICE. To convert to page units, the target is CVTC_PAGE. The two fields of the SIZEL structure (*cx* and *cy*) correspond to the two fields of a POINTL structure (*x* and *y*), so a pointer to the *sizlClient* need only be cast to a PPOINTL for the last parameter of *GpiConvert.* The function converts the dimensions in *sizlClient* to page units.

THE DEVICE TRANSFORM: A FIRST GUESS

I mentioned earlier that all the transforms can be represented by mathematical formulas. For example, the windowing transform formulas are

$$x_{media} = x_{device} + WX$$

$$y_{media} = y_{device} + WY$$

where the point (WX,WY) is the point in media space (the screen) that corresponds to the lower-left corner of the window. This is a type of tranform known as *translation.* Both device space and media space are in units of pixels, but device space is offset from media space by WX and WY.

The device transform that maps from the presentation page to device space is a little different. The device space is in units of pixels but the presentation page is in units indicated by the PU identifier you specify in the *GpiSetPS* function. This requires a type of transform known as *scaling.*

We might guess that the device transform probably looks something like this:

$$x_{device} = DX \cdot x_{page}$$

$$y_{device} = DY \cdot y_{page}$$

DX and DY are scaling factors, where:

DX = horizontal pixels per page unit

DY = vertical pixels per page unit

For example, if you run the DEVCAPS program from Chapter 5 on the VGA, you'll find that the resolution is 2667 pixels per meter, or about 68 pixels per inch both horizontally and vertically. If you set page units of PU_LOENGLISH (0.01 inches) on a window presentation space on the VGA, then GPI would set DX and DY to 0.68. Thus, the point (100,100) in presentation page space maps to the pixel at point (68,68) in device space.

This is certainly valid, but it's not the entire story. The device transform actually includes both scaling and translation, and GPI allows you to change it. Let's see how this works.

THE PAGE VIEWPORT RECTANGLE

When you set page units and a page size by calling *GpiSetPS*, GPI calculates a *page viewport* and maintains that as an attribute of the presentation space. GPI calculates the page viewport based on the page units and page size you specify, and the pixel dimensions and resolution of the output device.

The page viewport is a structure of type RECTL ("rectangle with LONG coordinates"), which (as review) is defined in PMGPI.H like this:

```
typedef struct _RECTL
     {
     LONG xLeft ;
     LONG yBottom ;
     LONG xRight ;
     LONG yTop ;
     }
RECTL ;
```

By convention a variable of type RECTL has a prefix of *rcl*. Notice that the RECTL structure can be seen as two POINTL structures stuck together; the first is the point at the lower-left corner of the rectangle and the second is the point at the upper-right corner.

You can obtain the page viewport rectangle by calling *GpiQueryPageViewport*:

```
GpiQueryPageViewport (hps, &rcl) ;
```

You can take a look at the page viewport rectangle that GPI calculates for you by defining a RECTL structure and calling the function.

Let's look at some concrete examples using a real output device, the Enhanced Graphics Adapter. The EGA does not have square pixels—that is, the pixel resolution is different in the horizontal and vertical directions—so this is a more "interesting" example than the VGA or 8514/A. The EGA is 640 pixels horizontally by 350 pixels vertically on a screen with an aspect ratio of 1.33 to 1. A square-pixel video adapter working with such a screen needs 640 by 480 pixels (like the VGA) or 1024 by 768 pixels (like the 8514/A), or a different pair of numbers in the ratio of 1.33 to 1.

Suppose you have an EGA and make the following calls for each of the seven PU identifiers:

```
sizl.cx = 0 ;
sizl.cy = 0 ;
GpiSetPS (hps, &sizl, PU_...) ;

GpiQueryPS (hps, &sizl) ;
GpiQueryPageViewport (hps, &rcl) ;
```

The following table shows the values you'll obtain from the *GpiQueryPS* and *GpiQueryPageViewport* functions. In all cases, the *xLeft* and *yBottom* fields of the page viewport are set to 0L and are not shown in this table.

	Page Size		**Page Viewport**	
Page Units	**sizl.cx**	**sizl.cy**	**rcl.xRight**	**rcl.yTop**
PU_PELS	640	350	640	350
PU_ARBITRARY	640	467	640	350
PU_LOMETRIC	2400	1750	640	350
PU_HIMETRIC	23997	17500	640	350
PU_LOENGLISH	945	689	640	350
PU_HIENGLISH	9448	6890	640	350
PU_TWIPS	13605	9921	640	350

In all cases the page viewport is a rectangle that describes the dimensions of the screen in device units (pixels). The values of 0L used in the SIZEL structure passed to *GpiSetPS* indicate a default presentation page that is the size of the screen in page units.

For example, when you call *GpiSetPS* for PU_LOMETRIC page units, the page is the size of the screen in 0.1 millimeters. This table indicates that the screen is 240 millimeters wide and 175 millimeters high. Similarly, for PU_LO-ENGLISH page units, the page is the size of the screen in 0.01 inches. The screen is 9.45 inches wide and 6.89 inches high.

Page units of PU_ARBITRARY require a bit more explanation. (Unfortunately, the word "arbitrary" seems to refer more to the naming of this identifier than to what it actually does.) For devices with the same pixel resolutions in the horizontal and vertical directions, PU_ARBITRARY has the same result as PU_PELS. Otherwise, GPI will create a device transform *close* to PU_PELS but with an adjustment so that page units are equal in both directions. This lets you draw round circles and square squares more easily on devices such as the EGA.

The presentation page and the page viewport are both rectangles the size of the screen. But the presentation page is specified in page units and the page viewport is in device units (pixels)—always 640 by 350.

Now let's try something a little different. We'll set the page size to 1000 by 1000 page units:

```
sizl.cx = 1000 ;
sizl.cy = 1000 ;
GpiSetPS (hps, &sizl, PU_...) ;

GpiQueryPS (hps, &sizl) ;
GpiQueryPageViewport (hps, &rcl) ;
```

Now you'll see the following values:

	Page Size		Page Viewport	
Page Units	**sizl.cx**	**sizl.cy**	**rcl.xRight**	**rcl.yTop**
PU_PELS	1000	1000	1000	1000
PU_ARBITRARY	1000	1000	467	350
PU_LOMETRIC	1000	1000	267	200
PU_HIMETRIC	1000	1000	27	20
PU_LOENGLISH	1000	1000	677	508
PU_HIENGLISH	1000	1000	68	51
PU_TWIPS	1000	1000	47	35

Although the page size is specified as 1000 by 1000, the physical size of the page is different because the page size is in page units. For PU_LOMETRIC, the page size is 1000 by 1000 in units of 0.1 millimeters, so the page is 100 millimeters square. For PU_HIENGLISH, the page is 1 inch square.

The page viewport rectangle indicates the pixel dimension of the presentation page. For example, the PU_LOMETRIC line tells us that the EGA has 267 pixels horizontally and 200 pixels vertically in the 100 millimeter square presentation page. Thus, the horizontal resolution is 2.67 pixels per millimeter, and the vertical resolution is 2.00 pixels per millimeter. (The DEVCAPS program reports the resolution of the EGA as 2667 and 2000 pixels per meter.)

The PU_HIENGLISH row tells us that the EGA has 68 pixels horizontally and 51 pixels vertically in the 1-inch square page. This means that the resolution of the EGA is 68 dots per inch horizontally and 51 dots per inch vertically.

PU_ARBITRARY works a little differently when you explicitly set the page size than it does when you don't. However, it still sets the device transform so that page units represent equal physical differences in the horizontal and vertical directions.

THE DEVICE TRANSFORM FORMULAS

The device transform maps points in presentation page space to points in device space. Earlier we guessed that the device transform formulas looked something like this:

$$x_{device} = DX \cdot x_{page}$$

$$y_{device} = DY \cdot y_{page}$$

where DX and DY are the horizontal and vertical pixels per page unit. But look at the tables of page sizes and page viewport rectangles shown above. DX and DY are simply the ratios of the page viewport to the page size:

$$x_{device} = \left(\frac{\text{rcl.xRight}}{\text{sizl.cx}}\right) \cdot x_{page}$$

$$y_{device} = \left(\frac{\text{rcl.yTop}}{\text{sizl.cy}}\right) \cdot y_{page}$$

The presentation page and page viewport rectangles are the same size, but are just expressed in different units. So the ratios are truly pixels per page unit. The four corners of the presentation page map to the four corners of the page viewport:

Page Coordinate	Device Coordinate
(0,0)	(0,0)
(sizl.cx,0)	(rcl.xRight,0)
(0,sizl.cy)	(0,rcl.yTop)
(sizl.cx,sizl.cy)	(rcl.xRight,rcl.yTop)

You can visualize this by imagining the lower-left corner of the page viewport as corresponding to the origin of the window. But, as mentioned, it's actually a little more complex than this. Why should the page viewport be a RECTL structure if the *xLeft* and *yBottom* fields are not used? Although GPI sets these to fields to 0L when you call *GpiCreatePS* or *GpiSetPS*, they enter the device transform formula.

The *real* device transform formulas are

$$x_{device} = \frac{x_{page}\,(rcl.xRight - rcl.xLeft)}{sizl.cx} + rcl.xLeft$$

$$y_{device} = \frac{y_{page}\,(rcl.yTop - rcl.yBottom)}{sizl.cy} + rcl.yBottom$$

These formulas still translate the four corners of the presentation page to the four corners of the page viewport rectangle, as shown in the following table:

Page Coordinate	Device Coordinate
(0,0)	(rcl.xLeft,rcl.yBottom)
(0,sizl.cy)	(rcl.xLeft,rcl.yTop)
(sizl.cx,0)	(rcl.xRight,rcl.yBottom)
(sizl.cx,sizl.cy)	(rcl.xRight,rcl.yTop)

Thus, the lower-left corner of the page viewport rectangle (and hence the presentation page) does not have to correspond with the lower-left corner of the window. If *rcl.xLeft* and *rcl.yBottom* are nonzero, the page viewport is offset from the window.

THE SIGNIFICANCE OF THE PAGE SIZE

The presentation page dimensions and the page viewport rectangle together define the device transform. Does the page size have any significance beyond that?

Not really. In theory, you could define any page size you want in the *GpiSetPS* function and GPI would calculate an appropriate page viewport rectangle for the device transform. The page size is simply part of a mathematical construct. It is not a clipping rectangle. You can draw outside the boundaries of the presentation page.

But keep in mind that the scaling operation of the device transform is a ratio of the page viewport size to presentation page size. If you set the page size very small, GPI attempts to set the page viewport appropriately and the ratio may be inaccurate. For example, imagine the table of page sizes and viewports for the EGA shown above with page sizes of 10 by 10 rather than 1000 by 1000. In some cases, the page viewport rectangle would have a width and height of zero!

In general, using the default page size (which GPI sets when you set the two fields of the SIZEL structure to 0) is the best approach.

WHY DO I NEED TO KNOW ALL THIS?

You may have been happy using the simple PU identifiers to set page units. Introducing the page viewport rectangle and the actual device transform formulas at first seems like an excessively detailed view into the inner workings of GPI. But the importance of the device transform formulas becomes apparent with the introduction of the following function:

```
GpiSetPageViewport (hps, &rcl) ;
```

The page size and page units you specify in the *GpiSetPS* functions merely provide GPI with information to set an initial page viewport rectangle. *GpiSetPageViewport* lets you alter the page viewport rectangle, and thus the device transform.

The page viewport rectangle is an attribute of the presentation space. It is saved with *GpiSavePS* and restored with *GpiRestorePS*, but it is not reset with a call to *GpiResetPS* (regardless of the *GpiResetPS* parameter). The only way to reset the page viewport to default values is with a call to *GpiSetPS* or, of course, by calling *GpiSetPageViewport* itself.

NONSTANDARD PAGE UNITS

Perhaps when you looked over the collection of seven PU identifiers, you were disappointed. You have an application where page units of 1/64 of an inch would be ideal. In fact, page units of 1/64 inch would have been useful for the RULER program in Chapter 5.

Using *GpiSetPageViewport*, you can indeed set the page viewport rectangle to give you page units of 1/64 inch. First set page units to Low English:

```
sizlPage.cx = 0 ;
sizlPage.cy = 0 ;
GpiSetPS (hab, &sizlPage, PU_LOENGLISH) ;
```

At this point the page viewport rectangle is constructed to transform units of 1/100 inch to pixels. You can obtain the page viewport rectangle and adjust the *xRight* and *yTop* fields like this:

```
GpiQueryPageViewport (hps, &rcl) ;
rcl.xRight = 100 * rcl.xRight / 64 ;
rcl.yTop   = 100 * rcl.yTop   / 64 ;
GpiSetPageViewport (hps, &rcl) ;
```

Keep in mind that the ratio of the page viewport rectangle to the page size represents the number of pixels per page unit. You increase the size of the page viewport rectangle because you want more pixels per page unit than PU_LOENGLISH.

Here's another example. You may be a real pro with PostScript. You live, think, and breathe in terms of PostScript's default coordinate system—1/72 inch, the printer's point size. Setting PU_TWIPS lets you work in units that are 1/20 of a point or 1/1440 inch. You could use that and multiply all your coordinates by 20. Or, you could let GPI do that multiplication for you by altering the page viewport:

```
sizl.cx = 0 ;
sizl.cy = 0 ;
GpiSetPS (hab, &sizl, PU_TWIPS) ;

GpiQueryPageViewport (hps, &rcl) ;
rcl.xRight *= 20 ;
rcl.yTop   *= 20 ;
GpiSetPageViewport (hps, &rcl) ;
```

ALTERING THE ORIGIN

Sometimes it's more convenient for the coordinate origin—the point (0,0)—to be somewhere other than the lower-left corner of the window. For example, you may want to have the origin in the center of the window and to use negative coordinates for drawing in the left and bottom halves of the window.

Let's take a look at the device transform again:

$$x_{device} = \frac{x_{page}\,(rcl.xRight - rcl.xLeft)}{sizl.cx} + rcl.xLeft$$

$$y_{device} = \frac{y_{page}\,(rcl.yTop - rcl.yBottom)}{sizl.cy} + rcl.yBottom$$

So far, all the examples we've seen have used values of zero for *rcl.xLeft* and *rcl.yBottom*. Change these values, and you change your origin.

For example, suppose you want an origin in the center of the client window. You've obtained the size of the client window during the WM_SIZE message and stored the dimensions in *cxClient* and *cyClient*. After using *GpiSetPS* to set the page units to what you want, here's the code to change the origin:

```
GpiQueryPageViewport (hps, &rcl) ;

rcl.xLeft   = cxClient / 2 ;
rcl.xRight += cxClient / 2 ;
rcl.yBottom = cyClient / 2 ;
rcl.yTop   += cyClient / 2 ;

GpiSetPageViewport (hps, &rcl) ;
```

Now the page coordinate (0,0) maps to the device point (*cxClient*/2,*cyClient*/2), the center of the window. Notice that we've had to increase the *xRight* and *yTop* fields as well as *xLeft* and *yBottom*, because it's the difference between these fields that affects the scaling factor.

Unfortunately, GPI won't let you set a page viewport rectangle with the *yTop* field less than the *yBottom* field. This would let you set up a system so that values on the y axis increase going down the screen (like the Windows default). But we'll see how to do that and more shortly.

STRETCHING THE IMAGE TO FIT

There are times when you may want to set up an arbitrary coordinate system (for example, the origin in the center and 1000 page units in each direction), and be assured that the image you draw will fit inside the window. You can do this by using the device transform.

Let's take a look at the CIRCLE program shown in Listing 7.4 with precisely the coordinate system I just described.

Listing 7.4: The CIRCLE program

The CIRCLE.MAK File

```
#----------------------
# CIRCLE.MAK make file
#----------------------

circle.exe : circle.obj circle.def
     $(PRGLINK) circle, circle, NUL, $(PRGLIB), circle

circle.obj : circle.c
     $(PRGCC) circle.c
```

The CIRCLE.C File

```
/*--------------------------------------
   CIRCLE.C -- Transform Demonstration
               (c) Charles Petzold, 1993
  --------------------------------------*/

#define INCL_WIN
#define INCL_GPI
#include <os2.h>

#define min(a,b)    ((a) < (b) ? (a) : (b))

MRESULT EXPENTRY ClientWndProc (HWND, ULONG, MPARAM, MPARAM) ;

int main (void)
     {
     static CHAR  szClientClass [] = "Circle" ;
     static ULONG flFrameFlags = FCF_TITLEBAR      | FCF_SYSMENU |
                                 FCF_SIZEBORDER    | FCF_MINMAX  |
                                 FCF_SHELLPOSITION | FCF_TASKLIST ;
     HAB          hab ;
     HMQ          hmq ;
     HWND         hwndFrame, hwndClient ;
     QMSG         qmsg ;

     hab = WinInitialize (0) ;
     hmq = WinCreateMsgQueue (hab, 0) ;

     WinRegisterClass (hab, szClientClass, ClientWndProc, CS_SIZEREDRAW, 0) ;

     hwndFrame = WinCreateStdWindow (HWND_DESKTOP, WS_VISIBLE,
                                     &flFrameFlags, szClientClass, NULL,
                                     0L, 0, 0, &hwndClient) ;

     while (WinGetMsg (hab, &qmsg, NULLHANDLE, 0, 0))
```

Listing 7.4: The CIRCLE program (Continued)

```
          WinDispatchMsg (hab, &qmsg) ;

     WinDestroyWindow (hwndFrame) ;
     WinDestroyMsgQueue (hmq) ;
     WinTerminate (hab) ;
     return 0 ;
     }

void DrawFigure (HPS hps)
     {
     POINTL ptl ;

     ptl.x = -1000 ;
     ptl.y = -1000 ;
     GpiMove (hps, &ptl) ;

     ptl.x = 1000 ;
     ptl.y = 1000 ;
     GpiBox (hps, DRO_OUTLINE, &ptl, 2000, 2000) ;
     }

MRESULT EXPENTRY ClientWndProc (HWND hwnd, ULONG msg, MPARAM mp1, MPARAM mp2)
     {
     static INT cxClient, cyClient ;
     HPS        hps ;
     POINTL     ptl ;
     RECTL      rcl ;
     SIZEL      sizel ;

     switch (msg)
          {
          case WM_SIZE:
               cxClient = SHORT1FROMMP (mp2) ;
               cyClient = SHORT2FROMMP (mp2) ;

               return 0 ;

          case WM_PAINT:
               hps = WinBeginPaint (hwnd, NULLHANDLE, NULL) ;
               GpiErase (hps) ;

                    // Draw ellipse

               sizel.cx = 1000 ;
               sizel.cy = 1000 ;
               GpiSetPS (hps, &sizel, PU_PELS) ;

               rcl.xLeft   = cxClient / 2 ;
               rcl.xRight  = cxClient ;
```

Listing 7.4: The CIRCLE program (Continued)

```
               rcl.yBottom = cyClient / 2 ;
               rcl.yTop    = cyClient ;

               GpiSetPageViewport (hps, &rcl) ;

               DrawFigure (hps) ;

                    // Draw circle

               sizel.cx = 1000 ;
               sizel.cy = 1000 ;
               GpiSetPS (hps, &sizel, PU_ARBITRARY) ;

               ptl.x = cxClient ;
               ptl.y = cyClient ;

               GpiConvert (hps, CVTC_DEVICE, CVTC_PAGE, 1, &ptl) ;

               ptl.x = ptl.y = min (ptl.x, ptl.y) ;

               GpiConvert (hps, CVTC_PAGE, CVTC_DEVICE, 1, &ptl) ;

               rcl.xLeft   = cxClient / 2 ;
               rcl.xRight  = (ptl.x + cxClient) / 2 ;
               rcl.yBottom = cyClient / 2 ;
               rcl.yTop    = (ptl.y + cyClient) / 2 ;

               GpiSetPageViewport (hps, &rcl) ;

               DrawFigure (hps) ;

               WinEndPaint (hps) ;
               return 0 ;
          }
     return WinDefWindowProc (hwnd, msg, mp1, mp2) ;
     }
```

The CIRCLE.DEF File

```
;------------------------------------
; CIRCLE.DEF module definition file
;------------------------------------

NAME           CIRCLE    WINDOWAPI

DESCRIPTION    'Transform Demonstration (c) Charles Petzold, 1993'
PROTMODE
```

This program uses two different device transforms to draw an ellipse that fills the client window, and to draw a circle that is as large as possible to fit within the client area without being distorted, even on devices that have unequal horizontal and vertical resolution. The *DrawFigure* function in CIRCLE draws both figures by specifying identical coordinates, namely (–1000,–1000) for the lower-left corner of the bounding rectangle and (1000,1000) for the upper-right corner. How these coordinates are interpreted depends upon the device transform.

For drawing the ellipse, we could set the page size to 2000 by 2000 and the page viewport size to the width and height of the client window with an origin in the center. But we don't have to. Because the device transform uses a ratio for scaling, we could use 1000 for the page size and half the width and height of the client window for the viewport rectangle. That's the approach I've taken. The CIRCLE program begins WM_PAINT processing by setting a page size of 1000 by 1000 units with PU_PELS page units. The page units don't really matter because the program changes the page viewport anyway—with a width and height of half the client window, offset to the center. You can think of the presentation page as corresponding to the upper-right quadrant of the client window.

Setting up a coordinate system for the circle is more complex because it needs to work on devices that have unequal horizontal and vertical pixel resolutions. The key is to set the page units to PU_ARBITRARY, again with a page size of 1000 by 1000. This sets a page viewport appropriate for the device, that is, compensating for possibly unequal horizontal and vertical pixel resolutions. But you would never use PU_ARBITRARY unless you plan to change the viewport rectangle. To what?

We can't set the page viewport based on the size of the client window, because then we'd be drawing an ellipse. Nor can we set the page viewport height and width to the minimum of the pixel height and width of the client window; that would work with square-pixel devices like the VGA, but it sure wouldn't work with the EGA.

Instead we must use *GpiConvert* to convert the pixel size of the client area to page units. These page units are equal in horizontal and vertical directions. The program finds the minimum of the two values (this will be the page size of the circle radius) and then converts that minimum back to device units (pixels), again using *GpiConvert.* This is what the program uses to set up the page viewport rectangle. The results are shown in Figure 7.6.

Code like this is very useful for drawing clocks or similar round images that should adjust their size to the client area but not degenerate into ellipses.

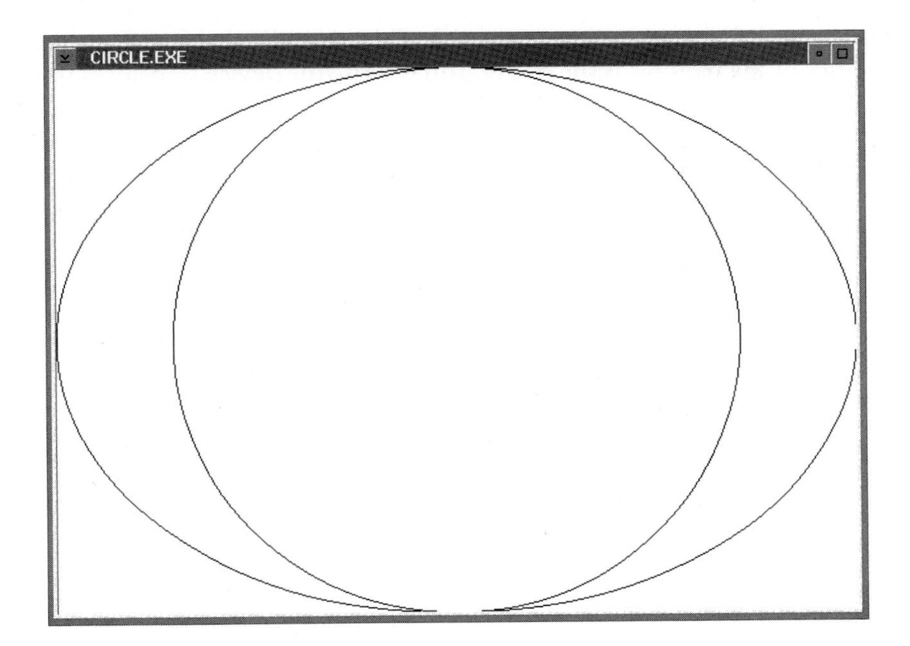

Figure 7.6: The CIRCLE display

CONSTRUCTING THE PICTURE

When drawing in GPI, conceptually you construct a picture on the presentation page, and the presentation page (or part of it) is displayed within the client window. As we've seen, a presentation page is of a particular size and particular units that you can set using *GpiSetPS* and *GpiSetPageViewport*.

As you construct a picture on the presentation page, you also have available two additional transforms: the modeling transform and the default viewing transform. The points you use in GPI functions are in world coordinate space. The modeling transform converts those points to model coordinate space. The default viewing transform converts the points in model space to the presentation page space.

The modeling and default viewing transforms are very similar and for some simple purposes they are interchangeable. But a general rule to follow is this: The transforms closest to the hardware (that is, the transforms at the bottom of Table 7.1) should be changed less frequently than the transforms furthest from the hardware. The simplest approach is to use the default viewing transform to apply to the whole picture and different modeling transforms to apply to pieces of the picture.

For example, suppose you want to work with a coordinate system in which the center of the window is the origin. You can use the device transform or the default viewing transform to accomplish that. Suppose you also want to draw a picture in which a particular object is drawn at several different places in the picture. You can draw these objects with different modeling transforms. The same points are passed to the GPI drawing functions, but the modeling transform causes those points to be transformed.

THE TRANSFORMATION MATRIX

Both the modeling transform and the default viewing transform are based on a standard two-dimensional *transformation matrix* common in many high-level graphics languages.

In GPI, you specify a transformation matrix as a structure of type MATRIXLF. (The LF part of the structure name stands for "LONG" and "FIXED," the two data types used for the structure fields.) The MATRIXLF structure is defined in the PMGPI.H header file like this:

```
typedef struct _MATRIXLF
     {
     FIXED fxM11 ;
     FIXED fxM12 ;
     LONG  lM13 ;
     FIXED fxM21 ;
     FIXED fxM22 ;
     LONG  lM23 ;
     LONG  lM31 ;
     LONG  lM32 ;
     LONG  lM33 ;
     }
MATRIXLF ;
```

At first glance, the jumble of numbers in the field names looks like a real mess. But it's actually quite simple. The nine fields of this structure are the nine elements of a 3-by-3 matrix:

$$\begin{vmatrix} fxM11 & fxM12 & lM13 \\ fxM21 & fxM22 & lM23 \\ lM31 & lM32 & lM33 \end{vmatrix}$$

The "M" in the field names stands for "matrix" and the numbers are simply the row and column positions of each field within the matrix.

The "l" prefix on some of the fields stands for LONG. The "fx" prefix stands for FIXED. The FIXED data type is a 32-bit signed long integer that is interpreted by GPI as a 16-bit signed integer and a 16-bit unsigned fraction. The FIXED data type allows GPI to use fractions without resorting to time-consuming floating-point operations. Here are some examples of FIXED values:

FIXED Value	Interpretation
0x00000001	1/65536
0x00002000	1/8
0x00010000	1
0x000AC000	10 3/4
0xFFF8F000	–7 1/16

In some of the examples that follow, I use normal decimal point notation for FIXED numbers. Keep in mind that these are really 32-bit integers.

You can convert a FIXED variable to a float or double variable by dividing by 65536.0:

```
dNumber = (fxNumber / 65536.0) ;
```

You can convert a float or double variable to FIXED by multiplying by 65536 and casting the result:

```
fxNumber = (FIXED) (65536 * dNumber) ;
```

The transformation matrix is actually slightly simpler than the version shown above. When you use a MATRIXLF structure in the GPI transformation functions, the *lM13* and *lM23* fields must be set equal to 0 and the *lM33* field must be set equal to 1:

$$\begin{vmatrix} fxM11 & fxM12 & 0 \\ fxM21 & fxM22 & 0 \\ lM31 & lM32 & 1 \end{vmatrix}$$

GPI uses a matrix multiplication to convert a point (x,y) to a point (x',y'). First, GPI constructs a 1-by-3 matrix from the original point (x,y) by appending a 1. Then that matrix is multiplied by the 3-by-3 transformation matrix. The resultant 1-by-3 matrix contains the points x', y', and 1:

$$\begin{vmatrix} x & y & 1 \end{vmatrix} \cdot \begin{vmatrix} fxM11 & fxM12 & 0 \\ fxM21 & fxM22 & 0 \\ lM31 & lM32 & 1 \end{vmatrix} = \begin{vmatrix} x' & y' & 1 \end{vmatrix}$$

If (x,y) is a point in world coordinate space, GPI applies the modeling transformation to determine the point (x',y') in model coordinate space. If (x,y) is a point in model coordinate space, GPI applies the default viewing transformation and the resultant point (x',y') is in presentation page units.

The matrix transformation can also be represented as a pair of formulas that describe the matrix multiplication:

$$x' = (fxM11)\,x + (fxM21)\,y + lM31$$

$$y' = (fxM12)\,x + (fxM22)\,y + lM32$$

Note that the points x' and y' are functions of both x and y. This is not the case in the device transform and windowing transform.

This type of transform is sometimes also called a *linear transform* because the x's and y's in the formulas above are simply multiplied by constants. There are no powers of x and y involved. Parallelograms always map to parallelograms and ellipses always map to ellipses. Still, however, the linear transform is quite powerful, allowing translation, scaling, skewing, and rotation.

For a new presentation space, the modeling and default viewing transformation matrices are both identity matrices. Only the *fxM11*, *fxM22*, and *lM33* fields are set to 1. The other fields are set to 0:

$$\begin{vmatrix} 1.0 & 0.0 & 0 \\ 0.0 & 1.0 & 0 \\ 0 & 0 & 1 \end{vmatrix}$$

Thus, the transformation formulas look like this:

$$x' = x$$

$$y' = y$$

Now let's look at some more interesting alternatives.

TRANSLATION

Suppose you have some code in your program that draws a little house 100 units wide and 100 units high firmly anchored (but not for long) at the origin. Figure 7.7 shows how the house looks normally.

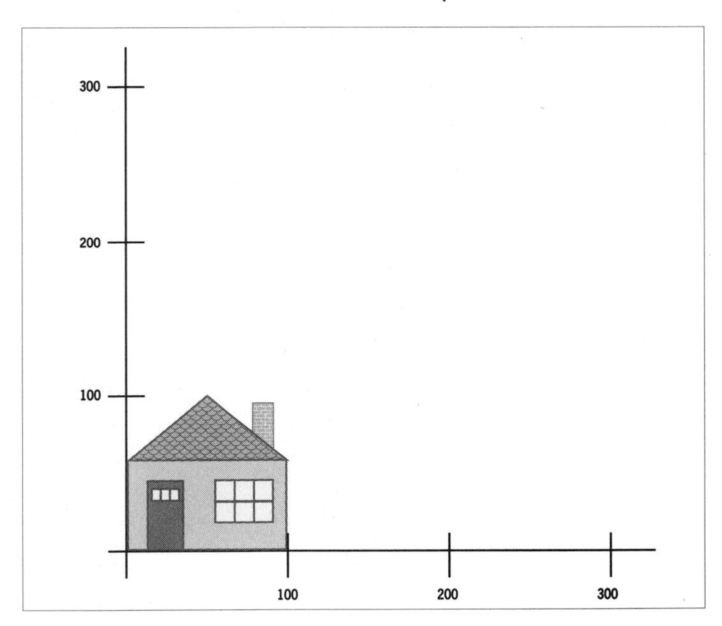

Figure 7.7: The house drawn with no transform

Perhaps you'd like to draw this house using the same code but have it appear in different places, or in different sizes, or even skewed or rotated. That's a perfect application for matrix transforms.

Nonzero values of the *lM31* and *lM32* elements in the transformation matrix cause an image to be shifted or translated from one place to another without any distortion of the image:

$$\begin{vmatrix} 1.0 & 0.0 & 0 \\ 0.0 & 1.0 & 0 \\ \mathrm{lM31} & \mathrm{lM32} & 1 \end{vmatrix}$$

The transformation formulas are

x' = x + lM31

y' = y + lM32

The matrix transform translates the point (0,0) to the point (lM31,lM32). If the matrix represents the default viewing transform, the point (0,0) in model coordinate space is the same as the point (lM31,lM32) in page coordinate space.

For example, suppose you want to move the house to the lot next door, 100 units to the right. You'd set *lM31* to 100 and *lM32* to 0. The result looks like what's shown in Figure 7.8.

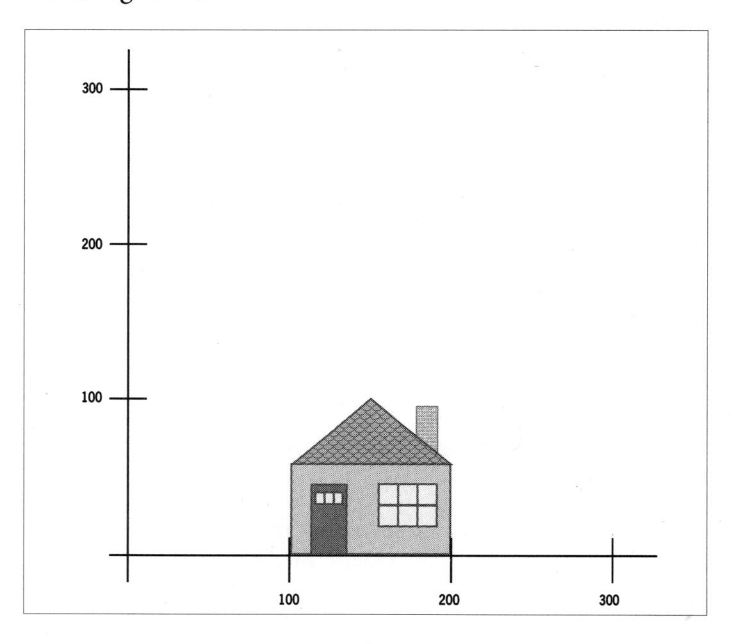

Figure 7.8: The house drawn with horizontal translation

Or you can elevate the house 50 units by setting lM31 to 0 and lM32 to 50, as shown in Figure 7.9. This could be Dorothy's house on its initial ascent to Oz.

You can use both fields of the structure to cause both effects at once. Negative values will move the house to the left or down.

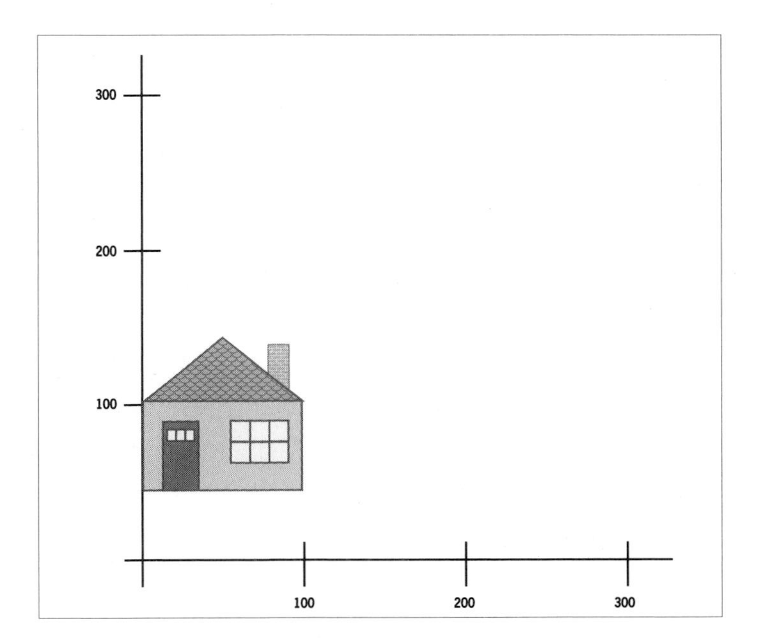

Figure 7.9: The house drawn with vertical translation

SCALING

The *fxM11* and *fxM22* fields of the MATRIXLF structure are the *scaling* fields. If *fxM11* is greater than 1.0, the resultant image is expanded along the x axis. Values less than 1.0 cause the width of the image to be compressed. Similarly, *fxM22* affects the height of the image.

If all other fields of the matrix are set to their default values, the transformation matrix for scaling is

$$\begin{vmatrix} \text{fxM11} & 0.0 & 0 \\ 0.0 & \text{fxM22} & 0 \\ 0 & 0 & 1 \end{vmatrix}$$

and the transformation formulas are

$$x' = (\text{fxM11})x$$

$$y' = (\text{fxM22})y$$

In general, scaling causes a square to be transformed into a rectangle. This is useful if the family is growing and you need to expand the house, for example,

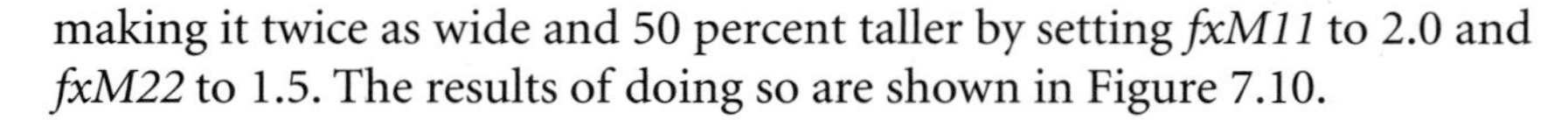

making it twice as wide and 50 percent taller by setting *fxM11* to 2.0 and *fxM22* to 1.5. The results of doing so are shown in Figure 7.10.

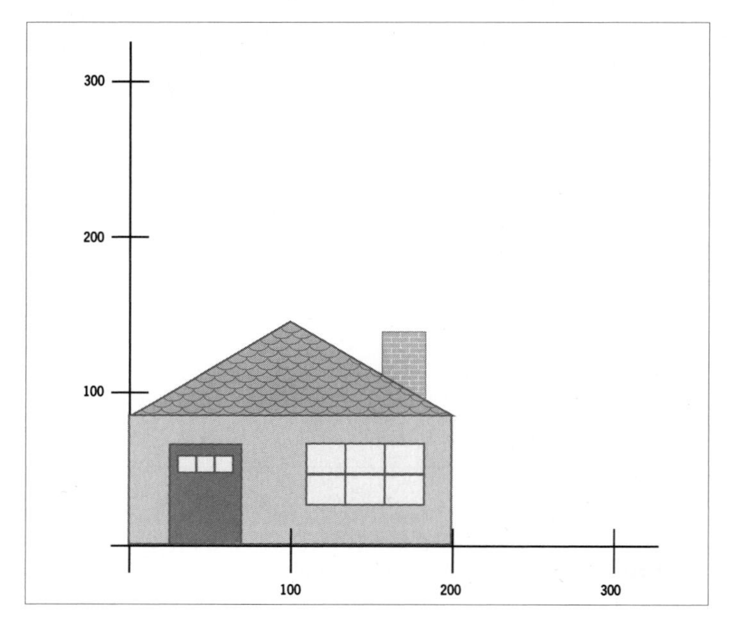

Figure 7.10: The house drawn with scaling

REFLECTION

Reflection is a form of scaling that uses negative scaling factors. Negative values of the *fxM11* and *fxM12* fields cause the image to be flipped horizontally or vertically.

For example, if you use this transformation matrix

$$\begin{vmatrix} -1.0 & 0.0 & 0 \\ 0.0 & 1.0 & 0 \\ 0 & 0 & 1 \end{vmatrix}$$

then the transformation formulas are

$$x' = -x$$

$$y' = y$$

This flips the image around the vertical axis, as shown in Figure 7.11.

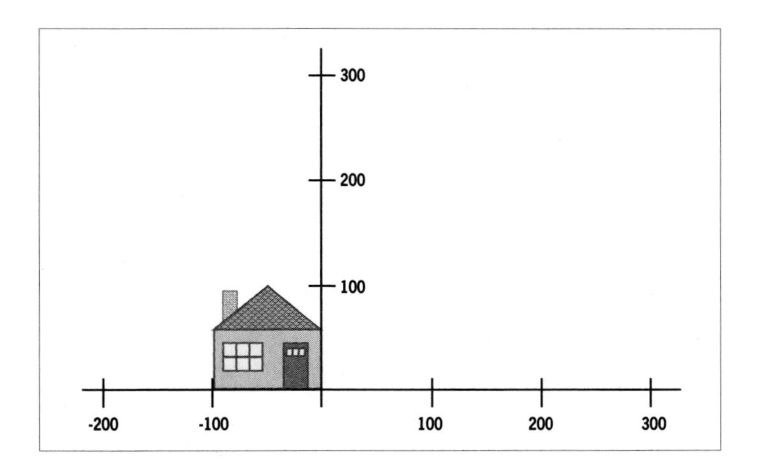

Figure 7.11: The house drawn with vertical reflection

Similary, this matrix

$$\begin{vmatrix} 1.0 & 0.0 & 0 \\ 0.0 & -1.0 & 0 \\ 0 & 0 & 1 \end{vmatrix}$$

causes a reflection around the horizontal axis and turns the object upside down, as you can see in Figure 7.12. This is what the house looks like if it's located in Australia. In either case, if our origin were at the lower-left corner of the client window, the image would be invisible.

SHEAR

The shear transformation effectively tilts one of the coordinate axes so that it is not at right angles to the other axis. The resultant drawing is distorted: A rectangle is mapped to a parallelogram.

A nonzero value of *fxM21* causes *x-shear*:

$$\begin{vmatrix} 1.0 & 0.0 & 0 \\ fxM21 & 1.0 & 0 \\ 0 & 0 & 1 \end{vmatrix}$$

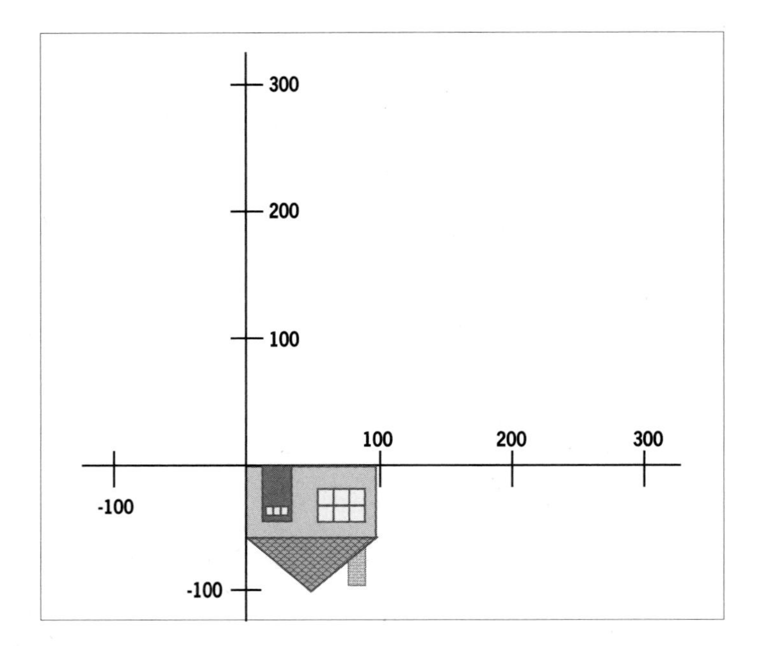

Figure 7.12: The house drawn with horizontal reflection

The transformation formulas are

$$x' = x + (fxM21)\,y$$

$$y' = y$$

This shifts a point left or right by an amount dependent upon the distance between the point and the horizontal axis. Figure 7.13 shows a "strong wind" effect on the house by using an x-shear value of 2.0.

Similarly, the *fxM12* field causes *y-shear.* The transformation matrix is

$$\begin{vmatrix} 1.0 & fxM12 & 0 \\ 0.0 & 1.0 & 0 \\ 0 & 0 & 1 \end{vmatrix}$$

Figure 7.14 shows our little house when the y-shear factor *fxM12* is set to 1.0. Shear sometimes suggests a three-dimensional view of an object. But because a square is always mapped to a parallelogram, there is no real depth perspective.

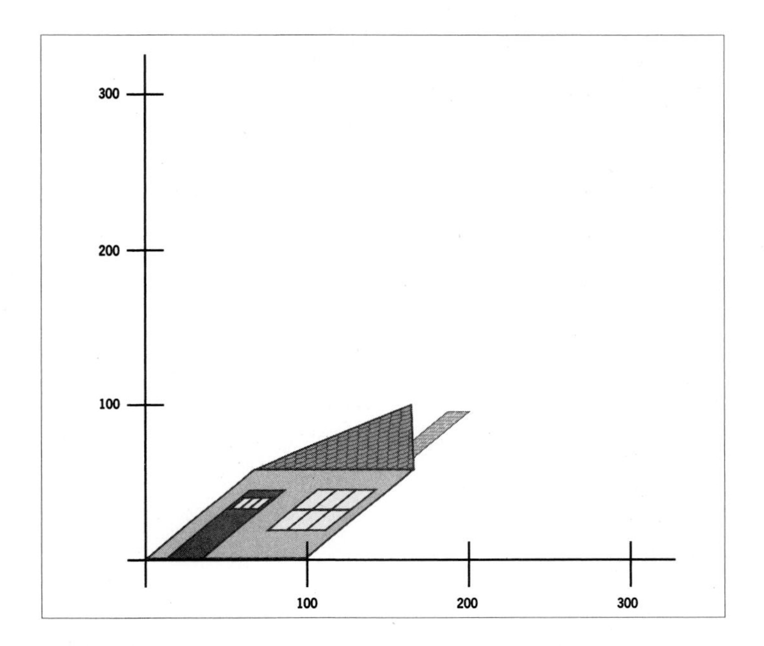

Figure 7.13: The house drawn with horizontal shear

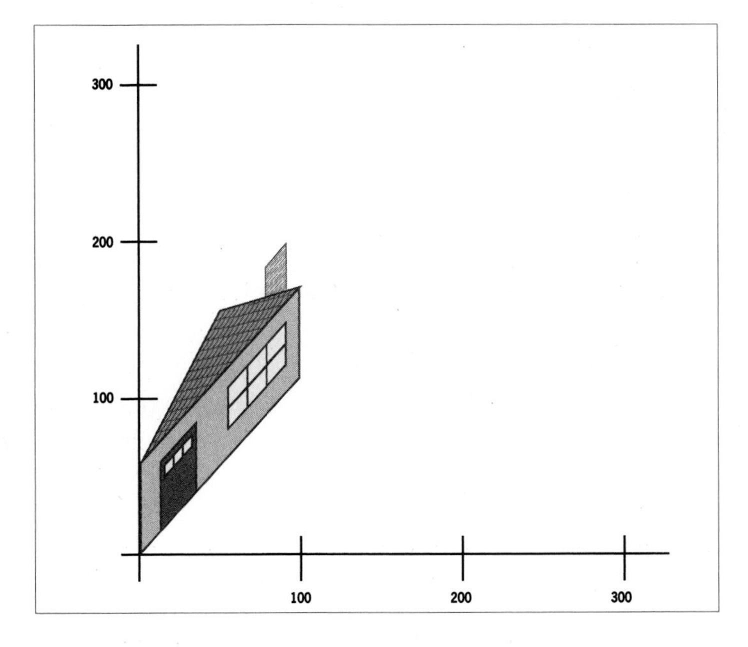

Figure 7.14: The house drawn with vertical shear

Now try this matrix that combines y-shear and negative x-shear:

$$\begin{vmatrix} 1.0 & 1.0 & 0 \\ -1.0 & 1.0 & 0 \\ 0 & 0 & 1 \end{vmatrix}$$

The result is shown in Figure 7.15. The image is rotated 45 percent counterclockwise and enlarged about 40 percent. This suggests that a combination of scaling and shear can produce rotation, which is exactly the case.

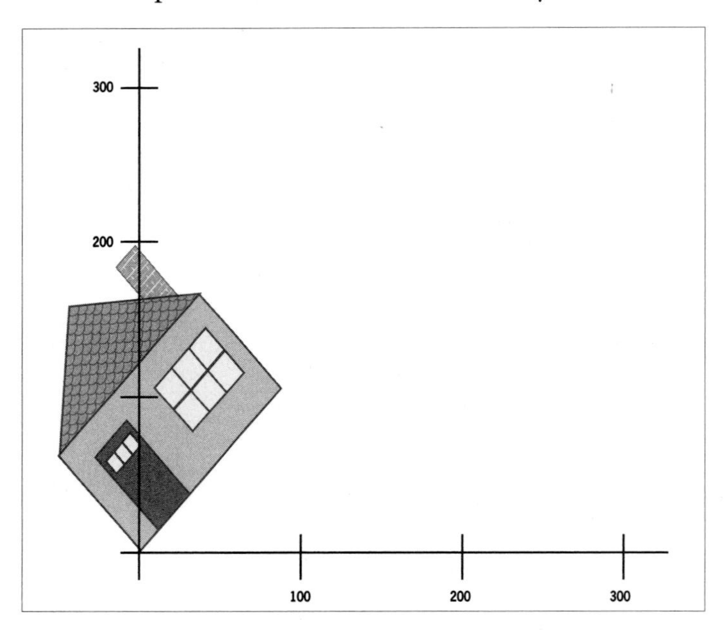

Figure 7.15: The house drawn with vertical and horizontal shear

ROTATION

From basic trigonometry we know that to rotate an image α degrees around the origin in a counterclockwise rotation requires the following formulas:

$$x' = x * \cos(\alpha) - y * \sin(\alpha)$$

$$y' = x * \sin(\alpha) + y * \cos(\alpha)$$

These formulas fit very nicely into the transformation matrix:

$$\begin{vmatrix} \cos(\alpha) & \sin(\alpha) & 0 \\ -\sin(\alpha) & \cos(\alpha) & 0 \\ 0 & 0 & 1 \end{vmatrix}$$

For example, to rotate an image 45 degrees counterclockwise around the origin, use

$$\begin{vmatrix} 0.707 & 0.707 & 0 \\ -0.707 & 0.707 & 0 \\ 0 & 0 & 1 \end{vmatrix}$$

and you get the results shown in Figure 7.16.

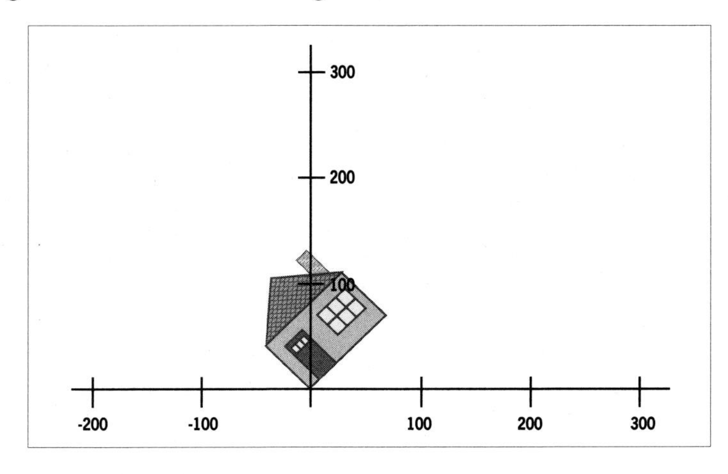

Figure 7.16: The house rotated

To rotate an image 90 degrees counterclockwise, use

$$\begin{vmatrix} 0.0 & 1.0 & 0 \\ -1.0 & 0.0 & 0 \\ 0 & 0 & 1 \end{vmatrix}$$

MATRIX MULTIPLICATION

One reason that matrices are used to represent graphics transforms is that the cumulative effect of two transformations is equivalent to the product of the two matrices. For example, suppose you want to double the height of an object and then rotate the object 45 degrees counterclockwise, as shown in Figure 7.17.

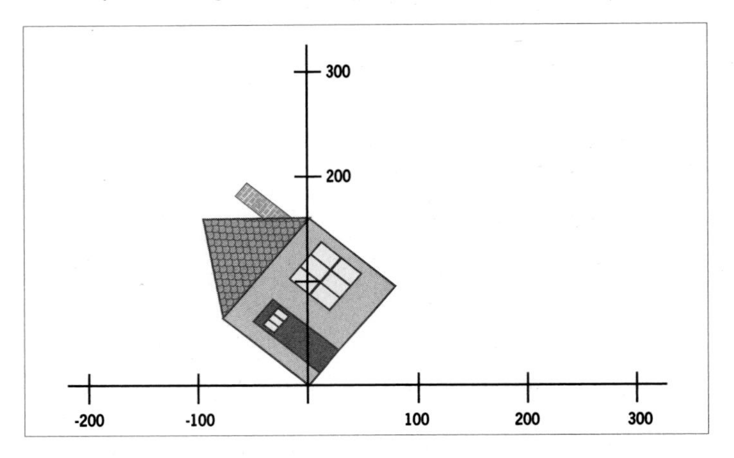

Figure 7.17: The house doubled in height and then rotated

You multiply the two matrices that describe these two transforms:

$$\begin{vmatrix} 1.0 & 0.0 & 0 \\ 0.0 & 2.0 & 0 \\ 0 & 0 & 1 \end{vmatrix} \bullet \begin{vmatrix} 0.707 & 0.707 & 0 \\ -0.707 & 0.707 & 0 \\ 0 & 0 & 1 \end{vmatrix} = \begin{vmatrix} 0.707 & 0.707 & 0 \\ -1.414 & 1.414 & 0 \\ 0 & 0 & 1 \end{vmatrix}$$

(A brief refresher on matrix multiplication: In the resultant matrix, the element in the ith row and jth column is the summation of element-by-element products of the ith row of the first matrix and the jth column of the second matrix.)

Matrix multiplication is associative but not commutative. If you want to first rotate an object 45 degrees and then double the height, as in Figure 7.18, the composite transformation matrix would be calculated like this:

$$\begin{vmatrix} 0.707 & 0.707 & 0 \\ -0.707 & 0.707 & 0 \\ 0 & 0 & 1 \end{vmatrix} \bullet \begin{vmatrix} 1.0 & 0.0 & 0 \\ 0.0 & 2.0 & 0 \\ 0 & 0 & 1 \end{vmatrix} = \begin{vmatrix} 0.707 & 1.414 & 0 \\ -0.707 & 1.414 & 0 \\ 0 & 0 & 1 \end{vmatrix}$$

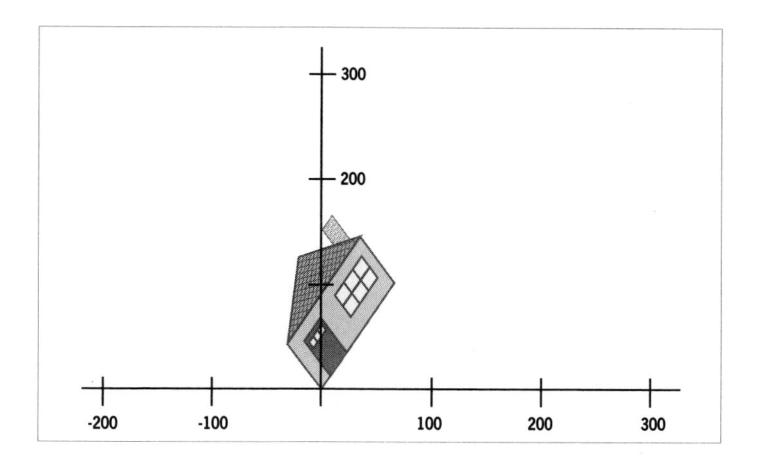

Figure 7.18: The house rotated and then doubled in height

A combination of matrices is often used with rotation to choose the point around which the object is rotated. For example, suppose you have stored a series of points that describes an object. You want to rotate this object 90 degrees around the point (100,100). This is equivalent to translating the object by -100 units on the x-axis and -100 units on the y-axis, rotating the image around the origin, and then translating it back 100 units on the x and y axes. The three matrices that describe these transforms are multiplied together in sequence:

$$\begin{vmatrix} 1.0 & 0.0 & 0 \\ 0.0 & 1.0 & 0 \\ -100 & -100 & 1 \end{vmatrix} \cdot \begin{vmatrix} 0.0 & 1.0 & 0 \\ -1.0 & 0.0 & 0 \\ 0 & 0 & 1 \end{vmatrix} \cdot \begin{vmatrix} 1.0 & 0.0 & 0 \\ 0.0 & 1.0 & 0 \\ 100 & 100 & 1 \end{vmatrix}$$

The result is

$$\begin{vmatrix} 0.0 & 1.0 & 0 \\ -1.0 & 0.0 & 0 \\ 200 & 0 & 1 \end{vmatrix}$$

This is the same as rotating the image 90 degrees and then translating it 200 units along the x axis, as shown in Figure 7.19. You do not have to do the matrix multiplication in your program. You can instead have GPI do the multiplications for you, as we'll see shortly.

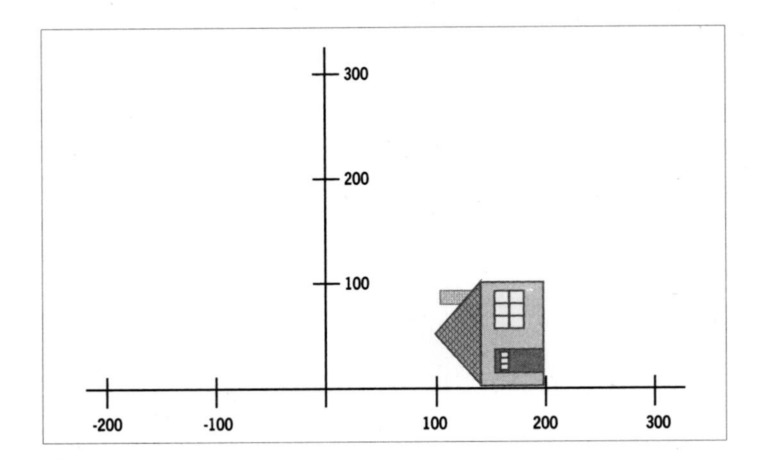

Figure 7.19: The house rotated and then translated

THE MATRIX TRANSFORM FUNCTIONS

So far I've been describing the matrix transforms in a rather abstract way. There are, of course, functions to set or alter the model and default viewing transforms:

```
GpiSetModelTransformMatrix (hps, lCount,&matlf, lOptions) ;
GpiSetDefaultViewMatrix (hps, lCount,&matlf, lOptions) ;
```

The third parameter is a pointer to a MATRIXLF structure and the second parameter is the number of elements in that structure, which is 9. You can use 0 to return the transform to the identify transform. The *lOptions* parameter is one of the following identifiers:

Transform Identifier	New Matrix
TRANSFORM_REPLACE	$M_{new} = M_{fnct}$
TRANSFORM_ADD	$M_{new} = M_{old} * M_{fnct}$
TRANSFORM_PREEMPT	$M_{new} = M_{fnct} * M_{old}$

The M_{new} matrix is the new transform matrix after the function, M_{fnct} is the matrix passed to the function, and M_{old} is the existing transform before the function is called. This is how you can force GDI to multiply matrices for you in the proper order.

DRAWING A FLOWER

We can put all this into practice by drawing a colorful flower using the FLOWER program shown in Listing 7.5.

Listing 7.5: The FLOWER program

The FLOWER.MAK File

```
#----------------------
# FLOWER.MAK make file
#----------------------

flower.exe : flower.obj flower.def
     $(PRGLINK) flower, flower, NUL, $(PRGLIB), flower

flower.obj : flower.c
     $(PRGCC) flower.c
```

The FLOWER.C File

```
/*---------------------------------------
   FLOWER.C -- Transform Demonstration
               (c) Charles Petzold, 1993
  ---------------------------------------*/

#define INCL_WIN
#define INCL_GPI
#include <os2.h>
#include <math.h>

#define TWOPI (2 * 3.14159)

MRESULT EXPENTRY ClientWndProc (HWND, ULONG, MPARAM, MPARAM) ;

int main (void)
     {
     static CHAR  szClientClass [] = "Flower" ;
     static ULONG flFrameFlags = FCF_TITLEBAR      | FCF_SYSMENU |
                                 FCF_SIZEBORDER    | FCF_MINMAX  |
                                 FCF_SHELLPOSITION | FCF_TASKLIST ;
     HAB          hab ;
     HMQ          hmq ;
     HWND         hwndFrame, hwndClient ;
     QMSG         qmsg ;

     hab = WinInitialize (0) ;
     hmq = WinCreateMsgQueue (hab, 0) ;

     WinRegisterClass (hab, szClientClass, ClientWndProc, CS_SIZEREDRAW, 0) ;
```

Listing 7.5: The FLOWER program (Continued)

```
     hwndFrame = WinCreateStdWindow (HWND_DESKTOP, WS_VISIBLE,
                                     &flFrameFlags, szClientClass, NULL,
                                     0L, 0, 0, &hwndClient) ;

     while (WinGetMsg (hab, &qmsg, NULLHANDLE, 0, 0))
          WinDispatchMsg (hab, &qmsg) ;

     WinDestroyWindow (hwndFrame) ;
     WinDestroyMsgQueue (hmq) ;
     WinTerminate (hab) ;
     return 0 ;
     }

VOID DrawPetal (HPS hps)
     {
     static AREABUNDLE ab = { CLR_RED } ;
     static LINEBUNDLE lb = { CLR_BLACK } ;
     static POINTL     aptl[] = {   0,    0,  125,  125,  475, 125,  600, 0,
                                  475, -125,  125, -125,    0,    0 } ;

     GpiSavePS (hps) ;
     GpiSetAttrs (hps, PRIM_AREA, ABB_COLOR, 0, (PBUNDLE) &ab) ;
     GpiSetAttrs (hps, PRIM_LINE, LBB_COLOR, 0, (PBUNDLE) &lb) ;

     GpiBeginArea (hps, BA_BOUNDARY | BA_ALTERNATE) ;

     GpiMove (hps, aptl) ;
     GpiPolySpline (hps, 6, aptl + 1) ;

     GpiEndArea (hps) ;
     GpiRestorePS (hps, -1) ;
     }

VOID DrawPetals (HPS hps)
     {
     static AREABUNDLE ab = { CLR_YELLOW } ;
     static LINEBUNDLE lb = { CLR_BLACK } ;
     static POINTL     aptl [2] = { -150, -150,  150, 150 } ;
     INT               i ;
     MATRIXLF          matlf ;

     GpiSavePS (hps) ;

     GpiQueryModelTransformMatrix (hps, 9, &matlf) ;

     for (i = 0 ; i < 8 ; i++)
          {
          matlf.fxM11 = (FIXED) (65536 *  cos (TWOPI * i / 8)) ;
```

Listing 7.5: The FLOWER program (Continued)

```
          matlf.fxM12 = (FIXED) (65536 *  sin (TWOPI * i / 8)) ;
          matlf.fxM21 = (FIXED) (65536 * -sin (TWOPI * i / 8)) ;
          matlf.fxM22 = (FIXED) (65536 *  cos (TWOPI * i / 8)) ;

          GpiSetModelTransformMatrix (hps, 9, &matlf, TRANSFORM_REPLACE) ;

          DrawPetal (hps) ;
          }

     GpiSetAttrs (hps, PRIM_AREA, ABB_COLOR, 0, (PBUNDLE) &ab) ;
     GpiSetAttrs (hps, PRIM_LINE, LBB_COLOR, 0, (PBUNDLE) &lb) ;

     GpiMove (hps, aptl) ;
     GpiBox (hps, DRO_OUTLINEFILL, aptl + 1, 300, 300) ;

     GpiRestorePS (hps, -1) ;
     }

VOID DrawFlower (HPS hps, INT cxClient, INT cyClient)
     {
     MATRIXLF matlf ;
     POINTL   ptl, aptl [4] ;

     GpiSavePS (hps) ;

     ptl.x = cxClient ;
     ptl.y = cyClient ;

     GpiConvert (hps, CVTC_DEVICE, CVTC_PAGE, 1, &ptl) ;

     aptl[0].x = 0 ;
     aptl[0].y = 0 ;

     aptl[1].x = 0 ;
     aptl[1].y = ptl.y / 4 ;

     aptl[2].x = 0 ;
     aptl[2].y = ptl.y ;

     aptl[3].x = ptl.x / 2 ;
     aptl[3].y = ptl.y / 2 ;

     GpiSavePS (hps) ;

     GpiSetLineWidthGeom (hps, 50) ;

     GpiBeginPath (hps, 1) ;
     GpiMove (hps, aptl) ;
     GpiPolySpline (hps, 3, aptl + 1) ;
```

Listing 7.5: The FLOWER program (Continued)

```
     GpiEndPath (hps) ;

     GpiStrokePath (hps, 1, 0) ;

     GpiRestorePS (hps, -1) ;

     GpiQueryDefaultViewMatrix (hps, 9, &matlf) ;

     matlf.lM31 = ptl.x / 2 ;
     matlf.lM32 = ptl.y / 2 ;

     GpiSetDefaultViewMatrix (hps, 9, &matlf, TRANSFORM_REPLACE) ;

     DrawPetals (hps) ;

     GpiRestorePS (hps, -1) ;
     }

MRESULT EXPENTRY ClientWndProc (HWND hwnd, ULONG msg, MPARAM mp1, MPARAM mp2)
     {
     static INT cxClient, cyClient ;
     HPS        hps ;
     SIZEL      sizel ;

     switch (msg)
          {
          case WM_SIZE:
               cxClient = SHORT1FROMMP (mp2) ;
               cyClient = SHORT2FROMMP (mp2) ;

               return 0 ;

          case WM_PAINT:
               hps = WinBeginPaint (hwnd, NULLHANDLE, NULL) ;
               GpiErase (hps) ;

               sizel.cx = 0 ;
               sizel.cy = 0 ;
               GpiSetPS (hps, &sizel, PU_LOMETRIC) ;

               DrawFlower (hps, cxClient, cyClient) ;

               WinEndPaint (hps) ;
               return 0 ;
          }
     return WinDefWindowProc (hwnd, msg, mp1, mp2) ;
     }
```

Listing 7.5: The FLOWER program (Continued)

The FLOWER.DEF File

```
;----------------------------------
; FLOWER.DEF module definition file
;----------------------------------

NAME          FLOWER    WINDOWAPI

DESCRIPTION   'Transform Demonstration (c) Charles Petzold, 1993'
PROTMODE
```

Many coordinate points are hard-coded in this program and based on PU_LOMETRIC page units. The page units are set during WM_PAINT processing and then the program then calls the *DrawFlower* function.

DrawFlower uses a path to stroke a Bézier spline with a 50-unit thick pen from the lower-left corner of the client window to the center. It then sets the default viewing matrix so the origin is in the center of the window and calls *DrawPetals.*

DrawPetals uses the model transform matrix to successively set a rotation angle of 0 degrees, 45 degrees, 90 degrees, and so forth. It then calls *DrawPetal* for each of the eight petals. *DrawPetal* again uses Bézier splines to draw each petal. The result is shown in Figure 7.20.

OUTLINE FONTS

Working with text and fonts is often the hairiest part of graphics programming. Most of the rest of computer graphics is basic analytic geometry—drawing lines, rectangles, ellipses, and other curves (such as Bézier splines) on a two-dimensional space. Even the nonvector parts of graphics programming (bitmaps and color) don't veer too far from solid mathematical foundations.

Fonts are different. To a typographer, fonts are art with a long history of sophisticated design. Designers of computer graphics systems that implement fonts with any degree of integrity must deal with classical typographical concepts, and application programmers must also learn about them.

Text is meant to be read, and fonts must be readable. This is the most important principle. There are subtleties in font design, font rendering, and page layout that affect readability even if they're not at all consciously noticeable to the average person. Moreover, text is not purely content; the style in which the text is printed on the page can affect the interpretation of the content, either positively or adversely. You don't want a wedding invitation to look like an office memorandum, or a doctoral thesis to look like advertising copy.

Figure 7.20: The FLOWER display

Before even approaching these issues, however, the graphics programmer must deal with function calls, data structures, font metrics, point sizes, baseline increments, leading, kerning, justification, and other concepts. Working with text just isn't like drawing lines, rectangles, and bitmaps.

When fonts first started appearing in printers, graphics applications, and graphical user interfaces such as the Macintosh and Windows, the fonts were almost always stored in a bitmap format. Basically, each character in the font is a tiny bitmap.

Bitmap fonts (also called image fonts or—my preferred term—raster fonts) can be designed for maximum readability and rendered very quickly. However, raster fonts have a very limiting disadvantage: They must be designed for a specific device resolution and font size. A particular raster font may be enlarged (generally in integral multiples) by duplicating rows and columns of pixels, but this creates noticeable jaggies. Conceivably, raster fonts could be decreased in size by deleting rows and columns of pixels, but with the danger of losing important information. For example, the horizontal arm of a capital "A" might disappear. That wouldn't be nice at all.

In more recent years, outline font technology has come to the personal computer. In outline fonts (also called vector fonts), each character is defined by an outline of straight lines and curves. The coordinate points that define the outline can be scaled to a specific size. The outline is then filled. The curves that make up the outline are generally quadratic or cubic splines. In particular, the Bézier spline has proven to be very useful for font design.

OUTLINE PROBLEMS AND SOLUTIONS

Because the characters in an outline font are defined by straight lines and curves, they are continuously scalable and can be manipulated like other graphics objects. Outline fonts can be rotated and skewed, and the outlines can even define clipping regions. Outline fonts also solve the long-frustrating problem of device dependency by being renderable on every type of output device.

There are a couple of problems with outline fonts, however. First, it is much faster to simply draw a bitmap than to algorithmically fill an area based upon on outline. For this reason, outline fonts implemented in printers and graphics systems are often initially converted to bitmaps at the time they are first needed and then cached in memory. This conversion is known as *rasterization.* Although the rasterization takes some time, once it's finished the display of the fonts can be as fast as the display of raster fonts.

A more serious problem involves rounding errors when the coordinate points are scaled. For example, in many fonts the two legs of a capital "H" should be the same width. During the scaling and rasterization process, one leg could become a pixel wider than the other. This is particularly noticeable on low-resolution devices such as video displays, and it severely affects readability. While not nearly as noticeable on 300 dots-per-inch laser printers, it can still affect the appearance of the text.

This was a real problem back in the days of OS/2 1.1, when the Presentation Manager supported a collection of simple outline fonts that clearly revealed these rounding errors in most disturbing ways. Moreover, the rasterized character bitmaps were not cached in memory, resulting in pure performance.

The solution to the rounding problem is to not blindly scale the outline coordinates, but to apply "hinting" algorithms that retain the correct proportions of the fonts. Thus, a hinted outline font is more like a little program than a collection of dumb data.

Adobe was the first company to bring hinted outline fonts to mainstream personal computers in a big way, albeit in PostScript printers rather than on video displays. Until a few years ago, programs still had to approximate printer fonts on the video display by using raster fonts. To fix this problem, the Adobe

Type Manager (ATM) program was released first for the Macintosh and later for Windows, and was also integrated into the Presentation Manager beginning with OS/2 1.3.

ATM supports Adobe "Type 1" outline fonts. These are hinted fonts, and the rasterized bitmaps are cached in memory. The outline fonts may be used on the video display, PostScript printers, and non-PostScript printers. The Adobe Type 1 font format used in ATM is now publicly documented, and thousands of Type 1 fonts are available from Adobe and other font manufacturers.

For this reason, the OS/2 Presentation Manager has evolved into an excellent platform for sophisticated text-based applications. The ATM support makes possible the on-screen WYSIWYG display of text destined for the printer, as well as many PostScript-like special effects.

RASTERS VERSUS OUTLINES

In Chapter 5, I discussed some text and font functions, but with a deliberate focus on the OS/2 raster fonts. Regardless of the flexibility of outline fonts, raster fonts give us the two things we value most when working with fonts on our personal computers: performance and appearance.

Raster fonts are faster than outline fonts. Before an outline font can be used, the characters must be rasterized and the character bitmaps stored in memory. This take time, even though the resultant bitmaps may potentially be as fast to display as raster fonts.

In theory at least, raster fonts can also look a little better on the screen. The characters in a raster font are individually designed by a human being for maximum legibility. This generally produces better results than a general-purpose outline font that is scaled to a particular point size.

When approaching the subject of fonts under the OS/2 Presentation Manager, raster fonts are a good place to start because they inherently limit what you can do with them. You can only use the font sizes that are available, and you don't have many options, so you can simply ignore many of the font and text manipulation functions. That's why I stuck to raster fonts in Chapter 5.

For strictly screen-based text that doesn't require character rotation and other special effects, raster fonts are fine. One problem, of course, is that you can't use the OS/2 raster fonts on most printers. But the worst thing about raster fonts is that they simply aren't as *fun* to use as outline fonts. We'll have some fun with outline fonts later in this chapter.

FAMILIES, FACES, AND POINTS

When working with outline fonts, it is necessary to delve more deeply into concepts of traditional typography. Traditionally, fonts have been identified simply by a typeface name and a size. Each typeface belongs to a type family. Type families have simple names such as Bookman, Helvetica, Garamond, and Times. Within each family, there are usually several variations:

- The strokes of the characters can be light or heavy in various degrees, giving us typeface names such as Helvetica Ultra Light, Helvetica Thin, Helvetica Light, Helvetica Medium, Helvetica Bold, Helvetica Heavy, and Helvetica Black.
- The widths of the characters can be narrower or wider than usual, for typeface names such as Helvetica Condensed, Helvetica Narrow, Helvetica Compressed, or Helvetica Extended.
- The characters can be slanted to the right, giving us typeface names such as Helvetica Italic or Helvetica Oblique. Strictly speaking, *oblique* refers to characters that are simply slanted, while *italic* implies that the characters are also stylistically somewhat different from the *Roman* or upright font.

These three variations can be combined in a single typeface name—for example, Helvetica Bold Extended Oblique. Typeface names can also include the copyright holder of the font and perhaps a code number meaningful only to the font manufacturer.

In recent times, three font families have become a minimum standard (of sorts) for font support on printers and personal computers. These are Courier, Times, and Helvetica in normal, bold, italic, and bold italic versions. Add a symbol font and you have the basic "PostScript 13" font collection, usually a minimum standard on PostScript printers.

Courier is a *fixed-pitch* font—that is, every character has the same width. Text printed in Courier looks like something that once came out of an obsolete piece of noncomputer hardware known as a typewriter. Today, Courier is mostly used for computer program listings and manuscripts submitted to book and magazine publishers. (I'll be printing this chapter in Courier before sending it to Ziff-Davis Press.)

Times is a very popular font for newspapers and magazines, and was originally designed for the *Times of London* in the 1930s. Helvetica is a *sans-serif* typeface, without the little turns at the ends of the letter strokes. Because serifs are believed to aid readability by guiding the eye horizontally across the letters, sans-serif fonts are usually restricted to short blocks of text.

Because typeface names are usually copyrighted and must be licensed from the copyright holder, font clones with different names are very common. For example, in the OS/2 Presentation Manager, raster fonts are named Tms Rmn (which I've heard pronounced "tims rimmin") and Helv (pronounced "helv"). The Times font clone in OS/2 is called Times New Roman.

Along with a typeface name, a font is identified by a size in *points.* In computer typography, a point is 1/72 of an inch. (In traditional typography, a point is actually somewhat smaller.) The point size is often defined as the maximum height of the characters, measured from the bottom of the longest descender to the top of the highest ascender of the upper- and lowercase alphabet, excluding any diacritical marks. However, that's really only an approximation; the actual size of the characters in a particular font of a particular point size is left up to the font designer.

NIX FIXED PITCH

Working with text in computer programs is simplified somewhat when the text uses fixed-pitch fonts (that is, fonts in which all the characters have the same width). However, fixed-pitch fonts are a typographical absurdity. Prior to the invention of the typewriter, it never occurred to anyone that a lowercase "i" should occupy the same amount of horizontal space as an uppercase "W." Many early computer printers had the same technological limitations as the typewriter, and character-mode video adapter boards were also limited to fixed-pitch fonts.

It's pretty well established now that fixed-pitch fonts are more difficult to read than variable-width fonts. One reasonable explanation is that people do not read individual letters, but instead read combinations of letters and even whole words at a glance. It helps a lot if these letters are in close proximity and form familiar patterns.

Fixed-pitch fonts are also more wasteful of display real estate. For a particular font height, more variable-width characters can fit into a line of text than fixed-width characters. Printed fixed-pitch text is also a problem. Because a whole printed page of fixed-pitch text is simply a grid of characters, the individual lines do not guide the reader's eye across the page. This is one reason why typewritten text is often double-spaced, wasting even more paper.

With the widespread use of graphical video adapters and printers, fixed-pitch fonts are no longer necessary or desirable, except for material that is not read in a conventional sense, such as hexadecimal dumps and program listings. It's more work on the programmer's part to use variable-width fonts, but it's worthwhile because it aids readability—and saves trees as well.

THE OS/2 OUTLINE FONTS

OS/2 is shipped with a standard set of 13 Adobe Type 1 fonts, as shown here:

Family Name	Face Names	File
Courier	Courier	COURIER.PSF
	Courier Italic	
	Courier Bold	
	Courier Bold Italic	
Helvetica	Helvetica	HELVETIC.PSF
	Helvetica Italic	
	Helvetica Bold	
	Helvetica Bold Italic	
Times New Roman	Times New Roman	TIMESNRM.PSF
	Times New Roman Italic	
	Times New Roman Bold	
	Times New Roman Bold Italic	
Symbol Set	Symbol Set	COURIER.PSF

The .PSF ("PostScript Font") files are not standard Adobe file formats. Instead, they are resource-only files in the OS/2 linear executable format. The files combine both the Adobe font metrics and the hinted outline code.

With raster fonts, the bold and italic versions are *synthesized*, meaning that a bold version of a raster font is created from the basic font by effectively displaying the character twice, the second time a little offset from the first. Similarly, italics are formed by tilting the bitmaps somewhat. With outline fonts, however, the italic, bold, and bold italic versions are separate and distinct, as in traditional typography.

OS/2 old-timers may remember the collection of unhinted outline fonts included first in OS/2 1.1. These had the family and face names shown here:

Family Name	Face Names
Courier	Courier
	Courier Italic
	Courier Bold
	Courier Bold Italic

Family Name	Face Names
Swiss	Helv
	Helv Italic
	Helv Bold
	Helv Bold Italic
Roman	Tms Rmn
	Tms Rmn Italic
	Tms Rmn Bold
	Tms Rmn Bold Italic

These unhinted outline fonts are not included in current versions of OS/2. However, programs that use these names to select outline fonts under OS/2 will obtain the corresponding Adobe Type 1 fonts. Programs that query all the fonts available in the system will find that the Presentation Manager reports the existence of a Tms Rmn outline font as well as a Times New Roman.

FACE NAMES VERSUS ATTRIBUTES

The early support of fonts in graphical environments such as the Macintosh, Windows, and the OS/2 Presentation Manager was not based very much on classical typography. You began with a face name such as Helvetica or Helv and then, for certain words or sections in your document, you'd apply an attribute such as boldface or italic. This is how the bitmap fonts in PM work.

The Type 1 outline fonts supported by ATM are more closely bound to classical typography. Rather than treating boldface and italics as attributes, these characteristic are part of the typeface name, such as Helvetica Bold, Helvetica Italic, and Helvetica Bold Italic.

This may seem like a trivial difference, but it's really not, for it determines how users select fonts for use in their documents. Some slanted fonts may include the word "Oblique" in their typeface names rather than "Italic." Some fonts may have different degrees of boldness, using words such as "Heavy," "Light," and "Dark." It's more complex than a simple matter of clicking a checkbox to turn on a boldface flag.

The conflict between full typeface names and attributes gets a little weirder in OS/2 because the italic and boldface attributes—normally used to simulate these effects on bitmap fonts—are still valid for outline fonts. You can indeed apply a boldface attribute to a Helvetica font. However, it will be a simulated boldface and not the same as the real Helvetica Bold font. You can also apply the boldface attribute to the Helvetica Bold font to get an even bolder font. The same goes for the italic attribute.

AN OVERVIEW OF FONT FUNCTIONS

There are several different aspects to working with text and fonts under the OS/2 Presentation Manager, some of which were presented in Chapter 5:

- One important job is querying available fonts on the video display and printer. This involves the *GpiQueryFonts* function, which returns information about all the fonts in an array of FONTMETRICS structures. These fonts could be presented to the user in a dialog box for selection. Beginning in OS/2 2.0, there's a built-in standard dialog box for font selection. This is invoked by the *WinFontDlg* function using a structure of type FONTDLG.
- To select a font for displaying text, you use the *GpiCreateLogFont* function with the FATTRS ("font attributes") structure to create a logical font and *GpiSetCharSet* to set the font in the presentation space.
- You can change certain attributes of the selected font using eight functions beginning with *GpiSetChar*. For outline fonts you must call *GpiSetCharBox* to set the size of the font. For outline fonts, you can also call *GpiSetCharAngle* to rotate the characters and *GpiSetCharShear* to give them a forward or backward tilt.
- To determine information about the font currently selected in the presentation space, call *GpiQueryFontMetrics* using a FONTMETRICS structure. This structure will give you much of the information you need to properly display the text.

Because outline fonts are defined by straight lines and Bézier curves, fonts can be manipulated and used like other lines in GPI. Fonts can be rotated and sheared, and the outlines of text characters can form part of a GPI path. You can use these techniques for several types of special effects. It's not something you'll want to do every day, but it's lots of fun and later in this chapter I'll demonstrate how it's done.

FONT ENUMERATION

Working with fonts sometimes reminds me of the Monty Python routine about the cheese shop. A customer at a cheese shop requests a kind of cheese, but the shop doesn't have it. He asks for another kind, and another, and another (eventually totalling over 40 kinds of cheese), but the shop doesn't have any of them. The customer finally shoots the shop's proprietor.

Similarly, I can imagine a font-hungry application running under the OS/2 Presentation Manager requesting specific fonts and coming up empty: Garamond? No. New Century Schoolbook? No. Goudy Old Style? No. New Baskerville? No. Avant Garde Gothic? No. Helvetica Narrow? No. This process might go on for quite awhile considering that there exist over 10,000 different font designs.

Of course, Times, Helvetica, and Courier are the Cheddar, Swiss, and American of fonts. But even these popular designs might not be available on some output devices under their licensed names. For example, the version of Times in OS/2 is called Times New Roman.

It's much more useful to first determine what fonts are available on an output device, and then to select from those. Determining available fonts is often called *font enumeration.* This is important stuff: The proprietor of that cheese shop might be alive today had he first properly enumerated the available cheeses to the customer.

Despite the importance of font enumeration, an OS/2 program *can* select different outline fonts without first enumerating them. You fill the fields of a FATTRS ("font attributes") structure and pass a pointer to this stucture to *GpiCreateLogFont.* Although this technique doesn't always work very well with raster fonts (because you must specify exactly the font height), it works much better with outline fonts.

All you really need to know for setting up the FATTRS structure to select an outline font is the font face name. You can hard-code the face names of the standard 13 OS/2 outline fonts in your program. You know their names because I listed them above. This might be a reasonable approach if you want to display richly formatted text that uses only Courier, Helvetica, and Times New Roman fonts in bold and italic versions.

USING GPIQUERYFONTS

The GPI function that enumerates fonts is *GpiQueryFonts.* The syntax of this function is a little awkward when examined out of the context of sample code. So let me show you first how the function is commonly used, and then we can look at the variations.

I'll assume you have a handle to a presentation space stored in a variable named *hps.* This presentation space is associated with a device context for either the video display or a printer. You want to get information about all the fonts available on that device. The information will be returned to you as an array of FONTMETRICS structures. The FONTMETRICS structure is one of the largest structures in OS/2. It has 52 fields, the last of which is another structure that has 11 fields.

The first step is to determine the *number* of fonts available on the device. You need a LONG variable; let's name it *lFonts*. First set *lFonts* equal to zero and then call *GpiQueryFonts* like so:

```
lFonts = 0 ;
lFonts = GpiQueryFonts (hps, QF_PUBLIC,NULL, &lFonts, 0, NULL) ;
```

Notice that a pointer to *lFonts* is passed to the function, and that *lFonts* also stores the function's return value. On return from *GpiQueryFonts*, *lFonts* will equal the total number of fonts available.

Step two is to allocate a block of memory sufficient for an array of this many FONTMETRICS structures. You first need a variable defined as a pointer to a FONTMETRICS structure:

```
PFONTMETRICS pfm ;
```

Then you can allocate the memory using your favorite memory allocation function:

```
pfm = (PFONTMETRICS) calloc (lFonts,sizeof (FONTMETRICS)) ;
```

Just to give you some idea of the size of this memory block, the FONTMETRICS structure is 228 bytes in length, and *lFonts* will be at least 41 when using a video presentation space. (The 41 fonts are the System Proportional font, the 4 System Monospaced fonts, the 3 Courier, 6 Tms Rmn, and 6 Helv bitmap fonts, the 13 Adobe Type 1 outline fonts, and the 4 Tms Rmn and 4 Helv face names that duplicate the Times New Roman and Helvetica Type 1 fonts.)

Step three is to call *GpiQueryFonts* a second time with the *pfm* pointer and the *lFonts* variable set in step one:

```
GpiQueryFonts (hps, QF_PUBLIC, NULL,
   &lFonts, sizeof (FONTMETRICS), pfm) ;
```

After this call, you can index the *pfm* pointer and access the fields of the FONTMETRICS structure for each font.

THE GENERAL SYNTAX

The general syntax of the *GpiQueryFonts* function is

```
lRemFonts = GpiQueryFonts (hps,flOptions, pszFacename,&lReqFonts, lMetricsLen, pfm)
```

The fourth parameter is a pointer to a LONG variable. This variable must be set to the number of requested fonts. If *lReqFonts* is greater than the number of available fonts, the function will set the variable equal to the actual number of fonts. (You could then call *realloc* to shrink the memory block pointed to by *pfm*.) If *lReqFonts* is less than the number of available fonts, the function returns the number of *remaining* fonts in *lRemFonts*. However, there's no way to find out about those remaining fonts unless you call the function again requesting *all* the fonts.

In the example I just showed, the *GpiQueryFonts* function was first called requesting 0 fonts. In this case, the last two parameters can be set to 0 and NULL. The function returns the number of remaining fonts, which is the total number of fonts.

The second parameter can be one or more flags beginning with the prefix QF. The QF_PUBLIC flag used in the example indicates that you want the fonts that are loaded by the OS/2 Presentation Manager during startup and which are available to all PM applications. (PM uses the *GpiLoadPublicFonts* function to load these fonts.) To have access to fonts that your application privately loads for its own purpose using *GpiLoadFonts*, you can use the flag QF_PRIVATE. You must use either the QF_PUBLIC or QF_PRIVATE flag, or both combined with the bitwise OR operator. Otherwise you won't get any fonts at all.

The second two flags you can use are QF_NO_DEVICE and QF_NO_GENERIC. These flags refer to device fonts and generic fonts. A device font is a font that is built into the graphics output device, such as fonts built into your printer. For video displays there are no device fonts. However, the default System Proportional font is considered to be a device font for purposes of this function call.

The generic fonts for the video display are the bitmap fonts (other than the System Proportional font) and the Adobe Type 1 fonts supported by the Adobe Type Manager. For a printer, generic fonts are the Type 1 fonts supported by ATM and whatever fonts are built into the printer. Don't use *both* the QF_NO_DEVICE and QF_NO_GENERIC flags, or you won't get any fonts at all.

The third parameter to *GpiQueryFonts* is normally set to NULL to enumerate fonts with all face names, but you can set this parameter to indicate a specific face name such as Tms Rmn or Helvetica. This facility was more useful back in the days when programs dealt mostly with bitmap fonts. For example, by specifying Tms Rmn a program could obtain all the sizes of Tms Rmn fonts available. However, it's much less useful with outline fonts or device fonts. If you specify Helvetica you'll only get one font. As mentioned, the bold, italic, and bold italic versions of the Helvetica font have different face names.

The second to last parameter is normally the size of a single FONTMETRICS structure, but it can be set to a smaller size if you're only interested in some of the fields in the beginning of the structure but not the later fields.

Now you may understand why I began with the example rather than the general syntax! For 95 percent of the times that you'll be using *GpiQueryFonts*, your code will look almost exactly like the code I showed in the example.

THE OUTFONTS PROGRAM

If you're now curious to see the outline fonts illustrated on the screen, let's take a look at the OUTFONTS program shown in Listing 7.6.

Listing 7.6: The OUTFONTS Program

The OUTFONTS.MAK File

```
#-----------------------
# OUTFONTS.MAK make file
#-----------------------

outfonts.exe : outfonts.obj outfonts.def
     $(PRGLINK) outfonts, outfonts, NUL, $(PRGLIB), outfonts

outfonts.obj : outfonts.c
     $(PRGCC) outfonts.c
```

The OUTFONTS.C File

```
/*-----------------------------------------
   OUTFONTS.C -- Displays OS/2 Outline Fonts
                 (c) Charles Petzold, 1993
  -----------------------------------------*/

#define INCL_WIN
#define INCL_GPI
#include <os2.h>
#include <stdlib.h>
#include <stdio.h>
#include <string.h>

#define LCID_FONT    1
#define PTSIZE      12

MRESULT EXPENTRY ClientWndProc (HWND, ULONG, MPARAM, MPARAM) ;

int main (void)
     {
     static CHAR  szClientClass [] = "OutFonts" ;
     static ULONG flFrameFlags = FCF_TITLEBAR      | FCF_SYSMENU  |
                                 FCF_SIZEBORDER    | FCF_MINMAX   |
                                 FCF_SHELLPOSITION | FCF_TASKLIST ;
     HAB          hab ;
```

Listing 7.6: The OUTFONTS Program (Continued)

```
     HMQ          hmq ;
     HWND         hwndFrame, hwndClient ;
     QMSG         qmsg ;

     hab = WinInitialize (0) ;
     hmq = WinCreateMsgQueue (hab, 0) ;

     WinRegisterClass (hab, szClientClass, ClientWndProc, CS_SIZEREDRAW, 0) ;

     hwndFrame = WinCreateStdWindow (HWND_DESKTOP, WS_VISIBLE,
                                     &flFrameFlags, szClientClass, NULL,
                                     0L, 0, 0, &hwndClient) ;

     while (WinGetMsg (hab, &qmsg, NULLHANDLE, 0, 0))
          WinDispatchMsg (hab, &qmsg) ;

     WinDestroyWindow (hwndFrame) ;
     WinDestroyMsgQueue (hmq) ;
     WinTerminate (hab) ;
     return 0 ;
     }

LONG GetAllOutlineFonts (HPS hps, PFONTMETRICS * ppfm)
     {
     LONG         l, lAllFnt, lOutFnt ;
     PFONTMETRICS pfmAll, pfmOut ;

               // Find number of fonts

     lAllFnt = 0 ;
     lAllFnt = GpiQueryFonts (hps, QF_PUBLIC, NULL, &lAllFnt, 0, NULL) ;

     if (lAllFnt ==  0)
          return 0 ;

               // Allocate memory for FONTMETRICS structures

     pfmAll = (PFONTMETRICS) calloc (lAllFnt, sizeof (FONTMETRICS)) ;

     if (pfmAll == NULL)
          return 0 ;

     pfmOut = (PFONTMETRICS) calloc (lAllFnt, sizeof (FONTMETRICS)) ;

     if (pfmOut == NULL)
          {
          free (pfmAll) ;
          return 0 ;
          }
```

Listing 7.6: The OUTFONTS Program (Continued)

```
               // Get all fonts

     GpiQueryFonts (hps, QF_PUBLIC, NULL, &lAllFnt,
                         sizeof (FONTMETRICS), pfmAll) ;

               // Get all the outline fonts

     lOutFnt = 0 ;

     for (l = 0 ; l < lAllFnt ; l++)
          if (pfmAll[l].fsDefn & FM_DEFN_OUTLINE)
               pfmOut [lOutFnt ++] = pfmAll [l] ;

               // Clean up

     free (pfmAll) ;
     pfmOut = (PFONTMETRICS) realloc (pfmOut, lOutFnt * sizeof (FONTMETRICS)) ;

     * ppfm = pfmOut ;

     return lOutFnt ;
     }

MRESULT EXPENTRY ClientWndProc (HWND hwnd, ULONG msg, MPARAM mp1, MPARAM mp2)
     {
     static FATTRS       fat ;
     static LONG         xRes, yRes, lFonts ;
     static PFONTMETRICS pfm ;
     static SHORT        cyClient ;
     CHAR                szBuffer [FACESIZE + 32] ;
     FONTMETRICS         fm ;
     HDC                 hdc ;
     HPS                 hps ;
     LONG                l ;
     POINTL              ptl ;
     SIZEF               sizef ;

     switch (msg)
          {
          case WM_CREATE:
                         // Get the array of FONTMETRICS structures

               hps = WinGetPS (hwnd) ;
               GpiQueryFontAction (hps, QFA_PUBLIC) ;
               lFonts = GetAllOutlineFonts (hps, & pfm) ;

                         // Get the font resolution of the device

               hdc = GpiQueryDevice (hps) ;
```

Listing 7.6: The OUTFONTS Program (Continued)

```
          DevQueryCaps (hdc, CAPS_HORIZONTAL_FONT_RES, 1, &xRes) ;
          DevQueryCaps (hdc, CAPS_VERTICAL_FONT_RES,   1, &yRes) ;
          WinReleasePS (hps) ;

          return Ø ;

     case WM_SIZE:
          cyClient = HIUSHORT (mp2) ;
          return Ø ;

     case WM_PAINT:
          hps = WinBeginPaint (hwnd, NULLHANDLE, NULL) ;

          GpiErase (hps) ;

               // Get new fonts if they've changed

          if (QFA_PUBLIC & GpiQueryFontAction (hps, QFA_PUBLIC))
               {
               free (pfm) ;
               lFonts = GetAllOutlineFonts (hps, & pfm) ;
               }

               // Set POINTL structure to upper left corner of client

          ptl.x = Ø ;
          ptl.y = cyClient ;

               // Set the character box for the point size

          sizef.cx = 65536 * xRes * PTSIZE / 72 ;
          sizef.cy = 65536 * yRes * PTSIZE / 72 ;

          GpiSetCharBox (hps, &sizef) ;

               // Loop through all the bitmap fonts

          for (l = Ø ; l < lFonts ; l++)
               {
                    // Define the FATTRS structure

               fat.usRecordLength  = sizeof (FATTRS) ;
               fat.fsSelection     = Ø ;
               fat.lMatch          = Ø ;

               strcpy (fat.szFacename, pfm[l].szFacename) ;

               fat.idRegistry      = pfm[l].idRegistry ;
               fat.usCodePage      = pfm[l].usCodePage ;
```

Listing 7.6: The OUTFONTS Program (Continued)

```
                    fat.lMaxBaselineExt = 0 ;
                    fat.lAveCharWidth   = 0 ;
                    fat.fsType          = FATTR_FONTUSE_OUTLINE |
                                          FATTR_FONTUSE_TRANSFORMABLE ;
                    fat.fsFontUse       = 0 ;

                         // Create the logical font and select it

                    GpiCreateLogFont (hps, NULL, LCID_FONT, &fat) ;
                    GpiSetCharSet (hps, LCID_FONT) ;

                         // Query the font metrics of the current font

                    GpiQueryFontMetrics (hps, sizeof (FONTMETRICS), &fm) ;

                         // Set up a text string to display

                    sprintf (szBuffer, " %s - %d points",
                             fm.szFacename, PTSIZE) ;

                         // Drop POINTL structure to baseline of font

                    ptl.y -= fm.lMaxAscender ;

                         // Display the character string

                    GpiCharStringAt (hps, &ptl, strlen (szBuffer), szBuffer) ;

                         // Drop POINTL structure down to bottom of text

                    ptl.y -= fm.lMaxDescender ;

                         // Select the default font; delete the logical font

                    GpiSetCharSet (hps, LCID_DEFAULT) ;
                    GpiDeleteSetId (hps, LCID_FONT) ;
                    }

               WinEndPaint (hps) ;
               return 0 ;

          case WM_DESTROY:
               if (lFonts > 0)
                    free (pfm) ;

               return 0 ;
          }
     return WinDefWindowProc (hwnd, msg, mp1, mp2) ;
     }
```

Listing 7.6: The OUTFONTS Program (Continued)

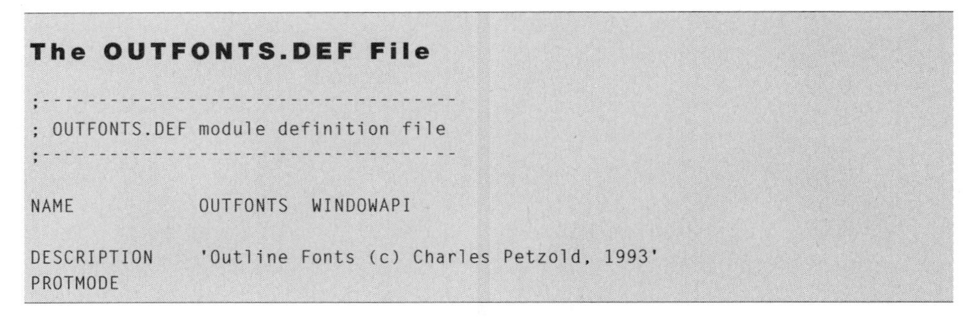

The OUTFONTS.DEF File

```
;-----------------------------------
; OUTFONTS.DEF module definition file
;-----------------------------------

NAME           OUTFONTS  WINDOWAPI

DESCRIPTION    'Outline Fonts (c) Charles Petzold, 1993'
PROTMODE
```

The *GetAllOutlineFonts* function in OUTFONTS uses *GpiQueryFonts* to determine the number of fonts on the video display, and then calls *GpiQueryFonts* again to obtain descriptions of them all as an array of FONTMETRICS structures. The function then loops through all the fonts and copies those with the FM_DEFN_OUTLINE flag set in the *fsDefn* field of the FONTMETRICS structure to another array of FONTMETRICS structures. These are the outline fonts. The function reallocates the memory for this second array and returns the array and the number of outline fonts. During the WM_PAINT message, OUTFONTS displays all the outline fonts. (I'll discuss the font selection code shortly.) Each font is displayed with a text string consisting of a space followed by the typeface name and point size. The results are shown in Figure 7.21.

The 21 lines in the display show the standard 13 Adobe fonts. The Helvetica and Helv fonts are the same: GPI has simply retained the Helv name used in OS/2 1.1 for the old unhinted outline fonts, but uses the Adobe Helvetica font instead. The same goes for the Times New Roman and Tms Rmn fonts. If you've installed other fonts from Adobe type packages, you'll also see those listed.

CREATING AND SELECTING THE FONT

Creating and selecting a logical outline font is much the same as creating and selecting a logical bitmap font. You first set up the fields of an FATTRS structure and pass it to the *GpiCreateLogFont* function. At this point, the logical font is associated with a local ID (often called an "lcid" and pronounced "el cid," but not to be confused with the Charlton Heston movie). You then use *GpiSetCharSet* to select that font—referenced by the local ID—into your presentation space.

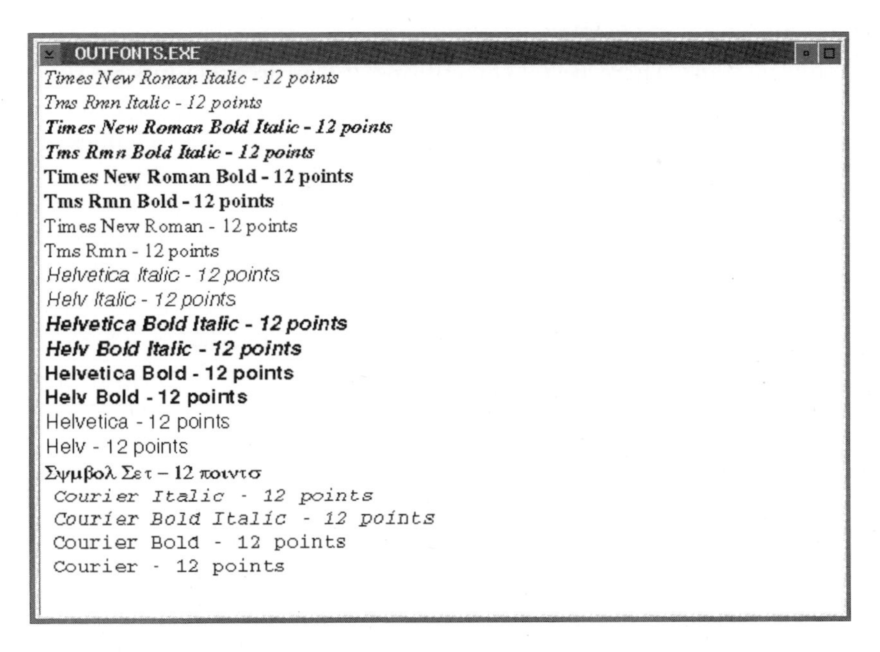

Figure 7.21: The OUTFONTS display

However, there are a couple of differences between selecting bitmap and outline fonts, as shown in the WM_PAINT processing in OUTFONTS.C. For outline fonts, you set the *lMaxBaselineExt* and *lAveCharWidth* fields of the FATTRS structure to zero. The size of the font is not specified here. Also, you set the *fsType* field to the combination of the FATTR_FONTUSE_OUTLINE and FATTR_FONTUSE_TRANSFORMABLE flags. The first flag ensures that you get an outline font. The second flag indicates that you want a font that is subject to graphics transforms. This is true of all outline fonts anyway, but I tend to include the second flag regardless.

You set the point size of the font using the *GpiSetCharBox* function:

```
GpiSetCharBox (hps, &sizef) ;
```

where the second parameter is a pointer to a SIZEF structure. The structure has two fields (*cx* and *cy*) that are treated as 32-bit fixed-point values. The high 16-bit part is an integer value and the lower 16 bits represent a fraction of 65,536. The *cy* field indicates something called the *em-height* of the font (which is equivalent to the point size) and the *cx* field indicates the *em-width*—the point size in horizontal coordinates.

Normally, the *cx* and *cy* fields are set to the same value, which is the point size in logical units. There are two exceptions: If your logical units are unequal in the horizontal and vertical directions—which is the case for the pixel resolution of the EGA—you can compensate for that by using unequal values of *cx* and *cy*. You can also use unequal values if you want the font to appear wider or narrower than normal.

It is customary to call *GpiSetCharBox* after the font has been selected in the presentation space. However, because the character box attribute applies to the presentation space, you can call it at any time while the presentation space handle is valid. Unless you later set it to a different value, it will apply to all outline fonts subsequently selected in the presentation space. To speed along the display of the fonts, I've chosen to call *GpiSetCharBox* once before looping through the font displays.

The tricky part here is converting a point size to pixels. During the WM_-CREATE message, I call *DevQueryCaps* to obtain the horizontal and vertical font resolution of the video display. As you may recall from Chapter 5, the font resolution is an "ideal" video display resolution. For the VGA, the font resolution is given as 96 pixels per inch, whereas the real resolution of the VGA is more like 68 pixels per inch. The use of the font resolution to size outline fonts results in larger character sizes, which are more readable on the screen.

When OUTFONTS calculates the *cx* and *cy* fields of the SIZEF structure, it multiplies the point size by the font resolution (in pixels per inch) and divides by 72—the number of points in an inch. This yields the size of the font in pixels. This pixel size is multiplied by 65,536 to convert to a fixed-point value. For a 12-point font on the VGA, for example, the pixel em-height and em-width are 16.

You can experiment with OUTFONTS by setting the *fsSelection* field of the FATTRS structure to FATTR_SEL_UNDERSCORE or FATTR_SEL_STRIKOUT. You can also use the FATTR_SEL_ITALIC or FATTR_SEL_BOLD attributes, but these are simulations applied to the font. A Times New Roman Italic font is not the same as a Times New Roman font with the italic attribute, and a Times New Roman Bold font is not the same as a Times New Roman font with the boldface attribute. This will be obvious when you see the difference in the lowercase "a" of the simulated italic version of the Times New Roman font and the real Times New Roman Italic font.

A fifth constant you can use with outline fonts (but not raster fonts) is FATTR_SEL_OUTLINE. This creates hollow characters consisting only of outlines. (Despite what IBM's documentation says, however, using this attribute does *not* result in faster display performance.)

SIMPLIFIED FONT SELECTION

Now it's time to encapsulate outline font selection in some easy-to-use functions that you can use in your own Presentation Manager programs. At the very simplest, selecting an outline font for use in a presentation space requires only that you specify the font face name. (Actually, that's not *precisely* true, as we shall see.) After selecting an outline font, you can then scale it to any desired size.

Listing 7.7 shows two files named OLF.H and OLF.C (OLF stands for "outline font"). To use the three functions in the OLF module, include OLF.H in your program, compile OLF.C, and link with OLF.OBJ.

Listing 7.7: The OLF Files

The OLF.H File

```
/*------------------------------------------
   OLF.H -- Easy access to OS/2 outline fonts
            (c) Charles Petzold, 1993
  ------------------------------------------*/

typedef struct
     {
     int  iNumFaces ;
     char szFacename [1] [FACESIZE] ;
     }
     FACELIST ;

typedef FACELIST * PFACELIST ;

PFACELIST GetAllOutlineFonts (HPS hps) ;

LONG CreateOutlineFont (HPS hps, LONG lcid, char * szFacename,
                        SHORT fsAttributes, SHORT usCodePage) ;

BOOL ScaleOutlineFont (HPS hps, int iPointSize, int iPointWidth) ;
```

The OLF.C File

```
/*------------------------------------------
   OLF.C -- Easy access to OS/2 outline fonts
            (c) Charles Petzold, 1993
  ------------------------------------------*/

#define INCL_GPI
#include <os2.h>
#include <stdlib.h>
#include <string.h>
```

Listing 7.7: The OLF Files (Continued)

```
#include "olf.h"

PFACELIST GetAllOutlineFonts (HPS hps)
     {
     static PFACELIST pfl ;
     LONG             l, lFonts ;
     PFONTMETRICS     pfm ;

               // Check for changed fonts

     if (!(QFA_PUBLIC & GpiQueryFontAction (hps, QFA_PUBLIC)) && pfl != NULL)
          return pfl ;

               // Delete old structure if necessary

     if (pfl != NULL)
          free (pfl) ;

               // Determine the number of fonts

     lFonts = 0 ;
     lFonts = GpiQueryFonts (hps, QF_PUBLIC, NULL, &lFonts, 0, NULL) ;

     if (lFonts == 0)
          return NULL ;

               // Allocate memory for FONTMETRICS structures

     pfm = (PFONTMETRICS) calloc (lFonts, sizeof (FONTMETRICS)) ;

     if (pfm == NULL)
          return NULL ;

               // Get all fonts

     GpiQueryFonts (hps, QF_PUBLIC, NULL, &lFonts,
                    sizeof (FONTMETRICS), pfm) ;

               // Allocate memory for FACELIST structure

     pfl = malloc (sizeof (FACELIST)) ;
     pfl->iNumFaces = 0 ;

               // Loop through all fonts

     for (l = 0 ; l < lFonts ; l++)
          {
                    // Check if outline font
```

Listing 7.7: The OLF Files (Continued)

```
          if (pfm[l].fsDefn & FM_DEFN_OUTLINE)
               {
                         // Reallocate FACELIST structure & store face name

               pfl = realloc (pfl, sizeof (FACELIST) +
                                   pfl->iNumFaces * FACESIZE) ;

               strcpy (pfl->szFacename[pfl->iNumFaces], pfm[l].szFacename) ;

               pfl->iNumFaces ++ ;
               }
          }

               // Clean up

     free (pfm) ;

     return pfl ;
     }

LONG CreateOutlineFont (HPS hps, LONG lcid, char * szFacename,
                        SHORT fsAttributes, SHORT usCodePage)
     {
     FATTRS fat ;
     LONG   lReturn ;

               // Set up FATTRS structure

     fat.usRecordLength  = sizeof (FATTRS) ;
     fat.fsSelection     = fsAttributes ;
     fat.lMatch          = 0 ;
     fat.idRegistry      = 0 ;
     fat.usCodePage      = usCodePage ;
     fat.lMaxBaselineExt = 0 ;
     fat.lAveCharWidth   = 0 ;
     fat.fsType          = FATTR_FONTUSE_OUTLINE |
                           FATTR_FONTUSE_TRANSFORMABLE ;
     fat.fsFontUse       = 0 ;

     strcpy (fat.szFacename, szFacename) ;

               // Create the font

     lReturn = GpiCreateLogFont (hps, NULL, lcid, &fat) ;

               // If no match, try a symbol code page

     if (lReturn == FONT_DEFAULT && usCodePage == 0)
          {
```

Listing 7.7: The OLF Files (Continued)

```
          fat.usCodePage = 65400 ;

          lReturn = GpiCreateLogFont (hps, NULL, lcid, &fat) ;
          }

     return lReturn ;
     }

BOOL ScaleOutlineFont (HPS hps, int iPointSize, int iPointWidth)
     {
     HDC    hdc ;
     LONG   xRes, yRes ;
     POINTL aptl[2] ;
     SIZEF  sizef ;

               // Get font resolution in pixels per inch

     hdc = GpiQueryDevice (hps) ;

     DevQueryCaps (hdc, CAPS_HORIZONTAL_FONT_RES, 1, &xRes) ;
     DevQueryCaps (hdc, CAPS_VERTICAL_FONT_RES,   1, &yRes) ;

               // Find desired font size in pixels

     if (iPointWidth == 0)
          iPointWidth = iPointSize ;

     aptl[0].x = 0 ;
     aptl[0].y = 0 ;
     aptl[1].x = (16 * xRes * iPointWidth + 360) / 720 ;
     aptl[1].y = (16 * yRes * iPointSize  + 360) / 720 ;

               // Convert to page coordinates

     GpiConvert (hps, CVTC_DEVICE, CVTC_PAGE, 2L, aptl) ;

               // Set the character box

     sizef.cx = (aptl[1].x - aptl[0].x) << 12 ;
     sizef.cy = (aptl[1].y - aptl[0].y) << 12 ;

     return GpiSetCharBox (hps, &sizef) ;
     }
```

The *GetAllOutlineFonts* function enumerates all the outline fonts and stores them in a structure of type FACELIST, which is defined in OLF.H. This structure consists simply of an integer value indicating the number of typeface names, followed by an array of zero-terminated 32-character face names. By now the font enumeration logic should look very familiar, so I won't bore you with the details.

The *CreateOutlineFont* function creates a logical outline font. The function takes five parameters. The *hps* parameter is the handle to the presentation space, and *lcid* is the local ID to be associated with the logical font. (A program later selects the font into the presentation space by calling *GpiSetCharSet.*) The next parameter is the font typeface name.

You use zero or more constants beginning with the FATTR_SEL prefix for the *fsAttributes* parameter. The final parameter to CreateOutlineFont is *usCodePage,* which you can set to 0 for the default code page.

The *ScaleOutlineFont* function scales a selected font to a particular point size. Because outline fonts can be scaled to fractional point sizes, the two sizing parameters (*iPointSize* and *iPointWidth*) are given in decipoints, which are 1/10 of a point. Thus, if you want a 12.5 point font, set *iPointSize* to 125.

For a normally proportioned font, you can set the *iPointWidth* parameter to the same value as *iPointSize,* or to 0. Or, you can make a narrower or wider font by using different values of *iPointSize* and *iPointWidth.* For example, if you set *iPointSize* to 120 and *iPointWidth* to 60, the 12-point font will be half the normal width. An *iPointWidth* value of 240 will give you a font that has double the normal width. Do not confuse the *iPointWidth* parameter with the average width of the font characters.

I decided to write *CreateOutlineFont* so that it was not dependent on the font information obtained by *GetAllOutlineFonts.* This means you can use *CreateOutlineFont* without first enumerating the fonts. Simply pass one of the 13 standard OS/2 typeface names to the function. These face names are Courier, Helvetica, and Times New Roman by themselves (or followed by Italic, Bold, or Bold Italic) plus Symbol Set.

The *CreateOutlineFont* function begins by setting up an FATTRS structure using the *szFacename, fsAttributes,* and *usCodePage* parameters to the function. The *fsType* field is set to the combination of FATTR_FONTUSE_OUTLINE and FATTR_FONTUSE_TRANSFORMABLE for creating an outline font. The function then calls *GpiCreateLogFont,* passing a pointer to the FATTRS structure.

There's only one little problem: This won't work for a font that consists of non-Latin characters, such as the Symbol Set font. To create a logical font with non-Latin characters, you must set the *usCodePage* field of the FATTRS function to 65400. Otherwise, *GpiCreateLogFont* will get the system default font and return the value FONT_DEFAULT.

If your program knows it wants to create a symbol font, you can pass 65400 as the *usCodePage* parameter to the *CreateOutlineFont* function. Otherwise,

CreateOutlineFont does the work for you. It checks if the return value from *GpiCreateLogFont* is FONT_DEFAULT, resets the *usCodePage* field to 65400, and calls *GpiCreateLogFont* again.

Of course, creating the logical font is only the first step. The font must later be selected in the presentation space by calling *GpiSetCharSet.* And, for outline fonts, the selected font must be scaled to a particular size by calling *GpiSetCharBox.* As we've seen, this function takes a parameter of type SIZEF, a structure that contains two fields for the desired em-height and em-width of the font. The em-height is the point size of the font measured in vertical coordinates, and the em-width is the point size of the font measured in horizontal coordinates. These two values are generally the same (at least in physical dimensions).

For typographers and other people who work with text, sizing a font by specifying the point size makes perfect sense. However, there are some programming problems in which text must fit within a particular fixed width or rectangle. In this case, choose a trial point size and measure the dimensions of the text using *GpiQueryTextBox.* Then scale the point size up or down. The OLFSTR1 and OLFSTR2 programs shown later in this chapter illustrate this technique.

As mentioned, the *ScaleOutlineFont* function in OLF.C takes a decipoint size directly. However, the character box dimensions passed to the *GpiSetCharBox* function must be given in world coordinates. This requires a calculation to convert the decipoint sizes passed to *ScaleOutlineFont.*

It's obvious that we want the *ScaleOutlineFont* function in OLF.C to work regardless of whether we're drawing in units of pixels, inches, or millimeters. That is, the physical size of a 12-point font on the screen or printer page should be independent of the device transform. This much is clear.

The default viewing and model transforms are often used to zoom into a graphics drawing and see it in a larger size. For example, you may want to make the drawing double the size. In such a zoomed-in image, you want a 12-point font to be displayed as twice the normal size. Thus, the physical size of the font should be affected by the default viewing and model transforms, but not the device transform.

Let's see how to solve this problem.

SCALING THE FONT

The function *ScaleOutlineFont* in OLF.C takes font sizes in decipoints and performs all the necessary conversions to pass values to *GpiSetCharBox.* It begins by using *DevQueryCaps* to obtain the horizontal and vertical font resolution (in dots per inch) of the output device. For the VGA, these values will be 96 dpi; for most laser printers, the resolution is 300 dpi.

The *ScaleOutlineFont* function defines an array of two POINTL structures. The *x* and *y* fields of the first are set to 0. The fields of the second are set to the point size in pixels. This is calculated by dividing the decipoint size by 720 to convert to inches, and multipling by the device resolution in pixels per inch. In the formulas in *ScaleOutlineFont*, the multiplication occurs first, then 360 is added for rounding, and the result is divided by 720.

You'll notice that the calculation also includes a multiplicative factor of 16. As you'll recall, the point sizes in the SIZEF structure are fixed point values—a 16-bit integer part and a 16-bit fractional part. In theory, I should be using 65536 rather than 16, but that might cause an overflow. I'll discuss my rationale for using 16 shortly.

Now we have the character box dimensions of the font in pixels. Next, the *ScaleOutlineFont* function passes the two POINTL functions to *GpiConvert*. The CVTC_DEVICE and CVTC_PAGE parameters indicate that we want device coordinates (pixels) converted to page coordinates. This is how the parameters to *ScaleOutlineFont* are made independent of the device transform but not the default page or model transforms.

Let's take an example: Suppose that your program has set page units to "high English," which means that coordinates are specified in 0.001 inches. You've also set a model transform that doubles coordinates and sizes. That is, you want the image to be visually twice as large as normal. You want a 12-point font. On the VGA, this font is 16 pixels tall. That's the font resolution of the VGA (96 dots per inch) times the decipoint size (120) divided by 720. (Let's ignore the multiplication by 16 in the calculations for this example.)

The *GpiConvert* function converts the 16-pixel device units to page units by multiplying by 7086 (the height of the VGA screen in 0.001 inches) and dividing by 480 (the height of the VGA in pixels) to get a height of 236. This means that the em-height of the 12-point font is 0.236 inches. (I realize that 0.236 seems to be the em-height for a 17-point font because 0.236 times 72 is about 17, but that's because we're using the video font resolution—higher than the actual resolution—for calculating the font size. I'll discuss an alternative later in this chapter.)

So, we now have a font with an em-height of 236 milli-inches. When it comes time to display the font, the model transform doubles the height of the font from 236 to 472. Then the device transform converts it to pixels by multiplying by 480 and dividing by 7086. That's 32 pixels. So, the 12-point font has been doubled in size by the model transform.

I still haven't finished discussing the *ScaleOutlineFont* function. After the *GpiConvert* call, the function subtracts the coordinates of the first POINTL structure (originally initialized to 0) from the second POINTL structure, and shifts the results left by 12 bits. Together with the earlier multiplication by 16, this converts an integer value into a fixed-point value in preparation for calling *GpiSetCharBox*.

The use of two POINTL structures—the first initialized to an origin of (0,0)—allows for cases where the device transform includes translation as well as scaling. This is only possible if a program has used *GpiSetPageViewport*, but it's something from which the *ScaleOutlineFont* function protects itself. The two POINTL structures ensure that an actual width and height are being calculated rather than just a point.

WORKING WITH FIXED POINT

Many traditional graphics programming systems use floating point extensively for coordinates and sizes. However, GPI sticks to integers for performance purposes. In cases where floating point might be more appropriate—such as the character box—32-bit fixed-point values are used, providing some of the precision of floating point but without the performance hit.

At first, it doesn't seem necessary to use a fixed-point value for the character box. Let's take an example with the EGA. (This stuff is easiest to illustrate with the EGA because the vertical font resolution is 72 dpi, and hence, a pixel is 1 point high.) Suppose you want a 12.25-point font. In theory (assuming device coordinates), you should specify the character box as 0x000C4000. But GPI eventually has to rasterize the font—that is, turn the characters into bitmaps that have distinct pixel dimensions. Because there is no such thing as a fractional pixel, the 12.25-point rasterized font will be no different than a 12.00-point font or an 11.75-point font.

The implication here is that fractional point sizes have no meaning on the EGA, and not much more on the VGA. And on 300 dpi laser printers, it doesn't make much sense to specify fonts with a resolution better than about a quarter of a point.

In reality, however, GPI *does* take fractional character box sizes into account. On the EGA, fonts with point sizes from 11.50 to 12.50 will all have an em-height of 12 pixels, but some of the character widths will be different, reflecting the different point sizes. We'll see an example of this in this chapter.

ScaleOutlineFont allows specifying the point size in decipoints. If we want this $^1/_{10}$th point resolution to be reflected in fonts displayed on the EGA and VGA, we must specify character box dimensions with fractional parts that also have at least a $^1/_{10}$th resolution. This is why the calculation of the pixel size of the font includes a multiplication by 16. If you're using device coordinates, the character box dimensions will have fractional parts of 0x0000, 0x1000, 0x2000, and so forth. Every distinct decipoint size passed to *ScaleOutlineFont* will produce a unique character box dimension.

Watch out when using fixed-point values, however: If you raise that value of 16 much higher, you run the risk of overflow, either in the calculation of the pixel dimensions of the font, or deep down in GPI in the *GpiConvert* function.

FONT RES OR REAL RES?

The *ScaleOutlineFont* shown in OLF.C uses the font resolution of the device (in pixels per inch) to convert the point size to a pixel size. The font resolution of video displays is normally higher than the actual resolution. For a VGA, for example, the font resolution is 96 dpi, while the actual resolution is closer to 68 dpi. (For printers, the font resolution is consistent with actual resolution.)

The video font resolution is a value set by the designers of the video device driver. It is chosen to accomplish three goals:

- First, it's easier to design bitmap fonts when there is a simple relationship between pixels and points. For example, the VGA font resolution of 96 dpi means that there are 4 pixels for every 3 points.
- Second, when using the video display to preview printer output, it is helpful if video fonts are slightly larger than printer fonts because the video display is usually viewed from farther away than people normally read text from paper.
- Third, video displays are usually wider than paper, so using slightly larger fonts on the screen takes better advantage of video real estate when the video display is used to preview printer output.

However, when displaying outline fonts on the video display, it is possible to scale them based on the actual resolution of the display rather than the font resolution. Here's how to modify *ScaleOutlineFont* to do it. First, instead of using the CAPS_HORIZONTAL_FONT_RES and CAPS_VERTICAL_FONT_RES parameters to *DevQueryCaps*, use CAPS_HORIZONTAL_RESOLUTION and CAPS_VERTICAL_RESOLUTION. These parameters give you the resolution of the device in the ungainly units of pixels per meter. For the VGA, the values are both 2667. Second, to calculate the pixel size of the font, use formulas similar to those shown in *ScaleOutlineFont*: Multiply the resolution by the point size, but divide by the magic number 28346. That's the number of decipoints in a meter (a number that rarely comes up in day-to-day life).

HAVING FUN

The most significant advantage of outline fonts over raster fonts is, of course, infinite scalability. You're not stuck with a few different discrete point sizes. You can simply scale the font to whatever point size you want. A second advantage is that the same outline fonts can be used on any graphics output device, so you get visual compatibility between the video display and the printer. The third advantage is that working (and playing) with outline fonts can be lots of fun. You begin with predefined character outlines and manipulate them in various ways to create sometimes very striking designs. It's now time to take that OLF module discussed earlier and put it to work with several sample programs.

Because these sample programs will simply process WM_PAINT messages, I've written a "shell" module (called OLFDEMO) that handles all the standard PM program overhead. This is shown in Listing 7.8.

Listing 7.8: The OLFDEMO files

The OLFDEMO.C File

```
/*-------------------------------------------------------
   OLFDEMO.C -- OS/2 Outline Fonts Demonstration Shell
                (c) Charles Petzold, 1993
  -------------------------------------------------------*/

#define INCL_WIN
#define INCL_GPI
#include <os2.h>

extern void PaintClient (HPS hps, SHORT cxClient, SHORT cyClient) ;

MRESULT EXPENTRY ClientWndProc (HWND, ULONG, MPARAM, MPARAM) ;

int main (void)
     {
     static CHAR  szClientClass [] = "OlfDemo" ;
     static ULONG flFrameFlags = FCF_TITLEBAR      | FCF_SYSMENU  |
                                 FCF_SIZEBORDER    | FCF_MINMAX   |
                                 FCF_SHELLPOSITION | FCF_TASKLIST ;
     HAB          hab ;
     HMQ          hmq ;
     HWND         hwndFrame, hwndClient ;
     QMSG         qmsg ;

     hab = WinInitialize (0) ;
     hmq = WinCreateMsgQueue (hab, 0) ;

     WinRegisterClass (hab, szClientClass, ClientWndProc, CS_SIZEREDRAW, 0) ;
```

Listing 7.8: The OLFDEMO files (Continued)

```
     hwndFrame = WinCreateStdWindow (HWND_DESKTOP, WS_VISIBLE,
                                    &flFrameFlags, szClientClass,
                                    NULL, ØL, NULLHANDLE, Ø, &hwndClient) ;

     while (WinGetMsg (hab, &qmsg, NULLHANDLE, Ø, Ø))
          WinDispatchMsg (hab, &qmsg) ;

     WinDestroyWindow (hwndFrame) ;
     WinDestroyMsgQueue (hmq) ;
     WinTerminate (hab) ;
     return Ø ;
     }

MRESULT EXPENTRY ClientWndProc (HWND hwnd, ULONG msg, MPARAM mp1, MPARAM mp2)
     {
     static SHORT cxClient, cyClient ;
     HPS          hps ;

     switch (msg)
          {
          case WM_SIZE:
               cxClient = LOUSHORT (mp2) ;
               cyClient = HIUSHORT (mp2) ;
               return Ø ;

          case WM_PAINT:
               hps = WinBeginPaint (hwnd, NULLHANDLE, NULL) ;

               GpiErase (hps) ;

               PaintClient (hps, cxClient, cyClient) ;

               WinEndPaint (hps) ;
               return Ø ;
          }
     return WinDefWindowProc (hwnd, msg, mp1, mp2) ;
     }
```

The OLFDEMO.DEF File

```
;-----------------------------------
; OLFDEMO.DEF module definition file
;-----------------------------------

NAME                          WINDOWAPI

DESCRIPTION    'OS/2 Outline Fonts Demo (c) Charles Petzold, 1993'
PROTMODE
```

To create a complete program, all we need is a make file and another module containing a routine called *PaintClient*, which is the function that OLFDEMO.C calls during the WM_PAINT mesage. The three parameters to *PaintClient* are the handle to the presentation space, and the width and height of the client window in pixels. This *PaintClient* function can also use functions in OLF.C to enumerate the outline fonts, create a logical font, and scale the font to a desired size. I'll be using the OLF and OLFDEMO files in all the remaining sample programs in this chapter.

LISTING THE FONTS

The first test of the OLF module is to list all the outline fonts in the client window. The OLFLIST.MAK and OLFLIST.C files shown in Listing 7.9 show how this is done.

Listing 7.9: The OLFLIST program

The OLFLIST.MAK File

```
#----------------------
# OLFLIST.MAK make file
#----------------------

olflist.exe : olflist.obj olfdemo.obj olf.obj olfdemo.def
     $(PRGLINK) olflist olfdemo olf, olflist, NUL, $(PRGLIB), olfdemo

olflist.obj : olflist.c olf.h
     $(PRGCC) olflist.c

olfdemo.obj : olfdemo.c
     $(PRGCC) olfdemo.c

olf.obj : olf.c olf.h
     $(PRGCC) olf.c
```

The OLFLIST.C File

```
/*---------------------------------------
   OLFLIST.C -- Lists OS/2 Outline Fonts
                (c) Charles Petzold, 1993
  ---------------------------------------*/

#define INCL_WIN
#define INCL_GPI
#include <os2.h>
#include <stdio.h>
#include <string.h>
```

Listing 7.9: The OLFLIST program (Continued)

```
#include "olf.h"

#define LCID_FONT     1
#define PTSIZE      120
#define PTWIDTH     120

void PaintClient (HPS hps, SHORT cxClient, SHORT cyClient)
     {
     CHAR         szBuffer [FACESIZE + 32] ;
     FONTMETRICS  fm ;
     int          i ;
     PFACELIST    pfl ;
     POINTL       ptl ;

          // Get pointer to FACELIST structure

     pfl = GetAllOutlineFonts (hps) ;

          // Set POINTL structure to upper left corner of client

     ptl.x = 0 ;
     ptl.y = cyClient ;

          // Loop through all the outline fonts

     for (i = 0 ; i < pfl->iNumFaces ; i++)
          {
               // Create the logical font and select it

          CreateOutlineFont (hps, LCID_FONT, pfl->szFacename[i], 0, 0) ;
          GpiSetCharSet (hps, LCID_FONT) ;

               // Scale the selected font

          ScaleOutlineFont (hps, PTSIZE, PTWIDTH) ;

               // Query the font metrics of the current font

          GpiQueryFontMetrics (hps, sizeof (FONTMETRICS), &fm) ;

               // Set up a text string to display

          sprintf (szBuffer, "%s - %d decipoints, width %d",
                   fm.szFacename, PTSIZE, PTWIDTH) ;

               // Drop POINTL structure to baseline of font

          ptl.y -= fm.lMaxAscender ;
```

Listing 7.9: The OLFLIST program (Continued)

```
                    // Display the character string

               GpiCharStringAt (hps, &ptl, strlen (szBuffer), szBuffer) ;

                    // Drop POINTL structure down to bottom of text

               ptl.y -= fm.lMaxDescender ;

                    // Select the default font; delete the logical font

               GpiSetCharSet (hps, LCID_DEFAULT) ;
               GpiDeleteSetId (hps, LCID_FONT) ;

               if (ptl.y < 0)
                    break ;
               }
     }
```

The *PaintClient* routine in OLFLIST.C first calls the function in OLF.C named *GetAllOutlineFonts*. This function returns a pointer to a pointer of type PFACELIST, a structure defined in OLF.H. This structure consists of an integer value indicating the number of outline font typeface names, followed by an array of these typeface names.

OLFLIST loops through all these typeface names, passing each face name to the OLF routine *CreateOutlineFont*. This function associates the font with a local ID. A call to *GpiSetCharSet* selects the font into the presentation space. OLFLIST then calls *ScaleOutlineFont* to scale the font to a particular point size in units of decipoints. In OLFLIST, the PTSIZE and PTWIDTH parameters passed to this function are both defined as 120, indicating a 12-point font.

Then OLFLIST calls *GpiQueryFontMetrics* to determine the pixel dimensions of the font. The POINTL structure named *ptl* is used to position the character string. It is initialized at the point (*0,cyClient*) which is the upper-left corner of the client window. The function decreases *ptl.y* by the the *lMaxAscender* field of the FONTMETRICS structure, displays the string, and then decreases *ptl.y* by the *lMaxDescender* field. The results are shown in Figure 7.22.

UNEQUAL HEIGHTS AND WIDTHS

Normally, the two size parameters to *ScaleOutlineFont* are set to the same value—the size of the font in decipoints. The second parameter indicates the height of the font, and the third parameter is the width. (Alternatively, a program can set the third parameter to 0, and the *ScaleOutlineFont* function will set the width to the same value as the height.)

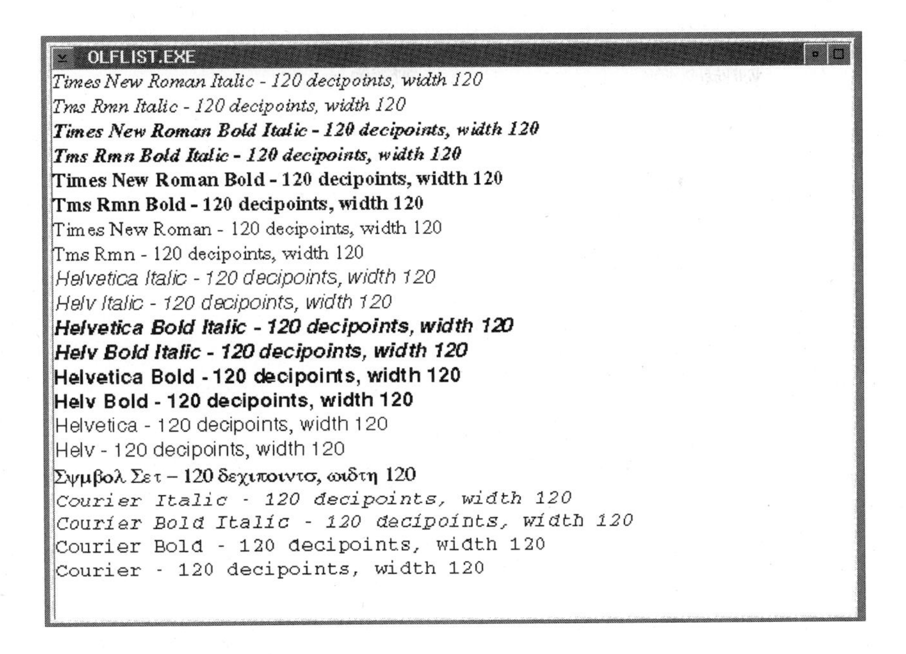

Figure 7.22: The OLFLIST display

You can experiment with different font height and width values by changing the PTSIZE and PTWIDTH constants defined in OLFLIST.C, and recompiling. For example, if you set PTWIDTH to 60, the 12-point font will have character widths appropriate for a 6-point font, as shown in Figure 7.23. Similarly, you can change PTWIDTH to 240, in which case the font characters will have widths appropriate for 24-point fonts, as shown in Figure 7.24.

SCALING THE FONTS

I wrote the *ScaleOutlineFont* function in OLF.C so that it accepts font sizes in units of decipoints. We should hope to see slightly different character sizes for each unique decipoint size. The OLFSIZE program shown in Listing 7.10 tests this hypothesis. This programs selects a Times New Roman Italic font and scales the font in decipoint increments beginning at 10 points. The results are shown in Figure 7.25.

After scaling the font, the program formats a character string consisting of the typeface name and the decipoint size. It then uses the *GpiQueryTextBox* function to determine the horizontal and vertical dimensions of this string (in pixels), and displays that information also.

OLFLIST.EXE
Times New Roman Italic - 120 decipoints, width 60
Tms Rmn Italic - 120 decipoints, width 60
Times New Roman Bold Italic - 120 decipoints, width 60
Tms Rmn Bold Italic - 120 decipoints, width 60
Times New Roman Bold - 120 decipoints, width 60
Tms Rmn Bold - 120 decipoints, width 60
Times New Roman - 120 decipoints, width 60
Tms Rmn - 120 decipoints, width 60
Helvetica Italic - 120 decipoints, width 60
Helv Italic - 120 decipoints, width 60
Helvetica Bold Italic - 120 decipoints, width 60
Helv Bold Italic - 120 decipoints, width 60
Helvetica Bold - 120 decipoints, width 60
Helv Bold - 120 decipoints, width 60
Helvetica - 120 decipoints, width 60
Helv - 120 decipoints, width 60
Courier Italic - 120 decipoints, width 60
Courier Bold Italic - 120 decipoints, width 60
Courier Bold - 120 decipoints, width 60
Courier - 120 decipoints, width 60

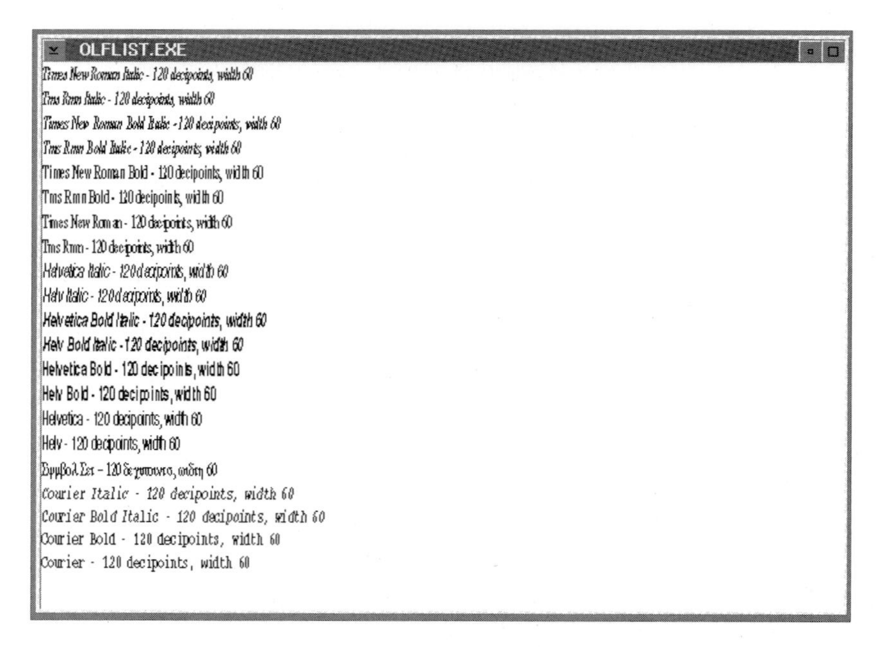

Figure 7.23: The OLFLIST display with 12-point font heights and 6-point font widths

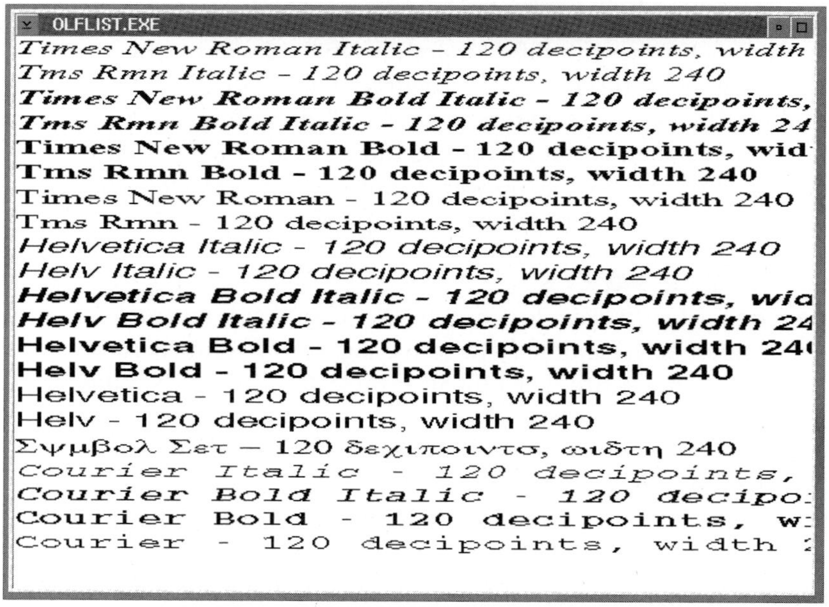

OLFLIST.EXE
Times New Roman Italic - 120 decipoints, width
Tms Rmn Italic - 120 decipoints, width 240
Times New Roman Bold Italic - 120 decipoints,
Tms Rmn Bold Italic - 120 decipoints, width 24
Times New Roman Bold - 120 decipoints, wid
Tms Rmn Bold - 120 decipoints, width 240
Times New Roman - 120 decipoints, width 240
Tms Rmn - 120 decipoints, width 240
Helvetica Italic - 120 decipoints, width 240
Helv Italic - 120 decipoints, width 240
Helvetica Bold Italic - 120 decipoints, wid
Helv Bold Italic - 120 decipoints, width 24
Helvetica Bold - 120 decipoints, width 24
Helv Bold - 120 decipoints, width 240
Helvetica - 120 decipoints, width 240
Helv - 120 decipoints, width 240
Σψμβολ Σετ — 120 δεχιποιντσ, ωιδτη 240
Courier Italic - 120 decipoints,
Courier Bold Italic - 120 decipo
Courier Bold - 120 decipoints, w
Courier - 120 decipoints, width

Figure 7.24: The OLFLIST display with 12-point font heights and 24-point font widths

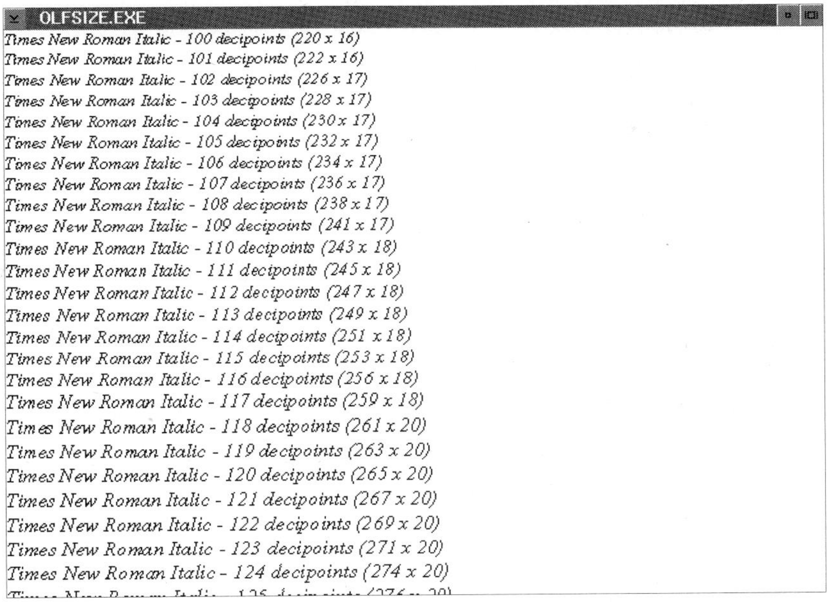

OLFSIZE.EXE

Times New Roman Italic - 100 decipoints (220 x 16)
Times New Roman Italic - 101 decipoints (222 x 16)
Times New Roman Italic - 102 decipoints (226 x 17)
Times New Roman Italic - 103 decipoints (228 x 17)
Times New Roman Italic - 104 decipoints (230 x 17)
Times New Roman Italic - 105 decipoints (232 x 17)
Times New Roman Italic - 106 decipoints (234 x 17)
Times New Roman Italic - 107 decipoints (236 x 17)
Times New Roman Italic - 108 decipoints (238 x 17)
Times New Roman Italic - 109 decipoints (241 x 17)
Times New Roman Italic - 110 decipoints (243 x 18)
Times New Roman Italic - 111 decipoints (245 x 18)
Times New Roman Italic - 112 decipoints (247 x 18)
Times New Roman Italic - 113 decipoints (249 x 18)
Times New Roman Italic - 114 decipoints (251 x 18)
Times New Roman Italic - 115 decipoints (253 x 18)
Times New Roman Italic - 116 decipoints (256 x 18)
Times New Roman Italic - 117 decipoints (259 x 18)
Times New Roman Italic - 118 decipoints (261 x 20)
Times New Roman Italic - 119 decipoints (263 x 20)
Times New Roman Italic - 120 decipoints (265 x 20)
Times New Roman Italic - 121 decipoints (267 x 20)
Times New Roman Italic - 122 decipoints (269 x 20)
Times New Roman Italic - 123 decipoints (271 x 20)
Times New Roman Italic - 124 decipoints (274 x 20)

Figure 7.25: The OLFSIZE display

Listing 7.10: The OLFSIZE program

The OLFSIZE.MAK File

```
#-----------------------
# OLFSIZE.MAK make file
#-----------------------

olfsize.exe : olfsize.obj olfdemo.obj olf.obj olfdemo.def
     $(PRGLINK) olfsize olfdemo olf, olfsize, NUL, $(PRGLIB), olfdemo

olfsize.obj : olfsize.c olf.h
     $(PRGCC) olfsize.c

olfdemo.obj : olfdemo.c
     $(PRGCC) olfdemo.c

olf.obj : olf.c olf.h
     $(PRGCC) olf.c
```

Listing 7.10: The OLFSIZE program (Continued)

The OLFSIZE.C File

```
/*---------------------------------------
   OLFSIZE.C -- OS/2 Outline Fonts Sizes
                (c) Charles Petzold, 1993
  ---------------------------------------*/

#define INCL_WIN
#define INCL_GPI
#include <os2.h>
#include <stdio.h>
#include <string.h>
#include "olf.h"

#define LCID_FONT    1
#define FACENAME     "Times New Roman Italic"

void PaintClient (HPS hps, SHORT cxClient, SHORT cyClient)
     {
     CHAR        szBuffer [FACESIZE + 32] ;
     FONTMETRICS fm ;
     int         i ;
     POINTL      aptlTextBox [TXTBOX_COUNT], ptl ;

          // Set POINTL structure to upper left corner of client

     ptl.x = 0 ;
     ptl.y = cyClient ;

          // Create the logical font and select it

     CreateOutlineFont (hps, LCID_FONT, FACENAME, 0, 0) ;
     GpiSetCharSet (hps, LCID_FONT) ;

          // Loop through the font sizes

     i = 100 ;

     while (ptl.y > 0)
          {
               // Scale the selected font

          ScaleOutlineFont (hps, i, i) ;

               // Query the font metrics of the current font

          GpiQueryFontMetrics (hps, sizeof (FONTMETRICS), &fm) ;
```

Listing 7.10: The OLFSIZE program (Continued)

```
          // Set up a text string to display

     sprintf (szBuffer, "%s - %d decipoints", fm.szFacename, i) ;

     GpiQueryTextBox (hps, strlen (szBuffer), szBuffer,
                      TXTBOX_COUNT, aptlTextBox) ;

     sprintf (szBuffer, "%s - %d decipoints (%d x %d)", fm.szFacename, i,
              aptlTextBox[TXTBOX_CONCAT].x,
              aptlTextBox[TXTBOX_TOPLEFT].y -
              aptlTextBox[TXTBOX_BOTTOMLEFT].y) ;

          // Drop POINTL structure to baseline of font

     ptl.y -= fm.lMaxAscender ;

          // Display the character string

     GpiCharStringAt (hps, &ptl, strlen (szBuffer), szBuffer) ;

          // Drop POINTL structure down to bottom of text

     ptl.y -= fm.lMaxDescender ;

     i++ ;
     }

     // Select the default font; delete the logical font

GpiSetCharSet (hps, LCID_DEFAULT) ;
GpiDeleteSetId (hps, LCID_FONT) ;
}
```

As you can see, the strings displayed in the client window are all of different lengths, even though the character heights often remain constant over a range of point sizes. For example, the 10.2-point font yields a character string that is 17 pixels high and 226 pixels wide. The 10.9-point font is also 17 pixels high, but 241 pixels wide. All these dimensions are rounded to the nearest pixel, of course, but it's obvious that the *ScaleOutlineFont* function in OLF.C is maintaining decipoint resolution in scaling the font, as I discussed earlier.

THE GPIQUERYTEXTBOX FUNCTION

Working with outline fonts often requires a good facility with using the *GpiQueryTextBox* function, so a quick review of this function is in order.

To use *GpiQueryTextBox*, you need an array of 5 POINTL structures. The TXTBOX_COUNT constant defined in the PMGPI.H header file is defined as 5, so you can use that:

```
POINTL aptl[TXTBOX_COUNT] ;
```

You call *GpiQueryTextBox* like so:

```
GpiQueryTextBox (hps, lStrLen,szString, TXTBOX_COUNT, aptl) ;
```

The function assumes that the string will be displayed with the baseline of the left side of the first character positioned at the origin, the point (0,0). You can use the constants TXTBOX_TOPLEFT, TXTBOX_BOTTOMLEFT, TXTBOX_-TOPRIGHT, and TXTBOX_BOTTOMRIGHT to index the array of POINTL structures and determine the relative coordinates of the four corners of a box that encloses the string. In addition, you can use the TXTBOX_CONCAT constant to determine that point at the baseline of the right side of the string.

Assuming the string will be displayed horizontally (that is, it will not be rotated by calls to *GpiSetCharAngle* or rotational transforms), the y coordinates of the POINTL structures are consistent with the *lMaxAscender* and *lMax-Descender* fields of the FONTMETRICS structure (although they may differ by a pixel or two, apparently because of rounding). However, even though *lMaxDescender* is usually a positive number (indicating a descent below the baseline), the y coordinates of the bottom-left and bottom-right POINTL structures will be less than zero.

Thus, you can determine the width of the string using

```
aptl[TXTBOX_CONCAT].x
```

The height of the string is

```
aptl[TXTBOX_TOPLEFT].y - aptl[TXTBOX_BOTTOMLEFT].y
```

Notice the negative sign to convert the bottom-left y coordinate to a positive number.

STRETCHING TO AN AREA

Sometimes it's necessary to make a character string fit within the confines of a fixed rectangle. This involves scaling the font to a particular point size, determining the character box dimensions, and then rescaling it. This is demonstrated in the OLFSTR1 ("outline font stretch 1") program shown in Listing 7.11.

Listing 7.11: The OLFSTR1 program

The OLFSTR1.MAK File

```
#----------------------
# OLFSTR1.MAK make file
#----------------------

olfstr1.exe : olfstr1.obj olfdemo.obj olf.obj olfdemo.def
     $(PRGLINK) olfstr1 olfdemo olf, olfstr1, NUL, $(PRGLIB), olfdemo

olfstr1.obj : olfstr1.c olf.h
     $(PRGCC) olfstr1.c

olfdemo.obj : olfdemo.c
     $(PRGCC) olfdemo.c

olf.obj : olf.c olf.h
     $(PRGCC) olf.c
```

The OLFSTR1.C File

```
/*-------------------------------------------
   OLFSTR1.C -- Stretched OS/2 Outline Fonts
                (c) Charles Petzold, 1993
  -------------------------------------------*/

#define INCL_WIN
#define INCL_GPI
#include <os2.h>
#include <string.h>
#include "olf.h"

#define LCID_FONT    1

void PaintClient (HPS hps, SHORT cxClient, SHORT cyClient)
     {
     static CHAR szText [] = "Hello!" ;
     FONTMETRICS fm ;
     int         iPtHt, iPtWd ;
     POINTL      ptl, aptl[TXTBOX_COUNT] ;

          // Create the logical font, select it, and scale it

     CreateOutlineFont (hps, LCID_FONT, "Helvetica", 0, 0) ;
     GpiSetCharSet (hps, LCID_FONT) ;
     ScaleOutlineFont (hps, 120, 120) ;

          // Scale font to client window size
```

Listing 7.11: The OLFSTR1 program (Continued)

```
GpiQueryTextBox (hps, strlen (szText), szText, TXTBOX_COUNT, aptl) ;

iPtHt = (int) (120 * cyClient / (aptl[TXTBOX_TOPLEFT].y -
                                 aptl[TXTBOX_BOTTOMLEFT].y)) ;
iPtWd = (int) (120 * cxClient /  aptl[TXTBOX_CONCAT].x) ;

ScaleOutlineFont (hps, iPtHt, iPtWd) ;

     // Display the text string

GpiQueryFontMetrics (hps, sizeof (FONTMETRICS), &fm) ;

ptl.x = 0 ;
ptl.y = cyClient - fm.lMaxAscender ;

GpiCharStringAt (hps, &ptl, strlen (szText), szText) ;

     // Select the default font; delete the logical font

GpiSetCharSet (hps, LCID_DEFAULT) ;
GpiDeleteSetId (hps, LCID_FONT) ;
}
```

The program displays the word "Hello!" scaled to the client window dimensions. It first scales the font to a 12-point size, and then obtains the character box dimension and calculates a new point height and point width for another call to *ScaleOutlineFont*. Of course, the word "Hello!" does not completely fill the client area because of the space required for descenders and accent marks.

Figure 7.26 shows three instances of OLFSTR1 running under OS/2 2.1, two very extreme (one very narrow and one very wide) and one about normal. This display demonstrates the flexibility of outline fonts; you can squeeze them and stretch them into any rectangular size.

If you wish to preserve correct dimensions of the font characters, you can use code similar to that shown in OLFSTR2 in Listing 7.12.

In this case, the point size is calculated as the minimum of the scaled point height and point width. The results are shown in Figure 7.27.

Notice that the character string is now centered in the client window, either horizontally or vertically, depending on the proportions of the client window. Centering the string horizontally is easy: You subtract the width of the string (available from the *GpiQueryTextBox* function) from the width of the client window and divide by 2. That's the starting position of the string from the client window.

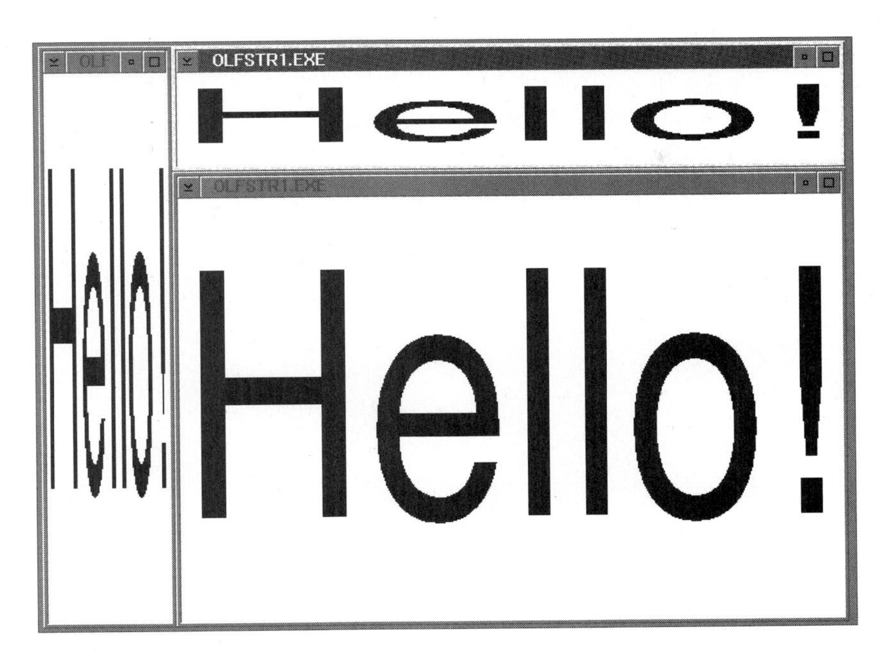

Figure 7.26: The OLFSTR1 display

Listing 7.12: The OLFSTR2 program

The OLFSTR2.MAK File

```
#-----------------------
# OLFSTR2.MAK make file
#-----------------------

olfstr2.exe : olfstr2.obj olfdemo.obj olf.obj olfdemo.def
     $(PRGLINK) olfstr2 olfdemo olf, olfstr2, NUL, $(PRGLIB), olfdemo

olfstr2.obj : olfstr2.c olf.h
     $(PRGCC) olfstr2.c

olfdemo.obj : olfdemo.c
     $(PRGCC) olfdemo.c

olf.obj : olf.c olf.h
     $(PRGCC) olf.c
```

Listing 7.12: The OLFSTR2 program (Continued)

The OLFSTR2.C File

```
/*-----------------------------------------
   OLFSTR2.C -- Stretched OS/2 Outline Fonts
             (c) Charles Petzold, 1993
  -----------------------------------------*/

#define INCL_WIN
#define INCL_GPI
#include <os2.h>
#include <stdlib.h>
#include <string.h>
#include "olf.h"

#define LCID_FONT    1

void PaintClient (HPS hps, SHORT cxClient, SHORT cyClient)
     {
     static CHAR szText [] = "Hello!" ;
     int         iPtHt, iPtWd, iPtSize ;
     POINTL      ptl, aptl[TXTBOX_COUNT] ;

          // Create the logical font, select it, and scale it

     CreateOutlineFont (hps, LCID_FONT, "Helvetica", 0, 0) ;
     GpiSetCharSet (hps, LCID_FONT) ;
     ScaleOutlineFont (hps, 120, 120) ;

          // Scale font to client window size

     GpiQueryTextBox (hps, strlen (szText), szText, TXTBOX_COUNT, aptl) ;

     iPtHt = (int) (120 * cyClient / (aptl[TXTBOX_TOPLEFT].y -
                                      aptl[TXTBOX_BOTTOMLEFT].y)) ;
     iPtWd = (int) (120 * cxClient /  aptl[TXTBOX_CONCAT].x) ;

     iPtSize = min (iPtHt, iPtWd) ;

     ScaleOutlineFont (hps, iPtSize, iPtSize) ;

          // Display the text string

     GpiQueryTextBox (hps, strlen (szText), szText, TXTBOX_COUNT, aptl) ;

     ptl.x = (cxClient - aptl[TXTBOX_CONCAT].x) / 2 ;
     ptl.y = (cyClient - aptl[TXTBOX_TOPLEFT].y
                       - aptl[TXTBOX_BOTTOMLEFT].y) / 2 ;
```

Listing 7.12: The OLFSTR2 program (Continued)

```
     GpiCharStringAt (hps, &ptl, strlen (szText), szText) ;

          // Select the default font; delete the logical font

     GpiSetCharSet (hps, LCID_DEFAULT) ;
     GpiDeleteSetId (hps, LCID_FONT) ;
     }
```

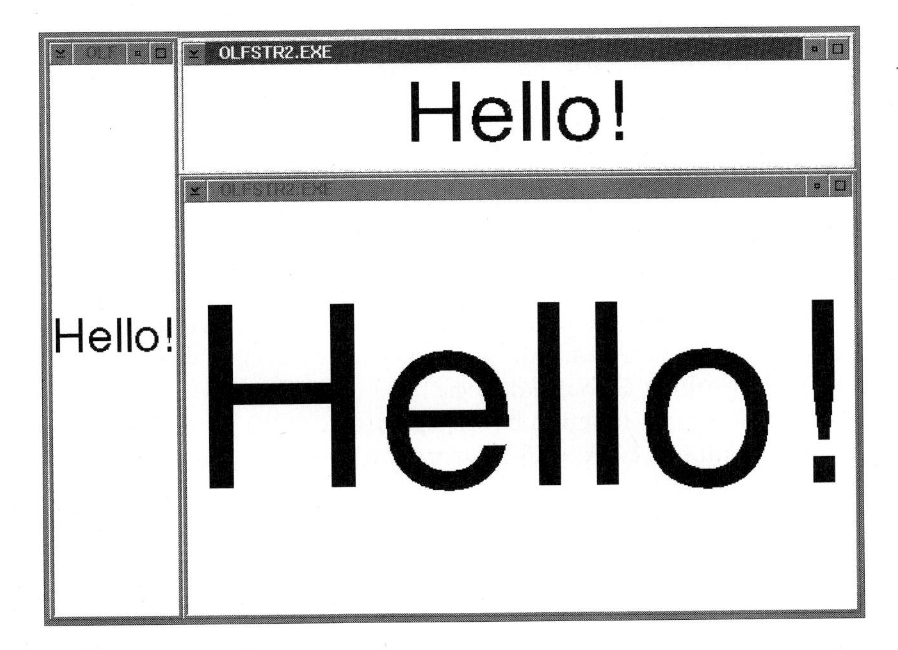

Figure 7.27: The OLFSTR2 display

Centering the string vertically required a bit of algebra before I actually wrote out the code. Let SP be the space above and below the text string, let TL be the y coordinate of the top-left corner of the text box, and let BL be the y coordinate of the bottom-left corner.

Thus, the height of the client window is

cyClient = 2 * SP + TL - BL

The negative sign before BL is necessary to make it a positive number. So, we can calculate SP like so:

SP = (cyClient - TL + BL) / 2

Keeping in mind that the GPI origin is the lower-left corner of the client window and that values of y increase going up, we can write a formula for the position of the baseline by subtracting SP and TL from *cyClient*:

ptl.y = cyClient - SP - TL

Substitute SP in the equation and you get this:

ptl.y = cyClient - (cyClient - TL + BL) / 2 - TL

This reduces to the following:

ptl.y = (cyClient - TL - BL) / 2

And that's the formula I use in OLFSTR2.C.

FONT ROTATION

Because Adobe outline fonts are defined internally by a series of Bézier splines, the characters can be easily rotated, either by using the default viewing or model transform, or by calling *GpiSetCharAngle*.

The *GpiSetCharAngle* function has two parameters: the presentation space handle and a point to a GRADIENTL structure. This structure has two fields named *x* and *y* that indicate a point relative to the origin. A line from the origin to this point defines the angle of the font baseline. For example, calling *GpiSetCharAngle* using a GRADIENTL structure with the point (1, 1) will cause character strings to be displayed with a baseline that is 45 degrees counterclockwise from the horizontal.

The OLFROT program shown in Listing 7.13 shows how to use the *GpiSetCharAngle* function to display the string "Rotated Font" with character angles progressively incremented by 22.5 degrees.

Listing 7.13: The OLFROT program

The OLFROT.MAK File

```
#---------------------
# OLFROT.MAK make file
#---------------------

olfrot.exe : olfrot.obj olfdemo.obj olf.obj olfdemo.def
     $(PRGLINK) olfrot olfdemo olf, olfrot, NUL, $(PRGLIB), olfdemo
```

Listing 7.13: The OLFROT program (Continued)

```
olfrot.obj : olfrot.c olf.h
     $(PRGCC) olfrot.c

olfdemo.obj : olfdemo.c
     $(PRGCC) olfdemo.c

olf.obj : olf.c olf.h
     $(PRGCC) olf.c
```

The OLFROT.C File

```
/*---------------------------------------
   OLFROT.C -- Rotated OS/2 Outline Fonts
               (c) Charles Petzold, 1993
  ---------------------------------------*/

#define INCL_WIN
#define INCL_GPI
#include <os2.h>
#include <math.h>
#include <string.h>
#include "olf.h"

#define LCID_FONT    1
#define TWO_PI       (2 * 3.14159)

void PaintClient (HPS hps, SHORT cxClient, SHORT cyClient)
     {
     static CHAR szText [] = "  Rotated Font" ;
     double      dAngle ;
     GRADIENTL   gradl ;
     POINTL      ptl ;

          // Set POINTL structure to center of client

     ptl.x = cxClient / 2 ;
     ptl.y = cyClient / 2 ;

          // Create the logical font, select it, and scale it

     CreateOutlineFont (hps, LCID_FONT, "Helvetica", 0, 0) ;
     GpiSetCharSet (hps, LCID_FONT) ;
     ScaleOutlineFont (hps, 240, 240) ;

          // Loop through the character angles

     for (dAngle = 0 ; dAngle < 360 ; dAngle += 22.5)
          {
```

Listing 7.13: The OLFROT program (Continued)

```
               // Set the character angle

          gradl.x = (LONG) (100 * cos (TWO_PI * dAngle / 360)) ;
          gradl.y = (LONG) (100 * sin (TWO_PI * dAngle / 360)) ;

          GpiSetCharAngle (hps, &gradl) ;

               // Display the character string

          GpiCharStringAt (hps, &ptl, strlen (szText), szText) ;
          }

          // Select the default font; delete the logical font

     GpiSetCharSet (hps, LCID_DEFAULT) ;
     GpiDeleteSetId (hps, LCID_FONT) ;
     }
```

The program sets the fields of a POINTL structure to the center of the client window. A pointer to this structure is later passed to *GpiCharStringAt* to indicate the starting position of the string relative to the baseline of the left side of the first character.

The program loops through angle values starting at 0 and incremented by 22.5 degrees. An angle of 0 indicates that the string is to be positioned normally with the baseline parallel to the horizontal axis. Each successive string has a baseline 22.5 degrees counterclockwise from the last. The program sets the two fields of the GRADIENTL structure by converting the angles to radians, passing the angles to the C *cos* and *sin* functions (for the *x* and *y* structure fields, respectively), and multiplying by 100 (to convert to a sufficiently large integer). The results are shown in Figure 7.28.

REFLECTED TEXT STRINGS

It may not have occurred to you, but you can use negative values in the SIZEF structure that you pass to *GpiSetCharBox*, and consequently, in the font point sizes you pass to *ScaleOutlineFont*. But what does it mean to have a negative point size?

If you set the character box with a negative *cx* field in the SIZEF structure, a character string displayed with *GpiCharStringAt* (or some other GPI text output function) will run from right to left rather than left to right. But it's not like the effect produced by the *GpiSetCharDirection* call: With a negative character box width, all the characters are flipped around the vertical axis. It's almost as if you held a mirror at the left side of the character string and looked at the reflection.

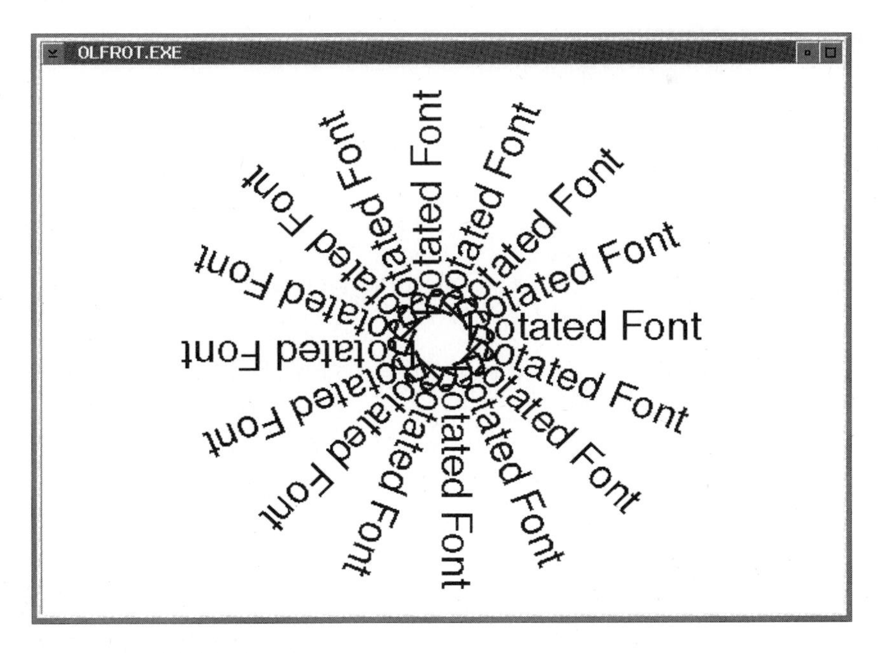

Figure 7.28: The OLFROT display

If the *cy* field of the SIZEF structure is negative, the text string is displayed upside down. All the characters are flipped around the horizontal axis, and appear as if you held a mirror along the baseline of the string. If both the *cx* and *cy* fields are negative, the string is displayed upside down and right to left with characters flipped around both the vertical and horizontal axes.

In all cases, the point specified in the *GpiSetCharStringAt* function indicates the baseline of the left side of the first character—even if the ascents of the characters are below the baseline, or if the left side of the first character is actually displayed at the right.

I know this can be confusing, so let's look at an example. The OLFREFL ("outline font reflection") program shown in Listing 7.14 displays the character string "Reflect" using the four combinations of positive and negative character box sizes.

The function shown in OLFREFL.C sets a POINTL structure to the center of the client window. This is the starting position of the displayed text. The function displays the character string with a 72-point Times New Roman font.

Listing 7.14: The OLFREFL program

The OLFREFL.MAK File

```
#-----------------------
# OLFREFL.MAK make file
#-----------------------

olfrefl.exe : olfrefl.obj olfdemo.obj olf.obj olfdemo.def
     $(PRGLINK) olfrefl olfdemo olf, olfrefl, NUL, $(PRGLIB), olfdemo

olfrefl.obj : olfrefl.c olf.h
     $(PRGCC) olfrefl.c

olfdemo.obj : olfdemo.c
     $(PRGCC) olfdemo.c

olf.obj : olf.c olf.h
     $(PRGCC) olf.c
```

The OLFREFL.C File

```
/*-------------------------------------------
   OLFREFL.C -- Reflected OS/2 Outline Fonts
                (c) Charles Petzold, 1993
  -------------------------------------------*/

#define INCL_WIN
#define INCL_GPI
#include <os2.h>
#include <string.h>
#include "olf.h"

#define LCID_FONT    1

void PaintClient (HPS hps, SHORT cxClient, SHORT cyClient)
     {
     static CHAR szText [] = "Reflect" ;
     int         i ;
     POINTL      ptl ;

          // Set POINTL structure to center of client

     ptl.x = cxClient / 2 ;
     ptl.y = cyClient / 2 ;

          // Create the logical font and select it

     CreateOutlineFont (hps, LCID_FONT, "Times New Roman", 0, 0) ;
     GpiSetCharSet (hps, LCID_FONT) ;
```

Listing 7.14: The OLFREFL program (Continued)

```
     for (i = 0 ; i < 4 ; i++)
          {
          ScaleOutlineFont (hps, (i > 1) ? -720 : 720,
                                 (i & 1) ? -720 : 720) ;

               // Display the character string

          GpiCharStringAt (hps, &ptl, strlen (szText), szText) ;
          }

          // Select the default font; delete the logical font

     GpiSetCharSet (hps, LCID_DEFAULT) ;
     GpiDeleteSetId (hps, LCID_FONT) ;
     }
```

The character string is displayed four times—the first using positive character box dimensions (displayed in the upper-right corner of the client window), the second using a negative width (displayed at the upper-left corner), the third using a negative height (lower-right corner), and the fourth using a negative width and height (lower-left corner). The results are shown in Figure 7.29.

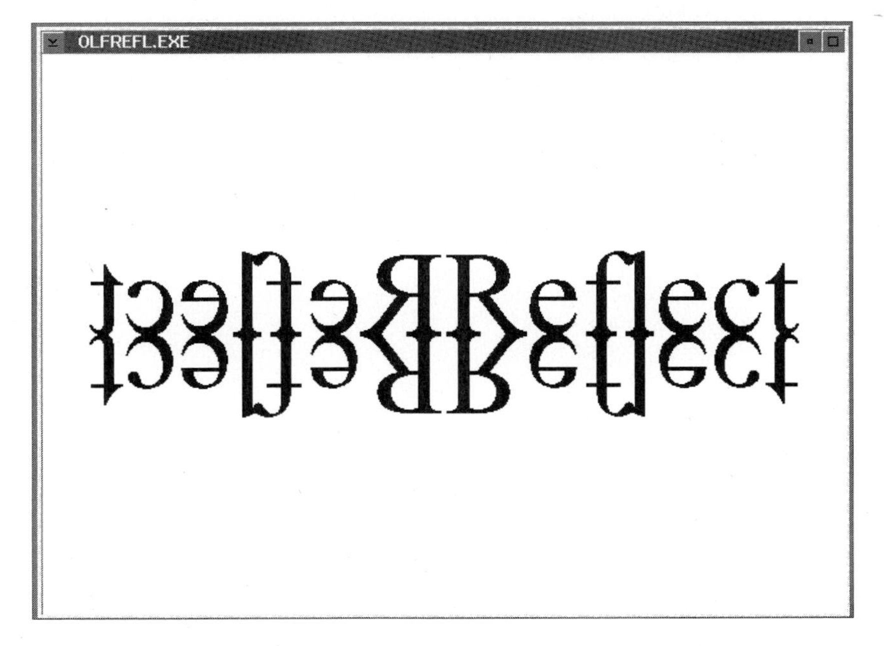

Figure 7.29: The OLFREFL display

COMBINING EFFECTS

In the OLFROT program shown earlier, I used the *GpiSetCharAngle* function to display text strings running at various angles around the screen. However, unlike negative character box values, the character angle does not change the actual appearance or ordering of the characters. If you tilted your monitor, the strings would still look normal.

You can combine character angles and negative character box dimensions. The OLFREFL2 program in Listing 7.15 shows an example of this.

Listing 7.15: The OLFREFL2 program

The OLFREFL2.MAK File

```
#------------------------
# OLFREFL2.MAK make file
#------------------------

olfrefl2.exe : olfrefl2.obj olfdemo.obj olf.obj olfdemo.def
     $(PRGLINK) olfrefl2 olfdemo olf, olfrefl2, NUL, $(PRGLIB), olfdemo

olfrefl2.obj : olfrefl2.c olf.h
     $(PRGCC) olfrefl2.c

olfdemo.obj : olfdemo.c
     $(PRGCC) olfdemo.c

olf.obj : olf.c olf.h
     $(PRGCC) olf.c
```

The OLFREFL2.C File

```
/*------------------------------------------------------
   OLFREFL2.C -- Reflected and Rotated OS/2 Outline Fonts
                 (c) Charles Petzold, 1993
  ------------------------------------------------------*/

#define INCL_WIN
#define INCL_GPI
#include <os2.h>
#include <string.h>
#include "olf.h"

#define LCID_FONT    1

void PaintClient (HPS hps, SHORT cxClient, SHORT cyClient)
     {
     static CHAR szText [] = "Reflect" ;
     GRADIENTL   gradl ;
```

Listing 7.15: The OLFREFL2 program (Continued)

```
     int         i ;
     POINTL      ptl ;

          // Set POINTL structure to center of client

     ptl.x = cxClient / 2 ;
     ptl.y = cyClient / 2 ;

          // Create the logical font and select it

     CreateOutlineFont (hps, LCID_FONT, "Times New Roman", 0, 0) ;
     GpiSetCharSet (hps, LCID_FONT) ;

          // Set character angle

     gradl.x = 1 ;
     gradl.y = 1 ;

     GpiSetCharAngle (hps, &gradl) ;

     for (i = 0 ; i < 4 ; i++)
          {
          ScaleOutlineFont (hps, (i > 1) ? -720 : 720,
                                 (i & 1) ? -720 : 720) ;

               // Display the character string

          GpiCharStringAt (hps, &ptl, strlen (szText), szText) ;
          }

          // Select the default font; delete the logical font

     GpiSetCharSet (hps, LCID_DEFAULT) ;
     GpiDeleteSetId (hps, LCID_FONT) ;
     }
```

The function in OLFREFL2.C is the same as that in OLFREFL.C except that it calls *GpiSetCharAngle* with *x* and *y* fields of the GRADIENTL structure set to 1. As you can see in Figure 7.30, the display looks a lot like OLFREFL except that everything is rotated 45 degrees counterclockwise.

THE CHARACTER SHEAR

Another way to manipulate outline fonts is by using the *GpiSetCharShear* function. This function determines the "shear" of the characters—that is, the extent to which they tilt to the right or left. For example, a small character shear to the right gives characters an oblique or italic appearance.

Figure 7.30: The OLFREFL2 display

It's important to understand the distinction between the character angle and the character shear. Setting a nondefault character angle simply rotates the characters without distorting them in any way. That is, the baseline becomes nonhorizontal. The character shear distorts the characters by tilting them. But the baseline is still horizontal (unless, of course, you also use *GpiSetCharAngle* or some transform function that performs rotation).

The *GpiSetCharShear* function requires a POINTL structure. A line drawn from (0,0) to the point (*x*,*y*) indicates the angle of the shear. The default is the point (0,1), which defines a vertical line indicating that the characters stand straight up with no shear. A character shear of (0,-1) produces the same effect. The character shear does not flip characters.

If the *y* field of the POINTL structure is 0, that would indicate an infinite shear to the right or the left. Characters would simply be flattened out on the baseline and proceed to infinity. For this reason, *y* fields of 0 raise an error. One exception is when both the *x* and *y* fields are set to 0, which sets the default character shear.

The OLFSHEAR program shown in Listing 7.16 demonstrates what different character shears look like.

Listing 7.16: The OLFSHEAR program

The OLFSHEAR.MAK File

```
#-----------------------
# OLFSHEAR.MAK make file
#-----------------------

olfshear.exe : olfshear.obj olfdemo.obj olf.obj olfdemo.def
     $(PRGLINK) olfshear olfdemo olf, olfshear, NUL, $(PRGLIB), olfdemo

olfshear.obj : olfshear.c olf.h
     $(PRGCC) olfshear.c

olfdemo.obj : olfdemo.c
     $(PRGCC) olfdemo.c

olf.obj : olf.c olf.h
     $(PRGCC) olf.c
```

The OLFSHEAR.C File

```
/*-----------------------------------------
   OLFSHEAR.C -- Sheared OS/2 Outline Fonts
                 (c) Charles Petzold, 1993
  -----------------------------------------*/

#define INCL_WIN
#define INCL_GPI
#include <os2.h>
#include <math.h>
#include <stdio.h>
#include <string.h>
#include "olf.h"

#define LCID_FONT    1
#define TWO_PI       (2 * 3.14159)

void PaintClient (HPS hps, SHORT cxClient, SHORT cyClient)
     {
     CHAR        szBuffer [32] ;
     double      dAngle ;
     FONTMETRICS fm ;
     POINTL      ptl, ptlShear ;

          // Set POINTL structure to near-left top of client

     ptl.x = cxClient / 8 ;
     ptl.y = cyClient ;
```

Listing 7.16: The OLFSHEAR program (Continued)

```
          // Create the logical font, select it, and scale it

     CreateOutlineFont (hps, LCID_FONT, "Helvetica", 0, 0) ;
     GpiSetCharSet (hps, LCID_FONT) ;
     ScaleOutlineFont (hps, 160, 160) ;

     GpiQueryFontMetrics (hps, sizeof (FONTMETRICS), &fm) ;

          // Loop through the shear angles

     for (dAngle = 0 ; dAngle <= 360 ; dAngle += 22.5)
          {
               // Set the shear angle

          ptlShear.x = (LONG) (100 * cos (TWO_PI * dAngle / 360)) ;
          ptlShear.y = (LONG) (100 * sin (TWO_PI * dAngle / 360)) ;

          GpiSetCharShear (hps, &ptlShear) ;

               // Display the character string

          ptl.y -= fm.lMaxAscender ;

          GpiCharStringAt (hps, &ptl,
               sprintf (szBuffer, "Character Shear (%.1f) degrees", dAngle),
                    szBuffer) ;

          ptl.y -= fm.lMaxDescender ;
          }

          // Select the default font; delete the logical font

     GpiSetCharSet (hps, LCID_DEFAULT) ;
     GpiDeleteSetId (hps, LCID_FONT) ;
     }
```

This program displays 17 character strings down the client window. The function in OLFSHEAR.C loops through 17 angles from 0 degrees through 360 degrees, measured counterclockwise from the horizontal. As in the OLFROT program shown earlier, these angles are converted to points by calling the C *sin* and *cos* functions. To avoid rounding problems, the points are scaled to 100 units.

Figure 7.31 shows the output from this program. The display looks almost as if someone had smeared it with their fingers.

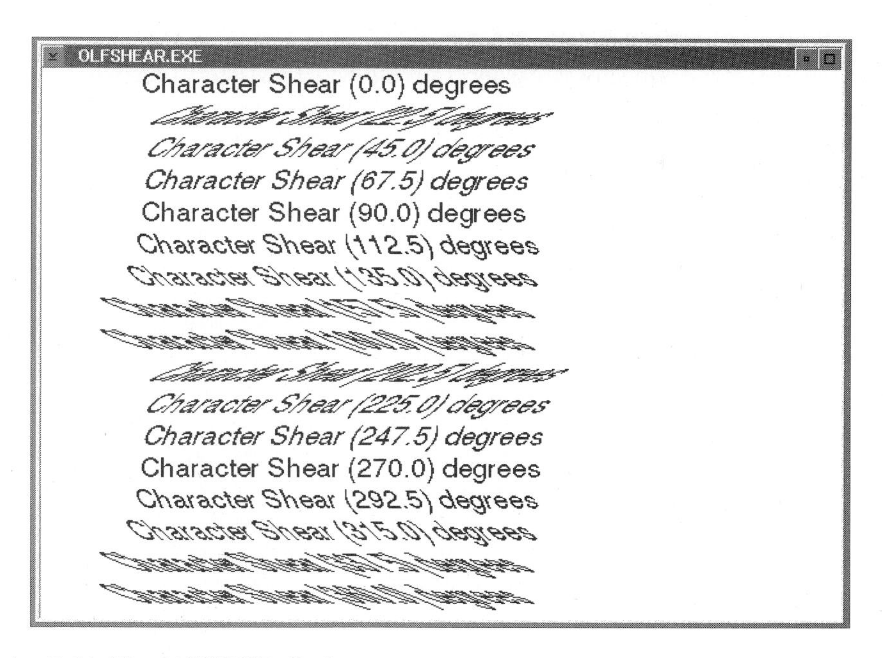

Figure 7.31: The OLFSHEAR display

Let's look a little closer. The first line of text uses an angle of zero degrees (measured counterclockwise from the horizontal) which is converted to the point (100,0). That indicates an infinite shear to the right, which is an error, so the text is displayed normally. The second line is a shear angle of 22.5 degrees. In this string, the vertical bar of the "h" is at an angle of 22.5 degrees from the horizontal.

The 90 degree line is the default. The point passed to the *GpiSetCharShear* function is (0,100). After this, the characters tilt progressively to the left. However, a character shear of 180 degrees raises an error, so the character shear is not changed and the line is displayed with the previous character shear of 157.5 degrees.

Character shears greater than 180 degrees produce the same effects as the angles 180 degrees less, so the display simply repeats itself. Character shears from 202.5 degrees through 337.5 degrees are the same as shears from 22.5 degrees through 157.5 degrees.

COMBINING EFFECTS, PART 2

The OLFROT program shown earlier used *GpiSetCharAngle* to display 16 strings rotated around the center of the client window. One interesting exercise is to combine the *GpiSetCharAngle* and *GpiSetCharShear* functions to create a display similar to OLFROT, but with the vertical bars of the characters always vertical. This is shown in the OLFROT2 program in Listing 7.17.

Listing 7.17: The OLFROT2 program

The OLFROT2.MAK File

```
#----------------------
# OLFROT2.MAK make file
#----------------------

olfrot2.exe : olfrot2.obj olfdemo.obj olf.obj olfdemo.def
     $(PRGLINK) olfrot2 olfdemo olf, olfrot2, NUL, $(PRGLIB), olfdemo

olfrot2.obj : olfrot2.c olf.h
     $(PRGCC) olfrot2.c

olfdemo.obj : olfdemo.c
     $(PRGCC) olfdemo.c

olf.obj : olf.c olf.h
     $(PRGCC) olf.c
```

The OLFROT2.C File

```
/*-----------------------------------------------------
   OLFROT2.C -- Rotated and Sheared OS/2 Outline Fonts
                (c) Charles Petzold, 1993
  -----------------------------------------------------*/

#define INCL_WIN
#define INCL_GPI
#include <os2.h>
#include <math.h>
#include <string.h>
#include "olf.h"

#define LCID_FONT    1
#define TWO_PI       (2 * 3.14159)

void PaintClient (HPS hps, SHORT cxClient, SHORT cyClient)
     {
     static CHAR szText [] = "  Rotated Font" ;
     double      dAngle ;
     GRADIENTL   gradl ;
```

Listing 7.17: The OLFROT2 program (Continued)

```
     POINTL       ptl, ptlShear ;

          // Set POINTL structure to center of client

     ptl.x = cxClient / 2 ;
     ptl.y = cyClient / 2 ;

          // Create the logical font, select it, and scale it

     CreateOutlineFont (hps, LCID_FONT, "Helvetica", 0, 0) ;
     GpiSetCharSet (hps, LCID_FONT) ;
     ScaleOutlineFont (hps, 240, 240) ;

          // Loop through the character angles

     for (dAngle = 11.25 ; dAngle < 360 ; dAngle += 22.5)
          {
               // Set the character angle

          gradl.x = (LONG) (100 * cos (TWO_PI * dAngle / 360)) ;
          gradl.y = (LONG) (100 * sin (TWO_PI * dAngle / 360)) ;

          GpiSetCharAngle (hps, &gradl) ;

               // Set the character shear

          ptlShear.x = (LONG) (100 * cos (TWO_PI * (90 - dAngle) / 360)) ;
          ptlShear.y = (LONG) (100 * sin (TWO_PI * (90 - dAngle) / 360)) ;

          GpiSetCharShear (hps, &ptlShear) ;

               // Display the character string

          GpiCharStringAt (hps, &ptl, strlen (szText), szText) ;
          }

          // Select the default font; delete the logical font

     GpiSetCharSet (hps, LCID_DEFAULT) ;
     GpiDeleteSetId (hps, LCID_FONT) ;
     }
```

To avoid infinite shear angles, I begin the angle loop at 11.25 degrees and increment by 22.5 degrees. This angle is used directly for computing the point passed to the *GpiSetCharAngle* function. To calculate a character shear that compensates for the character angle, I subtract the character angle from 90 degrees and use that to calculate the point passed to the *GpiSetCharShear* function.

As you can see in Figure 7.32, the vertical stroke of the "F" (and other characters, of course) is always vertical. Towards the center of the display, the shear is so extreme that the text is unreadable.

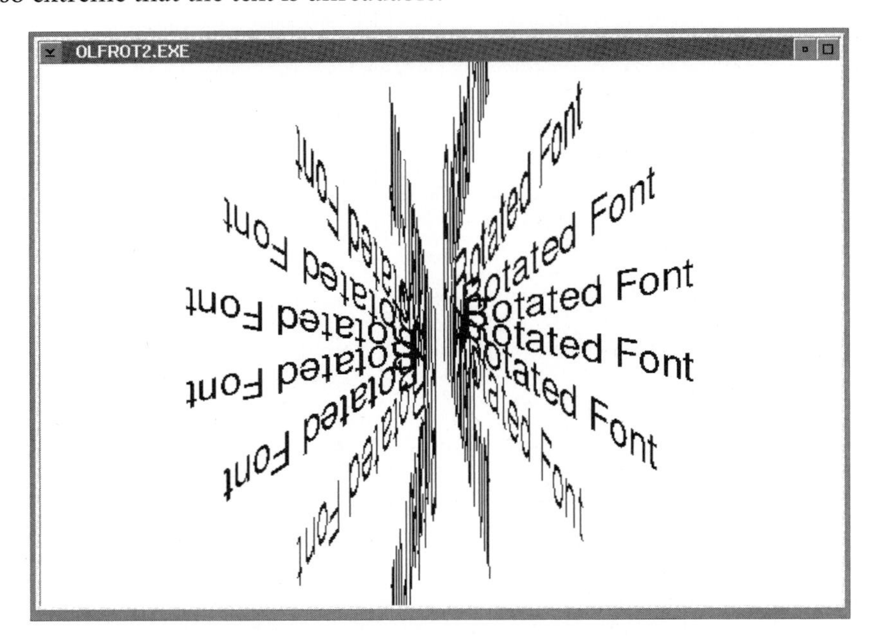

Figure 7.32: The OLFROT2 display

THREE-DIMENSIONAL EFFECTS

Look at the right side of Figure 7.32, avoiding the unreadable strings. Does it seem to you as if the top three character strings are going *into* the display and the bottom three are coming *out of* the display? Character shear that is somewhat more extreme than normal italic text can produce some interesting three-dimensional effects. The tilt of the characters makes it seem as if we're looking at the string from an angle.

The OLFSHAD ("outline font shadow") program shown in Listing 7.18 uses character shear to create a three-dimensional-like "shadow" for a character string.

The function in OLFSHAD.C begins by coloring the background of the client window blue. It then displays the string "Shadow" using a Times New Roman font in dark blue. This is the shadow. The font is scaled to 216 points, but with an em-width of 72 points. Thus, the font is three times as high as a normal 72-point font. The program sets the character shear point to (2,1).

Listing 7.18: The OLFSHAD program

The OLFSHAD.MAK File

```
#----------------------
# OLFSHAD.MAK make file
#----------------------

olfshad.exe : olfshad.obj olfdemo.obj olf.obj olfdemo.def
     $(PRGLINK) olfshad olfdemo olf, olfshad, NUL, $(PRGLIB), olfdemo

olfshad.obj : olfshad.c olf.h
     $(PRGCC) olfshad.c

olfdemo.obj : olfdemo.c
     $(PRGCC) olfdemo.c

olf.obj : olf.c olf.h
     $(PRGCC) olf.c
```

The OLFSHAD.C File

```
/*-----------------------------------------
   OLFSHAD.C -- Shadowed OS/2 Outline Font
                (c) Charles Petzold, 1993
  -----------------------------------------*/

#define INCL_WIN
#define INCL_GPI
#include <os2.h>
#include <string.h>
#include "olf.h"

#define LCID_FONT    1

void PaintClient (HPS hps, SHORT cxClient, SHORT cyClient)
     {
     static CHAR szText [] = "Shadow" ;
     POINTL      ptl, ptlShear ;

          // Color the client window

     GpiSetColor (hps, CLR_BLUE) ;

     ptl.x = 0 ;
     ptl.y = 0 ;
     GpiMove (hps, &ptl) ;

     ptl.x = cxClient ;
```

Listing 7.18: The OLFSHAD program (Continued)

```
     ptl.y = cyClient ;
     GpiBox (hps, DRO_FILL, &ptl, 0, 0) ;

          // Create the logical font

     CreateOutlineFont (hps, LCID_FONT, "Times New Roman", 0, 0) ;
     GpiSetCharSet (hps, LCID_FONT) ;

          // Display the shadow

     GpiSetColor (hps, CLR_DARKBLUE) ;

     ScaleOutlineFont (hps, 2160, 720) ;

     ptlShear.x = 2 ;
     ptlShear.y = 1 ;
     GpiSetCharShear (hps, &ptlShear) ;

     ptl.x = cxClient / 8 ;
     ptl.y = cyClient / 4 ;
     GpiCharStringAt (hps, &ptl, strlen (szText), szText) ;

          // Display the text

     GpiSetColor (hps, CLR_RED) ;

     ScaleOutlineFont (hps, 720, 720) ;

     ptlShear.x = 0 ;
     ptlShear.y = 1 ;
     GpiSetCharShear (hps, &ptlShear) ;

     GpiCharStringAt (hps, &ptl, strlen (szText), szText) ;

          // Select the default font; delete the logical font

     GpiSetCharSet (hps, LCID_DEFAULT) ;
     GpiDeleteSetId (hps, LCID_FONT) ;
     }
```

Next, the function displays the same string, with a point size of 72 points and no shear. The results are shown in Figure 7.33. As you can see, it looks as if the character string is standing up, throwing a tall, sheared shadow behind it.

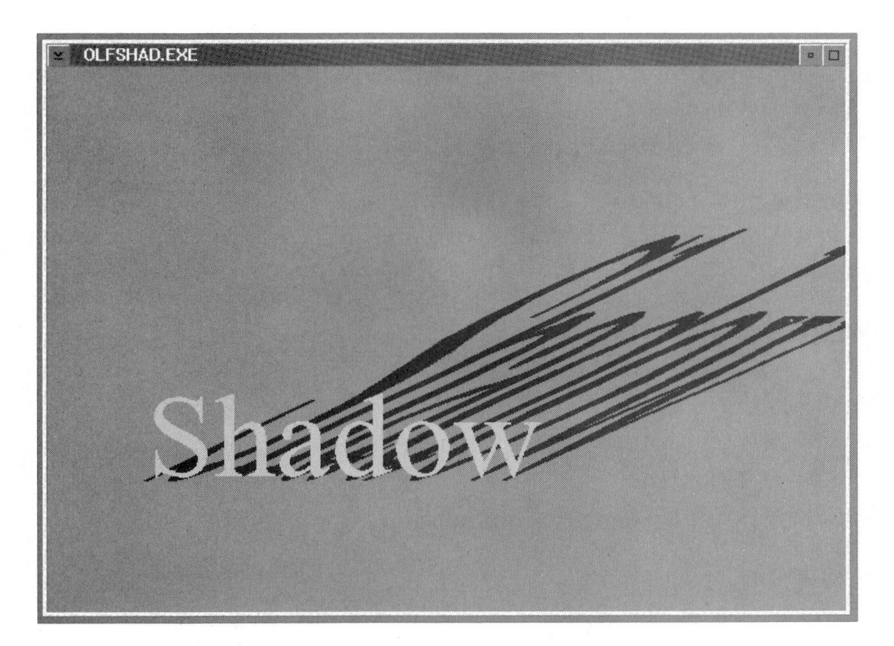

Figure 7.33: The OLFSHAD display

PATHS AND FONTS

As you saw earlier in this chapter, a path is a collection of line definitions stored internally in GPI. To create a path, you call line-drawing functions within a "path bracket," which is delimited by calls to *GpiBeginPath* and *GpiEndPath.* A Presentation Manager program can then use the path for outlining, stroking, filling, clipping, or converting to a region.

Outlining and stroking paths are in one way quite similar: In both cases, GPI draws the path as a series of lines. But there the similarity ends. An outlined path is basically the same as drawing the lines without using a path. The lines can have a style (such as being composed of dots and dashes) and a width. The width is limited to a normal width and a thick (that is, double) width. This is known as the "cosmetic" line width. It is not affected by any transforms that influence the size of other graphics objects.

GPI draws a stroked path using a line with a "geometric" width. The geometric width can be as wide as you want, and it is affected by transforms. GPI fills cosmetic lines with the current area-filling pattern, and also allows specifying different line ends and joins. It is not possible to draw geometric lines without using paths.

The connection between paths and outline fonts is very simple: When an outline font has been selected into a presentation space, you can call text output functions within the path bracket. The character outlines become part of the path.

OUTLINED CHARACTERS

Let's try it. The OLFLINE program shown in Listing 7.19 uses a path and the *GpiOutlinePath* function to draw outlined characters.

Listing 7.19: The OLFLINE program

The OLFLINE.MAK File

```
#----------------------
# OLFLINE.MAK make file
#----------------------

olfline.exe : olfline.obj olfdemo.obj olf.obj olfdemo.def
     $(PRGLINK) olfline olfdemo olf, olfline, NUL, $(PRGLIB), olfdemo

olfline.obj : olfline.c olf.h
     $(PRGCC) olfline.c

olfdemo.obj : olfdemo.c
     $(PRGCC) olfdemo.c

olf.obj : olf.c olf.h
     $(PRGCC) olf.c
```

The OLFLINE.C File

```
/*----------------------------------------
   OLFLINE.C -- Outlined OS/2 Outline Font
                (c) Charles Petzold, 1993
  ----------------------------------------*/

#define INCL_WIN
#define INCL_GPI
#include <os2.h>
#include <string.h>
#include "olf.h"

#define LCID_FONT    1

void PaintClient (HPS hps, SHORT cxClient, SHORT cyClient)
     {
     static CHAR szText [] = "Hello!" ;
     POINTL      ptl, aptlTextBox [TXTBOX_COUNT] ;
```

Listing 7.19: The OLFLINE program (Continued)

```
     // Create and size the logical font

CreateOutlineFont (hps, LCID_FONT, "Times New Roman Italic", 0, 0) ;
GpiSetCharSet (hps, LCID_FONT) ;
ScaleOutlineFont (hps, 1440, 1440) ;

     // Get the text box

GpiQueryTextBox (hps, strlen (szText), szText,
                 TXTBOX_COUNT, aptlTextBox) ;

     // Create the path

GpiBeginPath (hps, 1) ;

ptl.x = (cxClient - aptlTextBox [TXTBOX_CONCAT].x) / 2 ;
ptl.y = (cyClient - aptlTextBox [TXTBOX_TOPLEFT].y
                  - aptlTextBox [TXTBOX_BOTTOMLEFT].y) / 2 ;

GpiCharStringAt (hps, &ptl, strlen (szText), szText) ;

GpiEndPath (hps) ;

     // Outline the path

GpiSetLineWidth (hps, LINEWIDTH_THICK) ;
GpiOutlinePath (hps, 1, 0) ;

     // Select the default font; delete the logical font

GpiSetCharSet (hps, LCID_DEFAULT) ;
GpiDeleteSetId (hps, LCID_FONT) ;
}
```

The program begins by using the *CreateOutlineFont* and *ScaleOutlineFont* functions in OLF.C to create a Times New Roman Italic font and scale it to a 144-point size. It then uses *GpiQueryTextBox* to obtain the text box dimensions of the string "Hello!" This information is used to center the text string in the client window. The program begins the path bracket by calling *GpiBeginPath,* draws the character string by calling *GpiCharStringAt,* and ends the path bracket with *GpiEndPath.*

At this point, nothing has yet been drawn on the client window. OLFLINE.C calls *GpiSetLineWidth* to select a thick line, and then *GpiOutlinePath* to render the path on the window, as shown in Figure 7.34.

Figure 7.34: The OLFLINE display

Of course, you can get the same effect without a path by using the FATTR_-SEL_OUTLINE attribute when creating the font. However, if you wanted to use the normal filled font together with the outlined font, you'd have to create two fonts. Using the path, you only need one.

A DROP-SHADOW FONT

One case when you need both a normal font and an outline font is when drawing a text string with a "drop shadow." Earlier I drew a font shadow using an abnormally tall font tilted to one side using the *GpiSetCharShear* function. This made it appear as if the font were standing up perpendicular to the surface on which the shadow was thrown.

A drop shadow, on the other hand, makes the object appear as if it's suspended in front of the screen. By convention, such shadows are drawn as if the light source originates from the upper-left corner of the video display.

The OLFDROP program shown in Listing 7.20 shows how to draw an outlined font with a drop shadow.

Listing 7.20: The OLFDROP program

The OLFDROP.MAK File

```
#-----------------------
# OLFDROP.MAK make file
#-----------------------

olfdrop.exe : olfdrop.obj olfdemo.obj olf.obj olfdemo.def
     $(PRGLINK) olfdrop olfdemo olf, olfdrop, NUL, $(PRGLIB), olfdemo

olfdrop.obj : olfdrop.c olf.h
     $(PRGCC) olfdrop.c

olfdemo.obj : olfdemo.c
     $(PRGCC) olfdemo.c

olf.obj : olf.c olf.h
     $(PRGCC) olf.c
```

The OLFDROP.C File

```
/*--------------------------------------------
   OLFDROP.C -- Drop Shadow OS/2 Outline Font
                (c) Charles Petzold, 1993
  --------------------------------------------*/

#define INCL_WIN
#define INCL_GPI
#include <os2.h>
#include <string.h>
#include "olf.h"

#define LCID_FONT    1

void PaintClient (HPS hps, SHORT cxClient, SHORT cyClient)
     {
     static CHAR szText [] = "Hello!" ;
     POINTL      ptl, aptlTextBox [TXTBOX_COUNT] ;

          // Create and size the logical font

     CreateOutlineFont (hps, LCID_FONT, "Times New Roman Italic", 0, 0) ;
     GpiSetCharSet (hps, LCID_FONT) ;
     ScaleOutlineFont (hps, 1440, 1440) ;

          // Get the text box

     GpiQueryTextBox (hps, strlen (szText), szText,
                      TXTBOX_COUNT, aptlTextBox) ;
```

Listing 7.20: The OLFDROP program (Continued)

```
          // Display the font normally twice

     ptl.x = (cxClient - aptlTextBox [TXTBOX_CONCAT].x) / 2 ;
     ptl.y = (cyClient - aptlTextBox [TXTBOX_TOPLEFT].y
                       - aptlTextBox [TXTBOX_BOTTOMLEFT].y) / 2 ;

     GpiCharStringAt (hps, &ptl, strlen (szText), szText) ;

     ptl.x -= 10 ;
     ptl.y += 10 ;

     GpiSetColor (hps, CLR_BACKGROUND) ;
     GpiCharStringAt (hps, &ptl, strlen (szText), szText) ;

          // Create the path

     GpiBeginPath (hps, 1) ;
     GpiCharStringAt (hps, &ptl, strlen (szText), szText) ;
     GpiEndPath (hps) ;

          // Outline the path

     GpiSetColor (hps, CLR_NEUTRAL) ;
     GpiSetLineWidth (hps, LINEWIDTH_THICK) ;
     GpiOutlinePath (hps, 1, 0) ;

          // Select the default font; delete the logical font

     GpiSetCharSet (hps, LCID_DEFAULT) ;
     GpiDeleteSetId (hps, LCID_FONT) ;
     }
```

As in OLFLINE, the program creates a 144-point Times New Roman Italic font. The program then draws normal text centered in the client window; this is the shadow. The program switches to the background color by calling *GpiSetColor* with the CLR_BACKGROUND parameter. (By default, the background color is white, but it can be changed by the user.) The text is drawn again, offset 10 pixels from the left and bottom of the first text string. (This offset looks fine on a VGA, but in a real program you'll probably want to calculate the offset in a more device-independent manner.) This is the interior of the outlined font.

The program then creates a path containing the font outline, switches back to the foreground color using *GpiSetColor* with the CLR_NEUTRAL parameter (which indicates black by default), and calls *GpiOutlinePath*. The results are shown in Figure 7.35.

Figure 7.35: The OLFDROP display

Another approach to drawing a font with a three-dimensional appearance is shown in the OLFBLOK program in Listing 7.21.

Listing 7.21: The OLFBLOK program

The OLFBLOK.MAK File

```
#-----------------------
# OLFBLOK.MAK make file
#-----------------------

olfblok.exe : olfblok.obj olfdemo.obj olf.obj olfdemo.def
     $(PRGLINK) olfblok olfdemo olf, olfblok, NUL, $(PRGLIB), olfdemo

olfblok.obj : olfblok.c olf.h
     $(PRGCC) olfblok.c

olfdemo.obj : olfdemo.c
     $(PRGCC) olfdemo.c

olf.obj : olf.c olf.h
     $(PRGCC) olf.c
```

Listing 7.21: The OLFBLOK program (Continued)

The OLFBLOK.C File

```
/*---------------------------------------
   OLFBLOK.C -- Blocked OS/2 Outline Font
                (c) Charles Petzold, 1993
  ---------------------------------------*/

#define INCL_WIN
#define INCL_GPI
#include <os2.h>
#include <string.h>
#include "olf.h"

#define LCID_FONT    1

void PaintClient (HPS hps, SHORT cxClient, SHORT cyClient)
     {
     static CHAR szText [] = "Hello!" ;
     int         i ;
     POINTL      ptl, aptlTextBox [TXTBOX_COUNT] ;

          // Create and size the logical font

     CreateOutlineFont (hps, LCID_FONT, "Times New Roman Italic", 0, 0) ;
     GpiSetCharSet (hps, LCID_FONT) ;
     ScaleOutlineFont (hps, 1440, 1440) ;

          // Get the text box

     GpiQueryTextBox (hps, strlen (szText), szText,
                      TXTBOX_COUNT, aptlTextBox) ;

          // Display the font normally

     ptl.x = (cxClient - aptlTextBox [TXTBOX_CONCAT].x) / 2 ;
     ptl.y = (cyClient - aptlTextBox [TXTBOX_TOPLEFT].y
                       - aptlTextBox [TXTBOX_BOTTOMLEFT].y) / 2 ;

     for (i = 0 ; i < 16 ; i++)
          {
          GpiCharStringAt (hps, &ptl, strlen (szText), szText) ;

          ptl.x -- ;
          ptl.y ++ ;
          }

     GpiSetColor (hps, CLR_BACKGROUND) ;
     GpiCharStringAt (hps, &ptl, strlen (szText), szText) ;

          // Create the path
```

Listing 7.21: The OLFBLOK program (Continued)

```
     GpiBeginPath (hps, 1) ;
     GpiCharStringAt (hps, &ptl, strlen (szText), szText) ;
     GpiEndPath (hps) ;

          // Outline the path

     GpiSetColor (hps, CLR_NEUTRAL) ;
     GpiSetLineWidth (hps, LINEWIDTH_THICK) ;
     GpiOutlinePath (hps, 1, 0) ;

          // Select the default font; delete the logical font

     GpiSetCharSet (hps, LCID_DEFAULT) ;
     GpiDeleteSetId (hps, LCID_FONT) ;
     }
```

This program is very similar to OLFDROP, but instead of drawing just one normal black font, this program draws 16 of them, each progressively offset by one pixel up and to the left. This is capped off by a normal white font, and then an outlined black font. The result is shown in Figure 7.36. The characters appear as if they were carved blocks.

Figure 7.36: The OLFBLOK display

STROKING THE FONT

So far, we've been looking at effects possible with outlining a path by calling *GpiOutlinePath*. You can also render the path by calling *GpiStrokePath*, which draws the path as a geometric thick line filled with the current area-filling pattern.

The OLFWIDE program in Listing 7.22 demonstrates this.

Listing 7.22: The OLFWIDE program

The OLFWIDE.MAK File

```
#-----------------------
# OLFWIDE.MAK make file
#-----------------------

olfwide.exe : olfwide.obj olfdemo.obj olf.obj olfdemo.def
     $(PRGLINK) olfwide olfdemo olf, olfwide, NUL, $(PRGLIB), olfdemo

olfwide.obj : olfwide.c olf.h
     $(PRGCC) olfwide.c

olfdemo.obj : olfdemo.c
     $(PRGCC) olfdemo.c

olf.obj : olf.c olf.h
     $(PRGCC) olf.c
```

The OLFWIDE.C File

```
/*------------------------------------------
   OLFWIDE.C -- Wide-Lined OS/2 Outline Font
                (c) Charles Petzold, 1993
  ------------------------------------------*/

#define INCL_WIN
#define INCL_GPI
#include <os2.h>
#include <string.h>
#include "olf.h"

#define LCID_FONT    1

void PaintClient (HPS hps, SHORT cxClient, SHORT cyClient)
     {
     static CHAR szText [] = "Hello!" ;
     POINTL      ptl, aptlTextBox [TXTBOX_COUNT] ;

          // Create and size the logical font
```

Listing 7.22: The OLFWIDE program (Continued)

```
     CreateOutlineFont (hps, LCID_FONT, "Times New Roman Italic", 0, 0) ;
     GpiSetCharSet (hps, LCID_FONT) ;
     ScaleOutlineFont (hps, 1440, 1440) ;

          // Get the text box

     GpiQueryTextBox (hps, strlen (szText), szText,
                      TXTBOX_COUNT, aptlTextBox) ;

          // Create the path

     GpiBeginPath (hps, 1) ;

     ptl.x = (cxClient - aptlTextBox [TXTBOX_CONCAT].x) / 2 ;
     ptl.y = (cyClient - aptlTextBox [TXTBOX_TOPLEFT].y
                       - aptlTextBox [TXTBOX_BOTTOMLEFT].y) / 2 ;

     GpiCharStringAt (hps, &ptl, strlen (szText), szText) ;

     GpiEndPath (hps) ;

          // Stroke the path

     GpiSetLineWidthGeom (hps, 10) ;
     GpiSetPattern (hps, PATSYM_HATCH) ;
     GpiStrokePath (hps, 1, 0) ;

          // Create the path again

     GpiBeginPath (hps, 1) ;
     GpiCharStringAt (hps, &ptl, strlen (szText), szText) ;
     GpiEndPath (hps) ;

          // Modify and outline the path

     GpiModifyPath (hps, 1, MPATH_STROKE) ;
     GpiOutlinePath (hps, 1, 0) ;

          // Select the default font; delete the logical font

     GpiSetCharSet (hps, LCID_DEFAULT) ;
     GpiDeleteSetId (hps, LCID_FONT) ;
     }
```

As in the previous programs, the program creates a 144-point Times New Roman Italic font and draws the "Hello!" text string within a path bracket. OLFWIDE then calls *GpiSetLineWidthGeom* to set the geometric line width at

10 pixels. (In a real program, you'd want to use a more device-independent approach to setting that width.) The program then sets the area-filling pattern to PATSYM_HATCH—a pattern that is a series of horizontal and vertical lines—and calls *GpiStrokePath*. This renders the font outlines as a series of 10-pixel-wide lines filled with the PATSYM_HATCH pattern.

The OLFWIDE program then creates another path with the same text string, and calls *GpiModifyPath*. You'll recall from earlier that *GpiModifyPath* takes an existing path and replaces it with a new path that represents the outline of the geometrically thick line that would be rendered by calling *GpiStrokePath*. Thus, this modified path outlines the area-pattern just drawn. The program finishes up by calling *GpiOutlinePath* to outline that pattern. The results are shown in Figure 7.37.

Figure 7.37: The OLFWIDE display

To see the separate effects of stroking and outlining the modified path, you may want to comment out either the *GpiStrokePath* or *GpiOutlinePath* calls in OLFWIDE.C and recompile the program. In particular, if you remove the call to *GpiStrokePath*, you'll see rather strange-looking results. We saw some of this oddness in the PATHS program earlier in this chapter: When two lines in the path are joined at an angle, the modified path often has a little interior loop.

You'll also notice little lines in the interior of the path where the path curves. These are results of GPI's path-modification algorithm.

FILLING THE PATH

The third function that uses a path is called *GpiFillPath*, and as its name implies, it fills the interior of the path using the current area-filling pattern. This is different from *GpiStrokePath*, which strokes the path using the area-filling pattern.

However, the *GpiFillPath* and *GpiStrokePath* functions are related: *GpiStrokePath* is equivalent to *GpiModifyPath* followed by *GpiFillPath*. IBM's *Presentation Manager Programming Reference* indicates that *GpiStrokePath* "is provided to enable device drivers to optimize storage, if possible." What happens is that *GpiModifyPath* greatly increases the storage necessary to store the path. A device driver might be able to implement *GpiStrokePath* without requiring that additional storage.

Anyway, let's take a look at a sample program called OLFFILL, shown in Listing 7.23. The program is quite similar to OLFWIDE, but a little simpler. The program creates the path twice. With the first path, OLFFILL sets the area-filling pattern to PATSYM_HATCH and calls *GpiFillPath*. After creating the second path, the program calls *GpiOutlinePath*. The results (obviously much more normal looking than the OLFWIDE display) are shown in Figure 7.38.

Listing 7.23: The OLFFILL program

The OLFFILL.MAK File

```
#----------------------
# OLFFILL.MAK make file
#----------------------

olffill.exe : olffill.obj olfdemo.obj olf.obj olfdemo.def
     $(PRGLINK) olffill olfdemo olf, olffill, NUL, $(PRGLIB), olfdemo

olffill.obj : olffill.c olf.h
     $(PRGCC) olffill.c

olfdemo.obj : olfdemo.c
     $(PRGCC) olfdemo.c

olf.obj : olf.c olf.h
     $(PRGCC) olf.c
```

Listing 7.23: The OLFFILL program (Continued)

The OLFFILL.C File

```
/*--------------------------------------
   OLFFILL.C -- Filled OS/2 Outline Font
                (c) Charles Petzold, 1993
  --------------------------------------*/

#define INCL_WIN
#define INCL_GPI
#include <os2.h>
#include <string.h>
#include "olf.h"

#define LCID_FONT    1

void PaintClient (HPS hps, SHORT cxClient, SHORT cyClient)
     {
     static CHAR szText [] = "Hello!" ;
     POINTL      ptl, aptlTextBox [TXTBOX_COUNT] ;

          // Create and size the logical font

     CreateOutlineFont (hps, LCID_FONT, "Times New Roman Italic", 0, 0) ;
     GpiSetCharSet (hps, LCID_FONT) ;
     ScaleOutlineFont (hps, 1440, 1440) ;

          // Get the text box

     GpiQueryTextBox (hps, strlen (szText), szText,
                      TXTBOX_COUNT, aptlTextBox) ;

          // Create the path

     GpiBeginPath (hps, 1) ;

     ptl.x = (cxClient - aptlTextBox [TXTBOX_CONCAT].x) / 2 ;
     ptl.y = (cyClient - aptlTextBox [TXTBOX_TOPLEFT].y
                       - aptlTextBox [TXTBOX_BOTTOMLEFT].y) / 2 ;

     GpiCharStringAt (hps, &ptl, strlen (szText), szText) ;

     GpiEndPath (hps) ;

          // Fill the path

     GpiSetPattern (hps, PATSYM_HATCH) ;
     GpiFillPath (hps, 1, 0) ;
```

Listing 7.23: The OLFFILL program (Continued)

```
          // Create the path again

     GpiBeginPath (hps, 1) ;
     GpiCharStringAt (hps, &ptl, strlen (szText), szText) ;
     GpiEndPath (hps) ;

          // Outline the path

     GpiOutlinePath (hps, 1, 0) ;

          // Select the default font; delete the logical font

     GpiSetCharSet (hps, LCID_DEFAULT) ;
     GpiDeleteSetId (hps, LCID_FONT) ;
     }
```

Figure 7.38: The OLFFILL display

PATHS AND CLIPPING

When I first began learning graphics programming, the whole concept of clipping really mystified me. Most graphics programming environments support some type of clipping, but I couldn't understand why it was stressed so much—that is, why clipping was considered so important in the total feature list of a graphics programming system.

Clipping is basically instructing the graphics programming environment to restrict drawing to a particular area of the display (either the video screen or the printer page). When you set a clipping area, you are telling the graphics system not to draw outside of that area. Any graphics object you subsequently draw appears only within the area you set.

What mystified me about clipping is this: If you don't want to draw outside of a particular area, why not just avoid doing so?

Well, as every graphics programmer eventually learns, clipping is not usually strictly necessary, but it is often *very* convenient. Clipping makes certain things much easier than they would be otherwise. For example, GPI prohibits you from drawing outside the window with which the presentation space is associated. This is *very* convenient, because you don't have to worry about drawing on another program's window.

Just as GPI supports several levels of coordinate transforms, it also supports several levels of clipping. However, by far the most versatile clipping involves paths. After you create a path, you can use the path as a clipping area by calling

```
GpiSetClipPath (hps, lPath, lOption) ;
```

To set the clipping path, the *lPath* parameter must be equal to 1, as is normal with the path functions. The *lOption* parameter can be a combination of identifiers defined in PMGPI.H, beginning with the prefix SCP. These identifiers are defined like so:

```
#define SCP_ALTERNATE     0L
#define SCP_WINDING       2L
#define SCP_AND           4L
#define SCP_RESET         0L
```

You need to include SCP_AND when setting the clipping path. This causes the area defined by the path to be intersected with the current clipping path. The SCP_ALTERNATE and SCP_WINDING constants determine how overlapping areas are interpreted. To reset the presentation space to no clipping, use a 0 value for the *lPath* parameter, and an SCP_RESET value (also equal to 0) for the *lOption* parameter.

The OLFCLIP program in Listing 7.24 shows an example of using an outline font for clipping. The program uses the same path we've been using, but after calling *GpiSetClipPath*, it draws a series of colored Bézier splines. The results are shown in Figure 7.39. Now, try doing *that* without clipping.

Figure 7.39: The OLFCLIP display

Listing 7.24: The OLFCLIP program

The OLFCLIP.MAK File

```
#----------------------
# OLFCLIP.MAK make file
#----------------------

olfclip.exe : olfclip.obj olfdemo.obj olf.obj olfdemo.def
     $(PRGLINK) olfclip olfdemo olf, olfclip, NUL, $(PRGLIB), olfdemo

olfclip.obj : olfclip.c olf.h
     $(PRGCC) olfclip.c

olfdemo.obj : olfdemo.c
     $(PRGCC) olfdemo.c

olf.obj : olf.c olf.h
     $(PRGCC) olf.c
```

Listing 7.24: The OLFCLIP program (Continued)

The OLFCLIP.C File

```
/*--------------------------------------------
   OLFCLIP.C -- OS/2 Outline Font Clipping
                (c) Charles Petzold, 1993
  --------------------------------------------*/

#define INCL_WIN
#define INCL_GPI
#include <os2.h>
#include <string.h>
#include "olf.h"

#define LCID_FONT    1

void PaintClient (HPS hps, SHORT cxClient, SHORT cyClient)
     {
     static CHAR szText [] = "Hello!" ;
     int         i ;
     POINTL      ptl, aptl[3], aptlTextBox [TXTBOX_COUNT] ;

          // Create and size the logical font

     CreateOutlineFont (hps, LCID_FONT, "Times New Roman Italic", 0, 0) ;
     GpiSetCharSet (hps, LCID_FONT) ;
     ScaleOutlineFont (hps, 1440, 1440) ;

          // Get the text box

     GpiQueryTextBox (hps, strlen (szText), szText,
                      TXTBOX_COUNT, aptlTextBox) ;

          // Create the path

     GpiBeginPath (hps, 1) ;

     ptl.x = (cxClient - aptlTextBox [TXTBOX_CONCAT].x) / 2 ;
     ptl.y = (cyClient - aptlTextBox [TXTBOX_TOPLEFT].y
                       - aptlTextBox [TXTBOX_BOTTOMLEFT].y) / 2 ;

     GpiCharStringAt (hps, &ptl, strlen (szText), szText) ;

     GpiEndPath (hps) ;

          // Set the clipping path

     GpiSetClipPath (hps, 1, SCP_AND | SCP_ALTERNATE) ;
```

Listing 7.24: The OLFCLIP program (Continued)

```
          // Draw Bezier splines

     for (i = 0 ; i < cyClient ; i++)
          {
          GpiSetColor (hps, (i / 16) % 6 + 1) ;

          ptl.x = 0 ;
          ptl.y = i ;
          GpiMove (hps, &ptl) ;

          aptl[0].x = cxClient / 3 ;
          aptl[0].y = i + cyClient / 3 ;

          aptl[1].x = 2 * cxClient / 3 ;
          aptl[1].y = i - cyClient / 3 ;

          aptl[2].x = cxClient ;
          aptl[2].y = i ;

          GpiPolySpline (hps, 3, aptl) ;
          }

          // Select the default font; delete the logical font

     GpiSetCharSet (hps, LCID_DEFAULT) ;
     GpiDeleteSetId (hps, LCID_FONT) ;
     }
```

BACK TO WORK

Now that we've had some fun with outline fonts, it's time to get serious.

I don't know about you, but for me the idea of writing a modern word processor for a graphical environment such as the OS/2 Presentation Manager is downright scary. Users have come to expect both ease of use and sophistication from such software, and these goals are often at odds. Also, knowing the folks at *PC Magazine* who review word processors, I would be very hesitant about creating a product that could withstand *their* incisive scrutiny!

Still, however, one of the objectives of learning how to work with fonts under OS/2 is to understand how graphical word processors do what they do, and to imitate some of that in our own applications. That means we have to tackle the issue of formatted text.

CHARACTER AND PARAGRAPH FORMATTING

I mention word processors because they illustrate clearly many of the options you can use in displaying text. At the very least, word processors divide formatting into three major categories: character formatting, paragraph formatting, and page formatting.

If you look at the menus or dialog boxes of your word processor, you'll find that character formatting involves (at the very least) a selection of a font and point size, and the setting of character attributes—italics, boldface, underline, and strikeout. We've seen in this chapter how to do this. Of course, word processors often support other character attributes, specifically subscripting and superscripting, and perhaps small capitals (where a word is displayed entirely in capital letters but at a smaller size than normal). Because these attributes usually require changing the font point size by a specific percentage of the normal point size, you'll be spending a lot of time analyzing the information available in the FONTMETRICS structure before implementing these features.

Paragraph formatting determines how a paragraph is displayed. This involves such options as indentation, line spacing, and alignment. Here I'd like to illustrate how to implement line spacing and alignment options. Although many modern word processors (and to a greater extent, desktop publishing programs) allow very specific line spacing options, I'll be illustrating the traditional simple ones: single spacing, double spacing, and the compromise—spacing by 1.5 lines.

I'll also show how to do the four standard types of paragraph alignment: left, right, centered, and justified. Of course, you can probably guess that justified text (in which each line of text occupies the full space in the text column) is the most difficult. As we'll see, however, GPI provides a couple of functions that make displaying justified text a lot easier than it would be otherwise. The *GpiQueryTextBox* function plays a part, of course, but other functions help out also.

ALIGNING TEXT

You can use *GpiQueryTextBox* for determining the width of a character string using the *aptl[TXTBOX_CONCAT].x* value. This is what you use for breaking a paragraph into successive lines of text.

Let's assume you have a single paragraph of text stored in memory. For purposes of simplicity, none of the individual words in the paragraph contain any character formatting, and there are no hyphenated words or anything like that. The paragraph just consists of words separated by spaces. You need to display this paragraph in a rectangle. The top of the rectangle determines the vertical starting point of the text, and the width of the rectangle is the column width in which the text must fit.

Whether you want left, right, center, or justified alignment, the initial process is the same and conceptually quite simple. You begin with the beginning of the paragraph and search for the first space character. Then, using *GpiQueryTextBox*, you find the width of the string before that space character. This is the width of the first word of the paragraph. Most likely, this will be less than the column width. So, you search for the next space character, and find the width of the first two words (and the space between them) together. You keep doing this until the width of the text is greater than the column width. Then you back up one word and that's your line break.

Now you have the substring that will be displayed as the first line of the formatted paragraph, and you can continue with the second line.

Regardless of the character alignment you choose, any particular line in the formatted paragraph will have the same number of words. The width of the text in each line will be less than or equal to the column width. Let's call the difference the "surplus space." The only difference between the four character alignments is where this surplus space goes.

With left-aligned text, the surplus space appears at the right side of the column; with right-aligned text, it appears at the left; with centered text, it's divided equally between the left and right sides of the column. And with justified text, the surplus space is.... Well, let's think about it.

BREAK AND CHARACTER SPACE

For justified text, the immediate instinct might be to divide the surplus space between all the characters in the string. However, the publishing convention is to justify the text line by distributing the surplus space *not* between each individual character, but in the spaces between the words. That is, all the space characters in the text line are made slightly wider by an equal amount.

Fortunately, there's a GPI function that sets a device context attribute that performs precisely this job with a minimum of fuss:

```
GpiSetCharBreakExtra (hps, fxExtra) ;
```

The second parameter is a FIXED value. It's a fixed-point number with an integral part in the high 16 bits and a fractional part (that is, a fraction of 65536) in the low 16 bits. You calculate *fxExtra* by multiplying the surplus space by 65536 and dividing by the number of spaces in the text line. After you call this function, any text you display will have a space character that is wider by *fxExtra* than the normal space character.

Of course, there's always the possibility that only one word fits in the column. This can happen very easily when you're writing about the OS/2 Presentation Manager and bandy about such words as *GpiQuerySegmentTransformMatrix*. Sometimes such a word will be hyphenated and will straddle two columns, but all (or part) of it might nearly fill the full column width, preventing any other word from appearing there. You can't use *GpiSetCharBreakExtra* because there are no spaces in the line.

In this case, you need to insert extra spaces between the characters. And once again GPI provides a hassle-free function to do this:

```
GpiSetCharExtra (hps, fxExtra) ;
```

In this case you calculate *fxExtra* by multipling 65536 by the surplus space and dividing by the number of characters in the word less 1.

Interestingly enough, *GpiSetCharExtra* also solves the problem of a text line containing a single word that is too wide to fit in the column. This might happen if you're writing about *GpiQuerySegmentTransformMatrix* and haven't implemented any hyphenation logic. If the surplus space is negative, *fxExtra* becomes so also, and *GpiSetCharExtra* will scrunch up the text. It might not look that good, but at least it will still fit within the boundaries of the column.

THE SAMPLE PROGRAM

Now that we know the theory, let's look at a simple implementation. The OLFJUST program is shown in Listing 7.25. The OLFJUST.C file contains the sample paragraph used to illustrate paragraph formatting. It is the first paragraph of Mark Twain's *Adventures of Huckleberry Finn*, terminated by a zero byte.

Listing 7.25: The OLFJUST program

The OLFJUST.MAK File

```
#----------------------
# OLFJUST.MAK make file
#----------------------

olfjust.exe : olfjust.obj olfdemo.obj olf.obj olfdemo.def
     $(PRGLINK) olfjust olfdemo olf, olfjust, NUL, $(PRGLIB), olfdemo

olfjust.obj : olfjust.c olf.h
     $(PRGCC) olfjust.c

olfdemo.obj : olfdemo.c
     $(PRGCC) olfdemo.c

olf.obj : olf.c olf.h
     $(PRGCC) olf.c
```

Listing 7.25: The OLFJUST program (Continued)

The OLFJUST.C File

```
/*-----------------------------------------
   OLFJUST.C -- Justified OS/2 Outline Font
                (c) Charles Petzold, 1993
  -----------------------------------------*/

#define INCL_WIN
#define INCL_GPI
#include <os2.h>
#include "olf.h"

#define LCID_FONT         1
#define FACENAME          "Times New Roman"
#define PTWIDTH           200
#define PTHEIGHT          200

#define ALIGN_LEFT        1
#define ALIGN_RIGHT       2
#define ALIGN_CENTER      3
#define ALIGN_JUST        4

#define SPACE_SINGLE      1
#define SPACE_HALF        2
#define SPACE_DOUBLE      3

VOID Justify (HPS hps, PCHAR pText, PRECTL prcl, SHORT nAlign, SHORT nSpace)
     {
     int      iBreakCount, iSurplus ;
     PCHAR    pStart, pEnd ;
     POINTL   ptlStart, aptlTextBox [TXTBOX_COUNT] ;

     ptlStart.y = prcl->yTop ;

     do                                  // until end of text
          {
          iBreakCount = 0 ;

          while (*pText == ' ')          // Skip over leading blanks
               pText++ ;

          pStart = pText ;

          do                             // until line is known
               {
               while (*pText == ' ')     // Skip over leading blanks
                    pText++ ;

                                         // Find next break point
```

Listing 7.25: The OLFJUST program (Continued)

```
          while (*pText != '\xØØ' && *pText != ' ')
               pText++ ;

                                        // Determine text width

          GpiQueryTextBox (hps, pText - pStart, pStart,
                           TXTBOX_COUNT, aptlTextBox) ;

                         // Normal case: text less wide than column

          if (aptlTextBox[TXTBOX_CONCAT].x < (prcl->xRight - prcl->xLeft))
               {
               iBreakCount++ ;
               pEnd = pText ;
               }

                         // Text wider than window with only one word

          else if (iBreakCount == Ø)
               {
               pEnd = pText ;
               break ;
               }

                         // Text wider than window, so fix up and get out
          else
               {
               iBreakCount-- ;
               pText = pEnd ;
               break ;
               }
          }
     while (*pText != '\xØØ') ;

                         // Get the final text box

     GpiQueryTextBox (hps, pEnd - pStart, pStart,
                      TXTBOX_COUNT, aptlTextBox) ;

                         // Drop down by maximum ascender

     ptlStart.y -= aptlTextBox[TXTBOX_TOPLEFT].y ;

                         // Find surplus space in text line

     iSurplus = prcl->xRight - prcl->xLeft -
                aptlTextBox[TXTBOX_CONCAT].x ;

                        // Adjust starting position and
```

Listing 7.25: The OLFJUST program (Continued)

```
               // space and character spacing

     switch (nAlign)
          {
          case ALIGN_LEFT:
               ptlStart.x = prcl->xLeft ;
               break ;

          case ALIGN_RIGHT:
               ptlStart.x = prcl->xLeft + iSurplus ;
               break ;

          case ALIGN_CENTER:
               ptlStart.x = prcl->xLeft + iSurplus / 2 ;
               break ;

          case ALIGN_JUST:
               ptlStart.x = prcl->xLeft ;

               if (*pText == '\x00')
                    break ;

               if (iBreakCount > 0)
                    GpiSetCharBreakExtra (hps,
                         65536 * iSurplus /  iBreakCount) ;

               else if (pEnd - pStart - 1 > 0)
                    GpiSetCharExtra (hps,
                         65536 * iSurplus / (pEnd - pStart - 1)) ;
               break ;
          }

                    // Display the string & return to normal

     GpiCharStringAt (hps, &ptlStart, pEnd - pStart, pStart) ;
     GpiSetCharExtra (hps, 0) ;
     GpiSetCharBreakExtra (hps, 0) ;

                    // Drop down by maximum descender

     ptlStart.y += aptlTextBox[TXTBOX_BOTTOMLEFT].y ;

                    // Do additional line-spacing

     switch (nSpace)
          {
          case SPACE_HALF:
               ptlStart.y -= (aptlTextBox[TXTBOX_TOPLEFT].y -
                              aptlTextBox[TXTBOX_BOTTOMLEFT].y) / 2 ;
               break ;
```

Listing 7.25: The OLFJUST program (Continued)

```
          case SPACE_DOUBLE:
               ptlStart.y -= aptlTextBox[TXTBOX_TOPLEFT].y -
                             aptlTextBox[TXTBOX_BOTTOMLEFT].y ;
               break ;
          }
     }

     while (*pText != '\x00' && ptlStart.y > prcl->yBottom) ;
     }

void PaintClient (HPS hps, SHORT cxClient, SHORT cyClient)
     {
     static CHAR szText [] =

          "You don't know about me, without you have read a book by "
          "the name of \"The Adventures of Tom Sawyer,\" but that "
          "ain't no matter. That book was made by Mr. Mark Twain, "
          "and he told the truth, mainly. There was things which he "
          "stretched, but mainly he told the truth. That is nothing. "
          "I never seen anybody but lied, one time or another, "
          "without it was Aunt Polly, or the widow, or maybe Mary. "
          "Aunt Polly - Tom's Aunt Polly, she is - and Mary, and the "
          "Widow Douglas, is all told about in that book - which is "
          "mostly a true book; with some stretchers, as I said before." ;

     RECTL       rcl ;

          // Create and size the logical font

     CreateOutlineFont (hps, LCID_FONT, FACENAME, 0, 0) ;
     GpiSetCharSet (hps, LCID_FONT) ;
     ScaleOutlineFont (hps, PTWIDTH, PTHEIGHT) ;

          // Display the text

     rcl.xLeft   = 0 ;
     rcl.yBottom = 0 ;
     rcl.xRight  = cxClient ;
     rcl.yTop    = cyClient ;

     Justify (hps, szText, &rcl, ALIGN_JUST, SPACE_SINGLE) ;

          // Select the default font; delete the logical font

     GpiSetCharSet (hps, LCID_DEFAULT) ;
     GpiDeleteSetId (hps, LCID_FONT) ;
     }
```

To avoid using menus (which you have not yet learned about), the program is hard-coded to display the paragraph using a 24-point Times New Roman font. (You can change that in the program's *#define* statements and recompile if you wish.) The program displays the formatted paragraph using the full width of the window. The program is set up for a single-spaced justified display, but you can also change that with parameters to the program's *Justify* function call in *PaintClient*.

Figure 7.40 shows two instances of this program running under the Presentation Manager. The first instance shows the paragraph with a fairly normal width, and illustrates the text justification achieved by using *GpiSetCharBreakExtra*. The second instance at the right of the screen has an extremely narrow column width, and several lines in the paragraph show what *GpiSetCharExtra* can do for you. Most lines contain only one word with letters that are spread across the column. Further down, the word "Adventures" would normally be too wide to fit within the column, but *GpiSetCharExtra* caused the letters to be squeezed closer together.

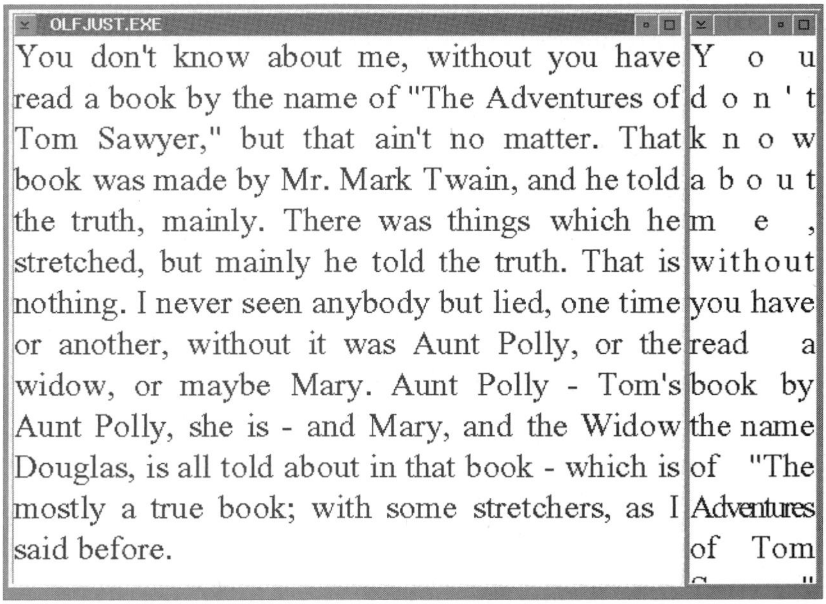

Figure 7.40: The JUSTIFY display

Justify begins by initializing the *y* field of the POINTL structure named *ptlStart* to the top of the display rectangle. This structure will later be used to indicate the starting position of each line of text. The code in the main *do* loop is executed once per line. The *iBreakCount* variable is used to store the number of break characters (spaces) in the line and is initialized to 0. After skipping over any leading spaces in the text pointed to by the *pText* variable, the function saves the pointer value in *pStart*, indicating the beginning of the text line.

The nested *do* loop is executed for each word in the line. Again, the function skips over any leading spaces pointed to by *pText*, and then searches for either a space (indicating the end of a word) or the concluding carriage return character. *GpiQueryTextBox* is used to determine the length of the string. There are three cases: If the text width is less than the column width, *iBreakCount* is incremented and the *pEnd* pointer is set to the end of the substring. If a single word is wider than the column, *pEnd* is also set to the end of the substring and the function breaks out of the *do* loop. Otherwise, a series of two or more words is wider than the column. That means that the substring contains one too many words. The *iBreakCount* variable is decremented and *pText* is set to the previously set *pEnd* in preparation for scanning the next line of text.

The *Justify* function then calls *GpiQueryTextBox* again to get the dimensions of the final text box for the line. The *y* field of the *ptlStart* structure is decremented to reflect the ascender part of the character height. The surplus space is calculated by subtracting the text width from the column width.

At this point, the function is ready to set the *x* field of *ptlStart* depending on the selected alignment. For left justification, it's simply the left side of the rectangle. For right justification, it's the left side of the rectangle plus the surplus space. For centered text, it's the left side of the rectangle plus half the surplus space.

For justified text, the text string also begins at the left side of the rectangle. For a positive *iBreakCount*, the function calls *GpiSetCharBreakExtra* as described earlier. Otherwise, the line contains one word and the function calls *GpiSetCharExtra*. At this time, *Justify* can display the line of text by calling *GpiCharStringAt*. The function then uses the height of the font and the selected line spacing to decrease the *y* field of the *ptlStart* structure in preparation for the next line.

DEALING WITH ADDED COMPLEXITIES

For purposes of clarity, *Justify* illustrates what is perhaps the simplest paragraph-formatting code possible. If the paragraph contains any words with character formatting (italics, boldface, underscores, or strikeouts), the function is not quite adequate.

The combination of paragraph formatting and character formatting adds complexities, but not insurmountable ones. Basically, as you scanned the paragraph looking for line breaks, you'd have to select different fonts based on the various character attributes. You can't use *GpiQueryTextBox* to find the total length of the string because the function is based on the font currently selected in the presentation space. You'll have to break the text down into pieces depending on which words (or letters) are formatted and which ones aren't.

If you want to display some words in color, you don't have exactly the same problems. You must still display the text in pieces, but because text color is an attribute of the presentation space instead of part of the font definition, you can still determine line breaks as shown in the *Justify* function.

Another complexity involves hyphens. There are actually several different ways in which hyphens must be treated.

Compound words such as "hurdy-gurdy" contain a hyphen that should appear whenever the word is displayed. If the "hurdy-" part of the word fits on the line but the "gurdy" part does not, the line can break between the two parts. Thus, you can treat the hyphen *almost* the same as a space character, except that a space character doesn't appear at the beginning or end of a line while the hyphen must appear at the end of the line.

Then there's the notorious "no break" hyphen. These appear in words such as "A-1." This word would look very strange if "A-" appeared at the end of one line and "1" appeared at the beginning of the next. In this case, you want all three characters to appear on the same line.

Long words can be broken at the end of a line by using a hyphen between syllables of the word. The hyphen should not appear otherwise. These hyphens can be inserted during text display using a dictionary or a good hyphenation algorithm, or the user can insert them manually.

This hyphen problem gets worse: Although the *Huckleberry Finn* paragraph shown in the program seems to contain a few hyphens, I'm not using them correctly. Hyphens should be used in words such as "hurdy-gurdy," but to separate a phrase in a sentence—such as this one right here—an "en dash" or "em dash" should be used instead. An en dash is half the width of an em dash, which is as wide as the point size of the font. The en dash is also used in place of the word "to" as when referring to "the Boston–New York shuttle."

WAIT—THERE'S MORE

There are still a few text functions I haven't discussed in this chapter. These allow very high control over the placement of characters in a string, and also determining where they appear.

The *GpiQueryCharStringPos* and *GpiQueryCharStringPosAt* functions fill up an array of POINTL structures with the starting positions of all the characters in a text string. These functions are useful for implementing "hit-testing"—that is, determining which character in a displayed string a user is clicking with the mouse.

If you're so inclined, you can do precise character-by-character positioning of a text string using the *GpiCharStringPos* and *GpiCharStringPosAt* functions. However, unless you want irregular character spacing, the *GpiSetCharExtra* and *GpiSetCharBreakExtra* functions are much easier to use.

The *GpiQueryWidthTable* function gives you the width of any (or all) of the characters in the current font, and *GpiQueryKerningPairs* gives you all the kerning pairs. These are pairs of letters (such as "To") that can be placed somewhat closer than normal to look a little better.

Exploration of these functions is—as teachers are wont to say after an exceptionally long lecture—left as an exercise for the student.

Part 3

Getting Input

Tapping into the Keyboard

THE KEYBOARD AND CODES

THE WM_CHAR MESSAGE

OTHER KEYBOARD MESSAGES AND FUNCTIONS

Chapter 8

Despite the sophisticated user interface of the Presentation Manager (including the mouse, menus, and dialog boxes), the keyboard is still the primary means of user input in most applications. Even if you write a Presentation Manager program that makes extensive use of the mouse, you should probably also include a keyboard interface that duplicates many of the common mouse functions.

A Presentation Manager program receives keyboard input in the form of messages. You process these keyboard messages in the same way you process other messages. In fact, because user input is closer to one's intuitive concept of a message, working with these keyboard messages should be easier in some ways than handling other types of messages.

As you've seen in previous programs, the Presentation Manager itself handles a large part of keyboard processing. The keystrokes involved in choosing an item from the system menu are handled outside the client window procedure, as are the keyboard accelerators that duplicate system menu options. Many child window controls (discussed in Chapter 11) have their own keyboard interface. The Presentation Manager also takes care of keyboard processing in a program's menu (Chapter 13) and dialog boxes (Chapter 14). But this isn't to say that keyboard handling is easy. The Presentation Manager delivers a lot of information to your program with the keyboard message. You need to recognize what is important and what you can safely ignore.

Keyboard processing becomes more complex if you want to ensure that your programs can survive the transition to a system with a foreign keyboard. By "foreign keyboard" I mean any type of keyboard that differs from the one on your desk. This includes a variety of European keyboards, keyboards used in Far Eastern countries that generate double-byte character codes, and even keyboards for non-PC computers that might someday run versions of the Presentation Manager. The Presentation Manager has a device-independent keyboard interface, but—as is the case with other device-independent interfaces—you have to help. You can even design your Presentation Manager programs so that they can be recompiled for a system with a keyboard that generates codes in the EBCDIC (Extended Binary Coded Decimal Interchange Code) character set used on IBM mainframes and minicomputers.

THE KEYBOARD AND CODES

A keyboard always generates numeric codes of various sorts. Within a program, you make an implicit assumption about how these codes relate to the keys that generate them.

You can think of the keyboard in one of two ways: as a collection of distinct physical keys or as a means of generating character codes. When you treat the keyboard as a collection of keys, any code generated by the keyboard must identify the key and indicate whether the key is being pressed or released. When you treat the keyboard as a character input device, a code generated by a particular keystroke identifies a unique character in a character set. For a U.S. keyboard on the PC, this character set is ASCII. For a European keyboard, however, it is an extended ASCII character set that includes accented letters and other symbols not in the standard ASCII character set. For a keyboard on an IBM mainframe, it is the EBCDIC character set. If you obtain a character code from the keyboard and echo it to the display, it should look the same as the character printed on the top of the key. That is, the visual appearance of the character on the screen shouldn't surprise the user. This requires that the keyboard driver and display driver are working with the same character set or *codepage*.

Because many of the keys on the keyboard aren't associated with character codes, you must usually treat the keyboard as both a collection of keys and a character generator. You can divide the keyboard into four general groups of keys:

- **Toggle keys** The Caps Lock, Num Lock, and Scroll Lock keys and possibly the Insert key. Pressing the key turns the state of the key on; pressing it again turns the state off.

- **Shift keys** The Shift, Ctrl, and Alt keys. The shift keys affect the interpretation of other keys.
- **Noncharacter keys** The function keys, the cursor movement keys, Pause, Escape, Delete, and possibly the Insert key. These keys aren't associated with characters but instead often direct a program to carry out a particular action.
- **Character keys** The letter, number, and symbol keys, the spacebar, the Tab key, Backspace, and Enter. (The Tab, Backspace, and Enter keys can also be treated as noncharacter keys.)

Often a single physical key can generate different character codes depending on the state of the shift keys. For example, the A key generates a lowercase "a" or an uppercase A depending on whether or not the Shift key is held down. Sometimes two different physical keys (such as the two Enter keys on an IBM enhanced keyboard) can generate the same character code.

The Presentation Manager handles the keyboard somewhat differently from other PC keyboard interfaces with which you may be more familiar. To put this into perspective, let's examine these other keyboard interfaces.

PRE-OS/2 KEYBOARD PROCESSING

The hardware of the keyboard on a PC generates a *hardware scan code.* This is an 8-bit code that identifies the physical key and indicates whether the key is being pressed or released. Hardware scan codes are generally numbered sequentially across the rows of keys.

In the DOS world, the PC BIOS processes each keystroke through its Interrupt 0x09 handler. For hardware scan codes corresponding to shift keys and toggle keys, the Interrupt 09H handler stores the current state of the key. For character keys, the hardware scan code is converted into an ASCII character code based on the state of the shift and toggle keys and is stored in a small buffer. For noncharacter keys, the hardware scan code is converted into an "extended keyboard code" and also stored in the buffer.

A program running under DOS can obtain keystrokes from the buffer through various DOS function calls or the BIOS Interrupt 0x16. For character keys, Interrupt 0x16 returns the ASCII character code and the hardware scan code. For noncharacter keys, the extended keyboard code is returned, and the ASCII code is set to 0.

In summary, the PC BIOS works with three types of codes:

- **Hardware scan code** Generated from keyboard hardware

- **Extended keyboard code** Identifies noncharacter keys in combination with the Shift, Ctrl, or Alt key
- **ASCII character code** Identifies character keys based on the Shift, Ctrl, or Caps Lock key

THE OS/2 KERNEL AND THE KEYBOARD

When OS/2 is running, the keyboard is handled by the OS/2 kernel rather than the PC BIOS. However, the OS/2 keyboard interface closely mimics the operation of the BIOS. A program running under the OS/2 kernel obtains keyboard input by calling the *DosRead*, *KbdCharIn*, or *KbdStringIn* function. The *KbdCharIn* function is the most general and is similar to Interrupt 0x16. The keyboard information from *KbdCharIn* is stored in a structure of type KBDKEYINFO.

Two fields of KBDKEYINFO identify the key. The *chChar* field contains an ASCII character code. If this field is 0, the *chScan* field contains an extended keyboard code. The *fsState* field is a 16-bit integer with flags that identify the current state of the shift and toggle keys.

Enter the Presentation Manager Rather than use *DosRead* or the *Kbd* functions to obtain keyboard input, a Presentation Manager program receives keyboard information in the form of messages. These messages contain more information about keyboard activity than is available from the OS/2 *KbdCharIn* function. When a key is pressed or released, the Presentation Manager decodes the key and stores the information about the keystroke in a system message queue. This keyboard message is later routed to the message queue of the window with the input focus (a concept discussed later in this chapter) and then retrieved by the program.

The Presentation Manager differs from other PC keyboard interfaces primarily in the treatment of the noncharacter keys. The Presentation Manager doesn't use the extended keyboard codes, which are too dependent on the specific hardware of the PC and would make little sense for versions of the Presentation Manager adapted for different hardware. Instead, an attempt has been made to virtualize the codes for noncharacter keys. A fourth type of keyboard code has been introduced: the *virtual key code.* Like the hardware scan code, the virtual key code generally identifies a physical key and isn't dependent on a particular shift state. (There are a few exceptions.)

Armed with this historical perspective, let's examine the Presentation Manager keyboard message.

THE WM_CHAR MESSAGE

In most cases a Presentation Manager program can obtain all the information it needs about keyboard input by processing the WM_CHAR message in the client window procedure. The information encoded in the *mp1* and *mp2* parameters is shown in Figure 8.1.

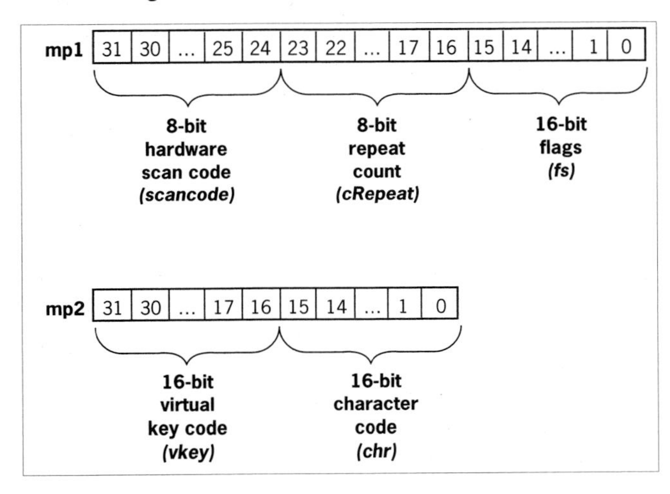

Figure 8.1: The WM_CHAR *mp1* and *mp2* parameters

You can use a variety of macros defined in PMWIN.H—such as SHORT1-FROMMP and CHAR3FROMMP—to extract each of these fields. Or you can use a macro called CHARMSG designed specifically for processing WM_CHAR messages. You use CHARMSG like this:

```
CHARMSG(&msg)->identifier
```

where *identifier* is one of the identifiers in parentheses shown in Figure 8.1. This macro references the *mp1* and *mp2* parameters to the window procedure from the stack. But watch out: If you want to use the CHARMSG macro in a subroutine called from the window procedure, the subroutine must be declared the same way as a window procedure, and you must pass *msg*, *mp1*, and *mp2* to the subroutine in that order.

The lower 16 bits of *mp1* contain a series of flags that further describe the keyboard message. The individual flags can be extracted using identifiers beginning with the letters KC defined in the PMWIN.H header file. These flags are shown in Figure 8.2.

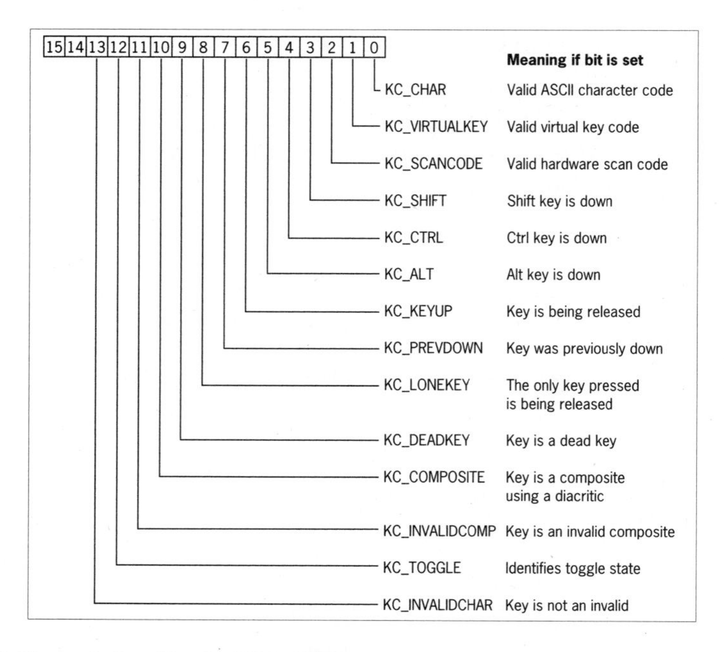

Figure 8.2: Flags defined in the WM_CHAR *mp1* parameter

You can test these flags with one of two expressions, for example:

```
SHORT1FROMMP (mp1) & KC_SHIFT
```

or

```
CHARMSG(&msg)->fs & KC_SHIFT
```

Both expressions return a nonzero value if the KC_SHIFT flag is set (meaning the Shift key is down) or 0 if the flag is 0 (meaning the Shift key is up).

LOOKING AT THE KEYS

As I discuss the various codes and flags in the *mp1* and *mp2* parameters, you may find it helpful to observe what the Presentation Manager actually gives your program in the WM_CHAR message when you press a particular key. To do this, you can use the KEYLOOK program, which is shown in Listing 8.1.

Listing 8.1: The KEYLOOK program

The KEYLOOK.MAK File

```
#-----------------------
# KEYLOOK.MAK make file
#-----------------------

keylook.exe : keylook.obj easyfont.obj keylook.def
     $(PRGLINK) keylook easyfont, keylook, NUL, $(PRGLIB), keylook

keylook.obj : keylook.c easyfont.h
     $(PRGCC) keylook.c

easyfont.obj : easyfont.c easyfont.h
     $(PRGCC) easyfont.c
```

The KEYLOOK.C File

```
/*---------------------------------------
   KEYLOOK.C -- Displays WM_CHAR Messages
                (c) Charles Petzold, 1993
  ---------------------------------------*/

#define INCL_WIN
#define INCL_GPI
#include <os2.h>
#include <stdio.h>
#include "easyfont.h"

#define LCID_FIXEDFONT 1L
#define MAX_KEYS       100

MRESULT EXPENTRY ClientWndProc (HWND, ULONG, MPARAM, MPARAM) ;

CHAR szClientClass [] = "KeyLook" ;

int main (void)
     {
     static ULONG flFrameFlags = FCF_TITLEBAR      | FCF_SYSMENU |
                                 FCF_SIZEBORDER    | FCF_MINMAX  |
                                 FCF_SHELLPOSITION | FCF_TASKLIST ;
     HAB          hab ;
     HMQ          hmq ;
     HWND         hwndFrame, hwndClient ;
     QMSG         qmsg ;

     hab = WinInitialize (0) ;
     hmq = WinCreateMsgQueue (hab, 0) ;
```

Listing 8.1: The KEYLOOK program (Continued)

```
     WinRegisterClass (hab, szClientClass, ClientWndProc, CS_SIZEREDRAW, 0) ;

     hwndFrame = WinCreateStdWindow (HWND_DESKTOP, WS_VISIBLE,
                                     &flFrameFlags, szClientClass, NULL,
                                     0L, 0, 0, &hwndClient) ;
     if (hwndFrame != NULLHANDLE)
          {
          while (WinGetMsg (hab, &qmsg, NULLHANDLE, 0, 0))
               WinDispatchMsg (hab, &qmsg) ;

          WinDestroyWindow (hwndFrame) ;
          }
     WinDestroyMsgQueue (hmq) ;
     WinTerminate (hab) ;
     return 0 ;
     }

MRESULT EXPENTRY ClientWndProc (HWND hwnd, ULONG msg, MPARAM mp1, MPARAM mp2)
     {
     static CHAR   szHeader [] = "Scan  Rept  IN TG IC CM DK LK PD KU"
                                 " AL CT SH SC VK CH  Virt  Char" ;
     static CHAR   szUndrLn [] = "----  ----  -- -- -- -- -- -- -- --"
                                 " -- -- -- -- -- --  ----  ----" ;
     static CHAR   szFormat [] = "%4X %4dx  %2d %2d %2d %2d %2d %2d %2d %2d"
                                 " %2d %2d %2d %2d %2d %2d  %4X  %4X  %c" ;

     static INT    cxChar, cyChar, cyDesc, cxClient, cyClient, iNextKey ;
     static struct {
                   MPARAM mp1 ;
                   MPARAM mp2 ;
                   BOOL   fValid ;
                   }
                   key [MAX_KEYS] ;
     CHAR          szBuffer [80] ;
     FONTMETRICS   fm ;
     HPS           hps ;
     INT           iKey, iIndex, iFlag ;
     POINTL        ptl ;
     RECTL         rcl, rclInvalid ;

     switch (msg)
          {
          case WM_CREATE:
               hps = WinGetPS (hwnd) ;
               EzfQueryFonts (hps) ;

               if (!EzfCreateLogFont (hps, LCID_FIXEDFONT, FONTFACE_MONO,
                                                        FONTSIZE_10, 0))
```

Listing 8.1: The KEYLOOK program (Continued)

```
                    {
                    WinReleasePS (hps) ;

                    WinMessageBox (HWND_DESKTOP, HWND_DESKTOP,
                         "Cannot find the System Monospaced font.",
                         szClientClass, Ø, MB_OK | MB_WARNING) ;

                    return MRFROMSHORT (1) ;
                    }

               GpiSetCharSet (hps, LCID_FIXEDFONT) ;

               GpiQueryFontMetrics (hps, sizeof fm, &fm) ;
               cxChar = fm.lAveCharWidth ;
               cyChar = fm.lMaxBaselineExt ;
               cyDesc = fm.lMaxDescender ;

               GpiSetCharSet (hps, LCID_DEFAULT) ;
               GpiDeleteSetId (hps, LCID_FIXEDFONT) ;
               WinReleasePS (hps) ;
               return Ø ;

          case WM_SIZE:
               cxClient = SHORT1FROMMP (mp2) ;
               cyClient = SHORT2FROMMP (mp2) ;
               return Ø ;

          case WM_CHAR:
               key [iNextKey].mp1 = mp1 ;
               key [iNextKey].mp2 = mp2 ;
               key [iNextKey].fValid = TRUE ;

               iNextKey = (iNextKey + 1) % MAX_KEYS ;

               WinSetRect (hwnd, &rcl,
                         Ø, 2 * cyChar, cxClient, cyClient - 2 * cyChar) ;

               WinScrollWindow (hwnd, Ø, cyChar, &rcl, &rcl, Ø, NULL,
                                                  SW_INVALIDATERGN) ;
               WinUpdateWindow (hwnd) ;
               return Ø ;

          case WM_PAINT:
               hps = WinBeginPaint (hwnd, NULLHANDLE, &rclInvalid) ;
               GpiErase (hps) ;
               EzfCreateLogFont (hps, LCID_FIXEDFONT, FONTFACE_MONO,
                                                       FONTSIZE_1Ø, Ø) ;
               GpiSetCharSet (hps, LCID_FIXEDFONT) ;
```

Listing 8.1: The KEYLOOK program (Continued)

```
          ptl.x = cxChar ;
          ptl.y = cyDesc ;
          GpiCharStringAt (hps, &ptl, sizeof szHeader - 1L, szHeader) ;

          ptl.y += cyChar ;
          GpiCharStringAt (hps, &ptl, sizeof szUndrLn - 1L, szUndrLn) ;

          for (iKey = 0 ; iKey < MAX_KEYS ; iKey++)
               {
               ptl.y += cyChar ;

               iIndex = (iNextKey - iKey - 1 + MAX_KEYS) % MAX_KEYS ;

               if (ptl.y > rclInvalid.yTop ||
                         ptl.y > cyClient - 2 * cyChar ||
                              !key [iIndex].fValid)
                    break ;

               mp1 = key [iIndex].mp1 ;
               mp2 = key [iIndex].mp2 ;

               iFlag = SHORT1FROMMP (mp1) ;

               GpiCharStringAt (hps, &ptl,
                    (LONG) sprintf (szBuffer, szFormat,
                              CHAR4FROMMP (mp1),  // scan code
                              CHAR3FROMMP (mp1),  // repeat count
                              iFlag & KC_INVALIDCHAR ? 1 : 0,
                              iFlag & KC_TOGGLE      ? 1 : 0,
                              iFlag & KC_INVALIDCOMP ? 1 : 0,
                              iFlag & KC_COMPOSITE   ? 1 : 0,
                              iFlag & KC_DEADKEY     ? 1 : 0,
                              iFlag & KC_LONEKEY     ? 1 : 0,
                              iFlag & KC_PREVDOWN    ? 1 : 0,
                              iFlag & KC_KEYUP       ? 1 : 0,
                              iFlag & KC_ALT         ? 1 : 0,
                              iFlag & KC_CTRL        ? 1 : 0,
                              iFlag & KC_SHIFT       ? 1 : 0,
                              iFlag & KC_SCANCODE    ? 1 : 0,
                              iFlag & KC_VIRTUALKEY  ? 1 : 0,
                              iFlag & KC_CHAR        ? 1 : 0,
                              SHORT2FROMMP (mp2),  // virtual key
                              SHORT1FROMMP (mp2),  // character
                              iFlag & KC_CHAR ? SHORT1FROMMP (mp2) : ' '),
                         szBuffer) ;
               }
          ptl.y = cyClient - cyChar + cyDesc ;
          GpiCharStringAt (hps, &ptl, sizeof szHeader - 1L, szHeader) ;
```

Listing 8.1: The KEYLOOK program (Continued)

```
               ptl.y -= cyChar ;
               GpiCharStringAt (hps, &ptl, sizeof szUndrLn - 1L, szUndrLn) ;

               GpiSetCharSet (hps, LCID_DEFAULT) ;
               GpiDeleteSetId (hps, LCID_FIXEDFONT) ;
               WinEndPaint (hps) ;
               return 0 ;
          }
     return WinDefWindowProc (hwnd, msg, mp1, mp2) ;
     }
```

The KEYLOOK.DEF File

```
;-----------------------------------
; KEYLOOK.DEF module definition file
;-----------------------------------

NAME           KEYLOOK   WINDOWAPI

DESCRIPTION    'Key Look Program (c) Charles Petzold, 1993'
PROTMODE
```

Compiling KEYLOOK also requires the EASYFONT.C and EASYFONT.H files from Chapter 5. KEYLOOK uses a fixed-pitch Courier font to ease the display of WM_CHAR information in the window. If a Courier font is not available, KEYLOOK displays a message box and returns 1 from the WM_CREATE message. This aborts creation of the program's window and causes the *WinCreateStdWindow* cell in main to return NULL. Figure 8.3 shows KEYLOOK running under the Presentation Manager after the word "Keyboard" has been typed.

KEYLOOK displays the contents of each WM_CHAR message it receives, starting with the high fields of *mp1* and working down. The heading in KEYLOOK uses abbreviations to identify this information:

Heading	Description
Scan	Hardware scan code in hexadecimal
Rept	Repeat count in decimal
IN	KC_INVALIDCHAR flag (0 or 1)
TG	KC_TOGGLE flag
IC	KC_INVALIDCOMP flag
CM	KC_COMPOSITE flag

```
KEYLOOK.EXE
Scan  Rept  IN TG IC CM DK LK PD KU AL CT SH SC VK CH  Virt  Char
----  ----  -- -- -- -- -- -- -- -- -- -- -- -- -- --  ----  ----

  2A   1x   0  1  0  0  0  0  0  0  0  0  1  1  1  0     9     0
  25   1x   0  0  0  0  0  0  0  0  0  0  1  1  0  1     0    4B  K
  25   1x   0  0  0  0  0  1  0  1  0  0  1  1  0  0     0  254B
  2A   1x   0  1  0  0  0  0  0  1  0  0  0  1  1  0     9     0
  12   1x   0  1  0  0  0  0  0  0  0  0  0  1  0  1     0    65  e
  12   1x   0  1  0  0  0  1  0  1  0  0  0  1  0  0     0  1265
  15   1x   0  0  0  0  0  0  0  0  0  0  0  1  0  1     0    79  y
  15   1x   0  0  0  0  0  1  0  1  0  0  0  1  0  0     0  1579
  30   1x   0  0  0  0  0  0  0  0  0  0  0  1  0  1     0    62  b
  30   1x   0  0  0  0  0  1  0  1  0  0  0  1  0  0     0  3062
  18   1x   0  1  0  0  0  0  0  0  0  0  0  1  0  1     0    6F  o
  18   1x   0  1  0  0  0  1  0  1  0  0  0  1  0  0     0  186F
  1E   1x   0  0  0  0  0  0  0  0  0  0  0  1  0  1     0    61  a
  1E   1x   0  0  0  0  0  1  0  1  0  0  0  1  0  0     0  1E61
  13   1x   0  1  0  0  0  0  0  0  0  0  0  1  0  1     0    72  r
  13   1x   0  1  0  0  0  1  0  1  0  0  0  1  0  0     0  1372
  20   1x   0  0  0  0  0  0  0  0  0  0  0  1  0  1     0    64  d
  20   1x   0  0  0  0  0  1  0  1  0  0  0  1  0  0     0  2064
----  ----  -- -- -- -- -- -- -- -- -- -- -- -- -- --  ----  ----
Scan  Rept  IN TG IC CM DK LK PD KU AL CT SH SC VK CH  Virt  Char
```

Figure 8.3: The KEYLOOK display

Heading	Description
DK	KC_DEADKEY flag
LK	KC_LONEKEY flag
PD	KC_PREVDOWN flag
KU	KC_KEYUP flag
AL	KC_ALT flag
CT	KC_CTRL flag
SH	KC_SHIFT flag
SC	KC_SCANCODE flag
VK	KC_VIRTUALKEY flag
CH	KC_CHAR flag
Virt	Virtual key code in hexadecimal
Char	ASCII character code in hexadecimal

Following the hexadecimal representation of the character code, KEYLOOK also displays the character itself.

THE THREE KEYBOARD CODES

The *mp1* and *mp2* parameters accompanying the WM_CHAR message contain three codes that identify the key or character. These are the hardware scan code, the virtual key code, and the character code.

Hardware scan code If the KC_SCANCODE bit is set, the upper 8 bits of *mp1* contain a valid hardware scan code. The KC_SCANCODE bit is set for all WM_CHAR messages you receive in a window procedure. The hardware scan code can be extracted with the expression

```
CHAR4FROMMP (mp1)
```

or

```
CHARMSG(& msg)->scancode
```

Presentation Manager programs usually ignore this code. The hardware scan codes will be quite different for non-PCs that may run a future version of the Presentation Manager. Using the scan code will guarantee that you'll have to modify your programs to run on these machines. You're also on your own here: There is no support in the header files for using the scan codes; you'll have to do some research on scan code values in the PC technical reference manuals.

Virtual key code If the KC_VIRTUALKEY bit is set, the upper 16 bits of *mp2* contain a valid virtual key code. The virtual key code can be extracted with the expression

```
SHORT2FROMMP (mp2)
```

or

```
CHARMSG(&msg)->vkey
```

If the KC_VIRTUALKEY flag is 0, the upper 16 bits of *mp2* are also set to 0. The virtual key code is used for keys that don't generate characters. The code generally identifies the key being pressed or released independent of the shift states. (The major exception is for the keyboard number pad.) I'll discuss the virtual key codes in detail later in this chapter.

Character code If the KC_CHAR flag is set, the lower 16 bits of *mp2* contain a valid character code. A character code is present in the WM_CHAR message only when the key is being pressed (that is, the KC_KEYUP flag is 0) and the key generates a character. While processing the WM_CHAR message, you can obtain the character code with the expression

```
SHORT1FROMMP (mp2)
```

or

```
CHARMSG(&msg)->chr
```

The character code reflects the state of the Shift key at the time the key is pressed. On IBM PCs and compatibles, this character code is usually from the ASCII character set. For European keyboards, however, the character code could have a value of 128 or above for letters and symbols not present in the ASCII character set. You can better code your programs for easy adaptation to other implementations of the Presentation Manager by making no assumptions about the character set.

If you run KEYLOOK and type a letter key in combination with the Ctrl key, you'll notice that the Presentation Manager sets neither KC_VIRTUALKEY nor KC_CHAR flag to 1 for the letter key.

This presents a problem for programs that need to recognize Ctrl-letter key combinations, such as modem communications programs that need to recognize Ctrl-letter combinations typed at the keyboard in order to send the ASCII control code to the communications port. For example, when the user types Ctrl-S to suspend incoming data, the program needs to convert that key combination to an ASCII code of 0x13 (known as XOFF).

These Ctrl-letter keys have to be handled as a special case: If the KC_VIRTUALKEY, KC_CHAR, and KC_KEYUP flags are set to 0, the KC_CTRL flag is set to 1, and the character code is not 0, the character code is the ASCII code of the letter being typed. You can convert that character code to an ASCII control code with this expression:

```
(CHARMSG(&msg)->chr) & 0x1F
```

PROCESSING VIRTUAL KEYS AND CHARACTERS

The processing of a WM_CHAR message in a window procedure is often divided into two parts: processing character keys and processing noncharacter keys. For a few keys (Enter, Backspace, spacebar, and Tab), both the KC_VIRTUALKEY and KC_CHAR flags are set. You can process these keys as virtual keys or character keys. The number pad generates both virtual codes and character codes if Num Lock is on. I'll discuss the number pad shortly.

The easiest approach is to examine the KC_CHAR flag first and process the character keys if the flag is set. You can then check the KC_VIRTUALKEY flag and process noncharacter keys. The code looks something like this:

```
case WM_CHAR:
          [ other program lines ]
     if (CHARMSG(&msg)->fs & KC_CHAR)
          {
          switch (CHARMSG(&msg)->chr)
               {
                    [ process character keys ]
               }
           }
     else if (CHARMSG(&msg)->fs & KC_VIRTUALKEY)
          {
          switch (CHARMSG(&msg)->vkey)
               {
                    [ process noncharacter keys ]
               }
          }
               [ other program lines ]
     return 1 ;
```

The two sections marked "process character keys" and "process noncharacter keys" each have a series of case statements for processing particular keys or characters.

A Closer Look at Virtual Key Codes When processing a virtual key, you use a switch and case construction to compare the virtual key code to identifiers beginning with VK_ defined in the PMWIN.H header file. The virtual key codes defined in PMWIN.H fall into several categories. Here is the group of identifiers for the function keys:

VK_F1	VK_F7	VK_F13	VK_F19
VK_F2	VK_F8	VK_F14	VK_F20
VK_F3	VK_F9	VK_F15	VK_F21
VK_F4	VK_F10	VK_F16	VK_F22
VK_F5	VK_F11	VK_F17	VK_F23
VK_F6	VK_F12	VK_F18	VK_F24

A machine that runs the Presentation Manager is required to have only the first ten function keys on the keyboard. The others are optional. The function keys don't generate character codes. The F10 key invokes the menu in Presentation Manager programs, so VK_MENU is defined to be the same as VK_F10.

The cursor movement keys generate the following virtual key codes:

VK_LEFT	VK_UP	VK_PAGEUP	VK_HOME
VK_RIGHT	VK_DOWN	VK_PAGEDOWN	VK_END

The Insert and Delete keys generate the following virtual key codes:

VK_INSERT VK_DELETE

The IBM enhanced keyboard has a set of dedicated cursor movement keys, as well as Insert and Delete. These keys always generate the virtual key codes just shown. The KC_CHAR flag is 0.

The number pad on IBM keyboards can be used for either typing numbers or for cursor movement, as well as for inserting or deleting. If Num Lock is toggled off, the number pad generates virtual key codes rather than character codes. If Num Lock is toggled on, the number pad generates the virtual key codes as well as character codes for numbers and the decimal point. For this reason, it's best to process character keys before virtual keys.

The Shift key reverses the meaning of Num Lock for the number pad keys. The virtual key codes for the number pad are important only if your program needs to differentiate between characters from the number pad and the same characters generated otherwise.

The spacebar, Tab, Enter, and Backspace keys generate both virtual codes and character codes. Their virtual key codes are as follows:

VK_SPACE	VK_NEWLINE
VK_TAB	VK_ENTER
VK_BACKSPACE	

The VK_NEWLINE code is generated from the Enter key on the main keyboard, and VK_ENTER is generated from the Enter key on the number pad of the IBM enhanced keyboard. You can process any of these five keys as virtual keys or character keys.

One slightly problematic key combination is Shift-Tab. This combination generates a virtual key code of VK_BACKTAB. But the character code is the same as for an unshifted Tab key. If you differentiate between a Tab and a Shift-Tab, you'll want to process the VK_BACKTAB virtual key before processing character keys. Or you can check the state of the KC_SHIFT flag while processing Tab as a character key.

Although an ASCII character code is defined for Escape, the Escape key generates only a virtual key code: VK_ESC.

The following virtual key code identifiers are for the shift and toggle keys:

K_SHIFT	VK_NUMLOCK
K_CTRL	VK_SCRLLOCK
K_ALT	VK_ALTGRAF
VK_CAPSLOCK	

The VK_ALTGRAF key is the right Alt key on some European versions of the IBM enhanced keyboard.

Certain key combinations generate these virtual key codes:

VK_BREAK	VK_PRINTSCRN
VK_PAUSE	VK_SYSRQ

Although the Presentation Manager does nothing with these key combinations, you may want to process them.

Finally, there are three virtual key codes that you never receive with a WM_CHAR message:

VK_BUTTON1   VK_BUTTON2   VK_BUTTON3

These refer to mouse buttons. I discuss how to use these identifiers in the next chapter.

GOING DOWN, GOING UP

If the user simply presses and releases a key, the window procedure usually receives two WM_CHAR messages. The KC_KEYUP flag in the WM_CHAR *mp1* parameter indicates whether the message signals a key press or release.

Action	**KC_KEYUP**
Key is pressed	0
Key is released	1

For character keys, the KC_CHAR flag is set (and the character code is valid) for key presses. For the Alt key, the window procedure receives only one WM_CHAR message for the key press. The frame window uses the release of the Alt key to activate the program's menu. For the F1 and F10 keys, the window procedure receives a WM_CHAR message only for the release. The window procedure receives a WM_HELP message for the F1 key press.

Often the key-down and key-up WM_CHAR messages come in pairs with nothing in between, but that's not always the case. For example, when the user presses the Shift key and a letter and then releases the letter and the Shift key, the program receives four WM_CHAR messages, in this order:

Action	KC_KEYUP	Virtual Key	Character
Press Shift	0	VK_SHIFT	0
Press A key	0	0	A
Release A key	1	0	A
Release Shift	1	VK_SHIFT	0

For most purposes, you can ignore these WM_CHAR messages when the KC_KEYUP bit is set to 1. Thus the processing of the WM_CHAR message can include logic like this:

```
case WM_CHAR:
          [ other program lines ]
     if (CHARMSG(&msg)->fs & KC_KEYUP)
          return Ø ;
          [ other program lines ]
```

If the user presses and holds down the key, the program receives a series of WM_CHAR messages because of the typematic action of the key. This is indicated by the KC_PREVDOWN flag:

Action	KC_KEYUP	KC_PREVDOWN
Key is pressed	0	0
Key is held down	0	1
Key is released	1	0

You receive one WM_CHAR message when the key is initially pressed, a series of messages as the key is held down, and a final WM_CHAR message when the key is released. A program can use the KC_PREVDOWN flag to distinguish between an initial key press and a typematic repeat of a key. Note that the KC_PREVDOWN flag is not set when the key is released, even though the key was previously down.

The *mp1* parameter also contains an 8-bit repeat count that you can extract with the expression

```
CHAR3FROMMP (mp1)
```

or

```
CHARMSG(&msg)->cRepeat
```

Most often, this value is 1. It can be greater than 1 only for a typematic repeat when the KC_KEYUP flag is 0 and KC_PREVDOWN is 1. A repeat count greater than 1 indicates that the keyboard hardware generated a typematic repeat of a keystroke while a WM_CHAR message for the same key was still in the message queue. What it really indicates is that your program can't keep up with the pace of typematic key repeats.

How you handle the repeat count requires some thought. We've all experienced the nuisance of "overscrolling" a word processing document or spreadsheet. By ignoring the repeat count, you avoid this problem. But you probably always want to use the repeat count when processing character input. This usually involves a simple *for* loop in the WM_CHAR processing:

```
for (i = 0 ; i < CHARMSG(&msg)->cRepeat ; i++)
     {
          [ process key ]
     }
```

The KC_LONEKEY flag is set only for a key release. It indicates that no other key was pressed between the time the key was pressed and released. You can ignore the KC_LONEKEY flag unless you think of a particular application for it.

THE SHIFT STATES

The KC_SHIFT, KC_CTRL, and KC_ALT flags in the WM_CHAR *mp1* parameter indicate the state of the Shift, Ctrl, and Alt keys at the time a key was pressed or released. When the flag is set to 1, the Shift key was pressed. You can also use the *WinGetKeyState* function (discussed later in this chapter) to obtain this information. When you process a character key, you don't have to look at the KC_SHIFT flag because the character code itself is based on the current state of the Shift key. The shift-state information is most useful during WM_CHAR messages for noncharacter keys, particularly the cursor movement keys.

The KC_TOGGLE flag is most useful for the Caps Lock, Num Lock, and Scroll Lock keys if your program displays the current state of these keys. The KC_TOGGLE flag is set if the keystroke is turning on the lock state. However, you can treat any key as a toggle key by examining this flag.

The KC_DEADKEY, KC_COMPOSITE, and KC_INVALIDCOMP flags are used with "dead keys" generated from some European keyboards. I'll discuss these flags in reference to the upcoming TYPEAWAY program.

OTHER KEYBOARD MESSAGES AND FUNCTIONS

Although processing the WM_CHAR message is the most important part of keyboard handling, it's not the only part: Several other important concepts, messages, and functions relate to the keyboard. We'll look at these and then apply this information in a program that illustrates several aspects of keyboard handling.

ACTIVE WINDOWS AND FOCUS WINDOWS

The keyboard must be shared among all applications running under the Presentation Manager. When a keyboard event occurs, the Presentation Manager stores the information about the event in the system message queue. The Presentation Manager later converts this event to a WM_CHAR message posted to a particular program message queue for a particular window. The window that gets the WM_CHAR message is the window with the "input focus," also called the "focus window."

The concept of input focus is closely related to the concept of active window. The *active window* is always a top-level window, that is, a child of the desktop window. The active window is positioned above all other top-level windows on the screen. A standard window frame indicates that it is active by highlighting its title bar. A dialog box indicates that it is active by highlighting its border. The user generally controls which window is active by using the Alt-Esc or Alt-Tab key combinations to switch from one window to another or by clicking on a particular window with the mouse.

The focus window (if any) is always the active window itself or a descendant of the active window. The Presentation Manager posts WM_CHAR messages to the focus window. When a program first creates a standard window, the frame window is the active window, and the client window is the focus window.

Thus, in a standard window without any additional child windows, the client window procedure always receives WM_CHAR messages when the frame window is active. (If the program creates some children of the client window, these child windows can get the input focus. We'll examine this subject in Chapter 11.) If a particular descendant of the active window has the input focus when the user changes the active window by pressing Alt-Esc or Alt-Tab, the same descendant regains the input focus when the frame window again becomes active.

The Presentation Manager sends a WM_SETFOCUS message to a window procedure when the window is gaining the input focus or losing the input focus. A program can determine which window has the input focus by calling the *WinQueryFocus* function. We'll use this message and function in the TYPE-AWAY program coming up soon.

I mentioned at the beginning of this section that the Presentation Manager first stores keyboard messages in a system message queue. It does this because one of these messages (an Alt-Tab key combination, for instance) could change the active window and hence the window with the input focus. The messages for the keys that follow the Alt-Tab must go to a different program. This wouldn't work properly if the messages were posted in a program's message queue when the keystrokes occurred.

GETTING KEYBOARD STATES

A program can obtain the state of a particular key at any time by calling

```
lKeyState = WinGetKeyState (HWND_DESKTOP, lVirtKey) ;
```

The *lVirtKey* parameter can be any of the virtual key identifiers beginning with VK. The *lKeyState* return value has the high bit set if the key is down. Because *WinGetKeyState* returns a signed long integer, you can determine if a key is down simply by testing if the return value is negative. The low bit is set if the key is toggled on. The low bit has little meaning for keys other than toggle keys, but it can allow you to treat any key as a toggle key.

WinGetKeyState is synchronized with the WM_CHAR messages. It reports that a particular key is pressed or released only if the WM_CHAR message for the press or release has already been retrieved from the message queue. This synchronization is to your advantage: If you call *WinGetKeyState* during processing of a WM_CHAR message, it reports the state of keys at the time of the keyboard action that resulted in the message. If you need to know the state of a key "right now" rather than as of the most recent WM_CHAR message, you can call the *WinGetPhysKeyState* function instead.

USING A CURSOR

When you process keystrokes, you often echo characters to the client window. To indicate where the next character will appear in the client window, a program can create a cursor.

Note: The terminology used in Microsoft Windows is different from the Presentation Manager terminology. The small bitmap on the screen that you move with the mouse is called the pointer. In Windows it is called the cursor. The Presentation Manager cursor is a small blinking box or line generally indicating an entry point for keyboard input. In Windows this is called the *caret.* There are no carets in the Presentation Manager. You point with the mouse and curse with the keyboard.

You create a cursor using the function

```
WinCreateCursor (hwnd, xPos, yPos, cxWidth, cyHeight, flFlags, &rclClip) ;
```

The *xPos* and *yPos* parameters indicate where the lower-left corner of the cursor is to appear relative to the lower-left corner of *hwnd.* Generally, the lower-left corner of the cursor will correspond to the lower-left corner of a character cell.

The *cxWidth* and *cyHeight* parameters are the size of the cursor. You can use 0 for either of the two parameters to set the size equal to the width of a thin border. These are the most common combinations of *cxWidth* and *cyHeight* (based on *cxChar* and *cyChar* character dimensions):

cxWidth	cyHeight	Cursor Form
cxChar	cyChar	Box
cxChar	0	Underline
0	cyChar	Vertical line

The box and underline cursors most closely mimic cursors in nongraphics programs. The vertical line cursor is the best suited for use with a font with variable character widths because you can position the vertical line between two adjacent characters. If you use a box or underline cursor with a variable-pitch font, you have to change the width of the cursor as it's moved over the characters. This requires that you destroy and recreate the cursor—a nuisance for you, and an annoyance to the user, who would be faced with a pulsating cursor.

The *flFlags* parameter can be CURSOR_SOLID (which equals 0, so it's the default) for a solid cursor or CURSOR_HALFTONE for a cursor with only half the bits present. You can use the C bitwise OR operator to include the CURSOR_FLASH flag and make a blinking cursor. If you create a box cursor, you can include the CURSOR_FRAME flag to draw only the frame of the cursor and not the interior.

The last parameter to *WinCreateCursor* is a pointer to a RECTL structure, which defines a clipping region relative to *hwnd.* The cursor won't be visible outside this rectangle. Specifying NULL for this parameter sets the clipping region equal to the entire area of the window at the time of the *WinCreate-Cursor* call.

When the cursor is first created, it is invisible. You can show it by calling

```
WinShowCursor (hwnd, TRUE) ;
```

You can hide the cursor by calling

```
WinShowCursor (hwnd, FALSE) ;
```

You need to hide the cursor when you write to the screen during a message other than WM_PAINT.

After the cursor is created, you can change the position with another call to *WinCreateCursor*:

```
WinCreateCursor (hwnd, xPos, yPos, 0, 0, CURSOR_SETPOS, NULL) ;
```

This is a special version of the *WinCreateCursor* call. The size and clipping region parameters are ignored. The only flag you can use is CURSOR_SETPOS. (Do not, however, use CURSOR_SETPOS when you are creating the cursor.)

Finally, to destroy the cursor, you call

```
WinDestroyCursor (hwnd) ;
```

When using a cursor, you must remember this very important rule: Only one cursor can be present in the Presentation Manager at any time. Do not create a cursor during the WM_CREATE message and destroy it during WM_DESTROY. Instead, you create the cursor when the window gets the input focus and destroy the cursor when the window loses the input focus. And take note of this: If the clipping region of the cursor depends on the size of the window (as it does if you specify NULL as the last parameter to *WinCreateCursor* when you create the cursor), you should destroy and re-create the cursor when you receive a WM_SIZE message. This is the only way to change the clipping region of the cursor.

The cursor logic can be tricky, so let's look at the code involved with maintaining a cursor in the context of a program that also does other keyboard handling.

SAMPLE KEYBOARD PROCESSING

The TYPEAWAY program, shown in Listing 8.2, demonstrates several of the concepts covered in this chapter. When TYPEAWAY's window first appears, the cursor is positioned in the upper-left corner of the client window. To use the program, simply type away. What you type is what you see.

TYPEAWAY uses a fixed-pitch Courier font and requires the EASYFONT.C and EASYFONT.H files shown in Chapter 5.

Listing 8.2: The TYPEAWAY program

The TYPEAWAY.MAK File

```
#-----------------------
# TYPEAWAY.MAK make file
#-----------------------

typeaway.exe : typeaway.obj easyfont.obj typeaway.def
     $(PRGLINK) typeaway easyfont, typeaway, NUL, $(PRGLIB), typeaway

typeaway.obj : typeaway.c easyfont.h
     $(PRGCC) typeaway.c

easyfont.obj : easyfont.c easyfont.h
     $(PRGCC) easyfont.c
```

The TYPEAWAY.C File

```
/*-----------------------------------------
   TYPEAWAY.C -- Typing Program
                 (c) Charles Petzold, 1993
  -----------------------------------------*/

#define INCL_WIN
#define INCL_GPI
#include <os2.h>
#include <stdio.h>
#include <stdlib.h>
#include "easyfont.h"

#define LCID_FIXEDFONT 1L
#define BUFFER(x,y) (*(pBuffer + y * xMax + x))

MRESULT EXPENTRY ClientWndProc (HWND, ULONG, MPARAM, MPARAM) ;

CHAR szClientClass [] = "TypeAway" ;
HAB  hab ;

int main (void)
     {
     static ULONG flFrameFlags = FCF_TITLEBAR      | FCF_SYSMENU |
                                 FCF_SIZEBORDER    | FCF_MINMAX  |
                                 FCF_SHELLPOSITION | FCF_TASKLIST ;
     HMQ          hmq ;
     HWND         hwndFrame, hwndClient ;
     QMSG         qmsg ;

     hab = WinInitialize (0) ;
```

Listing 8.2: The TYPEAWAY program (Continued)

```
     hmq = WinCreateMsgQueue (hab, 0) ;

     WinRegisterClass (hab, szClientClass, ClientWndProc, CS_SIZEREDRAW, 0) ;

     hwndFrame = WinCreateStdWindow (HWND_DESKTOP, WS_VISIBLE,
                                     &flFrameFlags, szClientClass, NULL,
                                     0L, 0, 0, &hwndClient) ;
     if (hwndFrame != NULLHANDLE)
          {
          while (WinGetMsg (hab, &qmsg, NULLHANDLE, 0, 0))
               WinDispatchMsg (hab, &qmsg) ;

          WinDestroyWindow (hwndFrame) ;
          }
     WinDestroyMsgQueue (hmq) ;
     WinTerminate (hab) ;
     return 0 ;
     }

VOID GetCharXY (HPS hps, INT *pcxChar, INT *pcyChar, INT *pcyDesc)
     {
     FONTMETRICS fm ;

     GpiQueryFontMetrics (hps, sizeof fm, &fm) ;
     *pcxChar = fm.lAveCharWidth ;
     *pcyChar = fm.lMaxBaselineExt ;
     *pcyDesc = fm.lMaxDescender ;
     }

MRESULT EXPENTRY ClientWndProc (HWND hwnd, ULONG msg, MPARAM mp1, MPARAM mp2)
     {
     static BOOL  fInsertMode = FALSE ;
     static CHAR  *pBuffer ;
     static INT   cxClient, cyClient, cxChar, cyChar, cyDesc,
                  xCursor, yCursor, xMax,  yMax ;
     BOOL         fProcessed ;
     CHAR         szBuffer [20] ;
     HPS          hps ;
     INT          iRep, i ;
     POINTL       ptl ;
     RECTL        rcl ;

     switch (msg)
          {
          case WM_CREATE:
               hps = WinGetPS (hwnd) ;
               EzfQueryFonts (hps) ;

               if (!EzfCreateLogFont (hps, LCID_FIXEDFONT, FONTFACE_MONO,
```

Listing 8.2: The TYPEAWAY program (Continued)

```
                                                        FONTSIZE_10, 0))
                    {
                    WinReleasePS (hps) ;

                    WinMessageBox (HWND_DESKTOP, HWND_DESKTOP,
                         "Cannot find the System Monospaced font.",
                         szClientClass, 0, MB_OK | MB_WARNING) ;

                    return MRFROMSHORT (1) ;
                    }

               GpiSetCharSet (hps, LCID_FIXEDFONT) ;

               GetCharXY (hps, &cxChar, &cyChar, &cyDesc) ;

               GpiSetCharSet (hps, LCID_DEFAULT) ;
               GpiDeleteSetId (hps, LCID_FIXEDFONT) ;
               WinReleasePS (hps) ;
               return 0 ;

          case WM_SIZE:
               cxClient = SHORT1FROMMP (mp2) ;
               cyClient = SHORT2FROMMP (mp2) ;

               xMax = cxClient / cxChar ;
               yMax = cyClient / cyChar - 2 ;

               if (pBuffer != NULL)
                    free (pBuffer) ;

               if (NULL == (pBuffer = malloc (xMax * yMax + 1)))
                    {
                    WinMessageBox (HWND_DESKTOP, hwnd,
                         "Cannot allocate memory for text buffer.\n"
                         "Try a smaller window.", szClientClass, 0,
                         MB_OK | MB_WARNING) ;

                    xMax = yMax = 0 ;
                    }
               else
                    {
                    for (i = 0 ; i < xMax * yMax ; i++)
                         BUFFER (i, 0) = ' ' ;

                    xCursor = 0 ;
                    yCursor = 0 ;
                    }

               if (hwnd == WinQueryFocus (HWND_DESKTOP))
```

Listing 8.2: The TYPEAWAY program (Continued)

```
          {
          WinDestroyCursor (hwnd) ;

          WinCreateCursor (hwnd, 0, cyClient - cyChar,
                           cxChar, cyChar,
                           CURSOR_SOLID | CURSOR_FLASH, NULL) ;

          WinShowCursor (hwnd, xMax > 0 && yMax > 0) ;
          }
     return 0 ;

case WM_SETFOCUS:
     if (SHORT1FROMMP (mp2))
          {
          WinCreateCursor (hwnd, cxChar * xCursor,
                           cyClient - cyChar * (1 + yCursor),
                           cxChar, cyChar,
                           CURSOR_SOLID | CURSOR_FLASH, NULL) ;

          WinShowCursor (hwnd, xMax > 0 && yMax > 0) ;
          }
     else
          WinDestroyCursor (hwnd) ;
     return 0 ;

case WM_CHAR:
     if (xMax == 0 || yMax == 0)
          return 0 ;

     if (CHARMSG(&msg)->fs & KC_KEYUP)
          return 0 ;

     if (CHARMSG(&msg)->fs & KC_INVALIDCHAR)
          return 0 ;

     if (CHARMSG(&msg)->fs & KC_INVALIDCOMP)
          {
          xCursor = (xCursor + 1) % xMax ;        // Advance cursor
          if (xCursor == 0)
               yCursor = (yCursor + 1) % yMax ;

          WinAlarm (HWND_DESKTOP, WA_ERROR) ;     // And beep
          }

     for (iRep = 0 ; iRep < CHARMSG(&msg)->cRepeat ; iRep++)
          {
          fProcessed = FALSE ;

          ptl.x = xCursor * cxChar ;
```

Listing 8.2: The TYPEAWAY program (Continued)

```
               ptl.y = cyClient - cyChar * (yCursor + 1) + cyDesc ;

                         /*--------------------------
                            Process some virtual keys
                           --------------------------*/

               if (CHARMSG(&msg)->fs & KC_VIRTUALKEY)
                    {
                    fProcessed = TRUE ;

                    switch (CHARMSG(&msg)->vkey)
                         {
                                   /*---------------
                                      Backspace key
                                     ---------------*/

                         case VK_BACKSPACE:
                              if (xCursor > 0)
                                   {
                                   WinSendMsg (hwnd, WM_CHAR,
                                        MPFROM2SHORT (KC_VIRTUALKEY, 1),
                                        MPFROM2SHORT (0, VK_LEFT)) ;

                                   WinSendMsg (hwnd, WM_CHAR,
                                        MPFROM2SHORT (KC_VIRTUALKEY, 1),
                                        MPFROM2SHORT (0, VK_DELETE)) ;
                                   }
                              break ;

                                   /*---------
                                      Tab key
                                     ---------*/

                         case VK_TAB:
                              i = min (8 - xCursor % 8, xMax - xCursor) ;

                              WinSendMsg (hwnd, WM_CHAR,
                                   MPFROM2SHORT (KC_CHAR, i),
                                   MPFROM2SHORT ((USHORT) ' ', 0)) ;
                              break ;

                                   /*------------------------
                                      Backtab (Shift-Tab) key
                                     ------------------------*/

                         case VK_BACKTAB:
                              if (xCursor > 0)
```

Listing 8.2: The TYPEAWAY program (Continued)

```
                              {
                              i = (xCursor - 1) % 8 + 1 ;

                              WinSendMsg (hwnd, WM_CHAR,
                                   MPFROM2SHORT (KC_VIRTUALKEY, i),
                                   MPFROM2SHORT (Ø, VK_LEFT)) ;
                              }
                         break ;

                              /*------------------------
                                 Newline and Enter keys
                                ------------------------*/

                    case VK_NEWLINE:
                    case VK_ENTER:
                         xCursor = Ø ;
                         yCursor = (yCursor + 1) % yMax ;
                         break ;

                    default:
                         fProcessed = FALSE ;
                         break ;
                    }
               }

                    /*------------------------
                       Process character keys
                      ------------------------*/

          if (!fProcessed && ((CHARMSG(&msg)->fs & KC_CHAR) ||
                              (CHARMSG(&msg)->fs & KC_DEADKEY)))
               {
                                        // Shift line if fInsertMode
               if (fInsertMode)
                    for (i = xMax - 1 ; i > xCursor ; i--)
                         BUFFER (i, yCursor) =
                              BUFFER (i - 1, yCursor) ;

                                        // Store character in buffer

               BUFFER (xCursor, yCursor) =
                                   (CHAR) CHARMSG(&msg)->chr ;

                                        // Display char or new line

               WinShowCursor (hwnd, FALSE) ;
               hps = WinGetPS (hwnd) ;

               EzfCreateLogFont (hps, LCID_FIXEDFONT,
```

Listing 8.2: The TYPEAWAY program (Continued)

```
                                    FONTFACE_MONO, FONTSIZE_10, 0) ;
                    GpiSetCharSet (hps, LCID_FIXEDFONT) ;
                    GpiSetBackMix (hps, BM_OVERPAINT) ;

                    if (fInsertMode)
                         GpiCharStringAt (hps, &ptl,
                                          (LONG) (xMax - xCursor),
                                          & BUFFER (xCursor, yCursor)) ;
                    else
                         GpiCharStringAt (hps, &ptl, 1L,
                                          (CHAR *) & CHARMSG(&msg)->chr) ;

                    GpiSetCharSet (hps, LCID_DEFAULT) ;
                    GpiDeleteSetId (hps, LCID_FIXEDFONT) ;
                    WinReleasePS (hps) ;
                    WinShowCursor (hwnd, TRUE) ;

                                             // Increment cursor

                    if (!(CHARMSG(&msg)->fs & KC_DEADKEY))
                         if (0 == (xCursor = (xCursor + 1) % xMax))
                              yCursor = (yCursor + 1) % yMax ;

                    fProcessed = TRUE ;
                    }

                         /*----------------------------------
                           Process remaining virtual keys
                           ----------------------------------*/

               if (!fProcessed && CHARMSG(&msg)->fs & KC_VIRTUALKEY)
                    {
                    fProcessed = TRUE ;

                    switch (CHARMSG(&msg)->vkey)
                         {
                                   /*----------------------
                                     Cursor movement keys
                                     ----------------------*/

                         case VK_LEFT:
                              xCursor = (xCursor - 1 + xMax) % xMax ;

                              if (xCursor == xMax - 1)
                                   yCursor = (yCursor - 1 + yMax) % yMax ;
                              break ;

                         case VK_RIGHT:
                              xCursor = (xCursor + 1) % xMax ;
```

Listing 8.2: The TYPEAWAY program (Continued)

```
          if (xCursor == 0)
               yCursor = (yCursor + 1) % yMax ;
          break ;

     case VK_UP:
          yCursor = max (yCursor - 1, 0) ;
          break ;

     case VK_DOWN:
          yCursor = min (yCursor + 1, yMax - 1) ;
          break ;

     case VK_PAGEUP:
          yCursor = 0 ;
          break ;

     case VK_PAGEDOWN:
          yCursor = yMax - 1 ;
          break ;

     case VK_HOME:
          xCursor = 0 ;
          break ;

     case VK_END:
          xCursor = xMax - 1 ;
          break ;

               /*------------
                 Insert key
                ------------*/

     case VK_INSERT:
          fInsertMode = fInsertMode ? FALSE : TRUE ;
          WinSetRect (hab, &rcl, 0, 0,
                           cxClient, cyChar) ;
          WinInvalidateRect (hwnd, &rcl, FALSE) ;
          break ;

               /*------------
                 Delete key
                ------------*/

     case VK_DELETE:
          for (i = xCursor ; i < xMax - 1 ; i++)
               BUFFER (i, yCursor) =
                    BUFFER (i + 1, yCursor) ;
```

Listing 8.2: The TYPEAWAY program (Continued)

```
                                        BUFFER (xMax, yCursor) = ' ' ;

                                        WinShowCursor (hwnd, FALSE) ;
                                        hps = WinGetPS (hwnd) ;
                                        EzfCreateLogFont (hps, LCID_FIXEDFONT,
                                                  FONTFACE_MONO, FONTSIZE_10, 0) ;
                                        GpiSetCharSet (hps, LCID_FIXEDFONT) ;
                                        GpiSetBackMix (hps, BM_OVERPAINT) ;

                                        GpiCharStringAt (hps, &ptl,
                                                  (LONG) (xMax - xCursor),
                                                  & BUFFER (xCursor, yCursor)) ;

                                        GpiSetCharSet (hps, LCID_DEFAULT) ;
                                        GpiDeleteSetId (hps, LCID_FIXEDFONT) ;
                                        WinReleasePS (hps) ;
                                        WinShowCursor (hwnd, TRUE) ;
                                        break ;

                                   default:
                                        fProcessed = FALSE ;
                                        break ;
                                   }
                              }
                         }
                    WinCreateCursor (hwnd, cxChar * xCursor,
                                           cyClient - cyChar * (1 + yCursor),
                                           0, 0, CURSOR_SETPOS, NULL) ;
                    return 0 ;

               case WM_PAINT:
                    hps = WinBeginPaint (hwnd, NULLHANDLE, NULL) ;
                    GpiErase (hps) ;
                    EzfCreateLogFont (hps, LCID_FIXEDFONT, FONTFACE_MONO,
                                                           FONTSIZE_10, 0) ;
                    GpiSetCharSet (hps, LCID_FIXEDFONT) ;

                    ptl.x = cxChar ;
                    ptl.y = cyDesc ;
                    GpiCharStringAt (hps, &ptl,
                                 (LONG) sprintf (szBuffer, "Insert Mode: %s",
                                                  fInsertMode ? "ON" : "OFF"),
                                 szBuffer) ;

                    ptl.x = 0 ;
                    ptl.y = 3 * cyChar / 2 ;
                    GpiMove (hps, &ptl) ;

                    ptl.x = cxClient ;
```

Listing 8.2: The TYPEAWAY program (Continued)

```
               GpiLine (hps, &ptl) ;

               if (xMax > 0 && yMax > 0)
                    {
                    for (i = 0 ; i < yMax ; i++)
                         {
                         ptl.x = 0 ;
                         ptl.y = cyClient - cyChar * (i + 1) + cyDesc ;

                         GpiCharStringAt (hps, &ptl, (LONG) xMax,
                                              & BUFFER (0, i)) ;
                         }
                    }
               GpiSetCharSet (hps, LCID_DEFAULT) ;
               GpiDeleteSetId (hps, LCID_FIXEDFONT) ;
               WinEndPaint (hps) ;
               return 0 ;

          case WM_DESTROY:
               if (pBuffer != NULL)
                    free (pBuffer) ;
               break ;
          }
     return WinDefWindowProc (hwnd, msg, mp1, mp2) ;
     }
```

The TYPEAWAY.DEF File

```
;-------------------------------------
; TYPEAWAY.DEF module definition file
;-------------------------------------

NAME           TYPEAWAY  WINDOWAPI

DESCRIPTION    'Typing Program (c) Charles Petzold, 1993'
PROTMODE
```

You can move the cursor to any position within the client window using the cursor movement keys. They work as follows:

Key	Cursor Movement
Right Arrow	One character right (wraps to next line)
Left Arrow	One character left (wraps to previous line)
Down Arrow	One line down

Key	Cursor Movement
Up Arrow	One line up
Home	Beginning of line
End	End of line
PgUp	Top line (same column position)
PgDn	Bottom line (same column position)

TYPEAWAY also processes the following keys:

Key	Action
Insert	Turn Insert mode on and off
Delete	Delete character at cursor position, move rest of line to left
Return	Move cursor to beginning of next line
Tab	Move cursor to next tab position based on 8-column increments
Shift-Tab	Move cursor to previous tab position
Backspace	Delete character to left of cursor, move rest of line to left

The characters you type are stored in a block of memory allocated using *malloc*. This allows TYPEAWAY to re-create the client window when the window procedure receives a WM_PAINT message. TYPEAWAY frees this memory block and allocates a new one whenever the size of the window changes. This means that the contents of the buffer aren't preserved following a WM_SIZE message.

Let's first isolate the cursor logic, because that is perhaps the trickiest to deal with. Cursor creation and destruction occur during processing of the WM_SETFOCUS message:

```
case WM_SETFOCUS:
     if (SHORT1FROMMP (mp2))
          {
          WinCreateCursor (hwnd, cxChar * xCursor,
               cyClient - cyChar * (1 + yCursor,
               cxChar, cyChar,
               CURSOR_SOLID | CURSOR_FLASH, NULL) ;

          WinShowCursor (hwnd, xMax > 0 && yMax > 0) ;
          }
     else
          WinDestroyCursor (hwnd) ;
     return 0 ;
```

The *mp2* parameter is nonzero if the window is getting the input focus and 0 if it's losing the input focus. These two types of WM_SETFOCUS messages are equally balanced during the lifetime of a window. This ensures that the program doesn't attempt to create a second cursor or destroy a nonexistent cursor. The window loses the input focus before it's destroyed, at which time the cursor will also be destroyed.

When the TYPEAWAY client window receives the input focus, it creates a solid blinking cursor which it positions based on the size of the client area, the size of a character, and the cursor position (in terms of a row and column) stored in the variables *xCursor* and *yCursor.* The *WinShowCursor* function normally requires TRUE as the second parameter to display the cursor. The *xMax* and *yMax* variables are the number of character columns and rows in the client window, so this code displays the cursor only if the client window can fit at least one character.

The cursor is also destroyed and re-created during processing of the WM_SIZE message. This is necessary to change the clipping region of the cursor when the window size changes. But note that TYPEAWAY does this only if the client window has the input focus. Otherwise, the cursor doesn't exist and will be re-created during the next WM_SETFOCUS message.

```
if (hwnd == WinQueryFocus (HWND_DESKTOP, FALSE))
     {
     WinDestroyCursor (hwnd) ;

     WinCreateCursor (hwnd, 0, cyClient - cyChar,
          cxChar, cyChar,
          CURSOR_SOLID | CURSOR_FLASH, NULL) ;

     WinShowCursor (hwnd, xMax > 0 && yMax > 0) ;
     }
```

The cursor is automatically hidden during a WM_PAINT message. This prevents a program from writing over the cursor. However, if you write on the window during messages other than WM_PAINT (as TYPEAWAY does), you must hide and show the cursor. TYPEAWAY writes on the window during WM_CHAR. Before calling *WinGetPS,* the cursor is hidden:

```
WinShowCursor (hwnd, FALSE) ;
```

After a call to *WinReleasePS,* the cursor is shown again:

```
WinShowCursor (hwnd, TRUE) ;
```

After the key has been processed and the character (if any) written to the client window, the cursor is repositioned:

```
WinCreateCursor (hwnd, cxChar * xCursor,
    cyClient - cyChar * (1 + yCursor),
     Ø, Ø, CURSOR_SETPOS, NULL) ;
```

The processing of the WM_CHAR message is fairly straightfoward and easy to follow because of the switch and case structure. The program first checks to see that at least one character can fit in the client window:

```
if (xMax == Ø || yMax == Ø)
     return Ø ;
```

It then checks to see that the message is for a key press:

```
if (CHARMSG(&msg)->fs & KC_KEYUP)
     return Ø ;
```

Most of the key processing logic is repeated based on the repeat count:

```
for (iRep = Ø ; iRep < CHARMSG(&msg)->cRepeat ; iRep++)
```

TYPEAWAY also throws away WM_CHAR messages whenever the KC_INVALIDCHAR flag is set. (This is rarely the case.)

I've chosen to process some virtual keys first. These are the Backspace, Tab, Shift-Tab, and Enter keys, which also generate character codes.

The Backspace, Tab, and Shift-Tab keys are processed by sending the window function other WM_CHAR messages. This simplifies the logic for these keys. The character keys are processed next by displaying the character at the current cursor position. Then, the remaining virtual keys (cursor movement keys, Insert, and Delete) are processed.

DEAD KEYS AND FOREIGN LANGUAGE KEYBOARDS

TYPEAWAY shows the correct processing of dead keys and composite keys. These keys are generated on some foreign language keyboards to create characters containing diacritics (sometimes called accent marks). These characters require two keystrokes. The first keystroke is the diacritic itself and is called a *dead key.* The second keystroke is a letter and is called a *composite key.* The letter is combined with the diacritic mark to form a composite character.

You can process dead keys and composite keys using the KC_DEADKEY, KC_COMPOSITE, and KC_INVALIDCOMP flags that accompany the WM_CHAR message. This will allow your program to be converted more easily to a foreign language. If foreign language conversion is not of concern to you, you can ignore these flags. A compromise approach is to throw away

WM_CHAR messages when the KC_DEADKEY flag is set. Near the beginning of your WM_CHAR processing, you'd have

```
if (CHARMSG(&msg)->fs & KC_DEADKEY)
     return 0 ;
```

But this doesn't give good feedback to the user or provide error processing of incorrect combinations of dead keys and letters.

If you add dead-key logic to your program, you'll need to test the logic. You must make the Presentation Manager believe that it is running on a foreign language keyboard that uses dead keys (for example, the German keyboard), by issuing the following statement from an OS/2 command line:

```
KEYB GR
```

You'll probably find that using this German keyboard is not easy. The Y and Z keys are reversed, and all the symbols are in different places. You can switch to the U.S. keyboard and codepage using the following OS/2 command:

```
KEYB US
```

Here's how dead keys work: A German user who wishes to type a letter with a diacritic first presses the dead key. The key corresponding to the + and = key on the U.S. keyboard generates dead keys on the German keyboard. When unshifted, the dead key is an acute diacritic (´). When shifted, the dead key is a grave diacritic (`). A Presentation Manager program should display this diacritic but not advance the cursor.

The user then follows this dead key with an uppercase or lowercase A, E, I, O, or U. The resultant character is the letter with the diacritic. The program displays this character and advances the cursor. If the user wants to type the acute or grave mark by itself, he or she follows the dead key by pressing the spacebar. A dead key followed by any other key is considered an error, and the program should indicate this by beeping. In this case, your program should advance the cursor past the diacritic and display the new key anyway, just as if the dead key were followed by the spacebar and then the new key.

The TYPEAWAY's code for correctly handling dead-key combinations is not very large. You can consider three cases:

- **Case 1** If the KC_CHAR and KC_DEADKEY flags are set, the character code is the code for the diacritic. You display this character, but do not advance the cursor. In TYPEAWAY, this is handled at the end of the section that processes character keys. The character is stored in the buffer and displayed, but the cursor is advanced only if the KC_DEADKEY flag is not set.

- **Case 2** If the KC_CHAR and KC_COMPOSITE flags are set, the character accompanying the message will be the composite character. (If the dead key is followed by a spacebar, the character code accompanying the WM_CHAR message for the spacebar is the previous dead-key character.) You display the character and advance the cursor. This is exactly how you process a normal character key, so you do not need to check the KC_COMPOSITE flag. TYPEAWAY ignores it.
- **Case 3** If the KC_INVALIDCOMP flag is set, the dead key was followed by a character or virtual key that cannot be combined with the dead key. You advance the cursor past the dead key and beep the speaker to indicate an error. Then you process the WM_CHAR message as usual. In TYPEAWAY, this is done near the beginning of the WM_CHAR message processing.

READING CHARACTER STRINGS

Because a program gets WM_CHAR messages one at a time, there doesn't seem to be anything in the Presentation Manager that corresponds to the *KbdStringIn* function to read an entire character string. In the Presentation Manager you do this a little differently. You create a child window control of the predefined WC_ENTRYFIELD class. This window accepts typed input, understands cursor movement keys, and can even scroll the input left and right if it's too long to fit in the window. We'll create such a child window control in Chapter 14.

Taming the Mouse

MOUSE AND POINTER BASICS

MOUSE BUTTONS AND HIT-TESTING

TRACKING AND CAPTURING

Chapter 9

All user input to a Presentation Manager program comes from the keyboard and the mouse. The keyboard is adequate for alphanumeric input and rudimentary cursor movement. The mouse provides a more intimate connection between the user and the objects on the screen. As an extension of the user's fingers, the mouse can point, grab, and move. As you've seen in the sample programs from previous chapters, the Presentation Manager takes care of all mouse input involving menus, scroll bars, and the moving and sizing of windows. Your programs will be concerned mostly with mouse activity that occurs within the client window.

When you program for the Presentation Manager, however, you should try to duplicate the most common mouse functions with a keyboard interface. Obviously, some programs (drawing programs and page-layout programs) become awkward when controlled *solely* from the keyboard, so in those cases you might feel justified in not providing a keyboard interface that duplicates all the mouse functions. That's up to you and what you feel your users require.

The Presentation Manager supports a mouse that has one, two, or three buttons. You must decide how many mouse buttons you'll use in your program. The easiest approach is to go for the lowest common denominator and use only one mouse button.

MOUSE AND POINTER BASICS

Let's begin with a few simple definitions, starting with the distinction between the mouse and the pointer. The mouse is the object that sits on the desk. The pointer is a small bitmapped picture on the screen. When you move the mouse with your hand, the Presentation Manager moves the pointer.

Clicking the mouse is pressing and releasing a mouse button. *Double-clicking* is pressing and releasing the mouse button twice in succession. For an action to qualify as a double click, both clicks must occur within a fixed period of time (by default, half a second) and with the pointer in approximately the same area of the screen (within an area about half the size of a system font character). *Dragging* the mouse is holding down the mouse button and moving the mouse. For example, you drag the mouse to change the position or size of a window.

MORE ABOUT THE POINTER

The Presentation Manager moves the pointer in response to mouse movements. The Presentation Manager includes several predefined pointer shapes, with the most familiar being the arrow pointer used by default on most windows. Four other predefined pointers (double-headed arrows of various types) are used on the sizing border. You can also create your own customized pointers, as described in Chapter 12.

The displayed size of the mouse pointer is dependent on the resolution of the video display. For example, on the VGA a pointer is 32 pixels wide and 32 pixels high. A program can obtain the dimensions of the pointer from *WinQuerySysValue* using the SV_CXPOINTER and SV_CYPOINTER parameters.

Every pointer has a *hot spot*, which is a single pixel position within the pointer bitmap. For the standard arrow pointer, the hot spot is the tip of the arrow. The Presentation Manager uses the hot spot as the position of the pointer.

THE POINTER POSITION

Programs that use the mouse for input must often determine the position of the pointer or, more precisely, the coordinates of the pointer's hot spot. Such programs can make this determination in three ways: by calling *WinQueryPointerPos*, by calling *WinQueryMsgPos*, or by processing WM_MOUSEMOVE messages.

THE *WINQUERYPOINTERPOS* FUNCTION

The *WinQueryPointerPos* function fills in the *x* and *y* fields of a POINTL structure with the current pointer position in screen coordinates, relative to the lower-left corner of the screen.

```
WinQueryPointerPos (HWND_DESKTOP, &ptl) ;
```

You can call this function at any time.

THE *WINQUERYMSGPOS* FUNCTION

You can use the second method, the *WinQueryMsgPos* function, while processing a message in a window procedure. This function reports the screen coordinates of the pointer at the time a message was last placed in the program's message queue:

```
WinQueryMsgPos (hab, &ptl) ;
```

If the window procedure calls this function while processing a nonqueued message, this pointer position could be long out of date. The pointer position obtained from *WinQueryMsgPos* is originally part of the QMSG structure that the Presentation Manager fills in when you retrieve a message from the message queue with *WinGetMsg*. However, the pointer position isn't passed to the window procedure along with the more important QMSG fields (the window handle, message number, *mp1*, and *mp2*). You use *WinQueryMsgPos* to get this field. This function is sometimes useful when you need to determine the pointer position at the time a key on the keyboard was pressed.

Both *WinQueryPointerPos* and *WinQueryMsgPos* return the pointer coordinates relative to the lower-left corner of the screen, but they don't necessarily return the same value. *WinQueryPointerPos* returns the pointer position at the time the function is called, whereas *WinQueryMsgPos* returns the position at the time the message currently being processed was posted in the message queue.

PROCESSING THE WM_MOUSEMOVE MESSAGE

The third way to obtain the pointer position is by processing the WM_MOUSEMOVE message in the window procedure. The pointer coordinates are stored in *mp1*. You can extract the *x* (horizontal) coordinate with the expression

```
xPointer = SHORT1FROMMP (mp1) ;
```

and extract the y (vertical) coordinate using

```
yPointer = SHORT2FROMMP (mp1) ;
```

The PMWIN.H header file also includes a MOUSEMSG macro that is similar to the CHARMSG macro discussed in Chapter 8. You can use MOUSEMSG to obtain the pointer position like this:

```
case WM_MOUSEMOVE:
     xPointer = MOUSEMSG(&msg)->x ;
     yPointer = MOUSEMSG(&msg)->y ;
```

Unlike the pointer position obtained from *WinQueryPointerPos* and *WinQueryMsgPos*, the pointer position in the WM_MOUSEMOVE message is in window coordinates relative to the lower-left corner of the window receiving the message. Under normal circumstances, a window procedure receives WM_MOUSEMOVE messages only when the pointer is positioned over the window. Thus, the coordinates in *mp1* won't be negative. (The exception is when a program "captures the mouse," a technique I'll discuss later in this chapter.)

You'll recall from Chapter 8 that a window procedure receives WM_CHAR messages when the window has the input focus. The mouse is handled differently: A window procedure receives WM_MOUSEMOVE messages when the pointer is positioned over the window, regardless of the active window and the focus window. If the mouse pointer is positioned over overlapping windows, the topmost window receives the WM_MOUSEMOVE message.

Processing WM_MOUSEMOVE messages is generally the easiest way for a program to determine the pointer position, for two reasons:

- The message notifies a window procedure when the mouse has moved.
- The coordinates of the pointer position are relative to the window rather than the screen.

WM_MOUSEMOVE MESSAGE DEFAULT PROCESSING

After processing most messages, the window procedure returns a 0. Any message that a window procedure does not process must be passed to *WinDefWindowProc* for default processing.

But WM_MOUSEMOVE messages should be handled a little differently. The Presentation Manager documentation recommends that a window procedure return 1 if it processes a WM_MOUSEMOVE message and 0 if it does not. But this is just a convention. The value you return from the window procedure is not used for anything important; it is simply returned from the *WinDispatchMsg* call that originally dispatched the WM_MOUSEMOVE message to the window procedure.

Rather than return a 0 or 1 from the window procedure, you'll probably want to conclude your WM_MOUSEMOVE processing with a *break* statement. This will cause *WinDefWindowProc* to be called for the same message. *WinDefWindowProc* processes WM_MOUSEMOVE messages by setting the pointer shape to the default tilted arrow.

If you had the source code to *WinDefWindowProc*, you'd probably find that it looked something like this:

```
MRESULT APIENTRY WinDefWindowProc (HPS hps, ULONG msg, MPARAM mp1, MPARAM mp2)
{
     [ .... ]
 switch (msg)
     {
```

```
          [ .... ]
     case WM_MOUSEMOVE:
          WinSetPointer (HWND_DESKTOP,
               WinQuerySysPointer (HWND_DESKTOP, SPTR_ARROW, FALSE)) ;
          return 0 ;
          [ .... ]
     }
return 0 ;
}
```

The *WinQuerySysPointer* function returns a handle to a system pointer. The SPTR_ARROW identifier refers to the tilted arrow pointer. The *WinSetPointer* call uses that pointer handle to set the pointer shape.

If you want a different pointer shape when the pointer is positioned on your client window, you can call *WinSetPointer* while you are processing WM_MOUSEMOVE and return from the window procedure without calling *WinDefWindowProc*. You can set the pointer to any of the system pointers (obtained from *WinQuerySysPointer* using the SPTR identifiers) or to a customized pointer (discussed in Chapter 12).

If you do not call *WinSetPointer* while processing the WM_MOUSEMOVE message, you should call *WinDefWindowProc* so the tilted arrow pointer is set. Otherwise, the pointer used by another window (for example, the double-headed arrows used by the sizing border window) may continue to be used when the pointer is inside the client window.

PROCESSING WM_MOUSEMOVE MESSAGES

The WEB program, shown in Listing 9.1, processes WM_MOUSEMOVE messages. Whenever this program receives a WM_MOUSEMOVE message, it draws a series of lines from the pointer position encoded in *mp1* to the four corners and four sides of the client window. The pattern looks like a web (Figure 9.1). As you move the mouse around the window, the center of the web follows. When you move the mouse outside the client window, the client window stops receiving WM_MOUSEMOVE messages; thus the web stops changing shape.

Listing 9.1: The WEB program

The WEB.MAK File

```
#------------------
# WEB.MAK make file
#------------------

web.exe : web.obj web.def
```

Listing 9.1: The WEB program (Continued)

```
     $(PRGLINK) web, web, NUL, $(PRGLIB), web

web.obj : web.c
     $(PRGCC) web.c
```

The WEB.C File

```
/*--------------------------------------
   WEB.C -- Mouse Movement Demo Program
            (c) Charles Petzold, 1993
  --------------------------------------*/

#define INCL_WIN
#define INCL_GPI
#include <os2.h>

MRESULT EXPENTRY ClientWndProc (HWND, ULONG, MPARAM, MPARAM) ;

int main (void)
     {
     static CHAR  szClientClass [] = "Web" ;
     static ULONG flFrameFlags = FCF_TITLEBAR      | FCF_SYSMENU |
                                 FCF_SIZEBORDER    | FCF_MINMAX  |
                                 FCF_SHELLPOSITION | FCF_TASKLIST ;
     HAB          hab ;
     HMQ          hmq ;
     HWND         hwndFrame, hwndClient ;
     QMSG         qmsg ;

     hab = WinInitialize (0) ;
     hmq = WinCreateMsgQueue (hab, 0) ;

     WinRegisterClass (hab, szClientClass, ClientWndProc,
                       CS_SIZEREDRAW | CS_SYNCPAINT, 0) ;

     hwndFrame = WinCreateStdWindow (HWND_DESKTOP, WS_VISIBLE,
                                     &flFrameFlags, szClientClass, NULL,
                                     0L, 0, 0, &hwndClient) ;

     while (WinGetMsg (hab, &qmsg, NULLHANDLE, 0, 0))
          WinDispatchMsg (hab, &qmsg) ;

     WinDestroyWindow (hwndFrame) ;
     WinDestroyMsgQueue (hmq) ;
     WinTerminate (hab) ;
     return 0 ;
     }
```

Listing 9.1: The WEB program (Continued)

```
VOID DrawWeb (HPS hps, POINTL *pptlPointerPos, POINTL *pptlClient)
     {
     POINTL ptl ;
                                   // Lower Left --> Pointer --> Upper Right
     ptl.x = 0 ;
     ptl.y = 0 ;
     GpiMove (hps, &ptl) ;
     GpiLine (hps, pptlPointerPos) ;
     GpiLine (hps, pptlClient) ;
                                   // Upper Left --> Pointer --> Lower Right
     ptl.x = 0 ;
     ptl.y = pptlClient->y ;
     GpiMove (hps, &ptl) ;
     GpiLine (hps, pptlPointerPos) ;

     ptl.x = pptlClient->x ;
     ptl.y = 0 ;
     GpiLine (hps, &ptl) ;
                                   // Lower Center --> Pointer --> Upper Center
     ptl.x = pptlClient->x / 2 ;
     ptl.y = 0 ;
     GpiMove (hps, &ptl) ;
     GpiLine (hps, pptlPointerPos) ;

     ptl.y = pptlClient->y ;
     GpiLine (hps, &ptl) ;
                                   // Left Center --> Pointer --> Right Center
     ptl.x = 0 ;
     ptl.y = pptlClient->y / 2 ;
     GpiMove (hps, &ptl) ;
     GpiLine (hps, pptlPointerPos) ;

     ptl.x = pptlClient->x ;
     GpiLine (hps, &ptl) ;
     }

MRESULT EXPENTRY ClientWndProc (HWND hwnd, ULONG msg, MPARAM mp1, MPARAM mp2)
     {
     static POINTL ptlClient, ptlPointerPos ;
     HPS           hps ;

     switch (msg)
          {
          case WM_SIZE:
               ptlClient.x = SHORT1FROMMP (mp2) ;
               ptlClient.y = SHORT2FROMMP (mp2) ;
               return 0 ;

          case WM_MOUSEMOVE:
```

Listing 9.1: The WEB program (Continued)

```
               hps = WinGetPS (hwnd) ;
               GpiSetMix (hps, FM_INVERT) ;

               DrawWeb (hps, &ptlPointerPos, &ptlClient) ;

               ptlPointerPos.x = MOUSEMSG(&msg)->x ;
               ptlPointerPos.y = MOUSEMSG(&msg)->y ;

               DrawWeb (hps, &ptlPointerPos, &ptlClient) ;

               WinReleasePS (hps) ;
               break ;                        // do default processing

          case WM_PAINT:
               hps = WinBeginPaint (hwnd, NULLHANDLE, NULL) ;
               GpiErase (hps) ;
               GpiSetMix (hps, FM_INVERT) ;

               DrawWeb (hps, &ptlPointerPos, &ptlClient) ;

               WinEndPaint (hps) ;
               return 0 ;
          }
     return WinDefWindowProc (hwnd, msg, mp1, mp2) ;
     }
```

THE WEB.DEF FILE

```
;-------------------------------
; WEB.DEF module definition file
;-------------------------------

NAME           WEB  WINDOWAPI

DESCRIPTION    'Mouse Movement Demo Program (c) Charles Petzold, 1993'
PROTMODE
```

ERASING AND REDRAWING

WEB draws lines using a series of *GpiMove* and *GpiLine* calls in the *DrawWeb* function. When WEB receives a WM_MOUSEMOVE message, it must erase the lines previously drawn and draw new lines based on the new mouse position. One way to erase the old lines is to write over them using a different mix mode. The default mix mode, called FM_OVERPAINT, causes any object you

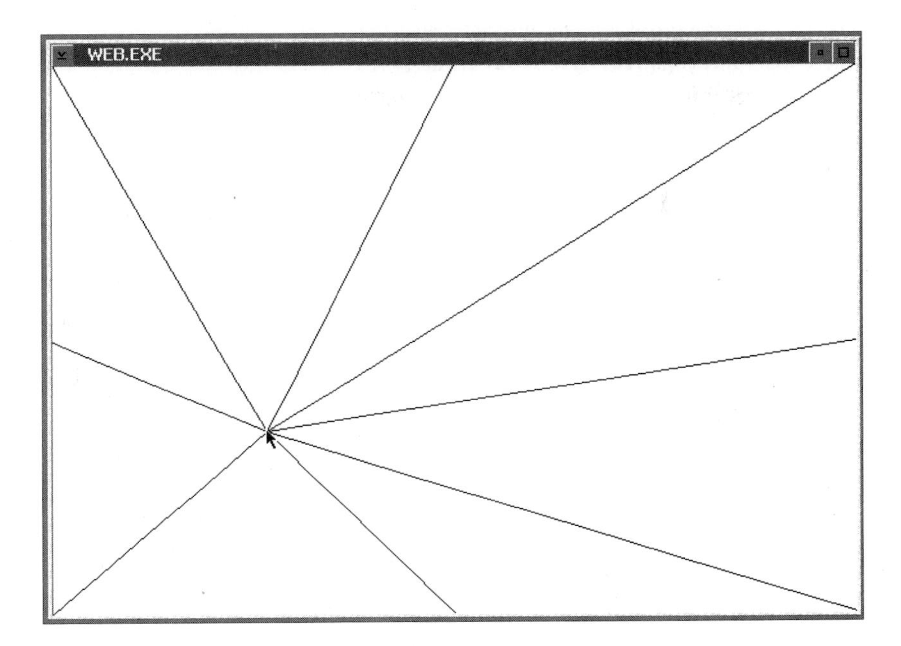

Figure 9.1: The WEB display

draw to overpaint whatever was previously in the client window. You can instead set a mix mode of FM_INVERT:

```
GpiSetMix (hps, FM_INVERT) ;
```

This causes the Presentation Manager to draw the lines by inverting the color of the client window background. Thus if you set the mix mode to FM_INVERT and draw over the old lines, the lines are effectively erased.

The WM_MOUSEMOVE code first sets the mix mode to FM_INVERT and then calls *DrawWeb* to erase the previous web:

```
case WM_MOUSEMOVE:
     hps = WinGetPS (hwnd) ;
     GpiSetMix (hps, FM_INVERT) ;

     DrawWeb (hps, &ptlPointerPos, &ptlClient) ;
```

The new position of the pointer is stored in *ptlPointerPos*, and the program calls *DrawWeb* again to draw the new web:

```
ptlPointerPos.x = MOUSEMSG (&msg) -> x ;
ptlPointerPos.y = MOUSEMSG (&msg) -> y ;
```

```
DrawWeb (hps, &ptlPointerPos, &ptlClient) ;

WinReleasePS (hps) ;
break ;
```

But there's a potential bug in this web. Both WM_MOUSEMOVE and WM_PAINT are queued messages. The WM_PAINT message is a low-priority message. If both a WM_MOUSEMOVE message and a WM_PAINT message are in the message queue, WM_MOUSEMOVE is retrieved first.

If the pointer is positioned over a window when the window is first created, the Presentation Manager places an initial WM_MOUSEMOVE message in the program's message queue even if the mouse isn't moving during that time. This is often the first queued message the window procedure receives. The WM_PAINT message is usually the second queued message. But the code in WEB assumes that the window procedure receives a WM_PAINT message (and draws an initial web) before the first WM_MOUSEMOVE message (which begins by erasing the previous web). The fix for this is relatively easy. The window class is given a CS_SYNCPAINT style:

```
WinRegisterClass (hab, szClientClass, ClientWndProc,
     CS_SIZEREDRAW | CS_SYNCPAINT, 0) ;
```

This class style makes WM_PAINT messages nonqueued. The window procedure receives a WM_PAINT message immediately whenever part of the window is invalid. The first WM_PAINT message then precedes the first WM_MOUSEMOVE message.

If you move the mouse quickly within WEB's client area, you'll notice a lag between the position of the pointer and the center of the web. This results from the delay between the time the WM_MOUSEMOVE message is posted and the time it is actually processed. You can force the web to follow the movement of the mouse more closely by replacing the following two statements:

```
ptlPointerPos.x = MOUSEMSG(&msg)->x ;
ptlPointerPos.y = MOUSEMSG(&msg)->y ;
```

with the following code:

```
WinQueryPointerPos (HWND_DESKTOP, &ptlPointerPos) ;
WinMapWindowPoints (HWND_DESKTOP, hwnd, &ptlPointerPos, 1) ;
```

The WM_MOUSEMOVE message continues to notify the window procedure of a change in the pointer position, but the program obtains a more up-to-date pointer position from the *WinQueryPointerPos* function. The position must be converted from screen coordinates to client window coordinates with *WinMapWindowPoints.*

You'll notice with both methods that no matter how quickly you move the mouse around the client window, the program never has to "catch up" to a stream of unprocessed WM_MOUSEMOVE messages. That's because the Presentation Manager doesn't fill up your message queue with multiple WM_MOUSEMOVE messages—it posts them only as quickly as you can process them. If the queue already contains a WM_MOUSEMOVE message when a new WM_MOUSEMOVE message is ready, the Presentation Manager replaces the message currently in the queue. Therefore, only one WM_MOUSEMOVE message exists at a time in the message queue.

MOUSE BUTTONS AND HIT-TESTING

A mouse can have one, two, or three buttons. A program can obtain the number of mouse buttons from *WinQuerySysValue*:

```
lNumButtons = WinQuerySysValue (HWND_DESKTOP, SV_CMOUSEBUTTONS) ;
```

If the return value is 0, no mouse is installed. A program can check for the presence of a mouse in this manner or by calling *WinQuerySysValue* with the SV_MOUSEPRESENT parameter.

The PMWIN.H header file defines several identifiers that you use in button-related functions and messages. These identifiers contain the words BUTTON1, BUTTON2, and BUTTON3 to refer to the three buttons. The following table shows how these identifiers normally correspond to the actual buttons on the mouse:

	Identifier		
Number of Mouse Buttons	**BUTTON1**	**BUTTON2**	**BUTTON3**
One	Center	--	--
Two	Left	Right	--
Three	Left	Center	Right

You can write your programs for a three-button mouse and then include special logic to mimic the third button for a two-button mouse and the second and third buttons for a one-button mouse. But the easiest approach is to assume that the mouse has only one button and to work entirely with the functions and messages that pertain to BUTTON1. The Presentation Manager's own window procedures for the menu, scroll bar, sizing border, title bar, push buttons, and so forth all work this way.

Left-handed users often prefer to use their index finger for the first button. For this reason, the Presentation Manager Control Panel allows the user to switch the orientation of the buttons, like this:

	Identifier		
Number of Mouse Buttons	**BUTTON1**	**BUTTON2**	**BUTTON3**
One	Center	--	--
Two	Right	Left	--
Three	Right	Center	Left

This swapping of the mouse buttons is transparent to your program; usually you needn't worry about it. The user knows which physical button is the first button, and that's all that's important. (But if you're writing a training program that draws a mouse on the screen and labels the buttons, you can determine if the mouse buttons have been swapped by calling *WinQuerySysValue* with the SV_SWAPBUTTON parameter.)

A program can determine whether a mouse button is currently pressed or released by calling *WinGetKeyState*, the function used in Chapter 8 to determine the state of keys on the keyboard:

```
lKeyState = WinGetKeyState (HWND_DESKTOP, VK_BUTTON1) ;
```

The high bit of *lKeyState* is set (that is, *lKeyState* is negative) if the first mouse button is currently held down. You can use the VK_BUTTON2 and VK_BUTTON3 identifiers to determine the state of the second and third buttons.

BUTTON MESSAGES

A window procedure is notified of button presses and releases by the following messages:

Button	Pressed	Released
1	WM_BUTTON1DOWN	WM_BUTTON1UP
2	WM_BUTTON2DOWN	WM_BUTTON2UP
3	WM_BUTTON3DOWN	WM_BUTTON3UP

If the user presses and releases the mouse button twice to qualify as a double click, the window procedure receives the two messages shown above for the first click and the following pair of messages for the second click:

Button	Pressed Again	Released
1	WM_BUTTON1DBLCLK	WM_BUTTON1UP
2	WM_BUTTON2DBLCLK	WM_BUTTON2UP
3	WM_BUTTON3DBLCLK	WM_BUTTON3UP

The Presentation Manager routes these messages to window procedures in the same way it routes the WM_MOUSEMOVE message: The window underneath the pointer at the time of the button action determines the window procedure that receives the message. The pointer position is stored in the *mp1* parameter, just as it is in the WM_MOUSEMOVE message.

WinDefWindowProc performs some important default processing of button down messages:

```
case WM_BUTTON1DOWN:
case WM_BUTTON2DOWN:
case WM_BUTTON3DOWN:
     WinSetActiveWindow (HWND_DESKTOP, hwnd) ;

     hwndOwner = WinQueryWindow (hwnd, QW_OWNER) ;

     if (hwndOwner != NULL)
          return WinSendMsg (hwndOwner, msg, mp1, mp2) ;
     else
          return 0 ;
```

The *WinSetActiveWindow* call sets the active window to *hwnd*. If *hwnd* is not a top-level window, then *hwnd* is a descendant of a top-level window and that top-level window becomes active. This allows the user to bring a window to the foreground by clicking the client area with the mouse. You should either include a call to *WinSetActiveWindow* in your button down processing or call *WinDefWindowProc*.

WinDefWindowProc also sends the message to the window's owner, under the assumption that, if the window is not interested in the message, the window's owner might be.

HIT-TESTING

When you draw graphic figures or text on the screen, you determine the coordinates of each object (whether figure or text) and call the appropriate GPI functions to draw it. Often a program uses a mouse interface to allow a user to point to and manipulate these graphic objects. But that means your program must work backward from the pointer coordinates to determine which of these objects the mouse is pointing to.

This process is called *hit-testing*. Hit-testing can be complex, particularly if your client window contains figures that overlap or text in a variable-pitch font. To help out, GPI includes a built-in facility to draw a series of objects and then determine which object coincides with a particular point. You'll want to use this facility for complex hit-testing, but for simple hit-testing, you can use the old-fashioned techniques, which I'll discuss in this section.

SIMPLE HIT-TESTING

The CHECKER1 program, shown in Listing 9.2, demonstrates some simple hit-testing logic. The program draws 25 rectangles in a 5-by-5 grid. When you click within one of these rectangles, CHECKER1 draws an X in it. When you click again, the X disappears.

Listing 9.2: The CHECKER1 program

The CHECKER1.MAK File

```
#-----------------------
# CHECKER1.MAK make file
#-----------------------

checker1.exe : checker1.obj checker1.def
     $(PRGLINK) checker1, checker1, NUL, $(PRGLIB), checker1

checker1.obj : checker1.c
     $(PRGCC) checker1.c
```

The CHECKER1.C File

```
/*------------------------------------------
   CHECKER1.C -- Mouse Hit-Test Demo Program
                 (c) Charles Petzold, 1993
  ------------------------------------------*/

#define INCL_WIN
#include <os2.h>

#define DIVISIONS 5

MRESULT EXPENTRY ClientWndProc (HWND, ULONG, MPARAM, MPARAM) ;
```

Listing 9.2: The CHECKER1 program (Continued)

```
int main (void)
     {
     static CHAR  szClientClass [] = "Checker1" ;
     static ULONG flFrameFlags = FCF_TITLEBAR      | FCF_SYSMENU |
                                 FCF_SIZEBORDER    | FCF_MINMAX  |
                                 FCF_SHELLPOSITION | FCF_TASKLIST ;
     HAB          hab ;
     HMQ          hmq ;
     HWND         hwndFrame, hwndClient ;
     QMSG         qmsg ;

     hab = WinInitialize (0) ;
     hmq = WinCreateMsgQueue (hab, 0) ;

     WinRegisterClass (hab, szClientClass, ClientWndProc, CS_SIZEREDRAW, 0) ;

     hwndFrame = WinCreateStdWindow (HWND_DESKTOP, WS_VISIBLE,
                                     &flFrameFlags, szClientClass, NULL,
                                     0L, 0, 0, &hwndClient) ;

     while (WinGetMsg (hab, &qmsg, NULLHANDLE, 0, 0))
          WinDispatchMsg (hab, &qmsg) ;

     WinDestroyWindow (hwndFrame) ;
     WinDestroyMsgQueue (hmq) ;
     WinTerminate (hab) ;
     return 0 ;
     }

VOID DrawLine (HPS hps, LONG x1, LONG y1, LONG x2, LONG y2)
     {
     POINTL ptl ;

     ptl.x = x1 ;  ptl.y = y1 ;  GpiMove (hps, &ptl) ;
     ptl.x = x2 ;  ptl.y = y2 ;  GpiLine (hps, &ptl) ;
     }

MRESULT EXPENTRY ClientWndProc (HWND hwnd, ULONG msg, MPARAM mp1, MPARAM mp2)
     {
     static BOOL  fBlockState [DIVISIONS] [DIVISIONS] ;
     static INT   xBlock, yBlock ;
     HPS          hps ;
     INT          x, y ;
     RECTL        rcl ;

     switch (msg)
          {
          case WM_SIZE:
```

Listing 9.2: The CHECKER1 program (Continued)

```
          xBlock = SHORT1FROMMP (mp2) / DIVISIONS ;
          yBlock = SHORT2FROMMP (mp2) / DIVISIONS ;
          return 0 ;

     case WM_BUTTON1DOWN:
     case WM_BUTTON1DBLCLK:
          if (xBlock > 0 && yBlock > 0)
               {
               x = MOUSEMSG(&msg)->x / xBlock ;
               y = MOUSEMSG(&msg)->y / yBlock ;

               if (x < DIVISIONS && y < DIVISIONS)
                    {
                    fBlockState [x][y] = !fBlockState [x][y] ;

                    rcl.xRight = xBlock + (rcl.xLeft   = x * xBlock) ;
                    rcl.yTop   = yBlock + (rcl.yBottom = y * yBlock) ;

                    WinInvalidateRect (hwnd, &rcl, FALSE) ;
                    }
               else
                    WinAlarm (HWND_DESKTOP, WA_WARNING) ;
               }
          else
               WinAlarm (HWND_DESKTOP, WA_WARNING) ;

          break ;                         // do default processing

     case WM_PAINT:
          hps = WinBeginPaint (hwnd, NULLHANDLE, NULL) ;
          GpiErase (hps) ;

          if (xBlock > 0 && yBlock > 0)
               for (x = 0 ; x < DIVISIONS ; x++)
                    for (y = 0 ; y < DIVISIONS ; y++)
                         {
                         rcl.xRight = xBlock + (rcl.xLeft   = x * xBlock);
                         rcl.yTop   = yBlock + (rcl.yBottom = y * yBlock);

                         WinDrawBorder (hps, &rcl, 1, 1,
                                        CLR_NEUTRAL, CLR_BACKGROUND,
                                        DB_STANDARD | DB_INTERIOR) ;

                         if (fBlockState [x][y])
                              {
                              DrawLine (hps, rcl.xLeft,  rcl.yBottom,
                                             rcl.xRight, rcl.yTop) ;

                              DrawLine (hps, rcl.xLeft,  rcl.yTop,
```

Listing 9.2: The CHECKER1 program (Continued)

```
                                                                rcl.xRight, rcl.yBottom) ;
                                               }
                                          }
                WinEndPaint (hps) ;
                return 0 ;
           }
     return WinDefWindowProc (hwnd, msg, mp1, mp2) ;
     }
```

The CHECKER1.DEF File

```
;-----------------------------------
; CHECKER1.DEF module definition file
;-----------------------------------

NAME           CHECKER1  WINDOWAPI

DESCRIPTION    'Mouse Hit-Test Program No. 1 (c) Charles Petzold, 1993'
PROTMODE
```

A sample CHECKER1 display is shown in Figure 9.2.

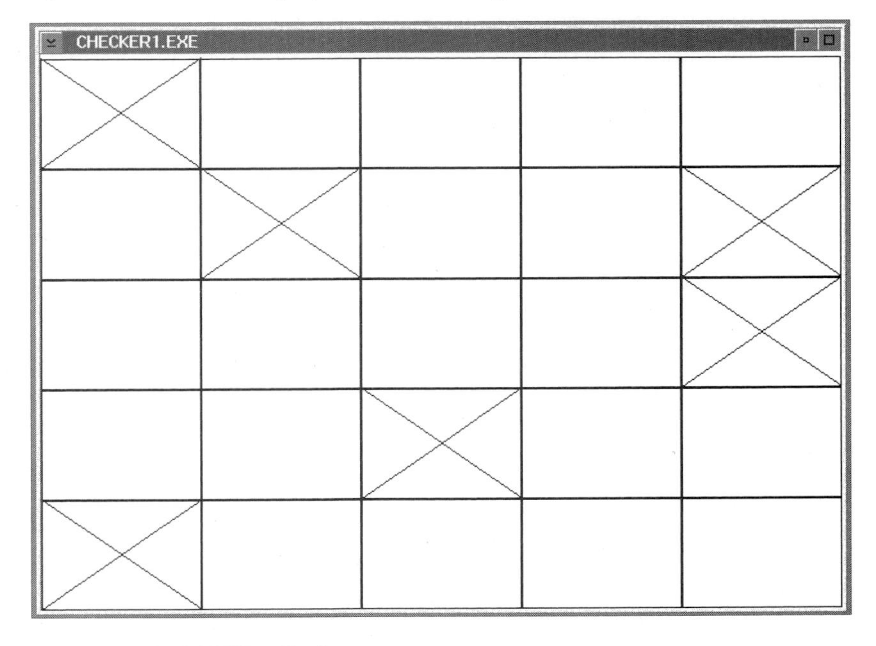

Figure 9.2: The CHECKER1 display

Each rectangle in CHECKER1 has the same width and height. The program determines the dimensions of the rectangles during the WM_SIZE message by dividing the client window width and height by 5. These dimensions are stored in *xBlock* and *yBlock*. The *fBlockState* array stores the state (checked or not checked) of each block. The state is TRUE if the rectangle contains an X and FALSE if it doesn't. The WM_PAINT message code tests the values in this array to determine if it should draw the Xs in the rectangles.

The WM_BUTTON1DOWN code must work backward from the pointer coordinates to determine the particular block being clicked on. Because all the blocks are the same height and width, this task is fairly trivial, requiring only that the pointer coordinates be divided by the rectangle size:

```
x = MOUSEMSG(&msg)->x / xBlock ;
y = MOUSEMSG(&msg)->y / yBlock ;
```

The values of *x* and *y* can range from 0 to 4, identifying the rectangle that the user clicked on. The value of *fBlockState* for that rectangle is inverted:

```
fBlockState [x][y] = !fBlockState [x][y] ;
```

The rectangle is then invalidated to generate a WM_PAINT message. If the width or height of the client window isn't evenly divisible by 5, the program leaves a strip across the right or top of the window that isn't covered by any of the rectangles. If the user clicks on that area, the *x* or *y* value (calculated as shown above) will be greater than 4, in which case CHECKER1 beeps to indicate the error.

Before we proceed to a more sophisticated hit-testing technique, let's add a keyboard interface to this program.

EMULATING THE MOUSE WITH THE KEYBOARD

I said at the outset of this chapter that you should try to write your Presentation Manager programs so they are usable with either a mouse or the keyboard. So far, I've been shamelessly ignoring that rule in order to concentrate on mouse logic. The CHECKER2 program, shown in Listing 9.3, adds a keyboard interface to CHECKER1. You can use the cursor movement keys to move the pointer from rectangle to rectangle. The spacebar or Enter key draws an X or removes the X in the rectangle under the pointer.

Listing 9.3: The CHECKER2 program

The CHECKER2.MAK File

```
#-----------------------
# CHECKER2.MAK make file
#-----------------------
```

Listing 9.3: The CHECKER2 program (Continued)

```
checker2.exe : checker2.obj checker2.def
     $(PRGLINK) checker2, checker2, NUL, $(PRGLIB), checker2

checker2.obj : checker2.c
     $(PRGCC) checker2.c
```

The CHECKER2.C File

```
/*-------------------------------------------------------------------
   CHECKER2.C -- Mouse Hit-Test Demo Program with Keyboard Interface
                 (c) Charles Petzold, 1993
  -------------------------------------------------------------------*/

#define INCL_WIN
#include <os2.h>
#include <stdlib.h>

#define DIVISIONS 5

MRESULT EXPENTRY ClientWndProc (HWND, ULONG, MPARAM, MPARAM) ;

int main (void)
     {
     static CHAR  szClientClass [] = "Checker2" ;
     static ULONG flFrameFlags = FCF_TITLEBAR      | FCF_SYSMENU |
                                 FCF_SIZEBORDER    | FCF_MINMAX  |
                                 FCF_SHELLPOSITION | FCF_TASKLIST ;
     HAB          hab ;
     HMQ          hmq ;
     HWND         hwndFrame, hwndClient ;
     QMSG         qmsg ;

     hab = WinInitialize (0) ;
     hmq = WinCreateMsgQueue (hab, 0) ;

     WinRegisterClass (hab, szClientClass, ClientWndProc, CS_SIZEREDRAW, 0) ;

     hwndFrame = WinCreateStdWindow (HWND_DESKTOP, WS_VISIBLE,
                                     &flFrameFlags, szClientClass, NULL,
                                     0L, 0, 0, &hwndClient) ;

     while (WinGetMsg (hab, &qmsg, NULLHANDLE, 0, 0))
          WinDispatchMsg (hab, &qmsg) ;

     WinDestroyWindow (hwndFrame) ;
     WinDestroyMsgQueue (hmq) ;
     WinTerminate (hab) ;
     return 0 ;
```

Listing 9.3: The CHECKER2 program (Continued)

```
     }

VOID DrawLine (HPS hps, INT x1, INT y1, INT x2, INT y2)
     {
     POINTL ptl ;

     ptl.x = x1 ;  ptl.y = y1 ;  GpiMove (hps, &ptl) ;
     ptl.x = x2 ;  ptl.y = y2 ;  GpiLine (hps, &ptl) ;
     }

MRESULT EXPENTRY ClientWndProc (HWND hwnd, ULONG msg, MPARAM mp1, MPARAM mp2)
     {
     static BOOL  fBlockState [DIVISIONS] [DIVISIONS] ;
     static INT   xBlock, yBlock ;
     HPS          hps ;
     INT          x, y ;
     POINTL       ptl ;
     RECTL        rcl ;

     switch (msg)
          {
          case WM_SIZE:
               xBlock = SHORT1FROMMP (mp2) / DIVISIONS ;
               yBlock = SHORT2FROMMP (mp2) / DIVISIONS ;
               return 0 ;

          case WM_BUTTON1DOWN:
          case WM_BUTTON1DBLCLK:
               if (xBlock > 0 && yBlock > 0)
                    {
                    x = MOUSEMSG(&msg)->x / xBlock ;
                    y = MOUSEMSG(&msg)->y / yBlock ;

                    if (x < DIVISIONS && y < DIVISIONS)
                         {
                         fBlockState [x][y] = !fBlockState [x][y] ;

                         rcl.xRight = xBlock + (rcl.xLeft   = x * xBlock) ;
                         rcl.yTop   = yBlock + (rcl.yBottom = y * yBlock) ;

                         WinInvalidateRect (hwnd, &rcl, FALSE) ;
                         }
                    else
                         WinAlarm (HWND_DESKTOP, WA_WARNING) ;
                    }
               else
                    WinAlarm (HWND_DESKTOP, WA_WARNING) ;

               break ;                      // do default processing
```

Listing 9.3: The CHECKER2 program (Continued)

```
          case WM_SETFOCUS:
               if (WinQuerySysValue (HWND_DESKTOP, SV_MOUSEPRESENT) == 0)
                    WinShowPointer (HWND_DESKTOP,
                                    SHORT1FROMMP (mp2) ? TRUE : FALSE) ;
               return 0 ;

          case WM_CHAR:
               if (xBlock == 0 || yBlock == 0)
                    break ;

               if (CHARMSG(&msg)->fs & KC_KEYUP)
                    break ;

               if (!(CHARMSG(&msg)->fs & KC_VIRTUALKEY))
                    break ;

               WinQueryPointerPos (HWND_DESKTOP, &ptl) ;
               WinMapWindowPoints (HWND_DESKTOP, hwnd, &ptl, 1) ;

               x = max (0, min (DIVISIONS - 1, ptl.x / xBlock)) ;
               y = max (0, min (DIVISIONS - 1, ptl.y / yBlock)) ;

               switch (CHARMSG(&msg)->vkey)
                    {
                    case VK_LEFT:
                         x-- ;
                         break ;

                    case VK_RIGHT:
                         x++ ;
                         break ;

                    case VK_DOWN:
                         y-- ;
                         break ;

                    case VK_UP:
                         y++ ;
                         break ;

                    case VK_HOME:
                         x = 0 ;
                         y = DIVISIONS - 1 ;
                         break ;

                    case VK_END:
                         x = DIVISIONS - 1 ;
                         y = 0 ;
```

Listing 9.3: The CHECKER2 program (Continued)

```
                    break ;

               case VK_NEWLINE:
               case VK_ENTER:
               case VK_SPACE:
                    WinSendMsg (hwnd, WM_BUTTON1DOWN,
                         MPFROM2SHORT (x * xBlock, y * yBlock), NULL) ;
                    break ;

               default:
                    return 0 ;
               }
          x = (x + DIVISIONS) % DIVISIONS ;
          y = (y + DIVISIONS) % DIVISIONS ;

          ptl.x = x * xBlock + xBlock / 2 ;
          ptl.y = y * yBlock + yBlock / 2 ;

          WinMapWindowPoints (hwnd, HWND_DESKTOP, &ptl, 1) ;
          WinSetPointerPos (HWND_DESKTOP, ptl.x, ptl.y) ;
          return 0 ;

     case WM_PAINT:
          hps = WinBeginPaint (hwnd, NULLHANDLE, NULL) ;
          GpiErase (hps) ;

          if (xBlock > 0 && yBlock > 0)
               for (x = 0 ; x < DIVISIONS ; x++)
                    for (y = 0 ; y < DIVISIONS ; y++)
                         {
                         rcl.xRight = xBlock + (rcl.xLeft   = x * xBlock);
                         rcl.yTop   = yBlock + (rcl.yBottom = y * yBlock);

                         WinDrawBorder (hps, &rcl, 1, 1,
                                        CLR_NEUTRAL, CLR_BACKGROUND,
                                        DB_STANDARD | DB_INTERIOR) ;

                         if (fBlockState [x][y])
                              {
                              DrawLine (hps, rcl.xLeft,  rcl.yBottom,
                                             rcl.xRight, rcl.yTop) ;

                              DrawLine (hps, rcl.xLeft,  rcl.yTop,
                                             rcl.xRight, rcl.yBottom) ;
                              }
                         }
          WinEndPaint (hps) ;
          return 0 ;
     }
```

Listing 9.3: The CHECKER2 program (Continued)

```
     return WinDefWindowProc (hwnd, msg, mp1, mp2) ;
     }
```

The CHECKER2.DEF File

```
;-----------------------------------
; CHECKER2.DEF module definition file
;-----------------------------------

NAME           CHECKER2  WINDOWAPI

DESCRIPTION    'Mouse Hit-Test Program No. 2 (c) Charles Petzold, 1993'
PROTMODE
```

The first problem to be solved in a program like the one in Listing 9.3 involves the pointer itself. If no mouse is installed, how can the program use the pointer? Well, it's easier than you may think. Even if a mouse isn't installed, the pointer still exists and has a position on the display. You can determine that position from *WinQueryPointerPos* and set the position by calling *WinSetPointerPos*. If there's no mouse, calling *WinSetPointerPos* is the only way to move the pointer. Obviously, a user without a mouse would be annoyed to have a pointer sitting in the center of the display, so the Presentation Manager hides the pointer to make it invisible.

The Presentation Manager maintains a value called the *pointer level*, which determines whether the pointer is visible. Initially, the pointer level is set to 0 if a mouse is installed and to 1 if a mouse isn't installed. To decrement the pointer level, call

```
WinShowPointer (HWND_DESKTOP, TRUE) ;
```

The Presentation Manager will not decrement the pointer level below zero. To increment the pointer level, make the following call:

```
WinShowPointer (HWND_DESKTOP, FALSE) ;
```

The Presentation Manager displays the pointer only if the pointer level is equal to 0. (You can obtain the current pointer level from *WinQuerySysValue* with the SV_POINTERLEVEL parameter.)

CHECKER2 shows how this works in practice. The program calls *WinShowPointer* in only one place—while processing the WM_SETFOCUS message:

```
case WM_SETFOCUS:
     if (WinQuerySysValue (HWND_DESKTOP, SV_MOUSEPRESENT) == 0)
          WinShowPointer (HWND_DESKTOP,
```

```
                    SHORT1FROMMP (mp2) ? TRUE : FALSE) ;
     return 0 ;
```

You'll recall from the discussion of WM_SETFOCUS in Chapter 8 that *mp2* is TRUE if the window is gaining the input focus and FALSE if the window is losing the input focus.

If a mouse isn't installed (indicated by a 0 value returned from *WinQuery-SysValue* with the SV_MOUSEPRESENT parameter), the initial pointer level is 1, and the pointer is hidden. When CHECKER2 gets the input focus, it decrements the pointer level to 0. The pointer becomes visible. When CHECKER2 loses the input focus, the pointer level is incremented back to 1 to hide the pointer again.

This logic allows CHECKER2 to display the pointer whenever it has the input focus. Normally, input focus has nothing to do with the pointer. But CHECKER2 uses the keyboard to mimic the action of the mouse. It only makes sense to display the pointer when CHECKER2 has the input focus, because that's when CHECKER2 gets WM_CHAR messages.

The button and repainting logic in *ClientWndProc* is the same as that in CHECKER1. The bulk of the new code is the addition of WM_CHAR processing. When CHECKER2 receives a WM_CHAR message, it obtains the position of the pointer in screen coordinates and converts the position to client window coordinates:

```
WinQueryPointerPos (HWND_DESKTOP, &ptl) ;
WinMapWindowPoints (HWND_DESKTOP, hwnd, &ptl, 1) ;
```

The pointer could be outside the client window entirely. The program determines the values of *x* and *y* (ranging from 0 to 4) that identify the rectangle closest to the pointer:

```
x = max (0, min (DIVISIONS - 1, ptl.x / xBlock)) ;
y = max (0, min (DIVISIONS - 1, ptl.y / yBlock)) ;
```

(The identifier DIVISIONS is defined as 5 near the top of the program.) These values of *x* and *y* are then incremented or decremented depending on the particular cursor movement key being pressed. The VK_NEWLINE, VK_ENTER, and VK_SPACE keys are processed by sending the window a WM_BUTTON1DOWN message to simulate a mouse button action.

The new *x* and *y* values must then be converted back to a pointer position. The following formulas calculate a point in window coordinates at the center of the rectangle identified by *x* and *y*:

```
ptl.x = x * xBlock + xBlock / 2 ;
ptl.y = y * yBlock + yBlock / 2 ;
```

CHECKER2 then converts that point to window coordinates and sets the new pointer position:

```
WinMapWindowPoints (hwnd, HWND_DESKTOP, &ptl, 1) ;
WinSetPointerPos (HWND_DESKTOP, ptl.x, ptl.y) ;
```

HIT-TESTING WITH CHILD WINDOWS

Now let's try a different approach to hit-testing—one that involves creating child windows that process WM_BUTTON1DOWN messages themselves. The CHECKER3 program is shown in Listing 9.4.

Listing 9.4: The CHECKER3 program

The CHECKER3.MAK File

```
#-----------------------
# CHECKER3.MAK make file
#-----------------------

checker3.exe : checker3.obj checker3.def
     $(PRGLINK) checker3, checker3, NUL, $(PRGLIB), checker3

checker3.obj : checker3.c
     $(PRGCC) checker3.c
```

The CHECKER3.C File

```
/*--------------------------------------------------------------
   CHECKER3.C -- Mouse Hit-Test Demo Program with Child Windows
                 (c) Charles Petzold, 1993
  --------------------------------------------------------------*/

#define INCL_WIN
#include <os2.h>

#define DIVISIONS 5

MRESULT EXPENTRY ClientWndProc (HWND, ULONG, MPARAM, MPARAM) ;
MRESULT EXPENTRY ChildWndProc  (HWND, ULONG, MPARAM, MPARAM) ;

HAB  hab ;

int main (void)
     {
     static CHAR  szClientClass [] = "Checker3" ;
     static ULONG flFrameFlags = FCF_TITLEBAR      | FCF_SYSMENU |
                                 FCF_SIZEBORDER    | FCF_MINMAX  |
```

Listing 9.4: The CHECKER3 program (Continued)

```
                                   FCF_SHELLPOSITION | FCF_TASKLIST ;
     HMQ          hmq ;
     HWND         hwndFrame, hwndClient ;
     QMSG         qmsg ;

     hab = WinInitialize (Ø) ;
     hmq = WinCreateMsgQueue (hab, Ø) ;

     WinRegisterClass (hab, szClientClass, ClientWndProc, CS_SIZEREDRAW, Ø) ;

     hwndFrame = WinCreateStdWindow (HWND_DESKTOP, WS_VISIBLE,
                                     &flFrameFlags, szClientClass, NULL,
                                     ØL, Ø, Ø, &hwndClient) ;

     while (WinGetMsg (hab, &qmsg, NULLHANDLE, Ø, Ø))
          WinDispatchMsg (hab, &qmsg) ;

     WinDestroyWindow (hwndFrame) ;
     WinDestroyMsgQueue (hmq) ;
     WinTerminate (hab) ;
     return Ø ;
     }

VOID DrawLine (HPS hps, LONG x1, LONG y1, LONG x2, LONG y2)
     {
     POINTL ptl ;

     ptl.x = x1 ;  ptl.y = y1 ;  GpiMove (hps, &ptl) ;
     ptl.x = x2 ;  ptl.y = y2 ;  GpiLine (hps, &ptl) ;
     }

MRESULT EXPENTRY ClientWndProc (HWND hwnd, ULONG msg, MPARAM mp1, MPARAM mp2)
     {
     static CHAR szChildClass [] = "Checker3.Child" ;
     static HWND hwndChild [DIVISIONS][DIVISIONS] ;
     INT         xBlock, yBlock, x, y ;

     switch (msg)
          {
          case WM_CREATE:
               WinRegisterClass (hab, szChildClass, ChildWndProc,
                                 CS_SIZEREDRAW, sizeof (USHORT)) ;

               for (x = Ø ; x < DIVISIONS ; x++)
                    for (y = Ø ; y < DIVISIONS ; y++)

                         hwndChild [x][y] =
                              WinCreateWindow (
                                        hwnd,          // Parent window
```

Listing 9.4: The CHECKER3 program (Continued)

```
                                   szChildClass,  // Window class
                                   NULL,          // Window text
                                   WS_VISIBLE,    // Window style
                                   Ø, Ø, Ø, Ø,    // Position & size
                                   hwnd,          // Owner window
                                   HWND_BOTTOM,   // Placement
                                   y << 8 | x,    // Child window ID
                                   NULL,          // Control data
                                   NULL) ;        // Pres. Params
               return Ø ;

          case WM_SIZE:
               xBlock = SHORT1FROMMP (mp2) / DIVISIONS ;
               yBlock = SHORT2FROMMP (mp2) / DIVISIONS ;

               for (x = Ø ; x < DIVISIONS ; x++)
                    for (y = Ø ; y < DIVISIONS ; y++)

                         WinSetWindowPos (hwndChild [x][y], Ø,
                              x * xBlock, y * yBlock, xBlock, yBlock,
                              SWP_MOVE | SWP_SIZE) ;
               return Ø ;

          case WM_BUTTON1DOWN:
          case WM_BUTTON1DBLCLK:
               WinAlarm (HWND_DESKTOP, WA_WARNING) ;
               break ;                       // do default processing

          case WM_ERASEBACKGROUND:
               return MRFROMSHORT (1) ;
          }
     return WinDefWindowProc (hwnd, msg, mp1, mp2) ;
     }

MRESULT EXPENTRY ChildWndProc (HWND hwnd, ULONG msg, MPARAM mp1, MPARAM mp2)
     {
     HPS   hps ;
     RECTL rcl ;

     switch (msg)
          {
          case WM_CREATE:
               WinSetWindowUShort (hwnd, Ø, Ø) ;
               return Ø ;

          case WM_BUTTON1DOWN:
          case WM_BUTTON1DBLCLK:
               WinSetActiveWindow (HWND_DESKTOP, hwnd) ;
               WinSetWindowUShort (hwnd, Ø, !WinQueryWindowUShort (hwnd, Ø)) ;
```

Listing 9.4: The CHECKER3 program (Continued)

```
               WinInvalidateRect (hwnd, NULL, FALSE) ;
               return Ø ;

          case WM_PAINT:
               hps = WinBeginPaint (hwnd, NULLHANDLE, NULL) ;

               WinQueryWindowRect (hwnd, &rcl) ;

               WinDrawBorder (hps, &rcl, 1, 1, CLR_NEUTRAL, CLR_BACKGROUND,
                                   DB_STANDARD | DB_INTERIOR) ;

               if (WinQueryWindowUShort (hwnd, Ø))
                    {
                    DrawLine (hps, rcl.xLeft,  rcl.yBottom,
                                   rcl.xRight, rcl.yTop) ;
                    DrawLine (hps, rcl.xLeft,  rcl.yTop,
                                   rcl.xRight, rcl.yBottom) ;
                    }
               WinEndPaint (hps) ;
               return Ø ;
          }
     return WinDefWindowProc (hwnd, msg, mp1, mp2) ;
     }
```

The CHECKER3.DEF File

```
;-----------------------------------
; CHECKER3.DEF module definition file
;-----------------------------------

NAME           CHECKER3  WINDOWAPI

DESCRIPTION    'Mouse Hit-Test Program No. 3 (c) Charles Petzold, 1993'
PROTMODE
```

While processing the WM_CREATE message, *ClientWndProc* registers another window class named "Checker3.Child." Windows that are created based on the "Checker3.Child" class use the *ChildWndProc* window procedure for message processing. CHECKER3 then creates 25 child windows based on the "Checker3.Child" class:

```
for (x = Ø ; x < DIVISIONS ; x++)
     for (y = Ø ; y < DIVISIONS ; y++)
               hwndChild [x] [y] =
               WinCreateWindow (
                    hwnd,          // Parent window
```

```
szChildClass,   // Window class
NULL,           // Window text
WS_VISIBLE,     // Window style
Ø, Ø, Ø, Ø,     // Position and size
hwnd,           // Owner window
HWND_BOTTOM,    // Placement
y << 8 | x,     // Child window ID
NULL,           // Control data
NULL) ;         // Pres. Params
```

You've seen *WinCreateWindow* before. I used it in the WELCOME 4 program in Chapter 3 to create three child windows based on predefined window classes. CHECKER3 uses *WinCreateWindow* to create windows based on the "Checker3.Child" class.

In the *WinCreateWindow* function, the size and position parameters for these 25 child windows are all set to 0. The windows must be sized and positioned based on the size of CHECKER3's client window. The sizing and positioning occur during the WM_SIZE message:

```
case WM_SIZE:
     xBlock = SHORT1FROMMP (mp2) / DIVISIONS ;
     yBlock = SHORT2FROMMP (mp2) / DIVISIONS ;

     for (x = Ø ; x < DIVISIONS ; x++)
          for (y = Ø ; y < DIVISIONS ; y++)
               WinSetWindowPos (hwndChild [x] [y], NULL,
                    x * xBlock, y * yBlock, xBlock, yBlock,
                    SWP_MOVE | SWP_SIZE) ;
     return Ø ;
```

Each child window is set to one-fifth the height and one-fifth the width of CHECKER3's client window. Basically, instead of drawing 25 rectangles, CHECKER3 creates 25 child windows of the same size and position as the rectangles in CHECKER1 and CHECKER2. *ClientWndProc* doesn't do much else except call *WinAlarm* when it receives a WM_BUTTON1DOWN message. *ClientWndProc* receives this message only if the mouse is clicked in an area of the client window not covered by one of the children.

Messages to the 25 child windows are processed in *ChildWndProc*. When CHECKER3 registers the "Checker3.Child" window class, it reserves 2 bytes of additional space (the size of a USHORT) for each window created based on that class:

```
WinRegisterClass (hab, szChildClass, ChildWndProc,
     CS_SIZEREDRAW, sizeof (USHORT)) ;
```

ChildWndProc can access that USHORT by calling the *WinSetWindowUShort* and *WinQueryWindowUShort* functions. It uses the space to store the current state (X or no X) of the window. *ChildWndProc* initializes the reserved USHORT to 0 (meaning no X) when it receives a WM_CREATE message:

```
case WM_CREATE:
     WinSetWindowUShort (hwnd, 0, 0) ;
     return 0 ;
```

ChildWndProc actually processes this code 25 times, once for each of the 25 child windows. For each WM_CREATE message, the value of *hwnd* is different. A different reserved USHORT is initialized to 0 with each message.

Each of the 25 child windows also receives a WM_PAINT message. Each window paints itself. The logic is somewhat simpler than in CHECKER1 and CHECKER2 because the rectangle and the lines encompass the entire area of the child window. For example, to paint the rectangle around the window, the child need only obtain its window rectangle from *WinQueryWindowRect* and use that RECT structure directly in *WinDrawBorder*:

```
WinQueryWindowRect (hwnd, &rcl) ;
WinDrawBorder (hps, &rcl, 1, 1, CLR_NEUTRAL, CLR_BACKGROUND,
     DB_STANDARD | DB_INTERIOR) ;
```

The processing of the WM_BUTTON1DOWN message is also quite simple:

```
case WM_BUTTON1DOWN:
case WM_BUTTON1DBLCLK:
     WinSetActiveWindow (HWND_DESKTOP, hwnd) ;
     WinSetWindowUShort (hwnd, 0, !WinQueryWindowUShort (hwnd, 0)) ;
     WinInvalidateRect (hwnd, NULL, FALSE) ;
     return 0 ;
```

A particular child window receives a WM_BUTTON1DOWN message if the child is underneath the pointer when the button is clicked. The code here obtains the value stored in the reserved USHORT using *WinQueryWindow-UShort*, inverts it, and then stores it again using *WinSetWindowUShort*. The entire area of the child window is then invalidated to generate a WM_PAINT message for that child.

CHECKER3.C is longer than CHECKER1.C, and my explanation of CHECKER3 is longer than my explanation of CHECKER1. Nevertheless, I claim that CHECKER3 is simpler than CHECKER1. The reason? There's no real hit-testing in this program. If the child gets hit with a mouse click, it changes its own state without even examining the pointer position. If the rectangles in CHECKER1 were all different sizes, the hit-testing in that program would obviously be much more complex. But if the child windows in CHECKER3 were all different sizes, the logic in *ChildWndProc* wouldn't have to be changed at all.

Just as you use subroutines to modularize your programs, you can use child windows to modularize the area of the client window and simplify mouse message processing.

TRACKING AND CAPTURING

So far we've seen a program that processes WM_MOUSEMOVE messages and a series of three programs that process WM_BUTTON1DOWN messages. However, you'll often have to use a combination of mouse movement and mouse button messages. You begin an action when a button is pressed, follow the movement of the mouse around the window, and then finish up when the button is released. This is sometimes called "tracking" the mouse, and some complexities are involved.

SIMPLE MOUSE TRACKING

The BLOKOUT1 program in Listing 9.5 uses simple mouse tracking logic.

Listing 9.5: The BLOKOUT1 program

The BLOKOUT1.MAK File

```
#-----------------------
# BLOKOUT1.MAK make file
#-----------------------

blokout1.exe : blokout1.obj blokout1.def
     $(PRGLINK) blokout1, blokout1, NUL, $(PRGLIB), blokout1

blokout1.obj : blokout1.c
     $(PRGCC) blokout1.c
```

The BLOKOUT1.C File

```
/*---------------------------------------
   BLOKOUT1.C -- Mouse Button Demo Program
                 (c) Charles Petzold, 1993
  ---------------------------------------*/

#define INCL_WIN
#define INCL_GPI
#include <os2.h>
```

Listing 9.5: The BLOKOUT1 program (Continued)

```
MRESULT EXPENTRY ClientWndProc (HWND, ULONG, MPARAM, MPARAM) ;

int main (void)
     {
     static CHAR  szClientClass [] = "BlokOut1" ;
     static ULONG flFrameFlags = FCF_TITLEBAR      | FCF_SYSMENU |
                                 FCF_SIZEBORDER    | FCF_MINMAX  |
                                 FCF_SHELLPOSITION | FCF_TASKLIST ;
     HAB          hab ;
     HMQ          hmq ;
     HWND         hwndFrame, hwndClient ;
     QMSG         qmsg ;

     hab = WinInitialize (0) ;
     hmq = WinCreateMsgQueue (hab, 0) ;

     WinRegisterClass (hab, szClientClass, ClientWndProc, CS_SIZEREDRAW, 0) ;

     hwndFrame = WinCreateStdWindow (HWND_DESKTOP, WS_VISIBLE,
                                     &flFrameFlags, szClientClass, NULL,
                                     0L, 0, 0, &hwndClient) ;

     while (WinGetMsg (hab, &qmsg, NULLHANDLE, 0, 0))
          WinDispatchMsg (hab, &qmsg) ;

     WinDestroyWindow (hwndFrame) ;
     WinDestroyMsgQueue (hmq) ;
     WinTerminate (hab) ;
     return 0 ;
     }

VOID DrawBoxOutline (HWND hwnd, POINTL *pptlStart, POINTL *pptlEnd)
     {
     HPS hps ;

     hps = WinGetPS (hwnd) ;
     GpiSetMix (hps, FM_INVERT) ;

     GpiMove (hps, pptlStart) ;
     GpiBox (hps, DRO_OUTLINE, pptlEnd, 0L, 0L) ;

     WinReleasePS (hps) ;
     }

MRESULT EXPENTRY ClientWndProc (HWND hwnd, ULONG msg, MPARAM mp1, MPARAM mp2)
     {
     static BOOL   fButtonDown, fValidBox ;
     static POINTL ptlStart, ptlEnd, ptlBoxStart, ptlBoxEnd ;
```

Listing 9.5: The BLOKOUT1 program (Continued)

```
     HPS          hps ;

     switch (msg)
          {
          case WM_BUTTON1DOWN:
               ptlStart.x = ptlEnd.x = MOUSEMSG(&msg)->x ;
               ptlStart.y = ptlEnd.y = MOUSEMSG(&msg)->y ;

               DrawBoxOutline (hwnd, &ptlStart, &ptlEnd) ;

               fButtonDown = TRUE ;
               break ;                          // do default processing

          case WM_MOUSEMOVE:
               if (fButtonDown)
                    {
                    DrawBoxOutline (hwnd, &ptlStart, &ptlEnd) ;

                    ptlEnd.x = MOUSEMSG(&msg)->x ;
                    ptlEnd.y = MOUSEMSG(&msg)->y ;

                    DrawBoxOutline (hwnd, &ptlStart, &ptlEnd) ;
                    }
               break ;                          // do default processing

          case WM_BUTTON1UP:
               if (fButtonDown)
                    {
                    DrawBoxOutline (hwnd, &ptlStart, &ptlEnd) ;

                    ptlBoxStart = ptlStart ;
                    ptlBoxEnd.x = MOUSEMSG(&msg)->x ;
                    ptlBoxEnd.y = MOUSEMSG(&msg)->y ;

                    fButtonDown = FALSE ;
                    fValidBox = TRUE ;
                    WinInvalidateRect (hwnd, NULL, FALSE) ;
                    }
               return 0 ;

          case WM_PAINT:
               hps = WinBeginPaint (hwnd, NULLHANDLE, NULL) ;
               GpiErase (hps) ;

               if (fValidBox)
                    {
                    GpiMove (hps, &ptlBoxStart) ;
                    GpiBox (hps, DRO_OUTLINEFILL, &ptlBoxEnd, 0L, 0L) ;
                    }
```

Listing 9.5: The BLOKOUT1 program (Continued)

```
               if (fButtonDown)
                    {
                    GpiSetMix (hps, FM_INVERT) ;

                    GpiMove (hps, &ptlStart) ;
                    GpiBox (hps, DRO_OUTLINE, &ptlEnd, 0L, 0L) ;
                    }
               WinEndPaint (hps) ;
               return 0 ;
          }
     return WinDefWindowProc (hwnd, msg, mp1, mp2) ;
     }
```

The BLOKOUT1.DEF File

```
;-----------------------------------
; BLOKOUT1.DEF module definition file
;-----------------------------------

NAME           BLOKOUT1  WINDOWAPI

DESCRIPTION    'Mouse Button Demo Program (c) Charles Petzold, 1993'
PROTMODE
```

You can use this program to block out a rectangular area within the client window. When you press button 1, BLOKOUT1 saves the pointer position and uses it as one corner of a rectangle. You then move the mouse with the button pressed down. The current position of the pointer is the opposite corner of the rectangle. As you move the mouse, BLOKOUT1 displays the rectangle outline. When you release the mouse button, the program draws the filled rectangle.

Figure 9.3 shows one rectangle already drawn and another rectangle in progress.

When *WndProc* receives a WM_BUTTON1DOWN message, it saves the position of the pointer in two static POINTL structures:

```
ptlStart.x = ptlEnd.x = MOUSEMSG(&msg)->x;
ptlStart.y = ptlEnd.y = MOUSEMSG(&msg)->y;
```

It then calls the function *DrawBoxOutline* to draw a rectangle using *GpiBox* with the FM_INVERT mix mode between these two points. (The rectangle will be only one pixel after this first call to *DrawBoxOutline*.) The *fButtonDown* variable is set to TRUE so that the program knows the button is down during subsequent messages.

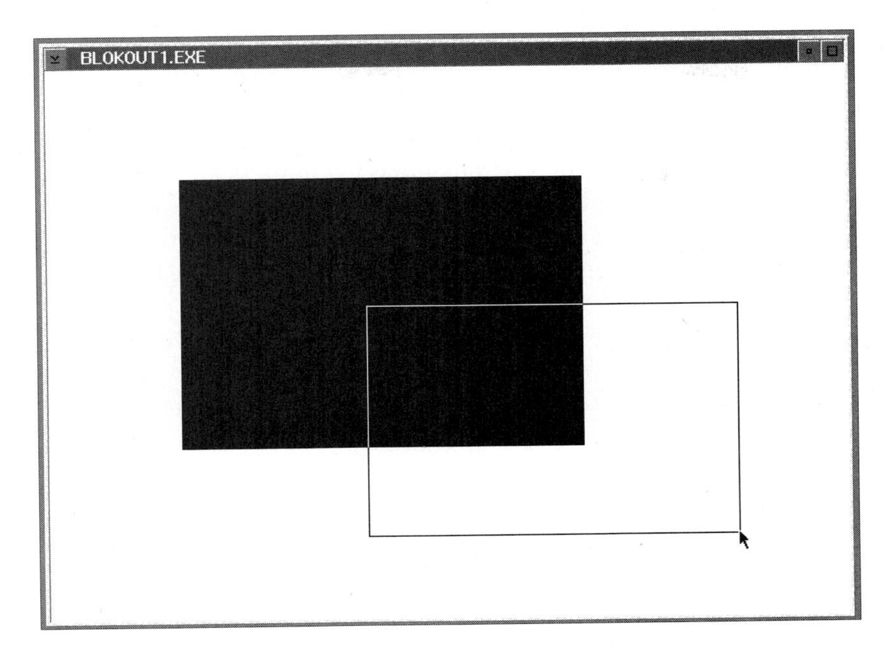

Figure 9.3: The BLOKOUT1 display

The WM_MOUSEMOVE message is processed only if *fButtonDown* is TRUE. *DrawBoxOutline* is called again to erase the previous box, the new pointer position is stored in *ptlEnd*, and the new rectangle outline is drawn.

The WM_BUTTON1UP message is also processed only if *fButtonDown* is TRUE. *ClientWndProc* first erases the previous rectangle and then saves the two opposite corners in the POINTL structures *ptlBoxStart* and *ptlBoxEnd*. The *fButtonDown* variable is set to FALSE and the client window is invalidated. The WM_PAINT processing draws a filled rectangle based on these two points.

At first, nothing seems to be wrong with this program. But a problem does exist.

THE PROBLEM

Try this: What happens if you press the mouse button within BLOKOUT1's client window but then move the pointer outside the window? BLOKOUT1 will stop receiving the WM_MOUSEMOVE messages. Now you release the mouse button. BLOKOUT1 doesn't get that WM_BUTTON1UP message because the pointer is outside the client window.

Now move the mouse pointer back within BLOKOUT1's client window. *ClientWndProc* still thinks the mouse button is pressed because *fButtonDown* is set to TRUE! This is clearly not good. The program doesn't know what's going on.

An alternative is to dispense with the *fButtonDown* variable and use *WinGetKeyState* to test the state of the button during the WM_MOUSEMOVE message. But this is also a problem. What happens if you press the mouse button outside of BLOKOUT1's client window and then move the pointer inside? *WinGetKeyState* will report that the mouse button is pressed, but BLOKOUT1 will not have a valid starting point for the rectangle because the button was pressed outside the client window.

How about using a combination of the *fButtonDown* logic and the *WinGetKeyState* function? You're welcome to try, but think a bit about what you really want to do here. You want the ability to follow the mouse pointer even when it ventures outside the client window. You want to process all of the WM_MOUSEMOVE messages between WM_BUTTON1DOWN and WM_BUTTON1UP, regardless of whether the mouse is inside or outside the client window.

You can do this. This process is called "capturing the mouse."

THE SOLUTION: CAPTURING THE MOUSE

Capturing the mouse is simpler than baiting a mousetrap. You simply call

```
WinSetCapture (HWND_DESKTOP, hwnd) ;
```

After you call *WinSetCapture*, all mouse messages will be directed to *hwnd*'s window procedure regardless of where the pointer is positioned. (Note that the coordinates of the pointer will still be relative to the lower-left corner of the window, so they could be negative.) To release the mouse, use the following call:

```
WinSetCapture (HWND_DESKTOP, NULL) ;
```

A window that has captured the mouse is called the *capture window*. Only one window can be the capture window at any time. You can obtain the window handle of the capture window by calling *WinQueryCapture*. The function returns NULL if there is no capture window, as is usually the case.

The BLOKOUT2 program, shown in Listing 9.6, demonstrates how to capture the mouse.

BLOKOUT2 captures the mouse on a WM_BUTTON1DOWN message. Rather than using the *fButtonDown* variable from BLOKOUT1, BLOKOUT2 uses an *fCapture* variable that it sets to TRUE when the mouse is captured.

Listing 9.6: The BLOKOUT2 program

The BLOKOUT2.MAK File

```
#-----------------------
# BLOKOUT2.MAK make file
#-----------------------

blokout2.exe : blokout2.obj blokout2.def
     $(PRGLINK) blokout2, blokout2, NUL, $(PRGLIB), blokout2

blokout2.obj : blokout2.c
     $(PRGCC) blokout2.c
```

The BLOKOUT2.C File

```
/*-------------------------------------------------
   BLOKOUT2.C -- Mouse Button & Capture Demo Program
                 (c) Charles Petzold, 1993
  -------------------------------------------------*/

#define INCL_WIN
#define INCL_GPI
#include <os2.h>

MRESULT EXPENTRY ClientWndProc (HWND, ULONG, MPARAM, MPARAM) ;

int main (void)
     {
     static CHAR  szClientClass [] = "BlokOut2" ;
     static ULONG flFrameFlags = FCF_TITLEBAR       | FCF_SYSMENU |
                                 FCF_SIZEBORDER     | FCF_MINMAX  |
                                 FCF_SHELLPOSITION  | FCF_TASKLIST ;
     HAB          hab ;
     HMQ          hmq ;
     HWND         hwndFrame, hwndClient ;
     QMSG         qmsg ;

     hab = WinInitialize (0) ;
     hmq = WinCreateMsgQueue (hab, 0) ;

     WinRegisterClass (hab, szClientClass, ClientWndProc, CS_SIZEREDRAW, 0) ;

     hwndFrame = WinCreateStdWindow (HWND_DESKTOP, WS_VISIBLE,
                                     &flFrameFlags, szClientClass, NULL,
                                     0L, 0, 0, &hwndClient) ;

     while (WinGetMsg (hab, &qmsg, NULLHANDLE, 0, 0))
          WinDispatchMsg (hab, &qmsg) ;
```

Listing 9.6: The BLOKOUT2 program (Continued)

```
     WinDestroyWindow (hwndFrame) ;
     WinDestroyMsgQueue (hmq) ;
     WinTerminate (hab) ;
     return 0 ;
     }

VOID DrawBoxOutline (HWND hwnd, POINTL *pptlStart, POINTL *pptlEnd)
     {
     HPS hps ;

     hps = WinGetPS (hwnd) ;
     GpiSetMix (hps, FM_INVERT) ;

     GpiMove (hps, pptlStart) ;
     GpiBox (hps, DRO_OUTLINE, pptlEnd, 0L, 0L) ;

     WinReleasePS (hps) ;
     }

MRESULT EXPENTRY ClientWndProc (HWND hwnd, ULONG msg, MPARAM mp1, MPARAM mp2)
     {
     static BOOL   fCapture, fValidBox ;
     static POINTL ptlStart, ptlEnd, ptlBoxStart, ptlBoxEnd ;
     HPS           hps ;

     switch (msg)
          {
          case WM_BUTTON1DOWN:
               ptlStart.x = ptlEnd.x = MOUSEMSG(&msg)->x ;
               ptlStart.y = ptlEnd.y = MOUSEMSG(&msg)->y ;

               DrawBoxOutline (hwnd, &ptlStart, &ptlEnd) ;

               WinSetCapture (HWND_DESKTOP, hwnd) ;
               fCapture = TRUE ;
               break ;                        // do default processing

          case WM_MOUSEMOVE:
               if (fCapture)
                    {
                    DrawBoxOutline (hwnd, &ptlStart, &ptlEnd) ;

                    ptlEnd.x = MOUSEMSG(&msg)->x ;
                    ptlEnd.y = MOUSEMSG(&msg)->y ;

                    DrawBoxOutline (hwnd, &ptlStart, &ptlEnd) ;
                    }
               break ;                        // do default processing
```

Listing 9.6: The BLOKOUT2 program (Continued)

```
          case WM_BUTTON1UP:
               if (fCapture)
                    {
                    DrawBoxOutline (hwnd, &ptlStart, &ptlEnd) ;

                    ptlBoxStart = ptlStart ;
                    ptlBoxEnd.x = MOUSEMSG(&msg)->x ;
                    ptlBoxEnd.y = MOUSEMSG(&msg)->y ;

                    WinSetCapture (HWND_DESKTOP, NULLHANDLE) ;
                    fCapture = FALSE ;
                    fValidBox = TRUE ;
                    WinInvalidateRect (hwnd, NULL, FALSE) ;
                    }
               return Ø ;

          case WM_CHAR:
               if (fCapture && CHARMSG(&msg)->fs   &  KC_VIRTUALKEY &&
                             !(CHARMSG(&msg)->fs   &  KC_KEYUP)     &&
                               CHARMSG(&msg)->vkey == VK_ESC)
                    {
                    DrawBoxOutline (hwnd, &ptlStart, &ptlEnd) ;

                    WinSetCapture (HWND_DESKTOP, NULLHANDLE) ;
                    fCapture = FALSE ;
                    }
               return Ø ;

          case WM_PAINT:
               hps = WinBeginPaint (hwnd, NULLHANDLE, NULL) ;
               GpiErase (hps) ;

               if (fValidBox)
                    {
                    GpiMove (hps, &ptlBoxStart) ;
                    GpiBox (hps, DRO_OUTLINEFILL, &ptlBoxEnd, ØL, ØL) ;
                    }
               if (fCapture)
                    {
                    GpiSetMix (hps, FM_INVERT) ;
                    GpiMove (hps, &ptlStart) ;
                    GpiBox (hps, DRO_OUTLINE, &ptlEnd, ØL, ØL) ;
                    }
               WinEndPaint (hps) ;
               return Ø ;
          }
     return WinDefWindowProc (hwnd, msg, mp1, mp2) ;
     }
```

Listing 9.6: The BLOKOUT2 program (Continued)

The BLOKOUT2.DEF File

```
;-----------------------------------
; BLOKOUT2.DEF module definition file
;-----------------------------------

NAME           BLOKOUT2  WINDOWAPI

DESCRIPTION    'Mouse Button & Capture Demo Program (c) Charles Petzold, 1993'
PROTMODE
```

If the size of the BLOKOUT2 window is less than the full screen, you'll notice that BLOKOUT2 continues to receive WM_MOUSEMOVE messages even when you move the pointer outside the client window. When you release the button (either while the pointer is inside or outside the client window), BLOKOUT2 releases the mouse.

BLOKOUT2 also processes the WM_CHAR message. If you press the Escape key while blocking out a rectangle, the program erases the rectangle you've been drawing and releases the mouse. This is how you can cancel the blockout. Otherwise, much of BLOKOUT2 is exactly the same as BLOKOUT1. Capturing the mouse adds very little overhead to mouse processing and helps out a great deal in many cases.

The Presentation Manager *WinTrackRect* function is also a big help in jobs that require a rectangle to be stretched or moved using the mouse and keyboard, particularly when the rectangle must be displayed outside the program's window. The title bar window and sizing border window use *WinTrackRect* to let you move and resize the standard window. I'll show you how to use *WinTrackRect* in the BLOWUP program in Chapter 15.

THE SKETCH PROGRAM

You've heard of CAD programs? You've heard of paint programs? The program in Listing 9.7 is neither of these. It's called SKETCH and is just about the most primitive drawing program possible.

To draw in SKETCH, you press button 1 and move the mouse. To erase (or, more precisely, to draw using the background color) you press button 2 and move the mouse. To clear the entire window, you... well, you have to end the program, load it again, and start all over. (I said that this is a primitive program, didn't I?) Figure 9.4 shows the SKETCH program with the word "Hello" drawn on the window, an homage to those early advertisements for the Apple Macintosh.

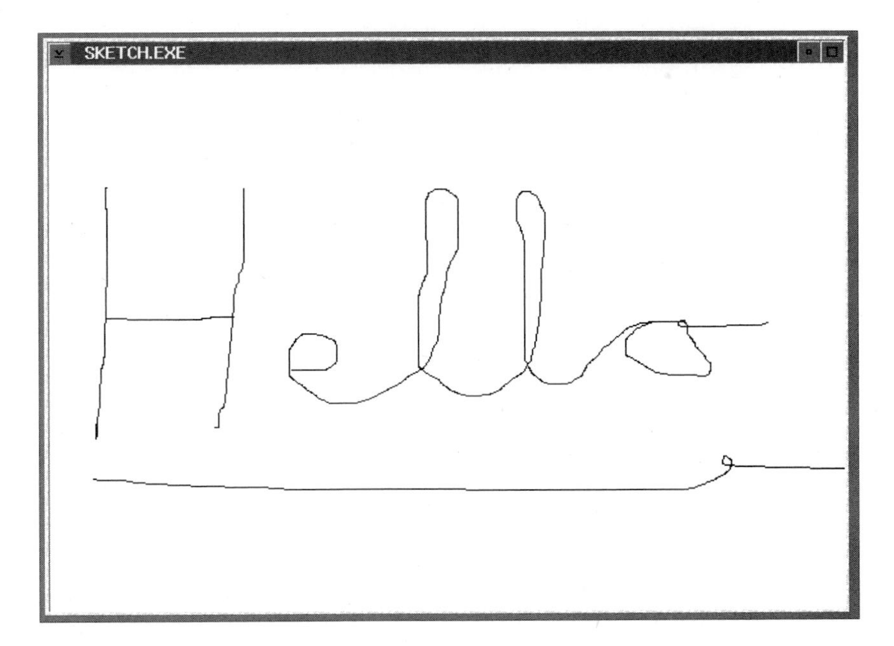

Figure 9.4: The SKETCH display

Listing 9.7: The SKETCH program

The SKETCH.MAK File

```
#---------------------
# SKETCH.MAK make file
#---------------------

sketch.exe : sketch.obj sketch.def
     $(PRGLINK) sketch, sketch, NUL, $(PRGLIB), sketch

sketch.obj : sketch.c
     $(PRGCC) sketch.c
```

The SKETCH.C File

```
/*----------------------------------------
   SKETCH.C -- Mouse Sketching Program
               (c) Charles Petzold, 1993
  ----------------------------------------*/
```

Listing 9.7: The SKETCH program (Continued)

```
#define INCL_WIN
#define INCL_GPI
#include <os2.h>

MRESULT EXPENTRY ClientWndProc (HWND, ULONG, MPARAM, MPARAM) ;

HAB  hab ;

int main (void)
     {
     static CHAR  szClientClass [] = "Sketch" ;
     static ULONG flFrameFlags = FCF_TITLEBAR       | FCF_SYSMENU |
                                 FCF_SIZEBORDER     | FCF_MINMAX  |
                                 FCF_SHELLPOSITION  | FCF_TASKLIST ;
     HMQ          hmq ;
     HWND         hwndFrame, hwndClient ;
     QMSG         qmsg ;

     hab = WinInitialize (0) ;
     hmq = WinCreateMsgQueue (hab, 0) ;

     WinRegisterClass (hab, szClientClass, ClientWndProc, CS_SIZEREDRAW, 0) ;

     hwndFrame = WinCreateStdWindow (HWND_DESKTOP, WS_VISIBLE,
                                     &flFrameFlags, szClientClass, NULL,
                                     0L, 0, 0, &hwndClient) ;

     if (hwndFrame == NULLHANDLE)
          WinMessageBox (HWND_DESKTOP, HWND_DESKTOP,
                         "Not enough memory to create the "
                         "bitmap used for storing images.",
                         szClientClass, 0, MB_OK | MB_WARNING) ;
     else
          {
          while (WinGetMsg (hab, &qmsg, NULLHANDLE, 0, 0))
               WinDispatchMsg (hab, &qmsg) ;

          WinDestroyWindow (hwndFrame) ;
          }

     WinDestroyMsgQueue (hmq) ;
     WinTerminate (hab) ;
     return 0 ;
     }

MRESULT EXPENTRY ClientWndProc (HWND hwnd, ULONG msg, MPARAM mp1, MPARAM mp2)
     {
     static BITMAPINFOHEADER2 bmp ;
     static BOOL              fButton1Down, fButton2Down ;
```

Listing 9.7: The SKETCH program (Continued)

```
     static HBITMAP          hbm ;
     static HDC              hdcMemory ;
     static HPS              hpsMemory ;
     static POINTL           ptlPointerPos, aptl [3] ;
     HPS                     hpsWindow ;
     LONG                    cxFullScrn, cyFullScrn ;
     SIZEL                   sizl ;

     switch (msg)
          {
          case WM_CREATE:
               cxFullScrn = WinQuerySysValue (HWND_DESKTOP, SV_CXFULLSCREEN) ;
               cyFullScrn = WinQuerySysValue (HWND_DESKTOP, SV_CYFULLSCREEN) ;

                         // Create Memory DC and PS

               hdcMemory = DevOpenDC (hab, OD_MEMORY, "*", ØL, NULL, Ø) ;

               sizl.cx = Ø ;
               sizl.cy = Ø ;
               hpsMemory = GpiCreatePS (hab, hdcMemory, &sizl,
                                        PU_PELS    | GPIF_DEFAULT |
                                        GPIT_MICRO | GPIA_ASSOC) ;

                         // Create monochrome bitmap, return 1 if cannot

               bmp.cbFix     = sizeof (BITMAPINFOHEADER2) ;
               bmp.cx        = cxFullScrn ;
               bmp.cy        = cyFullScrn ;
               bmp.cPlanes   = 1 ;
               bmp.cBitCount = 1 ;

               hbm = GpiCreateBitmap (hpsMemory, &bmp, ØL, ØL, NULL) ;

               if (hbm == Ø)
                    {
                    GpiDestroyPS (hpsMemory) ;
                    DevCloseDC (hdcMemory) ;
                    return MRFROMSHORT (1) ;
                    }

                         // Set bitmap in memory PS and clear it

               GpiSetBitmap (hpsMemory, hbm) ;

               aptl[1].x = cxFullScrn ;
               aptl[1].y = cyFullScrn ;
               GpiBitBlt (hpsMemory, Ø, 2L, aptl, ROP_ZERO, BBO_OR) ;
               return Ø ;
```

Listing 9.7: The SKETCH program (Continued)

```
          case WM_BUTTON1DOWN:
               if (!fButton2Down)
                    WinSetCapture (HWND_DESKTOP, hwnd) ;

               ptlPointerPos.x = MOUSEMSG(&msg)->x ;
               ptlPointerPos.y = MOUSEMSG(&msg)->y ;

               fButton1Down = TRUE ;
               break ;                          // do default processing

          case WM_BUTTON1UP:
               if (!fButton2Down)
                    WinSetCapture (HWND_DESKTOP, NULLHANDLE) ;

               fButton1Down = FALSE ;
               return Ø ;

          case WM_BUTTON2DOWN:
               if (!fButton1Down)
                    WinSetCapture (HWND_DESKTOP, hwnd) ;

               ptlPointerPos.x = MOUSEMSG(&msg)->x ;
               ptlPointerPos.y = MOUSEMSG(&msg)->y ;

               fButton2Down = TRUE ;
               break ;                          // do default processing

          case WM_BUTTON2UP:
               if (!fButton1Down)
                    WinSetCapture (HWND_DESKTOP, NULLHANDLE) ;

               fButton2Down = FALSE ;
               return Ø ;

          case WM_MOUSEMOVE:
               if (!fButton1Down && !fButton2Down)
                    break ;

               hpsWindow = WinGetPS (hwnd) ;

               GpiSetColor (hpsMemory, fButton1Down ? CLR_TRUE : CLR_FALSE) ;
               GpiSetColor (hpsWindow,
                            fButton1Down ? CLR_NEUTRAL : CLR_BACKGROUND) ;

               GpiMove (hpsMemory, &ptlPointerPos) ;
               GpiMove (hpsWindow, &ptlPointerPos) ;

               ptlPointerPos.x = MOUSEMSG(&msg)->x ;
```

Listing 9.7: The SKETCH program (Continued)

```
          ptlPointerPos.y = MOUSEMSG(&msg)->y ;

          GpiLine (hpsMemory, &ptlPointerPos) ;
          GpiLine (hpsWindow, &ptlPointerPos) ;

          WinReleasePS (hpsWindow) ;
          break ;                        // do default processing

     case WM_PAINT:
          hpsWindow = WinBeginPaint (hwnd, NULLHANDLE, (PRECTL) aptl) ;

          aptl[2] = aptl[0] ;

          GpiBitBlt (hpsWindow, hpsMemory, 3L, aptl, ROP_SRCCOPY,
                     BBO_OR) ;

          WinEndPaint (hpsWindow) ;
          return 0 ;

     case WM_DESTROY:
          GpiDestroyPS (hpsMemory) ;
          DevCloseDC (hdcMemory) ;
          GpiDeleteBitmap (hbm) ;
          return 0 ;
     }
return WinDefWindowProc (hwnd, msg, mp1, mp2) ;
}
```

The SKETCH.DEF File

```
;-----------------------------------
; SKETCH.DEF module definition file
;-----------------------------------

NAME           SKETCH    WINDOWAPI

DESCRIPTION    'Mouse Sketching Program (c) Charles Petzold, 1993'
PROTMODE
```

During the WM_CREATE message, SKETCH creates a monochrome bitmap the size of the maximized window. If this is not possible, SKETCH returns 1 from the WM_CREATE message. Returning 1 from WM_CREATE aborts the creation of the standard window. In *main*, SKETCH checks the value of *hwndFrame* to see if *WinCreateStdWindow* was successful. If not, SKETCH displays a message box informing the user of the problem.

This bitmap is used in a memory device context for saving any drawing you do and updating the window during the WM_PAINT message. A bitmap used in this way is sometimes called a *shadow bitmap.* Whenever SKETCH draws something on the window, it also draws the same thing on the bitmap. Consequently, WM_PAINT processing is very simple. All that's required is a *GpiBitBlt* call to update the window from the bitmap.

Setting the Timer

WHY THE TIMER IS NECESSARY

TIMER BASICS

THREE TIMER PROGRAMS

Chapter

10

The Presentation Manager timer is a form of input that periodically notifies a window procedure when a specific amount of time has elapsed. Your program specifies this time in the *WinStartTimer* function. The Presentation Manager then periodically posts WM_TIMER messages to the program's window procedure.

A clock is the most obvious application for a timer. The WM_TIMER messages tell the program to update the clock display. (Later in this chapter we'll tackle two clock programs that use the timer.) You can also use the timer to periodically update a status report (as is done in the FREEMEM program also shown in this chapter) or to pace screen activity for animation or computer-aided instruction.

Why the Timer Is Necessary

In previous chapters you've seen how the Presentation Manager provides alternatives to several categories of OS/2 kernel functions. For example, a Presentation Manager program doesn't use the OS/2 kernel VIO functions to write to the display. Instead, the program writes to the screen using the Presentation Manager GPI functions. Similarly, a Presentation Manager program doesn't use the OS/2 kernel KBD or MOU functions for keyboard or mouse input. Instead, the program processes keyboard and mouse input in the form of messages.

The Presentation Manager timer is also a substitute for OS/2 kernel functions—specifically those functions that involve suspending a thread of execution. For example, if you were to write a clock program for the OS/2 kernel, you would probably use the *DosSleep* function to suspend the thread for a set period of time. On return from *DosSleep*, the program would update the clock and call *DosSleep* again. But in a single-thread Presentation Manager program, *DosSleep* would suspend the normal processing of messages in that thread, even messages for such basic tasks as moving and resizing the window or selecting an item from the program's system menu. It's clear that for the Presentation Manager—which requires threads to process messages as quickly as possible—you shouldn't call functions such as *DosSleep* or wait on a semaphore in a message queue thread if you want optimum performance. That's why the Presentation Manager includes the timer. Message queue threads use the timer to regain periodic control in the absence of user input and other messages to the thread's windows. Chapter 17 discusses some alternatives to this use of the timer, including the use of multiple threads of execution.

TIMER BASICS

The timer is a fairly simple facility involving two functions and one message. The Presentation Manager defines two ways to set a timer. Both use the same *WinStartTimer* function but in a somewhat different format. The first method is by far the most common.

THE COMMON METHOD OF USING A TIMER

The BEEPER1 program, shown in Listing 10.1, demonstrates how to start a timer, process WM_TIMER messages, and stop the timer. BEEPER1 sets the timer to go off once every second. The window procedure responds to a WM_-TIMER message by beeping and changing the color of its client window, alternating between red and blue.

Listing 10.1: The BEEPER1 program

The BEEPER1.MAK File

```
#----------------------
# BEEPER1.MAK make file
#----------------------

beeper1.exe : beeper1.obj beeper1.def
     $(PRGLINK) beeper1, beeper1, NUL, $(PRGLIB), beeper1

beeper1.obj : beeper1.c
     $(PRGCC) beeper1.c
```

Listing 10.1: The BEEPER1 program (Continued)

The BEEPER1.C File

```
/*-----------------------------------------
   BEEPER1.C -- Timer Demo Program No. 1
                (c) Charles Petzold, 1993
  -----------------------------------------*/

#define INCL_WIN
#include <os2.h>

#define ID_TIMER 1

MRESULT EXPENTRY ClientWndProc (HWND, ULONG, MPARAM, MPARAM) ;

int main (void)
     {
     static char  szClientClass [] = "Beeper1" ;
     static ULONG flFrameFlags = FCF_TITLEBAR      | FCF_SYSMENU |
                                 FCF_SIZEBORDER    | FCF_MINMAX  |
                                 FCF_SHELLPOSITION | FCF_TASKLIST ;
     HAB          hab ;
     HMQ          hmq ;
     HWND         hwndFrame, hwndClient ;
     QMSG         qmsg ;

     hab = WinInitialize (0) ;
     hmq = WinCreateMsgQueue (hab, 0) ;

     WinRegisterClass (hab, szClientClass, ClientWndProc, 0L, 0) ;

     hwndFrame = WinCreateStdWindow (HWND_DESKTOP, WS_VISIBLE,
                                     &flFrameFlags, szClientClass, NULL,
                                     0L, 0, 0, &hwndClient) ;

     WinStartTimer (hab, hwndClient, ID_TIMER, 1000) ;

     while (WinGetMsg (hab, &qmsg, NULLHANDLE, 0, 0))
          WinDispatchMsg (hab, &qmsg) ;

     WinStopTimer (hab, hwndClient, ID_TIMER) ;

     WinDestroyWindow (hwndFrame) ;
     WinDestroyMsgQueue (hmq) ;
     WinTerminate (hab) ;
     return 0 ;
     }

MRESULT EXPENTRY ClientWndProc (HWND hwnd, ULONG msg, MPARAM mp1, MPARAM mp2)
```

Listing 10.1: The BEEPER1 program (Continued)

```
     {
     static BOOL fFlipFlop ;
     HPS         hps ;
     RECTL       rcl ;

     switch (msg)
          {
          case WM_TIMER:
               WinAlarm (HWND_DESKTOP, WA_NOTE) ;
               fFlipFlop = !fFlipFlop ;
               WinInvalidateRect (hwnd, NULL, FALSE) ;
               return 0 ;

          case WM_PAINT:
               hps = WinBeginPaint (hwnd, NULLHANDLE, NULL) ;

               WinQueryWindowRect (hwnd, &rcl) ;
               WinFillRect (hps, &rcl, fFlipFlop ? CLR_BLUE : CLR_RED) ;

               WinEndPaint (hps) ;
               return 0 ;
          }
     return WinDefWindowProc (hwnd, msg, mp1, mp2) ;
     }
```

The BEEPER1.DEF File

```
;-----------------------------------
; BEEPER1.DEF module definition file
;-----------------------------------

NAME           BEEPER1   WINDOWAPI

DESCRIPTION    'Timer Demo Program No. 1 (c) Charles Petzold, 1993'
PROTMODE
```

The general syntax of the *WinStartTimer* function is

```
WinStartTimer (hab, hwnd, idTimer, ulMsecInterval) ;
```

The *hwnd* parameter is the window handle that designates which window function receives the WM_TIMER messages. The *idTimer* parameter is a number you select to identify this particular timer.

The *ulMsecInterval* parameter specifies a time interval in milliseconds (msec). This is the rate at which the Presentation Manager posts the WM_TIMER messages in the message queue. Setting this parameter to 0 causes the system to deliver WM_TIMER messages as fast as the system clock. Although the parameter is a ULONG (and thus could theoretically represent a time interval of about 48 days), values over 65535 simply do not work. The maximum time interval is 65535 msec, or about 65½ seconds.

BEEPER1 starts a timer in *main* immediately following the *WinCreateStd-Window* call:

```
WinStartTimer (hab, hwndClient, ID_TIMER, 1000) ;
```

This tells the Presentation Manager to post a WM_TIMER message to *hwnd-Client* once every 1000 msec. The ID_TIMER identifier is defined near the top of the program:

```
#define ID_TIMER 1
```

The low USHORT of the *mp1* parameter that accompanies the WM_TIMER message is this ID number.

BEEPER1 processes the WM_TIMER messages in *ClientWndProc*:

```
case WM_TIMER:
     WinAlarm (HWND_DESKTOP, WA_NOTE) ;
     fFlipFlop = !fFlipFlop ;
     WinInvalidateRect (hwnd, NULL, FALSE) ;
     return 0 ;
```

The code simply beeps the speaker, inverts the value of the static BOOL variable *fFlipFlop*, and calls *WinInvalidateRect* to invalidate the entire client window and generate a WM_PAINT message. During the WM_PAINT message, BEEPER1 uses the *fFlipFlop* variable to determine the color (blue or red) used to paint the client window:

```
WinQueryWindowRect (hwnd, &rcl) ;
WinFillRect (hps, &rcl, fFlipFlop ? CLR_BLUE : CLR_RED) ;
```

The window procedure receives WM_TIMER messages during the entire time the window exists. Only when BEEPER1 exits the message queue in main on receipt of a WM_QUIT message does the program stop the timer:

```
WinStopTimer (hab, hwndClient, ID_TIMER) ;
```

BEEPER1 then terminates normally.

A program doesn't need to start and stop the timer in *main*. If the program doesn't need a timer for its entire duration, it can start or stop the timer from the window procedure. Although BEEPER1 causes its client window to be repainted once a second by calling *WinInvalidateRect*, a program can also call *WinGetPS* to do some painting while processing the WM_TIMER message.

The CLOCK program shown later in this chapter paints during the WM_-TIMER message.

TIMER IMPRECISION

If you can tolerate the program's incessant beeping, you can learn a lot about the timer by experimenting with BEEPER1 while running other Presentation Manager programs. The first discovery is that the timer is not a precise and regular clock tick. There are several reasons for this.

The resolution of the timer depends on the resolution of the hardware clock in the computer. Under OS/2, the hardware clock generates an interrupt every 31.25 msec, or 32 times per second. The rate of the WM_TIMER messages on a PC is always an integral multiple of 32 msec. You can't receive WM_TIMER messages more frequently than 32 msec.

The WM_TIMER message isn't sent directly to the window procedure but is instead placed in the program's message queue. WM_TIMER messages are low priority—*WinGetMsg* retrieves other queued messages (except WM_PAINT) before WM_TIMER messages. There can be a delay between the time the message is placed in the queue and the time the window procedure gets it. However, the Presentation Manager doesn't load a message queue with multiple WM_TIMER messages if the program can't process them. The message queue never contains more than one timer message of a particular timer ID.

LIMITED AVAILABILITY OF TIMERS

The Presentation Manager allows only a limited number of timers to be set throughout the system—specifically 40. A program can determine how many timers are still available in the Presentation Manager by calling

```
lAvailTimers = WinQuerySysValue (HWND_DESKTOP, SV_CTIMERS) ;
```

However, it's often easier simply to call *WinStartTimer*. If *WinStartTimer* returns 0, no timer was available.

If your program can't work properly without a timer (as is obviously the case for a clock application), the program has no choice but to terminate if no timer is available. You should display a message box informing the user of this problem. If you set the timer in *main* after the *WinCreateStdWindow* call, here is one way of dealing with the lack of an available timer:

```
hwndFrame = WinCreateStdWindow (...) ;

if (WinStartTimer (hab, hwndClient, ID_TIMER, 1000))
     {
     while (WinGetMsg (hab, &qmsg, NULL, 0, 0))
```

```
          WinDispatchMsg (hab, &qmsg) ;

     WinStopTimer (hab, hwndClient, ID_TIMER) ;
     }
else
     WinMessageBox (HWND_DESKTOP, hwndClient,
          "Too many clocks or timers",
          "Program Name", 0, MB_OK | MB_ICONEXCLAMATION) ;

WinDestroyWindow (hwndFrame) ;
```

If *WinStartTimer* returns a nonzero value, the program enters the message loop and later calls *WinStopTimer* when it exits the message loop. Otherwise, the program displays a message box, destroys the frame window, and terminates normally. You should perform this check in every program you write that uses a timer.

A ONE-SHOT TIMER

In some applications you may not need a timer that repeatedly sends WM_-TIMER messages. Instead, you may want to send only one WM_TIMER message after a specified period of time. In this case you can set the timer normally and call *WinStopTimer* during processing of the WM_TIMER message:

```
case WM_TIMER:
          [ other program lines ]
     WinStopTimer (hab, hwnd, ID_TIMER) ;
     return 0 ;
```

Calling *WinStopTimer* not only stops future WM_TIMER messages but also clears the message queue of any pending WM_TIMER messages. You'll never receive a stray WM_TIMER message after you call *WinStopTimer.*

A TIMER OVER 65½ SECONDS

The maximum timer interval is 65,535 msec, or 65½ seconds. If you need a timer interval greater than this (for example, 30 minutes), you can first set a static variable that contains the duration in minutes:

```
iMinuteWait = 30 ;
```

You then set a timer for 1 minute:

```
WinStartTimer (hab, hwnd, ID_TIMER, 60000) ;
```

During WM_TIMER processing, you decrement and test iMinuteWait:

```
case WM_TIMER:
     if (--iMinuteWait == 0)
          {
               [ other program lines ]
          }
     return 0 ;
```

An alternative method is to call *DosGetDateTime* to get the current time when you first start the timer. During the WM_TIMER message you can call *DosGetDateTime* again to determine if 30 minutes have elapsed.

The *WinGetCurrentTime* function can also be helpful here. This function returns the elapsed time in milliseconds since OS/2 was first booted. This is a ULONG value that rolls over to 0 about every 48 days. Let's assume again that you want to set a 30-minute timer interval. First, define a static ULONG variable:

```
static ULONG ulStartTime ;
```

Then call *WinGetCurrentTime* and *WinStartTimer*:

```
ulStartTime = WinGetCurrentTime (hab) ;
WinStartTimer (hab, hwnd, ID_TIMER, 60000) ;
```

During the WM_TIMER message, check to see if 30 minutes have elapsed:

```
case WM_TIMER:
     if (WinGetCurrentTime (hab) - ulStartTime > 30 * 60 * 1000)
          {
               [ other program lines ]
          }
     return 0 ;
```

RESETTING THE TIMER TIME

You may need to change the interval of the WM_TIMER messages. For example, you may have originally set the timer for 1-second intervals:

```
WinStartTimer (hab, hwnd, ID_TIMER, 1000) ;
```

If you later need to change that to 5-second intervals, you can simply call *WinStartTimer* again with the same timer ID and a different elapsed time:

```
WinStartTimer (hab, hwnd, ID_TIMER, 5000) ;
```

The next WM_TIMER message will now arrive in 5 seconds.

USING MULTIPLE TIMERS

If you like, you can set multiple timers in your program. Suppose you want one timer for 1-second intervals and another timer for 1-minute intervals. You first define two IDs:

```
#define ID_SECTIMER 1
#define ID_MINTIMER 2
```

To start the timers, make two *WinStartTimer* calls:

```
WinStartTimer (hab, hwnd, ID_SECTIMER,  1000) ;
WinStartTimer (hab, hwnd, ID_MINTIMER, 60000) ;
```

The processing of the WM_TIMER message can use a switch and case construction to do different processing based on the timer ID stored in *mp1*:

```
case WM_TIMER:
     switch (SHORT1FROMMP (mp1))
          {
          case ID_SECTIMER:
                    [ once-per-second processing ]
               return 0 ;

          case ID_MINTIMER:
                    [ once-per-minute processing ]
               return 0 ;
          }
     break ;
```

Before your program terminates, it stops both timers:

```
WinStopTimer (hab, hwnd, ID_SECTIMER) ;
WinStopTimer (hab, hwnd, ID_MINTIMER) ;
```

But considering that the Presentation Manager makes only a limited number of timers available, you should feel a little guilty about hogging system resources like this. A better approach is to set only one timer (the one with the shortest interval) and then derive longer intervals from that.

THE TIMERS YOU DON'T SET

Even if you never call *WinStartTimer* in your program, WM_TIMER messages may still be posted through your message queue and even dispatched to your client window procedure. Sometimes you need to make special provisions for these messages.

You'll recall that the TYPEAWAY program in Chapter 8 creates a blinking cursor. The blink is controlled by a timer. Because the client window procedure in TYPEAWAY doesn't explicitly process WM_TIMER messages, the messages are passed on to *WinDefWindowProc*. That's where the cursor-blinking logic is. If you add the following lines to TYPEAWAY's client window procedure, the cursor won't blink:

```
case WM_TIMER:
     return 0 ;
```

Child window scroll bars and edit fields (discussed in Chapters 11 and 14) also use the timer to blink their cursors. If you create a scroll bar or edit window, the WM_TIMER messages come through the program's message queue but are dispatched to the window procedure associated with the child window.

If you set a timer in a program that also creates a blinking cursor, you should process only those WM_TIMER messages with the ID number you use (for example, ID_TIMER). All other WM_TIMER messages should be passed on to *WinDefWindowProc*. The logic looks like this:

```
case WM_TIMER:
     if (SHORT1FROMMP (mp1) == ID_TIMER)
          {
               [ process timer message ]
          return 0 ;
          }
     break ;
```

If you set multiple timers, you can use *switch* and *case* statements and *break* for the default case, as shown earlier in the example of multiple timers.

The IDs for the cursor, scroll bar, and flashing window timers are defined in PMWIN.H using the identifiers TID_CURSOR, TID_SCROLL, and TID_-FLASHWINDOW. These are set equal to 0xFFFF, 0xFFFE, and 0xFFFD, so you should avoid using those IDs for any other timers.

THE UNCOMMON METHOD OF USING A TIMER

The examples in all of the preceding sections of this chapter use the following form of the *WinStartTimer* call:

```
WinStartTimer (hab, hwnd, idTimer, ulMsecInterval) ;
```

where *idTimer* is a predefined constant.

The second form of the *WinStartTimer* function requires that you first define a variable to store the timer ID:

```
ULONG idTimer ;
```

You then call the *WinStartTimer* function like this:

```
idTimer = WinStartTimer (hab, NULL, 0, ulMsecInterval) ;
```

The second parameter (normally set to the window handle) is set to NULL in this form of *WinStartTimer*. The Presentation Manager ignores the third parameter and instead returns a timer ID (or 0 if no timer was available) from the function. You use this ID when stopping the timer:

```
WinStopTimer (hab, NULL, idTimer) ;
```

This form of *WinStartTimer* requires that the WM_TIMER message be handled in a special way. Although the message is posted to the message queue associated with the thread, the window handle of the message is set to NULLHANDLE. This means that the message won't be dispatched to a window procedure. Instead, it must be processed after it is retrieved from the message queue. The BEEPER2 program, shown in Listing 10.2, illustrates how this is done.

Listing 10.2: The BEEPER2 program

The BEEPER2.MAK File

```
#----------------------
# BEEPER2.MAK make file
#----------------------

beeper2.exe : beeper2.obj beeper2.def
     $(PRGLINK) beeper2, beeper2, NUL, $(PRGLIB), beeper2

beeper2.obj : beeper2.c
     $(PRGCC) beeper2.c
```

The BEEPER2.C File

```
/*--------------------------------------
   BEEPER2.C -- Timer Demo Program No. 2
                (c) Charles Petzold, 1993
  --------------------------------------*/

#define INCL_WIN
#include <os2.h>

MRESULT EXPENTRY ClientWndProc (HWND, ULONG, MPARAM, MPARAM) ;

BOOL fFlipFlop ;

int main (void)
     {
```

Listing 10.2: The BEEPER2 program (Continued)

```
     static char  szClientClass [] = "Beeper2" ;
     static ULONG flFrameFlags = FCF_TITLEBAR       | FCF_SYSMENU |
                                 FCF_SIZEBORDER     | FCF_MINMAX  |
                                 FCF_SHELLPOSITION | FCF_TASKLIST ;
     HAB          hab ;
     HMQ          hmq ;
     HWND         hwndFrame, hwndClient ;
     QMSG         qmsg ;
     ULONG        idTimer ;

     hab = WinInitialize (0) ;
     hmq = WinCreateMsgQueue (hab, 0) ;

     WinRegisterClass (hab, szClientClass, ClientWndProc, CS_SIZEREDRAW, 0) ;

     hwndFrame = WinCreateStdWindow (HWND_DESKTOP, WS_VISIBLE,
                                     &flFrameFlags, szClientClass, NULL,
                                     0L, 0, 0, &hwndClient) ;

     idTimer = WinStartTimer (hab, NULLHANDLE, 0, 1000) ;

     while (WinGetMsg (hab, &qmsg, NULLHANDLE, 0, 0))
          {
          if (qmsg.msg == WM_TIMER && SHORT1FROMMP (qmsg.mp1) == idTimer)
               {
               WinAlarm (HWND_DESKTOP, WA_NOTE) ;
               fFlipFlop = !fFlipFlop ;
               WinInvalidateRect (hwndClient, NULL, FALSE) ;
               }
          else
               WinDispatchMsg (hab, &qmsg) ;
          }

     WinStopTimer (hab, NULLHANDLE, idTimer) ;

     WinDestroyWindow (hwndFrame) ;
     WinDestroyMsgQueue (hmq) ;
     WinTerminate (hab) ;
     return 0 ;
     }

MRESULT EXPENTRY ClientWndProc (HWND hwnd, ULONG msg, MPARAM mp1, MPARAM mp2)
     {
     HPS   hps ;
     RECTL rcl ;

     switch (msg)
          {
          case WM_PAINT:
               hps = WinBeginPaint (hwnd, NULLHANDLE, NULL) ;
```

Listing 10.2: The BEEPER2 program (Continued)

```
               WinQueryWindowRect (hwnd, &rcl) ;
               WinFillRect (hps, &rcl, fFlipFlop ? CLR_BLUE : CLR_RED) ;

               WinEndPaint (hps) ;
               return 0 ;
          }
     return WinDefWindowProc (hwnd, msg, mp1, mp2) ;
     }
```

The BEEPER2.DEF File

```
;-----------------------------------
; BEEPER2.DEF module definition file
;-----------------------------------

NAME           BEEPER2   WINDOWAPI

DESCRIPTION    'Timer Demo Program No. 2 (c) Charles Petzold, 1993'
PROTMODE
```

BEEPER2 doesn't process the WM_TIMER message in its client window procedure but instead has the timer logic within the message loop:

```
while (WinGetMsg (hab, &qmsg, NULLHANDLE, 0, 0))
     {
     if (qmsg.msg == WM_TIMER && SHORT1FROMMP (qmsg.mp1) == idTimer)
          {
          WinAlarm (HWND_DESKTOP, WA_NOTE) ;
          fFlipFlop = !fFlipFlop ;
          WinInvalidateRect (hwndClient, NULL, FALSE) ;
          }
      else
          WinDispatchMsg (hab, &qmsg) ;
     }
```

BEEPER2 checks to see if the *msg* field of the QMSG structure is equal to WM_TIMER and if the low USHORT of the *mp1* parameter is equal to the timer ID returned from *WinStartTimer*. If the check is successful, BEEPER2 proceeds like BEEPER1 when it received a WM_TIMER message. If not, BEEPER2 dispatches the message to the window procedure. This form of the *WinStartTimer* function might be appropriate for a program that creates several threads of execution and needs a timer in a thread that doesn't create any windows.

If you move or resize BEEPER2's window, or invoke the system menu, you'll notice that the WM_TIMER messages seemingly stop. These operations involve the use of a different message loop than the one in your program, so any WM_TIMER message in the queue is ignored.

THREE TIMER PROGRAMS

Now let's put what we've learned into practice by writing three useful programs: a free memory display and two clocks (one digital, one analog).

A FREE MEMORY DISPLAY

The FREEMEM program, shown in Listing 10.3, creates a tiny window and positions it in the lower-left corner of the display. The window displays, in bytes, the amount of free memory in OS/2. The display is updated every second. That's where the timer helps out.

Listing 10.3: The FREEMEM program

The FREEMEM.MAK File

```
#-----------------------
# FREEMEM.MAK make file
#-----------------------

freemem.exe : freemem.obj freemem.def
     $(PRGLINK) freemem, freemem, NUL, $(PRGLIB), freemem

freemem.obj : freemem.c
     $(PRGCC) freemem.c
```

The FREEMEM.C File

```
/*---------------------------------------
   FREEMEM.C -- Free Memory Display
                (c) Charles Petzold, 1993
  ---------------------------------------*/

#define INCL_WIN
#define INCL_GPI
#define INCL_DOS
#include <os2.h>
#include <string.h>

#define ID_TIMER 1

MRESULT EXPENTRY ClientWndProc (HWND, ULONG, MPARAM, MPARAM) ;
VOID    SizeTheWindow (HWND) ;
```

Listing 10.3: The FREEMEM program (Continued)

```
int main (void)
     {
     static CHAR  szClientClass[] = "FreeMem" ;
     static ULONG flFrameFlags = FCF_TITLEBAR | FCF_SYSMENU  |
                                 FCF_BORDER   | FCF_TASKLIST ;
     HAB          hab ;
     HMQ          hmq ;
     HWND         hwndFrame, hwndClient ;
     QMSG         qmsg ;

     hab = WinInitialize (Ø) ;
     hmq = WinCreateMsgQueue (hab, Ø) ;

     WinRegisterClass (hab, szClientClass, ClientWndProc, ØL, Ø) ;

     hwndFrame = WinCreateStdWindow (HWND_DESKTOP, WS_VISIBLE,
                                     &flFrameFlags, szClientClass, NULL,
                                     ØL, Ø, Ø, &hwndClient) ;
     SizeTheWindow (hwndFrame) ;

     if (WinStartTimer (hab, hwndClient, ID_TIMER, 1ØØØ))
          {
          while (WinGetMsg (hab, &qmsg, NULLHANDLE, Ø, Ø))
               WinDispatchMsg (hab, &qmsg) ;

          WinStopTimer (hab, hwndClient, ID_TIMER) ;
          }
     else
          WinMessageBox (HWND_DESKTOP, hwndClient,
                         "Too many clocks or timers",
                         szClientClass, Ø, MB_OK | MB_WARNING) ;

     WinDestroyWindow (hwndFrame) ;
     WinDestroyMsgQueue (hmq) ;
     WinTerminate (hab) ;
     return Ø ;
     }

VOID SizeTheWindow (HWND hwndFrame)
     {
     static CHAR szText [] = "1,234,567,89Ø bytes" ;
     HPS         hps ;
     POINTL      aptl[TXTBOX_COUNT] ;
     RECTL       rcl ;

     hps = WinGetPS (hwndFrame) ;
     GpiQueryTextBox (hps, sizeof szText - 1L, szText, TXTBOX_COUNT, aptl) ;
     WinReleasePS (hps) ;
```

Listing 10.3: The FREEMEM program (Continued)

```
     rcl.yBottom = 0 ;
     rcl.yTop    = 3 * (aptl[TXTBOX_TOPLEFT].y -
                        aptl[TXTBOX_BOTTOMLEFT].y) / 2 ;
     rcl.xLeft   = 0 ;
     rcl.xRight  = (sizeof szText + 1L) * (aptl[TXTBOX_BOTTOMRIGHT].x -
                   aptl[TXTBOX_BOTTOMLEFT].x) / (sizeof szText - 1L) ;

     WinCalcFrameRect (hwndFrame, &rcl, FALSE) ;

     WinSetWindowPos (hwndFrame, NULLHANDLE, rcl.xLeft, rcl.yBottom,
                      rcl.xRight - rcl.xLeft, rcl.yTop - rcl.yBottom,
                      SWP_SIZE | SWP_MOVE) ;
     }

VOID FormatNumber (CHAR *pchResult, ULONG ulValue)
     {
     BOOL  fDisplay = FALSE ;
     INT   iDigit ;
     ULONG ulQuotient, ulDivisor = 1000000000L ;

     for (iDigit = 0 ; iDigit < 10 ; iDigit++)
          {
          ulQuotient = ulValue / ulDivisor ;

          if (fDisplay || ulQuotient > 0 || iDigit == 9)
               {
               fDisplay = TRUE ;

               *pchResult++ = (CHAR) ('0' + ulQuotient) ;

               if ((iDigit % 3 == 0) && iDigit != 9)
                    *pchResult++ = ',' ;
               }
          ulValue -= ulQuotient * ulDivisor ;
          ulDivisor /= 10 ;
          }
     *pchResult = '\0' ;
     }

MRESULT EXPENTRY ClientWndProc (HWND hwnd, ULONG msg, MPARAM mp1, MPARAM mp2)
     {
     static RECTL rcl ;
     static ULONG ulFreeMem, ulPrevMem ;
     CHAR         szBuffer [24] ;
     HPS          hps;

     switch (msg)
          {
          case WM_SIZE:
```

Listing 10.3: The FREEMEM program (Continued)

```
               WinQueryWindowRect (hwnd, &rcl) ;
               return 0 ;

          case WM_TIMER:
               DosQuerySysInfo (QSV_TOTAVAILMEM, QSV_TOTAVAILMEM,
                                (PBYTE) &ulFreeMem, sizeof (ULONG)) ;

               if (ulFreeMem != ulPrevMem)
                    {
                    WinInvalidateRect (hwnd, NULL, FALSE) ;
                    ulPrevMem = ulFreeMem ;
                    }
               return 0 ;

          case WM_PAINT:
               hps = WinBeginPaint (hwnd, NULLHANDLE, NULL) ;

               FormatNumber (szBuffer, ulFreeMem) ;
               strcat (szBuffer, " bytes") ;

               WinDrawText (hps, -1, szBuffer, &rcl,
                            CLR_NEUTRAL, CLR_BACKGROUND,
                            DT_CENTER | DT_VCENTER | DT_ERASERECT) ;

               WinEndPaint (hps) ;
               return 0 ;
          }
     return WinDefWindowProc (hwnd, msg, mp1, mp2) ;
     }
```

The FREEMEM.DEF File

```
;-----------------------------------
; FREEMEM.DEF module definition file
;-----------------------------------

NAME           FREEMEM   WINDOWAPI

DESCRIPTION    'Free Memory Display (c) Charles Petzold, 1993'
PROTMODE
```

FREEMEM starts the timer in *main* and displays a message box if *WinStartTimer* returns 0. The processing of the WM_TIMER message in *ClientWndProc* is fairly simple. After obtaining the amount of free memory from the

DosQuerySysInfo function, the program invalidates the client area if the amount of memory has changed since the last timer message:

```
if (ulFreeMem != ulPrevMem)
     {
     WinInvalidateRect (hwnd, NULL, FALSE) ;
     ulPrevMem = ulFreeMem ;
     }
```

FREEMEM saves the previous free memory size in *ulPrevMem*. Only if that size differs from the current value returned from *DosQuerySysInfo* will FREEMEM invalidate the window to generate a WM_PAINT message. The WM_PAINT processing calls the function *FormatNumber* to convert the memory size into a text string with comma separators.

FREEMEM creates a window of a fixed size positioned in a set area of the display, so it is worthwhile to take a closer look at how this is done. The *WinCreateStdWindow* function in FREEMEM uses frame creation flags of FCF_TITLEBAR, FCF_SYSMENU, FCF_BORDER, and FCF_TASKLIST. The FCF_SIZEBORDER, FCF_MINMAX, and FCF_SHELLPOSITION flags are not used. Because the window doesn't contain the minimize/maximize menu, the Minimize and Maximize options on the system menu are grayed and disabled.

A program that does not use the the FCF_SHELLPOSITION flag when creating the standard window must call *WinSetWindowPos* to give the frame window a size and position. This is done in FREEMEM's *SizeTheWindow* function. Because the size of the client window must be based on the size of the text string it displays, the function first calls *GpiQueryTextBox* for a maximum possible string length. *SizeTheWindow* then defines the screen coordinates of a RECTL structure that contains the position and size of this client window.

The positioning of the client window in the lower-left corner of the screen is indicated by the *yBottom* and *xLeft* fields. To allow a little margin around the text, the client window rectangle is set to 1½ times the height of the text box, with a width sufficient for the string plus a slight margin.

That RECTL structure is the position and size of the client window. The *WinCalcFrameRect* function converts this rectangle to a frame window position and size:

```
WinCalcFrameRect (hwndFrame, &rcl, FALSE) ;
```

SizeTheWindow can then set the position and size of the frame window:

```
WinSetWindowPos (hwndFrame, NULLHANDLE, rcl.xLeft, rcl.yBottom,
     rcl.xRight - rcl.xLeft, rcl.yTop - rcl.yBottom,
     SWP_SIZE SWP_MOVE) ;
```

This window won't be the active window. Because the program's purpose is to display some information, FREEMEM needn't be the active window when it is first displayed. If we wanted FREEMEM to be the active window when it was first displayed, we could have included SWP_ACTIVATE among the last parameters to *WinSetWindowPos*.

Figure 10.1 shows FREEMEM running in the lower-left corner of Presentation Manager.

Figure 10.1: The FREEMEM display

A DIGITAL CLOCK

Listing 10.4 shows the DIGCLOCK program, a digital clock that occupies a small window positioned in the lower-right corner of the display. The clock displays the day of the week, the date (*month/day/year*), and the time. It is updated (with help from Presentation Manager timer) every second.

Listing 10.4: The DIGCLOCK program

The DIGCLOCK.MAK File

```
#-----------------------
# DIGCLOCK.MAK make file
#-----------------------

digclock.exe : digclock.obj digclock.def
     $(PRGLINK) digclock, digclock, NUL, $(PRGLIB), digclock

digclock.obj : digclock.c
     $(PRGCC) digclock.c
```

The DIGCLOCK.C File

```
/*----------------------------------------
   DIGCLOCK.C -- Digital Clock
                 (c) Charles Petzold, 1993
  ----------------------------------------*/
```

Listing 10.4: The DIGCLOCK program (Continued)

```
#define INCL_WIN
#define INCL_GPI
#define INCL_DOS
#include <os2.h>
#include <stdio.h>

#define ID_TIMER 1

MRESULT EXPENTRY ClientWndProc (HWND, ULONG, MPARAM, MPARAM) ;
VOID    SizeTheWindow (HWND) ;

int main (void)
     {
     static CHAR  szClientClass[] = "DigClock" ;
     static ULONG flFrameFlags = FCF_TITLEBAR | FCF_SYSMENU  |
                                 FCF_BORDER   | FCF_TASKLIST ;
     HAB          hab ;
     HMQ          hmq ;
     HWND         hwndFrame, hwndClient ;
     QMSG         qmsg ;

     hab = WinInitialize (0) ;
     hmq = WinCreateMsgQueue (hab, 0) ;

     WinRegisterClass (hab, szClientClass, ClientWndProc, 0L, 0) ;

     hwndFrame = WinCreateStdWindow (HWND_DESKTOP, WS_VISIBLE,
                                     &flFrameFlags, szClientClass, NULL,
                                     0L, 0, 0, &hwndClient) ;
     SizeTheWindow (hwndFrame) ;

     if (WinStartTimer (hab, hwndClient, ID_TIMER, 1000))
          {
          while (WinGetMsg (hab, &qmsg, NULLHANDLE, 0, 0))
               WinDispatchMsg (hab, &qmsg) ;

          WinStopTimer (hab, hwndClient, ID_TIMER) ;
          }
     else
          WinMessageBox (HWND_DESKTOP, hwndClient,
                         "Too many clocks or timers",
                         szClientClass, 0, MB_OK | MB_WARNING) ;

     WinDestroyWindow (hwndFrame) ;
     WinDestroyMsgQueue (hmq) ;
     WinTerminate (hab) ;
     return 0 ;
     }
```

Listing 10.4: The DIGCLOCK program (Continued)

```
VOID SizeTheWindow (HWND hwndFrame)
     {
     FONTMETRICS fm ;
     HPS         hps ;
     RECTL       rcl ;

     hps = WinGetPS (hwndFrame) ;
     GpiQueryFontMetrics (hps, (LONG) sizeof fm, &fm) ;
     WinReleasePS (hps) ;

     rcl.yBottom = 0 ;
     rcl.yTop    = 11 * fm.lMaxBaselineExt / 4 ;
     rcl.xRight  = WinQuerySysValue (HWND_DESKTOP, SV_CXSCREEN) ;
     rcl.xLeft   = rcl.xRight - 24 * fm.lAveCharWidth ;

     WinCalcFrameRect (hwndFrame, &rcl, FALSE) ;

     WinSetWindowPos (hwndFrame, NULLHANDLE, rcl.xLeft, rcl.yBottom,
                      rcl.xRight - rcl.xLeft, rcl.yTop - rcl.yBottom,
                      SWP_SIZE | SWP_MOVE) ;
     }

VOID UpdateTime (HWND hwnd, HPS hps)
     {
     static BOOL        fHaveCtryInfo = FALSE ;
     static CHAR        *szDayName [] = { "Sun", "Mon", "Tue", "Wed",
                                          "Thu", "Fri", "Sat" } ;
     static CHAR        szDateFormat [] = " %s  %d%s%02d%s%02d " ;
     static COUNTRYCODE ctryc = { 0, 0 } ;
     static COUNTRYINFO ctryi ;
     CHAR               szBuffer [20] ;
     DATETIME           dt ;
     RECTL              rcl ;
     ULONG              ulDataLength ;

               // Get Country Information, Date and Time

     if (!fHaveCtryInfo)
          {
          DosGetCtryInfo (sizeof ctryi, &ctryc, &ctryi, &ulDataLength) ;
          fHaveCtryInfo = TRUE ;
          }
     DosGetDateTime (&dt) ;
     dt.year %= 100 ;

               // Format Date
                                             // mm/dd/yy format
     if (ctryi.fsDateFmt == 0)
```

Listing 10.4: The DIGCLOCK program (Continued)

```
          sprintf (szBuffer, szDateFormat, szDayName [dt.weekday],
                             dt.month, ctryi.szDateSeparator,
                             dt.day,   ctryi.szDateSeparator, dt.year) ;

                                                 // dd/mm/yy format
     else if (ctryi.fsDateFmt == 1)

          sprintf (szBuffer, szDateFormat, szDayName [dt.weekday],
                             dt.day,   ctryi.szDateSeparator,
                             dt.month, ctryi.szDateSeparator, dt.year) ;

                                                 // yy/mm/dd format
     else
          sprintf (szBuffer, szDateFormat, szDayName [dt.weekday],
                             dt.year,  ctryi.szDateSeparator,
                             dt.month, ctryi.szDateSeparator, dt.day) ;

               // Display Date

     WinQueryWindowRect (hwnd, &rcl) ;
     rcl.yBottom += 5 * rcl.yTop / 11 ;
     WinDrawText (hps, -1, szBuffer, &rcl, CLR_NEUTRAL, CLR_BACKGROUND,
                  DT_CENTER | DT_VCENTER) ;

               // Format Time
                                                 // 12-hour format
     if ((ctryi.fsTimeFmt & 1) == 0)

          sprintf (szBuffer, " %d%s%02d%s%02d %cm ",
                             (dt.hours + 11) % 12 + 1, ctryi.szTimeSeparator,
                             dt.minutes, ctryi.szTimeSeparator,
                             dt.seconds, dt.hours / 12 ? 'p' : 'a') ;

                                                 // 24-hour format
     else
          sprintf (szBuffer, " %02d%s%02d%s%02d ",
                             dt.hours,   ctryi.szTimeSeparator,
                             dt.minutes, ctryi.szTimeSeparator, dt.seconds) ;

               // Display Time

     WinQueryWindowRect (hwnd, &rcl) ;
     rcl.yTop -= 5 * rcl.yTop / 11 ;
     WinDrawText (hps, -1, szBuffer, &rcl, CLR_NEUTRAL, CLR_BACKGROUND,
                  DT_CENTER | DT_VCENTER) ;
     }

MRESULT EXPENTRY ClientWndProc (HWND hwnd, ULONG msg, MPARAM mp1, MPARAM mp2)
```

Listing 10.4: The DIGCLOCK program (Continued)

```
     {
     HPS  hps;

     switch (msg)
          {
          case WM_TIMER:
               hps = WinGetPS (hwnd) ;
               GpiSetBackMix (hps, BM_OVERPAINT) ;

               UpdateTime (hwnd, hps) ;

               WinReleasePS (hps) ;
               return 0 ;

          case WM_PAINT:
               hps = WinBeginPaint (hwnd, NULLHANDLE, NULL) ;
               GpiErase (hps) ;

               UpdateTime (hwnd, hps) ;

               WinEndPaint (hps) ;
               return 0 ;
          }
     return WinDefWindowProc (hwnd, msg, mp1, mp2) ;
     }
```

The DIGCLOCK.DEF File

```
;-----------------------------------
; DIGCLOCK.DEF module definition file
;-----------------------------------

NAME           DIGCLOCK  WINDOWAPI

DESCRIPTION    'Digital Clock (c) Charles Petzold, 1993'
PROTMODE
```

To position and size the window, DIGCLOCK uses a technique similar to that used in FREEMEM. To allow a little margin around the two lines of text, I made the client window 2¾ times the height and 24 times the width of an average system font letter:

```
rcl.yBottom = 0 ;
rcl.yTop = 11 * fm.lMaxBaselineExt / 4 ;
rcl.xRight = WinQuerySysValue (HWND_DESKTOP, SV_CXSCREEN) ;
rcl.xLeft = rcl.xRight - 24 * fm.lAveCharWidth ;
```

During both the WM_TIMER and WM_PAINT messages, *ClientWndProc* calls the *UpdateTime* function to display the date and time. *UpdateTime* makes use of two OS/2 kernel functions: *DosGetDateTime* to obtain the date and time and *DosGetCtryInfo* to obtain information about the format of the date and time applicable for the country specified in the user's CONFIG.SYS file. Thus the format of the date and time in DIGCLOCK looks much like the format used in the OS/2 DATE, TIME, and DIR commands. The *UpdateTime* function is mostly a collection of various *sprintf* statements that format the date and time for display. The function writes the two lines of text to its client window using *WinDrawText*.

Figure 10.2 shows DIGCLOCK running in the lower-right corner of Presentation Manager.

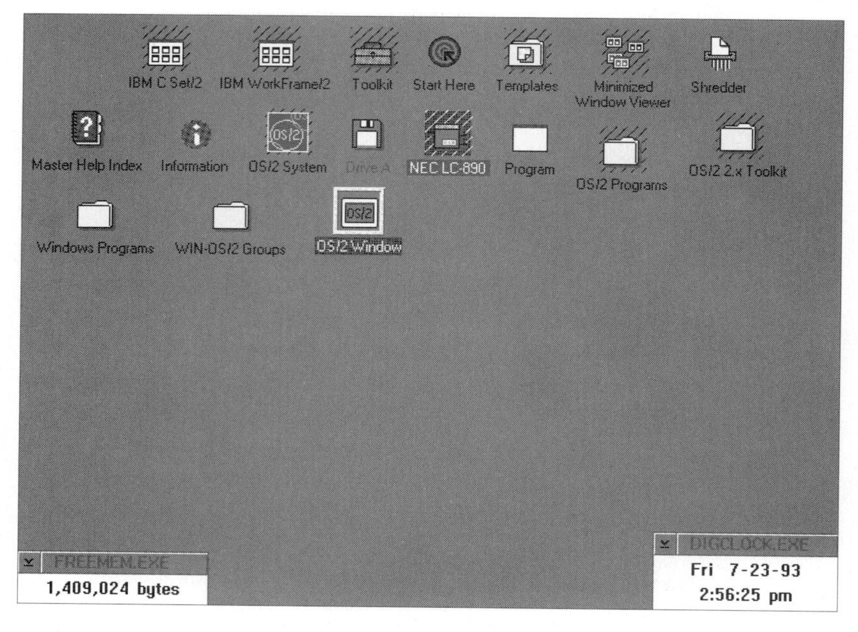

Figure 10.2: The DIGCLOCK display

AN ANALOG CLOCK

An analog clock program doesn't have to concern itself with different date and time formats, but the complexity of the graphics more than outweighs that convenience. The analog CLOCK program is shown in Listing 10.5. Most of the code in this program is devoted to displaying the face and hands of the clock, so that's what I'll discuss in this section.

Figure 10.3 shows CLOCK dominating the full Presentation Manager session.

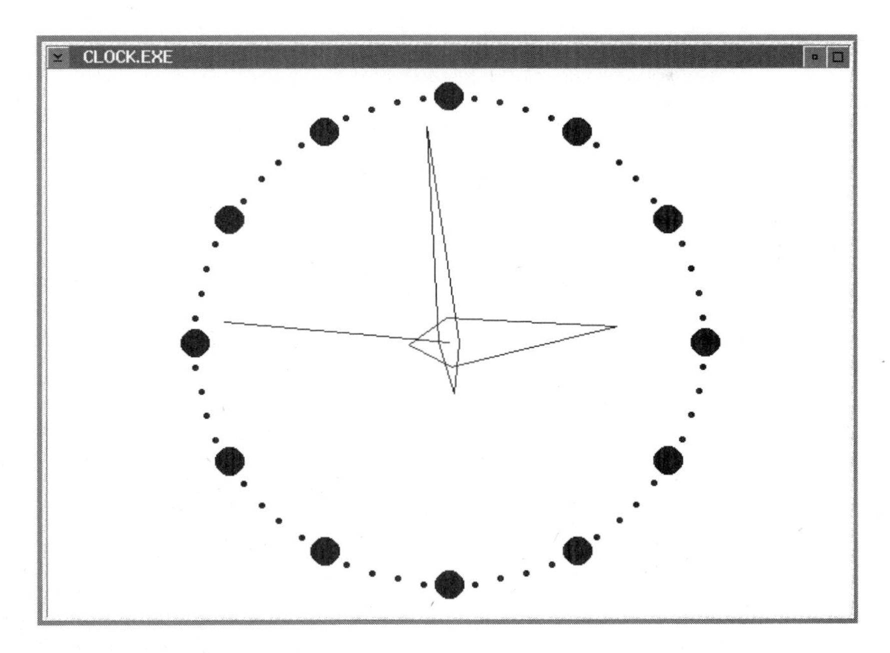

Figure 10.3: The CLOCK display

Listing 10.5: The CLOCK program

The CLOCK.MAK File

```
#---------------------
# CLOCK.MAK make file
#---------------------

clock.exe : clock.obj clock.def
     $(PRGLINK) clock, clock, NUL, $(PRGLIB), clock

clock.obj : clock.c
     $(PRGCC) clock.c
```

The CLOCK.C File

```
/*--------------------------------------
   CLOCK.C -- Analog Clock
              (c) Charles Petzold, 1993
  --------------------------------------*/
```

Listing 10.5: The CLOCK program (Continued)

```
#define INCL_WIN
#define INCL_GPI
#include <os2.h>
#include <stdlib.h>

#define ID_TIMER 1

typedef struct
     {
     INT cxClient ;
     INT cyClient ;
     INT cxPixelDiam ;
     INT cyPixelDiam ;
     }
     WINDOWINFO ;

typedef WINDOWINFO *PWINDOWINFO ;

MRESULT EXPENTRY ClientWndProc (HWND, ULONG, MPARAM, MPARAM) ;

int main (void)
     {
     static CHAR  szClientClass[] = "Clock" ;
     static ULONG flFrameFlags = FCF_TITLEBAR      | FCF_SYSMENU |
                                 FCF_SIZEBORDER    | FCF_MINMAX  |
                                 FCF_SHELLPOSITION | FCF_TASKLIST ;
     HAB          hab ;
     HMQ          hmq ;
     HWND         hwndFrame, hwndClient ;
     QMSG         qmsg ;

     hab = WinInitialize (0) ;
     hmq = WinCreateMsgQueue (hab, 0) ;

     WinRegisterClass (hab, szClientClass, ClientWndProc, CS_SIZEREDRAW, 0) ;

     hwndFrame = WinCreateStdWindow (HWND_DESKTOP, WS_VISIBLE,
                                     &flFrameFlags, szClientClass, NULL,
                                     0L, 0, 0, &hwndClient) ;

     if (WinStartTimer (hab, hwndClient, ID_TIMER, 1000))
          {
          while (WinGetMsg (hab, &qmsg, NULLHANDLE, 0, 0))
               WinDispatchMsg (hab, &qmsg) ;

          WinStopTimer (hab, hwndClient, ID_TIMER) ;
          }
     else
          WinMessageBox (HWND_DESKTOP, hwndClient,
```

Listing 10.5: The CLOCK program (Continued)

```
                         "Too many clocks or timers",
                         szClientClass, 0, MB_OK | MB_WARNING) ;

     WinDestroyWindow (hwndFrame) ;
     WinDestroyMsgQueue (hmq) ;
     WinTerminate (hab) ;
     return 0 ;
     }

VOID RotatePoint (POINTL aptl[], INT iNum, INT iAngle)
     {
     static INT iSin [60] =
                    {
                      0,  105,  208,  309,  407,  500,  588,  669,  743,  809,
                    866,  914,  951,  978,  995, 1000,  995,  978,  951,  914,
                    866,  809,  743,  669,  588,  500,  407,  309,  208,  105,
                      0, -104, -207, -308, -406, -499, -587, -668, -742, -808,
                   -865, -913, -950, -977, -994, -999, -994, -977, -950, -913,
                   -865, -808, -742, -668, -587, -499, -406, -308, -207, -104
                    } ;
     INT        iIndex ;
     POINTL     ptlTemp ;

     for (iIndex = 0 ; iIndex < iNum ; iIndex++)
          {
          ptlTemp.x = (aptl[iIndex].x * iSin [(iAngle + 15) % 60] +
                       aptl[iIndex].y * iSin [iAngle]) / 1000 ;

          ptlTemp.y = (aptl[iIndex].y * iSin [(iAngle + 15) % 60] -
                       aptl[iIndex].x * iSin [iAngle]) / 1000 ;

          aptl[iIndex] = ptlTemp ;
          }
     }

VOID ScalePoint (POINTL aptl[], INT iNum, PWINDOWINFO pwi)
     {
     INT iIndex ;

     for (iIndex = 0 ; iIndex < iNum ; iIndex++)
          {
          aptl[iIndex].x = aptl[iIndex].x * pwi->cxPixelDiam / 200 ;
          aptl[iIndex].y = aptl[iIndex].y * pwi->cyPixelDiam / 200 ;
          }
     }

VOID TranslatePoint (POINTL aptl[], INT iNum, PWINDOWINFO pwi)
     {
     INT iIndex ;
```

Listing 10.5: The CLOCK program (Continued)

```
     for (iIndex = 0 ; iIndex < iNum ; iIndex++)
          {
          aptl[iIndex].x += pwi->cxClient / 2 ;
          aptl[iIndex].y += pwi->cyClient / 2 ;
          }
     }

VOID DrawHand (HPS hps, POINTL aptlIn[], INT iNum, INT iAngle,
               PWINDOWINFO pwi)
     {
     INT    iIndex ;
     POINTL aptl [5] ;

     for (iIndex = 0 ; iIndex < iNum ; iIndex++)
          aptl [iIndex] = aptlIn [iIndex] ;

     RotatePoint    (aptl, iNum, iAngle) ;
     ScalePoint     (aptl, iNum, pwi) ;
     TranslatePoint (aptl, iNum, pwi) ;

     GpiMove (hps, aptl) ;
     GpiPolyLine (hps, iNum - 1L, aptl + 1) ;
     }

MRESULT EXPENTRY ClientWndProc (HWND hwnd, ULONG msg, MPARAM mp1, MPARAM mp2)
     {
     static DATETIME   dtPrevious ;
     static HDC        hdc ;
     static LONG       xPixelsPerMeter, yPixelsPerMeter ;
     static POINTL     aptlHour   [5] = { 0,-15, 10,0, 0,60, -10,0, 0,-15 },
                       aptlMinute [5] = { 0,-20,  5,0, 0,80,  -5,0, 0,-20 },
                       aptlSecond [2] = { 0,  0,  0,80 } ;
     static WINDOWINFO wi ;
     DATETIME          dt ;
     HPS               hps ;
     INT               iDiamMM, iAngle ;
     POINTL            aptl [3] ;

     switch (msg)
          {
          case WM_CREATE:
               hdc = WinOpenWindowDC (hwnd) ;

               DevQueryCaps (hdc, CAPS_VERTICAL_RESOLUTION,
                                  1L, &yPixelsPerMeter) ;
               DevQueryCaps (hdc, CAPS_HORIZONTAL_RESOLUTION,
                                  1L, &xPixelsPerMeter) ;
```

Listing 10.5: The CLOCK program (Continued)

```
          DosGetDateTime (&dtPrevious) ;
          dtPrevious.hours = (dtPrevious.hours * 5) % 60 +
                             dtPrevious.minutes / 12 ;
          return 0 ;

     case WM_SIZE:
          wi.cxClient = SHORT1FROMMP (mp2) ;
          wi.cyClient = SHORT2FROMMP (mp2) ;

          iDiamMM = min (wi.cxClient * 1000L / xPixelsPerMeter,
                         wi.cyClient * 1000L / yPixelsPerMeter) ;

          wi.cxPixelDiam = xPixelsPerMeter * iDiamMM / 1000 ;
          wi.cyPixelDiam = yPixelsPerMeter * iDiamMM / 1000 ;
          return 0 ;

     case WM_TIMER:
          DosGetDateTime (&dt) ;
          dt.hours = (dt.hours * 5) % 60 + dt.minutes / 12 ;

          hps = WinGetPS (hwnd) ;
          GpiSetColor (hps, CLR_BACKGROUND) ;

          DrawHand (hps, aptlSecond, 2, dtPrevious.seconds, &wi) ;

          if (dt.hours   != dtPrevious.hours ||
              dt.minutes != dtPrevious.minutes)
               {
               DrawHand (hps, aptlHour,   5, dtPrevious.hours,   &wi) ;
               DrawHand (hps, aptlMinute, 5, dtPrevious.minutes, &wi) ;
               }

          GpiSetColor (hps, CLR_NEUTRAL) ;

          DrawHand (hps, aptlHour,   5, dt.hours,   &wi) ;
          DrawHand (hps, aptlMinute, 5, dt.minutes, &wi) ;
          DrawHand (hps, aptlSecond, 2, dt.seconds, &wi) ;

          WinReleasePS (hps) ;
          dtPrevious = dt ;
          return 0 ;

     case WM_PAINT:
          hps = WinBeginPaint (hwnd, NULLHANDLE, NULL) ;
          GpiErase (hps) ;

          for (iAngle = 0 ; iAngle < 60 ; iAngle++)
               {
               aptl[0].x = 0 ;
```

Listing 10.5: The CLOCK program (Continued)

```
                    aptl[0].y = 90 ;

                    RotatePoint    (aptl, 1, iAngle) ;
                    ScalePoint     (aptl, 1, &wi) ;
                    TranslatePoint (aptl, 1, &wi) ;

                    aptl[2].x = aptl[2].y = iAngle % 5 ? 2 : 10 ;

                    ScalePoint (aptl + 2, 1, &wi) ;

                    aptl[0].x -= aptl[2].x / 2 ;
                    aptl[0].y -= aptl[2].y / 2 ;

                    aptl[1].x = aptl[0].x + aptl[2].x ;
                    aptl[1].y = aptl[0].y + aptl[2].y ;

                    GpiMove (hps, aptl) ;
                    GpiBox (hps, DRO_OUTLINEFILL, aptl + 1,
                                 aptl[2].x, aptl[2].y) ;
                    }
               DrawHand (hps, aptlHour,   5, dtPrevious.hours,   &wi) ;
               DrawHand (hps, aptlMinute, 5, dtPrevious.minutes, &wi) ;
               DrawHand (hps, aptlSecond, 2, dtPrevious.seconds, &wi) ;

               WinEndPaint (hps) ;
               return 0 ;
          }
     return WinDefWindowProc (hwnd, msg, mp1, mp2) ;
     }
```

The CLOCK.DEF File

```
;-----------------------------------
; CLOCK.DEF module definition file
;-----------------------------------

NAME           CLOCK     WINDOWAPI

DESCRIPTION    'Analog Clock (c) Charles Petzold, 1993'
PROTMODE
```

In the CLOCK program, I have chosen not to take advantage of the various transform functions I discussed in Chapter 7. Instead, all the translation, scaling, and rotation logic is done manually, so to speak.

To draw a round clock face, CLOCK defines its own coordinate system. The center of the clock (which is positioned in the center of the client window) is the point (0, 0) in this coordinate system. The horizontal and vertical axes both range from –100 to +100.

While processing the WM_CREATE message, CLOCK obtains two values from *DevQueryCaps* that report the horizontal and vertical resolution of the display in pixels per meter:

```
DevQueryCaps (hdc, CAPS_VERTICAL_RESOLUTION, 1L, &yPixelsPerMeter) ;
DevQueryCaps (hdc, CAPS_HORIZONTAL_RESOLUTION, 1L, &xPixelsPerMeter) ;
```

During the WM_SIZE message, the diameter of the clock face in millimeters is calculated based on the width and height of the client window:

```
iDiamMM = min (wi.cxClient * 1000L / xPixelsPerMeter,
               wi.cyClient * 1000L / yPixelsPerMeter) ;
```

This value is then converted to a diameter in pixels for both the horizontal and vertical axes:

```
wi.cxPixelDiam = xPixelsPerMeter * iDiamMM / 1000 ;
wi.cyPixelDiam = yPixelsPerMeter * iDiamMM / 1000 ;
```

As I noted above, CLOCK defines its own coordinates to range from –100 to +100 on the horizontal and vertical axes. Thus, on the horizontal axis, the width in pixels of the clock face is *cxPixelDiam*, but this corresponds to 200 units in CLOCK's coordinate system.

CLOCK has two functions to translate one or more POINTL structures from its own coordinate system to the window coordinates used in the GPI functions: *ScalePoint* and *TranslatePoint*.

ScalePoint uses the relationship between these two coordinate systems to convert a point in CLOCK's coordinate system to pixels:

```
aptl[iIndex].x = aptl[iIndex].x * pwi->cxPixelDiam / 200 ;
aptl[iIndex].y = aptl[iIndex].y * pwi->cyPixelDiam / 200 ;
```

CLOCK's coordinate system defines (0, 0) as the center of the client window. The point (0, 0) in window coordinates is the lower-left corner of the window. *TranslatePoint* converts the point accordingly:

```
aptl[iIndex].x += pwi->cxClient / 2 ;
aptl[iIndex].y += pwi->cyClient / 2 ;
```

The more complex aspect of CLOCK involves the rotation of points around the clock face. Let's look at an example. The hour hand of the clock is defined as an array of POINTL structures that specify a starting position and four line segments:

```
static POINTL aptlHour[5] = { 0,-15, 10,0, 0,60, -10,0, 0,-15 }
```

But these are the coordinates only when the hour hand points straight up, at midnight or noon. What are the coordinates of the hour hand at 3:00? To get those coordinates, the points have to be rotated 90 degrees clockwise around a circle. It's time for a trigonometry refresher: If the original point is (x, y) and the clockwise angle of rotation is α, then the new point (x', y') is calculated with the following formulas:

```
x' = x COS α + y SIN α
y' = y COS α - x SIN α
```

This is done in the *RotatePoint* function. Because a clock face is divided into 60 increments, all that's needed are 60 sine and cosine values in increments of 6 degrees. The cosines can be derived from the sines by offsetting the angle by 90 degrees.

To avoid introducing floating-point math in CLOCK (which would increase the CLOCK.EXE size), the *iSin* array in *RotatePoint* contains the 60 required sine values scaled by a factor of 1000. The rotation formulas in *RotatePoint* are

```
ptlTemp.x = (aptl[iIndex].x * iSin [(iAngle + 15) % 60 ] +
             aptl[iIndex].y * iSin [iAngle]) / 1000 ;

ptlTemp.y = (aptl[iIndex].y * iSin [(iAngle + 15) % 60 ] -
             aptl[iIndex].x * iSin [iAngle]) / 1000 ;

aptl[iIndex ] = ptlTemp ;
```

The *DrawHand* function in CLOCK is passed an array of points that define a clock hand at 12:00. It calls the *RotatePoint*, *ScalePoint*, and *TranslatePoint* functions to rotate the points and convert them from CLOCK's coordinate system to window coordinates. *DrawHand* then calls *GpiMove* and *GpiPolyLine* to draw the hand. During processing of the WM_PAINT message, CLOCK draws the face of the clock and the three hands at the current time. Processing during the WM_TIMER message updates the position of the clock hands based on the new time obtained from *DosGetDateTime*.

Control Windows: Putting the Children to Work

Control window basics

The button class

The scroll-bar class

Chapter 11

Control windows (sometimes called *child window controls* or simply *controls*) are child windows that take the form of objects such as buttons, scroll bars, list boxes, and text entry fields. A control window processes mouse and keyboard input and notifies its owner of significant input events. Although the input originates with the keyboard and the mouse, it is filtered through the control, so you can treat control windows as additional means of high-level input to your program.

For example, in a spreadsheet program you might want to display a small push button labeled "Recalculate" on your client window. You can do this in one of two ways. The first way requires the program itself to draw the push button on the client window. The client window procedure then has to process mouse messages and do some hit-testing to determine when the user clicks on the push button. But an easier approach is to create a push button control window that is a child of your client window. The window procedure for the push button window is inside the Presentation Manager.

That window procedure draws the button, processes the mouse messages, and sends your client window a message when the button is clicked. By putting child windows to work, your program can delegate the drawing and the mouse hit-testing jobs.

We've already explored some of the concepts involved in creating and using control windows. The WELCOME4 program in Chapter 3 created a push button, scroll bar, and text-entry field based on preregistered window classes. Creating each control window required only one *WinCreateWindow* call. (The only problem was that WELCOME4 didn't know quite what to do with these control windows after it created them.)

Although the control windows in WELCOME4 were based on preregistered window classes, you can also create your own classes of control windows. For example, the CHECKER3 program in Chapter 9 created 25 child windows on the surface of its client. These child windows processed mouse clicks by drawing or erasing an X mark on the child window. The child windows added a layer of processing between the user and CHECKER3's client window that simplified mouse input processing.

CHECKER3's client window was ignorant of the state (X or no X) of each of the 25 child windows. But it's not difficult to imagine each of the child windows sending messages to the client window whenever the child window was checked or unchecked. We might also have added a facility that allowed the client window to send the child window a message requesting information about the state of a particular rectangle. Had we done this in CHECKER3, the child windows would have been sophisticated enough to qualify as control windows.

Control windows appear most often in dialog boxes. You'll discover in Chapter 14 that defining the position and size of control windows in a dialog box is simplified by using a dialog box template. The dialog box logic within the Presentation Manager also assists greatly in much of the overhead involved with using controls, including shifting the keyboard input focus between the windows. However, it's a good exercise to create a few control windows yourself to get a better understanding of dialog boxes and a greater appreciation for the work the Presentation Manager assumes when you use dialog boxes.

CONTROL WINDOW BASICS

Using control windows involves three major jobs:

- You create a control window by calling *WinCreateWindow.* Most often, the window class has been preregistered by the Presentation Manager, which means that the window procedure for the class is in the Presentation Manager PMWIN.DLL dynamic link library. You specify the style, position, and size of the control window, and *WinCreateWindow* returns a handle to the window. The program can later adjust the position and size of the control by calling the *WinSetWindowPos* function.

- Your program can send messages to the control window using *WinSendMsg.* These messages can either set the state of a control or query the current state. The identifiers for the messages you send to controls begin with a prefix that indicates the type of control window that responds to the message. For example, messages that begin with BM are messages you send to button controls, and messages that begin with SBM are messages you send to scroll-bar controls.

- You receive notification messages from the control window when a significant input event occurs. This usually results from the user clicking on the control window with the mouse or—if the control window has the input focus—pressing a key that affects the control. The notification messages are usually WM_COMMAND and WM_CONTROL messages for most control windows and WM_VSCROLL and WM_HSCROLL messages for scroll bars.

CREATING THE WINDOW

You create a control window by calling the *WinCreateWindow* function, which generally looks like this:

```
hwnd = WinCreateWindow (
                hwndParent,          // Parent window
                szClass,             // Window class
                szText,              // Text
                WS_...,              // Window style
                xPosition,           // Position
                yPosition,
                cxWidth,             // Width
                cyHeight,            // Height
                hwndOwner,           // Owner window
                hwndPlacement,       // Placement
                id,                  // Child ID
                pCtrlData,           // Ctrl data
                pPresParams) ;       // Pres params
```

When you create a control window based on a preregistered window class, the last two parameters (far pointers to control data and presentation parameters) are often set to NULL. The other parameters are described in the following paragraphs.

THE PREDEFINED WINDOW CLASSES

In the CHECKER3 program in Chapter 9, the window class parameter in *WinCreateWindow* was a text string identifying a window class that the program registered. For control windows based on a preregistered window class, this parameter is an identifier beginning with the letters WC. These identifiers are as follows:

Preregistered Window Class	Type of Window
WC_FRAME	Standard frame window
WC_COMBOBOX	Combination edit field/list box
WC_BUTTON	Push button, check box, and so forth
WC_MENU	Menu (including system menu and min/max menu)
WC_STATIC	Static text string and rectangle
WC_ENTRYFIELD	Text entry field
WC_LISTBOX	List box
WC_SCROLLBAR	Scroll bar
WC_TITLEBAR	Standard title bar
WC_MLE	Multiline edit control
WC_SPINBUTTON	Scrollable choices
WC_CONTAINER	Object holder
WC_SLIDER	Value-modification
WC_VALUESET	Mutually exclusive choices
WC_NOTEBOOK	Page-oriented information

The WC_FRAME identifier isn't commonly used in the *WinCreateWindow* function because *WinCreateStdWindow* creates a frame window. The WC_MENU and WC_TITLEBAR identifiers refer to windows that are usually part of the standard window created with *WinCreateStdWindow.* Excluding those identifiers leaves us with the other control window classes. This chapter will discuss some of the most common controls, which are the WC_BUTTON, WC_STATIC, and WC_SCROLLBAR classes.

THE WINDOW STYLE

The window style parameter of *WinCreateWindow* is one or more identifiers that define the appearance and functionality of the window. The style identifiers you use depend on the window class. For example, when creating a scroll-bar control window, you specify either SBS_VERT or SBS_HORZ, depending on whether you want a vertical or horizontal scroll bar. When you create a button control, the window style identifies the button as a push button, a radio button, or a check box. The identifier WS_VISIBLE usually is included in the window style. If you omit it, the window is created but not displayed. You must later call *WinShowWindow* to display the window.

Some control windows (such as buttons) display text, which you specify in the text parameter to *WinCreateWindow*. You can later change the text using the *WinSetWindowText* function. The position parameters give the coordinates of the lower-left corner of the control relative to the lower-left corner of its parent window. The size parameters specify the control's width and height. You can change the position and size using the *WinSetWindowPos* function.

THE OWNER AND THE PARENT

When you create a child window, you assign it both a parent window and an owner window. The parent window determines where the control is positioned. The position parameters in *WinCreateWindow* specify the coordinates of the control window relative to the lower-left corner of the control's parent. If the parent window is moved, the child window is moved also. Like all child windows, a control window is clipped on the surface of its parent; it can't appear outside the area its parent occupies.

The control window sends notification messages not to its parent but to its owner. The window procedure associated with the owner window is responsible for interpreting these notification messages. Usually, the same window serves as both the parent and the owner of the control. For example, if you create a control window on the surface of your client window, the client window is usually both the parent and the owner of the control window. You can specify a different parent and owner if you want the notification messages to be processed by a window other than the one on which the control is located.

A third window handle can be passed to the *WinCreateWindow* function to specify how overlapping siblings appear on the screen. (This is identified as *hwndPlacement* in the *WinCreateWindow* call.) This parameter must be either a window handle of a sibling, HWND_TOP, or HWND_BOTTOM. The terminology often becomes confusing: An HWND_BOTTOM window obscures an HWND_TOP window if the two windows overlap. If you specify a handle of a sibling window, that sibling will be obscured by the new window if the windows overlap. If you create several sibling windows using HWND_TOP, the most recently created window will be obscured by the others. Specifying HWND_BOTTOM for several siblings causes the most recently created window to obscure the siblings that it overlaps.

If your child windows do not overlap, you can use either HWND_TOP or HWND_BOTTOM for all of them.

THE CHILD ID

The child ID is a very important parameter of the *WinCreateWindow* function. This ID number should be unique for each child of a particular window. The control window uses the ID to identify itself when it sends the owner a notification message. You can use any number you want for a child ID, but it's safest to use numbers less than 32,768 so as not to conflict with predefined IDs used by the frame window. If you create many control windows, you should choose IDs that let you conveniently determine which control is sending you a notification message and what you do with information from the control. For example, the sample programs in this chapter often use the IDs as indexes to arrays.

Although the *WinCreateWindow* function returns a handle to the child window, it's not essential that you save it. You can always determine the child window handle from the child ID by using the following function:

```
hwndChild = WinWindowFromID (hwnd, id) ;
```

The *hwnd* parameter is the window handle of the parent of *hwndChild*. The *id* parameter is the ID you specify when creating the child window.

Knowing the handle of a child window, you can also obtain the ID:

```
id = WinQueryWindowUShort (hwndChild, QWS_ID) ;
```

THE BUTTON CLASS

Let's begin with buttons, which are almost the simplest type of control window. (Static control windows are actually simpler because they don't process input at all.) When you create a button control window, you specify the WC_BUTTON window class in the *WinCreateWindow* function. The window style indicates the type of button. The most common button window styles are BS_PUSHBUTTON, BS_CHECKBOX, and BS_RADIOBUTTON.

A *push button* is a rectangle that contains text. When you click on the button or—if the button has the input focus—press the spacebar, the button flashes and sends a notification message to its owner. Push buttons generally signal simple actions: "Do this."

A *check box* is a small square (about the height of a character) followed by a text string. Clicking the button causes an X to appear in the box; clicking it again removes the X. A program often uses check boxes for various program options.

A *radio button* is a small circle followed by text. Like a check box, a radio button can be either checked or unchecked. Clicking on the radio button checks it, but clicking again doesn't uncheck it. Generally, a group of radio buttons is used to indicate mutually exclusive options. Checking one button unchecks all the other buttons in the same group, much as selecting one button on a car radio "unselects" any other selected buttons.

A PUSH BUTTON DEMONSTRATION PROGRAM

The BUTTONS1 program, shown in Listing 11.1, creates two push buttons, labeled "Smaller" and "Larger." These buttons appear in the center of the client window. When you click on the Smaller button, the program's window decreases in size by 10 percent. When you click on Larger, the window size increases by 10 percent.

Listing 11.1: The BUTTONS1 program

The BUTTONS1.MAK File

```
#-----------------------
# BUTTONS1.MAK make file
#-----------------------

buttons1.exe : buttons1.obj buttons1.def
     $(PRGLINK) buttons1, buttons1, NUL, $(PRGLIB), buttons1

buttons1.obj : buttons1.c
     $(PRGCC) buttons1.c
```

The BUTTONS1.C File

```
/*----------------------------------------
   BUTTONS1.C -- Push Button Demonstration
                 (c) Charles Petzold, 1993
  ----------------------------------------*/

#define INCL_WIN
#define INCL_GPI
#include <os2.h>

MRESULT EXPENTRY ClientWndProc (HWND, ULONG, MPARAM, MPARAM) ;

int main (void)
     {
     static CHAR  szClientClass[] = "Buttons1" ;
     static ULONG flFrameFlags = FCF_TITLEBAR      | FCF_SYSMENU |
                                 FCF_SIZEBORDER    | FCF_MINMAX  |
```

Listing 11.1: The BUTTONS1 program (Continued)

```
                                        FCF_SHELLPOSITION | FCF_TASKLIST ;
     HAB          hab ;
     HMQ          hmq ;
     HWND         hwndFrame, hwndClient ;
     QMSG         qmsg ;

     hab = WinInitialize (0) ;
     hmq = WinCreateMsgQueue (hab, 0) ;

     WinRegisterClass (hab, szClientClass, ClientWndProc, CS_SIZEREDRAW, 0) ;

     hwndFrame = WinCreateStdWindow (HWND_DESKTOP, WS_VISIBLE,
                                     &flFrameFlags, szClientClass, NULL,
                                     0L, 0, 0, &hwndClient) ;

     while (WinGetMsg (hab, &qmsg, NULLHANDLE, 0, 0))
          WinDispatchMsg (hab, &qmsg) ;

     WinDestroyWindow (hwndFrame) ;
     WinDestroyMsgQueue (hmq) ;
     WinTerminate (hab) ;
     return 0 ;
     }

MRESULT EXPENTRY ClientWndProc (HWND hwnd, ULONG msg, MPARAM mp1, MPARAM mp2)
     {
     static CHAR  *szButtonLabel[] = { "Smaller", "Larger" } ;
     static HWND  hwndFrame, hwndButton[2] ;
     static INT   cxClient, cyClient, cxChar, cyChar ;
     FONTMETRICS  fm ;
     HPS          hps ;
     INT          id ;
     RECTL        rcl ;

     switch (msg)
          {
          case WM_CREATE :
               hwndFrame = WinQueryWindow (hwnd, QW_PARENT) ;

               hps = WinGetPS (hwnd) ;
               GpiQueryFontMetrics (hps, sizeof fm, &fm) ;
               cxChar = fm.lAveCharWidth ;
               cyChar = fm.lMaxBaselineExt ;
               WinReleasePS (hps) ;

               for (id = 0 ; id < 2 ; id++)
                    hwndButton[id] = WinCreateWindow (
                                        hwnd,               // Parent
                                        WC_BUTTON,          // Class
```

Listing 11.1: The BUTTONS1 program (Continued)

```
                                   szButtonLabel[id],  // Text
                                   WS_VISIBLE |        // Style
                                       BS_PUSHBUTTON,
                                   0, 0,               // Position
                                   12 * cxChar,        // Width
                                   2 * cyChar,         // Height
                                   hwnd,               // Owner
                                   HWND_BOTTOM,        // Placement
                                   id,                 // ID
                                   NULL,               // Ctrl Data
                                   NULL) ;             // Pres Params
          return 0 ;

     case WM_SIZE :
          cxClient = SHORT1FROMMP (mp2) ;
          cyClient = SHORT2FROMMP (mp2) ;

          for (id = 0 ; id < 2 ; id++)
               WinSetWindowPos (hwndButton[id], NULLHANDLE,
                         cxClient / 2 + (14 * id - 13) * cxChar,
                         (cyClient - 2 * cyChar) / 2,
                         0, 0, SWP_MOVE) ;
          return 0 ;

     case WM_COMMAND:
          WinQueryWindowRect (hwnd, &rcl) ;
          WinMapWindowPoints (hwnd, HWND_DESKTOP, (PPOINTL) &rcl, 2) ;

          switch (COMMANDMSG(&msg)->cmd)              // Child ID
               {
               case 0:                                // "Smaller"
                    rcl.xLeft   += cxClient / 20 ;
                    rcl.xRight  -= cxClient / 20 ;
                    rcl.yBottom += cyClient / 20 ;
                    rcl.yTop    -= cyClient / 20 ;
                    break ;

               case 1:                                // "Larger"
                    rcl.xLeft   -= cxClient / 20 ;
                    rcl.xRight  += cxClient / 20 ;
                    rcl.yBottom -= cyClient / 20 ;
                    rcl.yTop    += cyClient / 20 ;
                    break ;
               }
          WinCalcFrameRect (hwndFrame, &rcl, FALSE) ;

          WinSetWindowPos (hwndFrame, NULLHANDLE,
                           rcl.xLeft, rcl.yBottom,
                           rcl.xRight - rcl.xLeft,
```

Listing 11.1: The BUTTONS1 program (Continued)

```
                              rcl.yTop    - rcl.yBottom,
                              SWP_MOVE | SWP_SIZE) ;
               return Ø ;

          case WM_ERASEBACKGROUND:
               return MRFROMSHORT (1) ;
          }
     return WinDefWindowProc (hwnd, msg, mp1, mp2) ;
     }
```

The BUTTONS1.DEF File

```
;-----------------------------------
; BUTTONS1.DEF module definition file
;-----------------------------------

NAME           BUTTONS1  WINDOWAPI

DESCRIPTION    'Push Button Demo (c) Charles Petzold, 1993'
PROTMODE
```

Figure 11.1 shows BUTTONS1 running under the Presentation Manager. The Larger button is in the process of being triggered by the mouse.

BUTTONS1 creates these two push buttons during processing of the WM_CREATE message in *ClientWndProc*:

```
for (id = Ø ; id < 2 ; id++)
     hwndButton [id] = WinCreateWindow (
          hwnd,                              // Parent
          WC_BUTTON,                         // Class
          szButtonLabel [id],                // Text
          WS_VISIBLE |                       // Style
               BS_PUSHBUTTON,
          Ø, Ø,                              // Position
          12 * cxChar,                       // Width
          2 * cyChar,                        // Height
          hwnd,                              // Owner
          HWND_BOTTOM,                       // Placement
          id,                                // ID
          NULL,                              // Ctrl data
          NULL) ;                            // Pres params
```

The window handles are saved in the *hwndButton* array. The two IDs are set to 0 and 1, as are the indexes to this array. The *szButton* Label array contains the two text strings that appear inside the buttons.

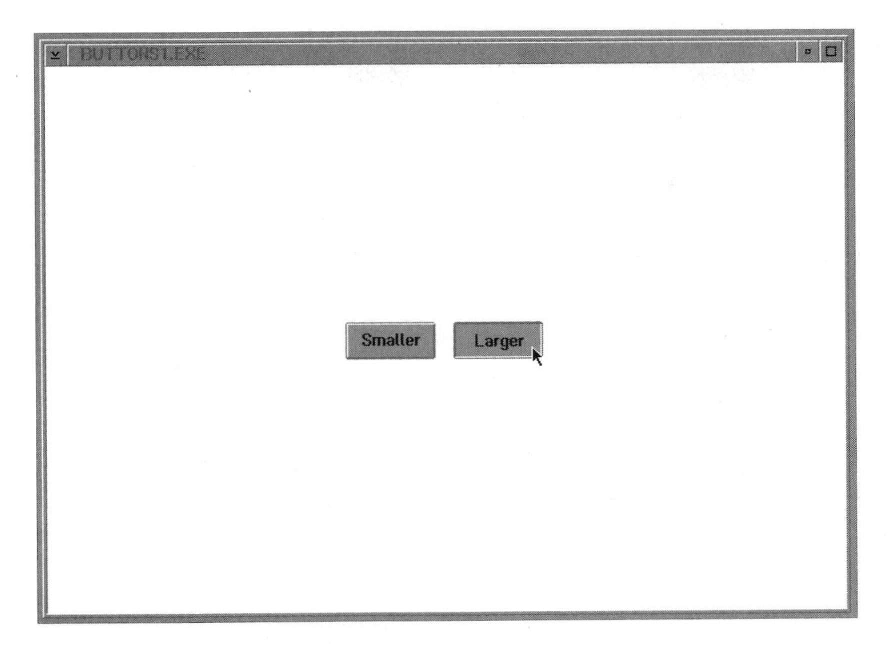

Figure 11.1: The BUTTONS1 display

The height of the buttons is set to two times the height of a character, which is a standard height for push buttons. The width of a push button should be at least the length of the text string inside the button plus two additional character widths. Twelve times the width of a character is adequate for the two buttons in this program.

The position parameters of *WinCreateWindow* are set to 0. Because the buttons will be positioned in the center of the client window, the position can be determined only when the program knows the size of the client window. This requires that *ClientWndProc* call *WinSetWindowPos* during the WM_SIZE message:

```
for (id = 0 ; id < 2 ; id++)
     WinSetWindowPos (hwndButton [id], NULLHANDLE,
          cxClient / 2 + (14 * id - 13) * cxChar,
          (cyClient - 2 * cyChar) / 2,
          0, 0, SWP_MOVE) ;
```

The third and fourth parameters give the position of the control relative to the lower-left corner of the client window. These messy looking formulas place the buttons side by side in the center of the client window. (Such formulas disappear when you work with controls in dialog boxes.)

Push buttons send WM_COMMAND messages to their owners when they are clicked on. The following *mp1* and *mp2* parameters accompany the WM_-COMMAND message:

WM_COMMAND Parameter	Meaning
SHORT1FROMMP (*mp1*)	Child ID
SHORT1FROMMP (*mp2*)	CMDSRC_PUSHBUTTON
SHORT2FROMMP (*mp2*)	Nonzero for mouse input; 0 for keyboard input

The CMDSRC_PUSHBUTTON identifier indicates that the WM_COMMAND message is sent by a push button. (As you'll see in Chapter 13, menus and keyboard accelerators also send WM_COMMAND messages to the client window. In these cases the low USHORT of *mp2* is either CMDSRC_MENU or CMDSRC_ACCELERATOR.) The only way to identify the push button sending the message is to examine the child ID in the low USHORT of *mp1*, which is why it's so important to give each push button a unique ID.

PMWIN.H contains a COMMANDMSG macro that you can use much as you'd use the CHARMSG and MOUSEMSG macros. The following expression returns the child window ID:

```
COMMANDMSG(&msg)->cmd
```

The following expression identifies the source of the message:

```
COMMANDMSG(&msg)->source
```

The following expression is TRUE if the mouse was used:

```
COMMANDMSG(&msg)->fMouse
```

In the BUTTONS1 program, the push button on the left (containing the text "Smaller") has an ID of 0. The push button with the text "Larger" has an ID of 1. The processing of the WM_COMMAND message in BUTTONS1.C is structured like this:

```
case WM_COMMAND:
     [other program lines]
     switch (COMMANDMSG(&msg)->cmd)
          {
          case 0:
               [process message from "Smaller" push button]
               break ;

          case 1:
```

```
            [process message from "Larger" push button]
            break ;
        }
    [other program lines]
    return 0 ;
```

When *ClientWndProc* receives a WM_COMMAND message, it must alter the size of the program's window. The program first obtains the client window's rectangle from *WinQueryWindowRect* and then translates the coordinates to window coordinates using *WinMapWindowPoints*. Depending on the ID of the push button that sent the message, BUTTONS1 adjusts the four fields of the rectangle to increase or decrease the size. It then determines the frame rectangle that corresponds to this client rectangle by calling *WinCalcFrameRect*. BUTTONS1 then sets the new size and position of the frame rectangle by calling *WinSetWindowPos*.

When BUTTONS1 calls *WinSetWindowPos*, the client window procedure receives a WM_SIZE message. As I've mentioned, BUTTONS1 responds to this by calling *WinSetWindowPos* to set the new position of the push button controls. Because the frame window is resized equally in all four directions and the push button controls are always positioned in the center of the window, the push buttons remain in the same position relative to the screen.

CONTROLS AND KEYBOARD INPUT FOCUS

When you click on one of the push buttons in BUTTONS1, the push button obtains the input focus, as indicated by a dotted line around the text of the button. Whenever a push button has the input focus, you can also press the spacebar to trigger the button. However, this is the only keystroke that the push button responds to in a meaningful way. When a dialog box contains push buttons and other controls, you can move the input focus between controls by using the Tab key and, sometimes, the cursor movement keys. The dialog box logic in the Presentation Manager adds this additional keyboard interface; it isn't part of the keyboard logic in individual control windows. In the COLORSCR program shown later in this chapter, we'll examine a way to add a keyboard interface to move the input focus between control windows.

RADIO BUTTONS TO INDICATE CHOICES

The BUTTONS1 program created two push button control windows. Now let's go a little further and write a program that has a few more controls. The DRAWLINE program, shown in Listing 11.2, creates 26 control windows: 24 radio buttons and 2 group boxes.

Listing 11.2: The DRAWLINE program

The DRAWLINE.MAK File

```
#-----------------------
# DRAWLINE.MAK make file
#-----------------------

drawline.exe : drawline.obj drawline.def
     $(PRGLINK) drawline, drawline, NUL, $(PRGLIB), drawline

drawline.obj : drawline.c
     $(PRGCC) drawline.c
```

The DRAWLINE.C File

```
/*---------------------------------------------
   DRAWLINE.C -- Draw line from radio buttons
                 (c) Charles Petzold, 1993
  ---------------------------------------------*/

#define INCL_WIN
#define INCL_GPI
#include <os2.h>

MRESULT EXPENTRY ClientWndProc (HWND, ULONG, MPARAM, MPARAM) ;

int main (void)
     {
     static CHAR  szClientClass[] = "DrawLine" ;
     static ULONG flFrameFlags = FCF_TITLEBAR      | FCF_SYSMENU |
                                 FCF_SIZEBORDER    | FCF_MINMAX  |
                                 FCF_SHELLPOSITION | FCF_TASKLIST ;
     HAB          hab ;
     HMQ          hmq ;
     HWND         hwndFrame, hwndClient ;
     QMSG         qmsg ;

     hab = WinInitialize (0) ;
     hmq = WinCreateMsgQueue (hab, 0) ;

     WinRegisterClass (hab, szClientClass, ClientWndProc, CS_SIZEREDRAW, 0) ;

     hwndFrame = WinCreateStdWindow (HWND_DESKTOP, WS_VISIBLE,
                                     &flFrameFlags, szClientClass, NULL,
                                     0L, 0, 0, &hwndClient) ;

     while (WinGetMsg (hab, &qmsg, NULLHANDLE, 0, 0))
          WinDispatchMsg (hab, &qmsg) ;
```

Listing 11.2: The DRAWLINE program (Continued)

```
     WinDestroyWindow (hwndFrame) ;
     WinDestroyMsgQueue (hmq) ;
     WinTerminate (hab) ;
     return 0 ;
     }

MRESULT EXPENTRY ClientWndProc (HWND hwnd, ULONG msg, MPARAM mp1, MPARAM mp2)
     {
     static CHAR   *szGroupText[] = { "Color", "Type" } ;
     static CHAR   *szColorText[] = { "Background", "Blue",       "Red",
                                      "Pink",       "Green",      "Cyan",
                                      "Yellow",     "Neutral",    "Dark Gray",
                                      "Dark Blue",  "Dark Red",   "Dark Pink",
                                      "Dark Green", "Dark Cyan",  "Brown",
                                      "Pale Gray" } ;
     static CHAR   *szTypeText [] = { "Dot",        "Short Dash",
                                      "Dash Dot",   "Double Dot",
                                      "Long Dash",  "Dash Double Dot",
                                      "Solid",      "Invisible" } ;
     static HWND   hwndGroup[2], hwndRadioColor[16], hwndRadioType[8] ;
     static INT    iCurrentColor = 7,    // Neutral
                   iCurrentType  = 6 ;   // Solid
     static POINTL aptl[5] ;
     FONTMETRICS   fm ;
     HPS           hps ;
     INT           i, id, cxChar, cyChar ;

     switch (msg)
          {
          case WM_CREATE :
               hps = WinGetPS (hwnd) ;
               GpiQueryFontMetrics (hps, sizeof fm, &fm) ;
               cxChar = fm.lAveCharWidth ;
               cyChar = fm.lMaxBaselineExt ;
               WinReleasePS (hps) ;

               for (i = 0 ; i < 2 ; i++)

                    hwndGroup[i] = WinCreateWindow (
                                        hwnd,                // Parent
                                        WC_STATIC,           // Class
                                        szGroupText[i],      // Text
                                        WS_VISIBLE |         // Style
                                             SS_GROUPBOX,
                                        (8 + 42 * i) * cxChar,
                                        4 * cyChar,          // Position
                                        (26 + 12 * (1 - i)) *
                                             cxChar,         // Width
```

Listing 11.2: The DRAWLINE program (Continued)

```
                                     14 * cyChar,         // Height
                                     hwnd,                // Owner
                                     HWND_TOP,            // Placement
                                     i + 24,              // ID
                                     NULL,                // Ctrl Data
                                     NULL) ;              // Pres Params

          for (i = Ø ; i < 16 ; i++)

               hwndRadioColor[i] = WinCreateWindow (
                                     hwnd,                // Parent
                                     WC_BUTTON,           // Class
                                     szColorText[i],      // Text
                                     WS_VISIBLE |         // Style
                                          BS_RADIOBUTTON,
                                     (1Ø + (i > 7 ? 18 : Ø))
                                          * cxChar,       // X Position
                                     (31 - 3 * (i % 8))
                                          * cyChar / 2,   // Y Position
                                     16 * cxChar,         // Width
                                     3 * cyChar / 2,      // Height
                                     hwnd,                // Owner
                                     HWND_BOTTOM,         // Placement
                                     i,                   // ID
                                     NULL,                // Ctrl Data
                                     NULL) ;              // Pres Params

          for (i = Ø ; i < 8 ; i++)

               hwndRadioType[i]  = WinCreateWindow (
                                     hwnd,                // Parent
                                     WC_BUTTON,           // Class
                                     szTypeText[i],       // Text
                                     WS_VISIBLE |         // Style
                                          BS_RADIOBUTTON,
                                     52 * cxChar,         // Position
                                     (31 - 3 * i) * cyChar / 2,
                                     22 * cxChar,         // Width
                                     3 * cyChar / 2,      // Height
                                     hwnd,                // Owner
                                     HWND_BOTTOM,         // Placement
                                     i + 16,              // ID
                                     NULL,                // Ctrl Data
                                     NULL) ;              // Pres Params

          WinSendMsg (hwndRadioColor[iCurrentColor],
                      BM_SETCHECK, MPFROMSHORT (1), NULL) ;

          WinSendMsg (hwndRadioType[iCurrentType],
```

Listing 11.2: The DRAWLINE program (Continued)

```
                    BM_SETCHECK, MPFROMSHORT (1), NULL) ;

          aptl[0].x = aptl[3].x = aptl[4].x = 4 * cxChar ;
          aptl[1].x = aptl[2].x = 80 * cxChar ;

          aptl[0].y = aptl[1].y = aptl[4].y = 2 * cyChar ;
          aptl[2].y = aptl[3].y = 20 * cyChar ;

          return 0 ;

     case WM_CONTROL:
          id = SHORT1FROMMP (mp1) ;

          if (id < 16)              // Color IDs
               {
               WinSendMsg (hwndRadioColor[iCurrentColor],
                           BM_SETCHECK, MPFROMSHORT (0), NULL) ;

               iCurrentColor = id ;

               WinSendMsg (hwndRadioColor[iCurrentColor],
                           BM_SETCHECK, MPFROMSHORT (1), NULL) ;
               }

          else if (id < 24)         // Line Type IDs
               {
               WinSendMsg (hwndRadioType[iCurrentType],
                           BM_SETCHECK, MPFROMSHORT (0), NULL) ;

               iCurrentType = id - 16 ;

               WinSendMsg (hwndRadioType[iCurrentType],
                           BM_SETCHECK, MPFROMSHORT (1), NULL) ;
               }
          WinInvalidateRect (hwnd, NULL, TRUE) ;
          return 0 ;

     case WM_PAINT:
          hps = WinBeginPaint (hwnd, NULLHANDLE, NULL) ;
          GpiErase (hps) ;

          GpiSetColor (hps, iCurrentColor) ;
          GpiSetLineType (hps, iCurrentType + LINETYPE_DOT) ;
          GpiMove (hps, aptl) ;
          GpiPolyLine (hps, 4L, aptl + 1) ;

          WinEndPaint (hps) ;
          return 0 ;
     }
```

Listing 11.2: The DRAWLINE program (Continued)

```
     return WinDefWindowProc (hwnd, msg, mp1, mp2) ;
     }
```

The DRAWLINE.DEF File

```
;-----------------------------------
; DRAWLINE.DEF module definition file
;-----------------------------------

NAME           DRAWLINE  WINDOWAPI

DESCRIPTION    'Draw Line from Radio Buttons (c) Charles Petzold, 1993'
PROTMODE
```

DRAWLINE displays two groups of mutually exclusive radio buttons. You specify a line color with one group and a line type (dotted, dashed, solid, and so forth) with the other group. DRAWLINE responds by drawing four-line segments (using the *GpiPolyLine* function) based on the color and line type you choose. Each group of radio buttons is enclosed in a *group box*, which is a control window of the WC_STATIC class. A group box looks like a box with some text at the top. The group box doesn't process keyboard and mouse input and doesn't send messages to its owner.

As in BUTTONS1, DRAWLINE creates the control windows in *ClientWndProc* during processing of the WM_CREATE message. The IDs for the first 16 radio buttons (those that specify the line color) are 0 through 15. The IDs for the eight line-type radio buttons are 16 through 23. The two group boxes have IDs of 24 and 25. DRAWLINE avoids processing the WM_SIZE message by positioning these control windows relative to the lower-left corner of the client window. This allows the position to be specified in the original *WinCreateWindow* function. When you first execute DRAWLINE, you may have to increase the size of the window to see all the controls. The DRAWLINE window is shown in Figure 11.2.

After DRAWLINE creates the 16 radio buttons, it sends BM_SETCHECK messages to 2 radio buttons:

```
WinSendMsg (hwndRadioColor [iCurrentColor],
          BM_SETCHECK, MPFROMSHORT (1), NULL) ;

WinSendMsg (hwndRadioType [iCurrentType],
          BM_SETCHECK, MPFROMSHORT (1), NULL) ;
```

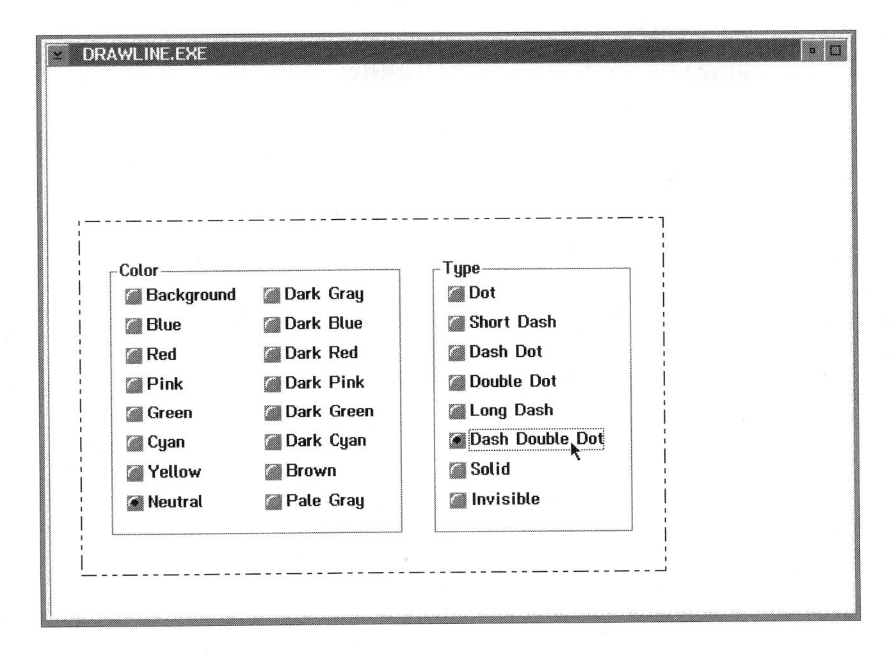

Figure 11.2: The DRAWLINE display

The BM_SETCHECK message tells a radio button to check or uncheck itself, depending on the value of *mp1*. These two statements cause a check to appear in the default radio button in each group—the buttons labeled "Neutral" and "Solid." The program keeps track of which radio button is checked in each group with the two static variables *iCurrentColor* and *iCurrentType*. When the program begins, the two variables are initialized to 7 and 6, which are the values of CLR_NEUTRAL and LINETYPE_SOLID.

When a radio button control is clicked, the control window sends its owner a WM_CONTROL message (not the WM_COMMAND message a push button sends its owner). The *mp1* and *mp2* parameters for radio buttons are

WM_CONTROL Parameter	Meaning
SHORT1FROMMP (*mp1*)	Child ID
SHORT2FROMMP (*mp1*)	Notification code
mp2	Control window handle

As in the WM_COMMAND message, the control window identifies itself by the child ID in the low USHORT of *mp1*. (Although the *mp2* parameter also identifies the control because it contains the control's window handle, some controls that send their owners WM_CONTROL messages use *mp2* for other purposes.)

The high USHORT of *mp1* is a notification code. Radio buttons send WM_CONTROL messages to their owners to indicate one of two occurrences, as follows:

Notification Code	Meaning
BN_CLICKED	Clicked with mouse
BN_DBLCLICKED	Double-clicked with mouse

DRAWLINE ignores the notification code and accepts either a single click or a double click.

DRAWLINE processes the WM_CONTROL message by first obtaining the ID number from *mp1*:

```
case WM_CONTROL:
     id = SHORT1FROMMP (mp1) ;
```

If the ID number is from 0 to 15, the radio button being clicked is in the first group of buttons—those that specify the line color. DRAWLINE must uncheck the currently checked radio button in the group and then check the radio button that has sent it the WM_CONTROL message:

```
if (id < 16)              // Color IDs
     {
     WinSendMsg (hwndRadioColor [iCurrentColor],
          BM_SETCHECK, MPFROMSHORT (0), NULL) ;

     iCurrentColor = id ;

     WinSendMsg (hwndRadioColor [iCurrentColor],
          BM_SETCHECK, MPFROMSHORT (1), NULL) ;
     }
```

Notice that the ID number is used as an array index and as the value stored in *iCurrentColor*. If the ID is from 16 to 23, the radio button is in the second group (line type):

```
else if (id < 24)         // Line type IDs
     {
     WinSendMsg (hwndRadioType [iCurrentType],
          BM_SETCHECK, MPFROMSHORT (0), NULL) ;
```

```
    iCurrentType = id - 16 ;

    WinSendMsg (hwndRadioType [iCurrentType],
         BM_SETCHECK, MPFROMSHORT (1), NULL) ;
    }
```

Here the ID must be adjusted by subtracting 16 before it's used as an array index and saved in *iCurrentType*. In either case, the client window is invalidated to generate a WM_PAINT message:

```
WinInvalidateRect (hwnd, NULL, TRUE) ;
```

During processing of WM_PAINT, DRAWLINE uses the *iCurrentColor* and *iCurrentType* variables to set the color and line type:

```
GpiSetColor (hps, iCurrentColor) ;
GpiSetLineType (hps, iCurrentType + LINETYPE_DOT) ;
```

It then draws the line in the specified color and type.

THE SCROLL-BAR CLASS

A program uses scroll bars to allow a user to specify a single value from a continuous range of integer values (even though the user may not think of using the scroll bar in quite this way). As you saw in the series of SYSVALS programs in Chapter 4, you can add a vertical and a horizontal scroll bar to the standard window by including the frame creation flags FCF_VERTSCROLL and FCF_-HORZSCROLL in the *WinCreateStdWindow* function. The vertical scroll bar is always positioned to the right of the client window, and the horizontal scroll bar is always positioned below the client window. (They are children of the frame window rather than the client window.) The scroll bars send messages to their owner (the frame window), which then passes the messages to the client window. You can also create vertical or horizontal scroll-bar control windows anywhere on your client window. These scroll bars send messages to their owner, which most often is the client.

The COLORSCR program, shown in Listing 11.3, shows how this is done. This program creates three vertical scroll bars—labeled "Red," "Green," and "Blue"—in the left half of its client window. Each has a range from 0 to 255. As you move the slider on each scroll bar, the right half of the client window uses the *WinFillRect* function to color itself with the composite color based on the red, green, and blue values.

Listing 11.3: The COLORSCR program

The COLORSCR.MAK File

```
#-----------------------
# COLORSCR.MAK make file
#-----------------------

colorscr.exe : colorscr.obj colorscr.def
     $(PRGLINK) colorscr, colorscr, NUL, $(PRGLIB), colorscr

colorscr.obj : colorscr.c
     $(PRGCC) colorscr.c
```

The COLORSCR.C File

```
/*----------------------------------------------------------
   COLORSCR.C -- Color Scroll using child window controls
                 (c) Charles Petzold, 1993
  ----------------------------------------------------------*/

#define INCL_WIN
#define INCL_GPI
#include <os2.h>
#include <stdio.h>
#include <stdlib.h>

MRESULT EXPENTRY ClientWndProc (HWND, ULONG, MPARAM, MPARAM) ;
MRESULT EXPENTRY ScrollProc (HWND, ULONG, MPARAM, MPARAM) ;

HWND  hwndScroll[3], hwndFocus ;
PFNWP pfnOldScroll[3] ;

int main (void)
     {
     static CHAR  szClientClass[] = "ColorScr" ;
     static ULONG flFrameFlags = FCF_TITLEBAR      | FCF_SYSMENU |
                                 FCF_SIZEBORDER    | FCF_MINMAX  |
                                 FCF_SHELLPOSITION | FCF_TASKLIST ;
     HAB          hab ;
     HMQ          hmq ;
     HWND         hwndFrame, hwndClient ;
     QMSG         qmsg ;

     hab = WinInitialize (0) ;
     hmq = WinCreateMsgQueue (hab, 0) ;

     WinRegisterClass (hab, szClientClass, ClientWndProc, CS_SIZEREDRAW, 0) ;

     hwndFrame = WinCreateStdWindow (HWND_DESKTOP, WS_VISIBLE,
                                     &flFrameFlags, szClientClass, NULL,
                                     0L, 0, 0, &hwndClient) ;
```

Listing 11.3: The COLORSCR program (Continued)

```
     WinSetFocus (HWND_DESKTOP, hwndFocus = hwndScroll[0]) ;

     while (WinGetMsg (hab, &qmsg, NULLHANDLE, 0, 0))
          WinDispatchMsg (hab, &qmsg) ;

     WinDestroyWindow (hwndFrame) ;
     WinDestroyMsgQueue (hmq) ;
     WinTerminate (hab) ;
     return 0 ;
     }

MRESULT EXPENTRY ClientWndProc (HWND hwnd, ULONG msg, MPARAM mp1, MPARAM mp2)
     {
     static CHAR  *apchColorLable[] = { "Red", "Green", "Blue" } ;
     static HWND  hwndLabel[3], hwndValue[3] ;
     static INT   cyChar, iColor[3] ;
     static LONG  alColorIndex[] = { CLR_RED, CLR_GREEN, CLR_BLUE } ;
     static RECTL rclRightHalf ;
     CHAR         szBuffer[10] ;
     FONTMETRICS  fm ;
     HPS          hps ;
     INT          i, id, cxClient, cyClient ;

     switch (msg)
          {
          case WM_CREATE :
               hps = WinGetPS (hwnd) ;
               GpiQueryFontMetrics (hps, (LONG) sizeof fm, &fm) ;
               cyChar = fm.lMaxBaselineExt ;
               WinReleasePS (hps) ;

               for (i = 0 ; i < 3 ; i++)
                    {
                    hwndScroll[i] = WinCreateWindow (
                                        hwnd,              // Parent
                                        WC_SCROLLBAR,      // Class
                                        NULL,              // Text
                                        WS_VISIBLE |       // Style
                                             SBS_VERT,
                                        0, 0,              // Position
                                        0, 0,              // Size
                                        hwnd,              // Owner
                                        HWND_BOTTOM,       // Placement
                                        i,                 // ID
                                        NULL,              // Ctrl Data
                                        NULL) ;            // Pres Params

                    hwndLabel[i]  = WinCreateWindow (
```

Listing 11.3: The COLORSCR program (Continued)

```
                                   hwnd,                 // Parent
                                   WC_STATIC,            // Class
                                   apchColorLable[i],    // Text
                                   WS_VISIBLE |          // Style
                                     SS_TEXT | DT_CENTER,
                                   Ø, Ø,                 // Position
                                   Ø, Ø,                 // Size
                                   hwnd,                 // Owner
                                   HWND_BOTTOM,          // Placement
                                   i + 3,                // ID
                                   NULL,                 // Ctrl Data
                                   NULL) ;               // Pres Params

               hwndValue[i]  = WinCreateWindow (
                                   hwnd,                 // Parent
                                   WC_STATIC,            // Class
                                   "Ø",                  // Text
                                   WS_VISIBLE |          // Style
                                     SS_TEXT | DT_CENTER,
                                   Ø, Ø,                 // Position
                                   Ø, Ø,                 // Size
                                   hwnd,                 // Owner
                                   HWND_BOTTOM,          // Placement
                                   i + 6,                // ID
                                   NULL,                 // Ctrl Data
                                   NULL) ;               // Pres Params

               pfnOldScroll[i] =
                         WinSubclassWindow (hwndScroll[i], ScrollProc) ;

               WinSetPresParam (hwndScroll [i], PP_FOREGROUNDCOLORINDEX,
                                sizeof (LONG), alColorIndex + i) ;

               WinSendMsg (hwndScroll[i], SBM_SETSCROLLBAR,
                           MPFROM2SHORT (Ø, Ø), MPFROM2SHORT (Ø, 255)) ;
               }
          return Ø ;

     case WM_SIZE :
          cxClient = SHORT1FROMMP (mp2) ;
          cyClient = SHORT2FROMMP (mp2) ;

          for (i = Ø ; i < 3 ; i++)
               {
               WinSetWindowPos (hwndScroll[i], NULLHANDLE,
                                (2 * i + 1) * cxClient / 14, 2 * cyChar,
                                cxClient / 14, cyClient - 4 * cyChar,
                                SWP_SIZE | SWP_MOVE) ;
```

Listing 11.3: The COLORSCR program (Continued)

```
               WinSetWindowPos (hwndLabel[i], NULLHANDLE,
                                (4 * i + 1) * cxClient / 28,
                                cyClient - 3 * cyChar / 2,
                                cxClient / 7, cyChar,
                                SWP_SIZE | SWP_MOVE) ;

               WinSetWindowPos (hwndValue[i], NULLHANDLE,
                                (4 * i + 1) * cxClient / 28, cyChar / 2,
                                cxClient / 7, cyChar,
                                SWP_SIZE | SWP_MOVE) ;
               }

          WinQueryWindowRect (hwnd, &rclRightHalf) ;
          rclRightHalf.xLeft = rclRightHalf.xRight / 2 ;
          return Ø ;

     case WM_VSCROLL :
          id = SHORT1FROMMP (mp1) ;          // ID of scroll bar

          switch (SHORT2FROMMP (mp2))
               {
               case SB_LINEDOWN :
                    iColor[id] = min (255, iColor[id] + 1) ;
                    break ;

               case SB_LINEUP :
                    iColor[id] = max (Ø, iColor[id] - 1) ;
                    break ;

               case SB_PAGEDOWN :
                    iColor[id] = min (255, iColor[id] + 16) ;
                    break ;

               case SB_PAGEUP :
                    iColor[id] = max (Ø, iColor[id] - 16) ;
                    break ;

               case SB_SLIDERTRACK :
                    iColor[id] = SHORT1FROMMP (mp2) ;
                    break ;

               default :
                    return Ø ;
               }
          WinSendMsg (hwndScroll[id], SBM_SETPOS,
                      MPFROM2SHORT (iColor[id], Ø), NULL) ;

          sprintf (szBuffer, "%d", iColor[id]) ;
          WinSetWindowText (hwndValue[id], szBuffer) ;
```

Listing 11.3: The COLORSCR program (Continued)

```
               WinInvalidateRect (hwnd, &rclRightHalf, FALSE) ;
               return 0 ;

          case WM_PAINT:
               hps = WinBeginPaint (hwnd, NULLHANDLE, NULL) ;

               GpiCreateLogColorTable (hps, LCOL_RESET, LCOLF_RGB,
                                        0L, 0L, NULL) ;

               WinFillRect (hps, &rclRightHalf, (ULONG) iColor[0] << 16 |
                                                (ULONG) iColor[1] <<  8 |
                                                (ULONG) iColor[2]) ;
               WinEndPaint (hps) ;
               return 0 ;

          case WM_ERASEBACKGROUND:
               return MRFROMSHORT (1) ;
          }
     return WinDefWindowProc (hwnd, msg, mp1, mp2) ;
     }

MRESULT EXPENTRY ScrollProc (HWND hwnd, ULONG msg, MPARAM mp1, MPARAM mp2)
     {
     INT id ;

     id = WinQueryWindowUShort (hwnd, QWS_ID) ;   // ID of scroll bar

     switch (msg)
          {
          case WM_CHAR:
               if (!(CHARMSG(&msg)->fs & KC_VIRTUALKEY))
                    break ;

               switch (CHARMSG(&msg)->vkey)
                    {
                    case VK_TAB:
                         if (!(CHARMSG(&msg)->fs & KC_KEYUP))
                              {
                              hwndFocus = hwndScroll[(id + 1) % 3] ;
                              WinSetFocus (HWND_DESKTOP, hwndFocus) ;
                              }
                         return MRFROMSHORT (1) ;

                    case VK_BACKTAB:
                         if (!(CHARMSG(&msg)->fs & KC_KEYUP))
                              {
                              hwndFocus = hwndScroll[(id + 2) % 3] ;
                              WinSetFocus (HWND_DESKTOP, hwndFocus) ;
                              }
```

Listing 11.3: The COLORSCR program (Continued)

```
                    return MRFROMSHORT (1) ;

               default:
                    break ;
               }
          break ;

     case WM_BUTTON1DOWN:
          WinSetFocus (HWND_DESKTOP, hwndFocus = hwnd) ;
          break ;
     }
return pfnOldScroll[id] (hwnd, msg, mp1, mp2) ;
}
```

The COLORSCR.DEF File

```
;-------------------------------------
; COLORSCR.DEF module definition file
;-------------------------------------

NAME           COLORSCR  WINDOWAPI

DESCRIPTION    'Color Scroll (c) Charles Petzold, 1993'
PROTMODE
```

COLORSCR creates nine control windows—three scroll-bar windows and six static text windows. Three static text windows are positioned on top of the scroll bars and display the labels "Red," "Green," and "Blue." The text windows on the bottom of each scroll bar display the current position (0 through 255) of the scroll bar. These values correspond directly to the red, green, and blue values used to create the composite color. The COLORSCR window is shown in Figure 11.3.

The nine windows are created during processing of the WM_CREATE message in *ClientWndProc*. The child IDs and the arrays the program uses for storing the window handles are as follows:

Window Type	Child ID	Window Handle Array
Scroll bar	0 to 2	*hwndScroll*
Static text	3 to 5	*hwndLabel*
Static text	6 to 8	*hwndValue*

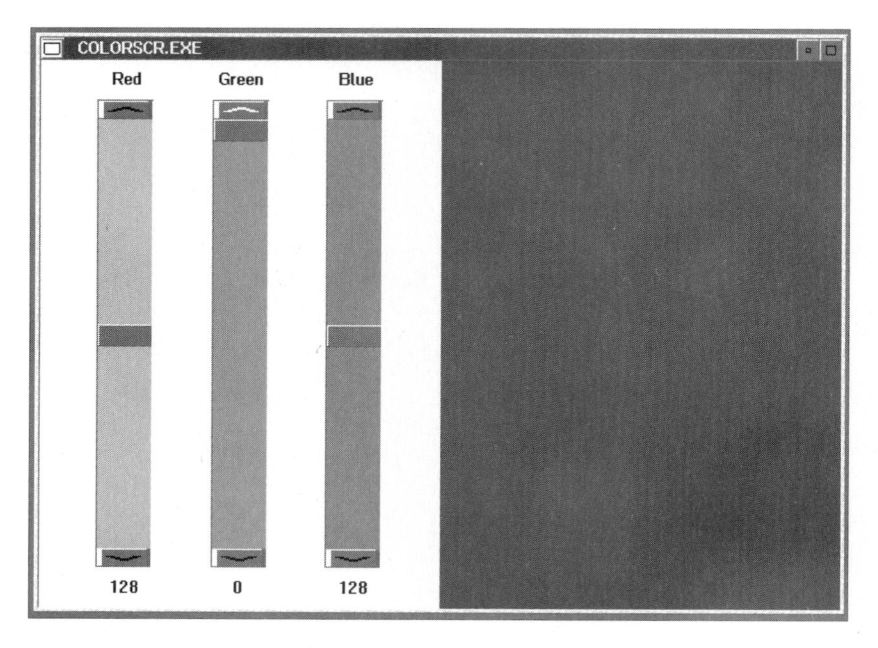

Figure 11.3: The COLORSCR display

The three scroll bars have the window class WC_SCROLLBAR and the window style WS_VISIBLE | SBS_VERT. The SBS_VERT style indicates that the scroll bars are vertical. COLORSCR gives the six static text windows the window style WS_VISIBLE | SS_TEXT | DT_CENTER. The SS_TEXT identifier is one of several window styles available for windows of the WC_STATIC class. The DT_CENTER identifier is normally used with the *WinDrawText* function, but you can also use it as a window style with SS_TEXT to center the text within the width of the window. The position and size parameters are set to 0 in the *WinCreateWindow* call. *ClientWndProc* positions and sizes the windows during the WM_SIZE message.

When you include scroll bars as part of the standard window, vertical scroll bars always have a standard width, and horizontal scroll bars always have a standard height. You can obtain these standard widths and heights from the *WinQuerySysValue* function using the SV_CXVSCROLL and SV_CYHSCROLL parameters. However, when you create scroll bars using the *WinCreateWindow* function, the scroll bars can be any size you want. You can make long, thin scroll bars or short, pudgy scroll bars. COLORSCR always sets the width of the three vertical scroll bars at one-fourteenth the width of the client window. This is done while processing the WM_SIZE message. If you want to use standard widths and heights for the scroll bars you create in your programs, get the values from *WinQuerySysValue*.

After creating the scroll bars during the WM_CREATE message, COLORSCR sends them a SBM_SETSCROLLBAR message to set the range and current position:

```
WinSendMsg (hwndScroll [i], SBM_SETSCROLLBAR,
     MPFROM2SHORT (0, 0), MPFROM2SHORT (0, 255)) ;
```

The SYSVALS programs in Chapter 4 use this same message.

PROCESSING THE SCROLL-BAR MESSAGES

The scroll bars in COLORSCR send WM_VSCROLL messages to the client window. WM_VSCROLL and WM_HSCROLL messages are accompanied by *mp1* and *mp2* parameters, as follows:

WM_*x*SCROLL Parameter	**Meaning**
SHORT1FROMMP (*mp1*)	Child ID
SHORT2FROMMP (*mp1*)	0
SHORT1FROMMP (*mp2*)	Slider position (for some commands)
SHORT2FROMMP (*mp2*)	Command

This is the same information used for scroll bars created in a standard window. The SYSVALS program didn't look at the control ID, because the program had only one vertical scroll bar and one horizontal scroll bar. If you include scroll bars as part of the standard window and then create additional scroll bars using *WinCreateWindow*, you can distinguish between the scroll bars by examining the ID number. The scroll bars that are part of the standard window have the predefined IDs FID_VERTSCROLL and FID_HORZSCROLL.

COLORSCR defines a static array named *iColor* to store the current position of each of the three scroll bars. The index to this array is the same as the scroll-bar ID. The processing of the WM_VSCROLL message thus begins by obtaining the ID number from *mp1*:

```
case WM_VSCROLL :
     id = SHORT1FROMMP (mp1) ;
```

COLORSCR then alters the appropriate value stored in *iColor* based on the scroll-bar command in the high USHORT of *mp2*:

```
switch (SHORT2FROMMP (mp2))
     {
     case SB_LINEDOWN :
```

```
          iColor [id] = min (255, iColor [id] + 1) ;
          break ;

     case SB_LINEUP :
          iColor [id] = max (Ø, iColor [id] - 1) ;
          break ;

     case SB_PAGEDOWN :
          iColor [id] = min (255, iColor [id] + 16) ;
          break ;

     case SB_PAGEUP :
          iColor [id] = max (Ø, iColor [id] - 16) ;
          break ;

     case SB_SLIDERTRACK :
          iColor [id] = SHORT1FROMMP (mp2) ;
          break ;

     default :
          return Ø ;
     }
```

The program sets a new position of the scroll-bar slider by sending it an SBM_SETPOS message. The window handle of the scroll bar is stored in the *hwndScroll* array that is also indexed by the ID number:

```
WinSendMsg (hwndScroll [id], SBM_SETPOS,
     MPFROM2SHORT (iColor [id], Ø), NULL) ;
```

COLORSCR must also change the text in the static control window displayed at the bottom of the scroll bar. It does this by first converting the number to its ASCII value by calling *sprintf* and then calling *WinSetWindowText.* The window handles are stored in the *hwndValue* array. The right half of the client window is then invalidated to generate a WM_PAINT message:

```
WinInvalidateRect (hwnd, &rclRightHalf, FALSE) ;
```

The *rclRightHalf* RECTL structure contains the coordinates of the right half of the client window. These are set during the WM_SIZE message.

The WM_PAINT processing is fairly simple. COLORSCR first calls *GpiCreateLogColorTable* to specify that color indexes are to be interpreted as 32-bit RGB values:

```
GpiCreateLogColorTable (hps, LCOL_RESET, LCOLF_RGB,
                        ØL, ØL, NULL) ;
```

The program then combines the current red, green, and blue color values stored in the *iColor* array into one ULONG and calls *WinFillRect* to color the right half of the client window with that color:

```
WinFillRect (hps, &rclRightHalf, (ULONG) iColor [0] << 16 |
             (ULONG) iColor [1] << 8 | (ULONG) iColor [2]) ;
```

CHANGING THE KEYBOARD INPUT FOCUS

Unlike BUTTONS1 and DRAWLINE, COLORSCR has a complete keyboard interface and doesn't require a mouse. You can move the position of the scroll-bar slider using the cursor-movement arrow keys, and you can move the keyboard input focus from one scroll bar to another using the Tab and Shift-Tab keys.

As you saw in the SYSVALS program in Chapter 4, the scroll bars include their own keyboard interface for the cursor movement keys. Once a scroll-bar window has the keyboard input focus, it can understand and interpret these keys. That's not the problem. The problem is that once a control window gets the input focus, it doesn't properly interpret the Tab key. We need to find a way to give a scroll bar the input focus (so that it uses the cursor movement keys) and then be able to take away the input focus when the Tab key is pressed. But how can *ClientWndProc* know that the Tab key is pressed when the scroll bar is getting all the WM_CHAR messages?

The solution involves a technique called *window subclassing*. Essentially, this technique allows your program to get first dibs on all messages sent to a particular window created by your program (but not to windows created by other programs). You can process some of these messages and then allow the window's normal window procedure to process the others. You can prevent the normal window procedure from receiving some messages, or you can alter messages before they get to the window procedure.

Let's look at COLORSCR to see how this works in practice. Toward the end of COLORSCR.C is a function called *ScrollProc* that is defined as if it were a normal window procedure. It is an EXPENTRY function, has a return value of MRESULT, and accepts the four parameters normally passed to window procedures.

After creating the three scroll-bar windows during processing of the WM_-CREATE message, COLORSCR calls *WinSubclassWindow* to specify that all messages to these three scroll-bar windows should be sent to *ScrollProc* instead:

```
pfnOldScroll[i] =
     WinSubclassWindow (hwndScroll[i], ScrollProc) ;
```

The *pfnOldScroll* array is a global variable defined near the top of COLORSCR.C:

```
PFNWP pfnOldScroll[3] ;
```

This array holds the addresses of the original window procedures for the three scroll bars.

Now let's look at *ScrollProc*. When a message is sent to any of the three scroll bars, *ScrollProc* gets the message rather than the normal scroll-bar window procedure. *ScrollProc* obtains the control ID associated with the scroll-bar window receiving the message:

```
id = WinQueryWindowUShort (hwnd, QWS_ID) ;
```

ScrollProc then checks to see if the message is WM_CHAR, if the message contains a valid virtual key code, if the key is being pressed, and if the virtual key is VK_TAB or VK_BACKTAB.

For VK_TAB, *ScrollProc* determines the window handle that is to receive the input focus:

```
hwndFocus = hwndScroll[(id + 1) % 3]
```

The new focus window is the scroll bar with the next highest ID. *ScrollProc* then uses this *hwndFocus* variable to set the new focus window:

```
WinSetFocus (HWND_DESKTOP, hwndFocus) ;
```

ScrollProc also sets the focus to one of the scroll bars when it receives a WM_-BUTTON1DOWN message.

ScrollProc sends all messages (except the VK_TAB and VK_BACKTAB keystrokes) to the old scroll-bar window procedure stored in *pfnOldScroll*:

```
return pfnOldScroll [id] (hwnd, msg, mp1, mp2) ;
```

This allows the normal processing in the scroll-bar window procedure to occur.

Of course, we must make sure that the first scroll bar gets the input focus when the program starts up. Following the *WinCreateStdWindow* call in *main*, COLORSCR sets the input focus to the first window:

```
WinSetFocus (HWND_DESKTOP, hwndFocus = hwndScroll [0]) ;
```

Without this statement, the first scroll bar wouldn't get the input focus until it was clicked.

CREATING YOUR OWN CONTROLS

In Chapter 9's CHECKER3 program, you created child windows that helped simplify mouse processing. These child windows were not really control windows because they had two deficiencies: They had no keyboard interface and they did not notify their owner when they were toggled. Now let's try something similar, but this time let's make the children full-fledged control windows.

In this exercise, we're going to reinvent the push button. While we're at it, we're going to make our push buttons look a little fancier than the ones built into the Presentation Manager. This new push button will have a more distinct three-dimensional appearance.

MOUSE CAPTURE AND INPUT FOCUS

You may want to experiment with BUTTONS1 (and with other programs that create control windows based on the predefined window classes) to help you understand what is going on in the window procedure for the control.

For example, you'll find in BUTTONS1 that triggering the button with the mouse requires that you both press and release the mouse button while the pointer is positioned within the control. If you press the mouse button when the pointer is within the control, the control is inverted. If you move the mouse pointer outside the control with the mouse button pressed, the control returns to normal. Moving the pointer back within the button inverts the button colors again.

Obviously, the window procedure is capturing the mouse (a concept discussed in Chapter 9). This is the only way the window procedure can determine that the mouse pointer has moved outside the control window.

Clicking the push button with the mouse causes a dotted outline to appear around the text. This indicates that the control has the input focus and requires that the window procedure give itself the input focus when the button is clicked. When the push button has the input focus, you can also trigger the button by pressing the spacebar. This requires that the window procedure for the control also process some keystrokes.

THE NEW BUTTON WINDOW PROCEDURE

Let's look first at the NEWBTN.C file shown in Listing 11.4.

Listing 11.4: The NEWBTN file

The NEWBTN.C File

```
/*----------------------------------------------------------------
   NEWBTN.C -- Contains window procedure for new 3D push button
               (c) Charles Petzold, 1993
  ----------------------------------------------------------------*/
```

Listing 11.4: The NEWBTN file (Continued)

```
#define INCL_WIN
#define INCL_GPI
#include <os2.h>
#include <stdlib.h>
#include <string.h>

#define LCID_ITALIC 1L

               /*--------------------------------------------------
                  Structure for storing data unique to each window
                 --------------------------------------------------*/
typedef struct
     {
     PSZ  pszText ;
     BOOL fHaveCapture ;
     BOOL fHaveFocus ;
     BOOL fInsideRect ;
     BOOL fSpaceDown ;
     }
     NEWBTN ;

typedef NEWBTN *PNEWBTN ;

MRESULT EXPENTRY NewBtnWndProc (HWND, ULONG, MPARAM, MPARAM) ;
VOID             DrawButton    (HWND, HPS, PNEWBTN) ;

          /*-----------------------------------------------------------
             RegisterNewBtnClass function available to other modules
            -----------------------------------------------------------*/

BOOL APIENTRY RegisterNewBtnClass (HAB hab)
     {
     return WinRegisterClass (hab, "NewBtn", NewBtnWndProc,
                              CS_SIZEREDRAW, sizeof (PNEWBTN)) ;
     }

          /*--------------------------------
             NewBtnWndProc window procedure
            --------------------------------*/

MRESULT EXPENTRY NewBtnWndProc (HWND hwnd, ULONG msg, MPARAM mp1, MPARAM mp2)
     {
     BOOL          fTestInsideRect ;
     HPS           hps ;
     CREATESTRUCT  *pcrst ;
     POINTL        ptl ;
     NEWBTN        *pNewBtn ;
     WNDPARAMS     *pwprm ;
     RECTL         rcl ;
```

Listing 11.4: The NEWBTN file (Continued)

```
pNewBtn = WinQueryWindowPtr (hwnd, 0) ;

switch (msg)
     {
     case WM_CREATE:
          pNewBtn = malloc (sizeof (NEWBTN)) ;

                    // Initialize structure

          pNewBtn->fHaveCapture = FALSE ;
          pNewBtn->fHaveFocus   = FALSE ;
          pNewBtn->fInsideRect  = FALSE ;
          pNewBtn->fSpaceDown   = FALSE ;

                    // Get window text from creation structure

          pcrst = (PCREATESTRUCT) PVOIDFROMMP (mp2) ;

          pNewBtn->pszText = malloc (1 + strlen (pcrst->pszText)) ;
          strcpy (pNewBtn->pszText, pcrst->pszText) ;

          WinSetWindowPtr (hwnd, 0, pNewBtn) ;
          return 0 ;

     case WM_SETWINDOWPARAMS:
          pwprm = (PWNDPARAMS) PVOIDFROMMP (mp1) ;

                    // Get window text from window parameter structure

          if (pwprm->fsStatus & WPM_TEXT)
               {
               free (pNewBtn->pszText) ;
               pNewBtn->pszText = malloc (1 + pwprm->cchText) ;
               strcpy (pNewBtn->pszText, pwprm->pszText) ;
               }
          return MRFROMSHORT (1) ;

     case WM_QUERYWINDOWPARAMS:
          pwprm = (PWNDPARAMS) PVOIDFROMMP (mp1) ;

                    // Set window parameter structure fields

          if (pwprm->fsStatus & WPM_CCHTEXT)
               pwprm->cchText = strlen (pNewBtn->pszText) ;

          if (pwprm->fsStatus & WPM_TEXT)
               strcpy (pwprm->pszText, pNewBtn->pszText) ;
```

Listing 11.4: The NEWBTN file (Continued)

```
          if (pwprm->fsStatus & WPM_CBPRESPARAMS)
               pwprm->cbPresParams = 0 ;

          if (pwprm->fsStatus & WPM_PRESPARAMS)
               pwprm->pPresParams = NULL ;

          if (pwprm->fsStatus & WPM_CBCTLDATA)
               pwprm->cbCtlData = 0 ;

          if (pwprm->fsStatus & WPM_CTLDATA)
               pwprm->pCtlData = NULL ;

          return MRFROMSHORT (1) ;

     case WM_BUTTON1DOWN:
          WinSetFocus (HWND_DESKTOP, hwnd) ;
          WinSetCapture (HWND_DESKTOP, hwnd) ;
          pNewBtn->fHaveCapture = TRUE ;
          pNewBtn->fInsideRect  = TRUE ;
          WinInvalidateRect (hwnd, NULL, FALSE) ;
          return 0 ;

     case WM_MOUSEMOVE:
          if (!pNewBtn->fHaveCapture)
               break ;

          WinQueryWindowRect (hwnd, &rcl) ;
          ptl.x = MOUSEMSG(&msg)->x ;
          ptl.y = MOUSEMSG(&msg)->y ;

                    // Test if mouse pointer is still in window

          fTestInsideRect = WinPtInRect (WinQueryAnchorBlock (hwnd),
                                         &rcl, &ptl) ;

          if (pNewBtn->fInsideRect != fTestInsideRect)
               {
               pNewBtn->fInsideRect = fTestInsideRect ;
               WinInvalidateRect (hwnd, NULL, FALSE) ;
               }
          break ;

     case WM_BUTTON1UP:
          if (!pNewBtn->fHaveCapture)
               break ;

          WinSetCapture (HWND_DESKTOP, NULLHANDLE) ;
          pNewBtn->fHaveCapture = FALSE ;
          pNewBtn->fInsideRect  = FALSE ;
```

Listing 11.4: The NEWBTN file (Continued)

```
          WinQueryWindowRect (hwnd, &rcl) ;
          ptl.x = MOUSEMSG(&msg)->x ;
          ptl.y = MOUSEMSG(&msg)->y ;

                    // Post WM_COMMAND if mouse pointer is in window

          if (WinPtInRect (WinQueryAnchorBlock (hwnd), &rcl, &ptl))
               WinPostMsg (WinQueryWindow (hwnd, QW_OWNER),
                    WM_COMMAND,
                    MPFROMSHORT (WinQueryWindowUShort (hwnd, QWS_ID)),
                    MPFROM2SHORT (CMDSRC_OTHER, TRUE)) ;

          WinInvalidateRect (hwnd, NULL, FALSE) ;
          return 0 ;

     case WM_ENABLE:
          WinInvalidateRect (hwnd, NULL, FALSE) ;
          return 0 ;

     case WM_SETFOCUS:
          pNewBtn->fHaveFocus = SHORT1FROMMP (mp2) ;
          WinInvalidateRect (hwnd, NULL, FALSE) ;
          return 0 ;

     case WM_CHAR:
          if (!(CHARMSG(&msg)->fs   &  KC_VIRTUALKEY) ||
                CHARMSG(&msg)->vkey != VK_SPACE       ||
                CHARMSG(&msg)->fs   &  KC_PREVDOWN)
               break ;

                    // Post WM_COMMAND when spacebar is released

          if (!(CHARMSG(&msg)->fs & KC_KEYUP))
               pNewBtn->fSpaceDown = TRUE ;
          else
               {
               pNewBtn->fSpaceDown = FALSE ;
               WinPostMsg (WinQueryWindow (hwnd, QW_OWNER),
                    WM_COMMAND,
                    MPFROMSHORT (WinQueryWindowUShort (hwnd, QWS_ID)),
                    MPFROM2SHORT (CMDSRC_OTHER, FALSE)) ;
               }
          WinInvalidateRect (hwnd, NULL, FALSE) ;
          return 0 ;

     case WM_PAINT:
          hps = WinBeginPaint (hwnd, NULLHANDLE, NULL) ;
          DrawButton (hwnd, hps, pNewBtn) ;
```

Listing 11.4: The NEWBTN file (Continued)

```
               WinEndPaint (hps) ;
               return 0 ;

          case WM_DESTROY:
               free (pNewBtn->pszText) ;
               free (pNewBtn) ;
               return 0 ;
          }
     return WinDefWindowProc (hwnd, msg, mp1, mp2) ;
     }

          /*---------------------------------------------------------
             Draws filled and outlined polygon (used by DrawButton)
            ---------------------------------------------------------*/

VOID Polygon (HPS hps, LONG lPoints, POINTL aptl[], LONG lColor)
     {
               // Draw interior in specified color

     GpiSavePS (hps) ;
     GpiSetColor (hps, lColor) ;

     GpiBeginArea (hps, BA_NOBOUNDARY | BA_ALTERNATE) ;
     GpiMove (hps, aptl) ;
     GpiPolyLine (hps, lPoints - 1, aptl + 1) ;
     GpiEndArea (hps) ;

     GpiRestorePS (hps, -1L) ;

               // Draw boundary in default color

     GpiMove (hps, aptl + lPoints - 1) ;
     GpiPolyLine (hps, lPoints, aptl) ;
     }

          /*---------------------
             Draws square button
            ---------------------*/

VOID DrawButton (HWND hwnd, HPS hps, PNEWBTN pNewBtn)
     {
     FATTRS      fat ;
     FONTMETRICS fm ;
     HDC         hdc ;
     LONG        lColor, lHorzRes, lVertRes, cxEdge, cyEdge ;
     POINTL      aptl[10], aptlTextBox[TXTBOX_COUNT], ptlShadow, ptlText ;
     RECTL       rcl ;

               // Find 2 millimeter edge width in pixels
```

Listing 11.4: The NEWBTN file (Continued)

```
hdc = GpiQueryDevice (hps) ;
DevQueryCaps (hdc, CAPS_HORIZONTAL_RESOLUTION, 1L, &lHorzRes) ;
DevQueryCaps (hdc, CAPS_VERTICAL_RESOLUTION,   1L, &lVertRes) ;

cxEdge = lHorzRes / 500 ;
cyEdge = lVertRes / 500 ;

          // Set up coordinates for drawing the button

WinQueryWindowRect (hwnd, &rcl) ;

aptl[0].x = 0 ;                      aptl[0].y = 0 ;
aptl[1].x = cxEdge ;                 aptl[1].y = cyEdge ;
aptl[2].x = rcl.xRight - cxEdge ;    aptl[2].y = cyEdge ;
aptl[3].x = rcl.xRight - 1 ;         aptl[3].y = 0 ;
aptl[4].x = rcl.xRight - 1 ;         aptl[4].y = rcl.yTop - 1 ;
aptl[5].x = rcl.xRight - cxEdge ;    aptl[5].y = rcl.yTop - cyEdge ;
aptl[6].x = cxEdge ;                 aptl[6].y = rcl.yTop - cyEdge ;
aptl[7].x = 0 ;                      aptl[7].y = rcl.yTop - 1 ;
aptl[8].x = 0 ;                      aptl[8].y = 0 ;
aptl[9].x = cxEdge ;                 aptl[9].y = cyEdge ;

          // Paint edges at bottom and right side

GpiSetColor (hps, CLR_BLACK) ;
lColor = (pNewBtn->fInsideRect || pNewBtn->fSpaceDown) ?
                         CLR_PALEGRAY : CLR_DARKGRAY ;
Polygon (hps, 4L, aptl + 0, lColor) ;
Polygon (hps, 4L, aptl + 2, lColor) ;

          // Paint edges at top and left side

lColor = (pNewBtn->fInsideRect || pNewBtn->fSpaceDown) ?
                         CLR_DARKGRAY : CLR_WHITE ;
Polygon (hps, 4L, aptl + 4, lColor) ;
Polygon (hps, 4L, aptl + 6, lColor) ;

          // Paint interior area

GpiSavePS (hps) ;
GpiSetColor (hps, (pNewBtn->fInsideRect || pNewBtn->fSpaceDown) ?
                         CLR_DARKGRAY : CLR_PALEGRAY) ;
GpiMove (hps, aptl + 1) ;
GpiBox (hps, DRO_FILL, aptl + 5, 0L, 0L) ;
GpiRestorePS (hps, -1L) ;
GpiBox (hps, DRO_OUTLINE, aptl + 5, 0L, 0L) ;

          // If button has focus, use italic font
```

Listing 11.4: The NEWBTN file (Continued)

```
GpiQueryFontMetrics (hps, (LONG) sizeof fm, &fm) ;

if (pNewBtn->fHaveFocus)
     {
     fat.usRecordLength  = sizeof fat ;
     fat.fsSelection     = FATTR_SEL_ITALIC ;
     fat.lMatch          = 0 ;
     fat.idRegistry      = fm.idRegistry ;
     fat.usCodePage      = fm.usCodePage ;
     fat.lMaxBaselineExt = fm.lMaxBaselineExt ;
     fat.lAveCharWidth   = fm.lAveCharWidth ;
     fat.fsType          = 0 ;
     fat.fsFontUse       = 0 ;
     strcpy (fat.szFacename, fm.szFacename) ;

     GpiCreateLogFont (hps, NULL, LCID_ITALIC, &fat) ;
     GpiSetCharSet (hps, LCID_ITALIC) ;
     }
          // Calculate text position

GpiQueryTextBox (hps, (LONG) strlen (pNewBtn->pszText), pNewBtn->pszText,
                      TXTBOX_COUNT, aptlTextBox) ;

ptlText.x = (rcl.xRight - aptlTextBox[TXTBOX_CONCAT].x) / 2 ;
ptlText.y = (rcl.yTop   - aptlTextBox[TXTBOX_TOPLEFT].y -
                          aptlTextBox[TXTBOX_BOTTOMLEFT].y) / 2 ;

ptlShadow.x = ptlText.x + fm.lAveCharWidth   / 3 ;
ptlShadow.y = ptlText.y - fm.lMaxBaselineExt / 8 ;

          // Display text shadow in black, and text in white

GpiSetColor (hps, CLR_BLACK) ;
GpiCharStringAt (hps, &ptlShadow, (LONG) strlen (pNewBtn->pszText),
                                  pNewBtn->pszText) ;
GpiSetColor (hps, CLR_WHITE) ;
GpiCharStringAt (hps, &ptlText, (LONG) strlen (pNewBtn->pszText),
                                pNewBtn->pszText) ;

          // X out button if the window is not enabled

if (!WinIsWindowEnabled (hwnd))
     {
     GpiMove (hps, aptl + 1) ;
     GpiLine (hps, aptl + 5) ;
     GpiMove (hps, aptl + 2) ;
     GpiLine (hps, aptl + 6) ;
     }
```

Listing 11.4: The NEWBTN file (Continued)

```
          // Clean up

     if (pNewBtn->fHaveFocus)
          {
          GpiSetCharSet (hps, LCID_DEFAULT) ;
          GpiDeleteSetId (hps, LCID_ITALIC) ;
          }
     }
```

This file contains several functions. Two functions are called from outside the module: *RegisterNewBtnClass* registers a window class called "NewBtn" that uses the window procedure *NewBtnWndProc*, another function in NEWBTN.C.

Often a program creates more than one child window based on the same window class. This means that you cannot use static variables to store information unique to each child window: These static variables would be shared by all windows that are based on that class and created within the same process. For this reason, only automatic variables (used during the course of processing a single message) are defined within *NewBtnWndProc*.

Information unique to each window is stored in a structure of type NEWBTN, defined in the NEWBTN.C file. When *RegisterNewBtnClass* registers the window class, the last parameter of *WinRegisterClass* is set to the size of a far pointer to the NEWBTN structure. This reserves some memory space that is unique to each window. During the WM_CREATE message, *NewBtnWndProc* calls *malloc* to allocate a block of memory the size of the NEWBTN structure. The pointer returned by *malloc* is stored in the variable *pNewBtn*. After the fields of this structure are initialized, the pointer is saved in the memory reserved by the *WinRegisterClass* function:

```
WinSetWindowPtr (hwnd, 0, pNewBtn) ;
```

The WM_CREATE message is the first message that the window procedure processes when creating a new window. For all other messages, the pointer stored in the reserved area will be valid. *NewBtnWndProc* obtains that pointer before processing any specific message:

```
pNewBtn = WinQueryWindowPtr (hwnd, 0) ;
```

This allows the window procedure to use the window-specific information stored in the structure.

Some windows have a *window text* that the window displays. For example, push buttons display their window text in the center of the button. Windows that have a window text must save the text themselves. This requires some additional processing in the WM_CREATE message. During WM_CREATE, a pointer to the initial window text of the window (which is the string passed as the window text parameter to *WinCreateWindow*) is stored in the *pszText* field of a CREATESTRUCT structure for the window.

The *mp2* message parameter contains a pointer to this structure. *NewBtnWndProc* must determine the length of this text, allocate memory for storing the text by calling *malloc*, copy the text into this memory, and save the pointer returned from *malloc* in the NEWBTN structure.

The window text can be changed by a call to *WinSetWindowText* and queried by a call to *WinQueryWindowText*. These functions send WM_SETWINDOWPARAMS and WM_QUERYWINDOWPARAMS messages, respectively, to the window procedure. This requires that *NewBtnWndProc* also process these two messages.

During the WM_BUTTON1DOWN message, *NewBtnWndProc* captures the mouse and sets the *fHaveCapture* field in the NEWBTN structure to TRUE. The window procedure tests this field during the WM_MOUSEMOVE and WM_BUTTON1UP message to determine if it can ignore the message. For both of these messages, *NewBtnWndProc* uses the *WinPtInRect* to determine if the mouse pointer is still within the area occupied by the control window. If the mouse pointer is within the window during a WM_BUTTON1UP message, *NewBtnWndProc* posts a WM_COMMAND message to its owner.

The WM_COMMAND message can also be posted during the WM_CHAR message. The window procedure posts this message when the spacebar is released. Because *NewBtnWndProc* will receive WM_CHAR messages only when the control has the input focus, it need not check that it has the input focus when processing the keystrokes.

During the WM_PAINT message, *NewBtnWndProc* calls *DrawButton* to draw the button. The processing is lengthy but does nothing we didn't see in Chapter 5 when exploring the GPI functions. Rather than outlining text to indicate the button's input focus, I decided to display italic text.

CREATING THE NEW BUTTONS

To test this new window class, we need a program that creates a couple of these new buttons. This is BUTTONS2, shown in Listing 11.5.

You'll notice that the BUTTONS2 make file compiles both NEWBTN.C and BUTTONS2.C and links them.

Listing 11.5: The BUTTONS2 program

The BUTTONS2.MAK File

```
#-----------------------
# BUTTONS2.MAK make file
#-----------------------

buttons2.exe : buttons2.obj newbtn.obj buttons2.def
     $(PRGLINK) buttons2 newbtn, buttons2, NUL, $(PRGLIB), buttons2

buttons2.obj : buttons2.c
     $(PRGCC) buttons2.c

newbtn.obj : newbtn.c
     $(PRGCC) newbtn.c
```

The BUTTONS2.C File

```
/*-----------------------------------------
   BUTTONS2.C -- New Button Demonstration
                 (c) Charles Petzold, 1993
  -----------------------------------------*/

#define INCL_WIN
#define INCL_GPI
#include <os2.h>

BOOL APIENTRY RegisterNewBtnClass (HAB) ;          // In NEWBTN.C

MRESULT EXPENTRY ClientWndProc (HWND, ULONG, MPARAM, MPARAM) ;

int main (void)
     {
     static CHAR  szClientClass[] = "Buttons2" ;
     static ULONG flFrameFlags = FCF_TITLEBAR      | FCF_SYSMENU |
                                 FCF_SIZEBORDER    | FCF_MINMAX  |
                                 FCF_SHELLPOSITION | FCF_TASKLIST ;
     HAB          hab ;
     HMQ          hmq ;
     HWND         hwndFrame, hwndClient ;
     QMSG         qmsg ;

     hab = WinInitialize (0) ;
     hmq = WinCreateMsgQueue (hab, 0) ;

     WinRegisterClass (hab, szClientClass, ClientWndProc, CS_SIZEREDRAW, 0) ;

     hwndFrame = WinCreateStdWindow (HWND_DESKTOP, WS_VISIBLE,
                                     &flFrameFlags, szClientClass, NULL,
```

Listing 11.5: The BUTTONS2 program (Continued)

```
                                       0L, 0, 0, &hwndClient) ;

     while (WinGetMsg (hab, &qmsg, NULLHANDLE, 0, 0))
          WinDispatchMsg (hab, &qmsg) ;

     WinDestroyWindow (hwndFrame) ;
     WinDestroyMsgQueue (hmq) ;
     WinTerminate (hab) ;
     return 0 ;
     }

MRESULT EXPENTRY ClientWndProc (HWND hwnd, ULONG msg, MPARAM mp1, MPARAM mp2)
     {
     static CHAR  *szButtonLabel[] = { "Smaller", "Larger" } ;
     static HWND  hwndFrame, hwndButton[2] ;
     static INT   cxClient, cyClient, cxChar, cyChar ;
     FONTMETRICS  fm ;
     HAB          hab ;
     HPS          hps ;
     INT          id ;
     RECTL        rcl ;

     switch (msg)
          {
          case WM_CREATE:
               hab = WinQueryAnchorBlock (hwnd) ;
               hwndFrame = WinQueryWindow (hwnd, QW_PARENT) ;

               hps = WinGetPS (hwnd) ;
               GpiQueryFontMetrics (hps, sizeof fm, &fm) ;
               cxChar = fm.lAveCharWidth ;
               cyChar = fm.lMaxBaselineExt ;
               WinReleasePS (hps) ;

               RegisterNewBtnClass (hab) ;

               for (id = 0 ; id < 2 ; id++)
                    hwndButton[id] = WinCreateWindow (
                                        hwnd,                // Parent
                                        "NewBtn",            // Class
                                        szButtonLabel[id],   // Text
                                        WS_VISIBLE,          // Style
                                        0, 0,                // Position
                                        12 * cxChar,         // Width
                                        2 * cyChar,          // Height
                                        hwnd,                // Owner
                                        HWND_BOTTOM,         // Placement
                                        id,                  // ID
                                        NULL,                // Ctrl Data
```

Listing 11.5: The BUTTONS2 program (Continued)

```
                                   NULL) ;              // Pres Params
          return 0 ;

     case WM_SIZE :
          cxClient = SHORT1FROMMP (mp2) ;
          cyClient = SHORT2FROMMP (mp2) ;

          for (id = 0 ; id < 2 ; id++)
               WinSetWindowPos (hwndButton[id], NULLHANDLE,
                         cxClient / 2 + (14 * id - 13) * cxChar,
                         (cyClient - 2 * cyChar) / 2,
                         0, 0, SWP_MOVE) ;
          return 0 ;

     case WM_COMMAND:
          WinQueryWindowRect (hwnd, &rcl) ;
          WinMapWindowPoints (hwnd, HWND_DESKTOP, (PPOINTL) &rcl, 2) ;

          switch (COMMANDMSG(&msg)->cmd)              // Child ID
               {
               case 0:                                // "Smaller"
                    rcl.xLeft   += cxClient / 20 ;
                    rcl.xRight  -= cxClient / 20 ;
                    rcl.yBottom += cyClient / 20 ;
                    rcl.yTop    -= cyClient / 20 ;
                    break ;

               case 1:                                // "Larger"
                    rcl.xLeft   -= cxClient / 20 ;
                    rcl.xRight  += cxClient / 20 ;
                    rcl.yBottom -= cyClient / 20 ;
                    rcl.yTop    += cyClient / 20 ;
                    break ;
               }
          WinCalcFrameRect (hwndFrame, &rcl, FALSE) ;

          WinSetWindowPos (hwndFrame, NULLHANDLE,
                           rcl.xLeft, rcl.yBottom,
                           rcl.xRight - rcl.xLeft,
                           rcl.yTop   - rcl.yBottom,
                           SWP_MOVE | SWP_SIZE) ;
          return 0 ;

     case WM_ERASEBACKGROUND:
          return MRFROMSHORT (1) ;
     }
return WinDefWindowProc (hwnd, msg, mp1, mp2) ;
}
```

Listing 11.5: The BUTTONS2 program (Continued)

The BUTTONS2.DEF File

```
;-----------------------------------
; BUTTONS2.DEF module definition file
;-----------------------------------

NAME          BUTTONS2  WINDOWAPI

DESCRIPTION   'New Button Demo (c) Charles Petzold, 1993'
PROTMODE
```

BUTTONS2 is almost identical to BUTTONS1. The only real difference is that *ClientWndProc* calls *RegisterNewBtnClass* during the WM_CREATE message. This is the routine in NEWBTN.C. The two push buttons are created based on the "NewBtn" class.

Figure 11.4 shows BUTTONS2 running under the Presentation Manager.

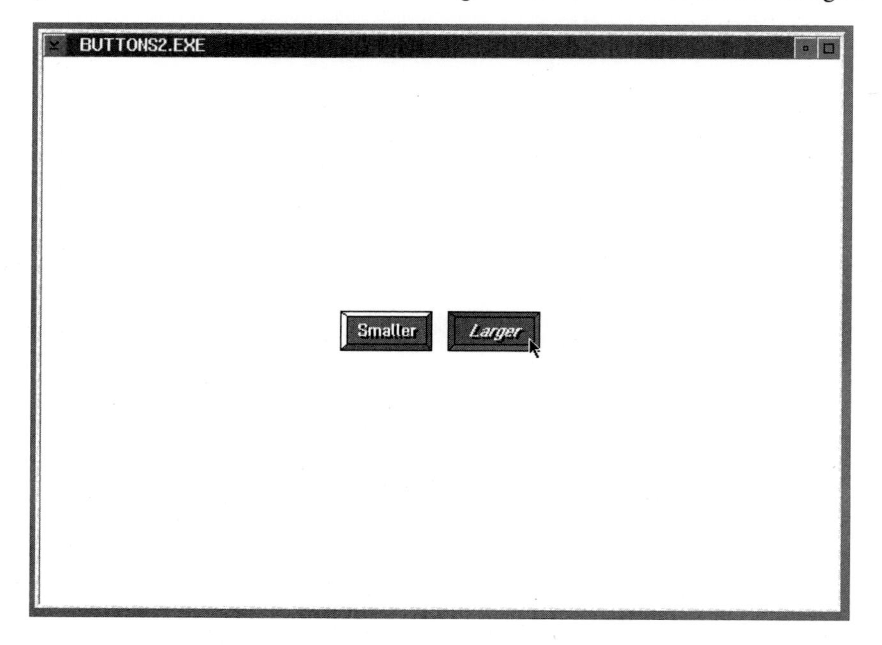

Figure 11.4: The BUTTONS2 display

You might like the look of these new push buttons and wonder if you could somehow use them in dialog boxes. We'll do exactly that in Chapter 14.

Part 4

Using Resources

BITMAPS, ICONS, POINTERS, AND STRINGS

MENUS AND KEYBOARD ACCELERATORS

DIALOG BOXES

Bitmaps, Icons, Pointers, and Strings

BASIC CONCEPTS

BITMAP RESOURCES

ICONS AND MOUSE POINTERS

THE STRING RESOURCE

PROGRAMMER-DEFINED RESOURCES

Chapter 12

Until now, our Presentation Manager programs have been missing a few features. The programs haven't included a menu bar across the top of the window, or dialog boxes invoked from menu items, or even a customized icon displayed when the program's window is minimized.

Icons, menus, and dialog boxes are all examples of program resources. *Resources* are read-only data objects that are stored in a program's .EXE file but that are not part of the program's normal code and data. In most cases, resources aren't loaded into memory when OS/2 runs the program; the resources reside on disk in the .EXE file until specifically needed. When resources are loaded into memory, the memory blocks they occupy are read-only. Thus OS/2 can allow the resources in memory to be shared by multiple instances of the same program. OS/2 can also discard resources if memory space is needed and then reload them from the .EXE file later.

The Presentation Manager BSEDOS.H header file defines 21 resource types, but only the first 10 are commonly used by programs. The identifiers for these resource types begin with the letters RT (as listed in the following table). You can also define your own resource types. This chapter covers bitmaps, icons and pointers, text strings, and programmer-defined resources. Menus and keyboard accelerator tables are covered in Chapter 13 and dialog boxes in Chapter 14.

Resource Type	Description
RT_POINTER	Icon or mouse pointer
RT_BITMAP	Bitmap

Resource Type	Description
RT_MENU	Menu template
RT_DIALOG	Dialog box template
RT_STRING	Text string
RT_FONTDIR	Font directory
RT_FONT	Font
RT_ACCELTABLE	Keyboard accelerator table
RT_RCDATA	Programmer-defined data
RT_MESSAGE	Message string

Using resources in your Presentation Manager programs is an option rather than a requirement. If you want, you can instead define menus, dialog boxes, icons, and so forth in the program's normal data area. However, you'll find that using resources is easier because OS/2 development tools help you create and edit resources. We'll examine one of these tools (the Icon Editor program) in this chapter.

BASIC CONCEPTS

A program's .EXE file (or a dynamic link library's .DLL file) is divided into several sections, as shown in Figure 12.1. Following the new .EXE header, the program's code and data objects occupy separate blocks in the .EXE file. Tables in the header allow OS/2 to identify the beginning of each block in the .EXE file, the size of the block, and characteristics of the block. Resources are organized similarly. They follow the normal code and data blocks in the .EXE file and likewise are identified by tables in the header section. You can thus think of an OS/2 program as consisting of code, data, and resources.

Each resource (with the exception of the RT_STRING and RT_MESSAGE types) occupies a separate block in the .EXE file. Text and message strings are stored with multiple strings in each block. Most of the resources are stored in a special format that is unique for that resource type. Your program doesn't need to know the format of the resource in the .EXE file, because the Presentation Manager usually loads the resource and takes care of any translation necessary to put it into a format suitable for use with other Presentation Manager functions.

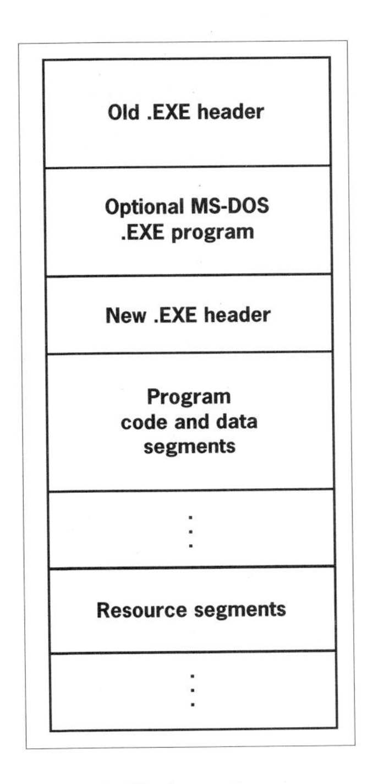

Figure 12.1: The OS/2 .EXE and .DLL file format

OS/2 KERNEL SUPPORT OF RESOURCES

Each resource in the program's .EXE file is identified by a type ID and a name ID, both of which are 32-bit numbers. The identifiers beginning with RT ("resource type") correspond to type IDs of 1 through 21. The Presentation Manager reserves type ID numbers up through 255 for its own use. You are free to use resource type IDs of 256 and above for programmer-defined resource types. The name ID uniquely identifies a particular resource of a particular type. For example, a .EXE file can have several bitmap resources, each of which occupies a different block in the .EXE file. They all have a type ID of RT_BITMAP, but each bitmap has a different name ID.

The OS/2 kernel includes a function called *DosGetResource* that allows a program to load resources from the .EXE file into memory. (For the moment, let's ignore the problem of how the resources get into the .EXE file in the first place.) Generally, a Presentation Manager program needs to use *DosGetResource* only for the programmer-defined resources. For the predefined resource types, the Presentation Manager includes other functions to load resources. But given that these Presentation Manager functions ultimately use the *DosGet-Resource* function to load the resource into memory, it's worthwhile to understand this function.

Before calling *DosGetResource*, you need several variables:

```
ULONG idType, idName ;
PVOID pResource ;
```

Based on the values of *idType* and *idName*, *DosGetResource* loads a resource from the program's .EXE file into memory and returns a pointer to the memory block containing the resource:

```
DosGetResource (NULL, idType, idName, &pResource) ;
```

The memory block belongs to your process. You can use *pResource* as a normal pointer to access the resource. But because the memory block is read-only, you can't write to it. Otherwise, it's a normal memory block. You can use *DosQueryMem* to find the size of the block and *DosFreeMem* to free the block from memory.

When the first parameter of *DosGetResource* is NULL, OS/2 loads the resource from the program's .EXE file. You can also load a resource from a dynamic link library. Let's assume the dynamic link library containing the resource is named MYLIB.DLL. You first need to define a variable of type HMODULE to hold the module handle:

```
HMODULE hmod ;
```

You then call *DosLoadModule* to obtain the module handle:

```
DosLoadModule (NULL, 0, "MYLIB.DLL", &hmod) ;
```

The first parameter of *DosLoadModule* can optionally be set to the address of a buffer area that OS/2 uses if it can't obtain the module handle. Generally, OS/2 will fill this buffer by using the name of the module that contributed to the failure of the function. The second parameter is the length of this buffer.

After you obtain the module handle, you can use it as the first parameter to *DosGetResource* to load a resource from the dynamic link library:

```
DosGetResource (hmod, idType, idName, &pResource) ;
```

After you free the resource and no longer need it, you can free the module handle:

```
DosFreeModule (hmod) ;
```

I'll discuss the use of dynamic link libraries in more depth in Chapter 16.

THE OS/2 KERNEL MESSAGE FACILITY

Although the *DosGetResource* function allows you to load resources of any type into memory, the only real use of resources within the OS/2 kernel is for *message strings.* These are text strings that contain replaceable parameters to display messages from OS/2 and the various OS/2 commands. The MKMSGF.EXE program creates a binary file with the extension .MSG based on an ASCII file containing message texts and codes. The MSGBIND.EXE program then adds these messages as resources to a program's .EXE file. An OS/2 program can either access a message from the .MSG file or load the message from its own .EXE file using the *DosGetMessage* function. If the message text has replaceable parameters (indicated by %1, %2, and so forth), the *DosGetMessage* function can insert other text (such as file names) into the message text. Because the messages aren't in the program's normal data block, OS/2 programs that use this messaging facility can be customized more easily for foreign-language markets.

THE RESOURCE SCRIPT

Although Presentation Manager programs can use the OS/2 message facility, they also need resources of other types. To add these resources to a program's .EXE file, the programmer first prepares an ASCII file called a *resource script.* By convention, this file has the extension .RC. The resource script file includes some resources in an ASCII format and can also reference other files that contain binary resources, such as icons, mouse pointers, and bitmaps. Listing 12.1 shows a sample resource script named SAMPLE.RC that contains a reference to an icon file, a menu template, a keyboard accelerator table, and a string table. It's not important right now that you understand the format of the statements in this file. We'll cover the details as we study each resource in depth.

Listing 12.1: The SAMPLE.RC file

```
/*-----------------------------------------
   SAMPLE.RC -- Sample Resource Script File
  -----------------------------------------*/

#include <os2.h>
#include "sample.h"

POINTER ID_RESOURCE sample.ico

MENU ID_RESOURCE
     {
     SUBMENU "~File",              IDM_FILE
          {
          MENUITEM "~New",                   IDM_NEW
```

Listing 12.1: The SAMPLE.RC file (Continued)

```
          MENUITEM "~Open...",                IDM_OPEN
          MENUITEM "~Save",                   IDM_SAVE
          MENUITEM "Save ~As...",             IDM_SAVEAS
          MENUITEM SEPARATOR
          MENUITEM "E~xit",                   IDM_EXIT
          MENUITEM "A~bout",                  IDM_ABOUT
          }
     SUBMENU "~Edit",               IDM_EDIT
          {
          MENUITEM "~Undo\tAlt+BkSp",         IDM_UNDO
          MENUITEM SEPARATOR
          MENUITEM "Cu~t\tShift+Delete",      IDM_CUT
          MENUITEM "~Copy\tCtrl+Insert",      IDM_COPY
          MENUITEM "~Paste\tShift+Insert",    IDM_PASTE
          MENUITEM SEPARATOR
          MENUITEM "C~lear\tDel",             IDM_CLEAR
          }
     MENUITEM "F1=Help",            IDM_HELP, MIS_HELP | MIS_BUTTONSEPARATOR
     }

ACCELTABLE ID_RESOURCE
     {
     VK_BACKSPACE, IDM_UNDO,  VIRTUALKEY, ALT
     VK_DELETE,    IDM_CUT,   VIRTUALKEY, SHIFT
     VK_INSERT,    IDM_COPY,  VIRTUALKEY, CONTROL
     VK_INSERT,    IDM_PASTE, VIRTUALKEY, SHIFT
     VK_DELETE,    IDM_CLEAR, VIRTUALKEY
     }

STRINGTABLE
     {
     IDS_APPNAME,   "Sample"
     IDS_TITLEBAR,  "Sample Titlebar Text"
     }
```

The keywords POINTER, MENU, ACCELTABLE, and STRINGTABLE all correspond to predefined resource types. The SAMPLE.ICO file referenced by the POINTER statement is a separate binary file containing a bitmap of the program's icon. The file also contains several identifiers beginning with the letters ID, IDM, IDS, and IDD. Some of these are resource name IDs. They are all constants defined in a separate header file, SAMPLE.H, shown in Listing 12.2. This header file must also be included in the program's C source code file so that the program can refer to these resources using the identifiers.

Listing 12.2: The SAMPLE.H file

```
/*---------------------------------------------
   SAMPLE.H - Sample Header File for Resource IDs
   ----------------------------------------------*/

#define ID_RESOURCE       1

     /*----------------
        IDM -- Menu IDs
        ----------------*/

#define IDM_FILE          10
#define IDM_NEW           11
#define IDM_OPEN          12
#define IDM_SAVE          13
#define IDM_SAVEAS        14
#define IDM_EXIT          15
#define IDM_ABOUT         16

#define IDM_EDIT          20
#define IDM_UNDO          21
#define IDM_CUT           22
#define IDM_COPY          23
#define IDM_PASTE         24
#define IDM_CLEAR         25

#define IDM_HELP          30

     /*------------------
        IDS -- String IDs
        ------------------*/

#define IDS_APPNAME       1
#define IDS_TITLEBAR      2
```

THE RESOURCE COMPILER

The ASCII resource script must be compiled to a binary form. By convention, the extension of the compiled resource file is .RES. The compiled resources must then be added to the program's .EXE file or to the dynamic link library's .DLL file. Both of these jobs—compiling the resources and adding them to the .EXE file—are handled by the RC.EXE resource compiler. You can do them separately or in a single step.

Compiling the resources To compile the ASCII.RC file into a binary .RES file without adding the resources to a .EXE file, use the command

```
RC -r SAMPLE
```

or

```
RC -r -i \BCOS2\INCLUDE SAMPLE
```

if you're using the Borland compiler. The .RC extension on SAMPLE is assumed. This command creates a SAMPLE.RES file.

Adding the resources to .EXE To add the compiled resources to the .EXE file, use the command

```
RC SAMPLE.RES
```

This adds the compiled resources in SAMPLE.RES to the SAMPLE.EXE file. (If the .EXE file contains any resources already, they are replaced with the new resources.) Optionally, you can include the name of the .EXE file if it's different from the .RES file:

```
RC SAMPLE.RES MYEXE.EXE
```

The .RES extension is required in this form of the command to differentiate it from the next form of the command.

Compiling and adding as a single step You can do both jobs in one step with the command:

```
RC SAMPLE
```

The .RC extension on SAMPLE is assumed. This command compiles the resources to create a SAMPLE.RES file and then adds the resources to the SAMPLE.EXE file. If the name of the .EXE file is different from the .RC file, you can use

```
RC SAMPLE MYEXE.EXE
```

Presentation Manager programmers usually set up their make files to compile the resources and add them to the .EXE file in two separate steps. This results in a faster edit-make-run cycle, because compiling the resources often takes much longer than adding them to the .EXE file. During development of a program, you'll generally make more changes to the C source code file than to the resource script file. You don't need to recompile the resources. Instead, you want to compile the C source code file, link it, and add the compiled resources. Typically, a make file for a program containing resources looks like SAMPLE.MAK, shown in Listing 12.3.

The first compile step indicates that SAMPLE.C and SAMPLE.H are dependent files for the creation of SAMPLE.OBJ. The header file defines constants used by the program to reference the resources. The second step in the make

Listing 12.3: The SAMPLE.MAK file

```
#---------------------
# SAMPLE.MAK make file
#---------------------

sample.exe : sample.obj sample.def sample.res
     $(PRGLINK) sample, sample, NUL, $(PRGLIB), sample
     rc sample.res

sample.obj : sample.c sample.h
     $(PRGCC) sample.c

sample.res : sample.rc sample.h
     $(PRGRC) sample
```

file runs RC.EXE with the -r parameter to compile the ASCII SAMPLE.RC file into a binary SAMPLE.RES file. This step also requires both SAMPLE.H and SAMPLE.ICO. The third step is executed if SAMPLE.OBJ, SAMPLE.DEF, or SAMPLE.RES is updated. This links the program and then adds the resources to the .EXE file using RC.EXE again.

Figure 12.2 shows the general procedure for creating a Presentation Manager program that uses resources. You create the source code files listed in the five boxes across the top of the diagram. The rest of the process is handled by the make file.

BITMAP RESOURCES

We learned about bitmaps in Chapter 6. A bitmap is a block of memory, organized by rows and columns, where the bits represent a graphical image. In a monochrome bitmap, each bit in the bitmap corresponds to a display pixel. A color bitmap requires multiple bits per pixel to contain color information. The Presentation Manager and Graphics Programming Interface include several functions for creating, manipulating, and displaying bitmaps. Although we were able to define a bitmap in a program by a series of bytes in Chapter 6, it's usually much easier to create the bitmap in the Icon Editor program supplied with IBM's C Developer's WorkSet/2 or in the Resource Workshop included with Borland's C++ for OS/2. These programs let you draw a bitmap, icon, or mouse pointer using the mouse, and let you save them in files. A bitmap has the file name extension .BMP.

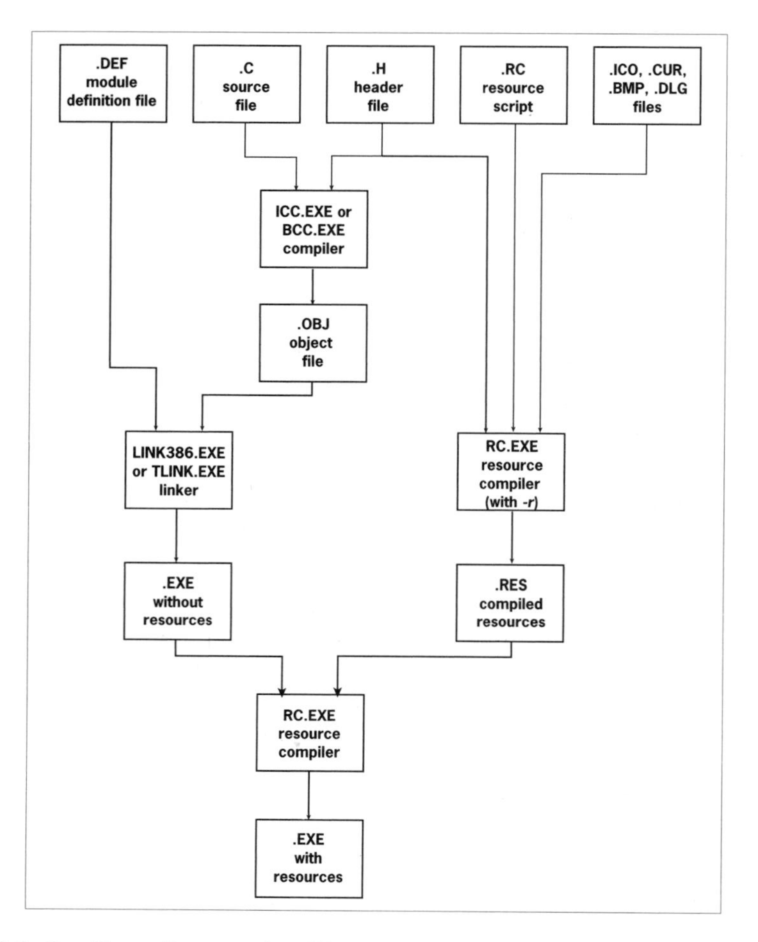

Figure 12.2: Creating a Presentation Manager program that uses resource

USING THE BITMAP RESOURCE IN A PROGRAM

After you create a bitmap file, you need to reference the bitmap file name in a resource script and assign the bitmap a name ID. In the program you use that name ID to load the bitmap into memory. Assuming the program's name is SAMPLE and the bitmap file is SAMPLE.BMP, the SAMPLE.RC resource script file contains the following statement to reference the bitmap file:

```
BITMAP idName sample.bmp
```

The *idName* value is simply an unsigned number or an identifier defined in a header file *#define* statement. BITMAP is a resource compiler keyword. When you compile the resource script and add the resources to the program's .EXE file, the .EXE file contains a resource with a type ID of RT_BITMAP and a name ID of *idName.*

A program loads a bitmap resource into memory using the *GpiLoadBitmap* function. First, the program must define a variable of type HBITMAP:

```
HBITMAP hbm ;
```

The *GpiLoadBitmap* function returns a handle to the bitmap:

```
hbm = GpiLoadBitmap (hps, hmod, idName, lWidth, lHeight) ;
```

The *GpiLoadBitmap* function works only with resources of the RT_BITMAP type. The name ID identifies the particular RT_BITMAP resource.

The *hps* parameter to *GpiLoadBitmap* is a handle to a presentation space. The Presentation Manager uses this handle for two purposes. The first is to convert the colors of the bitmap into a form suitable for the device context. (If you're working with a monochrome bitmap, the bitmap can be loaded without any color conversion.) The second purpose of the presentation space handle is to allow GPI to store the bitmap in an unused part of the display's memory. For a monochrome bitmap, you can set the parameter to NULL.

The *hmod* parameter is set to NULL if you're loading the bitmap from the program's .EXE file. Otherwise, this is the module handle of a dynamic link library file. The *idName* is the ID number of the bitmap you want to load. The *lWidth* and *lHeight* parameters indicate the resultant size of the bitmap when the Presentation Manager loads it into memory. The bitmap can be compressed or stretched. If you set both parameters to 0L, the bitmap will retain the size you specified when you created the bitmap file in the Icon Editor.

Before the program terminates, you delete the bitmap from memory:

```
GpiDeleteBitmap (hbm) ;
```

A SAMPLE PROGRAM

The LOADBMP1 program, shown in Listing 12.4, demonstrates how to include a bitmap as a resource in a program, load the bitmap into memory, and display it on the client window. The LOADBMP.BMP file is a 64-by-32-pixel bitmap file that was created in the Icon Editor program in about 10 seconds (and looks it).

Listing 12.4: The LOADBMP1 program

The LOADBMP1.MAK File

```
#-----------------------
# LOADBMP1.MAK make file
#-----------------------

loadbmp1.exe : loadbmp1.obj loadbmp1.def loadbmp.res
     $(PRGLINK) loadbmp1, loadbmp1, NUL, $(PRGLIB), loadbmp1
     rc loadbmp.res loadbmp1.exe

loadbmp1.obj : loadbmp1.c loadbmp.h
     $(PRGCC) loadbmp1.c

loadbmp.res : loadbmp.rc loadbmp.h loadbmp.bmp
     $(PRGRC) loadbmp
```

The LOADBMP1.C File

```
/*----------------------------------------------------
   LOADBMP1.C -- Loads a Bitmap Resource and Draws it
                 (c) Charles Petzold, 1993
  ----------------------------------------------------*/

#define INCL_WIN
#include <os2.h>
#include "loadbmp.h"

MRESULT EXPENTRY ClientWndProc (HWND, ULONG, MPARAM, MPARAM) ;

int main (void)
     {
     static CHAR  szClientClass [] = "LoadBmp1" ;
     static ULONG flFrameFlags = FCF_TITLEBAR       | FCF_SYSMENU |
                                 FCF_SIZEBORDER     | FCF_MINMAX  |
                                 FCF_SHELLPOSITION  | FCF_TASKLIST ;
     HAB          hab ;
     HMQ          hmq ;
     HWND         hwndFrame, hwndClient ;
     QMSG         qmsg ;

     hab = WinInitialize (0) ;
     hmq = WinCreateMsgQueue (hab, 0) ;

     WinRegisterClass (hab, szClientClass, ClientWndProc, CS_SIZEREDRAW, 0) ;

     hwndFrame = WinCreateStdWindow (HWND_DESKTOP, WS_VISIBLE,
                                     &flFrameFlags, szClientClass, NULL,
                                     0L, 0, 0, &hwndClient) ;
```

Listing 12.4: The LOADBMP1 program (Continued)

```
     while (WinGetMsg (hab, &qmsg, NULLHANDLE, 0, 0))
          WinDispatchMsg (hab, &qmsg) ;

     WinDestroyWindow (hwndFrame) ;
     WinDestroyMsgQueue (hmq) ;
     WinTerminate (hab) ;
     return 0 ;
     }

MRESULT EXPENTRY ClientWndProc (HWND hwnd, ULONG msg, MPARAM mp1, MPARAM mp2)
     {
     static INT cxClient, cyClient ;
     HBITMAP    hbm ;
     HPS        hps ;
     POINTL     ptl ;

     switch (msg)
          {
          case WM_SIZE:
               cxClient = SHORT1FROMMP (mp2) ;
               cyClient = SHORT2FROMMP (mp2) ;
               return 0 ;

          case WM_PAINT:
               hps = WinBeginPaint (hwnd, NULLHANDLE, NULL) ;
               GpiErase (hps) ;

               hbm = GpiLoadBitmap (hps, 0, IDB_HELLO, cxClient, cyClient) ;

               if (hbm)
                    {
                    ptl.x = 0 ;
                    ptl.y = 0 ;

                    WinDrawBitmap (hps, hbm, NULL, &ptl,
                                   CLR_BACKGROUND, CLR_NEUTRAL, DBM_NORMAL) ;

                    GpiDeleteBitmap (hbm) ;
                    }
               WinEndPaint (hps) ;
               return 0 ;
          }
     return WinDefWindowProc (hwnd, msg, mp1, mp2) ;
     }
```

Listing 12.4: The LOADBMP1 program (Continued)

The LOADBMP.RC File

```
/*--------------------------------
   LOADBMP.RC resource script file
  --------------------------------*/

#include "loadbmp.h"

BITMAP IDB_HELLO loadbmp.bmp
```

The LOADBMP.BMP Image

The LOADBMP.H File

```
/*----------------------
   LOADBMP.H header file
  ----------------------*/


#define IDB_HELLO 55
```

The LOADBMP1.DEF File

```
;-----------------------------------
; LOADBMP1.DEF module definition file
;-----------------------------------

NAME           LOADBMP1  WINDOWAPI

DESCRIPTION    'Loads Bitmap Resource and Draws it (c) Charles Petzold, 1993'
PROTMODE
```

I decided to give the bitmap a name ID of 55. The identifier IDB_HELLO is defined in LOADBMP.H for this purpose:

```
#define IDB_HELLO 55
```

The IDB prefix stands for "ID for a bitmap."

This statement in the LOADBMP.RC resource script file references the file containing the bitmap:

```
BITMAP IDB_HELLO loadbmp.bmp
```

The LOADBMP.RC resource script is compiled by the following command in the make file:

```
rc -r loadbmp
```

The resource compiler creates a binary LOADBMP.RES file that contains the entire LOADBMP.BMP file. When RC.EXE is run the second time in the make file, the bitmap resource in LOADBMP.RES is added to the LOADBMP1.EXE file:

```
rc loadbmp.res loadbmp1.exe
```

Following this step, the LOADBMP1.EXE file includes a resource block containing the entire bitmap. The header section of the .EXE file identifies the resource type ID (RT_BITMAP) and name ID (55). The program can then gain access to that resource.

During the WM_PAINT message in LOADBMP1.C, the bitmap resource is loaded into memory and stretched to fill the size of the client window:

```
hbm = GpiLoadBitmap (hps, NULL, IDB_HELLO, cxClient, cyClient) ;
```

Note that the second parameter is set to NULL to indicate that the resource is part of the program's .EXE file. The IDB_HELLO identifier is the name ID of the resource defined in LOADBMP.H. (Obviously, I could have dispensed with the LOADBMP.H file in this example and used 55 in place of IDB_HELLO in both the resource script and the program. But for more complex resources such as menus and dialog boxes, the header file becomes very important, so we might as well get accustomed to using it.)

GpiLoadBitmap returns NULL if the bitmap can't be loaded into memory. The rest of the WM_PAINT logic continues only if hbm isn't NULL:

```
if (hbm)
     {
     ptl.x = 0 ;
     ptl.y = 0 ;

     WinDrawBitmap (hps, hbm, NULL, &ptl,
```

```
                    CLR_BACKGROUND, CLR_NEUTRAL, DBM_NORMAL) ;

     GpiDeleteBitmap (hbm) ;
     }
```

This draws the bitmap on the client window and then deletes it from memory. The LOADBMP1 window is shown in Figure 12.3.

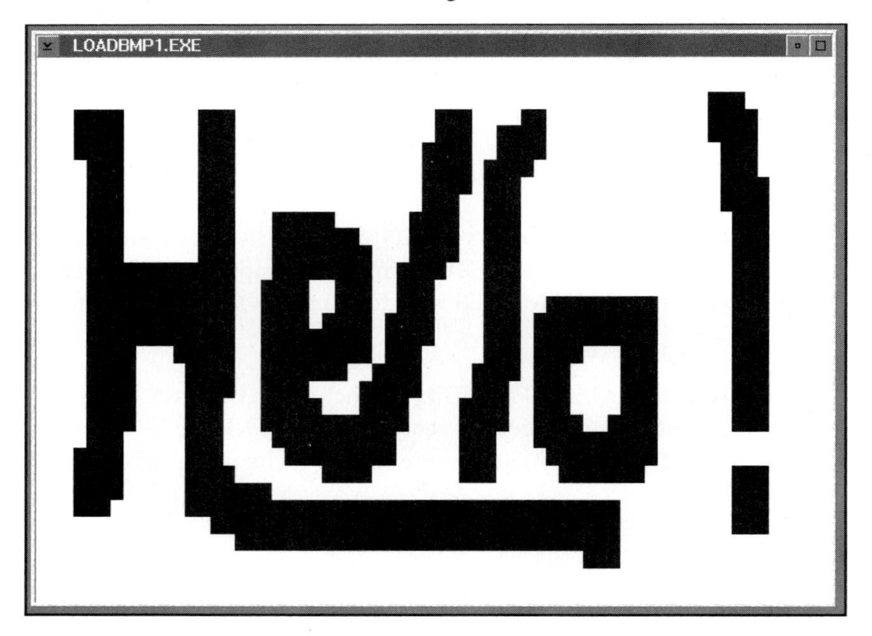

Figure 12.3: The LOADBMP1 display

AN ALTERNATIVE APPROACH TO LOADING BITMAPS

LOADBMP1 loads the bitmap and then deletes it whenever it needs to repaint the client window. Another approach is to load the bitmap during the WM_-CREATE message, keep it in memory for the duration of the program, and then delete it during the WM_DESTROY message.

The LOADBMP2 program, shown in Listing 12.5, illustrates this approach. The LOADBMP.H, LOADBMP.RC, and LOADBMP.BMP files from Listing 12.4 are also required to compile the program.

Listing 12.5: The LOADBMP2 program

The LOADBMP2.MAK File

```
#-----------------------
# LOADBMP2.MAK make file
#-----------------------

loadbmp2.exe : loadbmp2.obj loadbmp2.def loadbmp.res
     $(PRGLINK) loadbmp2, loadbmp2, NUL, $(PRGLIB), loadbmp2
     rc loadbmp.res loadbmp2.exe

loadbmp2.obj : loadbmp2.c loadbmp.h
     $(PRGCC) loadbmp2.c

loadbmp.res : loadbmp.rc loadbmp.h loadbmp.bmp
     $(PRGRC) loadbmp
```

The LOADBMP2.C File

```
/*----------------------------------------------------
   LOADBMP2.C -- Loads a Bitmap Resource and Draws it
                 (c) Charles Petzold, 1993
  ----------------------------------------------------*/

#define INCL_WIN
#include <os2.h>
#include "loadbmp.h"

MRESULT EXPENTRY ClientWndProc (HWND, ULONG, MPARAM, MPARAM) ;

int main (void)
     {
     static CHAR  szClientClass [] = "LoadBmp2" ;
     static ULONG flFrameFlags = FCF_TITLEBAR      | FCF_SYSMENU |
                                 FCF_SIZEBORDER    | FCF_MINMAX  |
                                 FCF_SHELLPOSITION | FCF_TASKLIST ;
     HAB          hab ;
     HMQ          hmq ;
     HWND         hwndFrame, hwndClient ;
     QMSG         qmsg ;

     hab = WinInitialize (0) ;
     hmq = WinCreateMsgQueue (hab, 0) ;

     WinRegisterClass (hab, szClientClass, ClientWndProc, CS_SIZEREDRAW, 0) ;

     hwndFrame = WinCreateStdWindow (HWND_DESKTOP, WS_VISIBLE,
                                     &flFrameFlags, szClientClass, NULL,
                                     0L, 0, 0, &hwndClient) ;
```

Listing 12.5: The LOADBMP2 program (Continued)

```
     while (WinGetMsg (hab, &qmsg, NULLHANDLE, 0, 0))
          WinDispatchMsg (hab, &qmsg) ;

     WinDestroyWindow (hwndFrame) ;
     WinDestroyMsgQueue (hmq) ;
     WinTerminate (hab) ;
     return 0 ;
     }

MRESULT EXPENTRY ClientWndProc (HWND hwnd, ULONG msg, MPARAM mp1, MPARAM mp2)
     {
     static HBITMAP hbm ;
     HPS            hps ;
     RECTL          rcl ;

     switch (msg)
          {
          case WM_CREATE:
               hps = WinGetPS (hwnd) ;
               hbm = GpiLoadBitmap (hps, 0, IDB_HELLO, 0L, 0L) ;
               WinReleasePS (hps) ;
               return 0 ;

          case WM_PAINT:
               hps = WinBeginPaint (hwnd, NULLHANDLE, NULL) ;
               GpiErase (hps) ;

               WinQueryWindowRect (hwnd, &rcl) ;

               if (hbm)
                    WinDrawBitmap (hps, hbm, NULL, (PPOINTL) &rcl,
                                   CLR_BACKGROUND, CLR_NEUTRAL, DBM_STRETCH) ;

               WinEndPaint (hps) ;
               return 0 ;

          case WM_DESTROY:
               if (hbm)
                    GpiDeleteBitmap (hbm) ;
               return 0 ;
          }
     return WinDefWindowProc (hwnd, msg, mp1, mp2) ;
     }
```

The LOADBMP2.DEF File

```
;-----------------------------------
; LOADBMP2.DEF module definition file
;-----------------------------------
```

Listing 12.5: The LOADBMP2 program (Continued)

```
NAME            LOADBMP2  WINDOWAPI

DESCRIPTION     'Loads Bitmap Resource and Draws it (c) Charles Petzold, 1993'
PROTMODE
```

In LOADBMP2.C, the last two parameters of *GpiLoadBitmap* are set to 0, so the bitmap isn't stretched when loaded into memory:

```
case WM_CREATE:
     hps = WinGetPS (hwnd) ;
     hbm = GpiLoadBitmap (hps, NULL, IDB_HELLO, 0L, 0L) ;
     WinReleasePS (hps) ;
     return 0 ;
```

The WM_PAINT logic stretches the bitmap in the *WinDrawBitmap* function:

```
WinQueryWindowRect (hwnd, &rcl) ;

if (hbm)
     WinDrawBitmap (hps, hbm, NULL, (PPOINTL) &rcl,
                    CLR_BACKGROUND, CLR_NEUTRAL, DBM_STRETCH) ;
```

LOADBMP2 deletes the bitmap while processing the WM_DESTROY message:

```
case WM_DESTROY:
     if (hbm)
          GpiDeleteBitmap (hbm) ;
     return 0 ;
```

It's OK to handle small bitmaps in this way, but you should be leery of keeping large bitmaps in memory for long periods. Even though the Presentation Manager can discard bitmaps from memory and reload them from the program's .EXE file, common courtesy requires that you not be greedy with memory space.

ICONS AND MOUSE POINTERS

Icons and customized mouse pointers are identical in structure and are often interchangeable. In fact, both icon and pointer resources are stored in the program's .EXE file with a resource type of RT_POINTER. Some Presentation Manager functions that seemingly apply to pointers (*WinLoadPointer* and *WinDestroyPointer*, for example) can also be used with icons.

You can use icons in your program in two ways: as a symbolic representation of the program when the program's top-level window is minimized, and as little pictures you can draw on the program's client window. You can create and use a customized mouse pointer in your program to substitute for the default mouse pointer. For example, the Icon Editor program itself has a customized mouse pointer that looks like a bucket of paint.

DESIGNING ICONS AND POINTERS

You use the Icon Editor or Resource Workshop to create icons and pointers. These are essentially bitmaps. Icon files have a .ICO extension, and pointer files have a .PTR extension.

When you create an icon or pointer in the Icon Editor, it has a dimension of 32 by 32 pixels and 16 colors. This is appropriate for a VGA display; for displays of higher or lower resolution, the Presentation Manager may expand or compress the image. A program can obtain the displayed dimensions of icons and pointers by calling the *WinQuerySysValue* function with parameters of SV_CXICON, SV_CYICON, SV_CXPOINTER, and SV_CYPOINTER. For most video display adapters, the Presentation Manager uses the same dimensions for both icons and pointers.

The icon and pointer files actually contain three bitmap images—two monochrome and one color. The two monochrome bitmaps allow two additional "colors" called "screen" and "inverse screen." The "screen" color is transparent. When the Presentation Manager displays the icon or pointer, whatever was originally behind it shows through. The "inverse screen" color inverts the background behind the image. A black background becomes white, white becomes black, and green becomes magenta.

Because an icon or pointer can be displayed against a background of almost any color, a few simple rules apply in designing the images: If the icon or pointer is mostly black, give it a white outline. If the icon or pointer is mostly white, give it a black outline. Use the "screen" color to make the icon or pointer nonrectangular (such as the common arrow pointer). Use "inverse screen" to add a dash of inverted color when the icon or pointer is displayed against a color background.

REFERENCING THE FILE IN THE RESOURCE SCRIPT

The statements in your resource script that reference the icon and pointer files are very similar to the statement used for bitmaps. You reference an icon file as a resource with the following statement:

```
POINTER idName sample.ico
```

You reference a pointer file with the following statement:

```
POINTER idName sample.ptr
```

POINTER is a keyword recognized by RC.EXE.

The use of the POINTER keyword for both icons and pointers may seem a little strange. As I mentioned earlier, icons and pointers are identical in structure and are in many ways interchangeable. Both icons and pointers are stored in a program's .EXE file with a resource type of RT_POINTER. If a different keyword (for example, ICON) were used to identify icons in a resource script, you might be tempted to use the same name ID for an icon resource and a pointer resource. The name IDs for any icons and pointers in a resource script must be unique.

FIVE STEPS FOR ADDING AN ICON TO A PROGRAM

By far the most common use of an icon is for a symbolic representation of a program when the window is minimized. You can add such an icon to a program by following these five steps:

1. Create an icon in the Icon Editor or Resource Workshop. Give the file the same name as your program but with a .ICO extension, for example, SAMPLE.ICO.
2. Create a SAMPLE.RC resource script file containing a POINTER statement. For example:

   ```
   POINTER 555 sample.ico
   ```

   This statement defines a pointer resource (which is actually an icon) with a name ID of 555.
3. Change your program's make file so that it looks like this:

   ```
   sample.exe : sample.obj sample.def sample.res
        $(PRGLINK) sample, sample, NUL, $(PRGLIB), sample
        rc sample.res

   sample.obj : sample.c
        $(PRGCC) sample.c

   sample.res : sample.rc sample.ico
        $(PRGRC) sample
   ```
4. Change the definition of *flFrameFlags* to include the FCF_ICON style:

   ```
   static ULONG flFrameFlags = FCF_TITLEBAR      | FCF_SYSMENU  |
                               FCF_SIZEBORDER    | FCF_MINMAX   |
   ```

```
                                     FCF_SHELLPOSITION | FCF_TASKLIST |
                                     FCF_ICON ;
```

5 Change the call to *WinCreateStdWindow* so the second-to-last parameter is the name ID of the bitmap:

```
hwndFrame = WinCreateStdWindow (HWND_DESKTOP, WS_VISIBLE,
                                &flFrameFlags, szClientClass, NULL,
                                ØL, NULL, 555, &hwndClient) ;
```

You're done. Remake the program.

As you'll see in the next chapter, the second-to-last parameter to *WinCreateStdWindow* is actually the name ID of three different resources. If you include the frame creation flag FCF_MENU, the Presentation Manager uses that same name ID to load the program's menu. If you include FCF_ACCELTABLE, the same name ID references the program's keyboard accelerator table.

You might want to use an identifier defined in a header file for the name ID of these three resources. In the programs in this chapter and the next two chapters, I use the identifier ID_RESOURCE for this purpose and define it to be equal to 1. In this case, a SAMPLE.H header file has the following statement:

```
#define ID_RESOURCE 1
```

The SAMPLE.RC resource script looks like this:

```
#include "sample.h"
POINTER ID_RESOURCE sample.ico
```

The SAMPLE make file is changed so that it recompiles the source code file and resource script file if the header file changes:

```
sample.exe : sample.obj sample.def sample.res
     $(PRGLINK) sample, sample, NUL, $(PRGLIB), sample
     rc sample.res

sample.obj : sample.c sample.h
     $(PRGCC) sample.c

sample.res : sample.rc sample.ico sample.h
     $(PRGRC) sample
```

The SAMPLE.C file includes the header file near the top of the program:

```
#include "sample.h"
```

and the second to last parameter of the *WinCreateStdWindow* function uses the defined name rather than a number:

```
hwndFrame = WinCreateStdWindow (HWND_DESKTOP, WS_VISIBLE,
                                &flFrameFlags, szClientClass, NULL,
                                    ØL, NULL, ID_RESOURCE, &hwndClient) ;
```

DRAWING ICONS AND SETTING POINTERS

Besides using an icon as a symbolic representation of a program, you can draw an icon on your client window. Because of the similarity between icons and pointers, the functions for loading and destroying icons are the same as those used for pointers.

You first define a handle of type HPOINTER to store a handle to the icon:

```
HPOINTER hIcon ;
```

You then load the icon into memory using the *WinLoadPointer* function:

```
hIcon = WinLoadPointer (HWND_DESKTOP, hmod, idName) ;
```

The *hmod* parameter is NULL if the icon is stored in the program's .EXE file. You can then display the icon on a presentation space using the function:

```
WinDrawPointer (hps, x, y, hIcon, iFlags) ;
```

where *x* and *y* are the coordinates of the presentation space corresponding to the lower-left corner of the icon. The *iFlags* parameter can be DP_NORMAL to draw the icon normally, DP_INVERTED to invert the icon, and DP_HALF-TONED to draw only every other bit of the icon. You might want to use icons in this way in a menu that you create and manage. You use the inverted icon when the user selects an option and the "halftoned" icon when a menu option is disabled.

Before your program terminates, you destroy the icon:

```
WinDestroyPointer (hIcon) ;
```

You can also use the *WinLoadPointer* and *WinDestroyPointer* functions with mouse pointers. If you create a customized mouse pointer and include it in your resource script, you can get a handle to the pointer in your program like this:

```
hptr = WinLoadPointer (HWND_DESKTOP, hmod, idName) ;
```

You'll probably do this during the WM _CREATE message. The *hptr* variable is defined as type HPOINTER.

The easiest way for your program to use this new pointer is to set the pointer during the WM_MOUSEMOVE message:

```
case WM_MOUSEMOVE:
     WinSetPointer (HWND_DESKTOP, hptr) ;
          [ other program lines ]
```

You can also test the coordinates of the mouse pointer during the WM_MOUSE-MOVE message and set a different pointer depending on where the pointer is located in the client area. If you divide your client area into several areas with the use of child windows, each child window might set its own pointer.

During processing of the WM_DESTROY message, you destroy the pointer:

```
WinDestroyPointer (hptr) ;
```

The RESOURCE program, shown in Listing 12.6, contains an icon and a pointer resource. The icon is a square pattern that shows four colors (black, white, "screen," and "inverse screen"). The program references the icon name ID in the *WinCreateStdWindow* call and while processing the WM_CREATE message. RESOURCE draws the icon on the four corners of its client window and shows what the "halftoned" and inverted icons look like. The customized pointer is displayed whenever the mouse is within RESOURCE's client window.

Listing 12.6: The RESOURCE program

The RESOURCE.MAK File

```
#-----------------------
# RESOURCE.MAK make file
#-----------------------

resource.exe : resource.obj resource.def resource.res
     $(PRGLINK) resource, resource, NUL, $(PRGLIB), resource
     rc resource.res

resource.obj : resource.c resource.h
     $(PRGCC) resource.c

resource.res : resource.rc resource.h resource.ico resource.ptr
     $(PRGRC) resource
```

The RESOURCE.C File

```
/*-----------------------------------------------
   RESOURCE.C -- Uses an Icon and Pointer Resource
                 (c) Charles Petzold, 1993
  -----------------------------------------------*/
```

Listing 12.6: The RESOURCE program (Continued)

```
#define INCL_WIN
#define INCL_GPI
#include <os2.h>
#include "resource.h"

MRESULT EXPENTRY ClientWndProc (HWND, ULONG, MPARAM, MPARAM) ;

int main (void)
     {
     static CHAR  szClientClass [] = "Resource" ;
     static ULONG flFrameFlags = FCF_TITLEBAR      | FCF_SYSMENU  |
                                 FCF_SIZEBORDER    | FCF_MINMAX   |
                                 FCF_SHELLPOSITION | FCF_TASKLIST |
                                 FCF_ICON ;
     HAB          hab ;
     HMQ          hmq ;
     HWND         hwndFrame, hwndClient ;
     QMSG         qmsg ;

     hab = WinInitialize (0) ;
     hmq = WinCreateMsgQueue (hab, 0) ;

     WinRegisterClass (hab, szClientClass, ClientWndProc, CS_SIZEREDRAW, 0) ;

     hwndFrame = WinCreateStdWindow (HWND_DESKTOP, WS_VISIBLE,
                                     &flFrameFlags, szClientClass, NULL,
                                     0L, 0, ID_RESOURCE, &hwndClient) ;

     while (WinGetMsg (hab, &qmsg, NULLHANDLE, 0, 0))
          WinDispatchMsg (hab, &qmsg) ;

     WinDestroyWindow (hwndFrame) ;
     WinDestroyMsgQueue (hmq) ;
     WinTerminate (hab) ;
     return 0 ;
     }

MRESULT EXPENTRY ClientWndProc (HWND hwnd, ULONG msg, MPARAM mp1, MPARAM mp2)
     {
     static HPOINTER hIcon, hptr ;
     static INT      cxClient, cyClient, cxIcon, cyIcon ;
     HPS             hps ;
     RECTL           rcl ;

     switch (msg)
          {
          case WM_CREATE:
               hIcon = WinLoadPointer (HWND_DESKTOP, 0, ID_RESOURCE) ;
```

Listing 12.6: The RESOURCE program (Continued)

```
               hptr   = WinLoadPointer (HWND_DESKTOP, 0, IDP_CIRCLE) ;

               cxIcon = WinQuerySysValue (HWND_DESKTOP, SV_CXICON) ;
               cyIcon = WinQuerySysValue (HWND_DESKTOP, SV_CYICON) ;
               return 0 ;

          case WM_SIZE:
               cxClient = SHORT1FROMMP (mp2) ;
               cyClient = SHORT2FROMMP (mp2) ;
               return 0 ;

          case WM_MOUSEMOVE:
               WinSetPointer (HWND_DESKTOP, hptr) ;
               return MRFROMSHORT (1) ;

          case WM_PAINT:
               hps = WinBeginPaint (hwnd, NULLHANDLE, NULL) ;

               WinQueryWindowRect (hwnd, &rcl) ;
               WinFillRect (hps, &rcl, CLR_CYAN) ;

               WinDrawPointer (hps, 0, 0, hIcon, DP_NORMAL) ;
               WinDrawPointer (hps, 0, cyClient - cyIcon, hIcon, DP_NORMAL) ;
               WinDrawPointer (hps, cxClient - cyIcon, 0, hIcon, DP_NORMAL) ;
               WinDrawPointer (hps, cxClient - cxIcon, cyClient - cyIcon,
                                    hIcon, DP_NORMAL) ;

               WinDrawPointer (hps, cxClient / 3, cyClient / 2, hIcon,
                                                       DP_HALFTONED) ;
               WinDrawPointer (hps, 2 * cxClient / 3, cyClient / 2, hIcon,
                                                       DP_INVERTED) ;
               WinEndPaint (hps) ;
               return 0 ;

          case WM_DESTROY:
               WinDestroyPointer (hIcon) ;
               WinDestroyPointer (hptr) ;
               return 0 ;
          }
     return WinDefWindowProc (hwnd, msg, mp1, mp2) ;
     }
```

The RESOURCE.RC File

```
/*-----------------------------------
   RESOURCE.RC resource script file
  -----------------------------------*/

#include "resource.h"
```

Listing 12.6: The RESOURCE program (Continued)

```
POINTER ID_RESOURCE resource.ico
POINTER IDP_CIRCLE  resource.ptr
```

The RESOURCE.ICO Image

The RESOURCE.PTR Image

Listing 12.6: The RESOURCE program (Continued)

The RESOURCE.H File

```
/*-----------------------
   RESOURCE.H header file
  -----------------------*/

#define ID_RESOURCE 1
#define IDP_CIRCLE  2
```

The RESOURCE.DEF File

```
;-----------------------------------
; RESOURCE.DEF module definition file
;-----------------------------------

NAME           RESOURCE  WINDOWAPI

DESCRIPTION    'Icon and Pointer Resources (c) Charles Petzold, 1993'
PROTMODE
```

THE STRING RESOURCE

For bitmaps, icons, and pointers, there are some clear advantages to using resources rather than defining the images in your program's source code file. The Icon Editor program lets you draw the image and save it as a binary file; you don't have to worry about the format of the bits and bytes. So the next type of resource—the text string—may initially seem a little strange. Rather than put text strings in your C source code file, you can instead include them in the program's resource script. But why on earth would you want to do this?

As you'll see in the next two chapters, a program's resource script also contains the program's menu and dialog box templates. If the resource script also contains all the text strings used by the program, converting the program to a foreign language requires that only the resource script (or files referenced by the resource script) be changed. The .C source code file doesn't even have to be recompiled. Of course, if your programs are intended only for yourself, a few friends, your corporation, or a domestic market, then using string resources provides no benefit, except perhaps—if the strings are handled properly—a slight saving in memory space when the program is running under the Presentation Manager.

DEFINING AND LOADING STRING RESOURCES

You include strings in a resource script using the STRINGTABLE block:

```
STRINGTABLE
     {
     idString1, "This little string went to market"
     idString2, "This little string stayed home"
          [ other string definitions ]
     }
```

A resource script can have only one string table that contains all the program's strings. Each string is one line long, with a maximum of 255 characters. You can use the keywords BEGIN and END rather than the curly braces if you're nostalgic for Pascal syntax.

In your program, you load a particular string into a character array with the following function:

```
WinLoadString (hab, hmod, idString, iBufferLen, achBuffer) ;
```

As in the previous resource-loading functions, *hmod* is NULL if the strings are resources in the program's .EXE file. The function copies up to (*iBufferLen*-1) characters into the character array addressed by *achBuffer* and appends a 0 character.

To use the *WinLoadString* function, you need a character array in your program large enough to hold the string:

```
CHAR achString [256] ;
     [ other program lines ]
WinLoadString (hab, NULL, idString, sizeof achString, achString) ;
```

Following this statement, *achString* contains the NULL-terminated string that was identified by *idString* in the resource script.

You probably want to load strings only when you need them for display purposes. In that case, make the string arrays local variables in functions so that the space is freed up when the function ends.

USING STRINGS FOR ERROR MESSAGES

Here's an example of how a program can use strings to display error messages in a message box. Suppose your program works with files and has three error messages: "File not found," "File too large to edit," and "File read-only." You first define three identifiers in the program's header file:

```
#define IDS_FILENOTFOUND 1
#define IDS_FILETOOBIG   2
#define IDS_FILEREADONLY 3
```

The string table in the resource script looks like this:

STRINGTABLE

```
     {
     IDS_FILENOTFOUND, "File %s not found."
     IDS_FILETOOBIG,   "File %s too large to edit."
     IDS_FILEREADONLY, "File %s is read-only."
     }
```

In your program you define a function that displays one of these messages with a particular file name:

```
VOID ErrorMessage (HWND hwnd, INT iError, CHAR * szFileName)
     {
     CHAR achString [40] ;
     CHAR achFormattedString [256] ;

     WinLoadString (hab, NULL, iError, sizeof achString, achString) ;

     sprintf (achFormattedString, achString, szFileName) ;

     WinMessageBox (HWND_DESKTOP, hwnd, achFormattedString,
                    NULL, 0, MB_OK MB_ICONEXCLAMATION) ;
     }
```

When the program needs to display the "File is not found" message, it calls the *ErrorMessage* function with the IDS_FILENOTFOUND identifier and the file name:

```
ErrorMessage (hwnd, IDS_FILENOTFOUND, szFileName) ;
```

PROGRAMMER-DEFINED RESOURCES

The programmer-defined resource provides a way for you to attach arbitrary data to your program's .EXE file and load it into memory during program execution. Perhaps this data is in a binary form, and it's inconvenient to make it part of the program's source code file. Or perhaps you have a large text file (for example, a file that contains reams of "help" text) that your program must access. Make it a programmer-defined resource.

The POEPOEM program, shown in Listing 12.7, shows how this is done. This program displays the text of Edgar Allan Poe's "Annabel Lee" in its client window. The text of the poem is a programmer-defined resource. The program's resource script also defines the text strings used in the program in a string table, as well as the program's icon.

Listing 12.7: The POEPOEM program

The POEPOEM.MAK File

```
#----------------------
# POEPOEM.MAK make file
#----------------------

poepoem.exe : poepoem.obj poepoem.def poepoem.res
     $(PRGLINK) poepoem, poepoem, NUL, $(PRGLIB), poepoem
     rc poepoem.res

poepoem.obj : poepoem.c poepoem.h
     $(PRGCC) poepoem.c

poepoem.res : poepoem.rc poepoem.ico poepoem.asc poepoem.h
     $(PRGRC) poepoem
```

The POEPOEM.C File

```
/*---------------------------------------------------------
   POEPOEM.C -- Demonstrates Programmer-Defined Resources
                (c) Charles Petzold, 1993
  ---------------------------------------------------------*/

#define INCL_WIN
#define INCL_GPI
#define INCL_DOS
#include <os2.h>
#include <stdlib.h>
#include "poepoem.h"

MRESULT EXPENTRY ClientWndProc (HWND, ULONG, MPARAM, MPARAM) ;

int main (void)
     {
     static CHAR  szClientClass [10] ;
     static CHAR  szTitleBar [64] ;
     static ULONG flFrameFlags = FCF_TITLEBAR      | FCF_SYSMENU  |
                                 FCF_SIZEBORDER    | FCF_MINMAX   |
                                 FCF_SHELLPOSITION | FCF_TASKLIST |
                                 FCF_VERTSCROLL    | FCF_ICON ;
     HAB          hab ;
     HMQ          hmq ;
     HWND         hwndFrame, hwndClient ;
     QMSG         qmsg ;

     hab = WinInitialize (0) ;
     hmq = WinCreateMsgQueue (hab, 0) ;
```

Listing 12.7: The POEPOEM program (Continued)

```
     WinLoadString (hab, 0, IDS_CLASS, sizeof szClientClass, szClientClass) ;
     WinLoadString (hab, 0, IDS_TITLE, sizeof szTitleBar,    szTitleBar) ;

     WinRegisterClass (hab, szClientClass, ClientWndProc, CS_SIZEREDRAW, 0) ;

     hwndFrame = WinCreateStdWindow (HWND_DESKTOP, WS_VISIBLE,
                                    &flFrameFlags, szClientClass, szTitleBar,
                                    0L, 0, ID_RESOURCE, &hwndClient) ;

     while (WinGetMsg (hab, &qmsg, NULLHANDLE, 0, 0))
          WinDispatchMsg (hab, &qmsg) ;

     WinDestroyWindow (hwndFrame) ;
     WinDestroyMsgQueue (hmq) ;
     WinTerminate (hab) ;
     return 0 ;
     }

MRESULT EXPENTRY ClientWndProc (HWND hwnd, ULONG msg, MPARAM mp1, MPARAM mp2)
     {
     static CHAR *pResource ;
     static HWND hwndScroll ;
     static INT  cyClient, cxChar, cyChar, cyDesc,
                 iScrollPos, iNumLines ;
     FONTMETRICS fm ;
     HPS         hps ;
     INT         iLineLength, iLine ;
     PCHAR       pText ;
     POINTL      ptl ;
     ULONG       ulMemSize, ulMemFlags ;

     switch (msg)
          {
          case WM_CREATE:

                    /*---------------------------------------
                       Load the resource, get size and address
                      ---------------------------------------*/

               DosGetResource (0, IDT_TEXT, IDT_POEM, (PPVOID) & pResource) ;
               DosQueryMem (pResource, &ulMemSize, &ulMemFlags) ;

                    /*---------------------------------------------
                       Determine how many text lines are in resource
                      ---------------------------------------------*/

               pText = pResource ;

               while (pText - pResource < ulMemSize)
```

Listing 12.7: The POEPOEM program (Continued)

```
          {
          if (*pText == '\0' || *pText == '\x1A')
               break ;

          if (*pText == '\r')
               iNumLines ++ ;

          pText++ ;
          }

          /*------------------------------------------
             Initialize scroll bar range and position
            ------------------------------------------*/

     hwndScroll = WinWindowFromID (
                       WinQueryWindow (hwnd, QW_PARENT),
                       FID_VERTSCROLL) ;

     WinSendMsg (hwndScroll, SBM_SETSCROLLBAR,
                             MPFROM2SHORT (iScrollPos, 0),
                             MPFROM2SHORT (0, iNumLines - 1)) ;

          /*---------------------
             Query character size
            ---------------------*/

     hps = WinGetPS (hwnd) ;

     GpiQueryFontMetrics (hps, (LONG) sizeof fm, &fm) ;
     cxChar = fm.lAveCharWidth ;
     cyChar = fm.lMaxBaselineExt ;
     cyDesc = fm.lMaxDescender ;

     WinReleasePS (hps) ;
     return 0 ;

case WM_SIZE:
     cyClient = SHORT2FROMMP (mp2) ;
     return 0 ;

case WM_CHAR:
     return WinSendMsg (hwndScroll, msg, mp1, mp2) ;

case WM_VSCROLL:
     switch (SHORT2FROMMP (mp2))
          {
          case SB_LINEUP:
               iScrollPos -= 1 ;
               break ;
```

Listing 12.7: The POEPOEM program (Continued)

```
                    case SB_LINEDOWN:
                         iScrollPos += 1 ;
                         break ;

                    case SB_PAGEUP:
                         iScrollPos -= cyClient / cyChar ;
                         break ;

                    case SB_PAGEDOWN:
                         iScrollPos += cyClient / cyChar ;
                         break ;

                    case SB_SLIDERPOSITION:
                         iScrollPos = SHORT1FROMMP (mp2) ;
                         break ;

                    default:
                         return 0 ;
                    }
               iScrollPos = max (0, min (iScrollPos, iNumLines - 1)) ;

               WinSendMsg (hwndScroll, SBM_SETPOS,
                           MPFROM2SHORT (iScrollPos, 0), NULL) ;

               WinInvalidateRect (hwnd, NULL, FALSE) ;
               return 0 ;

          case WM_PAINT:
               hps = WinBeginPaint (hwnd, NULLHANDLE, NULL) ;
               GpiErase (hps) ;

               pText = pResource ;

               for (iLine = 0 ; iLine < iNumLines ; iLine++)
                    {
                    iLineLength = 0 ;

                    while (pText [iLineLength] != '\r')
                         iLineLength ++ ;

                    ptl.x = cxChar ;
                    ptl.y = cyClient - cyChar * (iLine + 1 - iScrollPos)
                                     + cyDesc ;

                    GpiCharStringAt (hps, &ptl, (LONG) iLineLength, pText) ;

                    pText += iLineLength + 2 ;
                    }
```

Listing 12.7: The POEPOEM program (Continued)

```
               WinEndPaint (hps) ;
               return 0 ;

          case WM_DESTROY:
               DosFreeResource (pResource) ;
               return 0 ;
          }
     return WinDefWindowProc (hwnd, msg, mp1, mp2) ;
     }
```

The POEPOEM.RC File

```
/*---------------------------------
   POEPOEM.RC resource script file
  ---------------------------------*/

#include "poepoem.h"

POINTER ID_RESOURCE poepoem.ico

RESOURCE IDT_TEXT IDT_POEM poepoem.asc

STRINGTABLE
     {
     IDS_CLASS, "PoePoem"
     IDS_TITLE, "POEPOEM - ""Annabel Lee"" by Edgar Allan Poe"
     }
```

The POEPOEM.ICO Image

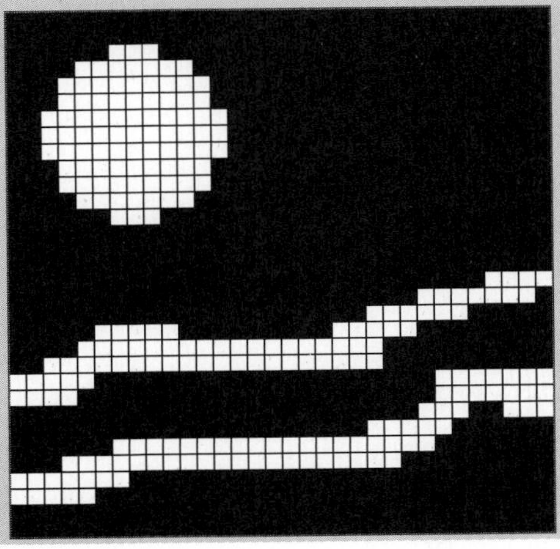

Listing 12.7: The POEPOEM program (Continued)

The POEPOEM.ASC File

```
It was many and many a year ago,
     In a kingdom by the sea,
That a maiden there lived whom you may know
     By the name of Annabel Lee;
And this maiden she lived with no other thought
     Than to love and be loved by me.

I was a child and she was a child
     In this kingdom by the sea,
But we loved with a love that was more than love --
     I and my Annabel Lee --
With a love that the winged seraphs of Heaven
     Coveted her and me.

And this was the reason that, long ago,
     In this kingdom by the sea,
A wind blew out of a cloud, chilling
     My beautiful Annabel Lee;
So that her highborn kinsmen came
     And bore her away from me,
To shut her up in a sepulchre
     In this kingdom by the sea.

The angels, not half so happy in Heaven,
     Went envying her and me --
Yes! that was the reason (as all men know,
     In this kingdom by the sea)
That the wind came out of the cloud by night,
     Chilling and killing my Annabel Lee.

But our love it was stronger by far than the love
     Of those who were older than we --
     Of many far wiser than we --
And neither the angels in Heaven above
     Nor the demons down under the sea
Can ever dissever my soul from the soul
     Of the beautiful Annabel Lee:

For the moon never beams, without bringing me dreams
     Of the beautiful Annabel Lee;
And the stars never rise, but I feel the bright eyes
     Of the beautiful Annabel Lee:
And so, all the night-tide, I lie down by the side
Of my darling -- my darling -- my life and my bride,
     In her sepulchre there by the sea --
     In her tomb by the sounding sea.

                                        [May, 1849]
```

Listing 12.7: The POEPOEM program (Continued)

The POEPOEM.H File

```
/*----------------------
   POEPOEM.H header file
  ----------------------*/

#define ID_RESOURCE      1

#define IDT_TEXT      1024
#define IDT_POEM         1

#define IDS_CLASS        00
#define IDS_TITLE        1
```

The POEPOEM.DEF File

```
;-----------------------------------
; POEPOEM.DEF module definition file
;-----------------------------------

NAME           POEPOEM   WINDOWAPI

DESCRIPTION    'Programmer-Defined Resource (c) Charles Petzold, 1993'
PROTMODE
```

The POEPOEM.ASC file contains the text of the poem. This text is made a programmer-defined resource by referencing it in the resource script with this statement:

```
RESOURCE IDT_TEXT IDT_POEM poepoem.asc
```

The IDT_TEXT and IDT_POEM identifiers are defined in POEPOEM.H:

```
#define IDT_TEXT 1024
#define IDT_POEM 1
```

IDT_TEXT is the resource type ID. Programmer-defined resources must have type IDs of 256 or greater. IDT_POEM is the name ID.

During processing of the WM_CREATE message, POEPOEM obtains a pointer to the resource by calling the OS/2 *DosGetResource* function:

```
DosGetResource (NULL, IDT_TEXT, IDT_POEM, (PPVOID) & pResource) ;
```

When OS/2 loads the resource into memory, it allocates a memory block and returns the pointer to the memory block in the *pResource* variable. A program can also use other OS/2 functions with this memory block, such as *DosQuery-Mem,* to find the size of the block. The only action that a program can't take is to write on this memory block. Resources loaded into memory using *DosGet-Resource* are always read-only. However, a program can allocate another memory block and copy the data for later modification.

During the WM_CREATE message, POEPOEM determines the number of lines of text in the poem and sets the range of a scroll bar accordingly. All WM_CHAR messages to the client window are sent to the scroll bar to give the program a complete keyboard interface. POEPOEM displays the text during the WM_PAINT message. The only assumption it makes is that each line of text is terminated by a carriage return and a line feed.

During the WM_DESTROY message, POEPOEM frees the memory block:

```
DosFreeResource(pResource) ;
```

You'll notice that POEPOEM.C itself contains no displayable text. The text used in the title bar is defined in the resource script. We've thus made it easier for translators to convert the program to a foreign-language version. Of course, they would also need to translate the text of "Annabel Lee," which I'm afraid would be a far more challenging job.

Menus and Keyboard Accelerators

CONVENTIONAL MENUS

OTHER APPROACHES TO MENUS

TWO GAMES

Chapter 13

The menu is an important part of the consistent user interface in Presentation Manager programs. Users learn a new program more quickly if the program has a menu that works like the menus in other Presentation Manager programs.

In one sense, putting a menu in a Presentation Manager program is fairly easy. You define the menu template in a resource script file, and you process WM_COMMAND messages from the menu in your client window procedure. The Presentation Manager takes care of all the keyboard and mouse processing involved with the menu. However, menus are also one of the more complex aspects of the Presentation Manager's windowing environment because they should be extensively tailored to the program's needs.

Let's nail down some terminology first. A *menu* is a control window created by *WinCreateStdWindow* as part of the standard window. A menu contains several items, each of which can be selected using either the mouse or the keyboard. The horizontal menu that appears below the window's title bar is called the program's *main menu* or *top-level menu* or the *action bar*. I'll generally use the term "top-level menu."

Some menu items invoke another menu called a *pop-up menu* or a *drop-down menu* or a *pull-down menu* or a *submenu*. I'll use the term "submenu" because that's the word used in several identifiers defined in the Presentation Manager header files. From the perspective of a program, each submenu is a separate window. Thus, when you create a top-level menu that invokes three submenus, you're actually creating four menu-control windows.

A Presentation Manager program also usually contains three other menu-control windows. One is the system menu, which contains one item: a little bitmapped picture to the left of the title bar. The system menu invokes a sub-menu. The minimize/maximize icon to the right of the title bar is also a menu. It contains two items, both of which are bitmaps.

Menu items can be *enabled* or *disabled*. A disabled menu item appears in gray text. Although the user can click on a disabled menu item or use the key-board to move a reverse-video bar to the menu item, the menu beeps and does not send a WM_COMMAND message to the program.

CONVENTIONAL MENUS

The CONVMENU program, shown in Listing 13.1, contains a conventional menu and demonstrates some sample menu processing. This program and the discussion that follows cover just about everything you'll need to know to implement a menu in most of your programs. The CONVMENU program also contains a keyboard accelerator table. Keyboard accelerators are key combinations that usually duplicate some menu items.

Listing 13.1: The CONVMENU program

The CONVMENU.MAK File

```
#-----------------------
# CONVMENU.MAK make file
#-----------------------

convmenu.exe : convmenu.obj convmenu.def convmenu.res
     $(PRGLINK) convmenu, convmenu, NUL, $(PRGLIB), convmenu
     rc convmenu.res

convmenu.obj : convmenu.c convmenu.h
     $(PRGCC) convmenu.c

convmenu.res : convmenu.rc convmenu.h
     $(PRGRC) convmenu
```

The CONVMENU.C File

```
/*---------------------------------------
   CONVMENU.C -- Conventional Menu Use
                 (c) Charles Petzold, 1993
  ---------------------------------------*/
```

Listing 13.1: The CONVMENU program (Continued)

```
#define INCL_WIN
#define INCL_GPI
#include <os2.h>
#include "convmenu.h"

#define ID_TIMER    1

MRESULT EXPENTRY ClientWndProc (HWND, ULONG, MPARAM, MPARAM) ;

CHAR szClientClass[] = "ConvMenu" ;
HAB  hab ;

int main (void)
     {
     static ULONG flFrameFlags = FCF_TITLEBAR      | FCF_SYSMENU  |
                                 FCF_SIZEBORDER    | FCF_MINMAX   |
                                 FCF_SHELLPOSITION | FCF_TASKLIST |
                                 FCF_MENU          | FCF_ACCELTABLE ;
     HMQ          hmq ;
     HWND         hwndFrame, hwndClient ;
     QMSG         qmsg ;

     hab = WinInitialize (Ø) ;
     hmq = WinCreateMsgQueue (hab, Ø) ;

     WinRegisterClass (hab, szClientClass, ClientWndProc, ØL, Ø) ;

     hwndFrame = WinCreateStdWindow (HWND_DESKTOP, WS_VISIBLE,
                                     &flFrameFlags, szClientClass, NULL,
                                     ØL, Ø, ID_RESOURCE, &hwndClient) ;

     while (TRUE)
          {
          while (WinGetMsg (hab, &qmsg, NULLHANDLE, Ø, Ø))
               WinDispatchMsg (hab, &qmsg) ;

          if (MBID_OK == WinMessageBox (HWND_DESKTOP, hwndClient,
                                        "Really want to end program?",
                                        szClientClass, Ø,
                                        MB_OKCANCEL | MB_QUERY))
               break ;

          WinCancelShutdown (hmq, FALSE) ;
          }

     WinDestroyWindow (hwndFrame) ;
     WinDestroyMsgQueue (hmq) ;
     WinTerminate (hab) ;
     return Ø ;
     }
```

Listing 13.1: The CONVMENU program (Continued)

```
MRESULT EXPENTRY ClientWndProc (HWND hwnd, ULONG msg, MPARAM mp1, MPARAM mp2)
     {
     static BOOL  fTimerGoing = FALSE ;
     static COLOR colBackground [] = {
                                     0xFFFFFFL, 0xC0C0C0L, 0x808080L,
                                     0x404040L, 0x000000L
                                     } ;
     static HWND  hwndMenu ;
     static INT   iCurrentBackground = IDM_WHITE ;
     HPS          hps ;
     RECTL        rcl ;

     switch (msg)
          {
          case WM_CREATE:
               hwndMenu = WinWindowFromID (
                              WinQueryWindow (hwnd, QW_PARENT),
                              FID_MENU) ;
               return 0 ;

          case WM_INITMENU:
               switch (SHORT1FROMMP (mp1))
                    {
                    case IDM_TIMER:
                         WinSendMsg (hwndMenu, MM_SETITEMATTR,
                                   MPFROM2SHORT (IDM_START, TRUE),
                                   MPFROM2SHORT (MIA_DISABLED,
                                             !fTimerGoing &&
                              WinQuerySysValue (HWND_DESKTOP, SV_CTIMERS) ?
                                             0 : MIA_DISABLED)) ;

                         WinSendMsg (hwndMenu, MM_SETITEMATTR,
                                   MPFROM2SHORT (IDM_STOP, TRUE),
                                   MPFROM2SHORT (MIA_DISABLED,
                                        fTimerGoing ? 0 : MIA_DISABLED)) ;
                         return 0 ;
                    }
               break ;

          case WM_COMMAND:
               switch (COMMANDMSG(&msg)->cmd)
                    {
                    case IDM_NEW:
                         WinMessageBox (HWND_DESKTOP, hwnd,
                                   "Bogus \"New\" Dialog",
                                   szClientClass, 0, MB_OK | MB_INFORMATION) ;
                         return 0 ;
```

Listing 13.1: The CONVMENU program (Continued)

```
          case IDM_OPEN:
               WinMessageBox (HWND_DESKTOP, hwnd,
                         "Bogus \"Open\" Dialog",
                         szClientClass, 0, MB_OK | MB_INFORMATION) ;
               return 0 ;

          case IDM_SAVE:
               WinMessageBox (HWND_DESKTOP, hwnd,
                         "Bogus \"Save\" Dialog",
                         szClientClass, 0, MB_OK | MB_INFORMATION) ;
               return 0 ;

          case IDM_SAVEAS:
               WinMessageBox (HWND_DESKTOP, hwnd,
                         "Bogus \"Save As\" Dialog",
                         szClientClass, 0, MB_OK | MB_INFORMATION) ;
               return 0 ;

          case IDM_EXIT:
               WinSendMsg (hwnd, WM_CLOSE, 0L, 0L) ;
               return 0 ;

          case IDM_START:
               if (WinStartTimer (hab, hwnd, ID_TIMER, 1000))
                    fTimerGoing = TRUE ;
               else
                    WinMessageBox (HWND_DESKTOP, hwnd,
                         "Too many clocks or timers",
                         szClientClass, 0,
                         MB_OK | MB_WARNING) ;
               return 0 ;

          case IDM_STOP:
               WinStopTimer (hab, hwnd, ID_TIMER) ;
               fTimerGoing = FALSE ;
               return 0 ;

          case IDM_WHITE:
          case IDM_LTGRAY:
          case IDM_GRAY:
          case IDM_DKGRAY:
          case IDM_BLACK:
               WinSendMsg (hwndMenu, MM_SETITEMATTR,
                           MPFROM2SHORT (iCurrentBackground, TRUE),
                           MPFROM2SHORT (MIA_CHECKED, 0)) ;

               iCurrentBackground = COMMANDMSG(&msg)->cmd ;

               WinSendMsg (hwndMenu, MM_SETITEMATTR,
```

Listing 13.1: The CONVMENU program (Continued)

```
                                        MPFROM2SHORT (iCurrentBackground, TRUE),
                                        MPFROM2SHORT (MIA_CHECKED, MIA_CHECKED)) ;

                           WinInvalidateRect (hwnd, NULL, FALSE) ;
                           return 0 ;

                      case IDM_HELP:
                           WinMessageBox (HWND_DESKTOP, hwnd,
                                          "Bogus \"Help\" Dialog",
                                          szClientClass, 0, MB_OK | MB_INFORMATION) ;
                           return 0 ;

                      case IDM_ABOUT:
                           WinMessageBox (HWND_DESKTOP, hwnd,
                                          "Bogus \"About\" Dialog",
                                          szClientClass, 0, MB_OK | MB_INFORMATION) ;
                           return 0 ;
                      }
                 break ;

            case WM_HELP:
                 WinMessageBox (HWND_DESKTOP, hwnd,
                                "Help not yet implemented",
                                szClientClass, 0, MB_OK | MB_WARNING) ;
                 return 0 ;

            case WM_TIMER:
                 WinAlarm (HWND_DESKTOP, WA_NOTE) ;
                 return 0 ;

            case WM_PAINT:
                 hps = WinBeginPaint (hwnd, NULLHANDLE, NULL) ;
                 GpiSavePS (hps) ;

                 GpiCreateLogColorTable (hps, 0L, LCOLF_RGB, 0L, 0L, NULL) ;

                 WinQueryWindowRect (hwnd, &rcl) ;

                 WinFillRect (hps, &rcl,
                              colBackground [iCurrentBackground - IDM_WHITE]) ;

                 GpiRestorePS (hps, -1L) ;
                 WinEndPaint (hps) ;
                 return 0 ;

            case WM_DESTROY:
                 if (fTimerGoing)
                      {
                      WinStopTimer (hab, hwnd, ID_TIMER) ;
```

Listing 13.1: The CONVMENU program (Continued)

```
                    fTimerGoing = FALSE ;
                    }
               return 0 ;
          }
     return WinDefWindowProc (hwnd, msg, mp1, mp2) ;
     }
```

The CONVMENU.RC File

```
/*-----------------------------------
   CONVMENU.RC resource script file
  -----------------------------------*/

#include <os2.h>
#include "convmenu.h"

MENU ID_RESOURCE
     {
     SUBMENU "~File",               IDM_FILE
          {
          MENUITEM "~New",                    IDM_NEW
          MENUITEM "~Open...",                IDM_OPEN
          MENUITEM "~Save\tShift+F3",         IDM_SAVE
          MENUITEM "Save ~As...",             IDM_SAVEAS
          MENUITEM SEPARATOR
          MENUITEM "E~xit\tF3",               IDM_EXIT
          }
     SUBMENU "~Timer",              IDM_TIMER
          {
          MENUITEM "~Start",                  IDM_START
          MENUITEM "S~top",                   IDM_STOP,,  MIA_DISABLED
          }
     SUBMENU "~Background",         IDM_BACKGROUND
          {
          MENUITEM "~White\tCtrl+W",          IDM_WHITE,, MIA_CHECKED
          MENUITEM "~Light Gray\tCtrl+L",     IDM_LTGRAY
          MENUITEM "~Gray\tCtrl+G",           IDM_GRAY
          MENUITEM "~Dark Gray\tCtrl+D",      IDM_DKGRAY
          MENUITEM "~Black\tCtrl+B",          IDM_BLACK
          }
     SUBMENU "~Help",               IDM_TOPHELP
          {
          MENUITEM "~Help...",                IDM_HELP, MIS_HELP
          MENUITEM SEPARATOR
          MENUITEM "~About...",               IDM_ABOUT
          }
     }
```

Listing 13.1: The CONVMENU program (Continued)

```
ACCELTABLE ID_RESOURCE
     {
     VK_F3, IDM_SAVE,   VIRTUALKEY, SHIFT
     VK_F3, IDM_EXIT,   VIRTUALKEY
     "w",   IDM_WHITE,  CONTROL
     "l",   IDM_LTGRAY, CONTROL
     "g",   IDM_GRAY,   CONTROL
     "d",   IDM_DKGRAY, CONTROL
     "b",   IDM_BLACK,  CONTROL
     }
```

The CONVMENU.H File

```
/*-------------------------
   CONVMENU.H header file
  -------------------------*/

#define ID_RESOURCE      1

#define IDM_FILE         1    // Top-level items
#define IDM_TIMER        2
#define IDM_BACKGROUND   3
#define IDM_TOPHELP      4

#define IDM_NEW          10   // "File" submenu
#define IDM_OPEN         11
#define IDM_SAVE         12
#define IDM_SAVEAS       13
#define IDM_EXIT         14

#define IDM_START        20   // "Timer" submenu
#define IDM_STOP         21

#define IDM_WHITE        30   // "Background" submenu
#define IDM_LTGRAY       31
#define IDM_GRAY         32        // Program logic assumes these
#define IDM_DKGRAY       33        // five numbers are consecutive
#define IDM_BLACK        34

#define IDM_HELP         40   // "Help" submenu
#define IDM_ABOUT        41
```

The CONVMENU.DEF File

```
;-----------------------------------
; CONVMENU.DEF module definition file
;-----------------------------------
```

Listing 13.1: The CONVMENU program (Continued)

```
NAME            CONVMENU  WINDOWAPI

DESCRIPTION     'Conventional Menu Demo (c) Charles Petzold, 1993'
PROTMODE
```

The File submenu in CONVMENU contains standard options that don't do anything in this program except display some message boxes. (In the next chapter you'll see how to invoke dialog boxes from menu items.) The Timer menu starts and stops the timer. The timer causes the program to beep once a second. When the timer is active, the Start option is disabled; when the timer is inactive, the Stop option is disabled. The Background menu changes the background color of the client window. This menu uses check marks to indicate the current color.

DEFINING THE MENU

You define a menu template in a resource script file. The menu template begins with the MENU statement, which indicates the resource name ID of the menu. The menu in CONVMENU.RC has a resource name ID of ID_RESOURCE, which is defined in CONVMENU.H. The actual definition of the menu is enclosed within a pair of curly braces:

```
MENU ID_RESOURCE
     {
          [ menu definition ]
     }
```

If you want to, you can use the BEGIN and END keywords rather than the curly braces.

Between the curly braces, you specify the items on the top-level menu with one or more MENUITEM or SUBMENU statements. The SUBMENU statement indicates a menu item that invokes a submenu, and the MENUITEM statement indicates a menu item that doesn't:

```
MENU ID_RESOURCE
     {
     SUBMENU "~File", IDM_FILE
          {
               [ definition of submenu ]
          }
     SUBMENU "~Timer", IDM_TIMER
          {
               [ definition of submenu ]
```

```
          }
     SUBMENU "~Background", IDM_BACKGROUND
          {
               [ definition of submenu ]
          }
     SUBMENU "~Help", IDM_TOPHELP
          {
               [ definition of submenu ]
          }
     }
```

Thus the top-level menu in CONVMENU contains the options "File," "Timer," "Background," and "Help."

The syntax of the MENUITEM and SUBMENU statements is the same. Each statement contains a text string and a menu item ID followed by optional style and attribute identifiers:

```
MENUITEM "Text", idMenuItem [,[style flags][, attribute flags]]
SUBMENU "Text", idMenuItem [,[style flags][, attribute flags]]
```

The text string is the text that appears in the menu. A tilde (~) character causes the letter that follows the tilde to be underlined when the text is displayed. A user can type that letter in combination with the Alt key to select the menu item from the keyboard. The underlined letters within the top-level menu and each submenu should be unique. It's recommended that you use the first letter, the first consonant, or a subsequent consonant.

The menu item ID is a 16-bit number that the Presentation Manager uses to identify the menu item in messages from the menu to your client window. You also use the menu item ID to send messages to the menu. The menu definition in CONVMENU.RC uses identifiers that are defined in CONVMENU.H and begin with the letters IDM ("ID for a menu item").

The optional styles and attributes are one or more identifiers beginning with the letters MIS ("menu item style") or MIA ("menu item attribute"). I'll describe these styles and attributes shortly.

The SUBMENU statement indicates a menu item that invokes a submenu. The submenu is defined by one or more MENUITEM statements within a pair of curly braces that follow the SUBMENU statement, like this:

```
SUBMENU "~Timer", IDM_TIMER
     {
     MENUITEM "~Start", IDM_START
     MENUITEM "S~top",  IDM_STOP,, MIA_DISABLED
     }
```

This indicates that the Timer item on the top-level menu invokes a submenu containing the items Start and Stop. Multiple levels of submenu nesting are also supported.

The text in submenu items can contain a tab character indicated by "\t." The text that follows the tab character appears to the right when the submenu is displayed. You generally use this to indicate the keyboard accelerator for the menu item, as in the submenu invoked by File:

```
SUBMENU "~File",          IDM_FILE
     {
     MENUITEM "~New",                 IDM_NEW
     MENUITEM "~Open...",             IDM_OPEN
     MENUITEM "~Save\tShift+F3",      IDM_SAVE
     MENUITEM "Save ~As...",          IDM_SAVEAS
     MENUITEM SEPARATOR
     MENUITEM "E~xit\tF3",            IDM_EXIT
     }
```

The F3 key in combination with the Shift key is a keyboard accelerator for Save. This text only indicates to the user what the keyboard accelerators are. I'll discuss later how you make these key combinations function as keyboard accelerators.

The ellipsis (...) in some text strings indicates that the item invokes a dialog box. The File submenu also includes the following line, which draws a horizontal line between the Save As and Exit menu items:

```
MENUITEM SEPARATOR
```

ID CONFUSION

We first worked with IDs in connection with child windows. A child window ID is assigned by the program when it creates a child window. The child window uses this ID to identify itself to its parent. In the last chapter we began working with resource type IDs and resource name IDs. These IDs identify unique resources within a program.

Now we have menu item IDs. Don't confuse these with resource name IDs or child window IDs. The menu item ID identifies a particular menu item within a top-level menu or a submenu. (However, the menu item IDs are sometimes related to child window IDs. For example, IDM_FILE is the menu item ID of the File item on CONVMENU's top-level menu. It is also the child window ID of the submenu invoked by the File item. But the submenu isn't a child window of the top-level menu. This is obvious, because the submenu is displayed outside the area occupied by the top-level menu.)

THE STYLES AND ATTRIBUTES

Every menu item has a style and an attribute, each of which is represented within the Presentation Manager by bit flags within a 16-bit integer. You can override the default style and attribute using identifiers beginning with MIS and MIA in the menu definition.

Menu item styles Styles fall into several groups of mutually exclusive options. The first four style bits determine the contents of the visible part of the menu item:

Style Bit	Description
MIS_TEXT	Text string
MIS_BITMAP	Bitmap
MIS_SEPARATOR	Horizontal dividing line in submenu
MIS_OWNERDRAW	Item that will be drawn by program

When you omit a style identifier for a menu item, RC.EXE uses the MIS_TEXT style as a default. In CONVMENU's menu, all menu items (except the separator bar in the File menu) have the MIS_TEXT style. In the GRAFMENU program shown later in this chapter, we'll use the MIS_BITMAP style. The MIS_SEPARATOR style serves as an alternative to using the MENUITEM SEPARATOR statement. The MIS_OWNERDRAW style requires that your program itself draw the item whenever the menu is displayed. The Presentation Manager sends the client window procedure WM_MEASUREITEM and WM_DRAWITEM messages when the item must be drawn.

The next group of style bits determines the organization of the menu items in rows and columns:

Style Bit	Description
MIS_BREAK	Menu item starts in a new row or column
MIS_BREAKSEPARATOR	Menu item starts in a new row or column with a line drawn between the rows or columns
MIS_BUTTONSEPARATOR	Menu item is separated by a bar—the user can't use the cursor movement keys to move to the item

The MIS_BREAK and MIS_BREAKSEPARATOR styles are used most often in submenus that contain a large number of items. These styles aren't required in top-level menus because the Presentation Manager automatically breaks the menu into multiple lines when the window is too narrow to display the menu as a single line.

The next set of style bits determines the message that the Presentation Manager sends the program when a menu item has been chosen by the user. Normally, the message is WM_COMMAND. These two bits override that:

Style Bit	Description
MIS_SYSCOMMAND	Choosing menu item generates a WM_SYSCOMMAND message
MIS_HELP	Choosing menu item generates a WM_HELP message

The WM_SYSCOMMAND message is usually reserved for system menu items. Because these items generate WM_SYSCOMMAND messages, you can process WM_COMMAND messages from the menu without worrying about receiving system menu messages.

Although these last two menu item styles have little to do with each other, in a practical sense they are mutually exclusive. In a resource script menu template, the MIS_SUBMENU style is assumed when you use the SUBMENU statement rather than a MENUITEM statement.

Style Bit	Description
MIS_SUBMENU	Item invokes a submenu
MIS_STATIC	Item can't be chosen

Menu item attributes These five identifiers determine the attribute of the menu item:

Attribute Bit	Description
MIA_NODISMISS	If item in submenu is chosen, the submenu remains down
MIA_FRAMED	Item is enclosed in a box (top-level menu only; used by Presentation Manager when item is selected)
MIA_CHECKED	Check mark appears to left of item (submenu only)
MIA_DISABLED	Item is shown in gray text and can't be chosen
MIA_HILITED	Item is shown in reverse video (used by Presentation Manager when item is selected)

The difference between a menu item style and a menu item attribute is fairly simple: A program can change an item's attribute but not its style (unless the entire item is replaced).

The MIA_CHECKED and MIA_DISABLED attributes are used in CONVMENU.RC for the White and Stop menu items respectively. You'll see shortly how a program can change these attributes.

INCLUDING THE MENU IN THE STANDARD WINDOW

You make the menu part of the standard window by including the FCF_MENU frame creation flag in the definition of *flFrameFlags*, just as you include the FCF_ICON flag discussed in the last chapter.

When the frame flags include FCF_MENU, the second-to-last parameter of *WinCreateStdWindow* must be set to the resource name ID of the menu, which, in CONVMENU.RC, is ID_RESOURCE. The Presentation Manager uses this same resource name ID to load the program's icon when the frame flags include FCF_ICON and to load the program's keyboard accelerator table when the frame flags include FCF_ACCELTABLE.

After the *WinCreateStdWindow* function returns, you can obtain the handle of the top-level menu by using the following function:

```
hwndMenu = WinWindowFromID (hwndFrame, FID_MENU) ;
```

Or, within the client window procedure, you can use

```
hwndMenu = WinWindowFromID (
          WinQueryWindow (hwnd, QW_PARENT),
          FID_MENU) ;
```

Often the client window procedure obtains the window handle of the menu during the WM_CREATE message and stores it in a static variable for later use.

RECEIVING MENU MESSAGES

The Presentation Manager sends the frame window procedure WM_COMMAND messages when the user chooses an enabled menu item from the menu. (This message will be WM_SYSCOMMAND or WM_HELP if the menu item style includes the MIS_SYSCOMMAND or MIS_HELP style bit.) The frame window passes the messages to the client window procedure. If a disabled menu item is chosen, no WM_COMMAND message is generated.

The *mp1* and *mp2* parameters that accompany a WM_COMMAND message are shown here:

WM_COMMAND Parameters	Description
SHORT1FROMMP (mp1)	Menu item ID
SHORT1FROMMP (mp2)	CMDSRC_MENU
SHORT2FROMMP (mp2)	Nonzero if selected by mouse, 0 if selected by keyboard

WM_COMMAND is the same message that a push button window sends its owner. For a push button, the low USHORT of *mp1* is the child window ID, and the low USHORT of *mp2* is CMDSRC_PUSHBUTTON. Keyboard accelerators send WM_COMMAND messages with the low USHORT of *mp1* equal to CMDSRC_ACCELERATOR. If you're receiving WM_COMMAND messages from menus, accelerators, and push buttons, it's easiest to ignore *mp2* and test only the low USHORT of *mp1*. You should thus make all ID numbers unique unless you deliberately want the program to process WM_COMMAND messages from two or more different sources in the same way. (This is often the case with keyboard accelerators, because you use them to duplicate menu items.) As you learned in Chapter 11, you can also use the COMMANDMSG macro for decoding the message parameters of a WM_COMMAND message. For example, the expression

```
COMMANDMSG (&msg) -> cmd
```

is the menu item ID.

In *ClientWndProc*, the processing of the WM_COMMAND message looks like this:

```
case WM_COMMAND:
     switch (COMMANDMSG (&msg) -> cmd)
          {
               [case statements for menu item IDs]
          }
     break ;
```

You'll note that the *switch* and *case* construction includes *case* statements only for IDs associated with menu items in the menu's MENUITEM statements. The window procedure never receives WM_COMMAND messages for the menu item IDs in SUBMENU statements because these items invoke submenus and aren't commands in themselves. The WM_COMMAND processing in CONVMENU.C also lacks a case statement for IDM_HELP because that menu item generates a WM_HELP message. In the WM_COMMAND message processing, the IDM_NEW, IDM_OPEN, IDM_SAVE, IDM_SAVEAS, and IDM_ABOUT items cause the program to display message boxes. Normally, these items would cause the program to create and display a dialog box.

WORKING WITH CHECKED MENU ITEMS

The submenu invoked by the Background item on CONVMENU's top-level menu allows the user to choose one of five colors that the program uses to color the background of the client window:

```
SUBMENU "~Background",      IDM_BACKGROUND
     {
     MENUITEM "~White\tCtrl+W",          IDM_WHITE,, MIA_CHECKED
     MENUITEM "~Light Gray\tCtrl+L",     IDM_LTGRAY
     MENUITEM "~Gray\tCtrl+G",           IDM_GRAY
     MENUITEM "~Dark Gray\tCtrl+D",      IDM_DKGRAY
     MENUITEM "~Black\tCtrl+B",          IDM_BLACK
     }
```

When the Presentation Manager first creates the window, the White item appears with a check mark to the left of the text. Check marks are used most often for mutually exclusive menu options, as is the case here.

Within *ClientWndProc*, the *iCurrentBackground* variable is initialized with the menu item ID of the checked item:

```
static INT iCurrentBackground = IDM_WHITE ;
```

When *ClientWndProc* receives a WM_COMMAND message for one of the five items in this submenu, it must remove the check mark from the item currently checked, add a check mark to the item that the user has chosen, and change the color of the client window.

Processing of the WM_COMMAND message is the same for all five items in this submenu:

```
case WM_COMMAND:
     switch (COMMANDMSG (&msg) -> cmd)
          {
               [other program lines]
          case IDM_WHITE:
          case IDM_LTGRAY:
          case IDM_GRAY:
          case IDM_DKGRAY:
          case IDM_BLACK:
```

To process these commands, CONVMENU first removes the check mark from the menu item that is currently checked. The ID of that menu item is stored in *iCurrentBackground.* The program can remove the check mark by sending the menu window a MM_SETITEMATTR message:

```
WinSendMsg (hwndMenu, MM_SETITEMATTR,
            MPFROM2SHORT (iCurrentBackground, TRUE),
            MPFROM2SHORT (MIA_CHECKED, 0)) ;
```

The *mp1* parameter of this message contains two USHORT values. The low USHORT of *mp1* has the ID of the menu item to be changed. However, you're sending this message to the window whose handle is *hwndMenu.* That's the window handle of the top-level window, not the submenu that contains the five color items. The high USHORT of *mp1* must be set to TRUE to tell the window procedure for the top-level menu to search through the submenus for a menu item with an ID equal to *iCurrentBackground.*

The low USHORT of *mp2* contains the attribute bit (or bits) to be changed. In this case, we want to change the MIA_CHECKED attribute bit. The high USHORT of *mp2* is set to the new value of these attribute bits, in this case 0. This removes the MIA_CHECKED attribute from the menu item.

CONVMENU sets *iCurrentBackground* equal to the item the user has chosen from the menu:

```
iCurrentBackground = COMMANDMSG (&msg) -> cmd ;
```

The program then sends the menu another MM_SETITEMATTR message. This is identical to the first message except that the high USHORT of *mp2* is set to MIA_CHECKED:

```
WinSendMsg (hwndMenu, MM_SETITEMATTR,
            MPFROM2SHORT (iCurrentBackground, TRUE),
            MPFROM2SHORT (MIA_CHECKED, MIA_CHECKED)) ;
```

The menu item chosen by the user now has the MIA_CHECKED attribute, and a check mark is drawn to the left of the item.

Most WM_COMMAND processing of mutually exclusive check-marked menu items requires little more than these three statements. Structurally, the code is very similar to that used in the DRAWLINE program in Chapter 11 to check and uncheck radio buttons. In CONVMENU, the only job left is to repaint the client window with the new color. This is accomplished by invalidating the window to generate a WM_PAINT message:

```
WinInvalidateRect (hwnd, NULL, FALSE) ;
```

During the WM_PAINT message, CONVMENU calls *GpiCreateLogColorTable* to use RGB color indices, obtains the dimensions of the client window, and uses *WinFillRect* to color it:

```
WinQueryWindowRect (hwnd, &rcl) ;
WinFillRect (hps, &rcl,
     colBackground [sCurrentBackground - IDM_WHITE]) ;
```

The *colBackground* array is initialized in *ClientWndProc* to contain the five color values corresponding to the five menu items:

```
static COLOR colBackground [] = {
                                 0xFFFFFFL, 0xC0C0C0L, 0x808080L,
                                 0x404040L, 0x000000L
                                 } ;
```

The only assumption the program logic makes is that the five menu item ID numbers are consecutive. The CONVMENU.H file contains a little note to this effect.

```
#define IDM_WHITE          30     // Background submenu
#define IDM_LTGRAY         31
#define IDM_GRAY           32            // Program logic assumes these
#define IDM_DKGRAY         33            // five numbers are consecutive
#define IDM_BLAC           34
```

ENABLING AND DISABLING MENU ITEMS

Another useful attribute of menu items is MIA_DISABLED. When a menu item is disabled, it appears in gray text. A disabled menu item doesn't generate a WM_COMMAND message.

CONVMENU uses disabled menu items on its Timer submenu. When the program begins, the Stop item is disabled, as indicated in the menu definition in CONVMENU.RC:

```
SUBMENU "~Timer",     IDM_TIMER
     {
     MENUITEM "~Start",    IDM_START
     MENUITEM "S~top",     IDM_STOP,, MIA_DISABLED
     }
```

It makes no sense to stop the timer when it hasn't been started yet. When you choose Start from the menu, CONVMENU disables the Start item and enables Stop.

We could handle this enabling and disabling in the same way that we removed and added the check mark, with some additional logic required for starting and stopping the timer. However, in CONVMENU, the processing of

WM_COMMAND messages for IDM_START and IDM_STOP doesn't alter the menu item attributes. Instead, IDM_START simply starts the timer, and IDM_STOP stops it:

```
case IDM_START:
     if (WinStartTimer (hab, hwnd, ID_TIMER, 1000))
          fTimerGoing = TRUE ;
     else
          WinMessageBox (HWND_DESKTOP, hwnd,
                         "Too many clocks or timers",
                         szClientClass, 0,
                         MB_OK | MB_ICONEXCLAMATION) ;
     return 0 ;

case IDM_STOP:
     WinStopTimer (hab, hwnd, ID_TIMER) ;
     fTimerGoing = FALSE ;
     return 0 ;
```

CONVMENU enables and disables the menu items while processing the WM_INITMENU message. The Presentation Manager sends a window procedure a WM_INITMENU message when it's about to display a submenu. The low USHORT of *mp1* is the ID of the top-level menu item that invokes the submenu. The program can take this opportunity to change the submenu. CONVMENU processes the WM_INITMENU message like this:

```
case WM_INITMENU:
     switch (SHORT1FROMMP (mp1))
          {
          case IDM_TIMER:
               WinSendMsg (hwndMenu, MM_SETITEMATTR,
                    MPFROM2SHORT (IDM_START, TRUE),
                    MPFROM2SHORT (MIA_DISABLED,
                         !fTimerGoing &&
                    WinQuerySysValue (HWND_DESKTOP, SV_CTIMERS) ?
                         0 : MIA_DISABLED)) ;

               WinSendMsg (hwndMenu, MM_SETITEMATTR,
                    MPFROM2SHORT (IDM_STOP, TRUE),
                    MPFROM2SHORT (MIA_DISABLED,
                         fTimerGoing? 0 : MIA_DISABLED)) ;
               return 0 ;
          }
     break ;
```

CONVMENU ignores WM_INITMENU messages unless they involve the Timer submenu.

The first *WinSendMsg* call sets the MIA_DISABLED bit on the Start item if the timer is already active (indicated by a TRUE value of *fTimerGoing*) or if no timers are available (which you can determine from the *WinQuerySysValue* function). The second *WinSendMsg* call sets the MIA_DISABLED bit on the Stop item if the timer isn't currently active.

HANDLING THE EXIT COMMAND

When *ClientWndProc* receives a WM_COMMAND message with the IDM_EXIT menu item ID, it sends itself a WM_CLOSE message:

```
case IDM_EXIT:
     WinSendMsg (hwnd, WM_CLOSE, 0L, 0L) ;
     return 0 ;
```

WM_CLOSE is the same message the system menu sends the window procedure when the user chooses Close from the system menu. Most of the programs I've written so far have not processed the WM_CLOSE message but have simply passed it on to *WinDefWindowProc*. *WinDefWindowProc* responds to the WM_CLOSE message by posting a WM_QUIT message to the program's message queue, which causes the message loop in *main* to end and the program to terminate. Some programs (those that work with files, for example) will want confirmation that the user really wants to end the program.

A program can be terminated not only from an Exit item on the program's menu or from the Close item on the system menu, but when the user shuts down the OS/2 system. In this case, the Presentation Manager posts a WM_QUIT message to the program's message queue.

To handle all of these cases, a program that needs to request confirmation from the user before terminating must do so after receiving a WM_QUIT message. This requires that you add some logic to the message loop. Here's how CONVMENU does it:

```
while (TRUE)
     {
     while (WinGetMsg (hab, &qmsg, NULL, 0, 0))
          WinDispatchMsg (hab, &qmsg) ;

     if (MBID_OK == WinMessageBox (HWND_DESKTOP, hwndClient,
                              "Really want to end program?",
                              szClientClass, 0,
                              MB_OKCANCEL | MB_ICONQUESTION))
```

```
          break ;
     WinCancelShutdown (hmq, FALSE) ;
     }
WinDestroyWindow (hwndFrame) ;
```

The WM_QUIT message causes *WinGetMsg* to return 0 and drop out of the message loop. CONVMENU then displays a message box with OK and Cancel buttons and asks if the user really wants to end the program. If the user answers by pressing OK, the break statement is executed and termination begins with *WinDestroyWindow.*

Otherwise, the program calls *WinCancelShutdown* (which halts any system shutdown that might have been initiated), ignores the WM_QUIT message, and goes back to the message loop.

In CONVMENU.RC, the Exit menu item is defined like this:

```
MENUITEM "E~xit ConvMenu\tF3", IDM_EXIT
```

It could have been defined like this:

```
MENUITEM "E~xit ConvMenu\tF3", SC_CLOSE, MIS_SYSCOMMAND
```

This causes the Exit item to generate a WM_SYSCOMMAND message with the low USHORT of *mp1* equal to SC_CLOSE. This is the same message generated from the system menu when the user selects Close. *WinDefWindowProc* processes this message by sending the window procedure a WM_CLOSE message. If I had used this, I wouldn't have required the IDM_EXIT identifier or the code to send the window procedure a WM_CLOSE message.

THE WM_HELP MESSAGE

The menu template in CONVMENU.RC includes this menu item:

```
MENUITEM "~Help...", IDM_HELP, MIS_HELP
```

The MIS_HELP style indicates that the menu item generates a WM_HELP message. The *mp1* and *mp2* parameters that accompany the WM_HELP message are the same as those for WM_COMMAND messages:

WM_HELP Parameters	Description
SHORT1FROMMP (mp1)	Menu item ID
SHORT1FROMMP (mp2)	CMDSRC_MENU
SHORT2FROMMP (mp2)	Nonzero if selected by mouse, 0 if selected by keyboard

A push button can also generate a WM_HELP message if it's given the style BS_HELP. For push buttons, the low USHORT of *mp1* is the child ID, and the low USHORT of *mp2* is CMDSRC_PUSHBUTTON. The WM_HELP message helps you consolidate all your help processing in one place. Regardless of the presence of a menu item for Help, pressing the F1 key always generates a WM_HELP message. F1 is a built-in keyboard accelerator. The *mp1* parameter is 0, and the low USHORT of *mp2* is CMDSRC_ACCELERATOR.

CONVMENU responds to the WM_HELP message by reporting that "Help is not yet implemented." In a real program, you can create a window that reads help text (probably from a programmer-defined resource) and display it.

THE KEYBOARD ACCELERATOR TABLE

CONVMENU.RC also includes a keyboard accelerator table, which lets the user duplicate menu items from the keyboard. The accelerator table is defined as shown here:

```
ACCELTABLE ID_RESOURCE
     {
     VK_F3, IDM_SAVE,    VIRTUALKEY, SHIFT
     VK_F3, IDM_EXIT,    VIRTUALKEY
     "w",   IDM_WHITE,   CONTROL
     "l",   IDM_LTGRAY,  CONTROL
     "g",   IDM_GRAY,    CONTROL
     "d",   IDM_DKGRAY,  CONTROL
     "b",   IDM_BLACK,   CONTROL
     }
```

Note that the resource name ID of the accelerator table is ID_RESOURCE, which is the same ID as the menu. The resource is loaded by the Presentation Manager because the window frame style bit of FCF_ACCELTABLE is included in the definition of *flFrameFlags.*

The first field in each line is the key, which is either a virtual key code or an ASCII code in quotes. These keys generate WM_COMMAND messages. The second field specifies the ID that accompanies the WM_COMMAND message. These are the same IDs used in the menu. Following the IDs are some options. The VIRTUALKEY keyword is required if the first field is a virtual key code. SHIFT specifies that the Shift key must be used; CONTROL specifies that the Control key must be used. Defining this table and including FCF_ACCEL-TABLE in the definition of *flFrameFlags* frame style is all that's required for keyboard accelerators that duplicate menu items.

OTHER APPROACHES TO MENUS

Now that we've studied the most common form of the Presentation Manager menu, let's look at a few unusual approaches and then complete this chapter with a couple of games.

ALTERING THE SYSTEM MENU

Small programs often need a menu for only one or two items—an About box and a Help screen, perhaps. If you would rather not give such programs their own menu, you can add the required menu items to the system menu. Although this practice isn't recommended, it illustrates some useful concepts involved with menu handling. The "poor person's menu" technique is shown in the POORMENU program in Listing 13.2.

Listing 13.2: The POORMENU program

The POORMENU.MAK File

```
#-----------------------
# POORMENU.MAK make file
#-----------------------

poormenu.exe : poormenu.obj poormenu.def
     $(PRGLINK) poormenu, poormenu, NUL, $(PRGLIB), poormenu

poormenu.obj : poormenu.c
     $(PRGCC) poormenu.c
```

The POORMENU.C File

```
/*---------------------------------------
   POORMENU.C -- Poor Person's Menu
                 (c) Charles Petzold, 1993
  ---------------------------------------*/

#define INCL_WIN
#include <os2.h>

#define IDM_ABOUT   10
#define IDM_HELP    11

MRESULT EXPENTRY ClientWndProc (HWND, ULONG, MPARAM, MPARAM) ;

CHAR szCaption [] = "Poor Person\'s Menu" ;

int main (void)
```

Listing 13.2: The POORMENU program (Continued)

```
     {
     static CHAR  szClientClass[] = "PoorMenu" ;
     static ULONG flFrameFlags = FCF_TITLEBAR       | FCF_SYSMENU |
                                 FCF_SIZEBORDER     | FCF_MINMAX  |
                                 FCF_SHELLPOSITION  | FCF_TASKLIST ;
     HAB          hab ;
     HMQ          hmq ;
     HWND         hwndFrame, hwndClient ;
     QMSG         qmsg ;

     hab = WinInitialize (0) ;
     hmq = WinCreateMsgQueue (hab, 0) ;

     WinRegisterClass (hab, szClientClass, ClientWndProc, 0L, 0) ;

     hwndFrame = WinCreateStdWindow (HWND_DESKTOP, WS_VISIBLE,
                                     &flFrameFlags, szClientClass, NULL,
                                     0L, 0, 0, &hwndClient) ;

     while (WinGetMsg (hab, &qmsg, NULLHANDLE, 0, 0))
          WinDispatchMsg (hab, &qmsg) ;

     WinDestroyWindow (hwndFrame) ;
     WinDestroyMsgQueue (hmq) ;
     WinTerminate (hab) ;
     return 0 ;
     }

MRESULT EXPENTRY ClientWndProc (HWND hwnd, ULONG msg, MPARAM mp1, MPARAM mp2)
     {
     static CHAR     *szMenuText [3] = { NULL,
                                         "A~bout PoorMenu...",
                                         "~Help..." } ;
     static MENUITEM mi [3] = {
                              MIT_END, MIS_SEPARATOR, 0, 0,         0, 0,
                              MIT_END, MIS_TEXT,      0, IDM_ABOUT, 0, 0,
                              MIT_END, MIS_TEXT,      0, IDM_HELP,  0, 0
                              } ;
     HWND            hwndSysMenu, hwndSysSubMenu ;
     INT             iItem, idSysMenu ;
     MENUITEM        miSysMenu ;

     switch (msg)
          {
          case WM_CREATE:
               hwndSysMenu = WinWindowFromID (
                                   WinQueryWindow (hwnd, QW_PARENT),
                                   FID_SYSMENU) ;
```

Listing 13.2: The POORMENU program (Continued)

```
          idSysMenu = SHORT1FROMMR (WinSendMsg (hwndSysMenu,
                                               MM_ITEMIDFROMPOSITION,
                                               NULL, NULL)) ;

          WinSendMsg (hwndSysMenu, MM_QUERYITEM,
                      MPFROM2SHORT (idSysMenu, FALSE),
                      MPFROMP (&miSysMenu)) ;

          hwndSysSubMenu = miSysMenu.hwndSubMenu ;

          for (iItem = 0 ; iItem < 3 ; iItem++)
               WinSendMsg (hwndSysSubMenu, MM_INSERTITEM,
                           MPFROMP (mi + iItem),
                           MPFROMP (szMenuText [iItem])) ;
          return 0 ;

     case WM_COMMAND:
          switch (COMMANDMSG(&msg)->cmd)
               {
               case IDM_ABOUT:
                    WinMessageBox (HWND_DESKTOP, hwnd,
                                   "(C) Charles Petzold, 1993",
                                   szCaption, 0, MB_OK | MB_INFORMATION) ;
                    return 0 ;

               case IDM_HELP:
                    WinMessageBox (HWND_DESKTOP, hwnd,
                                   "Help not yet implemented",
                                   szCaption, 0, MB_OK | MB_WARNING) ;
                    return 0 ;
               }
          break ;

     case WM_ERASEBACKGROUND:
          return MRFROMSHORT (1) ;
     }
return WinDefWindowProc (hwnd, msg, mp1, mp2) ;
}
```

The POORMENU.DEF File

```
;-----------------------------------
; POORMENU.DEF module definition file
;-----------------------------------

NAME           POORMENU  WINDOWAPI

DESCRIPTION    'The Poor Persons Menu (c) Charles Petzold, 1993'
PROTMODE
```

During processing of the WM_CREATE message in *ClientWndProc*, POORMENU obtains the window handle of the system menu:

```
hwndSysMenu = WinWindowFromID (
          WinQueryWindow (hwnd, QW_PARENT),
          FID_SYSMENU) ;
```

This is actually the handle to the top-level system menu—the single bitmap that is displayed to the left of the title bar. What we need is the handle to the system submenu.

Sending the system menu an MM_ITEMIDFROMPOSITION message obtains the menu item ID of the system menu bitmap. Because this bitmap is the only item in the system top-level menu, it's located at position 0:

```
idSysMenu = SHORT1FROMMR (WinSendMsg (hwndSysMenu,
                          MM_ITEMIDFROMPOSITION,
                          NULL, NULL)) ;
```

POORMENU then sends the system menu an MM_QUERYITEM message to fill in a MENUITEM structure with the characteristics of this menu item:

```
WinSendMsg (hwndSysMenu, MM_QUERYITEM,
            MPFROM2SHORT (idSysMenu, FALSE),
            MPFROMP (&miSysMenu)) ;
```

The MENUITEM structure is defined in PMWIN.H like this:

```
typedef struct _MENUITEM
     {
     SHORT iPosition ;
     ULONG afStyle ;
     ULONG afAttribute ;
     ULONG id ;
     HWND  hwndSubMenu ;
     ULONG hItem ;
     }
     MENUITEM ;
```

This contains all of the information about the particular menu item. The *hwndSubMenu* field has the window handle of the submenu:

```
hwndSysSubMenu = miSysMenu.hwndSubMenu ;
```

POORMENU then sends this submenu three MM_INSERTITEM messages to add three items to the system menu—a separator bar and two text strings:

```
for (iItem = 0 ; iItem < 3 ; iItem++)
     WinSendMsg (hwndSysSubMenu, MM_INSERTITEM,
```

```
                MPFROMP (mi + iItem),
                MPFROMP (szMenuText [iItem])) ;
```

The *mi* and *szMenuText* arrays are defined near the top of *ClientWndProc*. Figure 13.1 shows the new system menu in POORMENU.

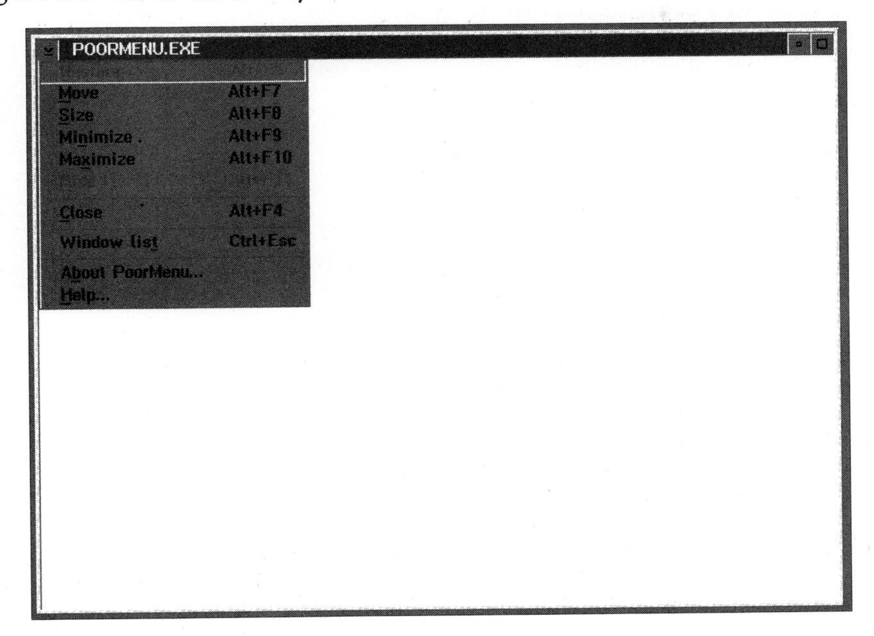

Figure 13.1: The POORMENU system menu

THE POP-UP MENU

Another unusual (but certainly not inadvisable) alternative is to display a menu somewhere other than near the top of the standard window, indeed anywhere within the client window. This is useful if your program requires a lot of mouse activity. In that case it would be more convenient for the user to invoke a menu without moving the mouse pointer to the top of the program's window. You could even have different menus depending on the area of the client window in which the user is working.

By convention, you invoke such detached pop-up menus using the right mouse button. This is because most Presentation Manager programs use the left mouse button for most mouse manipulations.

A special function—called *WinPopupMenu*—is available specifically for this purpose, and the POPMENU program shown in Listing 13.3 shows how to use it.

Listing 13.3: The POPMENU program

The POPMENU.MAK File

```
#----------------------
# POPMENU.MAK make file
#----------------------

popmenu.exe : popmenu.obj popmenu.def popmenu.res
     $(PRGLINK) popmenu, popmenu, NUL, $(PRGLIB), popmenu
     rc popmenu.res

popmenu.obj : popmenu.c popmenu.h
     $(PRGCC) popmenu.c

popmenu.res : popmenu.rc popmenu.h
     $(PRGRC) popmenu
```

The POPMENU.C File

```
/*-------------------------------------------
   POPMENU.C -- Popup Menu Demonstration
                (c) Charles Petzold, 1993
  -------------------------------------------*/

#define INCL_WIN
#include <os2.h>
#include "popmenu.h"

MRESULT EXPENTRY ClientWndProc (HWND, ULONG, MPARAM, MPARAM) ;
MRESULT EXPENTRY AboutDlgProc  (HWND, ULONG, MPARAM, MPARAM) ;

int main (void)
     {
     static CHAR  szClientClass[] = "PopMenu" ;
     static ULONG flFrameFlags = FCF_TITLEBAR      | FCF_SYSMENU  |
                                 FCF_SIZEBORDER    | FCF_MINMAX   |
                                 FCF_SHELLPOSITION | FCF_TASKLIST |
                                 FCF_MENU ;
     HAB          hab ;
     HMQ          hmq ;
     HWND         hwndFrame, hwndClient ;
     QMSG         qmsg ;

     hab = WinInitialize (0) ;
```

Listing 13.3: The POPMENU program (Continued)

```
     hmq = WinCreateMsgQueue (hab, 0) ;

     WinRegisterClass (hab, szClientClass, ClientWndProc, 0L, 0) ;

     hwndFrame = WinCreateStdWindow (HWND_DESKTOP, WS_VISIBLE,
                                     &flFrameFlags, szClientClass, NULL,
                                     0L, 0, ID_RESOURCE, &hwndClient) ;

     while (WinGetMsg (hab, &qmsg, NULLHANDLE, 0, 0))
          WinDispatchMsg (hab, &qmsg) ;

     WinDestroyWindow (hwndFrame) ;
     WinDestroyMsgQueue (hmq) ;
     WinTerminate (hab) ;
     return 0 ;
     }

MRESULT EXPENTRY ClientWndProc (HWND hwnd, ULONG msg, MPARAM mp1, MPARAM mp2)
     {
     static HWND hwndMenuPopup ;
     HPS         hps ;
     POINTL      ptlMouse ;

     switch (msg)
          {
          case WM_CREATE:
               hwndMenuPopup = WinLoadMenu (hwnd, 0, ID_RESOURCE) ;
               return 0 ;

          case WM_BUTTON2DOWN:
               ptlMouse.x = SHORT1FROMMP (mp1) ;
               ptlMouse.y = SHORT2FROMMP (mp1) ;

               WinMapWindowPoints (hwnd, HWND_DESKTOP, &ptlMouse, 1) ;

               WinPopupMenu (HWND_DESKTOP, hwnd, hwndMenuPopup,
                             ptlMouse.x, ptlMouse.y, 0,
                             PU_HCONSTRAIN   | PU_VCONSTRAIN   |
                             PU_MOUSEBUTTON1 | PU_MOUSEBUTTON2 |
                             PU_KEYBOARD) ;
               return 0 ;

          case WM_COMMAND:
               switch (COMMANDMSG(&msg)->cmd)
                    {
                    case IDM_ABOUT:
                         WinMessageBox (HWND_DESKTOP, hwnd,
                                        "PopMenu (c) Charles Petzold, 1993",
                                        "PopMenu", 0, MB_OK) ;
```

Listing 13.3: The POPMENU program (Continued)

```
                         return 0 ;
                         }
                    break ;

          case WM_PAINT:
                    hps = WinBeginPaint (hwnd, NULLHANDLE, NULL) ;
                    GpiErase (hps) ;
                    WinEndPaint (hps) ;
                    return 0 ;
          }
     return WinDefWindowProc (hwnd, msg, mp1, mp2) ;
     }
```

The POPMENU.RC File

```
/*----------------------------
   POPMENU.RC resource script
  ----------------------------*/

#include <os2.h>
#include "popmenu.h"

MENU ID_RESOURCE
     {
     SUBMENU "~File",                -1
          {
          MENUITEM "~New",                IDM_NEW
          MENUITEM "~Open",               IDM_OPEN
          MENUITEM "~Save",               IDM_SAVE
          MENUITEM "Save ~As",            IDM_SAVEAS
          MENUITEM SEPARATOR
          MENUITEM "A~bout PopMenu...", IDM_ABOUT
          }
     SUBMENU "~Edit",                -1
          {
          MENUITEM "Cu~t",                IDM_CUT
          MENUITEM "~Copy",               IDM_COPY
          MENUITEM "~Paste",              IDM_PASTE
          MENUITEM "C~lear",              IDM_CLEAR
          }
     SUBMENU "~Options",             -1
          {
          SUBMENU "~Color",          -1
               {
               MENUITEM "~Red",           IDM_RED
               MENUITEM "~Green",         IDM_GREEN
               MENUITEM "~Blue",          IDM_BLUE
               }
          SUBMENU "~Size",           -1
```

Listing 13.3: The POPMENU program (Continued)

```
              {
              MENUITEM "~Small",        IDM_SMALL
              MENUITEM "~Medium",       IDM_MEDIUM
              MENUITEM "~Large",        IDM_LARGE
              }
         SUBMENU "S~peed",         -1
              {
              MENUITEM "~Slow",         IDM_SLOW
              MENUITEM "~Medium",       IDM_MEDSPEED
              MENUITEM "~Fast",         IDM_FAST
              }
         }
    }
```

The POPMENU.H File

```
/*-----------------------
   POPMENU.H header file
  -----------------------*/

#define ID_RESOURCE       1

#define IDM_NEW           1
#define IDM_OPEN          2
#define IDM_SAVE          3
#define IDM_SAVEAS        4
#define IDM_ABOUT         5
#define IDM_CUT           6
#define IDM_COPY          7
#define IDM_PASTE         8
#define IDM_CLEAR         9
#define IDM_RED          10
#define IDM_GREEN        11
#define IDM_BLUE         12
#define IDM_SMALL        13
#define IDM_MEDIUM       14
#define IDM_LARGE        15
#define IDM_SLOW         16
#define IDM_MEDSPEED     17
#define IDM_FAST         18
```

The POPMENU.DEF File

```
;-----------------------------------
; POPMENU.DEF module definition file
;-----------------------------------

NAME           POPMENU   WINDOWAPI
```

Listing 13.3: The POPMENU program (Continued)

```
DESCRIPTION    'Popup Menu (c) Charles Petzold, 1993'
PROTMODE
```

The POPMENU.RC file has a single menu definition that the program uses for both the normal top-level menu and the detached pop-up menu. Note that the menu includes nested pop-ups. In a real program, you could have several detached pop-ups. *ClientWndProc* obtains the handle of this menu during the WM_CREATE message. When the program detects a WM_BUTTON2DOWN message, it obtains the mouse pointer coordinates and converts them to screen coordinates. This is necessary for the fourth and fifth parameters of *WinPopupMenu*. The last parameter is a series of flags. The PU_HCONSTRAIN and PU_VCONSTRAIN flags restrict the display of the menu to the client window. The PU_MOUSEBUTTON1, PU_MOUSEBUTTON2, and PU_KEYBOARD flags allow a variety of means for making a menu selection.

The detached pop-up menu is shown in Figure 13.2.

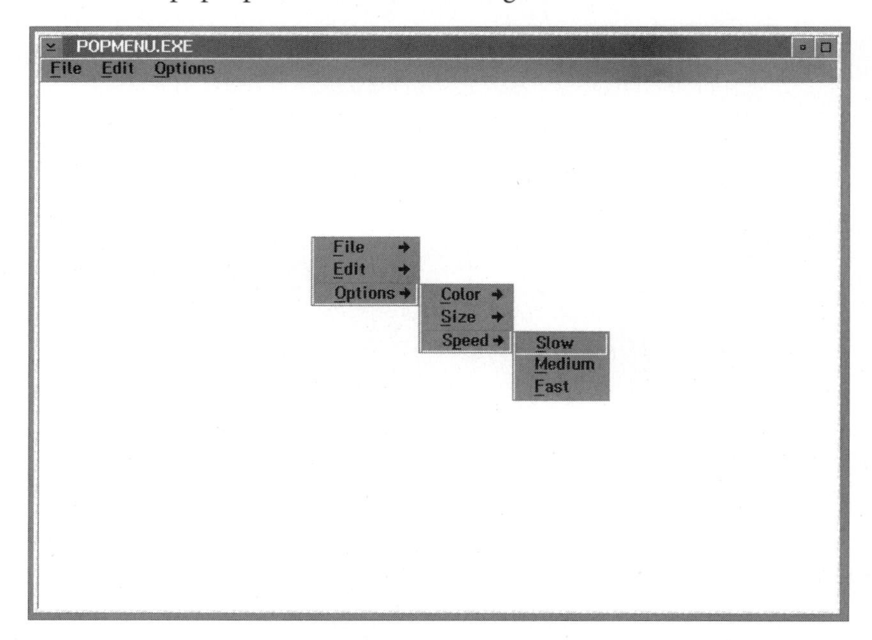

Figure 13.2: The POPMENU pop-up menu

USING GRAPHICS IN MENUS

You needn't always use text strings in menus; you can also use bitmaps. You either define these bitmaps as resources or create them right in the program. The GRAFMENU program, shown in Listing 13.4, takes the former approach.

Listing 13.4: The GRAFMENU program

The GRAFMENU.MAK File

```
#-----------------------
# GRAFMENU.MAK make file
#-----------------------

grafmenu.exe : grafmenu.obj grafmenu.def grafmenu.res
     $(PRGLINK) grafmenu, grafmenu, NUL, $(PRGLIB), grafmenu
     rc grafmenu.res

grafmenu.obj : grafmenu.c grafmenu.h
     $(PRGCC) grafmenu.c

grafmenu.res : grafmenu.rc grafmenu.h bighelp.bmp
     $(PRGRC) grafmenu
```

The GRAFMENU.C File

```
/*-----------------------------------------
   GRAFMENU.C -- A Menu with Graphics
                 (c) Charles Petzold, 1993
  -----------------------------------------*/

#define INCL_WIN
#define INCL_GPI
#include <os2.h>
#include "grafmenu.h"

MRESULT EXPENTRY ClientWndProc (HWND, ULONG, MPARAM, MPARAM) ;

CHAR szClientClass[] = "GrafMenu" ;

int main (void)
     {
     static ULONG flFrameFlags = FCF_TITLEBAR      | FCF_SYSMENU  |
                                 FCF_SIZEBORDER    | FCF_MINMAX   |
                                 FCF_SHELLPOSITION | FCF_TASKLIST |
                                 FCF_MENU ;
     HAB          hab ;
     HMQ          hmq ;
     HWND         hwndFrame, hwndClient ;
     QMSG         qmsg ;
```

Listing 13.4: The GRAFMENU program (Continued)

```
     hab = WinInitialize (0) ;
     hmq = WinCreateMsgQueue (hab, 0) ;

     WinRegisterClass (hab, szClientClass, ClientWndProc, 0L, 0) ;

     hwndFrame = WinCreateStdWindow (HWND_DESKTOP, WS_VISIBLE,
                                     &flFrameFlags, szClientClass, NULL,
                                     0L, 0, ID_RESOURCE, &hwndClient) ;

     while (WinGetMsg (hab, &qmsg, NULLHANDLE, 0, 0))
          WinDispatchMsg (hab, &qmsg) ;

     WinDestroyWindow (hwndFrame) ;
     WinDestroyMsgQueue (hmq) ;
     WinTerminate (hab) ;
     return 0 ;
     }

MRESULT EXPENTRY ClientWndProc (HWND hwnd, ULONG msg, MPARAM mp1, MPARAM mp2)
     {
     static MENUITEM miBigHelp = { 0,                         // iPosition
                                   MIS_BITMAP | MIS_HELP,     // afStyle
                                   0,                         // afAttribute
                                   IDM_HELP,                  // id
                                   NULLHANDLE,                // hwndSubMenu
                                   NULLHANDLE } ;             // hItem
     FONTMETRICS     fm ;
     HBITMAP         hbm ;
     HPS             hps ;
     HWND            hwndMenu ;

     switch (msg)
          {
          case WM_CREATE:

                    /*----------------------
                       Load bitmap resource
                      ----------------------*/

               hps = WinGetPS (hwnd) ;
               GpiQueryFontMetrics (hps, sizeof fm, &fm) ;
               hbm = GpiLoadBitmap (hps, 0, IDB_BIGHELP,
                                    64 * fm.lAveCharWidth / 3,
                                    64 * fm.lMaxBaselineExt / 8) ;
               WinReleasePS (hps) ;

                    /*-----------------------
                       Attach bitmap to menu
                      -----------------------*/
```

Listing 13.4: The GRAFMENU program (Continued)

```
          miBigHelp.hItem = (ULONG) hbm ;

          hwndMenu = WinWindowFromID (
                          WinQueryWindow (hwnd, QW_PARENT),
                          FID_MENU) ;

          WinSendMsg (hwndMenu, MM_SETITEM,
                      MPFROM2SHORT (0, TRUE), MPFROMP (&miBigHelp)) ;
          return 0 ;

     case WM_COMMAND:
          switch (COMMANDMSG(&msg)->cmd)
               {
               case IDM_NEW:
               case IDM_OPEN:
               case IDM_SAVE:
               case IDM_SAVEAS:
               case IDM_ABOUT:
                    WinAlarm (HWND_DESKTOP, WA_NOTE) ;
                    return 0 ;
               }
          break ;

     case WM_HELP:
          WinMessageBox (HWND_DESKTOP, hwnd,
                         "Help not yet implemented",
                         szClientClass, 0, MB_OK | MB_WARNING) ;
          return 0 ;

     case WM_ERASEBACKGROUND:
          return MRFROMSHORT (1) ;
     }
return WinDefWindowProc (hwnd, msg, mp1, mp2) ;
}
```

The GRAFMENU.RC File

```
/*---------------------------------
   GRAFMENU.RC resource script file
  ---------------------------------*/

#include <os2.h>
#include "grafmenu.h"

BITMAP IDB_BIGHELP bighelp.bmp

MENU ID_RESOURCE
     {
```

Listing 13.4: The GRAFMENU program (Continued)

```
    SUBMENU "~File",         IDM_FILE
         {
         MENUITEM "~New",                IDM_NEW
         MENUITEM "~Open...",            IDM_OPEN
         MENUITEM "~Save",               IDM_SAVE
         MENUITEM "Save ~As...",         IDM_SAVEAS
         MENUITEM SEPARATOR
         MENUITEM "A~bout GrafMenu...",IDM_ABOUT
         MENUITEM "",                    IDM_HELP
         }
    }
```

The BIGHELP.BMP Image

The GRAFMENU.H File

```
/*------------------------
   GRAFMENU.H header file
  ------------------------*/

#define ID_RESOURCE      1

#define IDB_BIGHELP      1

#define IDM_FILE         1

#define IDM_NEW          10
#define IDM_OPEN         11
#define IDM_SAVE         12
#define IDM_SAVEAS       13
#define IDM_ABOUT        14
#define IDM_HELP         15
```

Listing 13.4: The GRAFMENU program (Continued)

The GRAFMENU.DEF File

```
;------------------------------------
; GRAFMENU.DEF module definition file
;------------------------------------

NAME           GRAFMENU  WINDOWAPI

DESCRIPTION    'Graphics Menu (c) Charles Petzold, 1993'
PROTMODE
```

The BIGHELP.BMP file is a 64-by-64 bitmap created in the Icon Editor. In designing the bitmap, I tried to capture the frazzled emotions of a person attempting to learn a new program. The bitmap is included as a resource in GRAFMENU.RC and is given the resource name ID of IDB_BIGHELP. The definition of GRAFMENU's menu has an empty string as the last menu item:

```
MENU ID_RESOURCE
     {
     SUBMENU "~File",                IDM_FILE
          {
          MENUITEM "~New",                     IDM_NEW
          MENUITEM "~Open...",                 IDM_OPEN
          MENUITEM "~Save",                    IDM_SAVE
          MENUITEM "Save ~As...",              IDM_SAVEAS
          MENUITEM SEPARATOR
          MENUITEM "A~bout GrafMenu...",       IDM_ABOUT
          MENUITEM "",                         IDM_HELP
          }
     }
```

This is the menu item that will use the bitmap.

During the WM_CREATE message, GRAFMENU calls *WinQueryFontMetrics* to obtain the size of a system font character. When the bitmap is loaded into memory, it is stretched in proportion to the character size:

```
hbm = GpiLoadBitmap (hps, NULL, IDB_BIGHELP,
                     64 * fm.lAveCharWidth / 3,
                     64 * fm.lMaxBaselineExt / 8) ;
```

Thus, regardless of the video display resolution, the bitmap will appear in a size relative to the other text in the menu.

GRAFMENU defines a structure named *miBigHelp* of type MENUITEM that is already initialized with everything except the handle of the bitmap. Setting the *hItem* field to the bitmap handle requires an assignment statement:

```
miBigHelp.hItem = (ULONG) hbm ;
```

The program then obtains the window handle of its menu:

```
hwndMenu = WinWindowFromID (
                WinQueryWindow (hwnd, QW_PARENT),
                FID_MENU);
```

and sends the menu an MM_SETITEM message:

```
WinSendMsg (hwndMenu, MM_SETITEM,
            MPFROM2SHORT (Ø, TRUE), MPFROMP (&miBigHelp)) ;
```

When the user now pulls down the File menu, the big, bitmapped "Help" offers a comforting beacon of hope, as shown in Figure 13.3.

Figure 13.3: The GRAFMENU menu

In desperation the user chooses that option, and GRAFMENU responds by displaying the message box: "Help not yet implemented." Oh, well.

Two games

I don't know if you've realized it yet, but with the introduction of menus to our arsenal of Presentation Manager programming tools, we have reached the point where we can code up a few games.

Even if you're a hardcore corporate programmer with no time for frivolous activities, I hope you won't recoil at this thought. There is a reason why games are often some of the first programs to be written for graphical user interfaces. Games are heavily interactive, and they tend to be graphics-intensive and require fast feedback to the user. So, creating games is an excellent way for programmers to gain experience with the keyboard, mouse, and graphics.

JEU DE TAQUIN

The first example is not exactly a game, but more of a puzzle. It was invented in the 1870s, probably by the famous puzzle-maker Sam Loyd. For a while it was all the rage, particularly in Europe, and was known under various names, including the 15-puzzle, the 14-15 puzzle, and (in France) Jeu de Taquin, meaning "teasing game."

In its classic form, the puzzle consists of 15 square blocks, numbered 1 through 15. The squares are arranged in a 4-by-4 grid, leaving one blank space. You can move the squares around the grid by shifting a square horizontally or vertically into the blank space, which in turn opens a different blank space.

As Sam Loyd presented it, the numbered squares were arranged in consecutive order, except with the 14 and 15 reversed. He offered $1,000 to anyone who could find a way to shift the squares around to correct the order of the 14 and 15. No one collected the reward because, from that starting point, the puzzle is insolvable.

A mathematical analysis of the 14-15 puzzle appeared in an 1879 article in the *American Journal of Mathematics.* If you're interested, the underlying math is summarized in Volume 4 of *The World of Mathematics,* by James R. Newman (1956, republished in 1988 by Tempus Books, an imprint of Microsoft Press.)

This was one of the first puzzles created for the Apple Macintosh (where it was imaginatively called PUZZLE), and also appeared in early versions of the Microsoft Windows Software Development Kit, where it was called MUZZLE. (Trivia note: MUZZLE was the only program that demonstrated how to write for Windows using Microsoft Pascal.) Both these programs initially displayed the 15 squares in consecutive (solved) order and presented a menu option to scramble the squares. Using the mouse, you can attempt to restore the order of the squares or put them into different orders, such as going down the columns rather than across the rows.

I've called my PM version TAQUIN, and it's shown in Listing 13.5.

Listing 13.5: The TAQUIN program

The TAQUIN.MAK File

```
#----------------------
# TAQUIN.MAK make file
#----------------------

taquin.exe : taquin.obj taquin.def taquin.res
     $(PRGLINK) taquin, taquin, NUL, $(PRGLIB), taquin
     rc taquin.res

taquin.obj : taquin.c taquin.h
     $(PRGCC) taquin.c

taquin.res : taquin.rc taquin.h taquin.ico
     $(PRGRC) taquin
```

The TAQUIN.C File

```
/*--------------------------------------
   TAQUIN.C -- Jeu de Taquin
               (c) Charles Petzold, 1993
  --------------------------------------*/

#define INCL_WIN
#define INCL_GPI
#include <os2.h>
#include <stdlib.h>
#include <stdio.h>
#include "taquin.h"

#define NUMROWS        4       // greater than or equal to 2
#define NUMCOLS        4       // greater than or equal to 3
#define SCRAMBLEREP  100       // make larger if using more than 16 squares
#define SQUARESIZE    67       // in 1/100th inch

MRESULT EXPENTRY ClientWndProc (HWND, ULONG, MPARAM, MPARAM) ;

int main (void)
     {
     static CHAR  szClientClass[] = "Taquin" ;
     static ULONG flFrameFlags = FCF_SYSMENU  | FCF_TITLEBAR  |
                                 FCF_BORDER   | FCF_MINBUTTON |
                                 FCF_MENU     | FCF_ICON      |
                                 FCF_TASKLIST ;
     HAB          hab ;
```

Listing 13.5: The TAQUIN program (Continued)

```
     HMQ          hmq ;
     HWND         hwndFrame, hwndClient ;
     QMSG         qmsg ;

     hab = WinInitialize (0) ;
     hmq = WinCreateMsgQueue (hab, 0) ;

     WinRegisterClass (hab, szClientClass, ClientWndProc, 0L, 0) ;

     hwndFrame = WinCreateStdWindow (HWND_DESKTOP, WS_VISIBLE,
                                     &flFrameFlags, szClientClass, NULL,
                                     0L, 0, ID_RESOURCE, &hwndClient) ;

     while (WinGetMsg (hab, &qmsg, NULLHANDLE, 0, 0))
          WinDispatchMsg (hab, &qmsg) ;

     WinDestroyWindow (hwndFrame) ;
     WinDestroyMsgQueue (hmq) ;
     WinTerminate (hab) ;
     return 0 ;
     }

MRESULT EXPENTRY ClientWndProc (HWND hwnd, ULONG msg, MPARAM mp1, MPARAM mp2)
     {
     static INT aiPuzzle[NUMROWS][NUMCOLS],
                iBlankRow, iBlankCol, cxSquare, cySquare ;
     CHAR       szNum[10] ;
     HPS        hps ;
     HWND       hwndFrame ;
     INT        iRow, iCol, iMouseRow, iMouseCol, i ;
     POINTL     ptl ;
     RECTL      rcl, rclInvalid, rclIntersect ;
     SIZEL      sizl ;

     switch (msg)
          {
          case WM_CREATE:
                              // Calculate square size in pixels

               hps = WinGetPS (hwnd) ;
               sizl.cx = sizl.cy = 0 ;
               GpiSetPS (hps, &sizl, PU_LOENGLISH) ;
               ptl.x = SQUARESIZE ;
               ptl.y = SQUARESIZE ;
               GpiConvert (hps, CVTC_PAGE, CVTC_DEVICE, 1L, &ptl) ;
               WinReleasePS (hps) ;

               cxSquare = ptl.x ;
               cySquare = ptl.y ;
```

Listing 13.5: The TAQUIN program (Continued)

```
                              // Calculate client window size and position

          rcl.xLeft   = (WinQuerySysValue (HWND_DESKTOP, SV_CXSCREEN) -
                                        NUMCOLS * cxSquare) / 2 ;
          rcl.yBottom = (WinQuerySysValue (HWND_DESKTOP, SV_CYSCREEN) -
                                        NUMROWS * cySquare) / 2 ;
          rcl.xRight  = rcl.xLeft   + NUMCOLS * cxSquare ;
          rcl.yTop    = rcl.yBottom + NUMROWS * cySquare ;

                              // Set frame window position and size

          hwndFrame = WinQueryWindow (hwnd, QW_PARENT) ;
          WinCalcFrameRect (hwndFrame, &rcl, FALSE) ;
          WinSetWindowPos  (hwndFrame, NULLHANDLE,
                            rcl.xLeft, rcl.yBottom,
                            rcl.xRight - rcl.xLeft,
                            rcl.yTop - rcl.yBottom,
                            SWP_MOVE | SWP_SIZE | SWP_ACTIVATE) ;

                              // Initialize the aiPuzzle array

          WinSendMsg (hwnd, WM_COMMAND, MPFROMSHORT (IDM_NORMAL), NULL) ;
          return 0 ;

     case WM_PAINT:
          hps = WinBeginPaint (hwnd, NULLHANDLE, &rclInvalid) ;

                              // Draw the squares

          for (iRow = NUMROWS - 1 ; iRow >= 0 ; iRow--)
               for (iCol = 0 ; iCol < NUMCOLS ; iCol++)
                    {
                    rcl.xLeft   = cxSquare * iCol ;
                    rcl.yBottom = cySquare * iRow ;
                    rcl.xRight  = rcl.xLeft   + cxSquare ;
                    rcl.yTop    = rcl.yBottom + cySquare ;

                    if (!WinIntersectRect (0, &rclIntersect,
                                           &rcl, &rclInvalid))
                         continue ;

                    if (iRow == iBlankRow && iCol == iBlankCol)
                         WinFillRect (hps, &rcl, CLR_BLACK) ;
                    else
                         {
                         WinDrawBorder (hps, &rcl, 5, 5,
                                        CLR_PALEGRAY, CLR_DARKGRAY,
                                        DB_STANDARD | DB_INTERIOR) ;
```

Listing 13.5: The TAQUIN program (Continued)

```
                              WinDrawBorder (hps, &rcl, 2, 2,
                                             CLR_BLACK, ØL, DB_STANDARD) ;

                              sprintf (szNum, "%d", aiPuzzle[iRow][iCol]) ;

                              WinDrawText (hps, -1, szNum,
                                           &rcl, CLR_WHITE, CLR_DARKGRAY,
                                           DT_CENTER | DT_VCENTER) ;
                              }
                         }
               WinEndPaint (hps) ;
               return Ø ;

          case WM_BUTTON1DOWN:
               iMouseCol = MOUSEMSG(&msg)->x / cxSquare ;
               iMouseRow = MOUSEMSG(&msg)->y / cySquare ;

                              // Check if mouse was in valid area

               if ( iMouseRow < Ø          || iMouseCol < Ø          ||
                    iMouseRow >= NUMROWS   || iMouseCol >= NUMCOLS   ||
                   (iMouseRow != iBlankRow && iMouseCol != iBlankCol) ||
                   (iMouseRow == iBlankRow && iMouseCol == iBlankCol))
                         break ;

                              // Move a row right or left

               if (iMouseRow == iBlankRow)
                    {
                    if (iMouseCol < iBlankCol)
                         for (iCol = iBlankCol ; iCol > iMouseCol ; iCol--)
                              aiPuzzle[iBlankRow][iCol] =
                                   aiPuzzle[iBlankRow][iCol - 1] ;
                    else
                         for (iCol = iBlankCol ; iCol < iMouseCol ; iCol++)
                              aiPuzzle[iBlankRow][iCol] =
                                   aiPuzzle[iBlankRow][iCol + 1] ;
                    }
                              // Move a column up or down
               else
                    {
                    if (iMouseRow < iBlankRow)
                         for (iRow = iBlankRow ; iRow > iMouseRow ; iRow--)
                              aiPuzzle[iRow][iBlankCol] =
                                   aiPuzzle[iRow - 1][iBlankCol] ;
                    else
                         for (iRow = iBlankRow ; iRow < iMouseRow ; iRow++)
                              aiPuzzle[iRow][iBlankCol] =
```

Listing 13.5: The TAQUIN program (Continued)

```
                              aiPuzzle[iRow + 1][iBlankCol] ;
               }
                         // Calculate invalid rectangle

          rcl.xLeft   = cxSquare *  min (iMouseCol, iBlankCol) ;
          rcl.yBottom = cySquare *  min (iMouseRow, iBlankRow) ;
          rcl.xRight  = cxSquare * (max (iMouseCol, iBlankCol) + 1) ;
          rcl.yTop    = cySquare * (max (iMouseRow, iBlankRow) + 1) ;

                         // Set new array and blank values

          iBlankRow = iMouseRow ;
          iBlankCol = iMouseCol ;
          aiPuzzle[iBlankRow][iBlankCol] = 0 ;

                         // Invalidate rectangle

          WinInvalidateRect (hwnd, &rcl, FALSE) ;
          break ;

     case WM_CHAR:
          if (!(CHARMSG(&msg)->fs & KC_VIRTUALKEY) ||
                CHARMSG(&msg)->fs & KC_KEYUP)
                    return 0 ;

                         // Mimic a WM_BUTTON1DOWN message

          iMouseCol = iBlankCol ;
          iMouseRow = iBlankRow ;

          switch (CHARMSG(&msg)->vkey)
               {
               case VK_LEFT:   iMouseCol++ ;  break ;
               case VK_RIGHT:  iMouseCol-- ;  break ;
               case VK_UP:     iMouseRow-- ;  break ;
               case VK_DOWN:   iMouseRow++ ;  break ;
               default:        return 0 ;
               }
          WinSendMsg (hwnd, WM_BUTTON1DOWN,
                      MPFROM2SHORT (iMouseCol * cxSquare,
                                    iMouseRow * cySquare), NULL) ;
          return 0 ;

     case WM_COMMAND:
          switch (COMMANDMSG(&msg)->cmd)
               {
                         // Initialize aiPuzzle array

               case IDM_NORMAL:
```

Listing 13.5: The TAQUIN program (Continued)

```
               case IDM_INVERT:
                    for (iRow = Ø ; iRow < NUMROWS ; iRow++)
                         for (iCol = Ø ; iCol < NUMCOLS ; iCol++)
                              aiPuzzle[iRow][iCol] = iCol + 1 +
                                   NUMCOLS * (NUMROWS - iRow - 1) ;

                    if (COMMANDMSG(&msg)->cmd == IDM_INVERT)
                         {
                         aiPuzzle[Ø][NUMCOLS-2] = NUMCOLS * NUMROWS - 2 ;
                         aiPuzzle[Ø][NUMCOLS-3] = NUMCOLS * NUMROWS - 1 ;
                         }
                    aiPuzzle[iBlankRow = Ø][iBlankCol = NUMCOLS - 1] = Ø ;
                    WinInvalidateRect (hwnd, NULL, FALSE) ;
                    return Ø ;

                         // Randomly scramble the squares

               case IDM_SCRAMBLE:
                    WinSetPointer (HWND_DESKTOP, WinQuerySysPointer (
                                   HWND_DESKTOP, SPTR_WAIT, FALSE)) ;

                    srand ((int) WinGetCurrentTime (Ø)) ;

                    for (i = Ø ; i < SCRAMBLEREP ; i++)
                         {
                         WinSendMsg (hwnd, WM_BUTTON1DOWN,
                              MPFROM2SHORT (rand() % NUMCOLS * cxSquare,
                                   iBlankRow * cySquare), NULL) ;
                         WinUpdateWindow (hwnd) ;

                         WinSendMsg (hwnd, WM_BUTTON1DOWN,
                              MPFROM2SHORT (iBlankCol * cxSquare,
                                   rand() % NUMROWS * cySquare), NULL) ;
                         WinUpdateWindow (hwnd) ;
                         }
                    WinSetPointer (HWND_DESKTOP, WinQuerySysPointer (
                                   HWND_DESKTOP, SPTR_ARROW, FALSE));
                    return Ø ;
               }
          break ;
     }
return WinDefWindowProc (hwnd, msg, mp1, mp2) ;
}
```

The TAQUIN.RC File

```
/*---------------------------
   TAQUIN.RC resource script
  ---------------------------*/
```

Listing 13.5: The TAQUIN program (Continued)

```
#include <os2.h>
#include "taquin.h"

POINTER ID_RESOURCE taquin.ico

MENU ID_RESOURCE
     {
     SUBMENU  "~Options",                         -1
          {
          MENUITEM "~Normal Reset",               IDM_NORMAL
          MENUITEM "~Inverted Reset",             IDM_INVERT
          MENUITEM "~Scramble",                   IDM_SCRAMBLE
          }
     }
```

The TAQUIN.ICO File

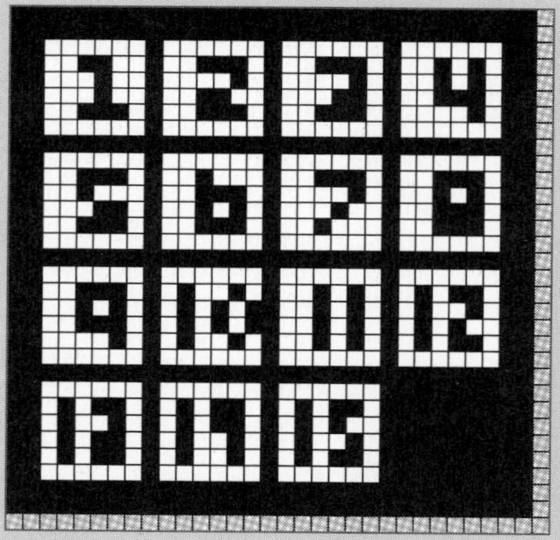

The TAQUIN.H File

```
/*---------------------
   TAQUIN.H header file
  ---------------------*/

#define ID_RESOURCE  1

#define IDM_NORMAL   1
#define IDM_INVERT   2
#define IDM_SCRAMBLE 3
```

Listing 13.5: The TAQUIN program (Continued)

The TAQUIN.DEF File

```
;----------------------------------
; TAQUIN.DEF module definition file
;----------------------------------

NAME           TAQUIN    WINDOWAPI

DESCRIPTION    'Jeu de Taquin (c) Charles Petzold, 1993'
PROTMODE
```

The menu is quite simple, listing just three options: resetting the squares, resetting them with the 14 and 15 reversed, and scrambling them. Beyond the menu processing, the program is mostly devoted to the graphics of drawing the puzzle and the mouse processing.

A LIFE PROGRAM

The game of Life was invented by Cambridge mathematician John Conway and popularized by Martin Gardner in his "Mathematical Games" columns in *Scientific American.* It has been a favorite of programmers ever since. Gardner's columns on Life are collected in his book *Wheels, Life, and Other Mathematical Amusements* (W. H. Freeman and Co., 1983). "Some Facts of Life," by David J. Buckingham (*Byte,* December 1978), is one of the best articles on the subject. *Hackers,* by Steven Levy (Anchor Press/Doubleday, 1984), has some good stories on early addictions to Life at MIT.

The Life playing board is a grid. Each cell in the grid can be either "alive" or "empty." You begin by defining a pattern of live cells. Then you take (or rather, the Life program takes) the grid through successive generations. For each new generation, a cell can die (change from alive to empty) or be born (change from empty to alive) based on the contents of the cell's eight immediate neighbors.

If a live cell has one or no neighbors, it dies from loneliness. If a live cell has four or more neighbors, it dies from overpopulation. If an empty cell has exactly three neighbors, a new cell is born.

The Presentation Manager version of Life is shown in Listing 13.6.

Listing 13.6: The LIFE program

The LIFE.MAK File

```
#-------------------
# LIFE.MAK make file
#-------------------

life.exe : life.obj life.def life.res
     $(PRGLINK) life, life, NUL, $(PRGLIB), life
     rc life.res

life.obj : life.c life.h
     $(PRGCC) life.c

life.res : life.rc life.h life.ico
     $(PRGRC) life
```

The LIFE.C File

```
/*--------------------------------------
   LIFE.C -- John Conway's Game of Life
             (c) Charles Petzold, 1993
  --------------------------------------*/

#define INCL_WIN
#define INCL_GPI
#include <os2.h>
#include <stdlib.h>
#include <stdio.h>
#include <string.h>
#include "life.h"

#define ID_TIMER    1
#define GRID(x,y)   (pbGrid [(y) * xNumCells + (x)])

MRESULT EXPENTRY ClientWndProc (HWND, ULONG, MPARAM, MPARAM) ;

CHAR szClientClass [] = "Life" ;

int main (void)
     {
     static ULONG flFrameFlags = FCF_TITLEBAR       | FCF_SYSMENU  |
                                 FCF_SIZEBORDER     | FCF_MINMAX   |
                                 FCF_SHELLPOSITION  | FCF_TASKLIST |
                                 FCF_MENU           | FCF_ICON ;
     HAB          hab ;
     HMQ          hmq ;
     HWND         hwndFrame, hwndClient ;
     QMSG         qmsg ;
```

Listing 13.6: The LIFE program (Continued)

```
     hab = WinInitialize (0) ;
     hmq = WinCreateMsgQueue (hab, 0) ;

     WinRegisterClass (hab, szClientClass, ClientWndProc, CS_SIZEREDRAW, 0) ;

     hwndFrame = WinCreateStdWindow (HWND_DESKTOP, WS_VISIBLE,
                                     &flFrameFlags, szClientClass, NULL,
                                     0L, 0, ID_RESOURCE, &hwndClient) ;

     while (WinGetMsg (hab, &qmsg, NULLHANDLE, 0, 0))
          WinDispatchMsg (hab, &qmsg) ;

     WinDestroyWindow (hwndFrame) ;
     WinDestroyMsgQueue (hmq) ;
     WinTerminate (hab) ;
     return 0 ;
     }

VOID ErrorMsg (HWND hwnd, CHAR *szMessage)
     {
     WinMessageBox (HWND_DESKTOP, hwnd, szMessage, szClientClass, 0,
                    MB_OK | MB_WARNING) ;
     }

VOID DrawCell (HPS hps, INT x, INT y, INT cxCell, INT cyCell, BYTE bCell)
     {
     RECTL rcl ;

     rcl.xLeft   = x * cxCell ;
     rcl.yBottom = y * cyCell ;
     rcl.xRight  = rcl.xLeft   + cxCell - 1 ;
     rcl.yTop    = rcl.yBottom + cyCell - 1 ;

     WinFillRect (hps, &rcl, (bCell & 1) ? CLR_NEUTRAL : CLR_BACKGROUND) ;
     }

VOID DoGeneration (HPS hps, PBYTE pbGrid, INT xNumCells, INT yNumCells,
                   INT cxCell, INT cyCell)
     {
     INT x, y, sSum ;

     for (y = 0 ; y < yNumCells - 1 ; y++)
          for (x = 0 ; x < xNumCells ; x++)
               {
               if (x == 0 || x == xNumCells - 1 || y == 0)
                    GRID (x,y) |= GRID (x,y) << 4 ;
               else
                    {
```

Listing 13.6: The LIFE program (Continued)

```
                    sSum = (GRID (x - 1, y     ) +              // Left
                            GRID (x - 1, y - 1) +              // Lower Left
                            GRID (x    , y - 1) +              // Lower
                            GRID (x + 1, y - 1)) >> 4 ;        // Lower Right

                    sSum += GRID (x + 1, y     ) +              // Right
                            GRID (x + 1, y + 1) +              // Upper Right
                            GRID (x    , y + 1) +              // Upper
                            GRID (x - 1, y + 1) ;              // Upper Left

                    sSum = (sSum | GRID (x, y)) & 0x0F ;

                    GRID (x, y) <<= 4 ;

                    if (sSum == 3)
                         GRID (x, y) |= 1 ;

                    if (GRID (x, y) != GRID (x, y) >> 4)
                         DrawCell (hps, x, y, cxCell, cyCell, GRID (x, y)) ;
                    }
               }
     }

VOID DisplayGenerationNum (HPS hps, INT xGen, INT yGen, INT iGeneration)
     {
     static CHAR szBuffer [24] = "Generation " ;
     POINTL      ptl ;

     ptl.x = xGen ;
     ptl.y = yGen ;

     sprintf (szBuffer + 11, "%d", iGeneration) ;

     GpiSavePS (hps) ;

     GpiSetBackMix (hps, BM_OVERPAINT) ;
     GpiCharStringAt (hps, &ptl, strlen (szBuffer), szBuffer) ;

     GpiRestorePS (hps, -1L) ;
     }

MRESULT EXPENTRY ClientWndProc (HWND hwnd, ULONG msg, MPARAM mp1, MPARAM mp2)
     {
     static BOOL  fTimerGoing ;
     static HAB   hab ;
     static HWND  hwndMenu ;
     static INT   iGeneration, cxChar, cyChar, cyDesc, cxClient, cyClient,
                  xGenNum, yGenNum, cxCell, cyCell, xNumCells, yNumCells,
                  iScaleCell = 2 ;
```

Listing 13.6: The LIFE program (Continued)

```
     static PBYTE pbGrid ;
     FONTMETRICS  fm ;
     HPS          hps ;
     INT          x, y ;
     POINTL       ptl ;

     switch (msg)
          {
          case WM_CREATE:
               hab = WinQueryAnchorBlock (hwnd) ;

               hps = WinGetPS (hwnd) ;
               GpiQueryFontMetrics (hps, sizeof fm, &fm) ;
               cxChar = fm.lAveCharWidth ;
               cyChar = fm.lMaxBaselineExt ;
               cyDesc = fm.lMaxDescender ;
               WinReleasePS (hps) ;

               hwndMenu = WinWindowFromID (
                                WinQueryWindow (hwnd, QW_PARENT),
                                FID_MENU) ;
               return 0 ;

          case WM_SIZE:
               if (pbGrid != NULL)
                    {
                    free (pbGrid) ;
                    pbGrid = NULL ;
                    }

               if (fTimerGoing)
                    {
                    WinStopTimer (hab, hwnd, ID_TIMER) ;
                    fTimerGoing = FALSE ;
                    }

               cxClient = SHORT1FROMMP (mp2) ;
               cyClient = SHORT2FROMMP (mp2) ;

               xGenNum = cxChar ;
               yGenNum = cyClient - cyChar + cyDesc ;

               cxCell = cxChar * 2 / iScaleCell ;
               cyCell = cyChar / iScaleCell ;

               xNumCells = cxClient / cxCell ;
               yNumCells = (cyClient - cyChar) / cyCell ;

               if (xNumCells <= 0 || yNumCells <= 0)
```

Listing 13.6: The LIFE program (Continued)

```
               ErrorMsg (hwnd, "Not enough room for even one cell.") ;

          else if (NULL == (pbGrid = calloc (xNumCells, yNumCells)))
               ErrorMsg (hwnd, "Not enough memory for this many cells.") ;

          WinEnableMenuItem (hwndMenu, IDM_SIZE,  TRUE) ;
          WinEnableMenuItem (hwndMenu, IDM_START, pbGrid != NULL) ;
          WinEnableMenuItem (hwndMenu, IDM_STOP,  FALSE) ;
          WinEnableMenuItem (hwndMenu, IDM_STEP,  pbGrid != NULL) ;
          WinEnableMenuItem (hwndMenu, IDM_CLEAR, pbGrid != NULL) ;

          iGeneration = 0 ;
          return 0 ;

     case WM_BUTTON1DOWN:
          x = MOUSEMSG(&msg)->x / cxCell ;
          y = MOUSEMSG(&msg)->y / cyCell ;

          if (pbGrid != NULL && !fTimerGoing && x < xNumCells &&
                                                 y < yNumCells)
               {
               hps = WinGetPS (hwnd) ;
               DrawCell (hps, x, y, cxCell, cyCell, GRID (x, y) ^= 1) ;
               WinReleasePS (hps) ;
               }
          else
               WinAlarm (HWND_DESKTOP, WA_WARNING) ;
          break ;

     case WM_COMMAND:
          switch (COMMANDMSG(&msg)->cmd)
               {
               case IDM_LARGE:
               case IDM_SMALL:
               case IDM_TINY:
                    WinCheckMenuItem (hwndMenu, iScaleCell, FALSE) ;
                    iScaleCell = COMMANDMSG(&msg)->cmd ;
                    WinCheckMenuItem (hwndMenu, iScaleCell, TRUE) ;

                    WinSendMsg (hwnd, WM_SIZE, NULL,
                                MPFROM2SHORT (cxClient, cyClient)) ;

                    WinInvalidateRect (hwnd, NULL, FALSE) ;
                    return 0 ;

               case IDM_START:
                    if (!WinStartTimer (hab, hwnd, ID_TIMER, 1))
                         ErrorMsg (hwnd, "Too many clocks or timers.") ;
                    else
```

Listing 13.6: The LIFE program (Continued)

```
                    {
                    fTimerGoing = TRUE ;

                    WinEnableMenuItem (hwndMenu, IDM_SIZE,  FALSE) ;
                    WinEnableMenuItem (hwndMenu, IDM_START, FALSE) ;
                    WinEnableMenuItem (hwndMenu, IDM_STOP,  TRUE) ;
                    WinEnableMenuItem (hwndMenu, IDM_STEP,  FALSE) ;
                    WinEnableMenuItem (hwndMenu, IDM_CLEAR, FALSE) ;
                    }
               return Ø ;

          case IDM_STOP:
               WinStopTimer (hab, hwnd, ID_TIMER) ;
               fTimerGoing = FALSE ;

               WinEnableMenuItem (hwndMenu, IDM_SIZE,  TRUE) ;
               WinEnableMenuItem (hwndMenu, IDM_START, TRUE) ;
               WinEnableMenuItem (hwndMenu, IDM_STOP,  FALSE) ;
               WinEnableMenuItem (hwndMenu, IDM_STEP,  TRUE) ;
               WinEnableMenuItem (hwndMenu, IDM_CLEAR, TRUE) ;
               return Ø ;

          case IDM_STEP:
               WinSendMsg (hwnd, WM_TIMER, NULL, NULL) ;
               return Ø ;

          case IDM_CLEAR:
               iGeneration = ØL ;
               memset (pbGrid, Ø, xNumCells * yNumCells) ;
               WinInvalidateRect (hwnd, NULL, FALSE) ;
               return Ø ;
          }
     break ;

case WM_TIMER:
     hps = WinGetPS (hwnd) ;

     DisplayGenerationNum (hps, xGenNum, yGenNum, ++iGeneration) ;
     DoGeneration (hps, pbGrid, xNumCells, yNumCells, cxCell, cyCell);

     WinReleasePS (hps) ;
     return Ø ;

case WM_PAINT:
     hps = WinBeginPaint (hwnd, NULLHANDLE, NULL) ;
     GpiErase (hps) ;

     if (pbGrid != NULL)
          {
          for (x = 1 ; x <= xNumCells ; x++)
```

Listing 13.6: The LIFE program (Continued)

```
                    {
                    ptl.x = cxCell * x - 1 ;
                    ptl.y = Ø ;
                    GpiMove (hps, &ptl) ;

                    ptl.y = cyCell * yNumCells - 1 ;
                    GpiLine (hps, &ptl) ;
                    }

               for (y = 1 ; y <= yNumCells ; y++)
                    {
                    ptl.x = Ø ;
                    ptl.y = cyCell * y - 1 ;
                    GpiMove (hps, &ptl) ;

                    ptl.x = cxCell * xNumCells - 1 ;
                    GpiLine (hps, &ptl) ;
                    }

               for (y = Ø ; y < yNumCells ; y++)
                    for (x = Ø ; x < xNumCells ; x++)
                         if (GRID (x, y) & 1)
                              DrawCell (hps, x, y, cxCell, cyCell,
                                             GRID (x, y)) ;

               DisplayGenerationNum (hps, xGenNum, yGenNum, iGeneration) ;
               }
          WinEndPaint (hps) ;
          return Ø ;

     case WM_DESTROY:
          if (fTimerGoing)
               WinStopTimer (hab, hwnd, ID_TIMER) ;

          if (pbGrid != NULL)
               free (pbGrid) ;

          return Ø ;
     }
return WinDefWindowProc (hwnd, msg, mp1, mp2) ;
}
```

The LIFE.RC File

```
/*------------------------------
   LIFE.RC resource script file
  ------------------------------*/

#include <os2.h>
```

Listing 13.6: The LIFE program (Continued)

```
#include "life.h"

POINTER ID_RESOURCE life.ico

MENU ID_RESOURCE
     {
     SUBMENU "~Cell-Size",     IDM_SIZE
          {
          MENUITEM "~Large",  IDM_LARGE
          MENUITEM "~Small",  IDM_SMALL,, MIA_CHECKED
          MENUITEM "~Tiny",   IDM_TINY
          }
     MENUITEM "~Start!",       IDM_START
     MENUITEM "S~top!",        IDM_STOP,,  MIA_DISABLED
     MENUITEM "Ste~p!",        IDM_STEP
     MENUITEM "C~lear!",       IDM_CLEAR
     }
```

The LIFE.ICO File

The LIFE.H File

```
/*--------------------
   LIFE.H header file
  --------------------*/

#define ID_RESOURCE       1

#define IDM_SIZE          10

#define IDM_LARGE         1          /* Values used in      */
```

Listing 13.6: The LIFE program (Continued)

```
#define IDM_SMALL          2          /*   program logic     */
#define IDM_TINY           4          /*   for cell size     */

#define IDM_CLEAR          20
#define IDM_START          21
#define IDM_STOP           22
#define IDM_STEP           23
```

The LIFE.DEF File

```
;-------------------------------
; LIFE.DEF module definition file
;-------------------------------

NAME          LIFE      WINDOWAPI

DESCRIPTION   'Game of Life Program (c) Charles Petzold, 1993'
PROTMODE
```

The LIFE.RC resource script defines one submenu that specifies the size of the cells, and four top-level items without submenus: Start, Stop, Step, and Clear. I made these items part of the top-level menu so you can more easily choose them with the mouse. By convention, items on the top-level menu that don't invoke submenus are followed by exclamation points.

You can use the mouse to toggle cells between an alive and an empty state. You start the program by choosing Start from the top-level menu. LIFE uses a timer to advance through the generations. You stop the timer by choosing Stop. You can advance through the generations manually with Step. The grid is cleared when you choose Clear from the top-level menu or when you change the cell size. Changing the size of the window also clears the grid.

I won't describe the workings of this program because little of the logic is related to menu processing. However, note that the program often enables and disables some menu items when the user chooses a menu item. The program can then avoid extensive testing during processing of the WM_COMMAND message. For example, when LIFE gets a WM_COMMAND message indicating that Start has been chosen from the menu, it doesn't have to check whether the timer is already going, because once the timer is going, the Start option is disabled. I think of this technique as an active rather than a passive approach to testing the validity of menu items. At the time a menu item becomes invalid, you send the menu a message to disable the item. Then you don't have to worry about getting WM_COMMAND messages for that menu item.

Dialog Boxes

THE SIMPLE "ABOUT" BOX

A MORE COMPLEX DIALOG BOX

MODELESS DIALOG BOXES

Chapter 14

We have already looked at several ways a Presentation Manager program can obtain input from the user. The most rudimentary is the direct processing of keyboard and mouse input to the program's client window. But we have also seen how a program can create child control windows (such as buttons, scroll bars, and menus) either implicitly as part of the standard window or explicitly with *WinCreateWindow* calls. These control windows provide a layer of processing between user input and the program.

Now we'll go one step further and create dialog boxes. A *dialog box* is a window that contains various child control windows. Programs generally use dialog boxes to obtain user input beyond that which can easily be handled in a menu. A menu item can indicate with an ellipsis (...) that it invokes a dialog box.

You define the layout of control windows in a dialog box by creating a dialog box template as part of the resource script file. In your program you create a dialog box window based on this template. You're essentially farming out to the Presentation Manager the job of creating, sizing, and positioning all control windows within the dialog box window.

In Chapter 11 we created control windows on the surface of the program's client window, and we encountered some difficulties in handling the keyboard interface. When you create a dialog box, these problems go away. The dialog box logic within the Presentation Manager implements a keyboard interface that allows the user to move the input focus between controls using the Tab key and the cursor movement keys.

Dialog boxes come in two flavors: modal and modeless. The modal dialog box is the most common. When a program creates a *modal dialog box*, the user can switch control to another window in the program only after the dialog box is destroyed. A *modeless dialog box* is more akin to a normal top-level window that you might create in your program (such as those in the WELCOME2 program in Chapter 3). The user can switch control between the dialog box and the program's client window. With one exception (the HEXCALC program), all of the dialog boxes in this chapter are modal dialog boxes.

THE SIMPLE "ABOUT" BOX

One simple modal dialog box is often called an "About" box. Traditionally, this dialog box is invoked when a user chooses the menu option About, usually from the Help submenu. (In the productivity tools included with OS/2 2.1, the menu item that invokes such a dialog box is called Product Information.) The dialog box usually contains a one- or two-line description of the program, a copyright notice, the program's icon, and a single push button labeled "OK." Pressing the spacebar or the Enter key destroys the dialog box. The ABOUT1 program, shown in Listing 14.1, does little but display a standard About box.

Figure 14.1 shows the ABOUT1 dialog box.

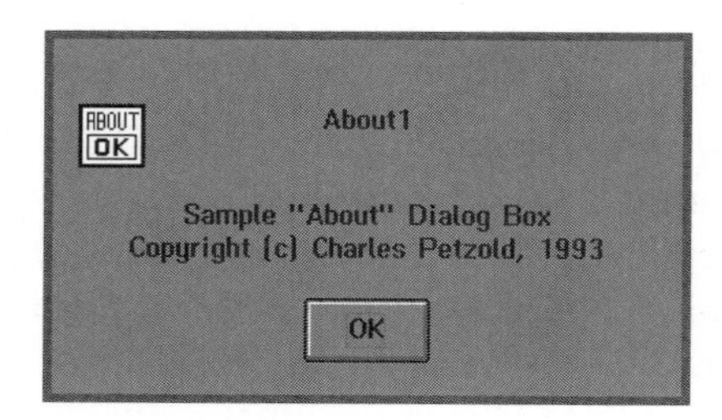

Figure 14.1: The ABOUT1 dialog box

THE DIALOG BOX TEMPLATE

The first step in adding a dialog box to a program is to create a template that describes the layout of child control windows within the dialog box window. You create a dialog box template in one of two ways. It's easiest to use the Dialog Editor program supplied as part of the IBM C Developer's WorkSet/2, or the Borland C+++ Resource Workshop. This programs can save a dialog box template as an ASCII file with the extension .DLG. You then include the DLG file in your RC resource script file using the following statement:

```
rcinclude mydialog.dlg
```

Listing 14.1: The ABOUT1 program

The ABOUT1.MAK File

```
#---------------------
# ABOUT1.MAK make file
#---------------------

about1.exe : about1.obj about1.def about1.res
     $(PRGLINK) about1, about1, NUL, $(PRGLIB), about1
     rc about1.res

about1.obj : about1.c about.h
     $(PRGCC) about1.c

about1.res : about1.rc about.h about.ico
     $(PRGRC) about1
```

The ABOUT1.C File

```
/*-----------------------------------------------------------
   ABOUT1.C -- Demonstration of About Box Dialog Procedure
               (c) Charles Petzold, 1993
  -----------------------------------------------------------*/

#define INCL_WIN
#include <os2.h>
#include "about.h"

MRESULT EXPENTRY ClientWndProc (HWND, ULONG, MPARAM, MPARAM) ;
MRESULT EXPENTRY AboutDlgProc  (HWND, ULONG, MPARAM, MPARAM) ;

int main (void)
     {
     static CHAR  szClientClass[] = "About1" ;
     static ULONG flFrameFlags = FCF_TITLEBAR      | FCF_SYSMENU |
                                 FCF_SIZEBORDER    | FCF_MINMAX  |
                                 FCF_SHELLPOSITION | FCF_TASKLIST |
                                 FCF_MENU          | FCF_ICON ;
     HAB          hab ;
     HMQ          hmq ;
     HWND         hwndFrame, hwndClient ;
     QMSG         qmsg ;

     hab = WinInitialize (0) ;
     hmq = WinCreateMsgQueue (hab, 0) ;

     WinRegisterClass (hab, szClientClass, ClientWndProc, 0L, 0) ;

     hwndFrame = WinCreateStdWindow (HWND_DESKTOP, WS_VISIBLE,
                                    &flFrameFlags, szClientClass, NULL,
```

Listing 14.1: The ABOUT1 program (Continued)

```
                                   ØL, Ø, ID_RESOURCE, &hwndClient) ;

     while (WinGetMsg (hab, &qmsg, NULLHANDLE, Ø, Ø))
          WinDispatchMsg (hab, &qmsg) ;

     WinDestroyWindow (hwndFrame) ;
     WinDestroyMsgQueue (hmq) ;
     WinTerminate (hab) ;
     return Ø ;
     }

MRESULT EXPENTRY ClientWndProc (HWND hwnd, ULONG msg, MPARAM mp1, MPARAM mp2)
     {
     switch (msg)
          {
          case WM_COMMAND:
               switch (COMMANDMSG(&msg)->cmd)
                    {
                    case IDM_NEW:
                    case IDM_OPEN:
                    case IDM_SAVE:
                    case IDM_SAVEAS:
                         WinAlarm (HWND_DESKTOP, WA_NOTE) ;
                         return Ø ;

                    case IDM_ABOUT:
                         WinDlgBox (HWND_DESKTOP, hwnd, AboutDlgProc,
                                    NULLHANDLE, IDD_ABOUT, NULL) ;
                         return Ø ;
                    }
               break ;

          case WM_ERASEBACKGROUND:
               return MRFROMSHORT (1) ;
          }
     return WinDefWindowProc (hwnd, msg, mp1, mp2) ;
     }

MRESULT EXPENTRY AboutDlgProc (HWND hwnd, ULONG msg, MPARAM mp1, MPARAM mp2)
     {
     switch (msg)
          {
          case WM_COMMAND:
               switch (COMMANDMSG(&msg)->cmd)
                    {
                    case DID_OK:
                    case DID_CANCEL:
                         WinDismissDlg (hwnd, TRUE) ;
                         return Ø ;
                    }
```

Listing 14.1: The ABOUT1 program (Continued)

```
               break ;
          }
     return WinDefDlgProc (hwnd, msg, mp1, mp2) ;
     }
```

The ABOUT1.H File

```
/*----------------------
   ABOUT1.H header file
  ----------------------*/

#define ID_RESOURCE      1

#define IDM_FILE         1

#define IDM_NEW          10
#define IDM_OPEN         11
#define IDM_SAVE         12
#define IDM_SAVEAS       13
#define IDM_ABOUT        14

#define IDD_ABOUT        1
```

The ABOUT1.RC File

```
/*-------------------------------
   ABOUT1.RC resource script file
  -------------------------------*/

#include <os2.h>
#include "about.h"

POINTER ID_RESOURCE about.ico

MENU ID_RESOURCE
     {
     SUBMENU "~File",          IDM_FILE
          {
          MENUITEM "~New",                IDM_NEW
          MENUITEM "~Open...",            IDM_OPEN
          MENUITEM "~Save",               IDM_SAVE
          MENUITEM "Save ~As...",         IDM_SAVEAS
          MENUITEM SEPARATOR
          MENUITEM "A~bout...",           IDM_ABOUT
          }
     }

DLGTEMPLATE IDD_ABOUT
  {
  DIALOG "", 0, 32, 32, 200, 88,, FCF_DLGBORDER
```

Listing 14.1: The ABOUT1 program (Continued)

```
     {
     CTEXT    "About1"                            -1, 10, 64, 180,  8
     ICON     ID_RESOURCE                         -1,  8, 56,   0,  0
     CTEXT    "Sample ""About"" Dialog Box"       -1, 10, 40, 180,  8
     CTEXT    "Copyright (c) Charles Petzold, 1993" -1, 10, 32, 180,  8
     DEFPUSHBUTTON "OK"                       DID_OK, 80,  8,  40, 16, WS_GROUP
     }
  }
```

The ABOUT.ICO Image

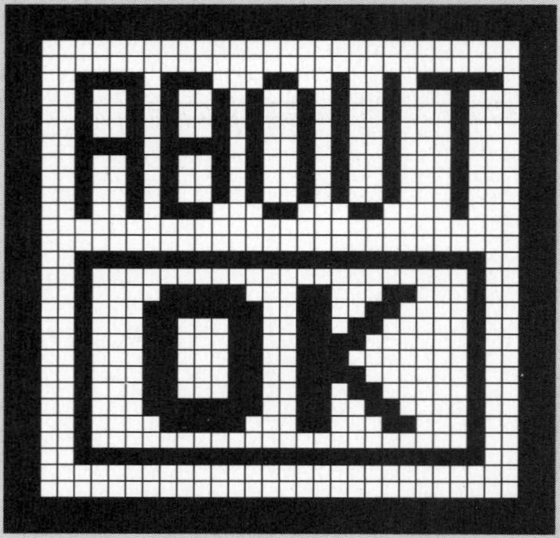

The ABOUT1.DEF File

```
;-----------------------------------
; ABOUT1.DEF module definition file
;-----------------------------------

NAME           ABOUT1    WINDOWAPI

DESCRIPTION    'Sample About Box Dialog Procedure (c) Charles Petzold, 1993'
PROTMODE
```

You can also create the dialog box template manually, right in the resource script file. This is what I've chosen to do. The dialog box template in ABOUT1.RC looks like this:

```
DLGTEMPLATE IDD_ABOUT
     {
     DIALOG "", 0, 32, 32, 200, 88,, FCF_DLGBORDER
```

```
        {
        CTEXT "ABOUT1"                             -1, 10, 64, 180, 8
        ICON ID_RESOURCE                           -1,  8, 56,   0, 0
        CTEXT "Sample ""About"" Dialog Box"        -1, 10, 40, 180, 8
        CTEXT "Copyright (C) Charles Petzold, 1993" -1, 10, 32, 180, 8
        DEFPUSHBUTTON "OK"                     DID_OK, 80,  8,  40,
             16, WS_GROUP
        }
    }
```

The keyword DLGTEMPLATE identifies this resource as a dialog box template. (You can use the keyword WINDOWTEMPLATE as a synonym for DLGTEMPLATE.) The resource compiler converts this template to a binary form and stores it in the program's EXE file with a resource type ID of RT_DIALOG. The IDD_ABOUT identifier, which is defined in ABOUT1.H as 1, is the resource name ID.

The definition of the dialog box is enclosed in a pair of curly brackets or between BEGIN and END statements. Within this first set of curly braces you define one (and only one) main window. In the ABOUT1 dialog box template, this window is specified by the DIALOG statement. The various child control windows within this dialog box are then nested in another set of curly braces following the DIALOG statement.

Using the DIALOG statement implies that the dialog box window is to be based on the WC_FRAME window class, the same window class used to create a standard frame window. The general format of the DIALOG statement is as follows:

```
DIALOG "text", ChildID, x, y, width, height [,window style] [,creation flags]
```

The "text" field is the text that would appear in the dialog box's title bar if it had one. (Some modal dialog boxes do; some do not.) Because the dialog box window will be a top-level window, the Child ID field isn't important, so in this example it's set to 0.

The next four fields specify the position and size of the dialog box window. The *x* and *y* values are the position of the lower-left corner of the dialog box window relative to the lower-left corner of its owner, which is usually the program's client window. These coordinates and sizes are *not* in units of pixels; they're in special units used only in dialog box templates. I'll describe the dialog box coordinate system in the next section.

The optional window style field of the DIALOG statement is a combination of identifiers beginning with WS ("window style"), just like the window style used in the *WinCreateStdWindow* function. WS_VISIBLE is not required for a modal dialog box. This is followed by creation flags beginning with FCF, like the *flFrameFlags* parameter passed to the *WinCreateStdWindow* function. The FCF_DLGBORDER flag is normal for a modal dialog box and causes the dialog box to have a normal dialog box border.

Following the DIALOG statement is a set of curly braces enclosing other statements that define all child control windows to be created on the surface of the dialog box window. In the ABOUT1 dialog box template, these statements begin with CTEXT, ICON, and DEFPUSHBUTTON, all of which are keywords recognized by the resource compiler. The CTEXT keyword stands for "centered text." CTEXT specifies a control window based on the WC_STATIC window class with the following window style:

```
SS_TEXT | DT_CENTER | WS_GROUP
```

This should look somewhat familiar, because we used the WC_STATIC class and the SS_TEXT window style in the COLORSCR program in Chapter 11. (I'll discuss the WS_GROUP identifier later in this chapter.) Our dialog box template has three CTEXT statements for the dialog box's three lines of centered text.

The CTEXT statement has a format similar to that of the DIALOG statement:

```
CTEXT "text", ChildID, x, y, width, height [, window style]
```

The "text" field is the window's text. In the ABOUT1 dialog box template, the *ChildID* field for the CTEXT control windows is set to –1 because the child ID isn't used by the program. The *x* and *y* fields specify the position of the lower-left corner of the control window relative to the lower-left corner of the dialog box window. For the optional window style field, you can use WS ("window style") or SS ("static style") identifiers to alter the default style of the control window.

The ICON statement specifies another window based on the WC_STATIC class, this one with a window style of

```
SS_ICON | WS_GROUP
```

The ICON statement has a format similar to the CTEXT statement, except that the first field is the resource name ID of an icon. The height and width fields are ignored because icons have a standard size based on the resolution of the display.

The DEFPUSHBUTTON statement specifies a push button based on the window class WC_BUTTON with the window style

```
BS_PUSHBUTTON | BS_DEFAULT | WS_TABSTOP
```

The BS_DEFAULT style makes this a default push button, which has a wider border than a normal button. I'll discuss the WS_TABSTOP style later in this chapter. The child ID of this push button is set to DID_OK. This is an identifier defined in PMWIN.H that is often used for default push buttons in dialog boxes.

The dialog box template in ABOUT1.RC thus defines six windows. The parent is based on the WC_DIALOG window class and has five children. Four of the children are based on the WC_STATIC window class, and the fifth is based on WC_BUTTON.

DIALOG BOX COORDINATES

The coordinates and sizes specified in the DIALOG, CTEXT, ICON, and DEFPUSHBUTTON statements are in special units used only within dialog box templates. The horizontal (*x*) coordinates and sizes are in units of one fourth the average width of a system font character; the vertical (*y*) coordinates and sizes are in units of one eighth the height of a system font character. Thus the ABOUT1 dialog box has a width of 50 characters (200 units) and a height of 11 characters (88 units). These special dialog box coordinates allow you to design dialog box templates that retain the same general appearance regardless of the resolution of the video display. Because a system font character is roughly twice as high as it is wide, the horizontal and vertical coordinates are about the same.

For the dialog box window itself, the position of the window is relative to the lower-left corner of its owner (which is generally the client window in the program that displays the dialog box). The positions of the control windows are relative to the lower-left corner of their parent, which is the dialog box window.

You'll note that the height of the CTEXT window controls in ABOUT1 is 8 units. That's one character. The height of the push button is 16 units (two characters) because the height must include the border of the button. For static text controls, the minimum width of the window in dialog box units must be four times the number of characters. To determine the minimum width of a push button, add 2 to the number of characters and then multiply by 4.

THE DIALOG PROCEDURE

A program that includes a dialog box must have a dialog procedure that processes messages to the dialog window. This dialog procedure looks a lot like a normal window procedure. The *AboutDlgProc* dialog procedure in ABOUT1.C looks like this:

```
MRESULT EXPENTRY AboutDlgProc (HWND hwnd, ULONG msg, MPARAM mp1, MPARAM mp2)
     {
     switch (msg)
          {
```

```
          case WM_COMMAND:
               switch (COMMANDMSG(&msg)->cmd)
                    {
                    case DID_OK:
                    case DID_CANCEL:
                         WinDismissDlg (hwnd, TRUE) ;
                         return Ø ;
                    }
                break ;
          }       return WinDefDlgProc (hwnd, msg, mp1, mp2) ;
     }
```

Within AboutDlgProc, the *hwnd* parameter is the window handle of the dialog box window.

Dialog procedures are often much simpler than client window procedures because they needn't worry about painting the window or processing keyboard or mouse input. Aside from possible initialization, a dialog procedure does little but process messages from child window controls on the dialog box window. *AboutDlgProc* processes only the WM_COMMAND message that the push button sends to its owner when the button is clicked on.

The dialog procedure calls *WinDefDlgProc* rather than *WinDefWindowProc* for all messages it doesn't process. This is one major difference between a dialog procedure and a window procedure. There are some other differences that I'll discuss in more detail later in this chapter. (For example, a dialog procedure doesn't receive a WM_CREATE message. Instead, you must do initialization during the special WM_INITDLG message.)

The dialog box destroys itself by calling *WinDismissDlg*. In *AboutDlgProc*, it does this when it receives a WM_COMMAND message with the low USHORT of *mp1* (the child window ID or *cmd* field when using the COMMANDMSG macro) equal to DID_OK or DID_CANCEL.

The push button window sends a WM_COMMAND message to its owner (the dialog box window) when the user clicks on the push button or presses the spacebar when the push button has the input focus. The low USHORT of *mp1* is the push button's child ID, which is DID_OK.

AboutDlgProc also calls *WinDismissDlg* when it receives a WM_COMMAND message with the low USHORT of *mp1* equal to DID_CANCEL. This message is generated by *WinDefDlgProc* when the user presses the Escape key. Thus, we're also allowing the user to get rid of the dialog box by pressing Escape. When the user presses the Enter key, *WinDefDlgProc* generates a WM_COMMAND message with the low USHORT of *mp1* equal to the child ID of the default push button in the dialog box. This is another part of the keyboard interface that the Presentation Manager adds to control windows organized in a dialog box. When this dialog box is displayed, the user can make it go away by pressing the spacebar, Enter key, or Escape key or by clicking the button with the mouse.

CREATING THE DIALOG BOX WINDOW

A program creates a modal dialog box window by calling *WinDlgBox*. ABOUT1 calls *WinDlgBox* from *ClientWndProc* when the user selects About from the program's menu:

```
WinDlgBox (HWND_DESKTOP, hwnd, AboutDlgProc,
           NULLHANDLE, IDD_ABOUT, NULL) ;
```

The parameter *AboutDlgProc* is the address of the dialog procedure; IDD_ABOUT is the resource name ID of the dialog box template. The *WinDlgBox* function creates the dialog box window and the child control windows based on the template and displays the dialog box. *AboutDlgProc* then processes messages to the dialog box window. When *AboutDlgProc* calls *WinDismissDlg*, the dialog box window is destroyed. Only then does the *WinDlgBox* function return control to *ClientWndProc*.

The general syntax of the *WinDlgBox* function is

```
ulResult = WinDlgBox (hwndParent, hwndOwner, lpfnDlgProc,
                      hmod, idResource, pCreateParams) ;
```

Dialog boxes are usually top-level windows, so *hwndParent* is set to HWND_DESKTOP. The dialog box is positioned relative to the lower-left corner of the window indicated by the *hwndOwner* parameter; this is usually the client window.

The *hmod* parameter is the module containing the dialog box template resource, and *idResource* is the resource name ID. As with all resources, specifying NULLHANDLE for *hmod* directs the Presentation Manager to load the resource from the program's EXE file. The *pCreateParams* parameter is a pointer that is passed to the dialog procedure during the WM_INITDLG message. (I'll explain how this works when we get to the PATTERNS program later in this chapter.)

The value returned from *WinDlgBox* is the second parameter passed to *WinDismissDlg* when the dialog window is destroyed. ABOUT1 doesn't check this value, but many dialog boxes contain two push buttons labeled OK and Cancel. Customarily, the dialog box procedure passes TRUE to *WinDismissDlg* when OK is clicked and FALSE when Cancel is clicked. Thus, the client window procedure can determine from the return value of *WinDlgProc* whether the dialog box was exited with OK or Cancel. (We'll find a use for this in the PATTERNS program.) Note also that the second parameter to *WinDismissDlg* and the return value from *WinDlgBox* are ULONGs, so this value need not be limited to a simple BOOL variable, and can indeed be a pointer.

The *WinDlgBox* function doesn't return until *WinDismissDlg* is called within the dialog procedure. While the dialog box is displayed, the program's other windows are disabled and can't receive user input. However, the client window procedure can still receive other messages such as WM_PAINT or WM_TIMER, so be alert to possible reentrance problems when you call *WinDlgBox*.

THE "NEW BUTTON" ABOUT BOX

You'll recall that in Chapter 11 you created your own window class for a new push button control. Let's use that new push button in a dialog box.

The statements in the ABOUT1.RC dialog box template beginning with the words CTEXT, ICON, and DEFPUSHBUTTON are simply convenient ways of defining what classes and styles of child window controls you want in the dialog box. Rather than use these keywords, you can use statements beginning with the keyword CONTROL or WINDOW. (The two keywords are synonymous.) The general syntax of a CONTROL statement is

```
CONTROL "text", ChildID, x, y, width, height, class [, style]
```

The second-to-last field is a window class. The last field (which is optional but almost always present) specifies the window style.

For example, rather than use

```
DEFPUSHBUTTON "OK", DID_OK, 80, 8, 40, 16, WS_GROUP
```

you can use

```
CONTROL "OK", DID_OK, 80, 8, 40, 16, WC_BUTTON,
     BS_PUSHBUTTON | BS_DEFAULT | WS_VISIBLE | WS_TABSTOP | WS_GROUP
```

These two statements are equivalent. With the exception of the WS_TABSTOP and WS_GROUP window styles (which I'll explain later in this chapter), the information in the CONTROL statement might clarify what the Presentation Manager does when it creates a dialog box. The various fields of the CONTROL statement translate into parameters used in a *WinCreateWindow* call: WC_BUTTON specifies the window class, BS_PUSHBUTTON and BS_DEFPUSHBUTTON are button styles, and WS_VISIBLE is a window style.

The DEFPUSHBUTTON keyword is recognized only by the resource compiler. The resource compiler constructs an entry in the binary RES file that contains all information explicitly indicated in the equivalent CONTROL statement. But one advantage of the CONTROL statement is that it lets you go beyond the predefined types of control keywords that the resource compiler recognizes.

For example, suppose you define a window class in your program with the name "NewBtn," as we did in Chapter 11. In that case you can use a CONTROL statement like this in a dialog box template:

```
CONTROL "OK", DID_OK, 80, 8, 40, 16, "NewBtn",
     WS_VISIBLE | WS_TABSTOP | WS_GROUP
```

Note that the "NewBtn" window class has replaced the WC_BUTTON identifier and that the BS_PUSHBUTTON and BS_DEFAULT identifiers have been removed. The only requirement is that you register the "NewBtn" class in the program before you call *WinDlgBox* for the first time.

To prove that this works, the ABOUT2 program shown in Listing 14.2 creates an About box with our new style of push button.

Listing 14.2: The ABOUT2 program

The ABOUT2.MAK File

```
#----------------------
# ABOUT2.MAK make file
#----------------------

about2.exe : about2.obj newbtn.obj about2.def about2.res
     $(PRGLINK) about2 newbtn, about2, NUL, $(PRGLIB), about2
     rc about2.res

about2.obj : about2.c about.h
     $(PRGCC) about2.c

newbtn.obj : newbtn.c
     $(PRGCC) newbtn.c

about2.res : about2.rc about.h about.ico
     $(PRGRC) about2
```

The ABOUT2.C File

```
/*------------------------------------------------------------
   ABOUT2.C -- Demonstration of About Box with New 3D Button
               (c) Charles Petzold, 1993
  ------------------------------------------------------------*/

#define INCL_WIN
#include <os2.h>
#include "about.h"

VOID APIENTRY RegisterNewBtnClass (HAB) ;         // In NEWBTN.C
```

Listing 14.2: The ABOUT2 program (Continued)

```
MRESULT EXPENTRY ClientWndProc (HWND, ULONG, MPARAM, MPARAM) ;
MRESULT EXPENTRY AboutDlgProc  (HWND, ULONG, MPARAM, MPARAM) ;

int main (void)
     {
     static CHAR  szClientClass[] = "About2" ;
     static ULONG flFrameFlags = FCF_TITLEBAR      | FCF_SYSMENU  |
                                 FCF_SIZEBORDER    | FCF_MINMAX   |
                                 FCF_SHELLPOSITION | FCF_TASKLIST |
                                 FCF_MENU          | FCF_ICON ;
     HAB          hab ;
     HMQ          hmq ;
     HWND         hwndFrame, hwndClient ;
     QMSG         qmsg ;

     hab = WinInitialize (0) ;
     hmq = WinCreateMsgQueue (hab, 0) ;

     RegisterNewBtnClass (hab) ;

     WinRegisterClass (hab, szClientClass, ClientWndProc, 0L, 0) ;

     hwndFrame = WinCreateStdWindow (HWND_DESKTOP, WS_VISIBLE,
                                     &flFrameFlags, szClientClass, NULL,
                                     0L, 0, ID_RESOURCE, &hwndClient) ;

     while (WinGetMsg (hab, &qmsg, NULLHANDLE, 0, 0))
          WinDispatchMsg (hab, &qmsg) ;

     WinDestroyWindow (hwndFrame) ;
     WinDestroyMsgQueue (hmq) ;
     WinTerminate (hab) ;
     return 0 ;
     }

MRESULT EXPENTRY ClientWndProc (HWND hwnd, ULONG msg, MPARAM mp1, MPARAM mp2)
     {
     switch (msg)
          {
          case WM_COMMAND:
               switch (COMMANDMSG(&msg)->cmd)
                    {
                    case IDM_NEW:
                    case IDM_OPEN:
                    case IDM_SAVE:
                    case IDM_SAVEAS:
                         WinAlarm (HWND_DESKTOP, WA_NOTE) ;
                         return 0 ;
```

Listing 14.2: The ABOUT2 program (Continued)

```
                    case IDM_ABOUT:
                         WinDlgBox (HWND_DESKTOP, hwnd, AboutDlgProc,
                                    NULLHANDLE, IDD_ABOUT, NULL) ;
                         return 0 ;
                    }
               break ;

          case WM_ERASEBACKGROUND:
               return MRFROMSHORT (1) ;
          }
     return WinDefWindowProc (hwnd, msg, mp1, mp2) ;
     }

MRESULT EXPENTRY AboutDlgProc (HWND hwnd, ULONG msg, MPARAM mp1, MPARAM mp2)
     {
     switch (msg)
          {
          case WM_COMMAND:
               switch (COMMANDMSG(&msg)->cmd)
                    {
                    case DID_OK:
                    case DID_CANCEL:
                         WinDismissDlg (hwnd, TRUE) ;
                         return 0 ;
                    }
               break ;
          }
     return WinDefDlgProc (hwnd, msg, mp1, mp2) ;
     }
```

The ABOUT2.RC File

```
/*-------------------------------
   ABOUT2.RC resource script file
  -------------------------------*/

#include <os2.h>
#include "about.h"

POINTER ID_RESOURCE about.ico

MENU ID_RESOURCE
     {
     SUBMENU "~File",          IDM_FILE
          {
          MENUITEM "~New",                IDM_NEW
```

Listing 14.2: The ABOUT2 program (Continued)

```
          MENUITEM "~Open...",            IDM_OPEN
          MENUITEM "~Save",               IDM_SAVE
          MENUITEM "Save ~As...",         IDM_SAVEAS
          MENUITEM SEPARATOR
          MENUITEM "A~bout...",           IDM_ABOUT
          }
     }

DLGTEMPLATE IDD_ABOUT
  {
  DIALOG "", 0, 32, 32, 200, 88,, FCF_DLGBORDER
    {
    CTEXT    "About2"                              -1, 10, 64, 180,  8
    ICON     ID_RESOURCE                           -1,  8, 56,   0,  0
    CTEXT    "Sample ""About"" Dialog Box"         -1, 10, 40, 180,  8
    CTEXT    "Copyright (c) Charles Petzold, 1993" -1, 10, 32, 180,  8
    CONTROL "OK"                               DID_OK, 80,  8,  40, 16,
                    "NewBtn", WS_VISIBLE | WS_TABSTOP | WS_GROUP
    }
  }
```

The ABOUT2.DEF File

```
;-----------------------------------
; ABOUT2.DEF module definition file
;-----------------------------------

NAME           ABOUT2    WINDOWAPI

DESCRIPTION    'About Box with New Button (c) Charles Petzold, 1993'
PROTMODE
```

Compiling this program requires the NEWBTN.C file from Chapter 11 and the ABOUT.H and ABOUT.ICO files from Listing 14.1.

The ABOUT2.RC resource script file is the same as ABOUT1.RC, except that a CONTROL statement specifying the "NewBtn" window class replaces the DEFPUSHBUTTON statement in ABOUT1.RC. The ABOUT2.C program is nearly the same as ABOUT1.C, except that ABOUT2 calls the *RegisterNewBtn-Class* function (in NEWBTN.C) from *main*. Figure 14.2 shows the dialog box created by ABOUT2.

Figure 14.2: The ABOUT2 dialog box

A MORE COMPLEX DIALOG BOX

Now that we've mastered the basics, we're ready to create dialog boxes with more than just a single button. In Chapter 11 we wrote a program called DRAWLINE that created some radio buttons on its client window and drew a line based on a specified line pattern and color. The PATTDLG program, shown in Listing 14.3, is similar except that it uses a dialog box.

Listing 14.3: The PATTDLG program

The PATTDLG.MAK File

```
#----------------------
# PATTDLG.MAK make file
#----------------------

pattdlg.exe : pattdlg.obj pattdlg.def pattdlg.res
     $(PRGLINK) pattdlg, pattdlg, NUL, $(PRGLIB), pattdlg
     rc pattdlg.res

pattdlg.obj : pattdlg.c pattdlg.h
     $(PRGCC) pattdlg.c

pattdlg.res : pattdlg.rc pattdlg.h
     $(PRGRC) pattdlg
```

The PATTDLG.C File

```
/*------------------------------------------------
   PATTDLG.C -- Select GPI Patterns from Dialog Box
                (c) Charles Petzold, 1993
  ------------------------------------------------*/

#define INCL_WIN
#define INCL_GPI
#include <os2.h>
```

Listing 14.3: The PATTDLG program (Continued)

```
#include "pattdlg.h"

typedef struct
     {
     INT  iPattern ;
     INT  iColor ;
     BOOL fBorder ;
     }
     PATTERNSDATA ;

typedef PATTERNSDATA *PPATTERNSDATA ;

MRESULT EXPENTRY ClientWndProc  (HWND, ULONG, MPARAM, MPARAM) ;
MRESULT EXPENTRY AboutDlgProc   (HWND, ULONG, MPARAM, MPARAM) ;
MRESULT EXPENTRY PatternDlgProc (HWND, ULONG, MPARAM, MPARAM) ;

#define WM_USER_QUERYSAVE (WM_USER + 1)

HAB  hab ;

int main (void)
     {
     static CHAR  szClientClass[] = "PattDlg" ;
     static ULONG flFrameFlags = FCF_TITLEBAR      | FCF_SYSMENU  |
                                 FCF_SIZEBORDER    | FCF_MINMAX   |
                                 FCF_SHELLPOSITION | FCF_TASKLIST |
                                 FCF_MENU ;
     HMQ          hmq ;
     HWND         hwndFrame, hwndClient ;
     QMSG         qmsg ;

     hab = WinInitialize (0) ;
     hmq = WinCreateMsgQueue (hab, 0) ;

     WinRegisterClass (hab, szClientClass, ClientWndProc, CS_SIZEREDRAW, 0) ;

     hwndFrame = WinCreateStdWindow (HWND_DESKTOP, WS_VISIBLE,
                                     &flFrameFlags, szClientClass, NULL,
                                     0L, 0, ID_RESOURCE, &hwndClient) ;

     while (WinGetMsg (hab, &qmsg, NULLHANDLE, 0, 0))
          WinDispatchMsg (hab, &qmsg) ;

     WinSendMsg (hwndClient, WM_USER_QUERYSAVE, NULL, NULL) ;

     WinDestroyWindow (hwndFrame) ;
     WinDestroyMsgQueue (hmq) ;
     WinTerminate (hab) ;
     return 0 ;
     }
```

Listing 14.3: The PATTDLG program (Continued)

```
MRESULT EXPENTRY ClientWndProc (HWND hwnd, ULONG msg, MPARAM mp1, MPARAM mp2)
     {
     static CHAR         szAppName [] = "PATTDLG" ;
     static CHAR         szKeyName [] = "SETTINGS" ;
     static INT          cxClient, cyClient ;
     static PATTERNSDATA pdCurrent = { IDD_DENSE1, IDD_BKGRND, TRUE } ;
     HPS                 hps ;
     POINTL              ptl ;
     ULONG               ulDataLength ;

     switch (msg)
          {
          case WM_CREATE:
               ulDataLength = sizeof pdCurrent ;

               PrfQueryProfileData (HINI_USERPROFILE, szAppName, szKeyName,
                                    &pdCurrent, & ulDataLength) ;
               return Ø ;

          case WM_SIZE:
               cxClient = SHORT1FROMMP (mp2) ;
               cyClient = SHORT2FROMMP (mp2) ;
               return Ø ;

          case WM_COMMAND:
               switch (COMMANDMSG(&msg)->cmd)
                    {
                    case IDM_PATTERNS:
                         if (WinDlgBox (HWND_DESKTOP, hwnd, PatternDlgProc,
                                        NULLHANDLE, IDD_PATTERNS, &pdCurrent))

                              WinInvalidateRect (hwnd, NULL, FALSE) ;
                         return Ø ;

                    case IDM_ABOUT:
                         WinDlgBox (HWND_DESKTOP, hwnd, AboutDlgProc,
                                    NULLHANDLE, IDD_ABOUT, NULL) ;
                         return Ø ;
                    }
               break ;

          case WM_PAINT:
               hps = WinBeginPaint (hwnd, NULLHANDLE, NULL) ;
               GpiErase (hps) ;

               GpiSetColor (hps, pdCurrent.iColor -
                                 IDD_BKGRND + CLR_BACKGROUND) ;

               GpiSetPattern (hps, pdCurrent.iPattern -
```

Listing 14.3: The PATTDLG program (Continued)

```
                                    IDD_DENSE1 + PATSYM_DENSE1) ;

               ptl.x = cxClient / 4 ;
               ptl.y = cyClient / 4 ;
               GpiMove (hps, &ptl) ;

               ptl.x *= 3 ;
               ptl.y *= 3 ;
               GpiBox (hps, pdCurrent.fBorder ? DRO_OUTLINEFILL : DRO_FILL,
                            &ptl, ØL, ØL) ;

               WinEndPaint (hps) ;
               return Ø ;

          case WM_USER_QUERYSAVE:
               if (MBID_YES == WinMessageBox (HWND_DESKTOP, hwnd,
                                   "Save current settings?", szAppName, Ø,
                                   MB_YESNO | MB_QUERY))

                    PrfWriteProfileData (HINI_USERPROFILE, szAppName, szKeyName,
                                        &pdCurrent, sizeof pdCurrent) ;
               return Ø ;
          }
     return WinDefWindowProc (hwnd, msg, mp1, mp2) ;
     }

MRESULT EXPENTRY AboutDlgProc (HWND hwnd, ULONG msg, MPARAM mp1, MPARAM mp2)
     {
     switch (msg)
          {
          case WM_COMMAND:
               switch (COMMANDMSG(&msg)->cmd)
                    {
                    case DID_OK:
                    case DID_CANCEL:
                         WinDismissDlg (hwnd, TRUE) ;
                         return Ø ;
                    }
               break ;
          }
     return WinDefDlgProc (hwnd, msg, mp1, mp2) ;
     }

MRESULT EXPENTRY PatternDlgProc (HWND hwnd, ULONG msg, MPARAM mp1, MPARAM mp2)
     {
     static PATTERNSDATA  pdLocal ;
     static PPATTERNSDATA ppdCurrent ;

     switch (msg)
          {
```

Listing 14.3: The PATTDLG program (Continued)

```
          case WM_INITDLG:
               ppdCurrent = PVOIDFROMMP (mp2) ;
               pdLocal = *ppdCurrent ;

               WinCheckButton (hwnd, pdLocal.iPattern, TRUE) ;
               WinCheckButton (hwnd, pdLocal.iColor,   TRUE) ;
               WinCheckButton (hwnd, IDD_BORDER,       pdLocal.fBorder) ;

               WinSetFocus (HWND_DESKTOP,
                            WinWindowFromID (hwnd, pdLocal.iPattern)) ;

               return MRFROMSHORT (1) ;

          case WM_CONTROL:
               if (SHORT1FROMMP (mp1) >= IDD_DENSE1 &&
                   SHORT1FROMMP (mp1) <= IDD_DIAGHATCH)
                    {
                    WinCheckButton (hwnd, pdLocal.iPattern, FALSE) ;
                    pdLocal.iPattern = SHORT1FROMMP (mp1) ;
                    WinCheckButton (hwnd, pdLocal.iPattern, TRUE) ;
                    }

               else if (SHORT1FROMMP (mp1) >= IDD_BKGRND &&
                        SHORT1FROMMP (mp1) <= IDD_PALEGRAY)
                    {
                    WinCheckButton (hwnd, pdLocal.iColor, FALSE) ;
                    pdLocal.iColor = SHORT1FROMMP (mp1) ;
                    WinCheckButton (hwnd, pdLocal.iColor, TRUE) ;
                    }
               return 0 ;

          case WM_COMMAND:
               switch (COMMANDMSG(&msg)->cmd)
                    {
                    case DID_OK:
                         pdLocal.fBorder = WinQueryButtonCheckstate
                                                  (hwnd, IDD_BORDER) ;
                         *ppdCurrent = pdLocal ;

                         WinDismissDlg (hwnd, TRUE) ;
                         return 0 ;

                    case DID_CANCEL:
                         WinDismissDlg (hwnd, FALSE) ;
                         return 0 ;
                    }
               break ;
          }
     return WinDefDlgProc (hwnd, msg, mp1, mp2) ;
     }
```

Listing 14.3: The PATTDLG program (Continued)

The PATTDLG.H File

```
/*----------------------
   PATTDLG.H header file
  ----------------------*/

#define ID_RESOURCE       1

#define IDM_SELECT        1

#define IDM_PATTERNS      10
#define IDM_ABOUT         11

#define IDD_ABOUT         1
#define IDD_PATTERNS      2

#define IDD_DENSE1        10
#define IDD_DIAGHATCH     (IDD_DENSE1 + 18)
#define IDD_BKGRND        30
#define IDD_PALEGRAY      (IDD_BKGRND + 15)
#define IDD_BORDER        50
```

The PATTDLG.RC File

```
/*--------------------------------
   PATTDLG.RC resource script file
  --------------------------------*/

#include <os2.h>
#include "pattdlg.h"

MENU ID_RESOURCE
     {
     SUBMENU "~Select",              IDM_SELECT
          {
          MENUITEM "~Pattern and Color...",  IDM_PATTERNS
          MENUITEM SEPARATOR
          MENUITEM "A~bout...",              IDM_ABOUT
          }
     }

DLGTEMPLATE IDD_ABOUT
  {
  DIALOG "", 0, 32, 32, 200, 88,, FCF_DLGBORDER
    {
    CTEXT "PattDlg"                             -1,  10, 64, 180,  8
    CTEXT "Select Patterns from Dialog Box"     -1,  10, 40, 180,  8
    CTEXT "Copyright (c) Charles Petzold, 1993" -1,  10, 32, 180,  8
```

Listing 14.3: The PATTDLG program (Continued)

```
    DEFPUSHBUTTON "OK"                    DID_OK,  80,  8,  40, 16, WS_GROUP
    }
  }

DLGTEMPLATE IDD_PATTERNS
  {
  DIALOG "", 0, 8, 8, 280, 194,, FCF_DLGBORDER
    {
    GROUPBOX      "Pattern"      -1,                  8,  30, 128, 158
    RADIOBUTTON   "Dense 1"      IDD_DENSE1 +  0,  12, 162,  56,  12, WS_GROUP
    RADIOBUTTON   "Dense 2"      IDD_DENSE1 +  1,  12, 148,  56,  12
    RADIOBUTTON   "Dense 3"      IDD_DENSE1 +  2,  12, 134,  56,  12
    RADIOBUTTON   "Dense 4"      IDD_DENSE1 +  3,  12, 120,  56,  12
    RADIOBUTTON   "Dense 5"      IDD_DENSE1 +  4,  12, 106,  56,  12
    RADIOBUTTON   "Dense 6"      IDD_DENSE1 +  5,  12,  92,  56,  12
    RADIOBUTTON   "Dense 7"      IDD_DENSE1 +  6,  12,  78,  56,  12
    RADIOBUTTON   "Dense 8"      IDD_DENSE1 +  7,  12,  64,  56,  12
    RADIOBUTTON   "Vert"         IDD_DENSE1 +  8,  12,  50,  56,  12
    RADIOBUTTON   "Horiz"        IDD_DENSE1 +  9,  12,  36,  56,  12
    RADIOBUTTON   "Diag 1"       IDD_DENSE1 + 10,  70, 162,  60,  12
    RADIOBUTTON   "Diag 2"       IDD_DENSE1 + 11,  70, 148,  60,  12
    RADIOBUTTON   "Diag 3"       IDD_DENSE1 + 12,  70, 134,  60,  12
    RADIOBUTTON   "Diag 4"       IDD_DENSE1 + 13,  70, 120,  60,  12
    RADIOBUTTON   "No Shade"     IDD_DENSE1 + 14,  70, 106,  60,  12
    RADIOBUTTON   "Solid"        IDD_DENSE1 + 15,  70,  92,  60,  12
    RADIOBUTTON   "Halftone"     IDD_DENSE1 + 16,  70,  78,  60,  12
    RADIOBUTTON   "Hatch"        IDD_DENSE1 + 17,  70,  64,  60,  12
    RADIOBUTTON   "Diag Hatch",  IDD_DENSE1 + 18,  70,  50,  60,  12
    GROUPBOX      "Color"        -1,              144,  58, 128, 130
    RADIOBUTTON   "Backgrnd"     IDD_BKGRND +  0, 148, 162,  56,  12, WS_GROUP
    RADIOBUTTON   "Blue"         IDD_BKGRND +  1, 148, 148,  56,  12
    RADIOBUTTON   "Red"          IDD_BKGRND +  2, 148, 134,  56,  12
    RADIOBUTTON   "Pink"         IDD_BKGRND +  3, 148, 120,  56,  12
    RADIOBUTTON   "Green"        IDD_BKGRND +  4, 148, 106,  56,  12
    RADIOBUTTON   "Cyan"         IDD_BKGRND +  5, 148,  92,  56,  12
    RADIOBUTTON   "Yellow"       IDD_BKGRND +  6, 148,  78,  56,  12
    RADIOBUTTON   "Neutral"      IDD_BKGRND +  7, 148,  64,  56,  12
    RADIOBUTTON   "Dk Gray"      IDD_BKGRND +  8, 212, 162,  56,  12
    RADIOBUTTON   "Dk Blue"      IDD_BKGRND +  9, 212, 148,  56,  12
    RADIOBUTTON   "Dk Red"       IDD_BKGRND + 10, 212, 134,  56,  12
    RADIOBUTTON   "Dk Pink"      IDD_BKGRND + 11, 212, 120,  56,  12
    RADIOBUTTON   "Dk Green"     IDD_BKGRND + 12, 212, 106,  56,  12
    RADIOBUTTON   "Dk Cyan"      IDD_BKGRND + 13, 212,  92,  56,  12
    RADIOBUTTON   "Brown"        IDD_BKGRND + 14, 212,  78,  56,  12
    RADIOBUTTON   "Pl Gray"      IDD_BKGRND + 15, 212,  64,  56,  12
    AUTOCHECKBOX  "Border"       IDD_BORDER,      148,  30,  56,  12, WS_GROUP
    DEFPUSHBUTTON "OK"           DID_OK,           66,   8,  52,  16, WS_GROUP
    PUSHBUTTON    "Cancel"       DID_CANCEL,      162,   8,  52,  16, WS_GROUP
    }
  }
```

Listing 14.3: The PATTDLG program (Continued)

The PATTDLG.DEF File

```
;-----------------------------------
; PATTDLG.DEF module definition file
;-----------------------------------

NAME          PATTDLG   WINDOWAPI

DESCRIPTION   'Select GPI Pattterns from Dialog Box (c) Charles Petzold, 1993'
PROTMODE
```

PATTDLG draws a filled rectangle in its client window using the *GpiBox* function. You use the dialog box to select the fill pattern and color and to choose whether you want a border. The dialog box (shown in Figure 14.3) contains one group of radio buttons for the pattern and another group for the color, one check box for the border, and the two push buttons OK and Cancel. Clicking the Cancel button destroys the dialog box without changing PATTERNS's client window.

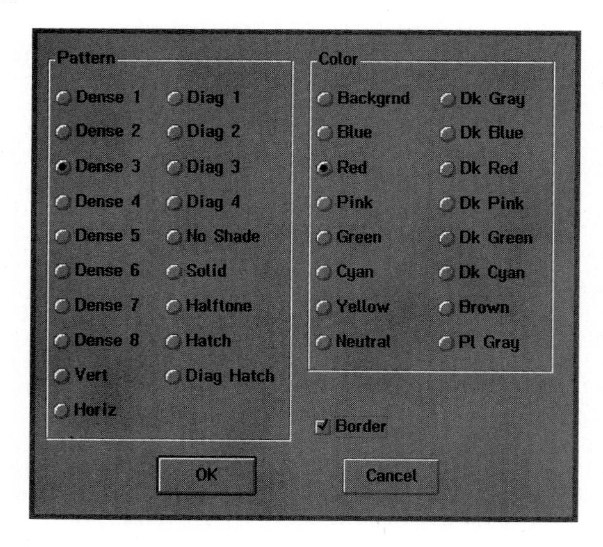

Figure 14.3: The PATTDLG dialog box

CREATION PARAMETERS

PATTDLG draws a box within its client window based on a pattern and color you select within the dialog box. Let's first examine how *ClientWndProc* and the *PatternDlgProc* dialog box procedure pass data between each other.

Near the top of PATTDLG.C is the definition of a structure named PATTERNS-DATA. This structure contains three fields (*iPattern*, *iColor*, and *fBorder*) that provide all the information *ClientWndProc* needs to draw the patterned box in the client window. Within *ClientWndProc*, a static variable of type PATTERNS-DATA is defined and initialized as

```
static PATTERNSDATA pdCurrent = { IDD_DENSE1, IDD_BKGRND, TRUE } ;
```

The IDD_DENSE1 and IDD_BKGRND identifiers are defined in PATTDLG.H and used in PATTDLG.RC for child window IDs of the radio buttons. These are the default values when you first run the program. During the WM_PAINT message, *ClientWndProc* uses the three fields of *pdCurrent* to set the color:

```
GpiSetColor (hps, pdCurrent.iColor -
             IDD_BKGRND + CLR_BACKGROUND) ;
```

and the pattern:

```
GpiSetPattern (hps, pdCurrent.iPattern -
               IDD_DENSE1 + PATSYM_DENSE1) ;
```

and to determine whether a border should be drawn:

```
GpiBox (hps, pdCurrent.fBorder ? DRO_OUTLINEFILL : DRO_FILL,
        &ptl, ØL, ØL) ;
```

When you select the Pattern and Color option from the menu, *ClientWnd-Proc* receives a WM_COMMAND message that has a *cmd* field of IDM_PAT-TERNS. Here's how it's processed:

```
case IDM_PATTERNS:
     if (WinDlgBox (HWND_DESKTOP, hwnd, PatternDlgProc,
                    NULLHANDLE, IDD_PATTERNS, &pdCurrent))

          WinInvalidateRect (hwnd, NULL, FALSE) ;
          return Ø ;
```

A pointer to the *pdCurrent* structure is passed as the last parameter to *WinDlgBox* when you invoke the dialog box. This is the "creation parameters" (*pCreateParams*) field of WinDlgBox. You use this field to pass data to the dialog box procedure.

Within *PatternDlgProc*, both a structure of type PATTERNSDATA and a pointer to a PATTERNSDATA structure are defined

```
static PATTERNSDATA  pdLocal ;
static PPATTERNSDATA ppdCurrent ;
```

During the WM_INITDLG message, *mp2* has been set equal to the last parameter of the *WinDlgBox* call that invoked the dialog box procedure. In *PatternDlgProc* the pointer is saved in *ppdCurrent*:

```
ppdCurrent = PVOIDFROMMP (mp2) ;
```

The entire structure is also copied to *pdLocal* with a simple assignment statement:

```
pdLocal = *ppdCurrent ;
```

I'll discuss the remainder of the WM_INITDLG message processing shortly.

As the dialog box is displayed and the user clicks the various radio buttons and so forth, *PatternDlgProc* uses *pdLocal* to store the selected values. However, if *ClientWndProc* needs to repaint its client window while the dialog box is still displayed, it continues to use the values stored in *pdCurrent*.

You can exit the dialog box by selecting the OK or Cancel button. When you select the OK button, *PatternDlgProc* copies the *pdLocal* structure back to the structure referenced by the pointer it obtained during the WM_INITDLG message:

```
*ppdCurrent = pdLocal ;
```

The *ppdCurrent* pointer points to the *pdCurrent* structure within *ClientWndProc*. *PatternDlgProc* then calls *WinDismissDlg* with a second parameter of TRUE:

```
WinDismissDlg (hwnd, TRUE) ;
```

If you select Cancel from the dialog box, the structure is not copied, and the second paramter of *WinDismissDlg* is set to FALSE:

```
WinDismissDlg (hwnd, FALSE) ;
```

In either case, the dialog box is destroyed, and the second parameter of *WinDismissDlg* is returned from the original call to *WinDlgBox* within *ClientWndProc*. If *WinDlgBox* returns TRUE, *ClientWndProc* invalidates the window:

```
if (WinDlgBox (HWND_DESKTOP, hwnd, PatternDlgProc,
               NULLHANDLE, IDD_PATTERNS, &pdCurrent))
     WinInvalidateRect (hwnd, NULL, FALSE) ;
```

This generates a WM_PAINT message and the client window is repainted with the new fields of *pdCurrent*.

You can simplify some of this logic somewhat by eliminating the PATTERNS-DATA structure and by using global variables to store the current pattern, color, and border used within *ClientWndProc*. During the WM_INITDLG message, *PatternDlgProc* would copy these variables to local static variables for use within the dialog box procedure. When you select OK, *PatternDlgProc* then assigns the global variables from the final values of the local variables.

This alternative using global variables may be simpler, but the approach used in PATTDLG is more structured. If you want to use the same dialog box procedure for more than one purpose (for example, if *ClientWndProc* displayed both a box and an ellipse and allowed you to change either from menu options), using the creation parameters is obviously preferable.

WORKING WITH RADIO BUTTONS

Each group of radio buttons in PATTDLG is enclosed in a group box, which is a WC_STATIC window that we also used in the DRAWLINE program in Chapter 11. In the dialog box template, this window style is indicated by the GROUPBOX statements. The first GROUPBOX statement in the dialog box template is followed by 19 RADIOBUTTON statements, which specify control windows based on the WC_BUTTON window class and the BS_RADIOBUTTON button style. The text fields of the 19 radio buttons correspond to the 19 GPI fill patterns.

A radio button width must accommodate the text plus two characters for the button itself. A height of 12 units is adequate for displaying the text and button along with a dotted line that surrounds the radio button text when it has the input focus. I use 14 units for spacing the radio buttons vertically.

The 19 radio buttons have child IDs ranging from IDD_DENSE1 to (IDD_-DENSE1 + 18). In PATTERNS.H I've defined identifiers for the first and last child IDs of these 19 controls:

```
#define IDD_DENSE1      10
#define IDD_DIAGHATCH  (IDD_DENSE1 + 18)
```

Painting logic in *ClientWndProc* requires that the child IDs of the push buttons be consecutive and in the same order as the corresponding PATSYM identifiers.

After *PatternDlgProc* copies the current settings to the *pdLocal* structure in the WM_INITDLG message, it must initialize the radio buttons by sending them BM_SETCHECK messages. Normally, if you want to send a message to a child window and you don't know the window handle, you first must call *WinWindowFromID* to get the window handle and then call *WinSendMsg*:

```
hwndChild = WinWindowFromID (hwnd, pdLocal.iPattern) ;

WinSendMsg (hwndChild, BM_SETCHECK,
            MPFROM2SHORT (TRUE, 0), NULL) ;
```

For these buttons, the *iPattern* field of *pdLocal* is a child ID of one of the radio buttons. When you're working with dialog boxes, there's a single function that sends a message based on the handle of its parent (which is *hwnd*) and the child ID of the control (*pdLocal.iPattern*):

```
WinSendDlgItemMsg (hwnd, pdLocal.iPattern, BM_SETCHECK,
                   MPFROM2SHORT (TRUE, 0), NULL) ;
```

The *WinSendDlgItemMsg* sends a message to a child window based on the handle of its parent (*hwnd*) and the child ID of the control (*pdLocal.iPattern*).

Even simpler is the macro:

```
WinCheckButton (hwnd, pdLocal.iPattern, TRUE) ;
```

The first time the dialog box is displayed, *pdLocal.iPattern* equals IDD_DENSE1, so the first button in the Patterns group is checked. When the user clicks a radio button, the button window sends its owner (in this case, the dialog box window) a WM_CONTROL message. The low USHORT of *mp1* is the child ID.

PatternDlgProc first determines if the child ID is within the range for the first 19 radio buttons:

```
case WM_CONTROL:
     if (SHORT1FROMMP(mp1) >= IDD_DENSE1 &&
         SHORT1FROMMP(mp1) <= IDD_DIAGHATCH)
          {
```

The function then uses the *WinCheckButton* macro to uncheck the currently checked button:

```
WinCheckButton (hwnd, pdLocal.iPattern, FALSE) ;
```

The *pdLocal.iPattern* variable is then set to the child ID of the button just pressed, and that button is sent a BM_SETCHECK message to turn the check on:

```
pdLocal.iPattern = SHORT1FROMMP (mp1) ;
WinCheckButton (hwnd, pdLocal.iPattern, TRUE) ;
```

This is similar to the way we handled radio buttons in the DRAWLINE program in Chapter 11.

Thus, *pdLocal.iPattern* always has the ID of the currently checked radio button. But only when the user selects OK is this copied to the *pdCurrent* structure in *ClientWndProc*:

```
*ppdCurrent = pdLocal ;
```

THE AUTORADIOBUTTON ALTERNATIVE

The processing of the WM_CONTROL messages from the radio buttons in PATTDLG is quite similar to that shown in the DRAWLINE program in Chapter 11. But for radio buttons in dialog boxes, you have an alternative that makes the processing easier.

First, replace all the RADIOBUTTON keywords in PATTDLG with AUTO-RADIOBUTTON. The radio buttons in the dialog box are then created with a style of BS_AUTORADIOBUTTON rather than BS_RADIOBUTTON. These buttons check themselves automatically when clicked and also uncheck all other radio buttons in the same group. Thus the processing of the WM_CONTROL message is reduced to this:

```
case WM_CONTROL:
     if (SHORT1FROMMP (mp1) >= IDD_DENSE1 &&
         SHORT1FROMMP (mp1) <= IDD_DIAGHATCH)
          {
          pdLocal.iPattern = SHORT1FROMMP (mp1) ;
          }
     else if (SHORT1FROMMP (mp1) >= IDD_BKGRND &&
              SHORT1FROMMP (mp1) <= IDD_PALEGRAY)
          {
          pdLocal.iColor = SHORT1FROMMP (mp1) ;
          }
     return 0 ;
```

This logic simply keeps track of the most recent button checked.

WORKING WITH CHECK BOXES

In addition to the radio buttons, the dialog box in PATTDLG contains a *check box*. This is a style of button that programs use to indicate an option that can be checked on or off. The check box in PATTDLG determines whether the rectangle drawn in the client window should include a border.

The child ID of the check box is IDD_BORDER. During processing of the WN_INITDLG message in *PatternsWndProc*, the state of the button (checked or unchecked) is set based on the value of the *fBorder* field of *pdLocal*:

```
WinCheckButton (hwnd, IDD_BORDER, pdLocal.fBorder) ;
```

This check box has the window style BS_AUTOCHECKBOX, which means that the check box window itself toggles the check mark on and off when clicked. Although the check box sends its owner WM_CONTROL messages, *PatternDlgProc* doesn't do anything with them. Instead, when the OK button is clicked, *PatternWndProc* obtains the current state of the check box by using a macro that sends the button a BM_QUERYCHECK message:

```
pdLocal.fBorder = WinQueryButtonCheckState (hwnd, IDD_BORDER) ;
```

TAB STOPS AND GROUPS

The dialog box in PATTDLG has a complete keyboard interface without any apparent effort on our part. You can use the Tab key to jump between the radio buttons, check box, and push buttons. Within each group of radio buttons, you can use the cursor movement keys to change the checked button. These two aspects of the keyboard interface are governed by the window styles called WS_TABSTOP and WS_GROUP. Some of the control windows have these styles by default; some don't. Sometimes you need to include one of these window styles in the definition for the control window. For example, in the dialog box template in PATTDLG.RC, the check box and push buttons are explicitly given the WS_GROUP style.

The WS_TABSTOP style determines how the input focus is transferred between control windows when the user presses the Tab key. Initially, the input focus is set to the first control in the dialog box (based on the order in which you define the controls in the template) that has the WS_TABSTOP style. When the user presses the Tab key, the input focus is transferred to the very next control that has the WS_TABSTOP style. After the last WS_TABSTOP control is reached, pressing the Tab key transfers the input focus to the first WS_TABSTOP control. PUSHBUTTON, DEFPUSHBUTTON, CHECKBOX, and AUTOCHECKBOX control windows all have a WS_TABSTOP style by default, as do the ENTRYFIELD and LISTBOX control windows used in the HEAD program shown later in this chapter.

The WS_GROUP style governs the way the input focus is transferred between controls when the user presses the Up and Down cursor movement keys. A range of controls in which the cursor movement keys transfer the input focus is called a *group*. The group ranges from the first control that has a WS_GROUP style up to (but not including) the next control that has a WS_-GROUP style. Static control windows defined with CTEXT, LTEXT, RTEXT, ICON, and GROUPBOX have a WS_GROUP style by default. However, these controls can't themselves receive the input focus, so the group really begins with the next control.

This is how the cursor movement keys work in the two groups of radio buttons in PATTDLG. The first radio button after each GROUPBOX window begins a group. The first group of radio buttons ends with the other GROUPBOX window that precedes the second group. The second group of radio buttons ends with the CHECKBOX window, which is explicitly given a WS_GROUP style. The buttons and check boxes in PATTDLG must be explicitly given a WS_GROUP style to prevent the cursor movement keys from doing anything when these windows have the input focus. If you remove the WS_GROUP style from the check box control window, you'll find that you can use the cursor movement keys to move between the check box and the radio buttons in the second group because the check box is no longer functioning as the end of the group.

Although radio buttons don't normally have a WM_TABSTOP style, a checked radio button functions as if it does. Thus, when you press the Tab key, the input focus transfers to the radio button that is currently checked in each group.

THE WM_INITDLG MESSAGE

The WM_INITDLG message is the first message the dialog procedure receives. You've already seen how the dialog procedure can use *mp2* to reference a pointer passed to *WinDlgBox* and perform initialization during the WM_INITDLG message. However, this message also has another function. The *mp1* parameter that accompanies the WM_INITDLG message contains the window handle of the control window that initially receives the input focus. This is generally the first control in the dialog box that has the WS_TABSTOP style. If this is satisfactory, you can either return 0 from the dialog procedure after processing WM_INITDLG or call *WinDefDlgProc* in lieu of processing WM_INITDLG.

In PATTDLG, the first control that has the WS_TABSTOP style is the check box. But it makes more sense for a radio button in the first group to get the input focus. When you want to set the input focus during WM_INITDLG, call *WinSetFocus* and return 1 from the dialog procedure. In *PatternDlgProc* the code looks like this:

```
WinSetFocus (HWND_DESKTOP,
     WinWindowFromID (hwnd, pdLocal.iPattern)) ;

return MRFROMSHORT (1) ;
```

If you don't return 1 after setting the input focus, the Presentation Manager will set the focus to the window indicated by the *mp1* parameter.

SAVING THE VALUES

When you end PATTDLG, a message box is displayed that asks "Save current settings?" If you check Yes on this message box, PATTDLG will use the last values of the pattern and color that you selected the next time you run the program.

The first question that you might ask is "Where is this information being saved?" The Presentation Manager maintains a file named OS2.INI that programs can use for storing configuration data. For example, a user of a Presentation Manager word processing program might prefer that the program be started with left margins of 1 inch and "insert mode" turned off. OS2.INI is an excellent place to store information like that. The Presentation Manager Control Panel uses OS2.INI to store your color and mouse preferences and your printer setups.

What makes this feature even better is that programs do not access OS2.INI directly. Instead they use Presentation Manager function calls beginning with the prefix *Prf* ("profile") to write to and read from the file.

Information in OS2.INI is accessed using two text strings: an "application" name, which is generally the same name as the program, and a "key" name, which identifies a particular piece of information that the program stores. For example, suppose the Presentation Manager word processing program I mentioned is called WORDPROC. To store the user's preference for insert mode and left margins, the program would use an application name of WORDPROC and key names of INSERTMODE and LEFTMARGIN.

For PATTDLG, the application name is PATTDLG, which is stored in the *szAppName* variable in *ClientWndProc.* To store the current settings, the program uses the key name SETTINGS, stored in *szKeyName.*

When you end PATTDLG and answer Yes to the message box displayed during the WM_DESTROY message, PATTDLG writes the current settings to OS2.INI by calling

```
PrfWriteProfileData (HINI_USERPROFILE, szAppName, szKeyName,
     &pdCurrent, sizeof pdCurrent) ;
```

You use this function to write binary data of any length to OS2.INI. In this case, PATTDLG writes the entire *pdCurrent* structure to the file. The last parameter is the size of this structure. You can also use *PrfWriteProfileString* to write a zero-terminated string.

During the WM_CREATE message, PATTDLG attempts to read the data from OS2.INI:

```
PrfQueryProfileData (HINI_USERPROFILE, szAppName, szKeyName,
     &pdCurrent, & ulDataLength) ;
```

If the Presentation Manager does not find a matching application and key name in OS2.INI, *PrfQueryProfileData* returns FALSE, but PATTDLG doesn't check for this. The *pdCurrent* structure already contains initialized default values, and these will not be altered by the *PrfQueryProfileData* function call.

You can read text strings from OS2.INI using *PrfQueryProfileString*. If the information you store using *PrfWriteProfileData* is a single integer, you can read it using *PrfQueryProfileInt*. The *PrfQueryProfileSize* function returns the size of the stored data for a particular application and key name.

THE FILE OPEN DIALOG BOX

One of the most complex—yet essential—modal dialog boxes is invoked by the menu's File Open option. Although there's a high-level function (called *WinFileDlg*) that helps you create one, it's a good exercise to try to roll your own.

The HEAD program, shown in Listing 14.4, is a Presentation Manager version of the UNIX head utility. The program shows the beginning of the file in its client window. To specify a file name, you can use the HEAD command line or the File Open dialog box.

Listing 14.4: The HEAD program

The HEAD.MAK File

```
#-------------------
# HEAD.MAK make file
#-------------------

head.exe : head.obj easyfont.obj head.def head.res
     $(PRGLINK) head easyfont, head, NUL, $(PRGLIB), head
     rc head.res

head.obj : head.c head.h easyfont.h
     $(PRGCC) head.c

easyfont.obj : easyfont.c
     $(PRGCC) easyfont.c

head.res : head.rc head.h
     $(PRGRC) head
```

Listing 14.4: The HEAD program (Continued)

The HEAD.C File

```
/*-------------------------------------
   HEAD.C -- Displays File Head
             (c) Charles Petzold, 1993
  -------------------------------------*/

#define INCL_WIN
#define INCL_GPI
#include <os2.h>
#include <stdio.h>
#include <stdlib.h>
#include <string.h>
#include "easyfont.h"
#include "head.h"

#define LCID_FIXEDFONT   1L
#define LCID_BOLDFONT    2L

MRESULT EXPENTRY ClientWndProc (HWND, ULONG, MPARAM, MPARAM) ;
MRESULT EXPENTRY AboutDlgProc  (HWND, ULONG, MPARAM, MPARAM) ;
MRESULT EXPENTRY OpenDlgProc   (HWND, ULONG, MPARAM, MPARAM) ;
INT              ParseFileName (CHAR *, CHAR *) ;

CHAR szClientClass [] = "Head" ;
CHAR szFileName [CCHMAXPATH] ;
HAB  hab ;

int main (int argc, char *argv[])
     {
     static ULONG flFrameFlags = FCF_TITLEBAR      | FCF_SYSMENU  |
                                 FCF_SIZEBORDER    | FCF_MINMAX   |
                                 FCF_SHELLPOSITION | FCF_TASKLIST |
                                 FCF_MENU ;
     HMQ          hmq ;
     HWND         hwndFrame, hwndClient ;
     QMSG         qmsg ;

               // Check for filename parameter and copy to szFileName

     if (argc > 1)
          ParseFileName (szFileName, argv [1]) ;

               // Continue normally

     hab = WinInitialize (0) ;
     hmq = WinCreateMsgQueue (hab, 0) ;
```

Listing 14.4: The HEAD program (Continued)

```
     WinRegisterClass (hab, szClientClass, ClientWndProc, CS_SIZEREDRAW, 0) ;

     hwndFrame = WinCreateStdWindow (HWND_DESKTOP, WS_VISIBLE,
                                     &flFrameFlags, szClientClass, NULL,
                                     0L, 0, ID_RESOURCE, &hwndClient) ;

     if (hwndFrame != NULLHANDLE)
          {
          while (WinGetMsg (hab, &qmsg, NULLHANDLE, 0, 0))
               WinDispatchMsg (hab, &qmsg) ;

          WinDestroyWindow (hwndFrame) ;
          }

     WinDestroyMsgQueue (hmq) ;
     WinTerminate (hab) ;
     return 0 ;
     }

MRESULT EXPENTRY ClientWndProc (HWND hwnd, ULONG msg, MPARAM mp1, MPARAM mp2)
     {
     static CHAR szErrorMsg [] = "File not found or could not be opened" ;
     static INT  cxClient, cyClient, cxChar, cyChar, cyDesc ;
     CHAR        *pcReadBuffer ;
     FILE        *fileInput ;
     FONTMETRICS fm ;
     HPS         hps ;
     INT         iLength ;
     POINTL      ptl ;

     switch (msg)
          {
          case WM_CREATE:
               hps = WinGetPS (hwnd) ;
               EzfQueryFonts (hps) ;

               if (!EzfCreateLogFont (hps, LCID_FIXEDFONT, FONTFACE_MONO,
                                                           FONTSIZE_10, 0))
                    {
                    WinReleasePS (hps) ;

                    WinMessageBox (HWND_DESKTOP, HWND_DESKTOP,
                         "Cannot find a fixed-pitch font.  Load the Courier "
                         "fonts from the Control Panel and try again.",
                         szClientClass, 0, MB_OK | MB_WARNING) ;

                    return MRFROMSHORT (1) ;
                    }
```

Listing 14.4: The HEAD program (Continued)

```
          GpiQueryFontMetrics (hps, (LONG) sizeof fm, &fm) ;
          cxChar = fm.lAveCharWidth ;
          cyChar = fm.lMaxBaselineExt ;
          cyDesc = fm.lMaxDescender ;

          GpiSetCharSet (hps, LCID_DEFAULT) ;
          GpiDeleteSetId (hps, LCID_FIXEDFONT) ;
          WinReleasePS (hps) ;
          return 0 ;

     case WM_SIZE:
          cxClient = SHORT1FROMMP (mp2) ;
          cyClient = SHORT2FROMMP (mp2) ;
          return 0 ;

     case WM_COMMAND:
          switch (COMMANDMSG(&msg)->cmd)
               {
               case IDM_OPEN:
                    if (WinDlgBox (HWND_DESKTOP, hwnd, OpenDlgProc,
                                   NULLHANDLE, IDD_OPEN, NULL))
                         WinInvalidateRect (hwnd, NULL, FALSE) ;
                    return 0 ;

               case IDM_ABOUT:
                    WinDlgBox (HWND_DESKTOP, hwnd, AboutDlgProc,
                               NULLHANDLE, IDD_ABOUT, NULL) ;
                    return 0 ;
               }
          break ;

     case WM_PAINT:
          hps = WinBeginPaint (hwnd, NULLHANDLE, NULL) ;
          GpiErase (hps) ;

          if (szFileName [0] != '\0')
               {
               EzfCreateLogFont (hps, LCID_FIXEDFONT, FONTFACE_MONO,
                                      FONTSIZE_10,    0) ;
               EzfCreateLogFont (hps, LCID_BOLDFONT,  FONTFACE_MONO,
                                      FONTSIZE_10,    FATTR_SEL_BOLD) ;

               GpiSetCharSet (hps, LCID_BOLDFONT) ;
               ptl.x = cxChar ;
               ptl.y = cyClient - cyChar + cyDesc ;
               GpiCharStringAt (hps, &ptl, strlen (szFileName),
                                szFileName) ;
               ptl.y -= cyChar ;
```

Listing 14.4: The HEAD program (Continued)

```
               if ((fileInput = fopen (szFileName, "r")) != NULL)
                    {
                    GpiSetCharSet (hps, LCID_FIXEDFONT) ;
                    pcReadBuffer = (PCHAR) malloc (cxClient / cxChar) ;

                    while ((ptl.y -= cyChar) > 0 &&
                           fgets (pcReadBuffer, cxClient / cxChar - 2,
                                  fileInput) != NULL)
                         {
                         iLength = strlen (pcReadBuffer) ;

                         if (pcReadBuffer [iLength - 1] == '\n')
                              iLength-- ;

                         if (iLength > 0)
                              GpiCharStringAt (hps, &ptl, iLength,
                                               pcReadBuffer) ;
                         }
                    free (pcReadBuffer) ;
                    fclose (fileInput) ;
                    }
               else           // file cannot be opened
                    {
                    ptl.y -= cyChar ;
                    GpiCharStringAt (hps, &ptl, strlen (szErrorMsg),
                                     szErrorMsg) ;
                    }
               GpiSetCharSet (hps, LCID_DEFAULT) ;
               GpiDeleteSetId (hps, LCID_FIXEDFONT) ;
               GpiDeleteSetId (hps, LCID_BOLDFONT) ;
               }
          WinEndPaint (hps) ;
          return 0 ;
     }
return WinDefWindowProc (hwnd, msg, mp1, mp2) ;
}

MRESULT EXPENTRY AboutDlgProc (HWND hwnd, ULONG msg, MPARAM mp1, MPARAM mp2)
     {
     switch (msg)
          {
          case WM_COMMAND:
               switch (COMMANDMSG(&msg)->cmd)
                    {
                    case DID_OK:
                    case DID_CANCEL:
                         WinDismissDlg (hwnd, TRUE) ;
                         return 0 ;
                    }
```

Listing 14.4: The HEAD program (Continued)

```
               break ;
          }
     return WinDefDlgProc (hwnd, msg, mp1, mp2) ;
     }

VOID FillDirListBox (HWND hwnd, CHAR *pcCurrentPath)
     {
     static CHAR  szDrive [] = "  :" ;
     FILEFINDBUF3 findbuf ;
     HDIR         hDir = HDIR_CREATE ;
     SHORT        sDrive ;
     ULONG        ulDriveNum, ulDriveMap, ulCurPathLen,
                  ulReturn, ulSearchCount = 1 ;

     DosQueryCurrentDisk (&ulDriveNum, &ulDriveMap) ;
     pcCurrentPath [0] = (CHAR) ulDriveNum + '@' ;
     pcCurrentPath [1] = ':' ;
     pcCurrentPath [2] = '\\' ;

     ulCurPathLen = CCHMAXPATH ;
     DosQueryCurrentDir (0, pcCurrentPath + 3, &ulCurPathLen) ;

     WinSetDlgItemText (hwnd, IDD_PATH, pcCurrentPath) ;
     WinSendDlgItemMsg (hwnd, IDD_DIRLIST, LM_DELETEALL, NULL, NULL) ;

     for (sDrive = 0 ; sDrive < 26 ; sDrive++)
          if (ulDriveMap & 1L << sDrive)
               {
               szDrive [1] = (CHAR) sDrive + 'A' ;

               WinSendDlgItemMsg (hwnd, IDD_DIRLIST, LM_INSERTITEM,
                                  MPFROM2SHORT (LIT_END, 0),
                                  MPFROMP (szDrive)) ;
               }

     ulReturn = DosFindFirst ("*.*", &hDir, FILE_DIRECTORY, &findbuf,
                             sizeof findbuf, &ulSearchCount, FIL_STANDARD) ;
     while (!ulReturn)
          {
          if (findbuf.attrFile & 0x0010 &&
                    (findbuf.achName [0] != '.' || findbuf.achName [1]))

               WinSendDlgItemMsg (hwnd, IDD_DIRLIST, LM_INSERTITEM,
                                  MPFROM2SHORT (LIT_SORTASCENDING, 0),
                                  MPFROMP (findbuf.achName)) ;

          ulReturn = DosFindNext (hDir, &findbuf, sizeof findbuf,
                                  &ulSearchCount) ;
          }
```

Listing 14.4: The HEAD program (Continued)

```
     DosFindClose (hDir) ;
     }

VOID FillFileListBox (HWND hwnd)
     {
     FILEFINDBUF3 findbuf ;
     HDIR         hDir = HDIR_CREATE ;
     ULONG        ulReturn, ulSearchCount = 1 ;

     WinSendDlgItemMsg (hwnd, IDD_FILELIST, LM_DELETEALL, NULL, NULL) ;

     ulReturn = DosFindFirst ("*.*", &hDir, FILE_NORMAL, &findbuf,
                              sizeof findbuf, &ulSearchCount, FIL_STANDARD) ;
     while (!ulReturn)
          {
          WinSendDlgItemMsg (hwnd, IDD_FILELIST, LM_INSERTITEM,
                             MPFROM2SHORT (LIT_SORTASCENDING, 0),
                             MPFROMP (findbuf.achName)) ;

          ulReturn = DosFindNext (hDir, &findbuf, sizeof findbuf,
                                  &ulSearchCount) ;
          }
     DosFindClose (hDir) ;
     }

MRESULT EXPENTRY OpenDlgProc (HWND hwnd, ULONG msg, MPARAM mp1, MPARAM mp2)
     {
     static CHAR szCurrentPath [CCHMAXPATH], szBuffer [CCHMAXPATH] ;
     INT         iSelect ;

     switch (msg)
          {
          case WM_INITDLG:
               FillDirListBox (hwnd, szCurrentPath) ;
               FillFileListBox (hwnd) ;

               WinSendDlgItemMsg (hwnd, IDD_FILEEDIT, EM_SETTEXTLIMIT,
                                  MPFROM2SHORT (CCHMAXPATH, 0), NULL) ;
               return 0 ;

          case WM_CONTROL:
               if (SHORT1FROMMP (mp1) == IDD_DIRLIST ||
                   SHORT1FROMMP (mp1) == IDD_FILELIST)
                    {
                    iSelect = (USHORT) WinSendDlgItemMsg (hwnd,
                                             SHORT1FROMMP (mp1),
                                             LM_QUERYSELECTION, 0L, 0L) ;
```

Listing 14.4: The HEAD program (Continued)

```
                    WinSendDlgItemMsg (hwnd, SHORT1FROMMP (mp1),
                                       LM_QUERYITEMTEXT,
                                       MPFROM2SHORT (iSelect, sizeof szBuffer),
                                       MPFROMP (szBuffer)) ;
                    }

               switch (SHORT1FROMMP (mp1))             // Control ID
                    {
                    case IDD_DIRLIST:
                         switch (SHORT2FROMMP (mp1))   // notification code
                              {
                              case LN_ENTER:
                                   if (szBuffer [0] == ' ')
                                        DosSetDefaultDisk (szBuffer [1] - '@');
                                   else
                                        DosSetCurrentDir (szBuffer) ;

                                   FillDirListBox (hwnd, szCurrentPath) ;
                                   FillFileListBox (hwnd) ;

                                   WinSetDlgItemText (hwnd, IDD_FILEEDIT, "") ;
                                   return 0 ;
                              }
                         break ;

                    case IDD_FILELIST:
                         switch (SHORT2FROMMP (mp1))   // notification code
                              {
                              case LN_SELECT:
                                   WinSetDlgItemText (hwnd, IDD_FILEEDIT,
                                                      szBuffer) ;
                                   return 0 ;

                              case LN_ENTER:
                                   ParseFileName (szFileName, szBuffer) ;
                                   WinDismissDlg (hwnd, TRUE) ;
                                   return 0 ;
                              }
                         break ;
                    }
               break ;

          case WM_COMMAND:
               switch (COMMANDMSG(&msg)->cmd)
                    {
                    case DID_OK:
                         WinQueryDlgItemText (hwnd, IDD_FILEEDIT,
                                              sizeof szBuffer, szBuffer) ;
```

Listing 14.4: The HEAD program (Continued)

```
                    switch (ParseFileName (szCurrentPath, szBuffer))
                         {
                         case 0:
                              WinAlarm (HWND_DESKTOP, WA_ERROR) ;
                              FillDirListBox (hwnd, szCurrentPath) ;
                              FillFileListBox (hwnd) ;
                              return 0 ;

                         case 1:
                              FillDirListBox (hwnd, szCurrentPath) ;
                              FillFileListBox (hwnd) ;
                              WinSetDlgItemText (hwnd, IDD_FILEEDIT, "") ;
                              return 0 ;

                         case 2:
                              strcpy (szFileName, szCurrentPath) ;
                              WinDismissDlg (hwnd, TRUE) ;
                              return 0 ;
                         }
                    break ;

               case DID_CANCEL:
                    WinDismissDlg (hwnd, FALSE) ;
                    return 0 ;
               }
          break ;
     }
     return WinDefDlgProc (hwnd, msg, mp1, mp2) ;
     }

INT ParseFileName (CHAR *pcOut, CHAR *pcIn)
     {
          /*-----------------------------------------------------------------
             Input:    pcOut -- Pointer to parsed file specification.
                       pcIn  -- Pointer to raw file specification.

             Returns:  0 -- pcIn had invalid drive or directory.
                       1 -- pcIn was empty or had no filename.
                       2 -- pcOut points to drive, full dir, and file name.

             Changes current drive and directory per pcIn string.
            -----------------------------------------------------------------*/

     CHAR   *pcLastSlash, *pcFileOnly ;
     ULONG  ulDriveNum, ulDriveMap, ulDirLen = CCHMAXPATH ;

     strupr (pcIn) ;

             // If input string is empty, return 1
```

Listing 14.4: The HEAD program (Continued)

```
if (pcIn [0] == '\0')
     return 1 ;

          // Get drive from input string or current drive

if (pcIn [1] == ':')
     {
     if (DosSetDefaultDisk (pcIn [0] - '@'))
          return 0 ;

     pcIn += 2 ;
     }
DosQueryCurrentDisk (&ulDriveNum, &ulDriveMap) ;

*pcOut++ = (CHAR) ulDriveNum + '@' ;
*pcOut++ = ':' ;
*pcOut++ = '\\' ;

          // If rest of string is empty, return 1

if (pcIn [0] == '\0')
     return 1 ;

          // Search for last backslash.  If none, could be directory.

if (NULL == (pcLastSlash = strrchr (pcIn, '\\')))
     {
     if (!DosSetCurrentDir (pcIn))
          return 1 ;

               // Otherwise, get current dir & attach input filename

     DosQueryCurrentDir (0, pcOut, &ulDirLen) ;

     if (strlen (pcIn) > 12)
          return 0 ;

     if (*(pcOut + strlen (pcOut) - 1) != '\\')
          strcat (pcOut++, "\\") ;

     strcat (pcOut, pcIn) ;
     return 2 ;
     }
          // If the only backslash is at beginning, change to root

if (pcIn == pcLastSlash)
     {
     DosSetCurrentDir ("\\") ;
```

Listing 14.4: The HEAD program (Continued)

```
          if (pcIn [1] == '\0')
               return 1 ;

          strcpy (pcOut, pcIn + 1) ;
          return 2 ;
          }
               // Attempt to change directory -- Get current dir if OK

     *pcLastSlash = '\0' ;

     if (DosSetCurrentDir (pcIn))
          return 0 ;

     DosQueryCurrentDir (0, pcOut, &ulDirLen) ;

               // Append input filename, if any

     pcFileOnly = pcLastSlash + 1 ;

     if (*pcFileOnly == '\0')
          return 1 ;

     if (*(pcOut + strlen (pcOut) - 1) != '\\')
          strcat (pcOut++, "\\") ;
          return 2 ;
          }
```

The HEAD.H File

```
/*-------------------
   HEAD.H header file
  -------------------*/

#define ID_RESOURCE      1

#define IDM_FILE         1
#define IDM_OPEN         10
#define IDM_ABOUT        11

#define IDD_OPEN         1
#define IDD_ABOUT        2

#define IDD_PATH         10
#define IDD_FILEEDIT     11
#define IDD_DIRLIST      12
#define IDD_FILELIST     13
```

Listing 14.4: The HEAD program (Continued)

The HEAD.RC File

```
/*-------------------------------
   HEAD.RC resource script file
  -------------------------------*/

#include <os2.h>
#include "head.h"

MENU ID_RESOURCE
     {
     SUBMENU "~File",              IDM_FILE
          {
          MENUITEM "~Open...",          IDM_OPEN
          MENUITEM SEPARATOR
          MENUITEM "A~bout...",         IDM_ABOUT
          }
     }

DLGTEMPLATE IDD_ABOUT
  {
  DIALOG "", 0, 32, 32, 200, 88,, FCF_DLGBORDER
    {
    CTEXT "Head"                                -1,  10, 64, 180,  8
    CTEXT "File Head Display"                   -1,  10, 40, 180,  8
    CTEXT "Copyright (c) Charles Petzold, 1993" -1,  10, 32, 180,  8
    DEFPUSHBUTTON "OK"                      DID_OK,  80,  8,  40, 16, WS_GROUP
    }
  }

DLGTEMPLATE IDD_OPEN
  {
  DIALOG "", 0, 8, 8, 240, 170,, FCF_DLGBORDER
    {
    CTEXT "Open File"              -1,             8, 154, 224,  8
    LTEXT "Use mouse to choose file, or type filename." -1, 8, 138, 224, 8
    LTEXT "Current Directory:"     -1,             8, 126,  80,  8
    LTEXT ""                       IDD_PATH,      88, 126, 144,  8
    LTEXT "Filename:"              -1,             8, 110,  48,  8
    ENTRYFIELD ""                  IDD_FILEEDIT,  56, 110, 176,  8, ES_MARGIN
    CTEXT "Directories"            -1,            16,  96,  92,  8
    CTEXT "Files"                  -1,           134,  96,  92,  8
    LISTBOX                        IDD_DIRLIST,   16,  32,  92, 64
    LISTBOX                        IDD_FILELIST, 134,  32,  92, 64
    DEFPUSHBUTTON "Open"           DID_OK,        32,   8,  64, 16, WS_GROUP
    PUSHBUTTON "Esc=Cancel"        DID_CANCEL,   144,   8,  64, 16, WS_GROUP
    }
```

Listing 14.4: The HEAD program (Continued)

```
}
```

The HEAD.DEF File

```
;-------------------------------
; HEAD.DEF module definition file
;-------------------------------

NAME          HEAD      WINDOWAPI

DESCRIPTION   'Displays File Head (c) Charles Petzold, 1993'
PROTMODE
```

You'll also need the EASYFONT.C and EASYFONT.H files from Chapter 5 to compile HEAD.

As I said, the File Open dialog box is one of the most complex you'll encounter and requires some messy code. To handle the box logic properly, you have to parse file specifications, separating the drive, directory, and file names. The *ParseFileName* function (the last function in HEAD.C) does a lot of the dirty work. You supply a file specification and *ParseFileName* determines the fully qualified file name with disk drive and directory. It returns a code indicating a possible error.

HEAD must retain this fully qualified file name because the File Open dialog box procedure often changes the current disk drive and directory. If you used HEAD to look at a file and then wanted to look at another file, you would invoke the File Open dialog box. After you changed the drive and directory, you might change your mind and decide to cancel the dialog box. If HEAD did not save the fully qualified file name or the original file, it might not be able to find the file again.

THE OVERALL STRUCTURE

One way to use HEAD is to specify a file name parameter when you run the program from on OS/2 command line, like this:

```
HEAD filename
```

The *main* function in HEAD declares the normal *argc* and *argv* parameters. If *argc* is greater than 1, *argv[1]* is passed to the *ParseFileName* function, which creates a fully qualified filename and stores it in the global variable *szFileName*.

During the WM_PAINT message in *ClientWndProc*, HEAD attempts to open this file (using normal C file I/O functions) and display as much of the file as can fit in the window. If this fails, HEAD displays the message "File not found or could not be opened" at the top of the client window. HEAD closes the file at the end of the WM_PAINT message. The file is opened and read only during the WM_PAINT message.

You can also select a file through HEAD's File Open dialog box, which uses the IDD_OPEN template in HEAD.RC and the *OpenDlgProc* function in HEAD.C. The dialog box is shown in Figure 14.4.

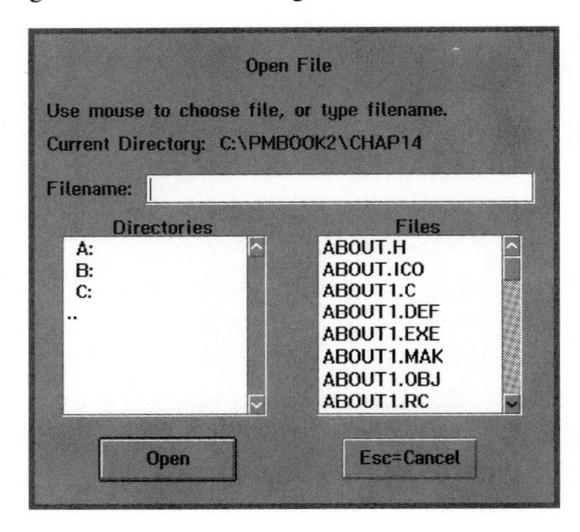

Figure 14.4: The HEAD dialog box

The dialog box contains several static text fields, one of which displays the current drive and directory. You can change the drive or directory—or select a file—by typing directly in a text entry field (the box following the text string "Filename"). The dialog box also contains two list boxes. The first displays all the disk drives and subdirectories of the current directory. You can change the drive or directory using this list box. The second list box lists all the files in the current directory. You can select a file by choosing it from the list box. Much of the complexity of the File Open dialog box stems from the interaction between the list boxes and the text entry field.

STATIC TEXT FIELDS

The File Open dialog box template in HEAD.RC has three static text fields of type CTEXT ("centered text") and four of type LTEXT ("left-justified text"). You'll notice that the third LTEXT statement in the dialog box template has a blank text field and a child ID of IDD_PATH. This is used to display the current disk drive and directory.

The text for this control is set in the *FillDirListBox* function. This function obtains the current disk drive by calling the OS/2 kernel function *DosQuery-CurrentDisk* and the current directory by calling *DosQueryCurrentDir.* The composite drive and directory is stored in the text string *pcCurrentPath.* The *WinSetDlgItemText* function sets the text for the IDD_PATH control:

```
WinSetDlgItemText (hwnd, IDD_PATH, pcCurrentPath) ;
```

This function is similar to the *WinSetWindowText* function we used in the COLORSCR program in Chapter 11 to set the text of a control window.

LIST BOXES

List boxes list text strings. The File Open dialog box template has two list boxes with child IDs of IDD_DIRLIST and IDD_FILELIST. The first lists disk drives and subdirectories; the second lists files in the current directory.

You can scroll through a list box using the cursor movement keys or a scroll bar. In the File Open dialog box, you change the current disk drive or directory by double-clicking an entry in the first list box or by pressing Enter when the list box has the input focus. You can select a file from the second list box in a similar fashion.

The *FillDirListBox* and *FillFileListBox* functions in HEAD.C fill the list boxes with text entries. These functions first delete all entries in the list box by sending the list box an LM_DELETEALL message. Here's the call in *FillDirListBox*:

```
WinSendDlgItemMsg (hwnd, IDD_DIRLIST, LM_DELETEALL, NULL, NULL) ;
```

The first list box is filled with all the valid disk drives and the subdirectories of the current directory. The *FillDirListBox* function uses the *DosQueryCurrent-Disk* function to obtain the valid disk drives and the *DosFindFirst* and *DosFind-Next* functions for the directories. To put a text string in a list box, you send the list box an LM_INSERTITEM message. The *mp2* parameter is a pointer to the text string. The *FillDirListBox* function sets the low USHORT of *mp1* to LIT_END to put the disk drives at the end of the list and LIT_SORT ASCENDING to put the subdirectories in the list box in alphabetical order.

The *FillFileListBox* function works similarly for the second list box. It finds all the files in the current directory using the OS/2 *DosFindFirst* and *DosFindNext* functions and sends the list box an LM_INSERTITEM message for each file.

OpenDlgProc first calls the *FillDirListBox* and *FillFileListBox* functions during the WM_INITDLG message and then awaits messages from the list boxes. A list box sends its owner a WM_CONTROL message. The low USHORT of *mp1* is the child ID; the high USHORT of *mp1* is a notification code. This notification code is either LN_SELECT (which means that the user has clicked an entry in the list box or moved the cursor to it) or LN_ENTER (which means the user has double-clicked an entry or pressed the Enter key).

OpenDlgProc processes the WM_CONTROL message by first sending the list box an LM_QUERYSELECTION message. This returns a number indicating the current list box selection. Sending the list box an LM_QUERYITEMTEXT message with this selection number obtains the text string of the selection.

For the first list box, an LN_ENTER notification code during a WM_CONTROL message indicates that the user wants to change the current drive or directory. *OpenDlgProc* changes the drive or directory and then calls *FillDirListBox* and *FillFileListBox* again to reflect this new selection. For the second list box, an LN_ENTER notification code indicates that the user is finished. *OpenDlgProc* calls *ParseFileName* for the current selection and ends the dialog box by calling *WinDismissDlg*.

TEXT ENTRY FIELDS

The File Open dialog box template also contains a text entry control in which the user can type a drive, directory, file name, or some combination of the three. The text entry field has a child ID of IDD_FILEEDIT. During the WM_INITDLG message, *OpenDlgProc* sends the text entry control an EM_SETTEXTLIMIT message with the low USHORT of *mp1* set to CCHMAXPATH (defined in BSEDOS.H as 260). This limits to 260 characters the amount of text the user can type in the field.

If you simply type something in this field and press Enter, *OpenDlgProc* receives a WM_COMMAND message with the *cmd* field set to DID_OK. This is not a message from the text entry control; when you press Enter, the *WinDefDlgProc* function generates a WM_COMMAND message that contains the child window ID of the default push button in the dialog box.

For a WM_COMMAND message of DID_OK, *OpenDlgProc* obtains the current text in the text entry field by calling *WinQueryDlgItemText* and passes the string to *ParseFileName*. The return value of *ParseFileName* is tested to determine whether the string is invalid (a 0 value), contains a new disk drive or directory (a 1 value), or a valid file name (a 2 value). In the last case, the dialog box is ended by calling *WinDismissDlg*.

The text entry control is also kept updated with the current file selected in the second list box. For a WM_CONTROL message with a child ID of IDD_FILELIST and notification code of LN_SELECT, *OpenDlgProc* calls *WinSetDlgItemText* to set the text in the text entry control.

MODELESS DIALOG BOXES

So far, the programs shown in this chapter have created modal dialog boxes. Although you can switch to other programs while a modal dialog box is displayed, you cannot switch to another window in the same program. However, a modeless dialog box works a little differently and is similar to a window that you create with *WinCreateStdWindow*. You can switch between the dialog box and other top-level windows in the program.

To create a modal dialog box, you call *WinDlgBox*. The function does not return until the dialog box destroys itself by calling *WinDismissDlg*. The *WinDlgBox* returns the second parameter passed to *WinDismissDlg*. To create a modeless dialog box, you call *WinLoadDlg*. The function returns after the dialog box is created, returning the handle of the dialog box window.

Perhaps the most interesting application of a modeless dialog box is to create a main window for your program. You create your program's window with *WinLoadDlg* rather than *WinCreateStdWindow*. Why would you want to do this? Simple: If you want to create a lot of child windows on your client, it's much easier to define them in a dialog box template than it is to call *WinCreateWindow* in your program.

THE HEXCALC PROGRAM

To demonstrate this, let's look at the HEXCALC program, which is shown in Listing 14.5.

Listing 14.5: The HEXCALC program

The HEXCALC.MAK File

```
#----------------------
# HEXCALC.MAK make file
#----------------------

hexcalc.exe : hexcalc.obj hexcalc.def hexcalc.res
     $(PRGLINK) hexcalc, hexcalc, NUL, $(PRGLIB), hexcalc
     rc hexcalc.res

hexcalc.obj: hexcalc.c hexcalc.h
     $(PRGCC) hexcalc.c

hexcalc.res : hexcalc.rc hexcalc.h
     $(PRGRC) hexcalc.rc
```

Listing 14.5: The HEXCALC program (Continued)

The HEXCALC.C File

```
/*---------------------------------------
   HEXCALC.C -- Hexadecimal Calculator
                (c) Charles Petzold, 1993
  ---------------------------------------*/

#define INCL_WIN
#include <os2.h>
#include <ctype.h>
#include <limits.h>
#include <stdio.h>
#include <string.h>
#include "hexcalc.h"

MRESULT EXPENTRY ClientWndProc (HWND, ULONG, MPARAM, MPARAM) ;

int main (void)
     {
     HAB  hab ;
     HMQ  hmq ;
     HWND hwndFrame ;
     QMSG qmsg ;

     hab = WinInitialize (0) ;
     hmq = WinCreateMsgQueue (hab, 0) ;

     WinRegisterClass (hab, CLIENTCLASS, ClientWndProc, 0L, 0) ;

     hwndFrame = WinLoadDlg (HWND_DESKTOP, HWND_DESKTOP,
                             NULL, NULLHANDLE, ID_HEXCALC, NULL) ;

     WinSendMsg (hwndFrame, WM_SETICON, (MPARAM)
                 WinLoadPointer (HWND_DESKTOP, 0, ID_ICON), NULL) ;

     WinSetFocus (HWND_DESKTOP, WinWindowFromID (hwndFrame, FID_CLIENT)) ;

     while (WinGetMsg (hab, &qmsg, NULLHANDLE, 0, 0))
          WinDispatchMsg (hab, &qmsg) ;

     WinDestroyWindow (hwndFrame) ;
     WinDestroyMsgQueue (hmq) ;
     WinTerminate (hab) ;
     return 0 ;
     }
```

Listing 14.5: The HEXCALC program (Continued)

```
void ShowNumber (HWND hwnd, ULONG ulNumber)
     {
     CHAR szBuffer [20] ;

     sprintf (szBuffer, "%lX", ulNumber) ;

     WinSetWindowText (WinWindowFromID (hwnd, ESCAPE), szBuffer) ;
     }

ULONG CalcIt (ULONG ulFirstNum, INT iOperation, ULONG ulNum)
     {
     switch (iOperation)
          {
          case '=' : return ulNum ;
          case '+' : return ulFirstNum +  ulNum ;
          case '-' : return ulFirstNum -  ulNum ;
          case '*' : return ulFirstNum *  ulNum ;
          case '&' : return ulFirstNum &  ulNum ;
          case '|' : return ulFirstNum |  ulNum ;
          case '^' : return ulFirstNum ^  ulNum ;
          case '<' : return ulFirstNum << ulNum ;
          case '>' : return ulFirstNum >> ulNum ;
          case '/' : return ulNum ? ulFirstNum / ulNum : ULONG_MAX ;
          case '%' : return ulNum ? ulFirstNum % ulNum : ULONG_MAX ;
          }
     return 0L ;
     }

MRESULT EXPENTRY ClientWndProc (HWND hwnd, ULONG msg, MPARAM mp1, MPARAM mp2)
     {
     static BOOL  fNewNumber = TRUE ;
     static INT   iOperation = '=' ;
     static ULONG ulNumber, ulFirstNum ;
     HWND         hwndButton ;
     INT          idButton ;

     switch (msg)
          {
          case WM_CHAR:
               if (CHARMSG(&msg)->fs & KC_KEYUP)
                    return 0 ;

               if (CHARMSG(&msg)->fs & KC_VIRTUALKEY)
                    switch (CHARMSG(&msg)->vkey)
                         {
                         case VK_LEFT:
                              if (!(CHARMSG(&msg)->fs & KC_CHAR))
                                   {
```

Listing 14.5: The HEXCALC program (Continued)

```
                                CHARMSG(&msg)->chr = '\b' ;
                                CHARMSG(&msg)->fs |= KC_CHAR ;
                                }
                           break ;

                      case VK_ESC:
                           CHARMSG(&msg)->chr = ESCAPE ;
                           CHARMSG(&msg)->fs |= KC_CHAR ;
                           break ;

                      case VK_NEWLINE:
                      case VK_ENTER:
                           CHARMSG(&msg)->chr = '=' ;
                           CHARMSG(&msg)->fs |= KC_CHAR ;
                           break ;
                      }

          if (CHARMSG(&msg)->fs & KC_CHAR)
               {
               CHARMSG(&msg)->chr = toupper (CHARMSG(&msg)->chr) ;

               hwndButton = WinWindowFromID (hwnd, CHARMSG(&msg)->chr) ;

               if (hwndButton != NULLHANDLE)
                    WinSendMsg (hwndButton, BM_CLICK, NULL, NULL) ;
               else
                    WinAlarm (HWND_DESKTOP, WA_ERROR) ;
               }
          return Ø ;

     case WM_COMMAND:
          idButton = COMMANDMSG(&msg)->cmd ;

          if (idButton == '\b')                         // backspace
               ShowNumber (hwnd, ulNumber /= 16) ;

          else if (idButton == ESCAPE)                  // escape
               ShowNumber (hwnd, ulNumber = ØL) ;

          else if (isxdigit (idButton))                 // hex digit
               {
               if (fNewNumber)
                    {
                    ulFirstNum = ulNumber ;
                    ulNumber = ØL ;
                    }
               fNewNumber = FALSE ;
```

Listing 14.5: The HEXCALC program (Continued)

```
                    if (ulNumber <= ULONG_MAX >> 4)
                         ShowNumber (hwnd,
                              ulNumber = 16 * ulNumber + idButton -
                                   (isdigit (idButton) ? '0' : 'A' - 10)) ;
                    else
                         WinAlarm (HWND_DESKTOP, WA_ERROR) ;
                    }
               else                                             // operation
                    {
                    if (!fNewNumber)
                         ShowNumber (hwnd, ulNumber =
                              CalcIt (ulFirstNum, iOperation, ulNumber)) ;
                    fNewNumber = TRUE ;
                    iOperation = idButton ;
                    }
               return 0 ;

          case WM_BUTTON1DOWN:
               WinAlarm (HWND_DESKTOP, WA_ERROR) ;
               break ;

          case WM_ERASEBACKGROUND:
               return MRFROMSHORT (1) ;
          }
     return WinDefWindowProc (hwnd, msg, mp1, mp2) ;
     }
```

The HEXCALC.H File

```
/*-----------------------
   HEXCALC.H header file
  -----------------------*/

#define ID_HEXCALC  1
#define ID_ICON     1

#define CLIENTCLASS "HexCalc"

#define ESCAPE      27
```

The HEXCALC.RC File

```
/*----------------------------
   HEXCALC.RC resource script
  ----------------------------*/
```

Listing 14.5: The HEXCALC program (Continued)

```
#include <os2.h>
#include "hexcalc.h"

POINTER ID_ICON hexcalc.ico

WINDOWTEMPLATE ID_HEXCALC
   {
   FRAME "", 0, 100, 40, 132, 122, WS_VISIBLE,
         FCF_TITLEBAR | FCF_SYSMENU | FCF_MINBUTTON | FCF_BORDER | FCF_TASKLIST
      {
      WINDOW "", FID_CLIENT, 0, 0, 132, 122, CLIENTCLASS, WS_VISIBLE
         {
         PUSHBUTTON "D",          68,   8,  84, 20, 14, BS_NOPOINTERFOCUS
         PUSHBUTTON "A",          65,   8,  68, 20, 14, BS_NOPOINTERFOCUS
         PUSHBUTTON "7",          55,   8,  52, 20, 14, BS_NOPOINTERFOCUS
         PUSHBUTTON "4",          52,   8,  36, 20, 14, BS_NOPOINTERFOCUS
         PUSHBUTTON "1",          49,   8,  20, 20, 14, BS_NOPOINTERFOCUS
         PUSHBUTTON "0",          48,   8,   4, 20, 14, BS_NOPOINTERFOCUS
         PUSHBUTTON "0",      ESCAPE,  32, 104, 68, 14, BS_NOPOINTERFOCUS
         PUSHBUTTON "E",          69,  32,  84, 20, 14, BS_NOPOINTERFOCUS
         PUSHBUTTON "B",          66,  32,  68, 20, 14, BS_NOPOINTERFOCUS
         PUSHBUTTON "8",          56,  32,  52, 20, 14, BS_NOPOINTERFOCUS
         PUSHBUTTON "5",          53,  32,  36, 20, 14, BS_NOPOINTERFOCUS
         PUSHBUTTON "2",          50,  32,  20, 20, 14, BS_NOPOINTERFOCUS
         PUSHBUTTON "Back",        8,  32,   4, 44, 14, BS_NOPOINTERFOCUS
         PUSHBUTTON "F",          70,  56,  84, 20, 14, BS_NOPOINTERFOCUS
         PUSHBUTTON "C",          67,  56,  68, 20, 14, BS_NOPOINTERFOCUS
         PUSHBUTTON "9",          57,  56,  52, 20, 14, BS_NOPOINTERFOCUS
         PUSHBUTTON "6",          54,  56,  36, 20, 14, BS_NOPOINTERFOCUS
         PUSHBUTTON "3",          51,  56,  20, 20, 14, BS_NOPOINTERFOCUS
         PUSHBUTTON "+",          43,  80,  84, 20, 14, BS_NOPOINTERFOCUS
         PUSHBUTTON "-",          45,  80,  68, 20, 14, BS_NOPOINTERFOCUS
         PUSHBUTTON "*",          42,  80,  52, 20, 14, BS_NOPOINTERFOCUS
         PUSHBUTTON "/",          47,  80,  36, 20, 14, BS_NOPOINTERFOCUS
         PUSHBUTTON "%",          37,  80,  20, 20, 14, BS_NOPOINTERFOCUS
         PUSHBUTTON "Equals",     61,  80,   4, 44, 14, BS_NOPOINTERFOCUS
         PUSHBUTTON "&",          38, 104,  84, 20, 14, BS_NOPOINTERFOCUS
         PUSHBUTTON "|",         124, 104,  68, 20, 14, BS_NOPOINTERFOCUS
         PUSHBUTTON "^",          94, 104,  52, 20, 14, BS_NOPOINTERFOCUS
         PUSHBUTTON "<",          60, 104,  36, 20, 14, BS_NOPOINTERFOCUS
         PUSHBUTTON ">",          62, 104,  20, 20, 14, BS_NOPOINTERFOCUS
         }
      }
   }
```

Listing 14.5: The HEXCALC program (Continued)

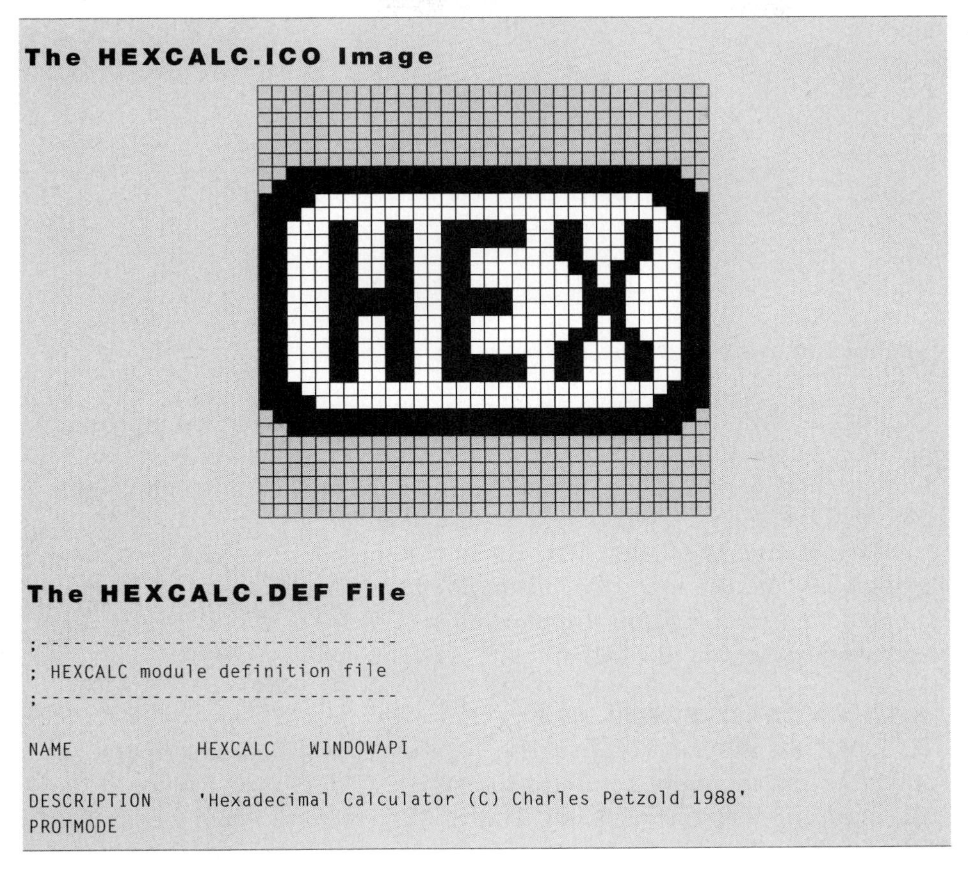

The HEXCALC.ICO Image

The HEXCALC.DEF File

```
;-------------------------------
; HEXCALC module definition file
;-------------------------------

NAME           HEXCALC   WINDOWAPI

DESCRIPTION    'Hexadecimal Calculator (C) Charles Petzold 1988'
PROTMODE
```

HEXCALC is a hexadecimal calculator with a complete keyboard and mouse interface. You can add, subtract, multiply, and divide 32-bit hexadecimal numbers, as well as perform the C remainder (%), left shift (<<), right shift (>>), and bitwise AND (&), OR (|), and exclusive-OR (^) operations.

The HEXCALC window is shown in Figure 14.5.

To use HEXCALC, type or click in the first number (up to eight hexadecimal digits) followed by the operation and then the second number. You can show the result by clicking the Equals button or by pressing either the keyboard equal key or the Enter key. To correct your entries, you can use either the Backspace key, the left arrow cursor movement key, or the Back button. Pressing Escape or clicking the result box clears the current entry.

Figure 14.5: The HEXCALC window

Results are always truncated to 32 bits, just as if you were performing the operation on two unsigned long integers in a C program. The only special handling is a check for division by zero before doing a division or remainder operation. In this case, HEXCALC sets the result to FFFFFFFF.

The client window of HEXCALC contains 29 push button controls, yet the program has not one call to *WinCreateStdWindow* or *WinCreateWindow*. Everything is defined in the dialog box template in HEXCALC.RC. All the windows are created by one call to *WinLoadDlg*.

THE HEXCALC TEMPLATE

The dialog box template shown in the HEXCALC.RC resource script describes the size, appearance, and structure of HEXCALC's main window. The template begins with the WINDOWTEMPLATE keyword, which is equivalent to the DLGTEMPLATE keyword used in the other templates shown in this chapter. The top-level window is denoted by a FRAME statement. The statement contains a window style of WS_VISIBLE and frame creation flags of FCF_TITLEBAR, FCF_SYSMENU, FCF_MINBUTTON, FCF_BORDER, and FCF_TASKLIST, such as you might use in a *WinCreateStdWindow* function.

The WINDOW statement that follows specifies a child of the frame window. This is the client window of HEXCALC. The child window ID is set to FID_CLIENT, and the class name is set to the identifier CLIENTCLASS, defined in HEXCALC.H as "HexCalc." This window class is registered in HEXCALC.C before the call to *WinLoadDlg*.

The template then defines 29 children of the client window with 29 PUSHBUTTON statements. The push buttons are given the style of BS_NOPOINTERFOCUS, which causes the push button not to get the input focus when clicked. I'll discuss the push button child window IDs shortly.

CREATING THE WINDOWS

The *main* function in HEXCALC.C looks as though it's missing something, and it is: It doesn't have a call to *WinCreateStdWindow*. Instead, the *WinLoadDlg* function creates a frame window, client window, and 29 push buttons based on the template in HEXCALC.RC. The frame window also creates a title bar, system menu, and minimize box based on the frame creation flags specified in the template.

Look at the call to *WinLoadDlg*:

```
hwndFrame = WinLoadDlg (HWND_DESKTOP, HWND_DESKTOP,
                        NULL, NULLHANDLE, ID_HEXCALC, NULL) ;
```

It doesn't even specify a window procedure for the dialog box. The only window procedure in HEXCALC is *ClientWndProc*, which is the window procedure for the "HexCalc" class registered in *main* and specified in the WINDOW statement in the template.

Following the call to *WinLoadDlg*, the windows in HEXCALC function as if they were created with a call to *WinCreateStdWindow* and 29 calls to *WinCreateWindow*. *ClientWndProc* gets WM_COMMAND messages from the push buttons and WM_CHAR messages from the keyboard.

CREATIVE USE OF CONTROL IDS

The programs developed so far in this chapter have used identifiers defined in a header file as the child window IDs of controls within a dialog box. The child window IDs of the push buttons in HEXCALC appear to be random, but they're not. The IDs have been set to the ASCII codes of the corresponding number, letter, or symbol that appears inside the push button.

This is an easy way to add a keyboard interface to the calculator. When the user clicks a child window button, the child window sends *ClientWndProc* a WM_COMMAND message with the *cmd* field equal to the control ID. When the user presses a character key on the keyboard, HEXCALC's main window receives a WM_CHAR message with the ASCII code of the character.

When *ClientWndProc* receives a WM_CHAR message, it first makes a few adjustments for the left cursor key, the Escape key, and the two Enter keys. Then it checks to see if a button exists with an ID equal to the typed character. If so, *ClientWndProc* sends the button a BM_CLICK message:

```
hwndButton = WinWindowFromID (hwnd, CHARMSG(&msg)->chr) ;

if (hwndButton != NULLHANDLE)
     WinSendMsg (hwndButton, BM_CLICK, NULL, NULL) ;
```

The BM_CLICK message causes the button to do two things: First, the button inverts itself briefly to appear as if it has been clicked. This gives the user visual feedback. Second, the button sends *ClientWndProc* a WM_COMMAND message—again—just as if it had been clicked with the mouse. This allows *ClientWndProc* to process both keyboard and mouse input as WM_COMMAND messages.

WINDOWS AND DIALOG BOXES

We've come full circle. We began creating standard windows in Chapter 2. Since Chapter 8 we've been looking at different ways that windows get input, first by processing keyboard and mouse input directly, then by using child window controls, and finally by moving to dialog boxes.

Now we've created a dialog box that seems to function just like a standard window! Of course, dialog boxes are normal windows, so it shouldn't be too surprising that we can do this.

Part 5

Miscellaneous Topics

Cut, Copy, and Paste: The Clipboard

Dynamic Link Libraries

Multithreaded Programming Techniques

Printing Graphics and Text

Cut, Copy, and Paste: The Clipboard

Transferring text with the clipboard

Transferring bitmaps with the clipboard

Chapter 15

The clipboard is a mechanism for transferring data between Presentation Manager applications. A program that makes use of the clipboard usually has an Edit menu with the options Cut, Copy, and Paste. The Cut and Copy options direct the program to transfer data to the clipboard, and the Paste option directs the program to transfer data from the clipboard to the program.

The clipboard is also useful for some operations that do not involve transferring data between applications. These operations most commonly occur in programs that work with documents—word processing programs, for example. Such programs use the clipboard as a storage area when moving text from one part of the document to another.

To move text within a word processing document, the user first selects part of the document to be moved. The user then selects Cut or Copy from the menu. Both commands copy the selection to the clipboard; the Cut command also deletes the selection from the document.

To use the Paste command in a word processing program, the user first moves the cursor to the point in the document where the text from the clipboard should be inserted. The user then selects the Paste command. The program copies the text from the clipboard to the document. In traditional word processing terminology, a "block copy" is a clipboard Copy command followed by a Paste command. A "block move" is a clipboard Cut command followed by a Paste command.

Of course, word processing programs have included block copy and block move operations for years without any help from a clipboard. But a

Presentation Manager program should use the clipboard for these operations rather than its own internal logic. Because all Presentation Manager programs have access to the same clipboard, a user can cut or copy data from one program and paste it into another program. The clipboard makes use of shared memory blocks to allow these interprocess transfers.

But the clipboard is really for the convenience of the user. The user controls what is copied to the clipboard by selecting menu commands from Presentation Manager programs. A program should copy data to the clipboard only on a Cut or Copy command; it should not use the clipboard as a form of temporary storage apart from these two commands.

Three standard data formats can be stored in the clipboard: text, bitmaps, and metafiles. (A *metafile* is a collection of GPI drawing commands.) This chapter discusses the text and bitmap formats.

TRANSFERRING TEXT WITH THE CLIPBOARD

A program that makes use of the clipboard generally has an Edit option on its top-level menu. The standard commands on the Edit submenu (in the order in which they usually appear) are as follows:

Menu Command	Keyboard Accelerator	Operation
Cut	Shift+Del	Copy selection to clipboard and delete selection from document
Copy	Ctrl+Ins	Copy selection to clipboard, but do not delete selection from document
Paste	Shift+Ins	Copy clipboard contents to document
Clear	Del	Delete selection from document but do not copy selection to clipboard

In some cases, you may not have all of these commands, but you'll probably include at least Copy and Paste. As you can see, the Clear option doesn't involve the clipboard at all. However, you'll want to write your Clear logic when you write your Cut logic because Cut is equivalent to a Copy followed by a Clear.

The most common format of clipboard data is a block of text in normal ASCII format. Each text line is terminated by the carriage return (\r) and line feed (\n) control characters. The text can contain tab characters (\t). The entire block is terminated by a zero byte.

A block of text that your program copies into the clipboard must be stored in a shared memory block allocated specifically for this purpose. To allocate this memory segment you use the OS/2 *DosAllocSharedMem* function with the OBJ_GIVEABLE option. This allows the Presentation Manager to call *DosGiveSharedMem* within its clipboard logic to give access rights to other programs that need to copy the text from the clipboard.

PREPARING THE SHARED MEMORY BLOCK

Let's suppose that the user of your program has selected a block of text in a document and chooses the Copy or Cut command to copy it to the clipboard. I'll assume your program has two variables named *pchText* (a pointer to the beginning of the character string to be copied to the clipboard) and *iTextLen* (the length of this string). In the general case, *pchText* is a pointer to a text string within a larger document, and the selected block of text will not itself be terminated by a zero byte.

In your program you define a variable of type PCHAR, a pointer to a character string:

```
PCHAR pchClipText ;
```

You first allocate a block of memory that is the length of the selected text string plus 1 byte (for the terminating zero). To do this, use the *DosAllocSharedMem* function with numerous flags:

```
DosAllocSeg ((PVOID) &pchClipText, NULL, iLen,
             PAG_COMMIT | PAG_READ | PAG_WRITE |
             OBJ_TILE | OBJ_GIVEABLE) ;
```

This function allocates a block of shareable memory and stores the pointer in *pchClipText.*

Now copy the text addressed by *pchText* to the memory block addressed by *pchClipText.* Don't forget to add the zero byte that terminates the text.

PUTTING TEXT IN THE CLIPBOARD

Now that you've prepared the shared memory block, you're ready to put the text in the clipboard. You use four Presentation Manager clipboard function calls to put text into the clipboard: *WinOpenClipbrd*, *WinEmptyClipbrd*, *WinSetClipbrdData*, and *WinCloseClipbrd.* First you open the clipboard and empty it of all data:

```
WinOpenClipbrd (hab) ;
WinEmptyClipbrd (hab) ;
```

Call *WinSetClipbrdData* to set the text string referenced by *pchClipText* into the clipboard:

```
WinSetClipbrdData (hab, (ULONG) pchClipText,CF_TEXT, CFI_POINTER) ;
```

Note that the second parameter is declared as a ULONG in the PMWIN.H header file, so you should cast the pointer to a ULONG to prevent compiler warning messages. The third parameter indicates the format of this data. In this case the format is CF_TEXT. (The CF prefix stands for "clipboard format.") The last parameter is the clipboard format information flag. You set this to CFI_POINTER to indicate that the second parameter is a pointer. Finally, close the clipboard:

```
WinCloseClipbrd (hab) ;
```

You're done.

Do not call *DosFreeMem* to free the block of memory you allocated using *DosAllocSharedMem*. (Nothing bad will happen if you do, but the *DosFreeMem* function will fail because the block has already been freed for your process by the Presentation Manager.) After you call *WinSetClipbrdData*, do not attempt to reference the text stored in this shared memory block. You allocated this block specifically for transferring the text to the clipboard; once you call *WinSetClipbrdData*, the text no longer belongs to your program.

GETTING TEXT FROM THE CLIPBOARD

When transferring data from the clipboard to your program (the Paste operation), you use three functions: *WinOpenClipbrd*, *WinQueryClipbrdData*, and *WinCloseClipbrd*. The *WinQueryClipbrdData* function gives your program temporary access to the shared memory block containing the data stored by the clipboard.

Again, you should define a variable of type PCHAR:

```
PCHAR pchClipText ;
```

You begin by opening the clipboard:

```
WinOpenClipbrd (hab) ;
```

You then obtain a pointer to the text block stored in the clipboard by calling *WinQueryClipbrdData*:

```
pchClipText = (PVOID) WinQueryClipbrdData (hab, CF_TEXT) ;
```

The return value of *WinQueryClipbrdData* is declared as a ULONG. To prevent compiler warning messages, you must cast this value to a pointer before assigning it to *pchClipText*. If there is no text in the clipboard, *WinQueryClipbrdData* returns a 0. In that case, you simply call *WinCloseClipbrd*.

The *pchClipText* pointer points to a shared memory block containing clipboard text contents. During the *WinQueryClipbrdData* call, the Presentation Manager calls *DosGiveSharedMem* to give your program access to this segment. You can reference this shared memory block only while the clipboard is still open. Do not alter the text in the clipboard. The block of text is terminated by a zero byte so you can use the *strlen* function to determine the length of the string.

What you do with this text depends on the program. For example, you may want to allocate a block of local memory and copy the contents of the clipboard to it. When you finish referencing the clipboard text, you close the clipboard:

```
WinCloseClipbrd (hab) ;
```

Do not attempt to use the *pchClipText* pointer after the clipboard is closed, because the block is freed for use by your process.

THE OPEN CLIPBOARD

Only one process can have the clipboard open at a time. If one program has the clipboard open and another program calls *WinOpenClipbrd*, the function will not return until the first program calls *WinCloseClipbrd*. For this reason, you should call *WinOpenClipbrd* and *WinCloseClipbrd* within the course of a single message.

You can also obtain information about the current contents of the clipboard without opening the clipboard. The following function call returns TRUE if the clipboard contains data in the CF_TEXT format and FALSE otherwise:

```
WinQueryClipbrdFmtInfo (hab, CF_TEXT, &ulfInfo)
```

On return from the function, the *ulfInfo* variable is set to CFI_POINTER if the clipboard contains data in the CF_TEXT format.

The *WinQueryClipbrdFmtInfo* function is also very handy during processing of the WM_INITMENU message. When the Edit submenu is invoked, the Presentation Manager sends your program a WM_INITMENU message with the low USHORT of *mp1* set to the menu ID of the Edit menu. You can take this opportunity to enable or disable the Cut, Copy, Paste, and Clear options. You disable the Cut, Copy, and Clear options if the user has not selected any text in the document. You disable the Paste option if *WinQueryClipbrdFmtInfo* returns FALSE. However, to be on the safe side, you should still check for a zero return value from *WinQueryClipbrdData* when you actually carry out the Paste command.

THE CLIPBOARD AND HEXCALC2

You'll recall the HEXCALC program from Chapter 14. A revised version, called HEXCALC2 (shown in Listing 15.1), uses the clipboard to read a string of hexadecimal numbers and symbols (such as + and –) from the clipboard and calculate the result.

Listing 15.1: The HEXCALC program

The HEXCALC2.MAK File

```
#------------------------
# HEXCALC2.MAK make file
#------------------------

hexcalc2.exe : hexcalc2.obj hexcalc2.def hexcalc.res
     $(PRGLINK) hexcalc2, hexcalc2, NUL, $(PRGLIB), hexcalc2
     rc hexcalc.res hexcalc2.exe

hexcalc2.obj: hexcalc2.c hexcalc.h
     $(PRGCC) hexcalc2.c

hexcalc.res : hexcalc.rc hexcalc.h
     $(PRGRC) hexcalc.rc
```

The HEXCALC2.C File

```
/*-------------------------------------------------------------------
   HEXCALC2.C -- Hexadecimal Calculator with Clipboard Cut and Paste
                 (c) Charles Petzold, 1993
  -------------------------------------------------------------------*/

#define INCL_WIN
#include <os2.h>
#include <ctype.h>
#include <limits.h>
#include <stdio.h>
#include <stdlib.h>
#include <string.h>
#include "hexcalc.h"

#define IDM_COPY    256
#define IDM_PASTE   257

MRESULT EXPENTRY ClientWndProc (HWND, ULONG, MPARAM, MPARAM) ;

int main (void)
     {
     HAB  hab ;
```

Listing 15.1: The HEXCALC program (Continued)

```
     HMQ  hmq ;
     HWND hwndFrame ;
     QMSG qmsg ;

     hab = WinInitialize (0) ;
     hmq = WinCreateMsgQueue (hab, 0) ;

     WinRegisterClass (hab, CLIENTCLASS, ClientWndProc, 0L, 0) ;

     hwndFrame = WinLoadDlg (HWND_DESKTOP, HWND_DESKTOP,
                             NULL, NULLHANDLE, ID_HEXCALC, NULL) ;

     WinSendMsg (hwndFrame, WM_SETICON, (MPARAM)
                 WinLoadPointer (HWND_DESKTOP, NULLHANDLE, ID_ICON), NULL) ;

     WinSetFocus (HWND_DESKTOP, WinWindowFromID (hwndFrame, FID_CLIENT)) ;

     while (WinGetMsg (hab, &qmsg, NULLHANDLE, 0, 0))
          WinDispatchMsg (hab, &qmsg) ;

     WinDestroyWindow (hwndFrame) ;
     WinDestroyMsgQueue (hmq) ;
     WinTerminate (hab) ;
     return 0 ;
     }

HACCEL AddItemsToSysMenu (HAB hab, HWND hwndFrame)
     {
     static CHAR     *szMenuText [3] = { NULL, "~Copy\tCtrl+Ins",
                                               "~Paste\tShift+Ins" } ;
     static MENUITEM mi [3] = {
                              MIT_END, MIS_SEPARATOR, 0, 0,         0, 0,
                              MIT_END, MIS_TEXT,      0, IDM_COPY,  0, 0,
                              MIT_END, MIS_TEXT,      0, IDM_PASTE, 0, 0
                              } ;
     ACCELTABLE      *pacct ;
     HACCEL          haccel ;
     HWND            hwndSysMenu, hwndSysSubMenu ;
     INT             idSysMenu, iItem ;
     MENUITEM        miSysMenu ;

                              // Add items to system menu

     hwndSysMenu = WinWindowFromID (hwndFrame, FID_SYSMENU) ;
     idSysMenu = SHORT1FROMMR (WinSendMsg (hwndSysMenu,
                                           MM_ITEMIDFROMPOSITION,
                                           NULL, NULL)) ;

     WinSendMsg (hwndSysMenu, MM_QUERYITEM,
```

Listing 15.1: The HEXCALC program (Continued)

```
                MPFROM2SHORT (idSysMenu, FALSE),
                MPFROMP (&miSysMenu)) ;

     hwndSysSubMenu = miSysMenu.hwndSubMenu ;

     for (iItem = 0 ; iItem < 3 ; iItem++)
          WinSendMsg (hwndSysSubMenu, MM_INSERTITEM,
                      MPFROMP (mi + iItem),
                      MPFROMP (szMenuText [iItem])) ;

                                // Create and set accelerator table

     pacct = malloc (sizeof (ACCELTABLE) + sizeof (ACCEL)) ;

     pacct->cAccel        = 2 ;    // Number of accelerators
     pacct->codepage      = 0 ;    // Not used

     pacct->aaccel[0].fs  = AF_VIRTUALKEY | AF_CONTROL ;
     pacct->aaccel[0].key = VK_INSERT ;
     pacct->aaccel[0].cmd = IDM_COPY ;

     pacct->aaccel[1].fs  = AF_VIRTUALKEY | AF_SHIFT ;
     pacct->aaccel[1].key = VK_INSERT ;
     pacct->aaccel[1].cmd = IDM_PASTE ;

     haccel = WinCreateAccelTable (hab, pacct) ;
     WinSetAccelTable (hab, haccel, hwndFrame) ;

     free (pacct) ;

     return haccel ;
     }

VOID EnableSysMenuItem (HWND hwnd, INT idItem, BOOL fEnable)
     {
     HWND hwndSysMenu ;

     hwndSysMenu = WinWindowFromID (WinQueryWindow (hwnd, QW_PARENT),
                                    FID_SYSMENU) ;

     WinSendMsg (hwndSysMenu, MM_SETITEMATTR,
                 MPFROM2SHORT ((USHORT) idItem, TRUE),
                 MPFROM2SHORT (MIA_DISABLED, fEnable ? 0 : MIA_DISABLED)) ;
     }

void ShowNumber (HWND hwnd, ULONG ulNumber)
     {
     CHAR szBuffer [20] ;
```

Listing 15.1: The HEXCALC program (Continued)

```
     sprintf (szBuffer, "%lX", ulNumber) ;

     WinSetWindowText (WinWindowFromID (hwnd, ESCAPE), szBuffer) ;
     }

ULONG CalcIt (ULONG ulFirstNum, INT iOperation, ULONG ulNum)
     {
     switch (iOperation)
          {
          case '=' : return ulNum ;
          case '+' : return ulFirstNum +  ulNum ;
          case '-' : return ulFirstNum -  ulNum ;
          case '*' : return ulFirstNum *  ulNum ;
          case '&' : return ulFirstNum &  ulNum ;
          case '|' : return ulFirstNum |  ulNum ;
          case '^' : return ulFirstNum ^  ulNum ;
          case '<' : return ulFirstNum << ulNum ;
          case '>' : return ulFirstNum >> ulNum ;
          case '/' : return ulNum ? ulFirstNum / ulNum : ULONG_MAX ;
          case '%' : return ulNum ? ulFirstNum % ulNum : ULONG_MAX ;
          }
     return 0L ;
     }

MRESULT EXPENTRY ClientWndProc (HWND hwnd, ULONG msg, MPARAM mp1, MPARAM mp2)
     {
     static BOOL   fNewNumber = TRUE ;
     static HAB    hab ;
     static HACCEL haccel ;
     static INT    iOperation = '=' ;
     static ULONG  ulNumber, ulFirstNum ;
     HWND          hwndButton ;
     INT           i, iLen, idButton ;
     PCHAR         pchClipText ;
     QMSG          qmsg ;

     switch (msg)
          {
          case WM_CREATE:
               hab = WinQueryAnchorBlock (hwnd) ;
               haccel = AddItemsToSysMenu (hab,
                              WinQueryWindow (hwnd, QW_PARENT)) ;
               return 0 ;

          case WM_CHAR:
               if (CHARMSG(&msg)->fs & KC_KEYUP)
                    return 0 ;

               if (CHARMSG(&msg)->fs & KC_VIRTUALKEY)
```

Listing 15.1: The HEXCALC program (Continued)

```
               switch (CHARMSG(&msg)->vkey)
                    {
                    case VK_LEFT:
                         if (!(CHARMSG(&msg)->fs & KC_CHAR))
                              {
                              CHARMSG(&msg)->chr = '\b' ;
                              CHARMSG(&msg)->fs |= KC_CHAR ;
                              }
                         break ;

                    case VK_ESC:
                         CHARMSG(&msg)->chr = ESCAPE ;
                         CHARMSG(&msg)->fs |= KC_CHAR ;
                         break ;

                    case VK_NEWLINE:
                    case VK_ENTER:
                         CHARMSG(&msg)->chr = '=' ;
                         CHARMSG(&msg)->fs |= KC_CHAR ;
                         break ;
                    }

          if (CHARMSG(&msg)->fs & KC_CHAR)
               {
               CHARMSG(&msg)->chr = toupper (CHARMSG(&msg)->chr) ;

               hwndButton = WinWindowFromID (hwnd, CHARMSG(&msg)->chr) ;

               if (hwndButton != NULLHANDLE)
                    WinSendMsg (hwndButton, BM_CLICK, NULL, NULL) ;
               else
                    WinAlarm (HWND_DESKTOP, WA_ERROR) ;
               }
          return Ø ;

     case WM_COMMAND:
          idButton = COMMANDMSG(&msg)->cmd ;

          if (idButton == IDM_COPY)                    // "Copy"
               {
               hwndButton = WinWindowFromID (hwnd, ESCAPE) ;
               iLen = WinQueryWindowTextLength (hwndButton) + 1 ;

               DosAllocSharedMem ((PVOID) &pchClipText, NULL, (ULONG) iLen,
                                   PAG_COMMIT | PAG_READ | PAG_WRITE |
                                   OBJ_TILE | OBJ_GIVEABLE) ;

               WinQueryWindowText (hwndButton, iLen, pchClipText) ;
```

Listing 15.1: The HEXCALC program (Continued)

```
          WinOpenClipbrd (hab) ;
          WinEmptyClipbrd (hab) ;
          WinSetClipbrdData (hab, (ULONG) pchClipText, CF_TEXT,
                             CFI_POINTER) ;
          WinCloseClipbrd (hab) ;
          }

     else if (idButton == IDM_PASTE)               // "Paste"
          {
          EnableSysMenuItem (hwnd, IDM_COPY,  FALSE) ;
          EnableSysMenuItem (hwnd, IDM_PASTE, FALSE) ;

          WinOpenClipbrd (hab) ;

          pchClipText = (PVOID) WinQueryClipbrdData (hab, CF_TEXT) ;

          if (pchClipText != 0)
               {
               for (i = 0 ; pchClipText[i] ; i++)
                    {
                    if (pchClipText[i] == '\r')
                         WinSendMsg (hwnd, WM_CHAR,
                                     MPFROM2SHORT (KC_CHAR, 1),
                                     MPFROM2SHORT ('=', 0)) ;

                    else if (pchClipText[i] != '\n' &&
                             pchClipText[i] != ' ')
                         WinSendMsg (hwnd, WM_CHAR,
                                     MPFROM2SHORT (KC_CHAR, 1),
                                     MPFROM2SHORT (pchClipText[i],
                                                   0)) ;

                    while (WinPeekMsg (hab, &qmsg, NULLHANDLE,
                                       0, 0, PM_NOREMOVE))
                         {
                         if (qmsg.msg == WM_QUIT)
                              {
                              WinCloseClipbrd (hab) ;
                              return 0 ;
                              }
                         else
                              {
                              WinGetMsg (hab, &qmsg, NULLHANDLE,
                                                   0, 0) ;
                              WinDispatchMsg (hab, &qmsg) ;
                              }
                         }
                    }
               }
```

Listing 15.1: The HEXCALC program (Continued)

```
                    WinCloseClipbrd (hab) ;

                    EnableSysMenuItem (hwnd, IDM_COPY,  TRUE) ;
                    EnableSysMenuItem (hwnd, IDM_PASTE, TRUE) ;
                    }

               else if (idButton == '\b')                 // backspace
                    ShowNumber (hwnd, ulNumber /= 16) ;

               else if (idButton == ESCAPE)               // escape
                    ShowNumber (hwnd, ulNumber = 0L) ;

               else if (isxdigit (idButton))              // hex digit
                    {
                    if (fNewNumber)
                         {
                         ulFirstNum = ulNumber ;
                         ulNumber = 0L ;
                         }
                    fNewNumber = FALSE ;

                    if (ulNumber <= ULONG_MAX >> 4)
                         ShowNumber (hwnd,
                              ulNumber = 16 * ulNumber + idButton -
                                   (isdigit (idButton) ? '0' : 'A' - 10)) ;
                    else
                         WinAlarm (HWND_DESKTOP, WA_ERROR) ;
                    }
               else                                       // operation
                    {
                    if (!fNewNumber)
                         ShowNumber (hwnd, ulNumber =
                              CalcIt (ulFirstNum, iOperation, ulNumber)) ;
                    fNewNumber = TRUE ;
                    iOperation = idButton ;
                    }
               return 0 ;

          case WM_BUTTON1DOWN:
               WinAlarm (HWND_DESKTOP, WA_ERROR) ;
               break ;

          case WM_ERASEBACKGROUND:
               return MRFROMSHORT (1) ;

          case WM_DESTROY:
               WinDestroyAccelTable (haccel) ;
               return 0 ;
          }
```

Listing 15.1: The HEXCALC program (Continued)

```
     return WinDefWindowProc (hwnd, msg, mp1, mp2) ;
     }
```

The HEXCALC2.DEF File

```
;-------------------------------
; HEXCALC2.DEF module definition file
;-------------------------------

NAME           HEXCALC2  WINDOWAPI

DESCRIPTION    'Hexadecimal Calculator With Clipboard (C) Charles Petzold 1993'
PROTMODE
```

Compiling HEXCALC2 also requires the HEXCALC.H, HEXCALC.RC, and HEXCALC.ICO files from Chapter 14.

The Copy and Paste options are located on HEXCALC2's System menu. You can copy the current result in HEXCALC2 (the number appearing in the topmost button) to the clipboard using Copy. But it is the Paste command that makes HEXCALC2 most useful. First enter the following text in a Presentation Manager text editor program such as the OS/2 System Editor:

```
123+234*8=
```

Select the text and use the editor's Copy command to copy it to the clipboard. Now invoke the Paste command in HEXCALC2. The buttons will quickly flash as the characters are entered. The result then appears: 1AB8. We've gone from a manual calculator to an automated one.

The *AddItemsToSysMenu* function in HEXCALC2.C adds the Copy and Paste options to the program's System menu using a technique discussed in Chapter 13. As you'll recall, both menus and buttons use WM_COMMAND messages to inform their owner of user input. HEXCALC2 makes use of buttons with IDs set to the ASCII codes of the button text. For this reason, the IDM_COPY and IDM_PASTE commands are given IDs of 256 and 257—out of the range of the ASCII codes.

The *AddItemsToSysMenu* function also defines an accelerator table for the two new menu items. First, it uses *malloc* to allocate storage for a structure of type ACCELTABLE. One field of the ACCELTABLE structure is an array of structures of type ACCEL. An ACCEL structure exists for each item in the accelerator table. (The definition of ACCELTABLE in PMWIN.H allocates space for an array of only one ACCEL structure; this is why memory for a larger ACCELTABLE structure must be allocated using *malloc*.)

After the fields of the structure are initialized, the accelerator table is created by a call to *WinCreateAccelTable*, which returns a handle to the table. The *WinSetAccelTable* function causes the frame window to use this accelerator table. The handle to the accelerator table is returned from *WinAddItemsToSysMenu* back to *ClientWndProc* so that the accelerator table can be destroyed during processing of the WM_DESTROY message.

The WM_COMMAND processing in HEXCALC2 is expanded to include the Copy and Paste commands. For Copy, HEXCALC2 needs to retrieve the text displayed in the result button and make a copy for the clipboard. The ID of this button is the ASCII Escape code, so the button handle can be obtained by calling

```
hwndButton = WinWindowFromID (hwnd, ESCAPE) ;
```

HEXCALC2 obtains the length of the button text by calling

```
iLen = WinQueryWindowTextLength (hwndButton) + 1 ;
```

Because this statement adds 1 to the window text length, *iLen* is large enough to accommodate a terminating zero byte. HEXCALC2 then allocates a block of shareable memory. Now it need only call *WinQueryWindowText* to copy the button text into the shareable memory:

```
WinQueryWindowText (hwndButton, iLen, pchClipText) ;
```

Finally, HEXCALC2 calls the four standard clipboard functions

```
WinOpenClipbrd (hab) ;
WinEmptyClipbrd (hab) ;
WinSetClipbrdData (hab, (ULONG) pchClipText, CF_TEXT,
                   CFI_POINTER) ;
WinCloseClipbrd (hab) ;
```

Processing of the Paste command is a bit different from the normal case. It starts out in a fairly standard fashion. HEXCALC2 opens the clipboard and obtains a pointer to the clipboard memory:

```
WinOpenClipbrd (hab) ;
pchClipText = (PVOID) WinQueryClipbrdData (hab, CF_TEXT) ;
```

But *ClientWndProc* doesn't need to store this text in local memory. Instead, the window procedure uses a *for* loop to go through the memory block and send the individual characters as WM_CHAR messages to itself. Any line feed characters or space characters are ignored (normally HEXCALC2 would beep at these invalid characters), and carriage returns are translated into equal signs, but otherwise the characters are translated directly into WM_CHAR messages:

```
WinSendMsg (hwnd, WM_CHAR,
            MPFROM2SHORT (KC_CHAR, 1),
            MPFROM2SHORT (pchClipText[i], 0)) ;
```

This is why the buttons in HEXCALC2 flash when you paste a numeric calculation from the clipboard into the program: The Paste logic mimics your fingers.

But think about the message traffic for a moment. *ClientWndProc* receives a WM_COMMAND message for IDM_PASTE when you select Paste from the System menu. The window procedure processes this message by sending itself WM_CHAR messages of the characters from the clipboard. The WM_CHAR processing in *ClientWndProc* obtains the window handle of the button that corresponds to the ASCII code in the WM_CHAR message and sends the button a BM_CLICK message. The button responds by flashing and posting a WM_COMMAND message to *ClientWndProc* with the button ID.

In response to the original WM_COMMAND message, the WM_CHAR and BM_CLICK messages are sent directly to the appropriate window procedure. But the WM_COMMAND message from the button (the final result of the Paste operation) is *posted* to the message queue. This is a problem because the message queue can store only a limited number of messages; it is quite possible that the queue will fill up with unprocessed WM_COMMAND messages from the buttons.

For this reason, the Paste processing in HEXCALC2 contains the following code, which is executed after each WM_CHAR message is sent:

```
while (WinPeekMsg (hab, &qmsg, NULLHANDLE,
                   0, 0, PM_NOREMOVE))
     {
     if (qmsg.msg == WM_QUIT)
          {
          WinCloseClipbrd (hab) ;
          return 0 ;
          }
     else
          {
          WinGetMsg (hab, &qmsg, NULLHANDLE,
                     0, 0) ;
          WinDispatchMsg (hab, &qmsg) ;
          }
     }
```

The *WinPeekMsg* function is similar to *WinGetMsg* but with two important differences. First, the last parameter to *WinPeekMsg* can be set to either PM_REMOVE or PM_NOREMOVE to remove or not remove the next message from the message queue. Second, if no message exists in the message queue, *WinGetMsg* will wait for one. *WinPeekMsg* returns immediately if there are no pending messages. The return value of *WinPeekMsg* is TRUE if a message was retrieved from the queue and FALSE otherwise.

In HEXCALC2, *WinPeekMsg* uses the PM_NOREMOVE option. If *WinPeekMsg* returns TRUE, the message is retrieved from the queue with *WinGetMsg* and dispatched to the window procedure with *WinDispatchMsg*. This applies for all messages except WM_QUIT—a case I'll discuss shortly.

The primary purpose of the *WinPeekMsg* function in HEXCALC2 is to retrieve WM_COMMAND messages posted by the buttons and prevent the message queue from overflowing. But this code also has some interesting side effects. If you paste a lengthy calculation into HEXCALC2, you can continue to use the mouse and keyboard with the program. For example, you can use the mouse to move the HEXCALC2 window in the middle of the paste operation. These mouse messages are queued, so *WinPeekMsg* returns TRUE when it encounters one, and the messages are retrieved and dispatched as usual.

You can also select Close from the System menu in the middle of the Paste operation. For this reason, the WM_QUIT command is checked explicitly following the *WinPeekMsg* call. The WM_QUIT message is not removed from the message queue. HEXCALC2 simply closes the clipboard and stops the Paste operation by returning from the window procedure.

Of course, if you can select Close from the System menu while a Paste operation is in progress, you could also select Copy or Paste. For this reason, HEXCALC2 calls the *EnableSysMenuItem* function to disable these two items before the Paste operation. When Paste is finished, HEXCALC2 calls the function again to enable the items.

I'll have more to say about the *WinPeekMsg* function in Chapter 17.

TRANSFERRING BITMAPS WITH THE CLIPBOARD

In some ways, transferring bitmaps to and from the clipboard is easier than transferring text. The only hard part is that you generally must make a copy of any bitmap you put in the clipboard if you want to continue using the bitmap in your program. You must also make a copy of a bitmap you get from the clipboard if you want to use the bitmap after the clipboard is closed. In the sample BLOWUP program used in this section, the *CopyBitmap* function does this.

TRANSFERRING FROM PROGRAM TO CLIPBOARD

Suppose you have a handle to a bitmap, and it is stored in the variable *hbm* of type HBITMAP. You want to keep this handle, but you want to transfer a copy of the bitmap to the clipboard.

First, you make a copy of the bitmap and store the handle in another variable (named *hbmClip*, for example) of type HBITMAP:

```
hbmClip = CopyBitmap (hbm) ;
```

If the copy operation is successful, you call the same four functions you use to transfer text into the clipboard:

```
WinOpenClipbrd (hab) ;
WinEmptyClipbrd (hab) ;
WinSetClipbrdData (hab, (ULONG) hbmClip, CF_BITMAP, CFI_HANDLE) ;
WinCloseClipbrd (hab) ;
```

Notice that the second parameter to *WinSetClipbrdData* is the handle of the bitmap copy rather than a pointer to shareable memory. This parameter is followed by the identifiers CF_BITMAP to indicate bitmap format and CFI_-HANDLE to indicate that a handle is being passed as the second parameter.

Following the *WinSetClipbrdData* call, do not use or delete *hbmClip*. This copy of the bitmap is specifically for the clipboard.

TRANSFERRING FROM CLIPBOARD TO PROGRAM

To transfer a bitmap from the clipboard into your program, first open the clipboard and obtain the bitmap handle:

```
WinOpenClipbrd (hab) ;
hbmClip = (HBITMAP) WinQueryClipbrdData (hab, CF_BITMAP) ;
```

The *WinQueryClipbrdData* function returns 0L if the clipboard does not contain a bitmap. Thus, *hbmClip* will be NULL. The *hbmClip* handle will be valid only when the clipboard is open. You'll probably want to make a copy of the bitmap and then close the clipboard:

```
if (hbmClip != NULL)
     hbm = CopyBitmap (hbmClip) ;
WinCloseClipbrd (hab) ;
```

I told you this was easy. Now all we need is that *CopyBitmap* function.

THE BLOWUP PROGRAM

The *CopyBitmap* function and some other goodies are shown in the BLOWUP program in Listing 15.2.

Listing 15.2: The BLOWUP program

The BLOWUP.MAK File

```
#----------------------
# BLOWUP.MAK make file
#----------------------

blowup.exe : blowup.obj blowup.def blowup.res
     $(PRGLINK) blowup, blowup, NUL, $(PRGLIB), blowup
     rc blowup.res

blowup.obj : blowup.c blowup.h
     $(PRGCC) blowup.c

blowup.res : blowup.rc blowup.h
     $(PRGRC) blowup
```

The BLOWUP.C File

```
/*---------------------------------------
   BLOWUP.C -- Screen Capture Program
               (c) Charles Petzold, 1993
  ---------------------------------------*/

#define INCL_WIN
#define INCL_GPI
#include <os2.h>
#include <string.h>
#include "blowup.h"

MRESULT EXPENTRY ClientWndProc (HWND, ULONG, MPARAM, MPARAM) ;
BOOL             BeginTracking (PRECTL) ;
HBITMAP          CopyScreenToBitmap (PRECTL) ;
HBITMAP          CopyBitmap (HBITMAP) ;
VOID             BitmapCreationError (HWND) ;

CHAR szClientClass [] = "BlowUp" ;
HAB  hab ;

int main (void)
     {
     static ULONG flFrameFlags = FCF_TITLEBAR      | FCF_SYSMENU  |
                                 FCF_SIZEBORDER    | FCF_MINMAX   |
                                 FCF_SHELLPOSITION | FCF_TASKLIST |
                                 FCF_MENU          | FCF_ACCELTABLE ;
     HMQ          hmq ;
     HWND         hwndFrame, hwndClient ;
     QMSG         qmsg ;
```

Listing 15.2: The BLOWUP program (Continued)

```
     hab = WinInitialize (0) ;
     hmq = WinCreateMsgQueue (hab, 0) ;

     WinRegisterClass (hab, szClientClass, ClientWndProc, CS_SIZEREDRAW, 0) ;

     hwndFrame = WinCreateStdWindow (HWND_DESKTOP, WS_VISIBLE,
                                     &flFrameFlags, szClientClass, NULL,
                                     0L, 0, ID_RESOURCE, &hwndClient) ;

     while (WinGetMsg (hab, &qmsg, NULLHANDLE, 0, 0))
          WinDispatchMsg (hab, &qmsg) ;

     WinDestroyWindow (hwndFrame) ;
     WinDestroyMsgQueue (hmq) ;
     WinTerminate (hab) ;
     return 0 ;
     }

MRESULT EXPENTRY ClientWndProc (HWND hwnd, ULONG msg, MPARAM mp1, MPARAM mp2)
     {
     static HBITMAP hbm ;
     static HWND    hwndMenu ;
     static INT     iDisplay = IDM_ACTUAL ;
     BOOL           bEnable ;
     HBITMAP        hbmClip ;
     HPS            hps ;
     RECTL          rclTrack, rclClient ;
     ULONG          ulfInfo ;

     switch (msg)
          {
          case WM_CREATE:
               hwndMenu = WinWindowFromID (
                               WinQueryWindow (hwnd, QW_PARENT),
                               FID_MENU) ;
               return 0 ;

          case WM_INITMENU:
               switch (SHORT1FROMMP (mp1))
                    {
                    case IDM_EDIT:
                         bEnable = (hbm != NULLHANDLE ? TRUE : FALSE) ;

                         WinEnableMenuItem (hwndMenu, IDM_CUT,   bEnable) ;
                         WinEnableMenuItem (hwndMenu, IDM_COPY,  bEnable) ;
                         WinEnableMenuItem (hwndMenu, IDM_CLEAR, bEnable) ;
                         WinEnableMenuItem (hwndMenu, IDM_PASTE,
                              WinQueryClipbrdFmtInfo (hab, CF_BITMAP,
                                                      &ulfInfo)) ;
```

Listing 15.2: The BLOWUP program (Continued)

```
                    return Ø ;
               }
          break ;

     case WM_COMMAND:
          switch (COMMANDMSG(&msg)->cmd)
               {
               case IDM_CUT:
                    if (hbm != NULLHANDLE)
                         {
                         WinOpenClipbrd (hab) ;
                         WinEmptyClipbrd (hab) ;
                         WinSetClipbrdData (hab, (ULONG) hbm,
                                             CF_BITMAP, CFI_HANDLE) ;
                         WinCloseClipbrd (hab) ;
                         hbm = NULLHANDLE ;
                         WinInvalidateRect (hwnd, NULL, FALSE) ;
                         }
                    return Ø ;

               case IDM_COPY:
                                   // Make copy of stored bitmap

                    hbmClip = CopyBitmap (hbm) ;

                                   // Set clipboard data to copy of bitmap

                    if (hbmClip != NULLHANDLE)
                         {
                         WinOpenClipbrd (hab) ;
                         WinEmptyClipbrd (hab) ;
                         WinSetClipbrdData (hab, (ULONG) hbmClip,
                                             CF_BITMAP, CFI_HANDLE) ;
                         WinCloseClipbrd (hab) ;
                         }
                    else
                         BitmapCreationError (hwnd) ;
                    return Ø ;

               case IDM_PASTE:
                                   // Get bitmap from clipboard

                    WinOpenClipbrd (hab) ;
                    hbmClip = (HBITMAP) WinQueryClipbrdData (hab,
                                                       CF_BITMAP) ;
                    if (hbmClip != NULLHANDLE)
                         {
                         if (hbm != NULLHANDLE)
                              GpiDeleteBitmap (hbm) ;
```

Listing 15.2: The BLOWUP program (Continued)

```
                         // Make copy of clipboard bitmap

                    hbm = CopyBitmap (hbmClip) ;

                    if (hbm == NULLHANDLE)
                         BitmapCreationError (hwnd) ;
                    }
               WinCloseClipbrd (hab) ;
               WinInvalidateRect (hwnd, NULL, FALSE) ;
               return 0 ;

          case IDM_CLEAR:
               if (hbm != NULLHANDLE)
                    {
                    GpiDeleteBitmap (hbm) ;
                    hbm = NULLHANDLE ;
                    WinInvalidateRect (hwnd, NULL, FALSE) ;
                    }
               return 0 ;

          case IDM_CAPTURE:
               if (BeginTracking (&rclTrack))
                    {
                    if (hbm != NULLHANDLE)
                         GpiDeleteBitmap (hbm) ;

                    hbm = CopyScreenToBitmap (&rclTrack) ;

                    if (hbm == NULLHANDLE)
                         BitmapCreationError (hwnd) ;

                    WinInvalidateRect (hwnd, NULL, FALSE) ;
                    }
               return 0 ;

          case IDM_ACTUAL:
          case IDM_STRETCH:
               WinCheckMenuItem (hwndMenu, iDisplay, FALSE) ;

               iDisplay = COMMANDMSG(&msg)->cmd ;

               WinCheckMenuItem (hwndMenu, iDisplay, TRUE) ;
               WinInvalidateRect (hwnd, NULL, FALSE) ;
               return 0 ;
          }
     break ;

case WM_PAINT:
```

Listing 15.2: The BLOWUP program (Continued)

```
               hps = WinBeginPaint (hwnd, NULLHANDLE, NULL) ;
               GpiErase (hps) ;

               if (hbm != NULLHANDLE)
                    {
                    WinQueryWindowRect (hwnd, &rclClient) ;

                    WinDrawBitmap (hps, hbm, NULL, (PPOINTL) &rclClient,
                                   CLR_NEUTRAL, CLR_BACKGROUND,
                                   iDisplay == IDM_STRETCH ?
                                        DBM_STRETCH : DBM_NORMAL) ;
                    }
               WinEndPaint (hps) ;
               return 0 ;

          case WM_DESTROY:
               if (hbm != NULLHANDLE)
                    GpiDeleteBitmap (hbm) ;
               return 0 ;
          }
     return WinDefWindowProc (hwnd, msg, mp1, mp2) ;
     }

BOOL BeginTracking (PRECTL prclTrack)
     {
     INT       cxScreen, cyScreen, cxPointer, cyPointer ;
     TRACKINFO ti ;

     cxScreen  = WinQuerySysValue (HWND_DESKTOP, SV_CXSCREEN) ;
     cyScreen  = WinQuerySysValue (HWND_DESKTOP, SV_CYSCREEN) ;
     cxPointer = WinQuerySysValue (HWND_DESKTOP, SV_CXPOINTER) ;
     cyPointer = WinQuerySysValue (HWND_DESKTOP, SV_CYPOINTER) ;

                                   // Set up track rectangle for moving

     ti.cxBorder = 1 ;                       // Border width
     ti.cyBorder = 1 ;
     ti.cxGrid = 0 ;                         // Not used
     ti.cyGrid = 0 ;
     ti.cxKeyboard = 4 ;                     // Pixel increment for keyboard
     ti.cyKeyboard = 4 ;

     ti.rclBoundary.xLeft   = 0 ;            // Area for tracking rectangle
     ti.rclBoundary.yBottom = 0 ;
     ti.rclBoundary.xRight  = cxScreen ;
     ti.rclBoundary.yTop    = cyScreen ;

     ti.ptlMinTrackSize.x = 1 ;              // Minimum rectangle size
     ti.ptlMinTrackSize.y = 1 ;
```

Listing 15.2: The BLOWUP program (Continued)

```
     ti.ptlMaxTrackSize.x = cxScreen ;       // Maximum rectangle size
     ti.ptlMaxTrackSize.y = cyScreen ;
                                             // Initial position

     ti.rclTrack.xLeft   = (cxScreen - cxPointer) / 2 ;
     ti.rclTrack.yBottom = (cyScreen - cyPointer) / 2 ;
     ti.rclTrack.xRight  = (cxScreen + cxPointer) / 2 ;
     ti.rclTrack.yTop    = (cyScreen + cyPointer) / 2 ;

     ti.fs = TF_MOVE | TF_STANDARD | TF_SETPOINTERPOS ;     // Flags

     if (!WinTrackRect (HWND_DESKTOP, NULLHANDLE, &ti))
          return FALSE ;
                                   // Switch to "sizing" pointer
     WinSetPointer (HWND_DESKTOP,
               WinQuerySysPointer (HWND_DESKTOP, SPTR_SIZENESW, FALSE)) ;

                                   // Track rectangle for sizing

     ti.fs = TF_RIGHT | TF_TOP | TF_STANDARD | TF_SETPOINTERPOS ;

     if (!WinTrackRect (HWND_DESKTOP, NULLHANDLE, &ti))
          return FALSE ;

     *prclTrack = ti.rclTrack ;    // Final rectangle

     return TRUE ;
     }

HBITMAP CopyScreenToBitmap (PRECTL prclTrack)
     {
     BITMAPINFOHEADER2 bmp ;
     HBITMAP           hbm ;
     HDC               hdcMemory ;
     HPS               hps, hpsMemory ;
     LONG              alBmpFormats[2] ;
     POINTL            aptl[3] ;
     SIZEL             sizl ;

                                   // Create memory DC and PS

     hdcMemory = DevOpenDC (hab, OD_MEMORY, "*", 0L, NULL, NULLHANDLE) ;

     sizl.cx = sizl.cy = 0 ;
     hpsMemory = GpiCreatePS (hab, hdcMemory, &sizl,
                              PU_PELS    | GPIF_DEFAULT |
                              GPIT_MICRO | GPIA_ASSOC) ;
```

Listing 15.2: The BLOWUP program (Continued)

```
                                        // Create bitmap for destination

     GpiQueryDeviceBitmapFormats (hpsMemory, 2L, alBmpFormats) ;

     memset (&bmp, 0, sizeof (BITMAPINFOHEADER2)) ;

     bmp.cbFix     = sizeof (BITMAPINFOHEADER2) ;
     bmp.cx        = prclTrack->xRight - prclTrack->xLeft ;
     bmp.cy        = prclTrack->yTop   - prclTrack->yBottom ;
     bmp.cPlanes   = (USHORT) alBmpFormats[0] ;
     bmp.cBitCount = (USHORT) alBmpFormats[1] ;

     hbm = GpiCreateBitmap (hpsMemory, &bmp, 0L, NULL, NULL) ;

                                        // Copy from screen to bitmap
     if (hbm != NULLHANDLE)
          {
          GpiSetBitmap (hpsMemory, hbm) ;
          hps = WinGetScreenPS (HWND_DESKTOP) ;

          aptl[0].x = 0 ;
          aptl[0].y = 0 ;
          aptl[1].x = bmp.cx ;
          aptl[1].y = bmp.cy ;
          aptl[2].x = prclTrack->xLeft ;
          aptl[2].y = prclTrack->yBottom ;

          WinLockVisRegions (HWND_DESKTOP, TRUE) ;

          GpiBitBlt (hpsMemory, hps, 3L, aptl, ROP_SRCCOPY, BBO_IGNORE);

          WinLockVisRegions (HWND_DESKTOP, FALSE) ;

          WinReleasePS (hps) ;
          }
                                        // Clean up
     GpiDestroyPS (hpsMemory) ;
     DevCloseDC (hdcMemory) ;

     return hbm ;
     }

HBITMAP CopyBitmap (HBITMAP hbmSrc)
     {
     BITMAPINFOHEADER2 bmp ;
     HBITMAP           hbmDst ;
     HDC               hdcSrc, hdcDst ;
     HPS               hpsSrc, hpsDst ;
     POINTL            aptl[3] ;
```

Listing 15.2: The BLOWUP program (Continued)

```
     SIZEL              sizl ;

                                   // Create memory DC's and PS's

     hdcSrc = DevOpenDC (hab, OD_MEMORY, "*", ØL, NULL, NULLHANDLE) ;
     hdcDst = DevOpenDC (hab, OD_MEMORY, "*", ØL, NULL, NULLHANDLE) ;

     sizl.cx = sizl.cy = Ø ;
     hpsSrc = GpiCreatePS (hab, hdcSrc, &sizl, PU_PELS    | GPIF_DEFAULT |
                                               GPIT_MICRO | GPIA_ASSOC) ;

     hpsDst = GpiCreatePS (hab, hdcDst, &sizl, PU_PELS    | GPIF_DEFAULT |
                                               GPIT_MICRO | GPIA_ASSOC) ;

                                   // Create bitmap

     bmp.cbFix = sizeof (BITMAPINFOHEADER2) ;
     GpiQueryBitmapInfoHeader (hbmSrc, &bmp) ;
     hbmDst = GpiCreateBitmap (hpsDst, &bmp, ØL, NULL, NULL) ;

                                   // Copy from source to destination

     if (hbmDst != NULLHANDLE)
          {
          GpiSetBitmap (hpsSrc, hbmSrc) ;
          GpiSetBitmap (hpsDst, hbmDst) ;

          aptl[Ø].x = aptl[Ø].y = Ø ;
          aptl[1].x = bmp.cx ;
          aptl[1].y = bmp.cy ;
          aptl[2]   = aptl[Ø] ;

          GpiBitBlt (hpsDst, hpsSrc, 3L, aptl, ROP_SRCCOPY, BBO_IGNORE) ;
          }
                                   // Clean up
     GpiDestroyPS (hpsSrc) ;
     GpiDestroyPS (hpsDst) ;
     DevCloseDC (hdcSrc) ;
     DevCloseDC (hdcDst) ;

     return hbmDst ;
     }

VOID BitmapCreationError (HWND hwnd)
     {
     WinMessageBox (HWND_DESKTOP, hwnd, "Cannot create bitmap.",
                    szClientClass, Ø, MB_OK | MB_WARNING) ;
     }
```

Listing 15.2: The BLOWUP program (Continued)

The BLOWUP.RC File

```
/*-------------------------------
   BLOWUP.RC resource script file
  -------------------------------*/

#include <os2.h>
#include "blowup.h"

MENU ID_RESOURCE
     {
     SUBMENU "~Edit",               IDM_EDIT
          {
          MENUITEM "Cu~t\tShift+Del",        IDM_CUT
          MENUITEM "~Copy\tCtrl+Ins",        IDM_COPY
          MENUITEM "~Paste\tShift+Ins",      IDM_PASTE
          MENUITEM "C~lear\tDel",            IDM_CLEAR
          }
     SUBMENU "~Display",            IDM_DISPLAY
          {
          MENUITEM "~Actual size",           IDM_ACTUAL,, MIA_CHECKED
          MENUITEM "~Stretch to window",     IDM_STRETCH
          }
     MENUITEM "~Capture!",          IDM_CAPTURE
     }

ACCELTABLE ID_RESOURCE
     {
     VK_DELETE, IDM_CUT,   VIRTUALKEY, SHIFT
     VK_INSERT, IDM_COPY,  VIRTUALKEY, CONTROL
     VK_INSERT, IDM_PASTE, VIRTUALKEY, SHIFT
     VK_DELETE, IDM_CLEAR, VIRTUALKEY
     }
```

The BLOWUP.H File

```
/*----------------------
   BLOWUP.H header file
  ----------------------*/

#define ID_RESOURCE      1

#define IDM_EDIT         10
#define IDM_CUT          11
#define IDM_COPY         12
#define IDM_PASTE        13
#define IDM_CLEAR        14

#define IDM_DISPLAY      20
```

Listing 15.2: The BLOWUP program (Continued)

```
#define IDM_ACTUAL        21
#define IDM_STRETCH       22

#define IDM_CAPTURE       30
```

The BLOWUP.DEF File

```
;----------------------------------
; BLOWUP.DEF module definition file
;----------------------------------

NAME           BLOWUP         WINDOWAPI

DESCRIPTION    'Bitmap Blowup Clipboard Program (c) Charles Petzold, 1993'
PROTMODE
```

You can use BLOWUP like a magnifying glass to explore areas of the Presentation Manager screen. First select Capture! from the menu. A little rectangle about the size of a mouse pointer appears in the middle of the screen. You can move it around with the mouse or the cursor movement keys. Move it to an area of the screen you want to enlarge, and press Enter or click the mouse button. You can then use the mouse or keyboard to adjust the upper-right corner of the rectangle. Press Enter or click the mouse button again.

BLOWUP then displays that area of the screen on its client window. By default, it is displayed at actual size. But you can select Stretch to Window from BLOWUP's Display menu to stretch the bitmap to the size of the client window. For example, Figure 15.1 shows the results of using BLOWUP to look at the minimize/maximize menu.

BLOWUP has an Edit menu with Copy and Paste options. You can copy a bitmap to the clipboard or paste a bitmap from the clipboard.

BLOWUP maintains a bitmap handle named *hbm* for displaying the bitmap on its client window. The clipboard logic in BLOWUP is almost exactly as I just described. The only substantial difference is that BLOWUP deletes the *hbm* handle it already has before pasting a bitmap from the clipboard.

```
case IDM_PASTE:
                    // Get bitmap from clipboard

     WinOpenClipbrd (hab) ;
     hbm = WinQueryClipbrdData (hab, CF_BITMAP) ;

     if (hbmClip != NULLHANDLE)
          {
```

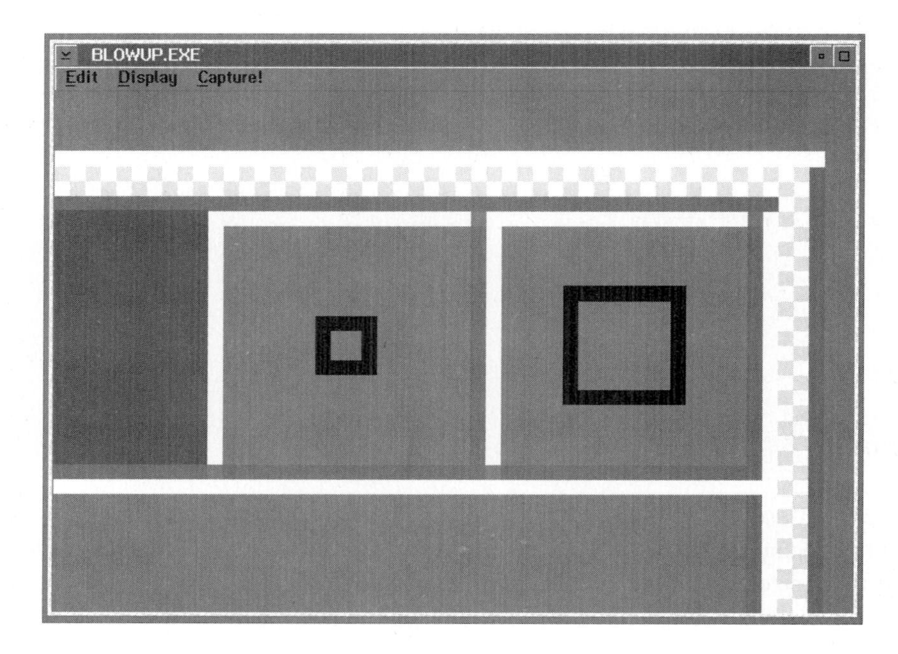

Figure 15.1: The BLOWUP display

```
          if (hbm != NULLHANDLE)
               GpiDeleteBitmap (hbm) ;

                    // Make copy of new bitmap

          hbm = CopyBitmap (hbmClip) ;

          if (hbm == NULLHANDLE)
               BitmapCreationError (hwnd) ;
          }
     WinCloseClipbrd (hab) ;
```

BLOWUP also processes the WM_INITMENU message to enable or disable the Copy and Paste options. The Copy option is enabled only if BLOWUP has a bitmap handle stored in *hbm*. Paste is enabled if the clipboard currently contains a bitmap.

The *CopyBitmap* function is fairly straightforward. The function opens two memory device contexts and creates two presentation spaces associated with these device contexts. *WinQueryBitmapInfoHeader* obtains the BITMAPINFOHEADER structure that describes the original bitmap. This structure is passed to *GpiCreateBitmap* to create a new bitmap of the same size and color organization.

The two bitmaps are set into the two presentation spaces, and *GpiBitBlt* copies the contents of the original bitmap to the new bitmap.

In its *BeginTracking* function, BLOWUP uses the powerful *WinTrackRect* function for capturing an area of the screen when you select the Capture! option from the menu. *WinTrackRect* is the same function that the title bar window uses when you move a window on the screen and the same function that the frame window uses when you resize a window. The function has its own keyboard and mouse interface.

To use *WinTrackRect*, you need to define a structure of type TRACKINFO:

```
TRACKINFO ti ;
```

The hard part of the job is setting all the fields of this structure. But once they're set, you just pass the structure to *WinTrackRect*:

```
WinTrackRect (HWND_DESKTOP, NULLHANDLE, &ti) ;
```

The second parameter to *WinTrackRect* is usually a handle to a presentation space, but the function can obtain a presentation space handle using the window handle passed as the first parameter. Because we want to capture anything on the screen, the first parameter is set to HWND_DESKTOP.

WinTrackRect displays a rectangle on the screen and allows it to be moved or sized with the keyboard or mouse. The function has its own message loop and will not return until the user presses the mouse button, the Enter key, or the Escape key. *WinTrackRect* returns FALSE if the user aborts the tracking operation by pressing Escape and returns TRUE otherwise.

BLOWUP calls *WinTrackRect* twice in its *BeginTracking* function, which is called from *ClientWndProc* when the Capture! menu option is selected. The first call to *WinTrackRect* lets you move the tracking rectangle to any area of the screen; the second call lets you change the size of the rectangle.

The TRACKINFO structure contains two fields that are RECTL structures. The first (called *rclBoundary*) indicates the area in which the rectangle can be moved. For BLOWUP, this is the entire screen. The second RECTL structure (called *rclTrack*) specifies the initial position and size of the rectangle when the function is called and specifies the final position and size of the rectangle when the function returns. (For the first call to *WinTrackRect*, BLOWUP makes the rectangle the size of a mouse pointer and places it in the center of the screen.) Two POINTL structures in the TRACKINFO structure specify the minimium and maximum allowable sizes of the rectangle. For BLOWUP, the minimum size is 1 pixel high and 1 pixel wide, and the maximum size is the dimension of the entire screen.

The *fs* field of the TRACKINFO structure specifies how the tracking is to work. For the first call to *WinTrackRect*, the *fs* field is set like this:

```
ti.fs = TF_MOVE | TF_STANDARD | TF_SETPOINTERPOS ;
```

The TF_MOVE flag indicates that the user can move the rectangle. The TF_-STANDARD flag indicates that the dimensions of the border given in the *cxBorder* and *cyBorder* fields are multiples of the standard border width. The TF_SETPOINTERPOS flag puts the mouse pointer in the center of the rectangle.

On the second call to WinTrackRect, the flags are set differently:

```
ti.fs = TF_RIGHT | TF_TOP | TF_STANDARD | TF_SETPOINTERPOS ;
```

The TF_RIGHT and TF_TOP flags allow the user to move the upper-right corner of the rectangle. The mouse pointer is positioned on that corner. Before this second call to *WinTrackRect*, BLOWUP sets the mouse pointer to the system pointer known as SPTR_SIZENESW:

```
WinSetPointer (HWND_DESKTOP,
     WinQuerySysPointer  (HWND_DESKTOP, SPTR_SIZENESW, FALSE)) ;
```

The letters "NESW" stand for "north-east-south-west." The pointer is a double-headed arrow that points to the upper-right and lower-left corners. This is the mouse pointer that appears when you resize a window by grabbing the upper-right or lower-left corner of the sizing border.

BLOWUP calls its *BeginTracking* function when the user selects Capture! from the menu. The *BeginTracking* function returns the final tracking rectangle. BLOWUP then calls *CopyScreenToBitmap* with this rectangle to create a bitmap and to copy the selected area of the screen. In *CopyScreenToBitmap*, the *GpiQueryDeviceBitmapFormats* function obtains the number of color planes and number of color bits per pixel used for the video display. This is required to create the bitmap. The bitmap is selected into a presentation space associated with a memory device context, and *GpiBitBlt* does the copy. Before and after the *GpiBitBlt* call, *CopyScreenToBitmap* makes calls to *WinLockVisRegions* to prevent the screen from changing while the copy is in progress.

If you have the CLOCK or DIGCLOCK program running when you use BLOWUP, you'll notice also that the screen is not updated during the calls to *WinTrackRect*. If the Presentation Manager allowed screen updates, another program might draw over the tracking rectangle or imprint part of the rectangle in its window when drawing in exclusive OR mode. This is one big advantage of using *WinTrackRect* rather than your own logic for tracking areas of the screen outside your window.

Dynamic Link Libraries

Dynamic link library basics

Libraries and window procedures

Resource-only libraries

Chapter 16

Dynamic linking is a process that lets your programs use functions or resources outside of their own .EXE files. Dynamic linking is one of the most interesting features of OS/2 and is very important to the overall structure of the operating system. Its degree of importance is reflected by the number of .DLL files you'll find on your hard disk. These files are dynamic link libraries or DLLs. They contain code, data, and resources, just as executable files do. However, a dynamic link library is *not* directly executed by the operating system. It is instead *used* by OS/2 executables and other dynamic link libraries.

When OS/2 1.0 was released in December 1987, it did not include the Presentation Manager, but it already included some dynamic link libraries providing access to the file system, memory, keyboard and mouse input, and video output. The Presentation Manager itself (first appearing in OS/2 1.1) is primarily a collection of additional dynamic link libraries. These libraries extend the functionality of the OS/2 kernel to include a windowing user interface and graphics.

Every operating system function that your program directly calls is in a dynamic link library. And even when you call C runtime library functions such as *malloc* and *fopen*, these functions eventually use (respectively) a memory-allocation function and a file-open function in a dynamic link library.

Two of the more important Presentation Manager libraries are PMWIN.DLL (which contains most functions with the "Win" prefix) and PMGPI.DLL (which contains most functions with the "Gpi" prefix). When you create a Presentation Manager program, the program's .EXE file contains no code for the various OS/2 and Presentation Manager functions called by the program. Instead, the *linker* builds tables in the .EXE file that identify these functions and the names of the dynamic link libraries where they are located. In the program itself, the actual calls to these functions contain dummy addresses.

When you run the program, OS/2 performs several important chores:

- It determines from the .EXE file which dynamic link libraries are required by the program.
- It maps the code and data blocks from the dynamic link library into the process's memory space.
- It replaces the dummy addresses in the program's code with the actual addresses of the entry points to the functions in the DLL code blocks.

This is what dynamic linking is all about.

Here's the really cool part: You can also write your own dynamic link libraries, as I'll demonstrate in this chapter. Code, read-only data, and resources in dynamic link libraries can be shared among all processes running under OS/2. Read-write data blocks associated with dynamic link libraries are usually private to each process. However, you can specify that some read-write data blocks in a dynamic link library be shared among all processes. This allows dynamic link libraries to assist in interprocess communication (IPC).

Because dynamic linking is a facility of the OS/2 kernel rather than the Presentation Manager, I won't discuss it in detail here. Instead, I'll concentrate on those aspects of dynamic linking that are most important to Presentation Manager programming.

Before we begin, you should know that OS/2 uses the directory paths specified in the LIBPATH statement in your CONFIG.SYS file to locate the library files. You should make sure that this list includes the directory path indicated by a single period. This causes OS/2 to search the current directory when a program requires a dynamic link library. That makes developing and testing the library somewhat easier. If you change your CONFIG.SYS file, you'll have to reboot to make the change effective. In the following discussions and examples, I'll assume you've done this.

DYNAMIC LINK LIBRARY BASICS

The word "library" is used in several different ways in OS/2 programming, so let's take a minute to examine these various meanings.

OBJECT AND IMPORT LIBRARIES

Normally when you link a program, you make use of *object libraries.* These are files with a .LIB extension that contain code and data. Linking with an object library is sometimes known as *static linking* to differentiate it from dynamic linking. Static linking is something we've been doing for years and years and years.

However, some files with a .LIB extension are not object libraries but *import libraries.* Import libraries are similar to object libraries because they contain information that the linker uses to construct a program's .EXE file. However, import libraries usually contain no code or data. Instead, the linker uses the import libraries to set up tables within the .EXE file that identify the dynamic link library functions used by the program.

For example, most Presentation Manager programs call the function *WinCreateStdWindow.* When you compile a Presentation Manager program, the .OBJ file produced by the compiler contains an unresolved reference to this function. When the linker links the program to create a .EXE file, it finds the *WinCreateStdWindow* function in an import library. This import library indicates that this function is located in the PMWIN.DLL dynamic link library module and has a particular *ordinal number* (a concept discussed later in this chapter). The linker then stores this information in the program's .EXE file. When OS/2 loads the program into memory, it can then determine both the name of the dynamic link library and the ordinal number within that library of the unresolved call to *WinCreateStdWindow.*

I'll show you how to create your own import libraries later in this chapter.

The object libraries and import libraries need to be present on the hard disk only when you *link* the program. The dynamic link library used by a program must be present when you *run* the program.

MODULES

Both programs (files with a .EXE extension) and dynamic link libraries (files with a .DLL extension) are sometimes called *modules.* The .EXE files are *program modules* and the .DLL files are *library modules.* Each module has a module name, which you must specify in the NAME statement (for program modules) or the LIBRARY statement (for library modules) of the module definition (.DEF) file.

A library module name must be the same as the file name, but without the .DLL extension; a program module name is usually the same as the file name (without the .EXE extension), but can be different.

EXPORTED FUNCTIONS

Most dynamic link libraries contain functions that can be called from executables or other dynamic link libraries. Such functions are said to be *exported* from the library. For example, the *WinCreateStdWindow* function is exported from the PMWIN.DLL dynamic link library. A function in a dynamic link library must be exported if it is to be used by another module.

You can get a list of functions exported from a particular dynamic link library by running the EXEHDR program (included with IBM's C Developer's WorkSet/2) like this:

```
EXEHDR C:\OS2\DLL\PMWIN.DLL
```

After displaying information stored in the file header, EXEHDR lists all of the code and data blocks in the module, followed by the exported functions. The "obj" and "offset" columns indicate the memory block and the offset within that block where the function begins. The "ord" column contains the ordinal number of the function. Each exported function has a unique positive ordinal number.

IMPORTED FUNCTIONS

When a program or library module makes use of functions in a library module, the functions are said to be *imported* to the module making the function call. You can get a list of the functions imported to a module by running EXEHDR with the -V ("verbose") switch. This displays a list of all addresses within the module that OS/2 must patch when loading the program into memory. Many of these are calls to functions in dynamic link library modules. You'll notice that imported functions are referred to by the module name (such as PMWIN and PMGPI) followed by a period and either a function name or an ordinal number.

Thus, dynamic linking is the process of connecting calls to functions imported to a program module with the functions exported from a dynamic link library module. Very often a library module imports functions from itself or from another library module, so OS/2 must also be able to dynamically link library modules.

SAME PROCESS, DIFFERENT MODULE

It's important to remember that a dynamic link library is not a process. Only an OS/2 executable file can become a process. Code that is executed in a dynamic link library (as a result of a call to a function within the library), is executed within the process that makes the call. Each process running under OS/2 has its own virtual memory space. When a process uses a library module, the code and data in that module are also included in the process's memory space.

In this sense, when a program calls a routine in a dynamic link library, it's no different from the program calling a routine in the program itself. The dynamic link library is an extension of the process. Everything the library does is done on behalf of the process. For example, a function in a dynamic link library can open a file or allocate a memory block. The open file or memory block belongs to the process that called the function in the library.

This is quite interesting when you think about it. We are accustomed to thinking about operating system code and program code as separate and distinct entities. A function such as *WinCreateStdWindow* is an operating system function call. Yet, when a Presentation Manager program calls *WinCreateStdWindow*, the function really executes as part of the process.

Is PMWIN.DLL an extension of the OS/2 operating system or an extension of a program running under Presentation Manager? Actually, it's both. Dynamic link libraries bridge the gap between program and operating system. Under OS/2, the concept of one module calling code located in another module is generalized. There is no real separation between program code and operating system code.

When you write your own dynamic link libraries, you may think of them as extensions of your programs. But you can also view them as extensions of the operating system. This explains why people say that OS/2 is easily and almost infinitely extensible.

WHY USE DYNAMIC LINK LIBRARIES?

Of course, the idea of writing an "extension" to OS/2 may be enough of a thrill to induce you to write dynamic link libraries. But there are more practical benefits.

Suppose you were developing an OS/2 accounting package that consisted of several programs. These programs would probably use a lot of the same code. In fact, under DOS you would probably isolate these common routines in separate source code files and put them in object libraries.

But if you did this, each program in the package would contain a copy of these common routines, increasing the total disk space required by the package. Moreover, if someone ran two or more of these programs under OS/2 at the same time, the common routines would also be duplicated in memory.

If you instead put these routines in a dynamic link library, the disk space required by the package would be reduced because only one copy of the routines is required. (And that copy is in the library module.) If two or more of the programs were run at the same time, the code in the library module would be shared among the programs that required it.

Moreover, when compiling and linking the separate programs, link time would be improved because the linker would no longer have to pull the routines from the object library and include them in the program's .EXE file. You could also someday improve the performance of the whole package by upgrading only the routines in the dynamic link library. The programs themselves would not even have to be relinked.

Dynamic link libraries can also be products in themselves. For example, suppose you write a collection of three-dimensional extensions to GPI graphics, put the functions in a dynamic link library, and call it GPI3D.DLL. You might be able to interest other software vendors in licensing this library from you for inclusion in their products. Users who own several products that use GPI3D.DLL would need only one copy of the library on their hard disks.

COMPILE AND LINK MECHANICS

Fortunately, the mechanics of creating dynamic link libraries have been eased by the 32-bit architecture of OS/2 2.0 and 2.1. The 16-bit segmented architecture of earlier versions of OS/2 had some messy implications for DLLs.

Nowadays, differences between creating executables and DLLs can be taken care of in the make files and module definition (.DEF) files. For convenience in compiling and linking DLLs, you can use the two command files shown in Listing 16.1, the first for the IBM compiler and the second for the Borland compiler.

Listing 16.1: Command files to set environment variables for creating dynamic link libraries

The IBMDLL.CMD File

```
REM ----------------------------------------------------------------------
REM  IBMDLL.CMD -- Set up DLL environment for IBM C Developer's WorkSet/2
REM ----------------------------------------------------------------------
SET DLLCC=icc -C -Kbcpr -Ss -Ge- -Fo
SET DLLLINK=link386
SET DLLLIB=
SET DLLRC=rc -r
```

The BORDLL.CMD File

```
REM ----------------------------------------------------------------
REM  BORDLL.CMD -- Set up DLL environment for Borland C++ for OS/2
REM ----------------------------------------------------------------
SET DLLCC=bcc -c -I\bcos2\include -sd -o
```

Listing 16.1: Command files to set environment variables for creating dynamic link libraries (Continued)

```
SET DLLLINK=tlink -c -x -v -L\bcos2\lib \bcos2\lib\c02d.obj
SET DLLLIB=c2 + os2
SET DLLRC=rc -r -i \bcos2\include
```

These command files set environment variables used in the make files in this chapter. You may want to compare them with the command files shown in Chapter 2. In particular, the IBMDLL.CMD file has a compiler switch of *-Ge-* (which translates as "don't create an executable"), and the BORDLL.CMD file has a compiler switch of *-sd* and startup code in the C02D.OBJ object module.

Notice also that the DLLCC environment variable ends with the *-Fo* flag (in IBMDLL.CMD) and the *-o* flag (in BORDLL.CMD). This allows you to specify an object file name different from the C source code name, which is sometimes useful if you're separating a source code module from a program into a DLL. I do that very thing with the NEWBTN source code from Chapter 11.

Functions exported from dynamic link libraries are declared with the APIENTRY identifier, the same identifier used with functions exported from all OS/2 DLLs. As I discussed in Chapter 2, the APIENTRY identifier is defined in OS2DEF.H like this for the IBM compiler:

```
#define APIENTRY _System
```

For the Borland compiler it's defined like this:

```
#define APIENTRY _syscall
```

These keywords indicate what conventions the compiler should use in generating the function call.

CREATING A DYNAMIC LINK LIBRARY

So let's get down to business and write a dynamic link library. Our first library is called HDRLIB ("Handy Drawing Routines Library") and is shown in Listing 16.2.

Listing 16.2: The HDRLIB library

The HDRLIB.MAK File

```
#---------------------
# HDRLIB.MAK make file
#---------------------

hdrlib.dll : hdrlib.obj hdrlib.def
     $(DLLLINK) hdrlib, hdrlib.dll, NUL, $(DLLLIB), hdrlib
```

Listing 16.2: The HDRLIB library (Continued)

```
hdrlib.obj : hdrlib.c hdrlib.h
     $(DLLCC)hdrlib.obj hdrlib.c
```

The HDRLIB.H File

```
/*-------------------------------------------------
   HDRLIB.H -- "Handy Drawing Routines" Header File
  -------------------------------------------------*/

INT  APIENTRY  HdrPuts    (HPS hps, PPOINTL pptl, PCHAR szText) ;
INT  APIENTRY  HdrPrintf  (HPS hps, PPOINTL pptl, PCHAR szFormat, ...) ;
LONG APIENTRY  HdrEllipse (HPS hps, LONG lOption, PPOINTL pptl) ;
```

The HDRLIB.C File

```
/*------------------------------------------------------------
   HDRLIB.C -- "Handy Drawing Routines" Dynamic Link Library
               (c) Charles Petzold, 1993
  ------------------------------------------------------------*/

#define INCL_GPI
#include <os2.h>
#include <stdio.h>
#include <stdarg.h>
#include <stdlib.h>
#include <string.h>
#include "hdrlib.h"

INT APIENTRY HdrPuts (HPS hps, PPOINTL pptl, PCHAR szText)
     {
     INT iLength = strlen (szText) ;

     if (pptl == NULL)
          GpiCharString (hps, iLength, szText) ;
     else
          GpiCharStringAt (hps, pptl, iLength, szText) ;

     return iLength ;
     }

INT APIENTRY HdrPrintf (HPS hps, PPOINTL pptl, PCHAR szFormat, ...)
     {
     static CHAR chBuffer [1024] ;
     INT         iLength ;
     va_list     pArguments ;

     va_start (pArguments, szFormat) ;
```

Listing 16.2: The HDRLIB library (Continued)

```
     iLength = vsprintf (chBuffer, szFormat, pArguments) ;

     if (pptl == NULL)
          GpiCharString (hps, iLength, chBuffer) ;
     else
          GpiCharStringAt (hps, pptl, iLength, chBuffer) ;

     va_end (pArguments) ;
     return iLength ;
     }

LONG APIENTRY HdrEllipse (HPS hps, LONG lOption, PPOINTL pptl)
     {
     POINTL ptlCurrent ;

     GpiQueryCurrentPosition (hps, &ptlCurrent) ;

     return GpiBox (hps, lOption, pptl, labs (pptl->x - ptlCurrent.x),
                                        labs (pptl->y - ptlCurrent.y)) ;
     }
```

The HDRLIB.DEF File

```
;----------------------------------
; HDRLIB.DEF module definition file
;----------------------------------

LIBRARY        HDRLIB    INITINSTANCE

DESCRIPTION    'Handy Drawing Routines DLL (c) Charles Petzold, 1993'
PROTMODE
DATA           NONSHARED

EXPORTS        HdrPuts
               HdrPrintf
               HdrEllipse
```

This library contains three functions that perform some common GPI tasks that would otherwise take more than one call to complete. *HdrPuts* displays a string starting at a specified position (or starting at the current position if the second parameter is set to NULL). The *HdrPrintf* function uses a technique shown in the *cprintf* function in Chapter 7 to let you write formatted text to your window. The *HdrEllipse* function is a version of the *Ellipse* function shown in Chapter 5. The function uses *GpiBox* to draw an ellipse.

HDRLIB.C contains the three functions. You'll notice that the HDRLIB.C file contains no *main* function. Although dynamic link libraries often do some initialization on the assembly language level, this is taken care of in startup code linked with the program by the linker.

THE MODULE DEFINITION FILE

The HDRLIB.DEF module definition file is different from module definition files used to create program modules. The first statement is not a NAME statement but a LIBRARY statement:

```
LIBRARY HDRLIB INITINSTANCE
```

A NAME statement indicates that the module is a program; a LIBRARY indicates a dynamic link library. This keyword is followed by the module name and INITINSTANCE. The INITINSTANCE keyword means that initialization code in the dynamic link library is executed for each process that links to the library.

This module definition file also contains a data statement:

```
DATA NONSHARED
```

This indicates that the data in the dynamic link library will not be shared among processes. Every time a process using HDRLIB.DLL begins, OS/2 creates a new data block for the dynamic link library.

The EXPORTS list names the three exported functions. These are the three functions in HDRLIB.DLL that are available to programs or other dynamic link libraries.

USING THE DYNAMIC LINK LIBRARY

We can test the dynamic link library with a program that calls the library functions. The HDRTEST program shown in Listing 16.3 does just that.

Listing 16.3: The HDRTEST program

The HDRTEST.MAK File

```
#----------------------
# HDRTEST.MAK make file
#----------------------

hdrtest.exe : hdrtest.obj hdrtest.def
     $(PRGLINK) hdrtest, hdrtest, NUL, $(PRGLIB), hdrtest

hdrtest.obj : hdrtest.c hdrlib.h
     $(PRGCC) hdrtest.c
```

Listing 16.3: The HDRTEST program (Continued)

The HDRTEST.C File

```
/*-----------------------------------------------------------------
   HDRTEST.C -- Program to Test HDRLIB.DLL Dynamic Link Library
                (c) Charles Petzold, 1993
  ----------------------------------------------------------------*/

#define INCL_WIN
#include <os2.h>
#include "hdrlib.h"

MRESULT EXPENTRY ClientWndProc (HWND, ULONG, MPARAM, MPARAM) ;

int main (void)
     {
     static CHAR  szClientClass [] = "HdrTest" ;
     static ULONG flFrameFlags = FCF_TITLEBAR      | FCF_SYSMENU |
                                 FCF_SIZEBORDER    | FCF_MINMAX  |
                                 FCF_SHELLPOSITION | FCF_TASKLIST ;
     HAB          hab ;
     HMQ          hmq ;
     HWND         hwndFrame, hwndClient ;
     QMSG         qmsg ;

     hab = WinInitialize (0) ;
     hmq = WinCreateMsgQueue (hab, 0) ;

     WinRegisterClass (hab, szClientClass, ClientWndProc, CS_SIZEREDRAW, 0) ;

     hwndFrame = WinCreateStdWindow (HWND_DESKTOP, WS_VISIBLE,
                                     &flFrameFlags, szClientClass, NULL,
                                     0L, 0, 0, &hwndClient) ;

     while (WinGetMsg (hab, &qmsg, NULLHANDLE, 0, 0))
          WinDispatchMsg (hab, &qmsg) ;

     WinDestroyWindow (hwndFrame) ;
     WinDestroyMsgQueue (hmq) ;
     WinTerminate (hab) ;
     return 0 ;
     }

MRESULT EXPENTRY ClientWndProc (HWND hwnd, ULONG msg, MPARAM mp1, MPARAM mp2)
     {
     static INT cxClient, cyClient ;
     HPS        hps;
     POINTL     ptl ;
```

Listing 16.3: The HDRTEST program (Continued)

```
     switch (msg)
       {
          case WM_SIZE:
               cxClient = SHORT1FROMMP (mp2) ;
               cyClient = SHORT2FROMMP (mp2) ;
               return 0 ;

          case WM_PAINT:
               hps = WinBeginPaint (hwnd, NULLHANDLE, NULL) ;
               GpiErase (hps) ;

               ptl.x = cxClient / 8 ;
               ptl.y = 3 * cyClient / 4 ;
               HdrPrintf (hps, &ptl, "Welcome to the %s",
                          "OS/2 2.0 Presentation Manager!") ;

               ptl.x = cxClient / 8 ;
               ptl.y = cyClient / 4 ;
               HdrPuts (hps, &ptl, "This line was displayed by a ") ;
               HdrPuts (hps, NULL, "routine in a dynamic link library.") ;

               ptl.x = 0 ;
               ptl.y = 0 ;
               GpiMove (hps, &ptl) ;

               ptl.x = cxClient - 1 ;
               ptl.y = cyClient - 1 ;
               HdrEllipse (hps, DRO_OUTLINE, &ptl) ;

               WinEndPaint (hps) ;
               return 0 ;
          }
     return WinDefWindowProc (hwnd, msg, mp1, mp2) ;
     }
```

The HDRTEST.DEF File

```
;-----------------------------------
; HDRTEST.DEF module definition file
;-----------------------------------

NAME           HDRTEST   WINDOWAPI

DESCRIPTION    'Test Program for HDRLIB.DLL (c) Charles Petzold, 1993'
PROTMODE

IMPORTS        HDRLIB.HdrPuts
               HDRLIB.HdrPrintf
               HDRLIB.HdrEllipse
```

You'll also need the HDRLIB.H header file from Listing 16.2 to compile this program. This file provides the declarations for the functions in the DLL used by the program.

And it works! Figure 16.1 shows the HDRTEST program running under the Presentation Manager.

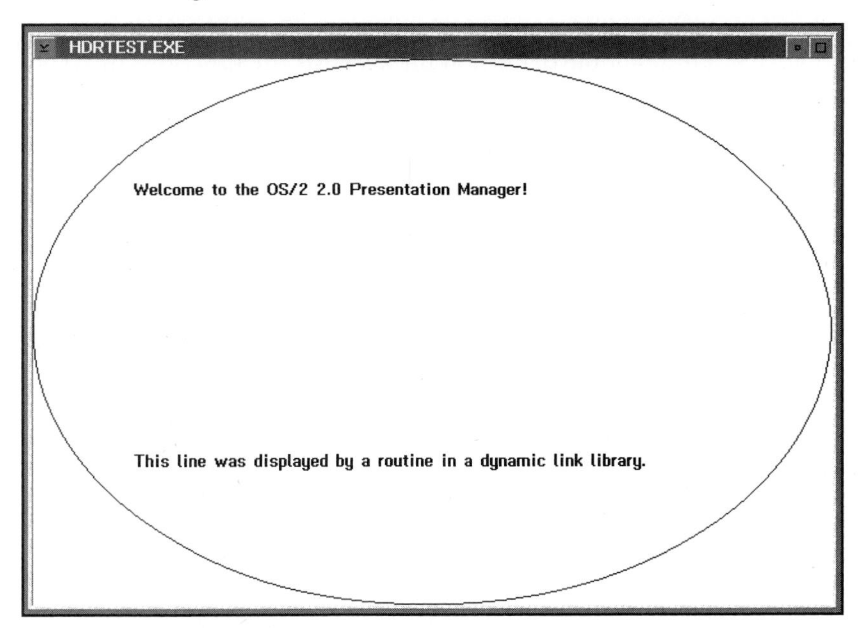

Figure 16.1: The HDRTEST display

The HDRTEST.DEF module definition file explicitly lists the three imported functions in an IMPORTS section:

```
IMPORTS HDRLIB.HdrPuts
        HDRLIB.HdrPrintf
        HDRLIB.HdrEllipse
```

If listing the imported functions in the module definition file annoys you, you'll be happy to know that we'll eliminate the IMPORTS list shortly.

ALTERNATE IMPORTS AND EXPORTS LISTS

The HDRLIB.DEF module definition file lists the functions exported from HDRLIB.DLL:

```
EXPORTS HdrPuts
        HdrPrintf
        HdrEllipse
```

The HDRTEST.DEF module definition file also lists the functions in HDRLIB-.DLL that are imported to HDRTEST:

```
IMPORTS HDRLIB.HdrPuts
        HDRLIB.HdrPrintf
        HDRLIB.HdrEllipse
```

Notice that each function in the IMPORTS list is identified by a module name and a function name. The linker uses this information in constructing the HDRTEST.EXE file.

This is not the only way to specify EXPORTS and IMPORTS. Another approach is to assign ordinals to each of the functions. *Ordinals* are unique positive integers that you assign in the module definition file for the library. You do this by preceding the number with an @ sign. You must change both module definition files. Here's the new EXPORTS list in HDRLIB.DEF:

```
EXPORTS HdrPuts    @1
        HdrPrintf  @2
        HdrEllipse @3
```

The IMPORTS list in HDRTEST.DEF then references these functions by specifying the ordinal numbers (without the @):

```
IMPORTS HdrPuts    = HDRLIB.1
        HdrPrintf  = HDRLIB.2
        HdrEllipse = HDRLIB.3
```

The advantage of this approach is that it can make the size of the .EXE file smaller if there are many imports involved. The .EXE file needs to contain only the ordinal numbers—not the names—of the imported functions. The big disadvantage to ordinals is that it's easy to mistakenly use the wrong number in the IMPORTS list. (This problem disappears when you use import libraries, as described in the next section.)

CREATING AN IMPORT LIBRARY

But why do we need an IMPORTS section at all in HDRTEST.DEF? After all, we've been using functions in dynamic link libraries such as PMWIN.DLL since Chapter 2, and this is the first time we've had to write an IMPORTS statement.

You can eliminate the need for the IMPORTS section by creating an import library. You'll use this import library in the same way you use (for example) BCOS2.LIB, which is an import library for all the OS/2 and Presentation Manager function calls included with the Borland compiler. The import library provides the same information to the linker as the IMPORTS section of a module definition file.

To create an import library for HDRLIB, you add a line to the HDRLIB.MAK make file. This line goes after the link command:

```
implib hdrlib.lib hdrlib.def
```

The IMPLIB.EXE program is included with the IBM and Borland C compilers. This program reads the module definition file used to create the library. From that file, IMPLIB obtains the module name and the names of the exported functions. (The EXPORTS section of HDRLIB.DEF can use either the names or ordinal numbers.) The IMPLIB.EXE program creates an import library called HDRLIB.LIB.

To use this import library when creating HDRTEST.EXE, first remove the IMPORTS list from HDRTEST.DEF. Then change the link step in the HDRTEST.MAK make file to

```
hdrtest.exe : hdrtest.obj hdrtest.def hdrlib.lib
     $(PRGLINK) hdrtest, hdrtest, NUL, $(PRGLIB) hdrlib, hdrtest
```

Notice the two changes: The HDRLIB.LIB file is now a dependent file for the link step. HDRLIB.LIB is also listed in the library field of the link parameters. (The .LIB extension is assumed.) Now you can remake HDRLIB.DLL (and, in the process, HDRLIB.LIB) and HDRTEST.EXE.

For just a few functions, using an explicit IMPORTS list in the program's .DEF file is satisfactory, but for a dynamic link library with lots of functions, the import library is definitely preferable. You'll want to specify ordinal numbers in the EXPORTS section of the library's .DEF file to save space in any .EXE file that uses the library.

LIBRARIES AND WINDOW PROCEDURES

The thing that makes Presentation Manager programs different from conventional programs is the messaging system. Window procedures send and receive messages. But can you put a window procedure in a dynamic link library?

Of course! All window classes that are predefined by the Presentation Manager (such as those for title-bar windows and scroll-bar windows) have window procedures in PMWIN.DLL. There's no reason why we can't also put a window procedure in a library module. Let's try it.

THE DLL VERSION OF NEW-BUTTON

In Chapter 11 you saw how to write a window procedure for a new style of push button; this was demonstrated in the BUTTONS2 program. Listing 16.4 shows some additional files to create NEWBTN.DLL, a dynamic link library that contains the new button window procedure.

Listing 16.4: The NEWBTN library

The NEWBTN.MAK File

```
#----------------------
# NEWBTN.MAK make file
#----------------------

newbtn.dll : newbtndl.obj newbtn.def
     $(DLLLINK) newbtndl, newbtn.dll, NUL, $(DLLLIB), newbtn
     implib newbtn.lib newbtn.def

newbtndl.obj : newbtn.c newbtn.h
     $(DLLCC)newbtndl.obj newbtn.c
```

The NEWBTN.H File

```
/*----------------------
   NEWBTN.H header file
  ----------------------*/

BOOL APIENTRY RegisterNewBtnClass (HAB hab) ;
```

The NEWBTN.DEF File

```
;----------------------------------
; NEWBTN.DEF module definition file
;----------------------------------

LIBRARY        NEWBTN    INITINSTANCE

DESCRIPTION    'New Button Dynamic Link Library (c) Charles Petzold, 1993'
PROTMODE
DATA           NONSHARED

EXPORTS        RegisterNewBtnClass
```

You'll also need the NEWBTN.C source code from Chapter 11. Notice that the EXPORTS section of the NEWBTN.DEF file lists *RegisterNewBtnClass*, which is the function that a program calls to register the window class. The make file reads NEWBTN.DEF to create an import library called NEWBTN.LIB.

RegisterNewBtnClass is defined as an APIENTRY function because it must be called from outside the dynamic link library. The declaration of this function is in NEWBNT.H, a header file that will be used in the BUTTONS3 program, shown next.

THE NEW BUTTONS PROGRAM

The BUTTONS3 program is shown in Listing 16.5. You'll also need the NEWBTN.H header file from Listing 16.4 to compile BUTTONS3.

Listing 16.5: The BUTTONS3 program

The BUTTONS3.MAK File

```
#-----------------------
# BUTTONS3.MAK make file
#-----------------------

buttons3.exe : buttons3.obj buttons3.def newbtn.lib
     $(PRGLINK) buttons3, buttons3, NUL, $(PRGLIB) newbtn, buttons3

buttons3.obj : buttons3.c newbtn.h
     $(PRGCC) buttons3.c

newbtn.lib : newbtn.c newbtn.h newbtn.def
     nmake newbtn.mak
```

The BUTTONS3.C File

```
/*----------------------------------------------
   BUTTONS3.C -- New Button Demonstration with DLL
                 (c) Charles Petzold, 1993
  ----------------------------------------------*/

#define INCL_WIN
#define INCL_GPI
#include <os2.h>
#include "newbtn.h"

MRESULT EXPENTRY ClientWndProc (HWND, ULONG, MPARAM, MPARAM) ;

int main (void)
     {
```

Listing 16.5: The BUTTONS3 program (Continued)

```
     static CHAR  szClientClass[] = "Buttons3" ;
     static ULONG flFrameFlags = FCF_TITLEBAR      | FCF_SYSMENU |
                                 FCF_SIZEBORDER    | FCF_MINMAX  |
                                 FCF_SHELLPOSITION | FCF_TASKLIST ;
     HAB          hab ;
     HMQ          hmq ;
     HWND         hwndFrame, hwndClient ;
     QMSG         qmsg ;

     hab = WinInitialize (0) ;
     hmq = WinCreateMsgQueue (hab, 0) ;

     WinRegisterClass (hab, szClientClass, ClientWndProc, CS_SIZEREDRAW, 0) ;

     hwndFrame = WinCreateStdWindow (HWND_DESKTOP, WS_VISIBLE,
                                     &flFrameFlags, szClientClass, NULL,
                                     0L, 0, 0, &hwndClient) ;

     while (WinGetMsg (hab, &qmsg, NULLHANDLE, 0, 0))
          WinDispatchMsg (hab, &qmsg) ;

     WinDestroyWindow (hwndFrame) ;
     WinDestroyMsgQueue (hmq) ;
     WinTerminate (hab) ;
     return 0 ;
     }

MRESULT EXPENTRY ClientWndProc (HWND hwnd, ULONG msg, MPARAM mp1, MPARAM mp2)
     {
     static CHAR *szButtonLabel [] = { "Smaller", "Larger" } ;
     static HWND hwndFrame, hwndButton [2] ;
     static INT  cxClient, cyClient, cxChar, cyChar ;
     FONTMETRICS fm ;
     HAB         hab ;
     HPS         hps ;
     INT         id ;
     RECTL       rcl ;

     switch (msg)
          {
          case WM_CREATE :
               hab = WinQueryAnchorBlock (hwnd) ;
               hwndFrame = WinQueryWindow (hwnd, QW_PARENT) ;

               hps = WinGetPS (hwnd) ;
               GpiQueryFontMetrics (hps, sizeof fm, &fm) ;
               cxChar = fm.lAveCharWidth ;
               cyChar = fm.lMaxBaselineExt ;
               WinReleasePS (hps) ;
```

Listing 16.5: The BUTTONS3 program (Continued)

```
          RegisterNewBtnClass (hab) ;

          for (id = 0 ; id < 2 ; id++)
               hwndButton [id] = WinCreateWindow (
                                   hwnd,                // Parent
                                   "NewBtn",            // Class
                                   szButtonLabel [id], // Text
                                   WS_VISIBLE,          // Style
                                   0, 0,                // Position
                                   12 * cxChar,         // Width
                                   2 * cyChar,          // Height
                                   hwnd,                // Owner
                                   HWND_BOTTOM,         // Placement
                                   id,                  // ID
                                   NULL,                // Ctrl Data
                                   NULL) ;              // Pres Params
          return 0 ;

     case WM_SIZE :
          cxClient = SHORT1FROMMP (mp2) ;
          cyClient = SHORT2FROMMP (mp2) ;

          for (id = 0 ; id < 2 ; id++)
               WinSetWindowPos (hwndButton [id], NULLHANDLE,
                         cxClient / 2 + (14 * id - 13) * cxChar,
                         (cyClient - 2 * cyChar) / 2,
                         0, 0, SWP_MOVE) ;
          return 0 ;

     case WM_COMMAND:
          WinQueryWindowRect (hwnd, &rcl) ;
          WinMapWindowPoints (hwnd, HWND_DESKTOP, (PPOINTL) &rcl, 2) ;

          switch (COMMANDMSG(&msg)->cmd)               // Child ID
               {
               case 0:                                 // "Smaller"
                    rcl.xLeft   += cxClient / 20 ;
                    rcl.xRight  -= cxClient / 20 ;
                    rcl.yBottom += cyClient / 20 ;
                    rcl.yTop    -= cyClient / 20 ;
                    break ;

               case 1:                                 // "Larger"
                    rcl.xLeft   -= cxClient / 20 ;
                    rcl.xRight  += cxClient / 20 ;
                    rcl.yBottom -= cyClient / 20 ;
                    rcl.yTop    += cyClient / 20 ;
                    break ;
```

Listing 16.5: The BUTTONS3 program (Continued)

```
               }
          WinCalcFrameRect (hwndFrame, &rcl, FALSE) ;

          WinSetWindowPos (hwndFrame, NULLHANDLE,
                           rcl.xLeft, rcl.yBottom,
                           rcl.xRight - rcl.xLeft,
                           rcl.yTop   - rcl.yBottom,
                           SWP_MOVE | SWP_SIZE) ;
          return 0 ;

     case WM_ERASEBACKGROUND:
          return MRFROMSHORT (1) ;
     }
return WinDefWindowProc (hwnd, msg, mp1, mp2) ;
}
```

The BUTTONS3.DEF File

```
;-------------------------------------
; BUTTONS3.DEF module definition file
;-------------------------------------

NAME           BUTTONS3  WINDOWAPI

DESCRIPTION    'New Button Demo with DLL (c) Charles Petzold, 1993'
PROTMODE
```

These three files are nearly identical to those used for the BUTTONS2 program except that the make file lists NEWBTN.LIB in the library field of the link step, and the declaration of *RegisterSqBtnClass* (which indicates that it's an APIENTRY function) is provided by the NEWBTN.H header file.

RESOURCE-ONLY LIBRARIES

You can also store resources in dynamic link libraries and access them from a program. The library module that contains these resources can also contain code and data. But it is possible to create a library module containing nothing but resources.

Why would you want to do this? As we saw in Chapter 12, you can create bitmaps in IBM's Icon Editor or Borland's Resource Workshop and store them as resources in a program. However, bitmaps are very dependent on the resolution of the device for which they are designed. If your program uses bitmaps within its client window, you might want to customize a set of bitmaps for each of the most common video display adapters. Each of these sets of bitmaps would be stored in a different resource-only dynamic link library. You could design an installation routine for your program to copy only the resource library for the user's video adapter to the user's hard disk. This is similar to what OS/2 itself does for raster fonts.

CREATING A BITMAP LIBRARY

The files shown in Listing 16.6 are used to create a resource-only library called BITLIB.DLL. This dynamic link library contains nine 32-by-32 bitmaps created in the Icon Editor. (The bitmap images are not shown here but are included on the floppy disk; they are simply nine bitmaps numbered one through nine.)

Listing 16.6: The BITLIB library

The BITLIB.MAK File

```
#---------------------
# BITLIB.MAK make file
#---------------------

bitlib.dll : bitlib.obj bitlib.def bitlib.res
     $(DLLLINK) bitlib, bitlib.dll, NUL, $(DLLLIB), bitlib
     rc bitlib.res bitlib.dll

bitlib.obj : bitlib.c
     $(DLLCC)bitlib.obj bitlib.c

bitlib.res : bitlib.rc bitmap1.bmp bitmap2.bmp bitmap3.bmp \
                       bitmap4.bmp bitmap5.bmp bitmap6.bmp \
                       bitmap7.bmp bitmap8.bmp bitmap9.bmp
     $(DLLRC) bitlib
```

The BITLIB.C File

```
/*--------------------------------------------
   BITLIB.C -- Dummy code for resource-only DLL
               (c) Charles Petzold, 1993
  --------------------------------------------*/
```

The BITLIB.RC File

```
/*------------------------------
   BITLIB.RC resource script file
  ------------------------------*/

BITMAP 1 bitmap1.bmp
BITMAP 2 bitmap2.bmp
```

Listing 16.6: The BITLIB library (Continued)

```
BITMAP 3 bitmap3.bmp
BITMAP 4 bitmap4.bmp
BITMAP 5 bitmap5.bmp
BITMAP 6 bitmap6.bmp
BITMAP 7 bitmap7.bmp
BITMAP 8 bitmap8.bmp
BITMAP 9 bitmap9.bmp
```

The BITLIB.DEF File

```
;-----------------------------------
; BITLIB.DEF module definition file
;-----------------------------------

LIBRARY        BITLIB

DESCRIPTION    'Bitmap Library for SHOWBIT (c) Charles Petzold, 1993'
PROTMODE
```

How about that C file? It has no source code, just a comment! But that's enough to create BITLIB.OBJ. All the linker needs is BITLIB.OBJ and BITLIB.-DEF. The BITLIB.RC resource script file lists the nine bitmap files and assigns them IDs of 1 through 9.

DLLS AND MODULE HANDLES

After you create BITLIB.DLL, you may wonder again whether loading resources from a library module into a program is possible. After all, when you load a bitmap using *GpiLoadBitmap*, how does OS/2 know whether you want to load the bitmap from your .EXE file or from a library module? And how does OS/2 know the library module from which to load the bitmap?

If you look again at the various functions that load resources into memory (such as *DosGetResource*, *WinCreateStdWindow*, *WinLoadString*, *WinLoadMessage*, *WinLoadDlg*, *WinDlgBox*, *WinLoadMenu*, *WinLoadAccelTable*, *WinLoadPointer*, and *GpiLoadBitmap*), you'll discover that each function has a parameter called the *module handle*. When a program wants to load a resource from its .EXE file, the program sets this parameter to NULL. When the program wants to load a resource from a dynamic link library, the parameter must be set to the module handle of the library.

To obtain a module handle, you first define a variable of type HMODULE:

```
HMODULE hmod ;
```

Then you call *DosLoadModule*:

```
DosLoadModule (NULL, 0, szModuleName, &hmod) ;
```

The first two parameters can be set to a character string and a length of the string to receive information if an error occurs, in which case *DosLoadModule* returns a nonzero value. The third parameter is the name of the dynamic link library file without the .DLL extension.

Besides making the dynamic link library available for use, the *DosLoadModule* function increments the "reference count" of the module. You should free the module before the program terminates:

```
DosFreeModule (hmod) ;
```

This decreases the reference count. When the reference count of a library module is zero, OS/2 can free the module from memory.

LOADING BITMAPS FROM THE DLL

With this ability to obtain a module handle, we're ready to load the bitmaps from BITLIB.DLL into memory and display them. The SHOWBIT program in Listing 16.7 shows how this is done.

Listing 16.7: The SHOWBIT program

The SHOWBIT.MAK File

```
#----------------------
# SHOWBIT.MAK make file
#----------------------

showbit.exe : showbit.obj showbit.def
     $(PRGLINK) showbit, showbit, NUL, $(PRGLIB), showbit

showbit.obj : showbit.c
     $(PRGCC) showbit.c
```

The SHOWBIT.C File

```
/*-----------------------------------------------------------------
   SHOWBIT.C -- Loads Bitmap Resources from BITLIB.DLL and Draws Them
                (c) Charles Petzold, 1993
  -----------------------------------------------------------------*/

#define INCL_DOS
#define INCL_WIN
#include <os2.h>
```

Listing 16.7: The SHOWBIT program (Continued)

```
MRESULT EXPENTRY ClientWndProc (HWND, ULONG, MPARAM, MPARAM) ;

int main (void)
     {
     static CHAR  szClientClass [] = "ShowBit" ;
     static ULONG flFrameFlags = FCF_TITLEBAR      | FCF_SYSMENU |
                                 FCF_SIZEBORDER    | FCF_MINMAX  |
                                 FCF_SHELLPOSITION | FCF_TASKLIST ;
     HAB          hab ;
     HMQ          hmq ;
     HWND         hwndFrame, hwndClient ;
     QMSG         qmsg ;

     hab = WinInitialize (0) ;
     hmq = WinCreateMsgQueue (hab, 0) ;

     WinRegisterClass (hab, szClientClass, ClientWndProc, CS_SIZEREDRAW, 0) ;

     hwndFrame = WinCreateStdWindow (HWND_DESKTOP, WS_VISIBLE,
                                     &flFrameFlags, szClientClass,
                                     "ShowBit -"
                                     " (Space bar or mouse click for next)",
                                     0L, 0, 0, &hwndClient) ;
     if (hwndFrame != NULLHANDLE)
          {
          while (WinGetMsg (hab, &qmsg, NULLHANDLE, 0, 0))
               WinDispatchMsg (hab, &qmsg) ;

          WinDestroyWindow (hwndFrame) ;
          }
     WinDestroyMsgQueue (hmq) ;
     WinTerminate (hab) ;
     return 0 ;
     }

MRESULT EXPENTRY ClientWndProc (HWND hwnd, ULONG msg, MPARAM mp1, MPARAM mp2)
     {
     static HMODULE hmodBitLib ;
     static INT     idBitmap = 1 ;
     HBITMAP        hbm ;
     HPS            hps ;
     RECTL          rcl ;

     switch (msg)
          {
          case WM_CREATE:
               if (DosLoadModule (NULL, 0, "BITLIB", &hmodBitLib))
                    {
                    WinMessageBox (HWND_DESKTOP, HWND_DESKTOP,
```

Listing 16.7: The SHOWBIT program (Continued)

```
                              "Cannot load BITLIB.DLL library",
                              "ShowBit", Ø, MB_OK | MB_WARNING) ;

                   return MRFROMSHORT (1) ;
                   }
              return Ø ;

         case WM_CHAR:
              if (  CHARMSG(&msg)->fs & KC_KEYUP ||
                  !(CHARMSG(&msg)->fs & KC_VIRTUALKEY) ||
                  !(CHARMSG(&msg)->vkey == VK_SPACE))
                        break ;

              if (++idBitmap == 1Ø)
                   idBitmap = 1 ;

              WinInvalidateRect (hwnd, NULL, FALSE) ;
              return Ø ;

         case WM_BUTTON1DOWN:
              if (++idBitmap == 1Ø)
                   idBitmap = 1 ;

              WinInvalidateRect (hwnd, NULL, FALSE) ;
              break ;

         case WM_PAINT:
              hps = WinBeginPaint (hwnd, NULLHANDLE, NULL) ;
              GpiErase (hps) ;

              hbm = GpiLoadBitmap (hps, hmodBitLib, idBitmap, ØL, ØL) ;

              if (hbm != NULLHANDLE)
                   {
                   WinQueryWindowRect (hwnd, &rcl) ;

                   WinDrawBitmap (hps, hbm, NULL, (PPOINTL) &rcl,
                                  CLR_NEUTRAL, CLR_BACKGROUND, DBM_STRETCH) ;

                   GpiDeleteBitmap (hbm) ;
                   }
              WinEndPaint (hps) ;
              return Ø ;

         case WM_DESTROY:
              DosFreeModule (hmodBitLib) ;
              return Ø ;
         }
    return WinDefWindowProc (hwnd, msg, mp1, mp2) ;
    }
```

Listing 16.7: The SHOWBIT program (Continued)

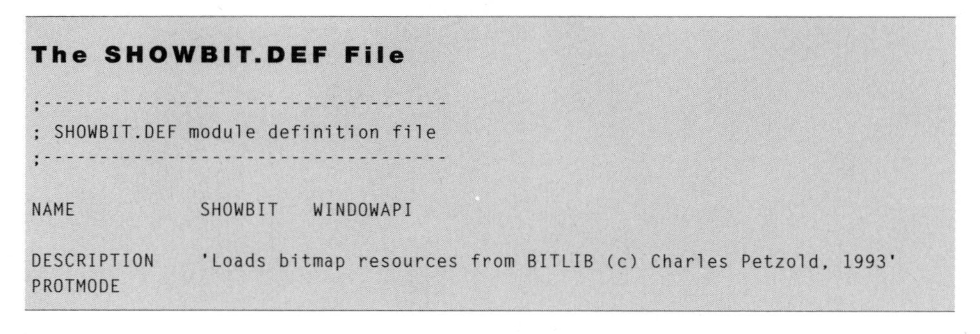

The SHOWBIT.DEF File

```
;-----------------------------------
; SHOWBIT.DEF module definition file
;-----------------------------------

NAME          SHOWBIT   WINDOWAPI

DESCRIPTION   'Loads bitmap resources from BITLIB (c) Charles Petzold, 1993'
PROTMODE
```

SHOWBIT calls *DosLoadModule* during the WM_CREATE message. If the function fails (probably because BITLIB.DLL is not in one of the directories listed in the user's LIBPATH), SHOWBIT displays a message box and returns 1 from the WM_CREATE message, which then causes the program to terminate.

If *DosLoadModule* is successful, *GpiLoadBitmap* loads the bitmap during the WM_PAINT message. The function requires the module handle and the bitmap ID. The module is freed during the WM_DESTROY message.

Multithreaded Programming Techniques

THE "BIG-JOB" PROBLEM

SINGLE-THREAD SOLUTIONS

MULTITHREADED SOLUTIONS

Chapter 17

OS/2 is a *preemptive multitasking operating system.* This means that OS/2 can run multiple programs concurrently and uses a priority-based scheduler to allocate time slices among them. The Presentation Manager is part of OS/2, so the programs running in the Presentation Manager session are also multitasked.

This is one of the most significant differences between the OS/2 Presentation Manager and the DOS-based versions of Microsoft Windows. Windows is a nonpreemptive multitasking environment. It does not perform the preemptive time-slicing we normally associate with a multitasking system. Instead, Windows multitasks programs based on the presence of messages in the programs' message queues.

When a Windows program calls the *GetMessage* function (equivalent to the Presentation Manager *WinGetMsg* function) to retrieve the next message from its message queue, and the message queue is empty, Windows suspends the program. Windows then switches to another program with a nonempty message queue. This causes that other program to return from its own *GetMessage* call to process the message. At any time, only one Windows program is running. The rest are suspended in the *GetMessage* function.

Windows programmers are well aware of the problems associated with this form of nonpreemptive multitasking. If a Windows program requires a long period of time to process a message, other programs running under Windows are effectively halted for the duration. Windows programmers must use special techniques when doing lengthy processing in order to prevent the program from suspending the rest of the system.

At first, the preemptive multitasking of OS/2 would seemingly eliminate the problems associated with the nonpreemptive nature of Windows. You might conclude that Presentation Manager programs can spend as much time as they need processing messages without worrying about suspending other programs.

Unfortunately, this is not so. As you'll see, a Presentation Manager program cannot spend a long time processing a message without affecting the environment as a whole. This problem results more from message-based architecture in general than from the preemptive or nonpreemptive nature of the multitasking system. The real difference between Microsoft Windows and the OS/2 Presentation Manager is that OS/2 provides a better solution to the problem of lengthy processing, specifically through the creation of multiple threads of execution.

Before we attempt to write a multithread Presentation Manager program, we'll examine the problem of lengthy processing jobs and explore some solutions that require only a single execution thread.

THE "BIG-JOB" PROBLEM

Presentation Manager programs can usually process most keyboard and mouse input very quickly. In a word processing program, for example, a character typed from the keyboard need only be inserted into the stored document and displayed on the screen. But many programs must also carry out commands that require more lengthy processing. Let's call this lengthy processing a "big job."

In a spreadsheet program, the big job is a recalculation of a large spreadsheet or the execution of a long macro. In a database program, the big job is a file sort or indexing. In a word processing program, it's a pagination or spelling check. In a CAD program, it's redrawing the screen. In a communications program, it's reading the serial port when an incoming character is not immediately available. And in almost any Presentation Manager program, printing is a big job.

THE ONE-TENTH OF A SECOND RULE

It is recommended that Presentation Manager programs take no more than one-tenth of a second to process a message. When a message is passed to a window procedure in your program, the window procedure should return control to the Presentation Manager within one-tenth of a second. (You'll see the reason for this shortly.) Hence, the definition of a big job is simple: It is anything your program needs to do that requires more than one-tenth of a second.

I'll be referring to this as the "one-tenth of a second rule," but it's really a guideline rather than a mandate. It's okay if a program violates this rule once in a while. For example, when a word processing program loads a document file into memory, it's not a serious problem if this requires a few seconds.

In fact, several of the programs shown in this book violate the one-tenth of a second rule. The WELCOME1 program in Chapter 2 spends eight-tenths of a second processing the WM_CREATE and WM_DESTROY messages because it plays a little tune by calling the *DosBeep* function. On a slow machine, the MINMAX2 program in Chapter 6 might take more than one-tenth of a second in the *GpiBitBlt* function. The HEAD program in Chapter 14 might take more than one-tenth of a second to load part of a file into memory if the file is in a large subdirectory on a floppy disk.

Don't get overly paranoid about violating the one-tenth of a second rule. On the other hand, if your program frequently violates this rule, you'll have to do something about it. For example, if a spreadsheet program spends more than one-tenth of a second in recalculations every time the user presses the Enter key, that's a problem. If the violation of the rule is infrequent (for example, if it occurs only when the program begins executing), then you can probably ignore the problem. But if you're spending 30 seconds or so initializing your program, you'll want to seek a solution.

Also keep in mind that it will be apparent when your program has a problem, because it will affect the performance of the entire Presentation Manager environment. Users will not look kindly on this type of behavior.

THE RULE VIOLATED

To examine the big-job problem, let's write a Presentation Manager program that does some lengthy processing in response to a WM_COMMAND message from a menu. This program is called BIGJOB1 and is shown in Listing 17.1.

Listing 17.1: The BIGJOB1 program

The BIGJOB1.MAK File

```
#----------------------
# BIGJOB1.MAK make file
#----------------------

bigjob1.exe : bigjob1.obj bigjob.obj bigjob1.def bigjob.res
     $(PRGLINK) bigjob1 bigjob, bigjob1, NUL, $(PRGLIB), bigjob1
     rc bigjob.res bigjob1.exe

bigjob1.obj : bigjob1.c bigjob.h
     $(PRGCC) bigjob1.c
```

Listing 17.1: The BIGJOB1 program (Continued)

```
bigjob.obj : bigjob.c
     $(PRGCC) bigjob.c

bigjob.res : bigjob.rc bigjob.h
     $(PRGRC) bigjob
```

The BIGJOB1.C File

```
/*---------------------------------------------------------
   BIGJOB1.C -- Naive approach to lengthy processing job
                (c) Charles Petzold, 1993
 ---------------------------------------------------------*/

#define INCL_DOS
#define INCL_WIN
#include <os2.h>
#include "bigjob.h"

int main (void)
     {
     return MainCode ("BigJob1", "BigJob1 - The Bad Program") ;
     }

MRESULT EXPENTRY ClientWndProc (HWND hwnd, ULONG msg, MPARAM mp1, MPARAM mp2)
     {
     static HAB   hab ;
     static HWND  hwndMenu ;
     static INT   iCurrentRep = IDM_10 ;
     static INT   iStatus = STATUS_READY ;
     static LONG  lCalcRep, lRepAmts [] = { 10, 100, 1000, 10000, 10000 } ;
     static ULONG ulElapsedTime ;
     double       A ;
     LONG         lRep ;

     switch (msg)
          {
          case WM_CREATE:
               hab = WinQueryAnchorBlock (hwnd) ;

               hwndMenu = WinWindowFromID (
                                WinQueryWindow (hwnd, QW_PARENT),
                                FID_MENU) ;
               return 0 ;

          case WM_COMMAND:
               switch (COMMANDMSG(&msg)->cmd)
                    {
                    case IDM_10:
```

Listing 17.1: The BIGJOB1 program (Continued)

```
          case IDM_100:
          case IDM_1000:
          case IDM_10000:
          case IDM_100000:
               WinCheckMenuItem (hwndMenu, iCurrentRep, FALSE) ;
               iCurrentRep = COMMANDMSG(&msg)->cmd ;
               WinCheckMenuItem (hwndMenu, iCurrentRep, TRUE) ;
               return 0 ;

          case IDM_START:
               WinEnableMenuItem (hwndMenu, IDM_START, FALSE) ;
               WinEnableMenuItem (hwndMenu, IDM_ABORT, TRUE) ;

               iStatus = STATUS_WORKING ;
               WinInvalidateRect (hwnd, NULL, FALSE) ;
               WinUpdateWindow (hwnd) ;

               WinSetPointer (HWND_DESKTOP,
                         WinQuerySysPointer (HWND_DESKTOP,
                                             SPTR_WAIT, FALSE)) ;

               if (WinQuerySysValue (HWND_DESKTOP, SV_MOUSEPRESENT)
                         == 0)
                    WinShowPointer (HWND_DESKTOP, TRUE) ;

               lCalcRep = lRepAmts [iCurrentRep - IDM_10] ;
               ulElapsedTime = WinGetCurrentTime (hab) ;

               for (A = 1.0, lRep = 0 ; lRep < lCalcRep ; lRep++)
                    A = Savage (A) ;

               ulElapsedTime = WinGetCurrentTime (hab) -
                               ulElapsedTime ;

               if (WinQuerySysValue (HWND_DESKTOP, SV_MOUSEPRESENT)
                         == 0)
                    WinShowPointer (HWND_DESKTOP, FALSE) ;

               WinSetPointer (HWND_DESKTOP,
                         WinQuerySysPointer (HWND_DESKTOP,
                                             SPTR_ARROW, FALSE)) ;
               iStatus = STATUS_DONE ;
               WinInvalidateRect (hwnd, NULL, FALSE) ;
               WinUpdateWindow (hwnd) ;

               WinEnableMenuItem (hwndMenu, IDM_START, TRUE) ;
               WinEnableMenuItem (hwndMenu, IDM_ABORT, FALSE) ;
               return 0 ;
```

Listing 17.1: The BIGJOB1 program (Continued)

```
                    case IDM_ABORT:     // Not much we can do here
                         return 0 ;
                    }
               break ;

          case WM_PAINT:
               PaintWindow (hwnd, iStatus, lCalcRep, ulElapsedTime) ;
               return 0 ;
          }
     return WinDefWindowProc (hwnd, msg, mp1, mp2) ;
     }
```

The BIGJOB.C File

```
/*----------------------------------------------------------
   BIGJOB.C -- Common functions used in BIGJOBx Programs
               (c) Charles Petzold, 1993
  ----------------------------------------------------------*/

#define INCL_DOS
#define INCL_WIN
#include <os2.h>
#include <math.h>
#include <stdio.h>
#include "bigjob.h"

int MainCode (CHAR *szClientClass, CHAR *szTitleBarText)
     {
     static ULONG flFrameFlags = FCF_TITLEBAR      | FCF_SYSMENU  |
                                 FCF_SIZEBORDER    | FCF_MINMAX   |
                                 FCF_SHELLPOSITION | FCF_TASKLIST |
                                 FCF_MENU ;
     HAB          hab ;
     HMQ          hmq ;
     HWND         hwndFrame, hwndClient ;
     QMSG         qmsg ;

     hab = WinInitialize (0) ;
     hmq = WinCreateMsgQueue (hab, 0) ;

     WinRegisterClass (hab, szClientClass, ClientWndProc, CS_SIZEREDRAW, 0) ;

     hwndFrame = WinCreateStdWindow (HWND_DESKTOP, WS_VISIBLE,
                                     &flFrameFlags, szClientClass,
                                     szTitleBarText,
                                     0L, 0, ID_RESOURCE, &hwndClient) ;

     while (WinGetMsg (hab, &qmsg, NULLHANDLE, 0, 0))
          WinDispatchMsg (hab, &qmsg) ;
```

Listing 17.1: The BIGJOB1 program (Continued)

```
     WinDestroyWindow (hwndFrame) ;
     WinDestroyMsgQueue (hmq) ;
     WinTerminate (hab) ;
     return 0 ;
     }

double Savage (double A)
     {
     return tan (atan (exp (log (sqrt (A * A))))) + 1.0 ;
     }

VOID PaintWindow (HWND hwnd, SHORT sStatus, LONG lCalcRep, ULONG ulTime)
     {
     static CHAR *szMessage [3] = { "Ready", "Working...",
                                    "%ld repetitions in %lu msec." } ;
     CHAR        szBuffer [60] ;
     HPS         hps ;
     RECTL       rcl ;

     hps = WinBeginPaint (hwnd, NULLHANDLE, NULL) ;
     WinQueryWindowRect (hwnd, &rcl) ;

     sprintf (szBuffer, szMessage [sStatus], lCalcRep, ulTime) ;
     WinDrawText (hps, -1, szBuffer, &rcl, CLR_NEUTRAL, CLR_BACKGROUND,
                  DT_CENTER | DT_VCENTER | DT_ERASERECT) ;

     WinEndPaint (hps) ;
     }
```

The BIGJOB.H File

```
/*----------------------
   BIGJOB.H header file
  ----------------------*/

#define ID_RESOURCE 1

#define IDM_REPS    1
#define IDM_ACTION  2
#define IDM_10      10
#define IDM_100     11
#define IDM_1000    12
#define IDM_10000   13
#define IDM_100000  14
#define IDM_START   20
#define IDM_ABORT   21

#define STATUS_READY     0
```

Listing 17.1: The BIGJOB1 program (Continued)

```
#define STATUS_WORKING   1
#define STATUS_DONE      2

#define WM_CALC_DONE     (WM_USER + 0)  // Used in BIGJOB4 and BIGJOB5
#define WM_CALC_ABORTED  (WM_USER + 1)  // Used in BIGJOB4 and BIGJOB5

#define STACKSIZE   4096                // Used in BIGJOB4 and BIGJOB5

typedef struct                          // Used in BIGJOB4 and BIGJOB5
     {
     HWND  hwnd ;
     LONG  lCalcRep ;
     BOOL  fContinueCalc ;
     HEV   hevTrigger ;                 // Used in BIGJOB5
     }
     CALCPARAM ;

typedef CALCPARAM *PCALCPARAM ;         // Used in BIGJOB4 and BIGJOB5

int     MainCode (CHAR *szClientClass, CHAR *szTitleBarText) ;
double  Savage (double A) ;
VOID    PaintWindow (HWND hwnd, SHORT sStatus, LONG lCalcRep, ULONG ulTime) ;
MRESULT EXPENTRY ClientWndProc (HWND hwnd, ULONG msg, MPARAM mp1, MPARAM mp2) ;
```

The BIGJOB.RC File

```
/*-------------------------------
   BIGJOB.RC resource script file
  -------------------------------*/

#include <os2.h>
#include "bigjob.h"

MENU ID_RESOURCE
     {
     SUBMENU "~Repetitions",  IDM_REPS
          {
          MENUITEM "~1.\a10",       IDM_10,,       MIA_CHECKED
          MENUITEM "~2.\a100",      IDM_100
          MENUITEM "~3.\a1,000",    IDM_1000
          MENUITEM "~4.\a10,000",   IDM_10000
          MENUITEM "~5.\a100,000",  IDM_100000
          }
     SUBMENU "~Action",       IDM_ACTION
          {
          MENUITEM "~Start",        IDM_START
          MENUITEM "~Abort",        IDM_ABORT,,    MIA_DISABLED
          }
```

Listing 17.1: The BIGJOB1 program (Continued)

```
     }
```

The BIGJOB1.DEF File

```
;----------------------------------
; BIGJOB1.DEF module definition file
;----------------------------------

NAME           BIGJOB1   WINDOWAPI

DESCRIPTION    'BigJob Program No. 1 (c) Charles Petzold, 1993'
PROTMODE
```

I've separated the source code for this program into two files, BIGJOB1.C and BIGJOB.C. The BIGJOB.C file contains subroutines that are also used in the next four programs in the BIGJOB series.

The BIGJOB.C file performs the functionality of the normal Presentation Manager *main* function, does WM_PAINT processing, and also contains a function called *Savage.* This function performs a floating-point calculation called the "savage" benchmark, which is sometimes used to test floating-point speed. The function increments its parameter in a roundabout way: It squares the parameter, then takes the square root, applies the *log* and then *exp* functions (which cancel each other out), then the *atan* and *tan* functions (which do the same), and finally adds 1.

The BIGJOB1 program allows you to repeat this calculation 10, 100, 1,000, 10,000, or 100,000 times based on a selection from the program's Repetitions menu. The time required for this job will depend on the speed of your machine and on whether you have a math coprocessor chip installed. A 16 MHz 386 machine with a math coprocessor requires about 30 seconds to execute the savage calculation 100,000 times—a clear violation of the one-tenth of a second rule.

You start the calculation from the Start option on the Action menu. When the calculation has finished, BIGJOB1 displays the number of repetitions and the calculation time in the client window. The program uses the *WinGetCurrentTime* function to calculate the elapsed time in milliseconds. The Action menu also has an Abort option to abort a calculation before it has finished. (This is not possible in BIGJOB1.)

Most of the code in BIGJOB1's client window procedure handles WM_COMMAND messages from the program's menu. When you select an option from the Repetitions menu, BIGJOB1 unchecks the currently selected option and checks the option you choose. When you select Start from the menu,

BIGJOB1 disables the Start option, enables the Abort option, and begins the calculation. After *ClientWndProc* is finished with the big job, the program re-enables the Start option and exits the window procedure.

BIGJOB1 is a bad program because it could spend many seconds processing a single WM_COMMAND message. If you run BIGJOB1 in the Presentation Manager, you'll easily see what's wrong with it.

STOP THE WORLD, I'M WORKING

While doing its big job, BIGJOB1 clogs up the rest of the Presentation Manager. You cannot switch to another program using the keyboard or the mouse. The whole system seemingly ignores all keyboard and mouse input until the calculation is finished. Although the Abort option is present on BIGJOB1's menu, you can't use the keyboard or mouse to select that option. Once you begin the big job, you have to wait until it's finished to do anything else.

At first, this is troubling. Aren't OS/2 and the Presentation Manager supposed to be multitasking? And if so, why does one program apparently cause the whole system to grind to a halt?

OS/2 *is* a multitasking operating system. What is happening with BIGJOB1 is a predictable result of the message-based architecture of the Presentation Manager. Let's examine why.

MESSAGE-BASED ARCHITECTURE: A REVIEW

BIGJOB1 creates a normal collection of windows in its call to *WinCreateStdWindow*. Each window in the collection has a window procedure that processes messages to these windows. The window procedure for BIGJOB1's client window is in the BIGJOB1 program. The other window procedures (such as those for the frame window, the title bar window, and the menu window) are contained in the Presentation Manager PMWIN.DLL dynamic link library.

BIGJOB1 also creates a message queue. Some of the messages for a window are stored in the program's message queue. (These messages are called *queued messages* and are said to be "posted to the queue.") Most of the queued messages report user input from the keyboard and mouse, such as WM_CHAR and WM_MOUSEMOVE. The queued messages are retrieved from the message queue when the program calls *WinGetMsg* and are dispatched to the window procedure by *WinDispatchMsg*.

Other messages are sent directly to the window procedure, bypassing the program's message queue. These *unqueued messages* result from calls to certain Presentation Manager functions. For example, *WinCreateStdWindow* sends WM_CREATE messages to window procedures of the windows it creates; *WinDestroyWindow* sends a WM_DESTROY message. A message can be sent directly to a window procedure by a call to *WinSendMsg*. The menu window uses *WinSendMsg* to send a WM_COMMAND message.

For most of the time that a typical Presentation Manager program is running, the program is suspended in the *WinGetMsg* function awaiting a message. Usually, the *WinGetMsg* function will return with a message that reports keyboard or mouse input. Sometimes the processing of this message will result in other messages being sent to the window procedure. For example, a WM_-COMMAND message from a menu is the result of keyboard or mouse input. While a program is awaiting a message in the *WinGetMsg* function, one of its window procedures can also be sent a message. In this case, the Presentation Manager will call the window procedure so that the window procedure can process the message.

PROCESSES AND THREADS

Multitasking in OS/2 is based on processes and threads within processes. An OS/2 program can consist of one or more processes, although most programs consist of only a single process. A process is started by a call to the *DosExecPgm* or *DosStartSession* function. Each process currently running under OS/2 is denoted by a unique process ID number. When a process allocates resources, such as open files and memory blocks, the resources are private to the process; that is, the process owns the resources.

A process running under OS/2 consists of one or more threads of execution. Each thread has a thread ID number that uniquely identifies the thread within the process. The thread that begins execution in the process always has an ID number of 1. A thread can create additional threads in the process by a call to *DosCreateThread*. All threads within a process share the process's resources (such as open files and memory blocks), but each thread has its own stack and its own set of CPU registers, including the instruction pointer. OS/2 multitasks among threads using a priority-based scheduler.

So far, all the programs shown in this book have consisted of a single process with a single execution thread. BIGJOB1 is no exception. When a thread running under the Presentation Manager program creates some windows, the messages for those windows must be processed by the thread that created them. This is true whether a message is posted to a message queue or sent directly to a window procedure, or whether the window's window procedure is contained in the program or in a dynamic link library.

A particular thread of execution can do only one task at a time. A thread cannot be multitasked with itself. While BIGJOB1 is busy doing its big job, no other code in BIGJOB1 can execute.

So here's the problem: When you select Start from BIGJOB1's menu, *Client-WndProc* begins the big job on response from the WM_COMMAND message. Now you try to use the Alt-Esc key combination to switch to another program. The window that must process this key combination is BIGJOB1's frame window. But the window procedure for the frame window runs in the same thread as the client window, and the client window is busy doing the big job. This means that the Alt-Esc keyboard message cannot be processed until BIGJOB1 finishes the calculation, exits *ClientWndProc*, and calls *WinGetMsg* to retrieve the message from the queue. This is why the Presentation Manager seemingly ignores keyboard input while BIGJOB1 is calculating.

SERIALIZATION OF USER INPUT

But maybe there's another way to switch programs while BIGJOB1 is doing its big job—a way that doesn't require window procedures in BIGJOB1 to process a message. As you know, you can use the mouse to make another window active. Maybe that will work.

To test this out, you first position the mouse pointer on top of another program's window and then use the keyboard to select Start from BIGJOB1's menu. While BIGJOB1 is calculating, you press the mouse button on this other window and...nothing happens.

Again, this is initially disturbing. Because the Presentation Manager is a true multitasking system, the other program should be able to read that mouse click even while BIGJOB1 is calculating. The Presentation Manager should also be able to change the active window from BIGJOB1 to the other program. But this does not happen.

This behavior results from the serialization of user input: All keyboard and mouse input is stored first in a system message queue. Keyboard and mouse messages are then passed—one message at a time—to an application's message queue. For keyboard messages, the destination of the message depends on which window has the input focus; for mouse messages, it's based on which window is underneath the mouse pointer or which window has captured the mouse.

The serialization of mouse and keyboard input in a system message queue is required to correctly handle "type ahead" and "mouse ahead" input from the user—input that occurs faster than it can be processed. One of the keystrokes or mouse clicks in the system message queue could have the effect of changing the active window and the focus window. Subsequent keyboard input must then go to that new window. Thus, a keyboard or mouse message cannot be posted to a particular application's message queue until the previous keyboard or mouse message has been entirely processed.

In this particular example (pressing the mouse button over another window while BIGJOB1 is working), another application cannot read a mouse message until BIGJOB1 processes all of its keyboard input. And BIGJOB1 has not processed the release of the key that caused the menu to send the WM_COMMAND message that started the calculation.

Thus, because BIGJOB1 renders itself resistant to keyboard or mouse input, it also prevents all other programs running under the Presentation Manager from receiving keyboard or mouse input.

But even if another program could read a mouse click, the Presentation Manager cannot change the input focus from BIGJOB1 to another program while BIGJOB1 is busy doing the calculation. To change the input focus, the Presentation Manager must send a WM_SETFOCUS message to the window losing the input focus. That WM_SETFOCUS message is blocked because the window that must receive the message is part of BIGJOB1's thread, and BIGJOB1 is busy doing the big job.

Messages are not like hardware interrupts! Although a window procedure can be sent a message as a result of calling *WinDefWindowProc*, and a window procedure can be sent a message as a result of calling some other Presentation Manager functions, these are examples of *recursion* in window procedures, not *interruption*. Messages do not preemptively interrupt a thread and start execution someplace else in the same thread.

Now that we've seen how BIGJOB1 effectively disables keyboard and mouse input in the Presentation Manager, the reason for the one-tenth of a second rule should be obvious. Presentation Manager programs must continually interact with the system, retrieving and processing their messages promptly.

BUT STILL THERE IS MULTITASKING

As bad as BIGJOB1 is, however, OS/2 can still multitask some Presentation Manager programs while BIGJOB1 is running. If you have one of the clock programs from Chapter 10 running when you begin the big job, you'll find that these programs continue to update the time every second. The WM_TIMER message is a queued message, but it does not need to be serialized like the keyboard and mouse messages. The clock programs can continue to receive WM_TIMER messages even if BIGJOB1 has clogged up keyboard and mouse input. Threads can also process WM_PAINT messages during this time.

But keep in mind that most messages are user input messages (such as WM_CHAR and WM_MOUSEMOVE), result directly from user input messages (such as WM_COMMAND and WM_CONTROL), or are sent from functions that are called in response to these messages. Most message traffic is initiated by user input. A program doing a big job is a program that's holding up traffic and preventing the user from getting to work.

THE INFAMOUS "WAIT" POINTER

Before BIGJOB1 begins its big job, it calls *WinQuerySysPointer* to obtain a handle to the SPTR_WAIT system mouse pointer and uses this handle in a call to *WinSetPointer.* (The program also displays the pointer by calling *WinShow-Pointer* if a mouse is not installed.) After the calculation is finished, it calls *WinQuerySysPointer* and *WinSetPointer* to display the normal SPTR_ARROW mouse pointer.

The SPTR_WAIT pointer looks like a little clock. This signals to the user that a big job is in progress and that the keyboard and mouse are effectively disabled. You should display the SPTR_WAIT pointer whenever you do a big job that requires more than a second or so.

As you probably know, users despise the wait pointer. It means they must wait for a piggish program to finish some work. None of the other programs in this chapter will require the wait pointer because these programs solve the big-job problem in various ways.

SINGLE-THREAD SOLUTIONS

Before we explore multithreaded Presentation Manager programs, let's look at two solutions that work with only a single thread: multitasking with the timer and peeking at messages.

MULTITASKING WITH THE TIMER

I noted a moment ago that clock programs continue to function normally while BIGJOB1 is working. This might have suggested the Presentation Manager timer as a possible solution. The Presentation Manager timer allows a program to break a big job into little pieces that are performed on receipt of a WM_TIMER message. This is the approach taken in the BIGJOB2 program shown in Listing 17.2.

Compiling BIGJOB2 also requires the BIGJOB.C, BIGJOB.H, and BIGJOB.RC files shown in Listing 17.1.

When you select the Start option from BIGJOB2's menu, BIGJOB2 calls *WinStartTimer* to start the timer. It disables the Start option, enables the Abort option, and initializes the *A* and *lRep* variables. The *Savage* function is called once for each WM_TIMER message. Thus, for 100 repetitions, the big job is finished after 100 WM_TIMER messages.

Listing 17.2: The BIGJOB2 Program

The BIGJOB2.MAK File

```
#----------------------
# BIGJOB2.MAK make file
#----------------------

bigjob2.exe : bigjob2.obj bigjob.obj bigjob2.def bigjob.res
     $(PRGLINK) bigjob2 bigjob, bigjob2, NUL, $(PRGLIB), bigjob2
     rc bigjob.res bigjob2.exe

bigjob2.obj : bigjob2.c bigjob.h
     $(PRGCC) bigjob2.c

bigjob.obj : bigjob.c
     $(PRGCC) bigjob.c

bigjob.res : bigjob.rc bigjob.h
     $(PRGRC) bigjob
```

The BIGJOB2.C File

```
/*-------------------------------------------------------
   BIGJOB2.C -- Timer approach to lengthy processing job
                (c) Charles Petzold, 1993
 --------------------------------------------------------*/

#define INCL_DOS
#define INCL_WIN
#include <os2.h>
#include "bigjob.h"

#define ID_TIMER 1

int main (void)
     {
     return MainCode ("BigJob2", "BigJob2 - The Timer") ;
     }

MRESULT EXPENTRY ClientWndProc (HWND hwnd, ULONG msg, MPARAM mp1, MPARAM mp2)
     {
     static double A ;
     static HAB    hab ;
     static HWND   hwndMenu ;
     static INT    iCurrentRep = IDM_10 ;
     static INT    iStatus = STATUS_READY ;
     static LONG   lRep, lCalcRep,
                   lRepAmts [] = { 10, 100, 1000, 10000, 100000 } ;
     static ULONG  ulElapsedTime ;
```

Listing 17.2: The BIGJOB2 Program (Continued)

```
     switch (msg)
          {
          case WM_CREATE:
               hab = WinQueryAnchorBlock (hwnd) ;

               hwndMenu = WinWindowFromID (
                                WinQueryWindow (hwnd, QW_PARENT),
                                FID_MENU) ;
               return 0 ;

          case WM_COMMAND:
               switch (COMMANDMSG(&msg)->cmd)
                    {
                    case IDM_10:
                    case IDM_100:
                    case IDM_1000:
                    case IDM_10000:
                    case IDM_100000:
                         WinCheckMenuItem (hwndMenu, iCurrentRep, FALSE) ;
                         iCurrentRep = COMMANDMSG(&msg)->cmd ;
                         WinCheckMenuItem (hwndMenu, iCurrentRep, TRUE) ;
                         return 0 ;

                    case IDM_START:
                         if (!WinStartTimer (hab, hwnd, ID_TIMER, 0))
                              {
                              WinAlarm (HWND_DESKTOP, WA_ERROR) ;
                              return 0 ;
                              }
                         WinEnableMenuItem (hwndMenu, IDM_START, FALSE) ;
                         WinEnableMenuItem (hwndMenu, IDM_ABORT, TRUE) ;

                         iStatus = STATUS_WORKING ;
                         WinInvalidateRect (hwnd, NULL, FALSE) ;

                         lCalcRep = lRepAmts [iCurrentRep - IDM_10] ;
                         ulElapsedTime = WinGetCurrentTime (hab) ;
                         A = 1.0 ;
                         lRep = 0 ;

                         return 0 ;

                    case IDM_ABORT:
                         WinStopTimer (hab, hwnd, ID_TIMER) ;

                         iStatus = STATUS_READY ;
                         WinInvalidateRect (hwnd, NULL, FALSE) ;
```

Listing 17.2: The BIGJOB2 Program (Continued)

```
                    WinEnableMenuItem (hwndMenu, IDM_START, TRUE) ;
                    WinEnableMenuItem (hwndMenu, IDM_ABORT, FALSE) ;
                    return 0 ;
                    }
               break ;

          case WM_TIMER:
               A = Savage (A) ;

               if (++lRep == lCalcRep)
                    {
                    ulElapsedTime = WinGetCurrentTime (hab) -
                                        ulElapsedTime ;

                    WinStopTimer (hab, hwnd, ID_TIMER) ;

                    iStatus = STATUS_DONE ;
                    WinInvalidateRect (hwnd, NULL, FALSE) ;

                    WinEnableMenuItem (hwndMenu, IDM_START, TRUE) ;
                    WinEnableMenuItem (hwndMenu, IDM_ABORT, FALSE) ;
                    }
               return 0 ;

          case WM_PAINT:
               PaintWindow (hwnd, iStatus, lCalcRep, ulElapsedTime) ;
               return 0 ;

          case WM_DESTROY:
               if (iStatus == STATUS_WORKING)
                    WinStopTimer (hab, hwnd, ID_TIMER) ;
               return 0 ;
          }
     return WinDefWindowProc (hwnd, msg, mp1, mp2) ;
     }
```

The BIGJOB2.DEF File

```
;------------------------------------
; BIGJOB2.DEF module definition file
;------------------------------------

NAME           BIGJOB2   WINDOWAPI

DESCRIPTION    'BigJob Program No. 2 (c) Charles Petzold, 1993'
PROTMODE
```

WM_TIMER messages are low-priority queued messages: Keyboard or mouse messages are retrieved from the queue and processed before a WM_-TIMER message. Thus BIGJOB2 continues to read keyboard and mouse input and allows the user to select Abort from BIGJOB2's menu, move or resize BIG-JOB2's window, or shift control to another program. The entire operating system—including BIGJOB2—continues to function normally while BIGJOB2 is doing the calculation. The timer is stopped when the calculation is finished or when you select Abort from the menu.

TIMER PROBLEMS

Although the timer approach is feasible for BIGJOB2, it's easy to imagine cases where the timer would be inadequate.

A program using the timer for a big job must enter and exit the processing loop with every WM_TIMER message. This is easy to structure when a single loop is involved (as in BIGJOB2), but it becomes a nightmare for more complex jobs with lots of nested loops.

The timer also slows down the big job. It simply isn't possible to receive WM_TIMER messages at a rate faster than that of the hardware clock. Under OS/2, this means the program receives a WM_TIMER message only once every 31.25 ms. But on most machines that run OS/2, BIGJOB2 spends only a fraction of this time processing the message. Because the calculation is paced by the timer, the calculation won't finish any faster on a faster computer!

Although the Presentation Manager timer can be of help in some big-job problems, as a general solution it must clearly be rejected.

PEEKING AT MESSAGES

The second solution involves the *WinPeekMsg* function. This function is similar in syntax and functionality to *WinGetMsg*. However, when a program calls *WinGetMsg*, the function does not return until it has a message from the message queue. If the message queue is empty, the *WinGetMsg* function waits. *WinPeekMsg*, on the other hand, always returns immediately. Thus, while doing the big job, a Presentation Manager program can periodically check for messages in the queue. These messages can be removed from the queue and processed normally.

This approach is used quite often in programs written for the DOS-based versions of Microsoft Windows, where the function is called *PeekMessage*. Windows is entirely a single-thread system—it multitasks among programs only when they call *GetMessage* or *PeekMessage*. Calling *PeekMessage* under Windows effectively yields control to other programs that might have messages in their message queues.

The syntax of *WinPeekMsg* is the same as that of *WinGetMsg* except that it has an options parameter:

```
WinPeekmsg (hab, &qmsg, hwnd, msgFirst, msgLast, fOptions)
```

The *fOptions* parameter can be either PM_REMOVE to remove the next message from the queue or PM_NOREMOVE to leave the message in the queue. *WinPeekMsg* returns FALSE if the message queue is empty and TRUE otherwise. (This is where it differs from *WinGetMsg*, which returns FALSE if the message retrieved from the queue is WM_QUIT and TRUE otherwise.) Thus, *WinPeekMsg* will not wait for a message; if no message is available, the function returns FALSE.

The BIGJOB3 program in Listing 17.3 shows how a program can use *WinPeekMsg* to retrieve and process messages while doing a big job.

Listing 17.3: The BIGJOB3 Program

The BIGJOB3.MAK File

```
#----------------------
# BIGJOB3.MAK make file
#----------------------

bigjob3.exe : bigjob3.obj bigjob.obj bigjob3.def bigjob.res
     $(PRGLINK) bigjob3 bigjob, bigjob3, NUL, $(PRGLIB), bigjob3
     rc bigjob.res bigjob3.exe

bigjob3.obj : bigjob3.c bigjob.h
     $(PRGCC) bigjob3.c

bigjob.obj : bigjob.c
     $(PRGCC) bigjob.c

bigjob.res : bigjob.rc bigjob.h
     $(PRGRC) bigjob
```

The BIGJOB3.C File

```
/*--------------------------------------------------------------
   BIGJOB3.C -- Peek Message approach to lengthy processing job
                (c) Charles Petzold, 1993
  --------------------------------------------------------------*/

#define INCL_DOS
#define INCL_WIN
#include <os2.h>
#include "bigjob.h"
```

Listing 17.3: The BIGJOB3 Program (Continued)

```
int main (void)
     {
     return MainCode ("BigJob3", "BigJob3 - Message Peeking") ;
     }

MRESULT EXPENTRY ClientWndProc (HWND hwnd, ULONG msg, MPARAM mp1, MPARAM mp2)
     {
     static BOOL   fContinueCalc = FALSE ;
     static HAB    hab ;
     static HWND   hwndMenu ;
     static INT    iStatus = STATUS_READY ;
     static INT    iCurrentRep = IDM_10 ;
     static LONG   lCalcRep, lRepAmts [] = { 10, 100, 1000, 10000, 10000 } ;
     static ULONG  ulElapsedTime ;
     double        A ;
     LONG          lRep ;
     QMSG          qmsg ;

     switch (msg)
          {
          case WM_CREATE:
               hab = WinQueryAnchorBlock (hwnd) ;

               hwndMenu = WinWindowFromID (
                                WinQueryWindow (hwnd, QW_PARENT),
                                FID_MENU) ;
               return 0 ;

          case WM_COMMAND:
               switch (COMMANDMSG(&msg)->cmd)
                    {
                    case IDM_10:
                    case IDM_100:
                    case IDM_1000:
                    case IDM_10000:
                    case IDM_100000:
                         WinCheckMenuItem (hwndMenu, iCurrentRep, FALSE) ;
                         iCurrentRep = COMMANDMSG(&msg)->cmd ;
                         WinCheckMenuItem (hwndMenu, iCurrentRep, TRUE) ;
                         return 0 ;

                    case IDM_START:
                         WinEnableMenuItem (hwndMenu, IDM_START, FALSE) ;
                         WinEnableMenuItem (hwndMenu, IDM_ABORT, TRUE) ;

                         iStatus = STATUS_WORKING ;
                         WinInvalidateRect (hwnd, NULL, FALSE) ;
```

Listing 17.3: The BIGJOB3 Program (Continued)

```
                    lCalcRep = lRepAmts [iCurrentRep - IDM_10] ;
                    fContinueCalc = TRUE ;
                    ulElapsedTime = WinGetCurrentTime (hab) ;

                    qmsg.msg = WM_NULL ;

                    for (A = 1.0, lRep = 0 ; lRep < lCalcRep ; lRep++)
                         {
                         A = Savage (A) ;

                         while (WinPeekMsg (hab, &qmsg, NULLHANDLE,
                                            0, 0, PM_NOREMOVE))
                              {
                              if (qmsg.msg == WM_QUIT)
                                   break ;

                              WinGetMsg (hab, &qmsg, NULLHANDLE, 0, 0) ;
                              WinDispatchMsg (hab, &qmsg) ;

                              if (!fContinueCalc)
                                   break ;
                              }
                         if (!fContinueCalc || qmsg.msg == WM_QUIT)
                              break ;
                         }
                    ulElapsedTime = WinGetCurrentTime (hab) -
                                             ulElapsedTime ;

                    if (!fContinueCalc || qmsg.msg == WM_QUIT)
                         iStatus = STATUS_READY ;
                    else
                         iStatus = STATUS_DONE ;

                    WinInvalidateRect (hwnd, NULL, FALSE) ;

                    WinEnableMenuItem (hwndMenu, IDM_START, TRUE) ;
                    WinEnableMenuItem (hwndMenu, IDM_ABORT, FALSE) ;
                    return 0 ;

               case IDM_ABORT:
                    fContinueCalc = FALSE ;
                    return 0 ;
               }
          break ;

     case WM_PAINT:
          PaintWindow (hwnd, iStatus, lCalcRep, ulElapsedTime) ;
          return 0 ;
     }
```

Listing 17.3: The BIGJOB3 Program (Continued)

```
     return WinDefWindowProc (hwnd, msg, mp1, mp2) ;
     }
```

The BIGJOB3.DEF File

```
;-----------------------------------
; BIGJOB3.DEF module definition file
;-----------------------------------

NAME           BIGJOB3   WINDOWAPI

DESCRIPTION    'BigJob Program No. 3 (c) Charles Petzold, 1993'
PROTMODE
```

BIGJOB3 also requires the BIGJOB.C, BIGJOB.H, and BIGJOB.RC files shown in Listing 17.1.

Like BIGJOB1, BIGJOB3 does the entire calculation in response to a WM_-COMMAND message. However, within the calculation loop, BIGJOB3 calls *WinPeekMsg* to check for messages in the message queue. BIGJOB3 first removes such messages with *WinGetMsg* and then dispatches them to a window procedure with *WinDispatchMsg*, just as in the normal message loop in *main*.

Notice that after the *WinGetMsg* and *WinDispatchMsg* calls, the value of *fContinueCalc* is checked. BIGJOB3 sets this to FALSE when it receives a WM_-COMMAND message indicating that the user has selected Abort from the menu.

You'll notice that special processing is required for the WM_QUIT message. This message is posted to the message queue by the Presentation Manager as a default response when the user selects Close from the system menu or when the program is terminated from the Presentation Manager Task Manager. The WM_QUIT message should not be removed from the queue within the window procedure. Instead, BIGJOB3 exits the window procedure so that the WM_QUIT message can be retrieved from the message queue in the *main* function.

RECEIVING UNQUEUED MESSAGES

If you've been thinking about queued and unqueued messages, the preceding code may have seemed incomplete. *WinPeekMsg* returns TRUE only when the message queue contains a message. Only then does BIGJOB3 retrieve the message from the queue and dispatch it.

But what happens when the user selects Abort from the menu? The menu window sends the WM_COMMAND message by calling *WinSendMsg*. The message is not posted to the queue. How, then, is BIGJOB3 able to process this message while doing its big job?

The answer is fairly simple. The WM_COMMAND message is initiated by user input through the keyboard or mouse. The keyboard and mouse messages are queued. *WinPeekMsg* detects their presence and allows *WinGetMsg* to retrieve them and *WinDispatchMsg* to send them to the appropriate window procedure. When the menu window determines that the user has selected the Abort option, it sends the WM_COMMAND message that *ClientWndProc* processes. Thus *ClientWndProc* receives this unqueued WM_COMMAND message while calling the *WinDispatchMsg* function for a queued mouse or keyboard message.

Here's a stickier problem: Let's assume you start BIGJOB3 calculating and you move the mouse pointer over the window of another program. You press the mouse button and the active window changes to the other program. The other program is processing this mouse input, not BIGJOB3. Yet, when the Presentation Manager changes the active window and the input focus, it must send BIGJOB3 a WM_SETFOCUS message. BIGJOB3's frame window responds by changing the color of the title bar window. But how can BIGJOB3 process an unqueued message initiated by a queued message outside BIGJOB3's message queue?

Although the purpose of *WinGetMsg* and *WinPeekMsg* is to retrieve messages from the message queue, these functions also allow a window procedure in the thread to process an unqueued message.

If another thread tries to send a message to BIGJOB3 by calling *WinSendMsg* (as happens with the WM_SETFOCUS message), and the recipient of the message is busy (doing a big job, for example), the *WinSendMsg* function is blocked until the recipient thread is free. But when the thread calls *WinGetMsg* or *WinPeekMsg*, the Presentation Manager checks to see if another thread is trying to send that thread a message. If so, the Presentation Manager lets that unqueued message be processed by calling the message procedure with the message. This happens before the Presentation Manager even checks the contents of the thread's message queue.

A window procedure can also receive an unqueued message while calling *WinSendMsg*. This is how the Presentation Manager prevents message deadlocks. For example, suppose a window procedure in one program calls *WinSendMsg* to send a message to a window procedure in a second program. Program 2 is doing something in its window procedure, so the *WinSendMsg* function is blocked. But then the window procedure in program 2 calls *WinSendMsg* to send a message to the window procedure in program 1. Uh oh—deadlock. The Presentation Manager resolves the deadlock by letting the message from program 1 be sent to program 2 and by then allowing the message from program 2 to be sent to program 1.

A DIFFERENT MESSAGE LOOP IN MAIN

In BIGJOB3 I used a normal message loop in *main* but called *WinPeekMsg*, *WinGetMsg*, and *WinDispatchMsg* in the window procedure. You can also alter the message loop in *main*, basing the loop on the *WinPeekMsg* function rather than on *WinGetMsg*. The normal message loop looks like this:

```
while (WinGetMsg (hab, &qmsg, NULLHANDLE, Ø, Ø))
     WinDispatchMsg (hab, &qmsg)
```

Here's the alternative message loop:

```
#define WM_DO_SOMETHING WM_USER
:
:
while (TRUE)
     {
     if (WinPeekMsg (hab, &qmsg, NULL, Ø, Ø, PM_REMOVE)) ;
          {
          if (qmsg.msg == WM_QUIT)
               break ;
          else
               WinDispatchMsg (hab, &qmsg) ;
          }
     else
     WinSendMsg (hwndClient, WM_DO_SOMETHING, NULL, NULL) ;
     }
```

Whenever *WinPeekMsg* returns FALSE (indicating that the message queue is empty), *WinSendMsg* is called to send a WM_DO_SOMETHING message to the client window. Note that the WM_QUIT message requires special handling.

This approach is good for demonstration programs that seemingly run forever. (One example is a program that displays a series of randomly sized and colored rectangles.) The client window procedure handles the WM_DO_-SOMETHING message in the same way it handles a WM_TIMER message. The advantage is that the WM_DO_SOMETHING messages come faster than 32 times per second.

This alternate message loop is not quite appropriate for handling the big-job problem in general. Although the client window could ignore the WM_-DO_SOMETHING messages when it's not doing the big job, you probably want a normal message loop in that case. This would require making the *sStatus* variable used in the BIGJOB programs (or its equivalent) a global variable and using the alternate message loop only when the value of *sStatus* is STATUS_WORKING.

PEEKING PROBLEMS

The most serious challenge you face with a program structured like BIGJOB3 is preventing reentrancy. You don't want to reenter the big-job calculation loop when you call *WinPeekMsg* or *WinDispatchMsg* from within that loop. BIGJOB3 prevents reentrancy by disabling the Start option on the menu before doing the big job.

Although message peeking usually works well in Presentation Manager programs, it's always a little messy for the programmer. Because the *WinPeekMsg* functions must be called frequently enough to give the system a good response time, an inordinate amount of code is required. If the big job must be aborted, it's sometimes difficult to get out of a calculation loop in a structured manner. You may even find yourself using *goto* statements!

MULTITHREADED SOLUTIONS

Let's now attack the big-job problem by creating a second thread of execution. When an OS/2 process contains multiple threads of execution, the threads run concurrently. All threads in a process share the program's resources (such as open files, memory, and semaphores), but each thread has its own CPU state, dispatching priority, and stack.

Within a program, the code used by a second thread of execution looks like a function. All local automatic variables in the thread function (or functions called from a thread) are private to each thread because they are stored on the thread's stack. Local static variables in the thread function (or functions called from each thread) can be shared by all threads that use the function.

THE TWO CATEGORIES OF THREADS

Threads used in Presentation Manager programs fall into two categories: *message queue threads* and *non-message queue threads.* A thread becomes a message queue thread when it calls *WinCreateMsgQueue.* The thread reverts to being a non-message queue thread upon a call to *WinDestroyMsgQueue.*

A Presentation Manager program always creates a message queue in at least one thread. A thread must create a message queue before it can create windows. The message queue is used to store messages for all windows created in the thread. Other threads in a Presentation Manager program need to create message queues only if they also create windows.

Although non-message queue threads have some advantages over message queue threads, they also have some disadvantages. Here's the good news: A non-message queue thread is not bound by the one-tenth of a second rule.

Because the thread does not receive or process messages, it needn't worry about clogging up the processing of messages in message queue threads. Thus, a non-message queue thread is often ideal for doing a big job.

But good news is not complete without the bad news: Non-message queue threads are restricted in the type of Presentation Manager functions they can call. Non-message queue threads

- Cannot create windows
- Cannot contain window procedures
- Cannot send messages to window procedures in a message queue thread
- Cannot call functions that cause messages to be sent to a window procedure

Some of these restrictions are obvious: A non-message queue thread cannot create a window or contain a window procedure because it has no queue to store messages for that window. However, a non-message queue thread can call some functions that affect windows created in message queue threads. For example, a non-message queue thread can obtain a presentation space handle for a window created in a message queue thread and is able to paint something on the surface of that window.

But non-message queue threads cannot send messages to message queue threads. The *WinSendMsg* function is not allowed. Nor can non-message queue threads call functions that cause messages to be sent. For example, *WinDestroy-Window* cannot be called from a non-message queue thread because it sends a window procedure a WM_DESTROY message.

Although a non-message queue thread cannot send a message using *Win-SendMsg*, the thread *can* post a message by calling *WinPostMsg*. The *WinPost-Msg* function places the message in a thread's message queue and returns immediately. Non-message queue threads often use the *WinPostMsg* function to signal a message queue thread when it has completed the big job.

THE MULTITHREAD RUNTIME LIBRARY

Writing multithread programs in C involves some additional problems caused by the C runtime library. Although many C functions are reentrant (that is, they can be called from multiple threads concurrently), not all of them are. Calling one of the nonreentrant functions from two threads concurrently could cause the threads to interfere with each other.

Fortunately, both the IBM and Borland C compilers have special multithread runtime libraries that avoid the reentrancy problems. To use the IBM multi-thread runtime library, you must specify the *-Gm* option when compiling the program. The compiler inserts the name of the multithread runtime library in the object module and the linker later uses that library. To use the Borland multithread runtime library, you must specify the *-sm* option when compiling, and link with C2MT.LIB rather than C2.LIB.

This means that we need new command files that set up different environment variables for our make files. The IBMMT.CMD and BORMT.CMD command files are shown in Listing 17.4. These define the PRGCCMT and PRGLIBMT environment variables that incorporate the differences for compiling and linking multithreaded programs.

Listing 17.4: Command files to set environment variables for multithreaded programs

The IBMMT.CMD File

```
REM ------------------------------------------------------------------
REM  IBMMT.CMD -- Multthreading environment for IBM C Developer's WorkSet/2
REM ------------------------------------------------------------------
SET PRGCCMT=icc -C -Kbcpr -Ss -Gm -Fo
SET PRGLINK=link386 /BASE:0x10000
SET PRGLIBMT=
SET PRGRC=rc -r
```

The BORMT.CMD File

```
REM ------------------------------------------------------------------
REM  BORMT.CMD -- Set up multithreading environment for Borland C++ for OS/2
REM ------------------------------------------------------------------
SET PRGCCMT=bcc -c -I\bcos2\include -sm -o
SET PRGLINK=tlink -c -x -v -L\bcos2\lib \bcos2\lib\c02.obj
SET PRGLIBMT=c2mt + os2
SET PRGRC=rc -r -i \bcos2\include
```

Notice also that the PRGCCMT environment variable ends with the *-Fo* flag (in IBMMT.CMD) and the *-o* flag (in BORMT.CMD). These flags allow specifying an object file name that is different than the C source code name. I've done this because I want to compile the BIGJOB.C file in a multithreaded version with an object file name of BIGJOBMT.OBJ.

Programs that use these multithreaded libraries must use the *_beginthread* function rather than *DosCreateThread* to create a new thread of execution. The *_beginthread* function is defined in the PROCESS.H header file. The code used by the thread looks like a function in the program. The *_beginthread* function also allows a pointer to be passed as a parameter to this function. If this is a pointer to a structure, the function that creates the thread and the thread function can share nonglobal data.

Unfortunately, the *_beginthread* function is defined a little differently in the IBM and Borland runtime libraries. The IBM version includes an extra parameter that is not used in OS/2 2.*x*, but was used in versions of OS/2 prior to 2.0 to specify the address of the thread's stack. In the next two programs shown in this chapter, I've solved the problem of the different function definitions by using an *#ifdef* statement with the __IBMC__ macro identifier. This identifier is defined only by the IBM compiler.

The BIGJOB4 program in Listing 17.5 uses the *_beginthread* function and the multithreaded runtime library.

The BIGJOB.C, BIGJOB.H, and BIGJOB.RC files from Listing 17.1 are required to create BIGJOB4.EXE.

PUTTING THE THREAD TO WORK

The function used for the second thread in BIGJOB4 is called *CalcThread* and is located near the bottom of BIGJOB4.C. The parameter to this function is a pointer of type CALCPARAM, which is defined in BIGJOB.H. This is a structure that *ClientWndProc* uses in order to pass information to the thread function.

When you select Start from BIGJOB4's menu, *ClientWndProc* sets the first three fields of the CALCPARAM structure and creates the thread by calling *_beginthread*. The *_beginthread* call requires the name of the thread function (*CalcThread*), the stack size, and a pointer to a parameter to pass to the thread function. The *_beginthread* function returns the thread ID. If this is -1, the thread could not be created. If *_beginthread* is successful, *ClientWndProc* disables the Start menu option and enables the Abort option.

After the second thread is created, the code in *CalcThread* runs concurrently with the code in the rest of the program. *CalcThread* gets the current time and then enters its calculation loop. Note that the *for* statement checks the *fContinueCalc* field of the CALCPARAM structure before each call to *Savage*. This field was initialized by *ClientWndProc* to TRUE. But when Abort is selected from the menu, *ClientWndProc* disables the Abort option and sets *fContinueCalc* to FALSE.

When *CalcThread* drops out of the *for* loop (because the calculation either is finished or has been aborted), it calls *DosEnterCritSec* (more on this shortly) and uses *WinPostMsg* to post either a WM_CALC_DONE or a WM_CALC_ABORTED message to the client window. (These two messages are defined in BIGJOB.H.) *CalcThread* obtains the handle of the client window from the *hwnd* field of the CALCPARAM structure. When *CalcThread* posts a WM_CALC_DONE message, it sets the *mp1* message parameter to the elapsed time. *CalcThread* then calls the *_endthread* function and is terminated.

Listing 17.5: The BIGJOB4 program

The BIGJOB4.MAK File

```
#-----------------------
# BIGJOB4.MAK make file
#-----------------------

bigjob4.exe : bigjob4.obj bigjobmt.obj bigjob4.def bigjob.res
     $(PRGLINK) bigjob4 bigjobmt, bigjob4, NUL, $(PRGLIBMT), bigjob4
     rc bigjob.res bigjob4.exe

bigjob4.obj : bigjob4.c bigjob.h
     $(PRGCCMT)bigjob4.obj bigjob4.c

bigjobmt.obj : bigjob.c
     $(PRGCCMT)bigjobmt.obj bigjob.c

bigjob.res : bigjob.rc bigjob.h
     $(PRGRC) bigjob
```

The BIGJOB4.C File

```
/*-----------------------------------------------------------------
   BIGJOB4.C -- Second thread approach to lengthy processing job
                (c) Charles Petzold, 1993
  -----------------------------------------------------------------*/

#define INCL_DOS
#define INCL_WIN
#include <os2.h>
#include <process.h>
#include <stdlib.h>
#include "bigjob.h"

VOID CalcThread (PVOID) ;

int main (void)
     {
     return MainCode ("BigJob4", "BigJob4 - A Second Thread") ;
     }

MRESULT EXPENTRY ClientWndProc (HWND hwnd, ULONG msg, MPARAM mp1, MPARAM mp2)
     {
     static CALCPARAM cp ;
     static HWND      hwndMenu ;
     static int       tidCalc ;
     static INT       iCurrentRep = IDM_10 ;
     static INT       iStatus = STATUS_READY ;
     static LONG      lRepAmts [] = { 10, 100, 1000, 10000, 100000 } ;
```

Listing 17.5: The BIGJOB4 program (Continued)

```
     static ULONG     ulElapsedTime ;

     switch (msg)
          {
          case WM_CREATE:
               hwndMenu = WinWindowFromID (
                                WinQueryWindow (hwnd, QW_PARENT),
                                FID_MENU) ;
               return 0 ;

          case WM_COMMAND:
               switch (COMMANDMSG(&msg)->cmd)
                    {
                    case IDM_10:
                    case IDM_100:
                    case IDM_1000:
                    case IDM_10000:
                    case IDM_100000:
                         WinCheckMenuItem (hwndMenu, iCurrentRep, FALSE) ;
                         iCurrentRep = COMMANDMSG(&msg)->cmd ;
                         WinCheckMenuItem (hwndMenu, iCurrentRep, TRUE) ;
                         return 0 ;

                    case IDM_START:
                         cp.hwnd = hwnd ;
                         cp.lCalcRep = lRepAmts [iCurrentRep - IDM_10] ;
                         cp.fContinueCalc = TRUE ;

                         if (-1 == (tidCalc = _beginthread (CalcThread,
#ifdef __IBMC__
                                                            NULL,
#endif
                                                            STACKSIZE, &cp)))
                              {
                              WinAlarm (HWND_DESKTOP, WA_ERROR) ;
                              return 0 ;
                              }

                         iStatus = STATUS_WORKING ;
                         WinInvalidateRect (hwnd, NULL, FALSE) ;
                         WinEnableMenuItem (hwndMenu, IDM_START, FALSE) ;
                         WinEnableMenuItem (hwndMenu, IDM_ABORT, TRUE) ;
                         return 0 ;

                    case IDM_ABORT:
                         cp.fContinueCalc = FALSE ;
                         WinEnableMenuItem (hwndMenu, IDM_ABORT, FALSE) ;
                         return 0 ;
                    }
```

Listing 17.5: The BIGJOB4 program (Continued)

```
               break ;

          case WM_CALC_DONE:
               iStatus = STATUS_DONE ;
               ulElapsedTime = LONGFROMMP (mp1) ;
               WinInvalidateRect (hwnd, NULL, FALSE) ;
               WinEnableMenuItem (hwndMenu, IDM_START, TRUE) ;
               WinEnableMenuItem (hwndMenu, IDM_ABORT, FALSE) ;
               return 0 ;

          case WM_CALC_ABORTED:
               iStatus = STATUS_READY ;
               WinInvalidateRect (hwnd, NULL, FALSE) ;
               WinEnableMenuItem (hwndMenu, IDM_START, TRUE) ;
               return 0 ;

          case WM_PAINT:
               PaintWindow (hwnd, iStatus, cp.lCalcRep, ulElapsedTime) ;
               return 0 ;

          case WM_DESTROY:
               if (iStatus == STATUS_WORKING)
                    DosKillThread (tidCalc) ;
               return 0 ;
          }
     return WinDefWindowProc (hwnd, msg, mp1, mp2) ;
     }

VOID CalcThread (PVOID pArg)
     {
     double     A ;
     HAB        hab ;
     LONG       lRep, lTime ;
     PCALCPARAM pcp ;

     hab = WinInitialize (0) ;
     pcp = (PCALCPARAM) pArg ;
     lTime = WinGetCurrentTime (hab) ;

     for (A = 1.0, lRep = 0 ; lRep < pcp->lCalcRep &&
                              pcp->fContinueCalc ; lRep++)
          A = Savage (A) ;

     DosEnterCritSec () ;     // So thread is dead when message retrieved

     if (pcp->fContinueCalc)
          {
          lTime = WinGetCurrentTime (hab) - lTime ;
          WinPostMsg (pcp->hwnd, WM_CALC_DONE, MPFROMLONG (lTime), NULL) ;
```

Listing 17.5: The BIGJOB4 program (Continued)

```
          }
     else
          WinPostMsg (pcp->hwnd, WM_CALC_ABORTED, NULL, NULL) ;

     WinTerminate (hab) ;
     _endthread () ;
     }
```

The BIGJOB4.DEF File

```
;-----------------------------------
; BIGJOB4.DEF module definition file
;-----------------------------------

NAME           BIGJOB4   WINDOWAPI

DESCRIPTION    'BigJob Program No. 4 (c) Charles Petzold, 1993'
PROTMODE
```

The *ClientWndProc* function responds to the WM_CALC_DONE and the WM_CALC_ABORTED messages by enabling the Start menu option.

Notice that the *CalcThread* function calls *WinInitialize* and *WinTerminate*. Every thread in your program should call *WinInitialize* before calling any other Presentation Manager function.

A FEW PRECAUTIONS

Threads within a single process must often communicate with each other in various ways. The execution of threads must be coordinated so that the threads don't step on each others' toes. Threads must also often signal each other and pass data among themselves. This requires some handshaking.

The handshaking is important. Don't make any assumptions about one thread being able to execute a certain block of code in its time slice before another thread does something to affect the first thread.

For example, the *CalcThread* function posts a WM_CALC_DONE or a WM_CALC_ABORTED message to *ClientWndProc* and then calls *_endthread*. You can't assume that *CalcThread* will finish processing the *_endthread* function and the thread be destroyed by the time *ClientWndProc* processes the posted message.

This is why *CalcThread* calls *DosEnterCritSec* ("enter critical section") before posting the message. *DosEnterCritSec* causes all other threads in the process to be suspended until the thread calls *DosExitCritSec* or until the thread terminates. *CalcThread* doesn't call *DosExitCritSec*, so the main thread in BIGJOB4 won't execute any code until the thread is terminated. When *ClientWndProc* processes the WM_CALC_DONE or WM_CALC_ABORTED message, it knows that the thread has terminated.

During processing of the WM_DESTROY message, *ClientWndProc* kills the second thread by calling *DosKillThread*. *ClientWndProc* receives the WM_-DESTROY message when BIGJOB4 calls *WinDestroyWindow* from main. The next call, after *WinDestroyWindow*, is to *WinDestroyMsgQueue*. You don't want *CalcThread* attempting to post a message to *ClientWndProc* after the window and the message queue have been destroyed.

USING SEMAPHORES TO TRIGGER THREADS

BIGJOB4 creates a thread each time it needs to do the big job. After the thread is finished, the thread terminates itself. This is a good approach for some big jobs, but other big jobs might benefit from a somewhat different structure.

For example, in a spreadsheet program you might want a second thread to perform the spreadsheet recalculation. Because this recalculation occurs quite frequently, it might be best to create the thread initially when the program first begins executing and trigger it whenever you need to do a recalculation. You can do this using semaphores.

This is the approach taken in the BIGJOB5 program shown in Listing 17.6.

Listing 17.6: The BIGJOB5 program

The BIGJOB5.MAK File

```
#----------------------
# BIGJOB5.MAK make file
#----------------------

bigjob5.exe : bigjob5.obj bigjobmt.obj bigjob5.def bigjob.res
     $(PRGLINK) bigjob5 bigjobmt, bigjob5, NUL, $(PRGLIBMT), bigjob5
     rc bigjob.res bigjob5.exe

bigjob5.obj : bigjob5.c bigjob.h
     $(PRGCCMT)bigjob5.obj bigjob5.c

bigjobmt.obj : bigjob.c
     $(PRGCCMT)bigjobmt.obj bigjob.c

bigjob.res : bigjob.rc bigjob.h
     $(PRGRC) bigjob
```

Listing 17.6: The BIGJOB5 program (Continued)

The BIGJOB5.C File

```
/*---------------------------------------------------
   BIGJOB5.C -- Second thread and semaphore trigger
                (c) Charles Petzold, 1993
  ---------------------------------------------------*/

#define INCL_DOS
#define INCL_WIN
#include <os2.h>
#include <process.h>
#include <stdlib.h>
#include "bigjob.h"

VOID CalcThread (PVOID) ;

int main (void)
     {
     return MainCode ("BigJob5", "BigJob5 - Second Thread with Semaphore") ;
     }

MRESULT EXPENTRY ClientWndProc (HWND hwnd, ULONG msg, MPARAM mp1, MPARAM mp2)
     {
     static CALCPARAM cp ;
     static HWND      hwndMenu ;
     static int       tidCalc ;
     static INT       iCurrentRep = IDM_10 ;
     static INT       iStatus = STATUS_READY ;
     static LONG      lRepAmts [] = { 10, 100, 1000, 10000, 100000 } ;
     static ULONG     ulElapsedTime ;

     switch (msg)
          {
          case WM_CREATE:
               hwndMenu = WinWindowFromID (
                                WinQueryWindow (hwnd, QW_PARENT),
                                FID_MENU) ;

               cp.hwnd = hwnd ;

               DosCreateEventSem (NULL, &cp.hevTrigger, 0L, FALSE) ;

               tidCalc = _beginthread (CalcThread,
#ifdef __IBMC__
                                       NULL,
#endif
                                       STACKSIZE, &cp) ;
               return 0 ;
```

Listing 17.6: The BIGJOB5 program (Continued)

```
          case WM_INITMENU:
               if (tidCalc == -1 && SHORT1FROMMP (mp1) == IDM_ACTION)
                    WinEnableMenuItem (hwnd, IDM_START, FALSE) ;
               return 0 ;

          case WM_COMMAND:
               switch (COMMANDMSG(&msg)->cmd)
                    {
                    case IDM_10:
                    case IDM_100:
                    case IDM_1000:
                    case IDM_10000:
                    case IDM_100000:
                         WinCheckMenuItem (hwndMenu, iCurrentRep, FALSE) ;
                         iCurrentRep = COMMANDMSG(&msg)->cmd ;
                         WinCheckMenuItem (hwndMenu, iCurrentRep, TRUE) ;
                         return 0 ;

                    case IDM_START:
                         cp.lCalcRep = lRepAmts [iCurrentRep - IDM_10] ;
                         cp.fContinueCalc = TRUE ;
                         DosPostEventSem (cp.hevTrigger) ;

                         iStatus = STATUS_WORKING ;
                         WinInvalidateRect (hwnd, NULL, FALSE) ;
                         WinEnableMenuItem (hwndMenu, IDM_START, FALSE) ;
                         WinEnableMenuItem (hwndMenu, IDM_ABORT, TRUE) ;
                         return 0 ;

                    case IDM_ABORT:
                         cp.fContinueCalc = FALSE ;
                         WinEnableMenuItem (hwndMenu, IDM_ABORT, FALSE) ;
                         return 0 ;
                    }
               break ;

          case WM_CALC_DONE:
               iStatus = STATUS_DONE ;
               ulElapsedTime = LONGFROMMP (mp1) ;
               WinInvalidateRect (hwnd, NULL, FALSE) ;
               WinEnableMenuItem (hwndMenu, IDM_START, TRUE) ;
               WinEnableMenuItem (hwndMenu, IDM_ABORT, FALSE) ;
               return 0 ;

          case WM_CALC_ABORTED:
               iStatus = STATUS_READY ;
               WinInvalidateRect (hwnd, NULL, FALSE) ;
               WinEnableMenuItem (hwndMenu, IDM_START, TRUE) ;
               return 0 ;
```

Listing 17.6: The BIGJOB5 program (Continued)

```
          case WM_PAINT:
               PaintWindow (hwnd, iStatus, cp.lCalcRep, ulElapsedTime) ;
               return 0 ;

          case WM_DESTROY:
               if (iStatus == STATUS_WORKING)
                    DosKillThread (tidCalc) ;
               return 0 ;
          }
     return WinDefWindowProc (hwnd, msg, mp1, mp2) ;
     }

VOID CalcThread (PVOID pArg)
     {
     double     A ;
     HAB        hab ;
     LONG       lRep, lTime ;
     PCALCPARAM pcp ;
     ULONG      ulPostCount ;

     hab = WinInitialize (0) ;
     pcp = (PCALCPARAM) pArg ;

     while (TRUE)
          {
          DosWaitEventSem (pcp->hevTrigger, SEM_INDEFINITE_WAIT) ;

          lTime = WinGetCurrentTime (hab) ;

          for (A = 1.0, lRep = 0 ; lRep < pcp->lCalcRep &&
                                   pcp->fContinueCalc ; lRep++)
               A = Savage (A) ;

          DosResetEventSem (pcp->hevTrigger, &ulPostCount) ;

          if (pcp->fContinueCalc)
               {
               lTime = WinGetCurrentTime (hab) - lTime ;
               WinPostMsg (pcp->hwnd, WM_CALC_DONE, MPFROMLONG (lTime), NULL) ;
               }
          else
               WinPostMsg (pcp->hwnd, WM_CALC_ABORTED, NULL, NULL) ;
          }

     WinTerminate (hab) ;
     _endthread () ;
     }
```

Listing 17.6: The BIGJOB5 program (Continued)

The BIGJOB5.DEF File

```
;-----------------------------------
; BIGJOB5.DEF module definition file
;-----------------------------------

NAME           BIGJOB5   WINDOWAPI

DESCRIPTION    'BigJob Program No. 5 (c) Charles Petzold, 1993'
PROTMODE
```

This program also requires the BIGJOB.C, BIGJOB.H, and BIGJOB.RC files from Listing 17.1.

During the WM_CREATE message, *ClientWndProc* calls *DosCreateEventSem* with a pointer to the *hevTrigger* field of the CALCPARAM structure. This field is an event semaphore handle and can be used to trigger the calculation thread into action. *ClientWndProc* then calls *_beginthread* to create the thread.

BIGJOB5 also processes the WM_INITMENU message. If the Action menu is being displayed, it checks to see if the thread ID originally returned from *_beginthread* is -1. If so, the Start option is disabled.

BIGJOB5 uses the event semaphore as a signaling mechanism. The semaphore can be either "set" (by calling the *DosResetEventSem* function) or "posted" (by calling the *DosPostEventSem* function). BIGJOB5 initially creates the semaphore as set using a last parameter of FALSE in the *DosCreateEventSem* function.

When a semaphore is set and a thread calls *DosWaitEventSem*, the thread is blocked until the semaphore is posted by another thread—that is, the *DosWait-EventSem* function will not return until the semaphore is posted. The thread is effectively suspended. If the semaphore is already posted when *DosWait-EventSem* is called, the thread returns from the function immediately and can continue. Actually, *DosWaitEventSem* has a second parameter that indicates a time-out value. If the semaphore is set, *DosWaitEventSem* can return when the specified time elapses. However, this parameter is set to the identifier SEM_INDEFINITE_WAIT (equal to –1) in BIGJOB5 to indicate an infinite wait.

CalcParam begins by entering an infinite loop. The first function it calls in this loop is *DosWaitEventSem* on the *hevTrigger* semaphore. Because *Client-WndProc* sets this semaphore when creating the thread, *CalcParam* will be suspended in the *DosWaitEventSem* function until the semaphore is posted.

When you select Start from the menu, *ClientWndProc* sets the *lCalcRep* and *fContinueCalc* fields of the CALCPARAM structure and posts the semaphore.

This allows *CalcThread* to start the calculation. As in BIGJOB4, *CalcThread* checks the value of *fContinueCalc* before each call to *Savage.*

After exiting the *for* loop, *CalcThread* calls *DosResetEventSem* to set the semaphore again and then posts the WM_CALC_DONE or WM_CALC_ABORTED message. When *CalcThread* returns to the top of the *while* loop, it again calls *DosWaitEventSem.* The semaphore is already set, so *CalcThread* can't proceed with a new calculation until Start is chosen again.

Note that the semaphore is used only for blocking and unblocking the non-message queue thread. A message queue thread should not be made to wait on a semaphore because of the possibility of violating the one-tenth of a second rule. If absolutely necessary, a non-message queue thread could suspend a message queue thread for very short periods of time by calling *DosSuspendThread* or *DosEnterCritSec,* as in BIGJOB4. This is sometimes helpful when both threads access common variables. (It's not necessary in BIGJOB4 or BIGJOB5 when the threads access *fContinueCalc,* because this variable can be accessed in one machine code instruction.)

In general, a message queue thread communicates to a non-message queue thread using semaphores. A non-message queue thread communicates to a message queue thread using posted messages. The two threads can also access common variables.

MESSAGE ORDERING

The *CalcThread* function in BIGJOB4 and BIGJOB5 used two *user-defined* messages called WM_CALC_DONE and WM_CALC_ABORTED to notify *ClientWndProc* that the job was completed or aborted. User-defined messages can be any value from WM_USER (defined in PMWIN.H as 0x1000 and above).

You might want a little more control over the priority of messages in the message queue. I've mentioned in earlier chapters that WM_PAINT and WM_TIMER messages are low-priority messages: If other messages appear in the message queue, they will be retrieved before WM_PAINT and WM_TIMER.

Four other messages have specific priorities in the message queue. These are WM_SEM1, WM_SEM2, WM_SEM3, and WM_SEM4. The priority of these messages is shown in the following table.

Message	Priority
WM_SEM4	Lowest
WM_PAINT	
WM_SEM3	

Message	Priority
WM_TIMER	
WM_SEM2	
All other messages	
WM_SEM1	Highest

For example, if you post a WM_SEM1 message to a message queue, it will be retrieved before any other message in the queue.

Only one of each of the four WM_SEM messages is allowed in the message queue at any time. If you post another, the Presentation Manager will perform a bitwise OR of the *mp1* parameter of the message already in the queue with the *mp1* parameter of the message you're posting. You can thus use the *mp1* parameter as a series of flags that combine messages in whatever way you want.

THINKING THREADS

A non-message queue thread is almost essential in Presentation Manager programs that must read input other than keyboard and mouse input.

For example, a communications program might have a client window in the message queue thread that processes keyboard messages, writes the characters to the communications port using *DosWrite*, and (if local echo is in effect) also writes the characters to the surface of the window.

The non-message queue thread reads the communications port with the *DosRead* function. Used most efficiently, this function returns only if a character has been read from the serial port. A message queue thread should not call *DosRead* to get input from the serial port because it might violate the one-tenth of a second rule. When the non-message queue thread reads a character, it can post either a user-defined message to the window containing that character or a pointer to a string of characters. The client window processes the message by displaying the character to the window.

A Presentation Manager program using queues (not Presentation Manager message queues, but the queues supported by the OS/2 kernel) for interprocess communication should also create a non-message queue thread for reading the queue. The non-message queue thread calls the *DosReadQueue* function with the "no wait" flag set to 0, thus blocking the thread until something is in the queue.

NO MORE WAIT POINTERS!

We started out looking at BIGJOB1, a program that did the job it was meant to do but did it in a way that was not advantageous for the user. Our immediate rejection of this program and our search for better ways of doing big jobs indicate some major changes in our perception of proper behavior in application programs.

In a traditional single-tasking nonwindowed environment, you accept the fact that you have to wait while your database program is sorting a file. When you start a file sort, it's time to take a coffee break.

In a traditional multitasking operating environment, you might be able to run the database program sort in the background while you work on another program.

However, in a multitasking windowing environment like the Presentation Manager, we are satisfied only when the user can continue to interact with a program even when it's doing a big job. Obviously, the complexities involved with structuring a program in this way require some extra work on the part of the programmer. But that makes the program better for the user.

Just as we can no longer tolerate programs that require the user to memorize scores of commands, we can no longer tolerate programs that display a wait pointer and require a user to wait until the program has finished its big job.

Printing Graphics and Text

Device independence

Printing and spooling

Printing a calendar

The printcal files

End of job

Chapter 18

Remember the "paperless office"? This was supposed to be one of the benefits of computers. The reality, of course, is that computers generate more paper than anyone could have possibly imagined. In fact, many computer applications—such as word processing, desktop publishing, business graphics, and computer-assisted drawing programs—exist primarily to prepare printed documents.

Maybe someday the paperless office will be a reality. Until then, we cannot lose sight of the importance of hard copy. Printer graphics may not be as much fun as the more immediate and interactive graphics possible on a video display, but graphics programming has to be useful as well as fun.

Whether you like it or not, there is no way to avoid the subject of printing under the OS/2 Presentation Manager. The only reason it's taken so long to get here is that printing is facilitated by multithreaded programming techniques, which were not covered until the previous chapter.

DEVICE INDEPENDENCE

The printer is the peripheral that we love to hate. Printers are awkward, cranky, obstinate, ugly pieces of hardware. Unfortunately, the problems with printers extend themselves into the software interfaces for controlling them.

In the early days under DOS, programs used the DOS (or more commonly, the BIOS) software interrupts for sending byte streams out to the printer. Very often these byte streams were simply strings of text and some control characters. As printers gained in graphics capabilities, DOS applications were faced with the problem of dealing with many incompatible graphics control sequences. For this reason, developers of these applications separated the device-dependent printer code from the main application and put that code into device drivers. As printers proliferated, it was not unusual for such DOS applications to be shipped with several disks containing nothing but printer drivers.

The good news with the OS/2 Presentation Manager is that developers of Presentation Manager applications need not write their own printer drivers. OS/2 itself is shipped with many printer drivers (actually, the official term is "presentation driver"), and applications can use printers in a device-independent manner. Information such as resolution and color capability can be obtained through functions such as *DevQueryCaps*. Otherwise programs use the same GPI functions for drawing on the video display and printing on a printer page.

This is of enormous benefit to programmers, users, and even hardware manufacturers. The programmer obviously benefits by avoiding the problem of supporting a huge variety of graphics output devices. The user benefits when upgrading to a new video display or printer. When a Presentation Manager driver for the output device is installed, all existing Presentation Manager programs can use the new device. This is true even if the device was invented after the programs were written.

Hardware manufacturers of video display equipment and printers also benefit. Although writing a presentation driver may be an initial hassle, it guarantees existing Presentation Manager applications can use the device. Hardware manufacturers can use their engineering creativity to create new graphics devices without worrying about compatibility with existing devices.

You might think that a device-independent graphics interface (such as the one included in the OS/2 Presentation Manager) would make printer graphics as easy as video graphics. This is not quite so. In reality, a printer is intrinsically different than a video display and definitely more difficult for both programmers and users. For example, have you ever had a video display run out of paper or get jammed or run out of toner?

The OS/2 Presentation Manager can use only one video display. But multiple printers can be installed on a single machine. The OS/2 installation program can usually determine which video display driver to use, but the installation of printer drivers is left up to the user. A Presentation Manager program must obtain information from OS2.INI and OS2SYS.INI to determine information about installed printers.

Here's another difference: A window on a video display is a reusable device that can be erased and redrawn. A printer prints a "document" that may comprise multiple pages. Thus, the Presentation Manager program must make use of function calls to start a document, end a document, and separate the pages.

Displaying graphics on a printer page generally takes longer than displaying graphics on a video display. As mentioned, this suggests that a Presentation Manager program should create a second thread of execution when using the printer.

Printing is never an easy job for a programmer, not under DOS and not under the Presentation Manager. Presentation Manager certainly simplifies some aspects of printing but introduces its own unique complications. Even Presentation Manager *users* don't get off the hook—the installation of printer drivers can be quite confusing.

PRINTING AND SPOOLING

The OS/2 Presentation Manager includes a print spooler program called the Print Manager. The OS/2 Print Manager captures printer output from all programs running under OS/2, even programs running in DOS compatibility mode. The printer output is saved to disk files. The program doing the printing is then free to do something else while the Print Manager shovels the printer output to the printer.

The printer presentation driver and the spooler work together. This is particularly true when a Presentation Manager program prints. The spooler can save the program's printer output to disk in two different formats: a device-independent format (called "standard" format) that must be translated by the printer driver on its way out to the printer, or a "raw" format, which contains the device-dependent control sequences that have already been generated by the printer driver.

PRINTER NAMES

One reason that printing is complex is because you can have several printers attached to your system through the parallel printer ports (LPT1, LPT2, and so on) and the serial ports (COM1, COM2, and so on). Indeed, you can even have multiple printers attached to a single port through a cable switch box. (You can also have printers available through a network, but I won't be getting into network issues here.) In addition, you want to be able to specify which of these printers is the default—the printer that should normally be used by Presentation Manager programs when they print.

Moreover, all of this information should be available to a Presentation Manager application in a manner that is transparent to the user. When you install and configure your printers, the information is stored in the OS2.INI and OS2-SYS.INI files so that applications can obtain it.

To help you identify the various printers you may have, the Presentation Manager introduces the concept of the *physical printer name.* It's tempting to say that "each printer you have on your system is identified by a printer name." But that's not true. If you happen to have multiple printers connected to a single port through a cable switch box, one printer name identifies them all.

It is correct to say that each printer name is associated with one unique parallel or serial port. You'll define one printer name for each parallel or serial port to which a printer is attached. Two different printer names cannot be associated with the same port.

Each printer name can be associated with one or more printer drivers (of which one is the default), but unless you have a cable switch box or you routinely swap printer cables, you'll generally associate only one printer driver with the printer name.

Finally, the user can select a default printer name, which in turn is associated with a default printer driver and a specific port.

THE DC AND PS

As you've known since Chapter 2, you need a handle to a presentation space (or PS) before you can draw on a window. The presentation space is mostly just a data structure internal to GPI that is used to store all the current drawing attributes.

Most of the Presentation Manager programs shown in this book obtain a handle to a presentation space by calling *WinGetPS* or *WinBeginPaint* with a NULL second parameter. The presentation space handle is the first parameter to virtually all GPI functions. These two functions obtain a cached micro-PS, which is a presentation space that has been precreated and ready for use.

Before you can use a presentation space for drawing, it must be associated with a device context (or DC). The device context refers to a physical output device and its driver. You don't have to worry about the device context when you use a cached micro-PS because the cached micro-PS is always associated with a device context for the video display.

Alternatively, a program can create its own presentation space by calling *GpiCreatePS.* You can associate this presentation space with a device context for either a window on the video display or a printer or bitmap memory (as we saw in Chapter 6). When you create a presentation space using *GpiCreatePS,* you must also open a device context and associate the PS with the DC.

Opening a device context for a window is simple. You call *WinOpenWindowDC*. The only parameter is a handle to a window. The function returns a handle to a device context for the window:

```
hdc = WinOpenWindowDC (hwnd) ;
```

Opening a device context for a printer is not so simple. The function you must call is *DevOpenDC*, but prior to calling *DevOpenDC* you must set up at least one (and possibly two) data structures describing the printer you want to use.

You set up these data structures using information stored in the OS2.INI and OS2SYS.INI files; you extract this information using the *PrfQueryProfileString* function, which I discussed in Chapter 14 in connection with the PATTDLG program.

THE DEFAULT PRINTER

Data stored in OS2.INI and OS2SYS.INI is referenced using two ASCII strings: an application name and a key name. The data can be either in ASCII or binary format. The data we need concerning printers is stored in an ASCII format. One reason that opening a device context for a printer is so difficult is that there are lots of options. I'll be showing you the most common way to open a device context for the default printer.

You can obtain the name of the default printer by calling *PrfQueryProfileString* with an application name of PM_SPOOLER and a key name of PRINTER. Strangely enough, the printer name is stored with an appended semicolon. The printer name can be 32 characters in length, so the semicolon and terminating zero byte require an array of 34 characters:

```
CHAR achDefPrnName[34] ;
```

You call *PrfQueryProfileString* with the following parameters:

```
PrfQueryProfileString (HINI_PROFILE, "PM_SPOOLER", "PRINTER", ";",
     achDefPrnName, sizeof achDefPrnName) ;
```

The second and third parameters are the application name and key name. The fourth parameter is a default string if the application name and key names cannot be found.

The terminating semicolon must be replaced with a zero byte. You can do that like this:

```
if ((pchDelimiter = strchr (achDefPrnName, ';')) != NULL)
     *pchDelimiter = '\0' ;
```

Now the printer name of the default printer is stored in *achDefPrnName* and we're ready to proceed.

THE PRINTER DATA STRING

OS/2 also stores important data on all the printer names in OS2SYS.INI using an application name of PM_SPOOLER_PRINTER and a key name which is the printer name. After you have obtained the name of the default printer, here's the code to obtain this data:

```
static CHAR achPrnData[256] ;

     ....

PrfQueryProfileString (HINI_PROFILE,
     "PM_SPOOLER_PRINTER", achDefPrnName, ";;;;",
     achPrnData, sizeof achPrnData) ;
```

Following this call, the *achPrnData* array will contain a zero-terminated character string that I'll be referring to as the *printer data string*. This string contains four items separated by semicolons. Any or all of the four items could be empty. In the most extreme case, the string could simply be four semicolons in a row. You'll note that this is the default string I've specified in the *PrfQueryProfileString* call if the application name or key name cannot be found in OS2-SYS.INI.

The first item in the printer data string is the physical output port to which the printer is connected. This is a standard OS/2 device name such as LPT1 or COM2. This item is generally ignored by a Presentation Manager program.

The second item contains the presentation driver file name without the .DRV extension. For example, if you have the IBM 5152 Graphics Printer installed as your default printer, the presentation driver would be IBM5152.DRV and the field would contain IBM5152. If the presentation driver supports more than one device (as the PostScript driver PSCRIPT.DRV does), the item contains the presentation driver name, a period, and a device name. For example, if your default printer were the NEC LC-890 (my PostScript printer), the field would contain PSCRIPT.NEC LC-890.

It is possible for the second item to list more than one presentation driver (or presentation driver and device name). If so, these are separated by commas.

If there are multiple presentation drivers associated with a printer name, the first one listed is the default.

The third item contains one or more queue names separated by commas. The first is the default. The fourth item contains network options. This field is generally ignored by the Presentation Manager program doing the printing.

THE *DEVOPENDC* FUNCTION

Now that we've seen what information is available from the OS2SYS.INI file, let's look at what the *DevOpenDC* function requires to open the printer device context.

DevOpenDC has six parameters. The first parameter is the anchor block handle returned from *WinInitialize*. The second is a constant beginning with the prefix OD. We'll be using OD_QUEUED. This indicates that the printer output is to be queued by the Presentation Manager spooler. The third parameter to *DevOpenDC* is not yet interpreted by OS/2. It is recommended that you use the character string "*" for this parameter.

The fourth parameter indicates the number of items (up to nine) supplied in the fifth parameter. The fifth parameter—although not exactly defined this way in the *DevOpenDC* function template—is a pointer to a structure of type DEVOPENSTRUC. This structure is defined like this:

```
typedef struct _DEVOPENSTRUC
     {
     PSZ      pszLogAddress ;          // logical address
     PSZ      pszDriverName ;          // driver name
     PDRIVDATA pdriv ;                 // DRIVDATA structure
     PSZ      pszDataType ;            // spooled data type
     PSZ      pszComment ;             // file description
     PSZ      pszQueueProcName ;       // queue processor name
     PSZ      pszQueueProcParams ;     // queue parameters
     PSZ      pszSpoolerParams ;       // spooler parameters
     PSZ      pszNetworkParams ;       // network parameters
     }
     DEVOPENSTRUC ;
```

In the *DevOpenDC* function template, the fifth parameter is actually defined as data of type PDEVOPENDATA, which is defined as an array of pointers to character strings. This is an alternative method of supplying the information.

Except for the *pdriv* field, all the fields in the DEVOPENSTRUC structure are pointers to character strings. The *pdriv* field is a pointer to another structure, this one of type DRIVDATA. This structure is defined like this:

```
typedef struct _DRIVDATA
   {
   LONG cb ;                      // size of structure in bytes
   LONG lVersion ;                // driver version
   CHAR szDeviceName[32] ;        // output device name
   CHAR abGeneralData[1] ;        // data specific to device
   }
   DRIVDATA ;
```

This structure is required only when using a presentation driver that supports more than one device (such as PSCRIPT.DRV).

The last parameter to *DevOpenDC* is a handle to a device context. When opening a printer device context, you set this parameter to 0. If all goes well, *DevOpenDC* returns a handle to an open device context. If an error occurs, *DevOpenDC* returns DEV_ERROR (which equals 0).

SETTING UP THE STRUCTURE FIELDS

In preparation for calling *DevOpenDC*, you need to define three variables:

```
DEVOPENSTRUC dop ;
DRIVDATA     driv ;
HDC          hdcPrinter ;
```

Using the information in the printer data string obtained from *PrfQueryProfileString*, you set the fields in the DEVOPENSTRUC and DRIVDATA structures and call *DevOpenDC* to open the printer device context. You need to set only the first four fields of the DEVOPENSTRUC structure. Thus, the *lCount* parameter to *DevOpenDC* is set to 4.

You set the first four DEVOPENSTRUC fields as follows:

- Set the *pszLogAddress* field to the queue name. This is the third item in the printer data string returned from *PrfQueryProfileString*. If there are multiple queue names, use the first.
- Set the *pszDriverName* field to the name of the presentation driver. This is the second item in the printer data string returned from *PrfQueryProfileString*. If there are multiple presentation drivers, use the first. If the presentation driver supports more than one device, the presentation driver name in the printer data string will be followed by a period and the device name. You use only the presentation driver name in the *pszDriverName* field of the DEVOPENSTRUC structure.

- If the presentation driver supports only one device, set the *pdriv* field to NULL. Otherwise, set it to a pointer to a DRIVDATA structure.
- Set the *pszDataType* field to the string "PM_Q_STD".

If the presentation driver supports more than one device, then you must also initialize a DRIVDATA structure:

- Set the *cb* field to the length of the DRIVDATA structure.
- Set the *lVersion* field to 0.
- Set the *szDeviceName* to the name of the device (for example, "NEC LC-890"). This is available in the second item of the printer data string returned from *PrfQueryProfileString*, separated by the preceding presentation driver name with a period.
- Set the *abGeneralData* field to contain a single zero byte.

After you have set the fields of the DEVOPENSTRUC and DRIVDATA structures, you call *DevOpenDC*:

```
hdcPrinter = DevOpenDC (hab, OD_QUEUED, "*", 4L,
                       (PDEVOPENDATA) &dop, ØL) ;
```

Notice that the pointer to the DEVOPENSTRUC structure is cast to a PDEVOPENDATA data type. This is how the fifth parameter is defined in the *DevOpenDC* function template, so the casting prevents a warning message from the C compiler.

THE PRINTDC.C FILE

The actual code to extract the information from the printer data string and use it for the structure fields involves some C string functions and pointer manipulation. This is shown in a function called *OpenDefaultPrinterDC* in the PRINTDC.C file in Listing 18.1.

Listing 18.1: The PRINTDC.C file

The PRINTDC.C File

```
/*----------------------------------------------------------------
   PRINTDC.C -- Function to open device context for default printer
                (c) Charles Petzold, 1993
  ----------------------------------------------------------------*/

#define INCL_WIN
#include <os2.h>
```

Listing 18.1: The PRINTDC.C file (Continued)

```
#include <string.h>
#pragma pack(1)          // align structure fields on 1-byte boundaries

HDC OpenDefaultPrinterDC (HAB hab)
     {
     static CHAR     achPrnData[256] ;
     static DRIVDATA driv = { sizeof (DRIVDATA) } ;
     CHAR            achDefPrnName[33], *pchDelimiter ;
     DEVOPENSTRUC    dop ;

               // Obtain default printer name and remove semicolon

     PrfQueryProfileString (HINI_PROFILE, "PM_SPOOLER",
                            "PRINTER", ";",
                            achDefPrnName, sizeof achDefPrnName) ;

     if ((pchDelimiter = strchr (achDefPrnName, ';')) != NULL)
          *pchDelimiter = '\0' ;

     if (achDefPrnName[0] == '\0')
          return DEV_ERROR ;

               // Obtain information on default printer

     PrfQueryProfileString (HINI_PROFILE, "PM_SPOOLER_PRINTER",
                            achDefPrnName, ";;;;",
                            achPrnData, sizeof achPrnData) ;

               // Parse printer information string

     if ((pchDelimiter = strchr (achPrnData, ';')) == NULL)
          return DEV_ERROR ;

     dop.pszDriverName = pchDelimiter + 1 ;

     if ((pchDelimiter = strchr (dop.pszDriverName, ';')) == NULL)
          return DEV_ERROR ;

     dop.pszLogAddress = pchDelimiter + 1 ;

     *(dop.pszLogAddress + strcspn (dop.pszLogAddress, ",;")) = '\0' ;
     *(dop.pszDriverName + strcspn (dop.pszDriverName, ",;")) = '\0' ;

               // Fill DRIVDATA structure if necessary

     if ((pchDelimiter = strchr (dop.pszDriverName, '.')) != NULL)
          {
          *pchDelimiter = '\0' ;
          strncpy (driv.szDeviceName, pchDelimiter + 1,
```

Listing 18.1: The PRINTDC.C file (Continued)

```
                              sizeof (driv.szDeviceName)) ;
          dop.pdriv = &driv ;
          }
     else
          dop.pdriv = NULL ;

               // Set data type to "std"

     dop.pszDataType = "PM_Q_STD" ;

               // Open printer device context

     return DevOpenDC (hab, OD_QUEUED, "*", 4L, (PDEVOPENDATA) &dop, 0L) ;
     }
```

In the *OpenDefaultPrinterDC* function in PRINTDC.C, the first *PrfQuery-ProfileString* call obtains the name of the default printer and stores it in *achDef-PrnName*. The second call to *PrfQueryProfileString* obtains the printer data string and stores it in *achPrnData*. The first item of this string (containing the physical device port) is ignored. The second item contains the presentation driver name. The function sets the *pszDriverName* field of the DEVOPEN-STRUC structure to point to this name. The third item is the queue name, and the function sets the *pszLogAddress* field of the DEVOPENSTRUC structure to point to this name. The fourth item is ignored.

A period following the presentation driver name indicates that the presentation driver supports more than one device. The function copies the name of this device to the *szDeviceName* field of the DRIVDATA structure using *strncpy*. (The *strncpy* function is needed because the *szDevicename* field is not a pointer to a character string but an array of characters.) The *pdriv* field of the DEVOPENSTRUC structure is set to point to the DRIVDATA structure.

Finally, the *OpenDefaultPrinterDC* function sets the *pszDataType* field of the DEVOPENSTRUC structure to the string "PM_Q_STD" and calls *DevOpenDC*.

PRINTING A CALENDAR

To demonstrate complete printing code, I'll show you a program called PRINT-CAL that prints a wall calendar, one month to a page. The graphics are fairly simple—just some lines and a GPI vector font.

When you first run PRINTCAL, it displays the calendar for the current month in its client window, as shown in Figure 18.1.

Figure 18.1: The PRINTCAL window

The program uses the GPI Helvetica vector font for both the month and year title at the top and for the day numbers. Using a vector font contributes greatly to a uniform appearance of the calendar on the screen and on various printers.

The calendar in the client window is just a static image, and you can't do anything with it. This window image is not necessary for the functioning of the program, but since the program requires a routine to draw the calendar on the printer page, it was fairly simple to add the visual display. Another advantage of device-independent graphics is that you can use the same functions for displaying graphics on both the screen and the printer.

The PRINTCAL menu has only one item: Calendar. This item invokes a submenu with two options: Print Calendar and About PrintCal. The About PrintCal option simply displays a dialog box with a copyright notice. The Print Calendar option lets you select a range of months within a particular year. You can type in a new year (from 1900 to 2099) and select a beginning and ending month. If you then press the Preview button, you'll see the first month of this range in the client window. If you press the Print button, the program will begin the job of printing the range of months.

THE PRINTING THREAD

PRINTCAL uses a second thread of execution to print. In any Presentation Manager program it's a good idea to create additional threads for handling lengthy processing jobs.

By way of review, you should remember that Presentation Manager programs begin execution with only one thread. This thread generally creates a message queue to receive messages posted to all the windows created in that thread. If the program starts a lengthy processing job, the thread can no longer receive messages until the job has been completed. The program usually displays the hourglass icon during this time to indicate that the user must wait. This is not good: Users hate the hourglass icon with a passion.

Although it's pretty obvious that a lengthy processing job prevents a Presentation Manager program from interacting with the user, a lengthy job also prevents the user from switching to another Presentation Manager program. When you switch to another program in the Presentation Manager session, the program you switch from must be notified through messages. These messages are blocked if the thread with the message queue is busy doing something else.

This means that any Presentation Manager program that does lengthy processing in its main message queue thread effectively halts all interaction between the user and all programs running in the Presentation Manager session. For this reason, it's recommended that a Presentation Manager program create additional threads for lengthy processing jobs. These additional threads do not create message queues and hence can run concurrently with the threads that process messages.

At first, you may think that printing from a Presentation Manager program would not require a separate thread. After all, the purpose of the Presentation Manager print spooler is to save application printer output to a file. This frees up the program while the printer output is later sent to the printer. But printing is really a two-stage process, and the print spooler only takes care of the second stage.

Although the second stage is generally slower than the first stage (particularly for slow devices like dot-matrix printers and pen plotters), the first stage could still require a considerable amount of time—perhaps a minute or so for some complex pages. In a multitasking windowing environment, that's a long time to force a user to wait. By putting the first stage of printing in a separate thread of execution, a Presentation Manager program can continue to interact with the user while the printer output is being prepared.

When you push the Print button in PRINTCAL's dialog box, the program creates the thread and displays a message box with the message "Print job successfully started." You'll see this message box almost immediately, and you'll start to see some disk output as the second thread prepares the printer output. While this is happening, you can print another range of months (perhaps on another printer), or you can switch to another program.

After the second thread has finished preparing the printer output, you'll see another message box saying either "Print job sent to spooler" or "Error encountered during printing." (The latter message probably indicates that the printer was not configured correctly.) If you get the first message, the print job will show up in the printer window and the Print Manager will send the output to the printer.

The dialog box in PRINTCAL allows you to select only a range of months within one year. If you want to print a range of months that stretches across two or more years (for example, July 1990 through June 1991), you'll have to select separate ranges in each year. But you can do this very quickly and have several printing threads running concurrently. You don't have to wait for one print job to finish before starting the next.

THE PRINTCAL FILES

Six files are required to create PRINTCAL.EXE. One of these files, PRINTDC.C, was shown earlier. Listing 18.2 shows the other five files.

Listing 18.2: The PRINTCAL files

The PRINTCAL.MAK File

```
#-------------------
# PRINTCAL.MAK make file
#-------------------

printcal.exe : printcal.obj printdc.obj printcal.def printcal.res
     $(PRGLINK) printcal printdc, printcal, NUL, $(PRGLIBMT), printcal
     rc printcal.res

printcal.obj : printcal.c
     $(PRGCCMT)printcal.obj printcal.c

printdc.obj : printdc.c
     $(PRGCCMT)printdc.obj printdc.c

printcal.res : printcal.rc
     $(PRGRC) printcal
```

Listing 18.2: The PRINTCAL files (Continued)

The PRINTCAL.C File

```
/*---------------------------------------
   PRINTCAL.C -- Print a calendar
                 (c) Charles Petzold, 1993
  ---------------------------------------*/

#define INCL_WIN
#define INCL_GPI
#define INCL_DEV
#define INCL_DOSPROCESS
#include <os2.h>
#include <stdio.h>
#include <stdlib.h>
#include <string.h>
#include <process.h>
#include "printcal.h"

#define LCID_CALFONT          1L
#define STACKSIZE             8192
#define WM_USER_PRINT_OK      (WM_USER + 0)
#define WM_USER_PRINT_ERROR   (WM_USER + 1)

typedef struct
     {
     SHORT iYear, iMonthBeg, iMonthEnd ;
     }
     CALPARAMS ;

typedef struct
     {
     CALPARAMS cp ;
     HWND      hwndNotify ;
     }
     THREADPARAMS ;

MPARAM EXPENTRY ClientWndProc (HWND, ULONG, MPARAM, MPARAM) ;
MPARAM EXPENTRY AboutDlgProc  (HWND, ULONG, MPARAM, MPARAM) ;
MPARAM EXPENTRY PrintDlgProc  (HWND, ULONG, MPARAM, MPARAM) ;
VOID            DisplayPage   (HPS, SIZEL *, INT, INT) ;
VOID            Message       (HWND, INT, CHAR *) ;
VOID            PrintThread   (VOID *) ;
HDC             OpenDefaultPrinterDC (HAB) ;          // in PRINTDC.C

UINT uiActiveThreads = 0 ;

int main (void)
     {
```

Listing 18.2: The PRINTCAL files (Continued)

```
     static CHAR  szClientClass[] = "PrintCal" ;
     static ULONG flFrameFlags = FCF_TITLEBAR       | FCF_SYSMENU |
                                 FCF_SIZEBORDER     | FCF_MINMAX  |
                                 FCF_MENU           |
                                 FCF_SHELLPOSITION  | FCF_TASKLIST ;
     HAB          hab ;
     HMQ          hmq ;
     HWND         hwndFrame, hwndClient ;
     QMSG         qmsg ;

     hab = WinInitialize (0) ;
     hmq = WinCreateMsgQueue (hab, 0) ;
     WinRegisterClass (hab, szClientClass, ClientWndProc, CS_SIZEREDRAW, 0) ;

     hwndFrame = WinCreateStdWindow (HWND_DESKTOP, WS_VISIBLE,
                                     &flFrameFlags, szClientClass, NULL,
                                     0L, 0L, ID_RESOURCE, &hwndClient) ;
     while (TRUE)
          {
          while (WinGetMsg (hab, &qmsg, NULLHANDLE, 0, 0))
               WinDispatchMsg (hab, &qmsg) ;

          if (uiActiveThreads == 0)
               break ;

          Message (hwndClient, MB_ICONEXCLAMATION,
                   "Printing thread still active.\n"
                   "Program cannot be closed now.") ;

          WinCancelShutdown (hmq, FALSE) ;
          }

     WinDestroyWindow (hwndFrame) ;
     WinDestroyMsgQueue (hmq) ;
     WinTerminate (hab) ;
     return 0 ;
     }

MPARAM EXPENTRY ClientWndProc (HWND hwnd, ULONG msg, MPARAM mp1, MPARAM mp2)
     {
     static CALPARAMS cp ;
     static HAB       hab ;
     static HPS       hps ;
     static SIZEL     sizlClient ;
     DATETIME         dt ;
     HDC              hdc ;
     INT              iResult ;
     SIZEL            sizlPage ;
     THREADPARAMS     *ptp ;
```

Listing 18.2: The PRINTCAL files (Continued)

```
switch (msg)
     {
     case WM_CREATE:
          hab = WinQueryAnchorBlock (hwnd) ;
          hdc = WinOpenWindowDC (hwnd) ;
          sizlPage.cx = 0 ;
          sizlPage.cy = 0 ;
          hps = GpiCreatePS (hab, hdc, &sizlPage,
                             PU_ARBITRARY | GPIF_DEFAULT |
                             GPIT_MICRO   | GPIA_ASSOC) ;

          DosGetDateTime (&dt) ;
          cp.iYear     = dt.year ;
          cp.iMonthBeg = dt.month - 1 ;
          cp.iMonthEnd = dt.month - 1 ;
          return 0 ;

     case WM_SIZE:
          sizlClient.cx = SHORT1FROMMP (mp2) ;
          sizlClient.cy = SHORT2FROMMP (mp2) ;

          GpiConvert (hps, CVTC_DEVICE, CVTC_PAGE, 1L,
                      (PPOINTL) &sizlClient) ;
          return 0 ;

     case WM_PAINT:
          WinBeginPaint (hwnd, hps, NULL) ;

          GpiErase (hps) ;
          DisplayPage (hps, &sizlClient, cp.iYear, cp.iMonthBeg) ;

          WinEndPaint (hps) ;
          return 0 ;

     case WM_COMMAND:
          switch (COMMANDMSG(&msg)->cmd)
               {
               case IDM_ABOUT:
                    WinDlgBox (HWND_DESKTOP, hwnd, AboutDlgProc,
                               0, IDD_ABOUT, NULL) ;
                    return 0 ;

               case IDM_PRINT:
                    iResult = WinDlgBox (HWND_DESKTOP, hwnd, PrintDlgProc,
                                         0, IDD_PRINT, &cp) ;

                    if (iResult == DID_CANCEL)
                         return 0 ;
```

Listing 18.2: The PRINTCAL files (Continued)

```
                         WinInvalidateRect (hwnd, NULL, FALSE) ;

                         if (iResult == IDD_PREVIEW)
                              return 0 ;

                         if ((ptp = malloc (sizeof (THREADPARAMS))) == NULL)
                              {
                              Message (hwnd, MB_ICONEXCLAMATION,
                                  "Cannot allocate memory for print thread!") ;
                              return 0 ;
                              }

                         ptp->cp         = cp ;
                         ptp->hwndNotify = hwnd ;

                         if (-1 == _beginthread (PrintThread,
#ifdef __IBMC__
                                                 NULL,
#endif
                                                 STACKSIZE, ptp))
                              {
                              free (ptp) ;
                              Message (hwnd, MB_ICONEXCLAMATION,
                                       "Cannot create print thread!") ;
                              return 0 ;
                              }

                         uiActiveThreads++ ;
                         Message (hwnd, MB_ICONASTERISK,
                                  "Print job successfully started.") ;
                         return 0 ;
                    }
               break ;

          case WM_USER_PRINT_OK:
               ptp = PVOIDFROMMP (mp1) ;
               free (ptp) ;
               uiActiveThreads-- ;
               Message (hwnd, MB_ICONASTERISK,
                        "Print job sent to spooler.") ;
               return 0 ;

          case WM_USER_PRINT_ERROR:
               ptp = PVOIDFROMMP (mp1) ;
               free (ptp) ;
               uiActiveThreads-- ;
               Message (hwnd, MB_ICONEXCLAMATION,
                        "Error encountered during printing.") ;
```

Listing 18.2: The PRINTCAL files (Continued)

```
               return 0 ;

          case WM_DESTROY:
               GpiDestroyPS (hps) ;
               return 0 ;
          }
     return WinDefWindowProc (hwnd, msg, mp1, mp2) ;
     }

MRESULT EXPENTRY AboutDlgProc (HWND hwnd, ULONG msg, MPARAM mp1, MPARAM mp2)
     {
     switch (msg)
          {
          case WM_COMMAND:
               switch (COMMANDMSG(&msg)->cmd)
                    {
                    case DID_OK:
                    case DID_CANCEL:
                         WinDismissDlg (hwnd, TRUE) ;
                         return 0 ;
                    }
               break ;
          }
     return WinDefDlgProc (hwnd, msg, mp1, mp2) ;
     }

MRESULT EXPENTRY PrintDlgProc (HWND hwnd, ULONG msg, MPARAM mp1, MPARAM mp2)
     {
     static CALPARAMS cpLocal, *pcpCurrent ;

     switch (msg)
          {
          case WM_INITDLG:
               pcpCurrent = PVOIDFROMMP (mp2) ;
               cpLocal = *pcpCurrent ;

               WinSendDlgItemMsg (hwnd, IDD_MONTHBEG + cpLocal.iMonthBeg,
                                  BM_SETCHECK, MPFROM2SHORT (TRUE, 0), NULL) ;

               WinSendDlgItemMsg (hwnd, IDD_MONTHEND + cpLocal.iMonthEnd,
                                  BM_SETCHECK, MPFROM2SHORT (TRUE, 0), NULL) ;

               WinSendDlgItemMsg (hwnd, IDD_YEAR, EM_SETTEXTLIMIT,
                                  MPFROM2SHORT (4, 0), NULL) ;

               WinSetDlgItemShort (hwnd, IDD_YEAR, cpLocal.iYear, FALSE) ;
               return 0 ;

          case WM_CONTROL:
```

Listing 18.2: The PRINTCAL files (Continued)

```
          if (SHORT1FROMMP (mp1) >= IDD_MONTHBEG &&
              SHORT1FROMMP (mp1) <  IDD_MONTHBEG + 12)

               cpLocal.iMonthBeg = SHORT1FROMMP (mp1) - IDD_MONTHBEG ;

          else if (SHORT1FROMMP (mp1) >= IDD_MONTHEND &&
                   SHORT1FROMMP (mp1) <  IDD_MONTHEND + 12)

               cpLocal.iMonthEnd = SHORT1FROMMP (mp1) - IDD_MONTHEND ;

          return 0 ;

     case WM_COMMAND:
          switch (COMMANDMSG(&msg)->cmd)
               {
               case DID_OK:
               case IDD_PREVIEW:
                    WinQueryDlgItemShort (hwnd, IDD_YEAR,
                                          &cpLocal.iYear, FALSE) ;

                    if (cpLocal.iYear < 1900 || cpLocal.iYear > 2099)
                         {
                         Message (hwnd, MB_ICONEXCLAMATION,
                                  "Year must be between 1900 and 2099!") ;
                         WinSetFocus (HWND_DESKTOP,
                                      WinWindowFromID (hwnd, IDD_YEAR)) ;
                         return 0 ;
                         }

                    if (cpLocal.iMonthBeg > cpLocal.iMonthEnd)
                         {
                         Message (hwnd, MB_ICONEXCLAMATION,
                                  "Begin month cannot be later "
                                  "than end month!") ;
                         WinSetFocus (HWND_DESKTOP,
                              WinWindowFromID (hwnd,
                                   IDD_MONTHBEG + cpLocal.iMonthBeg)) ;
                         return 0 ;
                         }

                    *pcpCurrent = cpLocal ;
                                                  // fall through
               case DID_CANCEL:
                    WinDismissDlg (hwnd, COMMANDMSG(&msg)->cmd) ;
                    return 0 ;
               }
          break ;
     }
return WinDefDlgProc (hwnd, msg, mp1, mp2) ;
```

Listing 18.2: The PRINTCAL files (Continued)

```
     }

VOID DisplayPage (HPS hps, SIZEL *psizlPage, INT iYear, INT iMonth)
     {
     static CHAR  *apszMonths[]  = { "January", "February", "March",
                                     "April",   "May",      "June",
                                     "July",    "August",   "September",
                                     "October", "November", "December" } ;
     static INT   aiMonthLen[]   = { 31, 28, 31, 30, 31, 30,
                                     31, 31, 30, 31, 30, 31 } ;
     static INT   aiMonthStart[] = {  0,  3,  3,  6,  1,  4,
                                      6,  2,  5,  0,  3,  5 } ;
     CHAR         szBuffer[16] ;
     BOOL         fLeap ;
     FATTRS       fat ;
     INT          iDayStart, iDay, iExtraDay ;
     LONG         lLength ;
     POINTL       ptl, aptlTextBox[TXTBOX_COUNT] ;
     SIZEF        sizfx ;
     SIZEL        sizlCell ;

     GpiSavePS (hps) ;

               // Determine size of day cell

     sizlCell.cx = (psizlPage->cx - 1) / 7 ;
     sizlCell.cy = (psizlPage->cy - 1) / 7 ;

               // Create the vector font and use it in the PS

     fat.usRecordLength  = sizeof fat ;
     fat.fsSelection     = 0 ;
     fat.lMatch          = 0 ;
     fat.idRegistry      = 0 ;
     fat.usCodePage      = GpiQueryCp (hps) ;
     fat.lMaxBaselineExt = 0 ;
     fat.lAveCharWidth   = 0 ;
     fat.fsType          = 0 ;
     fat.fsFontUse       = FATTR_FONTUSE_OUTLINE |
                           FATTR_FONTUSE_TRANSFORMABLE ;

     strcpy (fat.szFacename, "Helvetica") ;

     GpiCreateLogFont (hps, NULL, LCID_CALFONT, &fat) ;
     GpiSetCharSet (hps, LCID_CALFONT) ;

               // Scale the font for the month and year name

     lLength = sprintf (szBuffer, " %s %d ", apszMonths[iMonth], iYear) ;
```

Listing 18.2: The PRINTCAL files (Continued)

```
     GpiQueryTextBox (hps, lLength, szBuffer, TXTBOX_COUNT, aptlTextBox) ;
     GpiQueryCharBox (hps, &sizfx) ;

     sizfx.cx = sizlCell.cx * sizfx.cx /  aptlTextBox[TXTBOX_CONCAT].x * 7 ;
     sizfx.cy = sizlCell.cy * sizfx.cy / (aptlTextBox[TXTBOX_TOPLEFT].y -
                                          aptlTextBox[TXTBOX_BOTTOMLEFT].y) ;

     sizfx.cx = sizfx.cy = min (sizfx.cx, sizfx.cy) ;
     GpiSetCharBox (hps, &sizfx) ;
     GpiQueryTextBox (hps, lLength, szBuffer, TXTBOX_COUNT, aptlTextBox) ;

               // Display month and year at top of page

     ptl.x = (psizlPage->cx - aptlTextBox[TXTBOX_CONCAT].x) / 2 ;
     ptl.y =  6 * sizlCell.cy - aptlTextBox[TXTBOX_BOTTOMLEFT].y ;
     GpiCharStringAt (hps, &ptl, lLength, szBuffer) ;

               // Set font size for day numbers

     sizfx.cx = sizfx.cy = MAKEFIXED (min (sizlCell.cx, sizlCell.cy) / 4, 0) ;
     GpiSetCharBox (hps, &sizfx) ;

               // Calculate some variables for showing days in month

     fLeap = (iYear % 4 == 0) && ((iYear % 100 != 0) || (iYear % 400 == 0)) ;
     iExtraDay = fLeap && iMonth == 1 ? 1 : 0 ;

     iDayStart  = 1 + iYear - 1900 + (iYear - 1901) / 4 ;
     iDayStart += aiMonthStart[iMonth] + (fLeap && iMonth > 1 ? 1 : 0) ;
     iDayStart %= 7 ;

               // Loop through days

     for (iDay = 0 ; iDay < aiMonthLen[iMonth] + iExtraDay ; iDay++)
          {
          ptl.x =      (iDayStart + iDay) % 7  * sizlCell.cx ;
          ptl.y = (5 - (iDayStart + iDay) / 7) * sizlCell.cy ;
          GpiMove (hps, &ptl) ;

          ptl.x += sizlCell.cx ;
          ptl.y += sizlCell.cy ;
          GpiBox (hps, DRO_OUTLINE, &ptl, 0L, 0L) ;

          lLength = sprintf (szBuffer, " %d", iDay + 1) ;
          GpiQueryTextBox (hps, lLength, szBuffer, TXTBOX_COUNT, aptlTextBox) ;

          GpiQueryCurrentPosition (hps, &ptl) ;
          ptl.y += sizlCell.cy - aptlTextBox[TXTBOX_TOPLEFT].y ;
          GpiCharStringAt (hps, &ptl, lLength, szBuffer) ;
```

Listing 18.2: The PRINTCAL files (Continued)

```
          }
               // Clean up

     GpiSetCharSet (hps, LCID_DEFAULT) ;
     GpiDeleteSetId (hps, LCID_CALFONT) ;
     GpiRestorePS (hps, -1L) ;
     }

VOID Message (HWND hwnd, INT sIcon, CHAR *pszMessage)
     {
     WinMessageBox (HWND_DESKTOP, hwnd, pszMessage, "PrintCal",
                    0, sIcon | MB_OK | MB_MOVEABLE) ;
     }

VOID PrintThread (VOID * pArg)
     {
     HAB            hab ;
     HDC            hdcPrinter ;
     HPS            hpsPrinter ;
     INT            msgReturn ;
     INT            iMonth ;
     SIZEL          sizlPage ;
     THREADPARAMS * ptp ;

     ptp = (THREADPARAMS *) pArg ;

     hab = WinInitialize (0) ;

     if ((hdcPrinter = OpenDefaultPrinterDC (hab)) != DEV_ERROR)
          {
                    // Create the presentation space for the printer

          sizlPage.cx = 0 ;
          sizlPage.cy = 0 ;
          hpsPrinter = GpiCreatePS (hab, hdcPrinter, &sizlPage,
                                    PU_ARBITRARY | GPIF_DEFAULT |
                                    GPIT_MICRO   | GPIA_ASSOC) ;

          GpiQueryPS (hpsPrinter, &sizlPage) ;

                    // Start the document

          if (DevEscape (hdcPrinter, DEVESC_STARTDOC,
                         8L, "Calendar", NULL, NULL) != DEVESC_ERROR)
               {
                    // Loop through months

               for (iMonth  = ptp->cp.iMonthBeg ;
                    iMonth <= ptp->cp.iMonthEnd ; iMonth++)
```

Listing 18.2: The PRINTCAL files (Continued)

```
                    {
                    DisplayPage (hpsPrinter, &sizlPage, ptp->cp.iYear, iMonth);

                    DevEscape (hdcPrinter, DEVESC_NEWFRAME,
                               0L, NULL, NULL, NULL) ;
                    }

                         // End the document

               DevEscape (hdcPrinter, DEVESC_ENDDOC, 0L, NULL, NULL, NULL) ;
               msgReturn = WM_USER_PRINT_OK ;
               }
          else
               msgReturn = WM_USER_PRINT_ERROR ;

                    // Clean up

          GpiDestroyPS (hpsPrinter) ;
          DevCloseDC (hdcPrinter) ;
          }
     else
          msgReturn = WM_USER_PRINT_ERROR ;

               // Post message to client window and end thread

     DosEnterCritSec () ;
     WinPostMsg (ptp->hwndNotify, msgReturn, MPFROMP (ptp), NULL) ;
     WinTerminate (hab) ;
     _endthread () ;
     }
```

The PRINTCAL.RC File

```
/*----------------------------
   PRINTCAL.RC resource script
  ----------------------------*/

#include <os2.h>
#include "printcal.h"

MENU ID_RESOURCE
     {
     SUBMENU "~Calendar",                   -1
          {
          MENUITEM "~Print Calendar...",     IDM_PRINT
          MENUITEM SEPARATOR
          MENUITEM "A~bout PrintCal...",     IDM_ABOUT
          }
     }
```

Listing 18.2: The PRINTCAL files (Continued)

```
DLGTEMPLATE IDD_PRINT
  {
  DIALOG "Print Calendar", 0, 16, 16, 160, 220,, FCF_DLGBORDER | FCF_TITLEBAR
    {
    LTEXT   "Year (1900-2099):"  -1,                8, 200, 80,   8,
    EDITTEXT         ""          IDD_YEAR,         92, 200, 24,   8, ES_MARGIN

    GROUPBOX         "Begin"      -1,                8,  30, 68, 160
    AUTORADIOBUTTON "January"    IDD_MONTHBEG +  0, 12, 168, 60,  12, WS_GROUP
    AUTORADIOBUTTON "February"   IDD_MONTHBEG +  1, 12, 156, 60,  12
    AUTORADIOBUTTON "March"      IDD_MONTHBEG +  2, 12, 144, 60,  12
    AUTORADIOBUTTON "April"      IDD_MONTHBEG +  3, 12, 132, 60,  12
    AUTORADIOBUTTON "May"        IDD_MONTHBEG +  4, 12, 120, 60,  12
    AUTORADIOBUTTON "June"       IDD_MONTHBEG +  5, 12, 108, 60,  12
    AUTORADIOBUTTON "July"       IDD_MONTHBEG +  6, 12,  96, 60,  12
    AUTORADIOBUTTON "August"     IDD_MONTHBEG +  7, 12,  84, 60,  12
    AUTORADIOBUTTON "September"  IDD_MONTHBEG +  8, 12,  72, 60,  12
    AUTORADIOBUTTON "October"    IDD_MONTHBEG +  9, 12,  60, 60,  12
    AUTORADIOBUTTON "November"   IDD_MONTHBEG + 10, 12,  48, 60,  12
    AUTORADIOBUTTON "December"   IDD_MONTHBEG + 11, 12,  36, 60,  12

    GROUPBOX         "End"        -1,               84,  30, 68, 160
    AUTORADIOBUTTON "January"    IDD_MONTHEND +  0, 88, 168, 60,  12, WS_GROUP
    AUTORADIOBUTTON "February"   IDD_MONTHEND +  1, 88, 156, 60,  12
    AUTORADIOBUTTON "March"      IDD_MONTHEND +  2, 88, 144, 60,  12
    AUTORADIOBUTTON "April"      IDD_MONTHEND +  3, 88, 132, 60,  12
    AUTORADIOBUTTON "May"        IDD_MONTHEND +  4, 88, 120, 60,  12
    AUTORADIOBUTTON "June"       IDD_MONTHEND +  5, 88, 108, 60,  12
    AUTORADIOBUTTON "July"       IDD_MONTHEND +  6, 88,  96, 60,  12
    AUTORADIOBUTTON "August"     IDD_MONTHEND +  7, 88,  84, 60,  12
    AUTORADIOBUTTON "September"  IDD_MONTHEND +  8, 88,  72, 60,  12
    AUTORADIOBUTTON "October"    IDD_MONTHEND +  9, 88,  60, 60,  12
    AUTORADIOBUTTON "November"   IDD_MONTHEND + 10, 88,  48, 60,  12
    AUTORADIOBUTTON "December"   IDD_MONTHEND + 11, 88,  36, 60,  12

    DEFPUSHBUTTON   "Print"      DID_OK,             8,   8, 40,  16, WS_GROUP
    PUSHBUTTON      "Preview"    IDD_PREVIEW,       61,   8, 40,  16
    PUSHBUTTON      "Cancel"     DID_CANCEL,       114,   8, 40,  16
    }
  }

DLGTEMPLATE IDD_ABOUT
  {
  DIALOG "", 0, 32, 32, 200, 88,, FCF_DLGBORDER
    {
    CTEXT "PrintCal"                              -1, 10, 64, 180,  8
    CTEXT "Calendar Printing Program"             -1, 10, 48, 180,  8
    CTEXT "Copyright (c) Charles Petzold, 1993" -1, 10, 32, 180,  8
```

Listing 18.2: The PRINTCAL files (Continued)

```
     DEFPUSHBUTTON "OK"                          DID_OK, 80,  8,  40, 16, WS_GROUP
     }
   }
```

The PRINTCAL.H File

```
/*------------------------
   PRINTCAL.H header file
  ------------------------*/

#define ID_RESOURCE       1

#define IDM_PRINT         1
#define IDM_ABOUT         2

#define IDD_PRINT         1
#define IDD_ABOUT         2

#define IDD_YEAR          10
#define IDD_MONTHBEG      20
#define IDD_MONTHEND      40
#define IDD_PREVIEW       60
```

The PRINTCAL.DEF File

```
;-----------------------------------
; PRINTCAL.DEF module definition file
;-----------------------------------

NAME           PRINTCAL  WINDOWAPI

DESCRIPTION    'Prints monthly calendar (c) 1993, Charles Petzold'
PROTMODE
```

The PRINTCAL program demonstrates the basics of how to print from a Presentation Manager program. So that you don't lose sight of the forest while examining the trees, here are the steps involved in printing a document:

1. Open a device context for the printer. This requires the *OpenDefault-PrinterDC* function (or something equivalent) in the PRINTDC.C file.
2. Create a presentation space associated with that device context by calling *GpiCreatePS*.
3. Begin a document by calling *DevEscape* with the DEVESC_STARTDOC parameter.

4. Draw a page of text and graphics by calling GPI functions.
5. End the page by calling *DevEscape* with the DEVESC_NEWFRAME parameter.
6. Repeat steps 4 and 5 for each page in the document.
7. End the document by calling *DevEscape* with the DEVESC_ENDDOC parameter.
8. Clean up by destroying the printer presentation space (*GpiDestroyPS*) and closing the device context (*DevCloseDC*).

All of these steps should be performed in a second thread of execution to avoid forcing the user to wait for the program to finish these steps. This requires that the main thread and printing thread communicate in some way.

DRAWING THE CALENDAR PAGE

I'll start with the *DisplayPage* function that begins about two-thirds of the way into the PRINTCAL.C listing. This function is used to display one month of the calendar on the program's window and on a printer page. None of the overhead involved in printing is in this function. This is pure, unadulterated device-independent graphics programming.

There are four *DisplayPage* parameters: a handle to a presentation space (this is required for all the GPI drawing functions and will reference either a window or printer presentation space), a SIZEL structure with the horizontal and vertical dimensions of the drawing surface (either the window or the printer page), a year (from 1900 to 2099), and a month (0 through 11).

DisplayPage begins by calculating the two fields of the *sizlCell* variable. This is another SIZEL structure that describes the horizontal and vertical dimensions of the box containing each day. These dimensions are both one-seventh of the horizontal and vertical dimensions of the page.

The *GpiCreateLogFont* function obtains a GPI vector font, the font identified by the "Helvetica" facename. The *GpiSetCharSet* function sets this font in the presentation space for subsequent text. As we saw in Chapter 7, a GPI vector font must be scaled to a desired size using the *GpiSetCharBox* function. The second parameter to this function is a SIZEF structure with two fields denoting the horizontal and vertical sizes of the characters. The vertical size is the distance from the top of the uppercase letters to the bottom of lowercase descenders, not including leading used for diacritic marks and to space lines of text. The vertical size should be set to the same physical dimension as the horizontal size for a normal-looking font.

I use the *GpiQueryTextBox* function (which determines the dimensions of a box in which a text string is enclosed) together with the default character box to determine the character box required to make the month and year heading as large as possible while maintaining equal horizontal and vertical character box dimensions. The heading is displayed at the top of the page (or screen) using *GpiCharStringAt*.

The *DisplayPage* function then sets the dimensions of the character box to the lesser of one-quarter of the width and height of the day cell. This character box size is used for the numbers of each day. After the function calculates a few variables to determine the day of the week on which the month begins, a *for* loop cycles through all the days. The *GpiMove* and *GpiBox* functions draw a box and *GpiCharStringAt* displays the day of the month.

Now let's examine PRINTCAL from the top down to see how the program uses this routine to draw the calendar page on both its window and a printer page.

WINDOW PAINTING

The *main* function in PRINTCAL is fairly normal. The only oddity is that the message loop (the *WinGetMsg* and *WinDispatchMsg* functions) are enclosed within a *while* block. I'll discuss the significance of this later.

During the WM_CREATE message, *ClientWndProc* calls *GpiCreatePS* to create a presentation space associated with the window. I use *GpiCreatePS* in this program because the same function is required to create a presentation space for the printer. I thought it would be helpful to compare and contrast the two usages. To create a presentation space for a window, you must first call *WinOpenWindowDC* to obtain a device context handle for the window. The presentation space is associated with that device context.

During the WM_CREATE message, *ClientWndProc* also obtains the current year and month by calling *DosGetDateTime*. The results are stored in a CALPARAMS structure (defined near the top of PRINTCAL.C) called *cp*.

When *ClientWndProc* receives a WM_SIZE message, the size of the window is reported in units of pixels. These must be converted to the selected page units of the presentation space using the *GpiConvert* function. The result is saved in a SIZEL structure.

With everything in place, WM_PAINT processing is simple: It begins with a call to *WinBeginPaint* with the second parameter set to the presentation space handle. (If you want *WinBeginPaint* to obtain a cached micro presentation space, this parameter must be set to NULL, and the function returns the presentation space handle.) The *GpiErase* function erases the window. The presentation space handle, the size of the client window stored in the SIZEL structure, and the year and month stored in the CALPARAMS structure are passed to *DisplayPage* to show the month in the program's window.

MENUS AND DIALOG BOXES

The WM_COMMAND messages that *ClientWndProc* processes indicate that the user has selected one of the two menu options: About PrintCal (the IDM_ABOUT command) or Print Calendar (the IDM_PRINT command).

For IDM_ABOUT, *ClientWndProc* calls *WinDlgBox* using the IDD_ABOUT dialog box template (contained in the PRINTCAL.RC resource script) and the *AboutDlgProc* dialog box procedure. This is a standard dialog box procedure for an About box.

For the IDM_PRINT command, *ClientWndProc* calls *WinDlgBox* using the IDD_PRINT dialog box template and the *PrintDlgBox* dialog box procedure. Notice that the last parameter to *WinDlgBox* is a pointer to the CALPARAMS structure that initially contains the current year and month.

Let's now skip down to *PrintDlgProc* to see what goes on when the dialog box is invoked. During the WM_INITDLG message, the *mp2* message parameter is set to the last parameter of the *WinDlgBox* call that invoked the dialog box. This is the pointer to the CALPARAMS structure. The dialog procedure saves this pointer in the *pcpCurrent* variable and also copies it to the *cpLocal* variable. The text box and radio buttons in the dialog box are initialized with the year and month values of the *cpLocal* structure.

A WM_CONTROL message to *PrintDlgProc* indicates that a user has changed one of the radio buttons. This change is recorded in the *cpLocal* structure. When the user triggers one of the pushbuttons, *PrintDlgProc* receives a WM_-COMMAND message. For the Print (DID_OK) and Preview (IDD_PREVIEW) buttons, the dialog procedure verifies that the selected year and months are valid, and then copies the values of *cpLocal* back to *pcpCurrent* (which points to the CALPARAMS structure stored in *ClientWndProc*).

PrintDlgProc then passes the button ID as the second parameter to *WinDismiss-Dlg*, the function that destroys the dialog box. This parameter is returned from the *WinDlgBox* call in *ClientWndProc*.

If *WinDlgBox* returns DID_CANCEL, *ClientWndProc* is done processing the Print Calendar menu command and simply returns 0. Otherwise, the window procedure assumes that the user changed the year or month and invalidates the window with a call to *WinInvalidateRect*. This generates a WM_PAINT message to repaint the client window. If the user selected the Preview button (IDD_PREVIEW) from the dialog box, *ClientWndProc* is finished.

Otherwise, a print job is in the works. First, a structure of type THREADPARAMS must be allocated. This structure is defined near the top of PRINTCAL.C and contains fields for the handle of the client window, and a CALPARAMS structure for the selected year and month range. The *_beginthread* function starts a second thread of execution that begins at the *PrintThread* function. The last parameter to *_beginthread* is a pointer to the THREADPARAMS structure containing information the thread needs to print the calendar.

ClientWndProc then finishes processing the menu command by incrementing the value of *usActiveThreads* (a global variable defined near the top of PRINTCAL.C that I'll describe later) and displaying the message box "Print job successfully started."

THE SECOND THREAD

The *PrintThread* function (located near the bottom of PRINTCAL.C) is now running concurrently with the rest of the program. The variable passed as the last parameter to *_beginthread* (in this case a pointer to the THREADPARAMS structure) appears as a parameter to the thread function.

PrintThread obtains a handle to the device context of the default printer by calling *OpenDefaultPrinterDC*, located in the PRINTDC.C file. A presentation space associated with the printer device context is created by calling *GpiCreatePS*. This call is basically the same as the call used to create a presentation space for the program's window.

The SIZEL structure passed as the third parameter to *GpiCreatePS* indicates the size of the presentation page, which is the drawing surface for the presentation space. By setting the two fields of the structure to zero, the program can obtain a presentation page of default size. This default size is equal to the size of the printable area of the page. A call to *GpiQueryPS* then obtains the real size of the page.

A call to *DevEscape* with the DEVESC_STARTDOC parameter begins the document. The *DevEscape* function is similar in concept to the *DosDevIOCtl* function. It is used to pass information to (or obtain information from) a Presentation Manager presentation driver. In the future, *DevEscape* could be used to access special features of the device that are not supported in GPI. *DevEscape* is customarily used for controlling the printing of documents.

A *for* loop cycles through the range of selected months. For each month, a call to *DisplayPage* prints the calendar on the page. This is followed by another *DevEscape* call (this time with the DEVESC_NEWFRAME parameter) to end the page and begin a new page. After all pages are finished, a third *DevEscape* call (with a DEVESC_ENDDOC parameter) ends the document. *GpiDestroyPS* destroys the printer presentation space and *DevCloseDC* closes the printer device context.

If all went well, the value of *msgReturn* in *PrintThread* is set to WM_USER_-PRINT_OK; otherwise it's set to WM_USER_PRINT_ERROR. These are two user-defined messages defined near the top of PRINTCAL.C. *PrintThread* calls *DosEnterCritSec* (a function I discussed in the previous chapter) and then uses *WinPostMsg* to post the *msgReturn* message to the client window. The pointer to the THREADPARAMS structure passed to *PrintThread* is passed back to the client window in this message as the first message parameter. The thread then terminates.

ClientWndProc processes the two possible messages from *PrintThread* near the bottom of the window procedure. In both cases, the memory allocated for the THREADPARAMS structure is freed, the global *usActiveThreads* variable is decremented, and a message box is displayed denoting the status of the print job.

What happens if you terminate the PRINTCAL program while one of the printing threads is still active? Well, that's not such a hot idea. The *usActive-Threads* variable is intended to avoid this problem. The variable is incremented whenever a printing thread is begun and decremented when a thread has terminated. In PRINTCAL's *main* function, if a WM_QUIT message is fetched from the message queue (which causes *WinGetMsg* to return 0), the value of *usActiveThreads* is checked. If the variable is nonzero, PRINTCAL displays a message box saying the program can't be terminated. It then calls *WinCan-celShutdown* and goes back into the message loop.

END OF JOB

Printing from the Presentation Manager certainly isn't as easy as using the old BIOS or DOS interrupts. Then again, the printing of device-independent graphics in the background isn't exactly one of the strengths of the BIOS and DOS.

As is typical in Presentation Manager programming, I think the results are worth the effort. Adding printing to your Presentation Manager programs may not be easy, but when done right, it's something of which you can be legitimately proud.

Appendix: About the Accompanying Disk

The disk at the back of this book contains 99 complete executable programs and 3 dynamic link libraries. This appendix explains how to install these files to your hard disk, answers questions about the benefits and appropriate use of the programs, and lists the files.

Installing and Using the Files

The installation program that copies these files to your hard disk is called INSTALL.CMD. This OS/2 batch file assumes that your 3½-inch high-density disk drive is A and your hard disk is C. If this is not the case with your system, you can run the unarchiving program (PKUNZIP) stored on the disk manually. INSTALL.CMD creates a directory on your hard disk named PMBOOK. If you don't like that name—or if you already have a directory called PMBOOK—you also need to run the unarchiving program manually.

To install the programs manually from an OS/2 command line, switch to the hard disk where you want the files to be stored, make a directory using the MD command, change to that directory using the CD command, and run:

```
x:PKUNZIP -d x:PMBOOK.ZIP
```

where x is the drive letter of your 3½-inch disk drive.

Whether you perform the installation manually or with INSTALL.CMD, PKUNZIP will create subdirectories of the PMBOOK directory (or whatever you decide to call it) named CHAP02 through CHAP18 for the chapters that contain code. The PMBOOK directory will also contain 6 batch files, 3 of which you need to run before remaking the programs. If you have the IBM compiler installed, you need to run IBM.CMD, IBMDLL.CMD and IBM-MT.DLL. If you're using the Borland compiler, run BOR.CMD, BORDLL.CMD, and BORMT.CMD.

Questions sometimes arise about using sample code in books such as this for your own commercial or corporate programs. The basic rule is this: You cannot distribute the sample programs on the disk. That's equivalent to photocopying the pages of this book and distributing them, which is clearly a violation of copyright laws.

However, you can certainly use chunks of code from the samples in your own commercial or corporate programs. That's one of the primary purposes of this book. It makes no sense if I show you how to do something and then prohibit you from doing the same thing!

I sincerely hope that when you get stuck on a problem with one of your own Presentation Manager programs, you find a solution in this book and simply copy the code that does the trick. That would make me very happy. Think of it this way: Buying this book is equivalent to getting a license agreement for using chunks of the sample code in your own programs. So don't feel guilty about sampling my code, OK?

Here is a list of the files that are copied to your hard disk.

\PMBOOK
- IBM.CMD
- BOR.CMD
- IBMDLL.CMD
- BORDLL.CMD
- IBMMT.CMD
- BORMT.CMD

\PMBOOK\CHAP02
- W.MAK
- W.C
- W.DEF
- W.EXE
- WE.MAK
- WE.C
- WE.DEF
- WE.EXE
- WEL.MAK
- WEL.C
- WEL.DEF
- WEL.EXE
- WELC.MAK
- WELC.C
- WELC.DEF
- WELC.EXE
- WELCO.MAK
- WELCO.C
- WELCO.DEF
- WELCO.EXE
- WELCOM.MAK
- WELCOM.C
- WELCOM.DEF
- WELCOM.EXE
- WELCOME.MAK
- WELCOME.C
- WELCOME.DEF
- WELCOME.EXE

\PMBOOK\CHAP03
- WELCOME2.MAK
- WELCOME2.C
- WELCOME2.DEF
- WELCOME2.EXE
- WELCOME3.MAK
- WELCOME3.C
- WELCOME3.DEF
- WELCOME3.EXE
- WELCOME4.MAK
- WELCOME4.C
- WELCOME4.DEF
- WELCOME4.EXE

\PMBOOK\CHAP04
- SYSVALS1.MAK
- SYSVALS1.C
- SYSVALS.H
- SYSVALS1.DEF
- SYSVALS1.EXE
- SYSVALS2.MAK
- SYSVALS2.C
- SYSVALS2.DEF
- SYSVALS2.EXE
- SYSVALS3.MAK
- SYSVALS3.C
- SYSVALS3.DEF
- SYSVALS3.EXE
- SYSVALS.MAK
- SYSVALS.C
- SYSVALS.DEF
- SYSVALS.EXE

\PMBOOK\CHAP05
- STAR5.MAK
- STAR5.C
- STAR5.DEF
- STAR5.EXE
- SPIRAL.MAK
- SPIRAL.C
- SPIRAL.DEF
- SPIRAL.EXE
- LINETYPE.MAK
- LINETYPE.C
- LINETYPE.DEF
- LINETYPE.EXE
- DEVCAPS.MAK
- DEVCAPS.C
- DEVCAPS.H
- DEVCAPS.DEF
- DEVCAPS.EXE
- RULER.MAK
- RULER.C
- RULER.DEF
- RULER.EXE
- PATTERNS.MAK
- PATTERNS.C
- PATTERNS.DEF
- PATTERNS.EXE
- STARFILL.MAK
- STARFILL.C
- STARFILL.DEF
- STARFILL.EXE
- ALTWIND.MAK
- ALTWIND.C
- ALTWIND.DEF
- ALTWIND.EXE
- COLORS.MAK
- COLORS.C
- COLORS.DEF
- COLORS.EXE
- EASYFONT.H
- EASYFONT.C
- FONTS.MAK
- FONTS.C
- FONTS.DEF
- FONTS.EXE

IMAGECAT.MAK
IMAGECAT.C
IMAGECAT.DEF
IMAGECAT.EXE

\PMBOOK\CHAP06

MINMAX1.MAK
MINMAX1.C
MINMAX1.DEF
MINMAX1.EXE
MINMAX2.MAK
MINMAX2.C
MINMAX2.DEF
MINMAX2.EXE
MINMAX3.MAK
MINMAX3.C
MINMAX3.DEF
MINMAX3.EXE
BITCAT1.MAK
BITCAT1.C
BITCAT.H
BITCAT1.DEF
BITCAT1.EXE
BITCAT2.MAK
BITCAT2.C
BITCAT2.DEF
BITCAT2.EXE
HELLOBIT.MAK
HELLOBIT.C
HELLOBIT.DEF
HELLOBIT.EXE
BRICKS.MAK
BRICKS.C
BRICKS.DEF
BRICKS.EXE

\PMBOOK\CHAP07

BEZIER.MAK
BEZIER.C
BEZIER.DEF
BEZIER.EXE
ENDJOIN.MAK
ENDJOIN.C
ENDJOIN.DEF
ENDJOIN.EXE
PATHS.MAK
PATHS.C
PATHS.DEF
PATHS.EXE
CIRCLE.MAK
CIRCLE.C
CIRCLE.DEF
CIRCLE.EXE
FLOWER.MAK
FLOWER.C
FLOWER.DEF
FLOWER.EXE
OUTFONTS.MAK
OUTFONTS.C
OUTFONTS.DEF
OUTFONTS.EXE
OLF.H
OLF.C
OLFDEMO.C
OLFDEMO.DEF
OLFLIST.MAK
OLFLIST.C
OLFLIST.EXE
OLFSIZE.MAK
OLFSIZE.C
OLFSIZE.EXE
OLFSTR1.MAK
OLFSTR1.C
OLFSTR1.EXE
OLFSTR2.MAK
OLFSTR2.C
OLFSTR2.EXE
OLFROT.MAK
OLFROT.C
OLFROT.EXE
OLFREFL.MAK
OLFREFL.C
OLFREFL.EXE
OLFREFL2.MAK
OLFREFL2.C
OLFREFL2.EXE
OLFSHEAR.MAK
OLFSHEAR.C
OLFSHEAR.EXE
OLFROT2.MAK
OLFROT2.C
OLFROT2.EXE
OLFSHAD.MAK
OLFSHAD.C
OLFSHAD.EXE
OLFLINE.MAK
OLFLINE.C
OLFLINE.EXE
OLFDROP.MAK
OLFDROP.C
OLFDROP.EXE
OLFBLOK.MAK
OLFBLOK.C
OLFBLOK.EXE
OLFWIDE.MAK
OLFWIDE.C
OLFWIDE.EXE
OLFFILL.MAK
OLFFILL.C
OLFFILL.EXE
OLFCLIP.MAK
OLFCLIP.C
OLFCLIP.EXE
OLFJUST.MAK
OLFJUST.C
OLFJUST.EXE

\PMBOOK\CHAP08

KEYLOOK.MAK

KEYLOOK.C
KEYLOOK.DEF
KEYLOOK.EXE
EASYFONT.C
EASYFONT.H
TYPEAWAY.MAK
TYPEAWAY.C
TYPEAWAY.DEF
TYPEAWAY.EXE

\PMBOOK\CHAP09

WEB.MAK
WEB.C
WEB.DEF
WEB.EXE
CHECKER1.MAK
CHECKER1.C
CHECKER1.DEF
CHECKER1.EXE
CHECKER2.MAK
CHECKER2.C
CHECKER2.DEF
CHECKER2.EXE
CHECKER3.MAK
CHECKER3.C
CHECKER3.DEF
CHECKER3.EXE
BLOKOUT1.MAK
BLOKOUT1.C
BLOKOUT1.DEF
BLOKOUT1.EXE
BLOKOUT2.MAK
BLOKOUT2.C
BLOKOUT2.DEF
BLOKOUT2.EXE
SKETCH.MAK
SKETCH.C
SKETCH.DEF
SKETCH.EXE

\PMBOOK\CHAP10

BEEPER1.MAK
BEEPER1.C
BEEPER1.DEF
BEEPER1.EXE
BEEPER2.MAK
BEEPER2.C
BEEPER2.DEF
BEEPER2.EXE
FREEMEM.MAK
FREEMEM.C
FREEMEM.DEF
FREEMEM.EXE
DIGCLOCK.MAK
DIGCLOCK.C
DIGCLOCK.DEF
DIGCLOCK.EXE
CLOCK.MAK
CLOCK.C
CLOCK.DEF
CLOCK.EXE

\PMBOOK\CHAP11

BUTTONS1.MAK
BUTTONS1.C
BUTTONS1.DEF
BUTTONS1.EXE
DRAWLINE.MAK
DRAWLINE.C
DRAWLINE.DEF
DRAWLINE.EXE
COLORSCR.MAK
COLORSCR.C
COLORSCR.DEF
COLORSCR.EXE
NEWBTN.C
BUTTONS2.MAK
BUTTONS2.C
BUTTONS2.DEF
BUTTONS2.EXE

\PMBOOK\CHAP12

LOADBMP1.MAK
LOADBMP1.C
LOADBMP.RC
LOADBMP.BMP
LOADBMP.H
LOADBMP1.DEF
LOADBMP1.EXE
LOADBMP2.MAK
LOADBMP2.C
LOADBMP2.DEF
LOADBMP2.EXE
RESOURCE.MAK
RESOURCE.C
RESOURCE.RC
RESOURCE.ICO
RESOURCE.PTR
RESOURCE.H
RESOURCE.DEF
RESOURCE.EXE
POEPOEM.MAK
POEPOEM.C
POEPOEM.RC
POEPOEM.ICO
POEPOEM.ASC
POEPOEM.H
POEPOEM.DEF
POEPOEM.EXE

\PMBOOK\CHAP13

CONVMENU.MAK
CONVMENU.C
CONVMENU.RC
CONVMENU.H
CONVMENU.DEF
CONVMENU.EXE
POORMENU.MAK
POORMENU.C
POORMENU.DEF
POORMENU.EXE

POPMENU.MAK
POPMENU.C
POPMENU.RC
POPMENU.H
POPMENU.DEF
POPMENU.EXE
GRAFMENU.MAK
GRAFMENU.C
GRAFMENU.RC
BIGHELP.BMP
GRAFMENU.H
GRAFMENU.DEF
GRAFMENU.EXE
TAQUIN.MAK
TAQUIN.C
TAQUIN.RC
TAQUIN.ICO
TAQUIN.H
TAQUIN.DEF
TAQUIN.EXE
LIFE.MAK
LIFE.C
LIFE.RC
LIFE.ICO
LIFE.H
LIFE.DEF
LIFE.EXE

\PMBOOK\CHAP14

ABOUT1.MAK
ABOUT1.C
ABOUT.H
ABOUT1.RC
ABOUT.ICO
ABOUT1.DEF
ABOUT1.EXE
ABOUT2.MAK
ABOUT2.C
ABOUT2.RC
ABOUT2.DEF
ABOUT2.EXE
NEWBTN.C
PATTDLG.MAK
PATTDLG.C
PATTDLG.H
PATTDLG.RC
PATTDLG.DEF
PATTDLG.EXE
HEAD.MAK
HEAD.C
HEAD.H
HEAD.RC
HEAD.DEF
HEAD.EXE
EASYFONT.C
EASYFONT.H
HEXCALC.MAK
HEXCALC.C
HEXCALC.H
HEXCALC.RC
HEXCALC.ICO
HEXCALC.DEF
HEXCALC.EXE

\PMBOOK\CHAP15

HEXCALC2.MAK
HEXCALC2.C
HEXCALC.RC
HEXCALC.H
HEXCALC.ICO
HEXCALC2.DEF
HEXCALC2.EXE
BLOWUP.MAK
BLOWUP.C
BLOWUP.RC
BLOWUP.H
BLOWUP.DEF
BLOWUP.EXE

\PMBOOK\CHAP16

HDRLIB.MAK
HDRLIB.H
HDRLIB.C
HDRLIB.DEF
HDRLIB.DLL
HDRTEST.MAK
HDRTEST.C
HDRTEST.DEF
HDRTEST.EXE
NEWBTN.MAK
NEWBTN.H
NEWBTN.C
NEWBTN.DEF
NEWBTN.DLL
BUTTONS3.MAK
BUTTONS3.C
BUTTONS3.DEF
BUTTONS3.EXE
BITLIB.MAK
BITLIB.C
BITLIB.RC
BITMAP1.BMP
BITMAP2.BMP
BITMAP3.BMP
BITMAP4.BMP
BITMAP5.BMP
BITMAP6.BMP
BITMAP7.BMP
BITMAP8.BMP
BITMAP9.BMP
BITLIB.DEF
BITLIB.DLL
SHOWBIT.MAK
SHOWBIT.C
SHOWBIT.DEF
SHOWBIT.EXE

\PMBOOK\CHAP17

BIGJOB1.MAK
BIGJOB1.C
BIGJOB.C
BIGJOB.H
BIGJOB.RC
BIGJOB1.DEF
BIGJOB1.EXE
BIGJOB2.MAK
BIGJOB2.C
BIGJOB2.DEF
BIGJOB2.EXE
BIGJOB3.MAK
BIGJOB3.C
BIGJOB3.DEF
BIGJOB3.EXE
BIGJOB4.MAK
BIGJOB4.C
BIGJOB4.DEF
BIGJOB4.EXE
BIGJOB5.MAK
BIGJOB5.C
BIGJOB5.DEF
BIGJOB5.EXE

\PMBOOK\CHAP18

PRINTCAL.MAK
PRINTCAL.C
PRINTDC.C
PRINTCAL.RC
PRINTCAL.H
PRINTCAL.DEF
PRINTCAL.EXE

INDEX

A

B

E

F

G

M

P

Q

R

S

U

V

W

Imagination. Innovation. Insight.

The How It Works Series from Ziff-Davis Press

"... a magnificently seamless integration of text and graphics ..."

Larry Blasko, The Associated Press, reviewing *PC/Computing How Computers Work*

ISBN: 094-7 Price: $22.95

No other books bring computer technology to life like the *How It Works* series from Ziff-Davis Press. Lavish, full-color illustrations and lucid text from some of the world's top computer commentators make *How It Works* books an exciting way to explore the inner workings of PC technology.

PC/Computing How Computers Work

A worldwide blockbuster that hit the general trade bestseller lists! *PC/Computing* magazine executive editor Ron White dismantles the PC and reveals what really makes it tick.

ISBN: 129-3 Price: $24.95

How Networks Work

Two of the most respected names in connectivity showcase the PC network, illustrating and explaining how each component does its magic and how they all fit together.

ISBN: 146-3 Price: $24.95

How Macs Work

A fun and fascinating voyage to the heart of the Macintosh! Two noted *MacUser* contributors cover the spectrum of Macintosh operations from startup to shutdown.

ISBN: 184-6 Price: $17.95

ISBN: 133-1 Price: $24.95

How Software Works

This dazzlingly illustrated volume from Ron White peeks inside the PC to show in full-color how software breathes life into the PC. Covers Windows™ and all major software categories.

How to Use Your Computer

Conquer computerphobia and see how this intricate machine truly makes life easier. Dozens of full-color graphics showcase the components of the PC and explain how to interact with them.

ISBN: 155-2 Price: $22.95

All About Computers

This one-of-a-kind visual guide for kids features numerous full-color illustrations and photos on every page, combined with dozens of interactive projects that reinforce computer basics, making this an exciting way to learn all about the world of computers.

ISBN: 166-8 Price: $15.95

How To Use Word

Make Word 6.0 for Windows Work for You!

A uniquely visual approach puts the basics of Microsoft's latest Windows-based word processor right before your eyes. Colorful examples invite you to begin producing a variety of documents, quickly and easily. Truly innovative!

How To Use Excel Make Excel 5.0 for Windows Work for You!

Covering the latest version of Excel, this visually impressive resource guides beginners to spreadsheet fluency through a full-color graphical approach that makes powerful techniques seem plain as day. Hands-on "Try It" sections give you a chance to sharpen newfound skills.

HOW TO USE EXCEL — ERIC STONE

ISBN: 185-4 Price: $17.95

Available at all fine bookstores or by calling 1-800-688-0448, ext. 100.

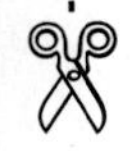

Ziff-Davis Press Survey of Readers

Please help us in our effort to produce the best books on personal computing. For your assistance, we would be pleased to send you a FREE catalog featuring the complete line of Ziff-Davis Press books.

1. How did you first learn about this book?

Recommended by a friend	☐	-1 (5)
Recommended by store personnel	☐	-2
Saw in Ziff-Davis Press catalog	☐	-3
Received advertisement in the mail	☐	-4
Saw the book on bookshelf at store	☐	-5
Read book review in: ____________	☐	-6
Saw an advertisement in: ____________	☐	-7
Other (Please specify): ____________	☐	-8

2. Which THREE of the following factors most influenced your decision to purchase this book? (Please check up to THREE.)

Front or back cover information on book	☐	-1 (6)
Logo of magazine affiliated with book	☐	-2
Special approach to the content	☐	-3
Completeness of content	☐	-4
Author's reputation	☐	-5
Publisher's reputation	☐	-6
Book cover design or layout	☐	-7
Index or table of contents of book	☐	-8
Price of book	☐	-9
Special effects, graphics, illustrations	☐	-0
Other (Please specify): ____________	☐	-x

3. How many computer books have you purchased in the last six months? ______ (7-10)

4. On a scale of 1 to 5, where 5 is excellent, 4 is above average, 3 is average, 2 is below average, and 1 is poor, please rate each of the following aspects of this book below. (Please circle your answer.)

Depth/completeness of coverage	5	4	3	2	1	(11)
Organization of material	5	4	3	2	1	(12)
Ease of finding topic	5	4	3	2	1	(13)
Special features/time saving tips	5	4	3	2	1	(14)
Appropriate level of writing	5	4	3	2	1	(15)
Usefulness of table of contents	5	4	3	2	1	(16)
Usefulness of index	5	4	3	2	1	(17)
Usefulness of accompanying disk	5	4	3	2	1	(18)
Usefulness of illustrations/graphics	5	4	3	2	1	(19)
Cover design and attractiveness	5	4	3	2	1	(20)
Overall design and layout of book	5	4	3	2	1	(21)
Overall satisfaction with book	5	4	3	2	1	(22)

5. Which of the following computer publications do you read regularly; that is, 3 out of 4 issues?

Byte	☐	-1 (23)
Computer Shopper	☐	-2
Corporate Computing	☐	-3
Dr. Dobb's Journal	☐	-4
LAN Magazine	☐	-5
MacWEEK	☐	-6
MacUser	☐	-7
PC Computing	☐	-8
PC Magazine	☐	-9
PC WEEK	☐	-0
Windows Sources	☐	-x
Other (Please specify): ____________	☐	-y

Please turn page.

6. What is your level of experience with personal computers? With the subject of this book?

	With PCs		With subject of book	
Beginner.	☐	-1 (24)	☐	-1 (25)
Intermediate.	☐	-2	☐	-2
Advanced.	☐	-3	☐	-3

7. Which of the following best describes your job title?

Officer (CEO/President/VP/owner).	☐	-1 (26)
Director/head.	☐	-2
Manager/supervisor.	☐	-3
Administration/staff.	☐	-4
Teacher/educator/trainer.	☐	-5
Lawyer/doctor/medical professional.	☐	-6
Engineer/technician.	☐	-7
Consultant.	☐	-8
Not employed/student/retired.	☐	-9
Other (Please specify): ________________	☐	-0

8. What is your age?

Under 20.	☐	-1 (27)
21-29.	☐	-2
30-39.	☐	-3
40-49.	☐	-4
50-59.	☐	-5
60 or over.	☐	-6

9. Are you:

Male.	☐	-1 (28)
Female.	☐	-2

Thank you for your assistance with this important information! Please write your address below to receive our free catalog.

Name: ______________________________

Address: ____________________________

City/State/Zip: _______________________

Fold here to mail.

1234-08-05

NO POSTAGE NECESSARY IF MAILED IN THE UNITED STATES

BUSINESS REPLY MAIL

FIRST CLASS MAIL PERMIT NO. 1612 OAKLAND, CA

POSTAGE WILL BE PAID BY ADDRESSEE

Ziff-Davis Press
5903 Christie Avenue
Emeryville, CA 94608-1925
Attn: Marketing

■ TO RECEIVE 5 1/4-INCH DISK(S)

The Ziff-Davis Press software contained on the 3 1/2-inch disk included with this book is also available in 5 1/4-inch format. If you would like to receive the software in the 5 1/4-inch format, please return the 3 1/2-inch disk with your name and address to:

Disk Exchange
Ziff-Davis Press
5903 Christie Avenue
Emeryville, CA 94608

■ END-USER LICENSE AGREEMENT